TASTE OF THE STATES

Designed by Marilyn F. Appleby.

Edited by Melissa E. Barranco, Claudia J. Garthwait, Ross A. Howell, Jr., and Kathleen D. Valenzi.

The publisher gratefully acknowledges the museums, galleries, and artists for permission to print their work in this book.

Printed in Hong Kong.

Published by Howell Press, Inc., 1147 River Road, Bay 2, Charlottesville, VA 22901, telephone 804-977-4006.

Library of Congress Cataloging in Publication Data

Lee, Hilde Gabriel
Taste of the states: a food history of America / Hilde Gabriel Lee.
p. cm.
Includes bibliographical references and index
ISBN 0-943231-56-6

1. Cookery, American. 2. Cookery—United States.
3. United States—History.
I. Title. II. Title: A food history of America.

TX715.L5 1992   641.5973
        QB192-10612

First printing

HOWELL PRESS

(Above and cover) *THE SCYTHERS* by N.C. Wyeth, oil, 37 ½ x 26 ¾ inches, courtesy of The University of Arizona Museum of Art, Tucson, Arizona, gift of Mr. and Mrs. Samuel L. Kingan.

TASTE OF THE STATES
A FOOD HISTORY OF AMERICA

HILDE GABRIEL LEE

ILLUSTRATIONS FROM AMERICAN ART

FRUIT FEST by Rene Rickabaugh, watercolor, 11 x 14 inches, courtesy of The Laura Russo Gallery, Inc., Portland, Oregon.

CONTENTS

INTRODUCTION

Oh beautiful for spacious skies,
For amber waves of grain,
For purple mountain's majesty,
Above the fruited plain....

Hearing those words sung by Tony Bennett on the radio on the Fourth of July, 1988, while my husband and I drove through the parched fields of Kansas at dusk brought tears streaming down my cheeks. Listening to *America the Beautiful* being broadcast from the Mall in Washington, D.C., evoked strong emotions in me as I watched people hurriedly harvesting wheat that was half as tall as usual because of the drought that had prevailed all summer in the Midwest. I had just started working on this book and had become very aware of how important Kansas wheat had become to our nation.

After six more trips across the country by car, visiting historic farms, interviewing personnel at the department of agriculture of each state, and talking with various food producers, I came to realize what a tremendous contribution the farmers and food producers have made to the development of our nation. Consequently, I have dedicated this book to the farmers and food producers of America.

The farms in this country are the result of generations of hard labor. They were carved out of raw, primeval land, frequently from rocky mountainsides or prairie hardpan. In many regions of the country, settlers had to fell trees and pull up stumps before they could farm. These pioneering settlers tamed the land and prepared it for those who followed.

Urban America was able to develop because farmers learned to raise their productivity above the subsistence level. America was founded as an agricultural country and now produces more agricultural products than any other country in the world. In colonial days 85 percent of the population lived on farms. Today, less than 5 percent does. Early settlers barely produced enough food to feed their families. Now each farm worker grows enough food for himself and 30 other people. As recently as 1930 one acre of land produced only 30 bushels of corn, while today that same acre produces 140 bushels. None of this improvement would have been significant if the nation had not been blessed with soils and climates that were receptive to growing the widest variety of foods found anywhere in the world.

Each of the 50 states has unique foods and food ingredients that make its cuisine distinctive. The most southerly states provide the country with tropical and subtropical fruits, such as papaya and citrus, while the most northerly ones have bountiful crops of grain and potatoes. States on both coasts yield a myriad of seafoods, while those on the vast lands of the Midwest and Southwest yield various types of red meats, including beef, pork, and lamb. These are just a few examples of the diversity of foods that this country produces and which permits us to enjoy a culinary heritage derived from our diverse population. American cooking is the most unusual in the world, because it is a melding of many different cuisines.

The native Indians taught the settlers how to cook many of the unique foods indigenous to the New World. They showed them how to bake beans in a pit in the ground and how to cook lobster in a bed of seaweed. It was not long before the settlers adapted the new foods to their own style of cooking and combined them with familiar foods that they had begun growing in their gardens. There are still popular dishes that were originally created by Native Americans and passed along to the European settlers.

As settlers from other European countries came to America, they added their recipes to the meld of cookery. In colonial days English cooking prevailed. Over the years French, Spanish, German, Scandinavian, Eastern European, Italian, and Mexican cooking were combined with English and Anglo-American cookery. When the settlers moved from the East to the West seeking new land, they established farms and homes and began cooking dishes familiar to them. Many adapted their native cuisine to the unique ingredients they found in their new homeland. In the latter part of the nineteenth century, the Chinese and Japanese immigrants added yet another dimension to American cooking.

As a cookbook author and weekly food columnist, I have always been interested in America's food heritage. Part of my interest stems from the fact that I came to this country as a child with my parents from Germany to escape the Holocaust. Over the years I have always been grateful for everything American, including its food. Finding regional specialties around the country that were clearly of German origin and which reminded me of my own heritage further tweaked my interest in learning more about how various regional specialties came into being.

This book is the product of my searchings. It focuses on the food history of each state in the Union and on the individual foods associated with each state. While many multi-state regional similarities exist, I found that important state-related variations have developed within the regions. A case in point: while there are many states in the Midwest that produce corn, only Indiana has become known for its popcorn and has built it into a multi-million dollar business. In the Upper South and Deep South, the methods and ingredients used to cure country hams vary from state to state. Their ultimate taste depends on the quantity of salt, sugar, and pepper used in the curing mix, and if the ham is smoked, what type of wood is burned in the smokehouse.

To enable the reader to try some of the unusual recipes and foods of America, I have included recipes of various traditional foods mentioned in the book, as well as recipes that include the unique foods produced in the states. The traditional recipes have been adapted to today's ingredients and methods of preparation where the original recipes can no longer be used.

During my travels around the country doing research for this book, I became enamored with the rich treasures of American art that focus on food-related subjects. Therefore, to illustrate the book I have chosen paintings by contemporary and historical American artists that illustrate events related to our food history.

I hope readers will enjoy this book as much as I did in putting it together. When I am preparing and eating a meal where I know the history of the foods and ingredients, the food is more enjoyable. In a way it adds another "course" to the meal. I hope the reader will experience the same benefit.

I want to thank the departments of agriculture of the 50 states for their help and cooperation in providing information about their foods. I also want to express my appreciation to Ross Howell, my publisher, for his patience and assistance in the long process of preparing the final manuscript, and to Kathleen Valenzi, who helped edit the final work. And last but, by no means least, I want to express my gratitude to my husband, Allan, for his help, encouragement, and continuous support of this project.

I also want to express my deep appreciation to the museums, art galleries, and artists listed below.

Hilde Gabriel Lee

HOPI BLUE CORN HARVEST *by Ray Swanson, oil, 30 x 44 inches, courtesy of Miner's Gallery Americana, Carmel, California.*

MUSEUMS:
Anglo-American Art Museum
University of Arizona Museum of Art
The Chrysler Museum
Gilcrease Museum
The Mariners' Museum
P. Buckley Moss Museum
National Gallery of Art
Abby Aldrich Rockefeller Folk Art Center
The Rockwell Museum
Timken Museum of Art

GALLERIES:
Babcock Galleries
Nicky Boehme Gallery
Hastings Art, Ltd.
Kertesz Fine Art Galleries

Legacy Galleries
Midtown Payson Galleries
Miner's Gallery Americana, Inc.
Mongerson Wunderlich Galleries, Ltd.
Montgomery Gallery
Thomas Nygard, Inc.
Peregrine Galleries
Michael Rosenfeld Gallery
The Laura Russo Gallery, Inc.
George Stern, Fine Arts
Taggart & Jorgensen Gallery
Virginia Arts
Richard York Gallery

ARTISTS:
Virginia Paul
Mary Ann Vessey

SCHOONER SAILING, VINALHAVEN ISLE, MAINE by Nicky Boehme, oil, 22 x 30 inches, courtesy of Nicky Boehme Gallery, Mendocino, California.

Designed by Marilyn F. Appleby.

Edited by Melissa E. Barranco, Claudia J. Garthwait, Ross A.
Howell, Jr., and Kathleen D. Valenzi.

The publisher gratefully acknowledges the museums, galleries,
and artists for permission to print their work in this book.

Printed in Hong Kong.

Published by Howell Press, Inc., 1147 River Road, Bay 2,
Charlottesville, VA 22901, telephone 804-977-4006.

Library of Congress Cataloging in Publication Data

Lee, Hilde Gabriel
Taste of the states: a food history of America / Hilde Gabriel Lee.
p. cm.
Includes bibliographical references and index
ISBN 0-943231-56-6

1. Cookery, American. 2. Cookery—United States.
3. United States—History.
I. Title. II. Title: A food history of America.

TX715.L5 1992   641.5973
QB192-10612

First printing

HOWELL PRESS

(Above and cover) *THE SCYTHERS by N.C. Wyeth, oil, 37 ½ x
26 ¾ inches, courtesy of The University of Arizona Museum of Art,
Tucson, Arizona, gift of Mr. and Mrs. Samuel L. Kingan.*

TASTE OF THE STATES

NEW ENGLAND

DURING MUCH of the sixteenth century, European fishermen, explorers, and fur traders plied the seas off the northeast coast of America. They feared the treacherous rocks along the coast, the fierce-looking natives, and most of all, the biting cold and blizzards of winter. Before 1620 the only settlements were temporary shore camps of European fishermen.

In 1620 the first permanent settlers, the Pilgrims, came to this area seeking religious freedom. They were followed in the late 1620s by several groups of Puritans, who also sought freedom from religious persecution. For many decades these people in the area, which became known as New England, were held together by a religious bond and common English heritage. Eventually splinter religious groups left the core and founded their own settlements. Other European immigrants, seeking a better life, also settled in New England.

The name New England was given to the region by John Smith, who explored and mapped its coast in 1614. Traditionally, it encompasses the six states of Massachusetts, Maine, Rhode Island, Connecticut, New Hampshire, and Vermont. Except for Vermont, five of the six New England states face the food-abundant sea.

Unfortunately, the original New Englanders, the Pilgrims and Puritans, were mainly tradesmen, artisans, and landowners, who knew nothing about fishing. However, a great variety of seafood was so abundant along the shore that they could fish with their bare hands. The settlers built wooden frames for drying fish, particularly cod, and found a market for the dried fish among New Englanders, as well as in England and Spain.

As the settlers moved inland, they began to farm the land, adopting the communal style of farming that was practiced in England. Each family was assigned a garden plot in the community garden, and their livestock was collected daily by a common herdsman and taken to pasture. Houses, stables, and gardens were clustered close together for protection. As the herds of livestock increased and needed more pasture, the farmers moved further inland and established individual farms. By 1629 the settlers had imported apple seedlings and established orchards.

The first colonists, the Pilgrims at Plymouth, Massachusetts, were amazed to find the Indians growing a wide variety of beans. The Indians taught the colonists how to bake beans in pots in the earth, how to cook them green in the summer, and how to dry them for winter storage. They also taught the settlers that beans and corn (known by the English as maize) have an affinity for each other and could be cooked together. The settlers called the dish "succotash," a variation of the original Indian name, *msickquatash*.

After living in Plymouth for a year, the Pilgrims had a celebration of Thanksgiving to thank God and their Indian friends for their survival in the new land. The meal featured an abundance of food—venison and turkey, oysters and eels, nuts, fruits, and vegetables—and was shared with Chief Massasoit and his Wampanoag tribe. The Indians contributed much of the food and its preparation, while the Pilgrim women prepared some of their English dishes with native American ingredients. This was one of the first meldings of native and English food traditions.

Game was plentiful but difficult for the early settlers to obtain, since few knew how to shoot a gun. In England hunting was a sport for the wealthy. The settlers soon learned, however, and the white-tailed deer and wild turkeys became their principal meat supply. As these types of wild game meat became scarce, the settlers also hunted birds.

After the Pilgrims had passed through a few hard winters, they learned the pattern of the seasons and what the soil and sea would yield in each. They sowed and harvested corn, domesticated the wild turkey, and found cod, mackerel, lobster, and crabs plentiful along the shore and in the ocean. They raised apples and pears, hybridized the wild grapes, and made use of the native cranberry. Dairy and beef cattle that they imported from Europe soon provided meat, milk, and cheese.

As New England developed the settlers cut trees and built trading vessels, which brought back exotic ingredients for their cooking. Teas and spices arrived from China; wines, brandy, and raisins were imported from the Mediterranean; and molasses, the staple of New England cooking, came from the West Indies.

Since winters were harsh in New England, the colonists spent time in the summer preserving and storing food for the long winter. Surplus meat was stored in the salt barrel, and salt pork, salt cod, and corned beef became the center of colonial New England meals. Some pork was also smoked. The settlers preserved fruits, as well as meats. These were used in pies, which became staples during long winter months.

Most farms had an icehouse where perishable foods were stored in the summer. Ice was cut from a pond by hand during the winter and stored in the ice house covered with straw.

The dour beliefs of the Puritans,

who settled the Boston area in 1628-30, were reflected in their cooking. The Puritans disdained the "French trickery" of rich sauces. Most of their food was roasted, boiled, or stewed, a tradition of New England cooking that exists today. Many of the traditional recipes used in New England originally came from England or were adaptations of Indian foods.

The kitchen hearth was the heart of the early New England home. During the day meals were cooked in the six to ten-foot fireplace, and at night the family gathered around it for warmth. After the ashes were raked up and the fire was banked, the warmth of the fireplace kept any pots of leftovers hot for breakfast. In the morning the fire was rekindled before sunup, and breakfast was started. The warmth of the hearth helped raise bread dough in a big wooden trough placed in front of it. A crane suspended in the fireplace held large pots for stews or soups.

Once or twice a week, the brick oven at the side of the fireplace was used for dishes that required slow cooking or baking, such as baked beans, Indian puddings, pies, breads, and cakes. Brick ovens in colonial New England were rated as to their pie-baking capacity, typically from 10-pie ovens to 20-pie ovens.

Baking bread in the oven required making yeast to raise the bread, either from hops and potatoes or from the dregs of the empty beer kegs. *Ryaninjun* was the standard bread for brick-oven baking. No pans were used, and the dome-shaped loaves were baked on the oven floor. The dough was made of equal parts of rye flour and cornmeal mixed with milk, sweetened with stewed pumpkin, and raised with homemade yeast. Corn bread was baked in a Dutch oven or skillet in the fireplace.

White flour was scarce in colonial New England and was used only for the finest pastries. If wheat was available, the farmer took it to the local gristmill to be ground. These mills also ground white corn into a fine meal that was almost as white as wheat flour.

Three hundred years ago, New England housewives often baked cakes in large batches, enough to last for three to four months. Sometimes yeast was used in cake batters, but more frequently the cook laboriously beat air into the batter to produce a light cake. (Baking powder was not invented until the 1800s.) Colonial cooks had no way of testing the oven's temperature except by hand. If the heat scorched the hand, then the oven was too hot for the cake.

New England women made pound cakes using two old English recipes called *Simnel* and Nun's Cake. *Simnel* was made with raisins, currants, and citron while Nun's Cake used spices, such as caraway seeds and cinnamon. The settlers served pound cake with tea and often offered this treat to important guests, like the minister. Fruitcakes were made with molasses, spices, raisins, figs, and other dried fruits. After baking, the cakes were wrapped in homespun and stored in stone crocks or boxes, because these rich fruit cakes grew more palatable as they aged.

Pies with a suet pastry crust encased both fruit and meat fillings and became a New England specialty. They were eaten at almost every meal, including breakfast. It was not unusual for the housewife to bake enough pies for a week at one time and store them in a pie chest or a cold storage room. In the winter she placed the baked pies in the snow to freeze. They were then thawed in front of the fireplace and warmed for each meal as needed.

One of the standard desserts was apple pie, prepared in many different ways—with thin sliced apples, with applesauce, or with dried apple slices or rings. The most popular spices in apple pies were cinnamon and nutmeg. Cran-

berries, or other berries, added tartness when imported lemons were not available. Fresh wild-blueberry pie also became a favorite in New England, particularly in Maine.

Many New Englanders considered mincemeat pie, whose origin goes back to Europe, to be the king of dessert pies. The pioneer women made mincemeat with tiny pieces of beef and suet to which raisins, chopped apples, candied fruit, and spices were added. They moistened the mincemeat with brandy or hard cider, which acted as a preservative. The mincemeat was then stored in a stone crock until it was aged and ready for use.

New England meals often included meat pies. Beef steak and kidney pie was an old English favorite and remained so with New Englanders. *Tourtière*, the famous French-Canadian pork pie made with ground pork, also became well known in New England and was often eaten cold. When going to a church supper, New Englanders usually took a chicken pot pie with either a biscuit or pastry topping.

The early settlers rarely ate fresh meat in the summer but preserved and stored it for winter meals. Salt, smoke, and snow or ice were the most common meat preservatives in New England. Brine from the pork barrel, smoke from corncob fires, and the icy chill of winter cold rooms preserved meats for a variety of dishes. Hog killing, or "pigsticking" as it was called, became an annual affair and resulted in the smoking of hams and bacon and the making of sausage. Beef was salted, corned, or frozen. A protected place such as the cold room next to the kitchen was used to freeze the meat.

"Come for pudding time," in colonial New England meant, "Come in time for dinner." Pies, cakes, and fruits were served at the end of the meal, but fragrant, steaming puddings preceded the main dish. To serve the pudding first was an English custom, which continued well into the nineteenth century. The first Thanksgiving, for example, started with a huge baked Indian whortleberry pudding. The early settlers called their puddings "grunts," "slumps," and "flummeries." Puddings even entered the political arena in the late 1700s. The Federalists, like their colonial ancestors, ate their puddings first, while the more-progressive Democrats preferred to begin their dinners with meat.

Modern New England cooking comprises a mixture of ethnic heritages. Scots and Welsh settled in Maine, New Hampshire, and Vermont, and their descendents still bake scones, oatmeal bread, and grow leeks in their gardens. The French who moved down from Canada contributed split pea soup, as well as various forms of pork pies to New England cuisine. They also brought with them recipes for their native *cassoulet,* which they modified in New England by using the region's traditional baked-bean recipes and adding bay leaves, thyme, and sausages. Germans, who settled in Massachusetts and Maine more than four generations ago, have been making their own kind of sausage and sauerkraut ever since. The Portuguese, who settled along the Massachusetts and Rhode Island coasts, brought new fish recipes and kale soup to New England cookery, while the Italians contributed pasta and broccoli.

New England produced the first genuine American cookbook, *American Cookery.* It was written by a New England cook, Amelia Simmons, and published by a Connecticut printer in 1796. The book detailed for the first time the methods of cooking squash, corn, pumpkins, and other American produce. Recipes for Indian Pudding and Johnnycake were also included, and later editions contained recipes for Election

MINCEMEAT PIE

New England is famous for its pies. Food historians have noted that New Englanders not only make the best pies in the country but also the greatest variety of pies.

Shortly after the Puritans settled Boston, they banned Christmas mincemeat pie. The pie was baked in a dish that had come to symbolize the Christ Child's manger, and the spices used in the pie had come to represent the gifts of the Wise Men. The Puritans considered these symbols to be sacrilegious and passed laws not only outlawing the pie but also all Christmas celebrations. Years later mincemeat pie staged a comeback in the common round pie plate.

Early New Englanders made their own mincemeat, while today mincemeat is available already prepared. This mincemeat pie filling contains additional spices and candied fruit.

Serves 8

Filling

1 jar (29 ounces) mincemeat

1 Pippin apple, peeled and shredded

3 tablespoons diced candied citron

3 tablespoons diced candied orange peel

3 tablespoons diced candied fruit cake mix

1/2 teaspoon nutmeg

1/2 teaspoon cinnamon

1/2 teaspoon coriander

3 tablespoons orange juice

1 tablespoon lemon juice

3 tablespoons brandy

2 tablespoons dry sherry

■

Combine all of the filling ingredients in a bowl and cover tightly with plastic wrap. Let macerate for 24 hours to meld flavors.

Pastry

2 cups all-purpose flour

5 tablespoons butter or margarine

4 tablespoons solid vegetable shortening

4 to 5 tablespoons ice water

■

Place the flour in a bowl. Cut in the butter and shortening until the flour mixture has the texture of coarse crumbs. Add the water, a tablespoon at a time, and mix with a fork until the dough can be formed into a ball. Wrap dough in plastic wrap and chill for at least 1 hour.

Roll out half the dough and fit it into a 9-inch pie plate. Add the mincemeat filling. Roll out the remaining pastry and cut it into 10 strips. Place the strips on top of the filling in a lattice pattern. Bake in a preheated 425° F. oven for 35 to 40 minutes or until the crust is brown and the filling is bubbly.

Cake and Federal Cake.

New England, being one of the first regions to be settled in America, has contributed many dishes to our cuisine. Recipes for New England cooking traveled with settlers from New England to the "new" regions of the Great Lakes and the Midwest. Boiled dinners, stews, baked beans, brown bread, pies, and Indian Pudding remain New England's enduring contributions to American cuisine.

11

CONNECTICUT

IN THE EARLY 1630s both the English of the Massachusetts Bay Colony and the Dutch of the New Amsterdam Colony eyed the wide, fertile Connecticut Valley as a possibility for settlement, agriculture, and fur trading. In June 1633 the Hollanders built a fort at what was to become Hartford. In the fall of 1634, John Oldham and ten others left Watertown in the Massachusetts Colony to establish a permanent settlement at Wethersfield, south of Hartford.

Members of the John Oldham group became the first Europeans to plant seeds in the soil of Connecticut. They sowed rye in a fallow Indian field. The next year several more groups came from Massachusetts and brought cattle and hogs. The harsh winters, however, drove most of these early settlers back to their Massachusetts homes. By the end of the 1630s, those who remained had created productive farms, started the mercantile town of New Haven, and established an independent government.

The early Dutch settlers in the Hartford area did likewise. They planted apple orchards, appointed a committee to select superior calves for breeding stock, and developed a dairy industry. By the 1640s the efforts of both the English and Dutch settlers had made the new territory of Connecticut virtually self-sufficient.

In the 1700s as towns were established, Connecticut became urbanized, and manufacturing became its heartbeat. During the Revolutionary War Connecticut iron foundries forged the cannons for the Continental Army. Following the war, its metalsmiths and clockmakers sent their wares with Yankee peddlers to the frontier.

As the population of Connecticut increased, so did farming. The variety of crops expanded to include many vegetables, as well as berries and tree fruits.

In the early 1800s the demand for fresh vegetables in Boston and New York helped create a market-garden farm industry. To extend their growing season in the spring and fall, Connecticut farmers built glass greenhouses. They were among the first American farmers to do so. Farmers placed fermenting horse manure under their greenhouses to augment the heating from sunlight. This enabled the farmers to raise radishes, lettuce, cucumbers, and even melons out of season. The early Connecticut farmers also dug underground pits where they stored cabbages, squash, potatoes, and other root vegetables for winter and spring selling.

Fishing has always been an important part of the Connecticut economy. Shad fishing along the Connecticut River, in particular, has been a tradition since colonial times. The Narragansett Indians knew that when the Juneberry bloomed in clusters of white flowers, shad would be coming up the river to spawn. When the English first settled in the Connecticut River Valley, the numerous shad were despised as food. Eating shad meant that a person was almost destitute or had exhausted his supply of salt pork. In 1743 an enterprising man named Ebenezer Hunt praised the virtues of shad and succeeded in making it popular.

When George Washington and his troops occupied the North River in 1776 and established a rather precarious position in White Plains, New York, the army subsisted on thousands of barrels of shad. Packing shad for the troops became a wartime industry in Connecticut and lasted through the following four seasons of shad runs.

Shad, like salmon, hatch in fresh water but live in the sea, returning to their birthplace to spawn. At one time all the rivers along the East Coast were clogged each spring with shad fighting their way upstream. Dams and pollution took their toll, and by 1900 shad runs in Connecticut had become almost a memory. Fortunately, efforts to clean the rivers, shifts in the economy, and the construction of fish ladders have brought shad back into the rivers of Connecticut and New England in recent years. Shad runs on the Connecticut River and its tributaries are so heavy now that a ton of shad is taken by fishermen each day in May!

In Essex, Connecticut, the first Saturday in June has been the traditional Shad Bake Day for generations. Nearby Windsor, Connecticut, also has an annual shad festival. Men of the local civic clubs prepare the fish by pinning the fillets to hardwood planks tilted toward an open fire. The wives make potato salad and apple pie for the traditional shad feast.

Also interested in fishing were Portuguese settlers who came mainly from the Azores and settled in the coastal towns of Connecticut. They adapted their cooking to the ingredients of the new land. Accustomed to white bread but finding white flour scarce, they used white cornmeal for most of their bread baking. Portuguese communities in Connecticut observe the Sunday before Labor Day as the traditional Feast of the Holy Ghost with Portuguese specialties such as marrowbone soup, dried codfish in a spicy sauce, and sweet breads.

Lobster rolls, said to have been invented at Palisades Park in New Haven, are probably the height of

BREAD AND FRUIT by Luigi Lucioni, oil, 14 x 18 ¹/2 inches, courtesy of Richard York Gallery, New York, New York.

elegance in fast food. They consist of a toasted frankfurter roll filled with cooked, chopped lobster meat that has been mixed with chopped celery, chopped onions, lemon juice, and mayonnaise and topped with shredded lettuce. Lobster rolls are served with a side order of onion rings.

The hamburger, the most popular sandwich in America, was born in 1900 at Louis' Lunch, a small lunch wagon in New Haven. It seems that the establish-ment was known for its steak sandwiches. The owner always took the steak trim-mings home and ground them up for patties to be eaten by his family. As the business grew so did the trimmings. The logical solution was to sell the by-product at the lunch wagon. Louis broiled the hamburger patties and served them on a plate with a slice of onion and some home-fries, creating a hamburger plate. Unfortunately, this took more time to eat than his regular steak sandwiches. One of his customers solved the problem one day when he said, "Put that patty between two slices of bread, and let me get out of here."

Like other coastal states in New England, most Connecticut food contin-ues to be heavily oriented toward prod-ucts of the sea. Nevertheless, the state still retains its agricultural heritage through its apple orchards, dairies, and poultry farms, although much of the rich diversity of years past has disappeared.

MAINE

EUROPEAN FISHERMEN discovered the fishing grounds off the coast of Maine almost 50 years before permanent settlers arrived in New England. These fishermen came mainly from France, Spain, Portugal, and later, England. They sought out the protected inlets along the rocky Maine coast and established temporary settlements during fishing season. These fishermen stayed only long enough to cure their fish and repair their oft-battered boats before the long voyage back to Europe. The native Indians of Maine, the Penobscots, resented the intrusion of the white man into their fishing grounds and frequently raided and destroyed these early fishing stations.

Permanent English settlers began to arrive in Maine in the mid-1620s. They regarded the European fishermen as a rough and rowdy lot and exploiters of Maine fishing grounds. The settlers complained to King Charles I of England, who issued restrictions against the foreign fishermen. As a result the fishermen moved their activities to the offshore islands.

By 1630 the settlers had established their own permanent fishing stations along the coast of Maine, and until the mid-1700s cod fishing was their principal industry. Maine fishing spawned shipbuilding, which also became a vital industry, contributing not only to fishing but also to world trade.

Periodic British blockades of the Maine coast during the Revolutionary War and through the War of 1812 brought chaos to Maine's fishing industry. The Treaty of Ghent, signed in December of 1814, finally stopped the blockades. By 1818 both deep-sea and inshore commercial fishing were rapidly expanding along the Maine coast.

As the popularity of cod declined in the mid-1800s, mackerel became more important. Large catches of herring soon followed, which required the establishment of smokehouses. Preserving fish by smoking was an Old World method, and herring lent itself particularly well to the process. Maine's smoked-herring business continued to expand until the 1880s, when canning supplanted smoking as the primary method of preserving fish.

The development of the canning industry in 1873 expanded the market for Maine fish. The Maine canned-sardine industry had its beginnings as a result of the Franco-Prussian War of 1870, when French oil-fried sardines became difficult to obtain. The Maine sardine proved to be a very suitable substitute for the French one.

Great schools of silvery sardines along the Maine coast were first harvested by the American Indians, who captured them with brushwood traps or weirs in shallow waters. Early Maine commercial fishermen continued to use the same technique. Today, with modern technology, Maine fisherman harvest sardines

BAKED BRIE WITH LOBSTER

Traditional Maine lobster is the main ingredient of a salad that is served on top of a warmed wheel of Brie. The combination makes an elegant and unique hors d'oeuvre or first course.

Serves 8 to 10 as hors d'oeuvres or 4 as a first course

1 1/2 cups cooked lobster meat, cut into bite-size cubes

2 scallions, finely chopped

1/2 teaspoon celery seeds

1/4 teaspoon white pepper

1/2 cup mayonnaise

1 small wheel of Brie (weighing about 14 ounces) at room temperature

Lettuce leaves, for garnish

■

Combine the lobster meat, scallions, celery seeds, pepper, and mayonnaise in a bowl. Refrigerate until ready to serve.

Just before serving, place the Brie on a non-stick baking sheet and top with the lobster salad. Bake in a preheated 350° F. oven for 3 minutes or until the salad is lukewarm and the cheese begins to soften.

Serve on lettuce leaves. Cut the cheese into wedges and serve as an hors d'oeuvres with crackers or as a first course with slices of French bread.

in deep water with large sea-going boats, depth recorders, and sounding devices.

Haddock has traditionally been another prime commercial fish of Maine, and today the demand exceeds the supply. With the shortage of haddock, Maine fishermen are promoting hake and cusk. Both are plentiful and have many of the same properties as haddock. Corned hake, boiled potatoes, butter gravy, and buttered beets have become a Maine specialty.

Lobster

When we think of Maine, we immediately think of lobster. These ungainly nocturnal creatures live on the rocky bottom of the cold Maine bays where there is abundant kelp for shelter and natural food.

Lobster was a favorite food of the coastal Indians. These Native Americans also used lobster for fertilizer and fashioned pipes from the larger claws. When the first European settlers arrived, lobsters weighing five to six pounds were the norm and some reached 25 pounds. The Penobscots taught the settlers how to steam lobsters and other shellfish in a variation of the cooking method we know today as a "clambake."

The method was simple. Stones were heated with wood fires, and when the stones became hot enough, the Penobscots covered them with wet seaweed. They put lobsters and clams on the seaweed and covered them with another layer of seaweed. Steam from the seaweed cooked the lobsters and clams. Often corn was added to this steaming seafood.

Commercial lobster fishing began in

LOBSTER SEASON by Nicky Boehme, oil, 18 x 27 inches, courtesy of Nicky Boehme Gallery, Mendocino, California.

the late 1800s, when canneries were built to process the daily lobster catches. Before then lobsters were so plentiful that they could be picked up by hand along the shore at low tide. After a particularly bad storm, lobsters might be found piled two feet high on the beaches. Before they became a national delicacy, lobsters were so plentiful that Mainers served them at almost every meal.

Lobsters are caught today by the same type of traps or "pots" as were used 100 years ago. These wooden or mesh boxes are baited with fish or fish heads and attached with a nylon rope to brightly painted buoys bearing the distinctive markings of each individual fisherman. Large fishing operations may have as many as 100 traps strung together.

Lobstermen (or women, as nine percent of Maine's lobster fishermen are

women) are independent operators who own their boats and gear. Each lobsterman has his or her own state-designated fishing territory off the coast of Maine, which extends 30 to 40 miles into the Atlantic Ocean. Encroachment on another's territory is punishable by law.

A typical lobster boat measures about 35 feet long and has a crew of two. Trips usually last for two to three days, during which, with the aid of hydraulic winches, lobstermen can haul in and re-bait about 500 traps. After harvesting the traps, the lobstermen take their catches to the Portland Fish Auction. There they are sold, wrapped in seaweed, and transported by air to distribution points around the country. A lobster can live in a bed of seaweed for approximately 18 hours; then, when put into a tank, it can survive for up to two weeks.

THE HERRING DIPPER by Philip Little, oil, 50 x 40 inches, courtesy of The Mariners' Museum, Newport News, Virginia.

Other Maine Shellfish

In addition to deep-sea fish and lobster, Maine is noted for its mussels, producing 60 percent of the mussels consumed in the United States. Mussel farmers gather seed (eggs) from crowded tidal beds and spread the seeds out thinly on areas of the sea floor leased from the state. After one or two growing seasons, the mussels are harvested with a special drag towed behind a boat. This "bottom-culture" fish farming was developed in Holland and is also used to grow clams and oysters.

Some Maine mussel farmers grow mussels on ropes suspended from floating rafts. Although this technique is more labor-intensive than bottom-culture, it yields mussels free of grit and pearls.

Maine sea urchins, whose salmon-colored roe is eaten raw from the shell as an appetizer, have become a chic food in some New England restaurants. The roe is the only part of the sea urchin that is eaten. It is also used in pasta sauces and is featured as a delicacy in sushi bars. Sea-urchin roe is exported in large quantities to Japan, where it has become very popular.

Most of Maine's fish and shellfish are sold at the Portland Fish Auction. The auction is held daily in a tempera-ture-controlled warehouse, where fishermen place their iced catches in brightly colored cartons. Usually one fish from each carton is displayed on top to indicate its species and quality. The auction takes less than an hour, and then the fish are immediately transported by refrigerated trucks or planes to domestic markets and overseas.

Maine Specialties

While the early settlers focused initially on harvesting the plentiful seafood off Maine's rocky shores, they also extracted necessary food crops from the rocky soil. Potatoes became an important crop in the 1800s, and Maine led the nation in potato production into the 1950s. A small, uniformly sized (about two inches) gourmet baking potato, called "Baby Maine," is now being grown.

Ninety-eight percent of the "wild" blueberries used in the United States are grown in Washington and Hancock Counties in eastern Maine. These small, very flavorful berries, also known as "lowbush" blueberries, have grown wild for centuries. Today, they are grown in controlled areas, known as "blueberry barrens," on a two-year cycle. Half of the estimated 50,000 acres under cultiva-tion is harvested each year, while the other half is mowed or burned-over to encourage growth in the following year. Lowbush blueberries cannot be mechani-cally harvested and are therefore picked with hand-held rakes that comb the berries from the bushes. Micmac Indians from Nova Scotia assist local residents each harvest season in picking about 20 million pounds of blueberries.

Lowbush berries are sold to bakeries for fresh muffins and to large food processors for muffin and pancake mixes. Surveys have indicated that consumers prefer these items with little dots of blue instead of big ones from cultivated blueberries.

Maine also grows the highbush, or cultivated variety of blueberries, which can be mechanically harvested several times during the growing season. Most of these are marketed as fresh-packed blueberries. Recently, new blueberry products, such as freeze-dried blueberry raisins, have been developed to make use of the cultivated blueberries.

The young tender unfurled fronds of the fiddlehead fern are a specialty of Maine. The Indians taught the early settlers how to gather them in the forests in the spring and how to cook them. Indian women hunted for the first green shoots to peek through the ground. Whole villages have been known to participate in fiddlehead hunts. Today, fiddleheads are sold fresh and frozen, as well as canned. Their flavor is a combination of asparagus, broccoli, and artichokes. They can be served hot with a hollandaise sauce or cold with a vinaigrette. They are now also being used in soups, quiches, and stir-frys.

Maine Beans

The early settlers of Maine learned to plant and cook beans from the Indians. The Jacob's Cattle, Yellow Eye, and Soldier varieties of dried beans have been well known in Maine since colonial times. Agricultural experts claim that the cool climate and rocky soil give these beans a particularly fine flavor.

The Indians taught the settlers how to cook beans in a pit in the ground called a "bean hole." A fire was started in the pit, and when it burned down, the coals were removed. A pot of beans was put into the pit, and the coals were piled back on top. Then earth was shoveled

BLUEBERRY TART

Although blueberries still grow wild in Maine, this tart is best when made with the larger, cultivated variety. Fresh and baked blueberries are combined in a moist tart, which may be topped with whipped cream, if desired.

Serves 8

6 cups blueberries

1 cup plus 1 $1/2$ tablespoons all-purpose flour

$1/4$ cup plus 2 tablespoons sugar

$1/2$ cup margarine

1 tablespoon white wine vinegar

3 tablespoons ice water

$1/8$ teaspoon cinnamon

■

Rinse the blueberries and let them drain.

Combine the 1 cup of flour and the 2 tablespoons of sugar in a bowl. Cut in the margarine until crumbly. Sprinkle the mixture with the vinegar and mix with a fork. Add 1 tablespoon of ice water at a time until a dough is formed and can be shaped into a ball. (1 or 2 more tablespoons of ice water may be needed.) Press the dough into the bottom and 1 inch up the sides of a 9-inch, ungreased springform pan.

Add 4 cups of the blueberries to the dough-lined pan. Combine the 1 $1/2$ tablespoons of flour, the $1/4$ cup of sugar, and the cinnamon, and sprinkle evenly over the top of the blueberries. Bake in a preheated 400° F. oven for 50 minutes. Remove from the oven and immediately cover the filling with the remaining 2 cups of fresh blueberries. Cool the tart on a wire rack. Remove the springform rim and serve.

over the pit, and the beans were left to cook slowly for a day and a night. Later, cooks in lumber camps used this method. Old-timers still insist that the bean-hole method of cooking beans is far superior to oven-baking.

Bean porridge was often served in early nineteenth-century farmhouses. It consisted of dried beans stewed with salt pork and corn. In the winter, after the mixture was cooked, it was set outdoors in bowls until frozen, then slipped from the molds and hung by string loops from the rafters of the kitchen shed. Slices were sawed off and reheated as needed. Bean porridge was considered best when slightly aged.

The heritage of Maine food stems from its people, as well as its natural resources. While the majority of Maine's early settlers were English and French-Canadian, German colonists settled in Maine about 30 years before the Revolutionary War and greatly influenced "Down East" cooking. Even now in the fall and winter months, fresh sauerkraut from Waldoboro can be found in the local markets.

While Maine's blueberries, potatoes, and other agricultural crops continue to be important, the true "taste of Maine" will always come from the sea.

MASSACHUSETTS

CONTRARY TO what the fish markets and restaurants would have us believe, there is no such fish as scrod. The name "scrod" was invented in the nineteenth century by the maitre d' hôtel of the Parker House in Boston to assure his clientele that they were eating the freshest fish possible.

At that time fishing vessels spent up to ten days at the Great Banks off the coasts of Maine and Massachusetts. The first day's catch was gutted and iced down in the bottom of the boat. Subsequent days' catches were put on top until the vessel was full. The ship then sped to the Boston Fish Pier, where the catch was auctioned.

The Parker House chef insisted on buying only the freshest fish from the top layer. Since the maitre d' had to get his menus printed a day in advance, and since he could not predict what fish would be on top, he coined the word "scrod." Today, scrod has come to mean a small fish of the cod family—cod, haddock, hake, or pollock—weighing one and a half to two and a half pounds.

In spite of the publicity scrod has received over the years, it is the Atlantic cod that is recognized as the symbol of the Commonwealth's natural heritage. This species of fish is so entwined in the early history of Massachusetts that a wooden replica of the cod, referred to as the "Sacred Cod," hangs in the statehouse. Cape Cod received its name in 1602 from English explorer Bartholomew Gosnold because of the great abundance of cod in the waters surrounding the peninsula. Starting with the first settlers, cod-fishing has been the mainstay of the Massachusetts economy for almost 300 years.

The port of Boston, which was founded in 1630 by the Puritans, soon became famous world-wide as a commercial fishing center. Boston fishermen ventured further and further from shore and began to harvest a wider variety of fish, bringing back haddock, halibut, and mackerel, as well as cod. Some of the fish were eaten fresh, but most were preserved by salting and drying or smoking. In 1640 the Pilgrim colonists exported more than 300,000 dried codfish, mostly to England.

The colonists found their fish trade limited by restrictive English laws. In 1677 Massachusetts sent King Charles II a handsome gift of ten barrels of cranberries, two barrels of cornmeal mush, and 3,000 dried codfish. Along with this gift was sent the request that His Majesty's Massachusetts subjects be represented in Parliament and that there be relief from the restrictive trade laws. These requests were not granted, but the king did give the colonists permission to sell dried cod in the Mediterranean and Caribbean, as well as to the southern colonies.

Cod was sent to the Mediterranean countries, where the fish had long been savored. Once empty of fish, the ships brought back citrus and other fruits grown on the shores of the Mediterranean. Ships with cod sent to the Caribbean brought back molasses for the New England rum distilleries. The rum was sent to Africa and traded for slaves, which, in turn, were sold in the South or in the West Indies for more molasses. Over time, cod made many New Englanders so rich that they became known as the "codfish aristocracy."

At home the thrifty New Englanders found dozens of uses for cod, either fresh

or dried and salted. They used cod to make fish cakes, chowder, boiled dinners, and fish hash. The hash was served at breakfast with oatmeal, eggs, hot bread, and sometimes fried ham. In the 1700s a typical Sunday breakfast in Boston consisted of codfish cakes or creamed codfish, baked beans, and brown bread.

Cape Cod Turkey was the name

THE CRANBERRY HARVEST, ISLAND OF NANTUCKET by Eastman Johnson, oil, 27 1/2 x 54 5/8 inches, courtesy of Putman Foundation, Timken Museum of Art, San Diego, California.

given to a dish consisting of a large, freshly caught codfish baked with bits of pork, served with an egg sauce, and accompanied by boiled potatoes and beets cooked with melted butter. Sailing-ship captains brought back recipes for *Kedgeree,* an East Indian dish that combined salt cod with rice, hard-cooked eggs, and parsley in a cream sauce.

Baked Beans and Chowders

Perhaps the most famous Massachusetts food tradition is the cooking of baked beans on Saturday night. This typical Saturday night supper originated in Puritan Boston. The Sabbath started at sundown Saturday, and according to Puritan belief, no work was to be done until sundown Sunday. Therefore, the bean pot was put in the low heat of the fireplace oven on Saturday morning so that the beans would be ready by suppertime. The slowly baking pot gave off fragrant aromas of onions, salt pork, and molasses all day. The leftovers from supper were kept warm in the fireplace and served for Sunday breakfast.

BAKED BEANS

This old-fashioned method of preparing baked beans is similar to one used by the early settlers of New England. The molasses keeps the beans from becoming too soft during the slow cooking process.

Serves 6

2 1/3 cups (1 pound) navy beans

7 cups water

1 medium onion, halved, and 1 large
   onion, thinly sliced

1/3 cup molasses

1/4 cup dark brown sugar

1 teaspoon dry mustard

3/4 teaspoon ground ginger

1/4 pound lean salt pork, cut into 4 pieces

3 tablespoons light brown sugar

■

Rinse and pick over the beans. Place them in a bowl, add the water, and soak overnight.

The next day drain the beans, reserving the liquid, and place them in a Dutch oven. Add enough water to the reserved liquid to measure 7 1/3 cups. Pour the liquid over the beans and add the halved onion. Bring to a boil over medium-high heat and skim off the white foam. Cover and simmer for 20 to 25 minutes or until the beans are barely tender. After discarding the onion, drain the beans and reserve the liquid.

Combine 1 1/2 cups of the liquid with the molasses, brown sugar, mustard, and ginger in a large bowl. Add the beans, gently stirring to coat them with the liquid.

Place half of the sliced onions in the bottom of a 2-quart casserole and add half of the bean mixture. Cover the beans with the remaining sliced onions and top with the remaining beans. Score the rind of the pork pieces and push them into the beans, rind side down. Add a sufficient amount of the reserved liquid to cover the beans by 1/2 inch. Cover the casserole with aluminum foil and then with the lid. Bake in a preheated 300° F. oven for 1 1/4 hours. Remove the casserole from the oven and discard the aluminum foil. If there is no liquid covering the beans, add some of the reserved liquid. Continue baking the beans, covered, for another 3 1/2 hours, occasionally adding more liquid if necessary to just keep the beans covered.

Remove the lid and sprinkle the top of the beans with the light brown sugar. Bake them uncovered for 45 minutes more so that a thin crust forms on top of the beans.

When the recipe for baked beans was first developed, maple sugar or syrup was used as a sweetener. After trade developed with the West Indies, less-expensive molasses was added to the beans. Many preferred maple sugar, however, because too much molasses tended to make the beans tough.

Eventually other foods were added to the Saturday night suppers. A moist, dark-brown bread of cornmeal, rye flour, molasses, buttermilk, and raisins was steamed in cylindrical molds and served with the baked beans. Coleslaw, pickles, and applesauce were also traditional accompaniments. Indian Pudding, which shared the fireplace oven with the beans in the last hours of baking, was also served on Saturday night. This pudding was made with milk, molasses, and, when they could be obtained, cinnamon and nutmeg. For special occasions an egg was added, as well as raisins and diced apples. Before serving, Indian Pudding was topped with cream.

Chowder is another food attributed to Massachusetts. The word probably comes from the French *"chaudière,"* meaning iron pot. This type of soup was introduced to Massachusetts by the Channel Islanders, natives of Guernsey and Jersey, who settled along the north shore of Massachusetts more than 300 years ago. They had traditionally combined food from the sea with milk from their cows in an iron cooking pot. Other settlers, after tasting this combination, soon concocted chowders with whatever ingredients they had on hand—seafood, chicken, beef, corn, potatoes, and even eggs. Corn in the consistency of a thin gruel also became the basis of chowders to which fish, shellfish, or meat was added. Later, salt pork enhanced the flavor of the corn chowders.

Cranberries

The cranberry is one of the few native American fruits, along with the blueberry and some grape varieties. Long before the Pilgrims arrived, the Massachuset Indians combined crushed cranberries with dried deer meat and melted fat to make pemmican. The Indians believed that the cranberry had medicinal properties; cranberry tea was used to draw poison from arrow wounds. Later, American sailors ate cranberries to prevent scurvy while at sea. Indian women used cranberry juice to dye their rugs and blankets.

The Cape Cod Nauset Indians called the little red berry *ibimi* or bitter berry. The Pilgrims called it cranberry, a contraction of "crane berry," since the little blossom resembled the head of a crane.

Cranberry cultivation began in Massachusetts on Cape Cod in 1816, when Henry Hall, an early resident, found that the berries grew larger where the soil was covered with a layer of sand. He found that acidic peat soil, sand, and a fresh water supply were necessary requirements for cranberry growing. Most of the cranberry bogs in Massachusetts, therefore, are built on former peat swamps.

Retired sea captains took a special interest in the cranberry bogs, and some of them financed their acreage as they had financed their ships—by selling 64th interests in them. To this day there are cranberry bogs on Cape Cod that belong to many different owners, some of them heirs of the seafaring men who bought one or more "64ths" at the time the bogs were cleared and planted.

The growing of cranberries became commercialized on Cape Cod in about

CRANBERRY SALAD

Most New England cranberries are grown on Cape Cod in Massachusetts. Cranberry harvest traditionally begins right after Labor Day and continues throughout the fall. In early years cranberries were picked by hand, with whole communities turning out to help in the harvest. In 1773 one Cape Cod community decreed a dollar fine for anyone found picking more than a quart of cranberries before the 20th of September. In addition to losing a dollar, anyone found who had jumped the gun also lost his or her cranberries.

Cranberry sauce is a traditional accompaniment to the Thanksgiving turkey. In this recipe the cranberry sauce is used in a molded salad, to which pears are added as a flavor contrast.

Serves 8

1 small package (3 1/2 ounces) strawberry gelatin
1 cup boiling water
1 can (16 ounces) whole berry cranberry sauce
1 cup fresh or frozen cranberries
2 tablespoons sugar
3/4 cup finely sliced celery
1 large Bartlett pear, peeled, cored, and coarsely chopped
1/2 cup chopped pecans

■

Place the strawberry gelatin in a medium-size bowl and add the boiling water. Stir to dissolve the gelatin. Add the cranberry sauce and stir until well blended. Place the cranberries, sugar, and 1/4 cup water in a 1-quart microwavable bowl, cover with vented plastic wrap, and microwave on high for 5 minutes or until the berries start to pop. (To cook cranberries on top of the stove, place them with the sugar and 1/3 cup of water in a small saucepan. Cook over medium heat until they start to pop.) Add the cooked berries to the gelatin mixture and cool to room temperature.

Then add the celery, chopped pear, and pecans. Pour the mixture into a 6-cup, oiled ring mold and refrigerate for at least 4 hours.

To serve, unmold the salad on lettuce leaves and fill the center with additional pieces of pear, if desired.

1840, when granulated sugar became affordable so that the New England housewife could liberally use it to sweeten her tart cranberries. Although there are approximately 100 different varieties of cranberries, only four—Early Black, Howes, Searles, and McFarlins—are now grown commercially.

Harvesting cranberries is a colorful process. Cranberry bogs are wet-harvested by mechanical water reels, also called "egg beaters." They stir up the water with sufficient force to dislodge the ripe berries from their vines. The berries float to the surface, forming a brilliant red mass. They are then guided to the shore, where conveyer belts transport the berries to waiting trucks.

Massachusetts is currently number one in the nation in cranberry production. About 80 percent of the state's 400 cranberry growers belong to the Ocean Spray Cooperative. Most cranberry farms are relatively small, producing about 1,000 barrels, each weighing 100 pounds. The average yield is about 105 barrels per acre, so that the typical farm is less than ten acres.

When Ocean Spray was first formed in 1930 under the name of Cranberry Canners, the product line was simple—canned whole and jellied cranberry sauce and cranberry-juice cocktail. In 1939 Ocean Spray Cran was introduced, which is a concentrated cranberry juice designed to be mixed with alcoholic beverages. This was followed by dehydrated cranberries and cranberry-orange marmalade in the early 1940s. Today, cranberries are also grown in Wisconsin, Oregon, and Washington and sold under the Ocean Spray label.

La Belle Chocolatière

Chocolate became a Northeastern pantry staple in 1765, when James Hannon, an Irish immigrant, started milling chocolate in Dorchester, Massachusetts. (The Boston Tea Party caused many colonists to switch to chocolate, giving a further boost to its use.) Hannon was encouraged and helped financially by Dr. James Baker, a young Harvard graduate who had started a country store in Dorchester. In 1780, after Hannon was lost at sea, Dr. Baker took over the mill and made it a family enterprise. When Baker's grandson started managing the business, the company became the Walter Baker Company.

Walter Baker's chocolate appeared on store shelves all over the country and was also used by commercial cake makers. In 1852 Baker introduced a new kind of chocolate, Baker's German's Sweet Chocolate. Baker named the chocolate for Samuel German, who had come from England, worked as Walter Baker's coachman, and then helped perfect this delicate, sweet chocolate. With the coming of the industrial age, advances were made in processing, and the first chocolate-wrapping machines in America were introduced at the Baker factory. In 1927 Walter Baker & Company, Limited, became a division of General Foods.

There is an interesting story connected with the little chocolate waitress that has been used as the symbol of the company since approximately 1880. An Austrian prince once fell in love with a waitress in a Vienna chocolate shop. After overcoming royal obstacles, they were married, and the Prince had his bride's portrait painted in her chocolate waitress costume. The painting later hung in the Dresden Museum in Dresden, Germany. Henry Pierce, who had become head of the Baker Company after Walter Baker's death, was enchanted with the portrait and decided to use it as the corporate symbol.

The Well-Traveled Cheese

Probably the largest, most famous, and well-traveled cheese ever made in America was produced in Massachusetts in 1801. Many of the dairy farmers in Cheshire, Massachusetts, were supporters of Thomas Jefferson. John Leland, an elder of the town of Cheshire, suggested that each farmer from the community donate one day's milk for a huge cheese

that would be sent to Jefferson to celebrate his presidency. The farmers agreed, and on July 20, 1801, wagons arrived from all directions with the milk.

After the cheese was made, it was left in the press for one month and then removed to a cheese house for aging. When the cheese was finally ready at the beginning of December, it measured four and a half feet in diameter, was one and a half feet thick, and weighed 1,600 pounds. The first part of the cheese's journey to Washington was by sled to Hudson, New York. There the cheese was transferred to a boat for the trip to New York City, where it was loaded into a wagon drawn by six horses and transported to Washington. The journey took three weeks, and on December 29, 1801, in the East Room of the White House President Jefferson took knife in hand and cut into this Massachusetts cheese.

Another symbol of dairying in Massachusetts is Elsie the cow, who in 1939 traveled from her dairy farm, Elm Hill Farm in Brookfield, to the New York World's Fair. She has become the symbol of the Borden Company.

Crackers

It should come as no surprise, given their ancestry, that crackers were invented in Massachusetts, a sea-oriented state. The cracker is the direct descendent of "hardtack," the staple carried aboard sea-going ships in lieu of bread in the 1700s. While this hard biscuit made from an unleavened mixture of flour and water was an important part of a sailor's diet at sea, it was seldom eaten on land because of its hardness and lack of taste.

In 1801 a Milton, Massachusetts, sea captain named Josiah Bent developed the first crisp, light biscuit that was acceptable to the general public. While his wife and children did the baking in the family kitchen, Bent sold the biscuits throughout the state, riding from town to town on horseback and carrying the biscuits in his saddlebag. Captain Bent is credited with creating the name "cracker" for his biscuit, presumably desiring to capture the crunchy sound it makes when it is eaten.

Four years later, in 1805, Artemas Kennedy established a rival company, Kennedy Biscuit, in nearby Arlington, Massachusetts. By the late 1800s Kennedy's company had become the largest baked-goods manufacturer in the country. The Kennedy Biscuit Company was the creator of the fig-jam cakes called Fig Newtons, named after a town in Massachusetts near the Kennedy factory.

Both the Bent and Kennedy companies became the nucleus for the creation of the National Biscuit Company in 1898. During the next five decades, the National Biscuit Company introduced many new crackers and cookies, including Graham Crackers and Ritz Crackers.

In 1902 the National Biscuit Company created Barnum's Animal Crackers, a set of crackers shaped like 17 of the animals in the P.T. Barnum Circus. The packaging of the product was unique in that it resembled a circus cage filled with animals. The crackers became popular as learning experiences for children, since few local zoos at the time contained the exotic circus animals shown on the crackers.

Fruits and Vegetables

In 1605 the explorer Samuel de Champlain found that the Indians on Cape Ann, Massachusetts, cultivated a tuber that tasted like the heart of an

GINGERBREAD WITH APRICOT GLAZE

In colonial Massachusetts gingerbread was always sold on Muster Day. When the companies of the militia met on that occasion, people came from every outlying farm and hamlet. Peddlers set up booths and went through the crowd selling their wares, including the most popular of all—hard gingerbread. Everyone brought the squares and munched on them while watching the militias train.

Two kinds of gingerbread were made at Molly Saunder's Bakeshop in Salem, Massachusetts, during colonial times. The plain, hard one sold for two cents a square, and the moister one with a maple sugar and butter topping sold for three cents. Molly Saunder's gingerbread squares were always of uniform size, since she rolled the dough flat on tin sheets and printed it with corrugated squares made especially for that purpose.

This moist, light gingerbread is topped with an apricot-sherry glaze.

Serves 10 to 12

Gingerbread

1/2 cup sugar

1/2 teaspoon ground ginger

1/4 teaspoon cinnamon

1/4 teaspoon ground cloves

1/4 teaspoon nutmeg

1/2 cup vegetable oil

1/2 cup dark molasses

1 teaspoon baking soda

1/4 cup boiling water

1/4 cup cream sherry

1 1/4 cups all-purpose flour

1 egg, beaten

■

Combine the sugar and spices in a bowl. Stir in the oil and molasses, blending well. Mix together the soda and the boiling water in a small bowl and stir into the sugar mixture. Then add the cream sherry and pour in the flour in a gradual stream, stirring constantly to prevent lumps. Add the beaten egg and mix well. Pour the batter into a well-greased 8-inch square pan and bake in a preheated 350° F. oven for 30 to 35 minutes.

Spoon the apricot glaze over the warm cake and serve at room temperature.

Apricot Glaze

1 cup apricot jam

1/3 cup water

1 teaspoon grated orange zest

2 tablespoons cream sherry

1/2 cup chopped walnuts

■

Combine the apricot jam, water, and orange zest in a small saucepan. Bring to a boil and simmer for 5 minutes, stirring constantly. Remove from the heat and stir in the sherry and walnuts.

NEW ENGLAND FISH CHOWDER

Every New England girl who lived within the sound of the sea in the 1600s and 1700s counted the chowder kettle as part of her dowry. When a bride left the family homestead, she carried with her a huge iron kettle in which to make hearty fish chowder. Long before her banns were cried, a seacoast bride had learned all of the tricks to making chowder. Clam chowder always ran fish chowder a close second.

Serves 6

1/4 pound salt pork, diced

2 large onions, sliced thin

3 cups thinly sliced potatoes

3 cups boiling water

2 pounds fresh cod, pollock, or haddock
    fillets, cut into 2-inch pieces

2 cups milk

1 cup half-and-half

Salt and pepper, to taste

Soda crackers, for garnish

■

Fry the salt pork in a Dutch oven until crisp and golden brown. Remove the pork and set aside. Discard all but 2 tablespoons of the fat. Add the onions and sauté them until soft, but not brown. Add the potatoes and boiling water. Bring to a boil and cook over medium heat until the potatoes are tender, 12 to 15 minutes. Add the fish and continue cooking for 10 to 12 minutes or until the fish flakes easily with a fork. Add the milk and half-and-half; season with salt and pepper, to taste; and heat, but do not let the chowder boil. Garnish each serving with some of the reserved pork and crumbled crackers.

Fish and the Fish Auctions

The Massachusetts fishing industry, which started with the Pilgrims and Puritans more than 350 years ago, continues to grow and prosper. Out of the historic ports of Massachusetts, fishermen, whose ancestors were the early English, Portuguese, Norwegian, and Italian fishermen, still fish the Great Bank off the Maine and Massachusetts coasts.

Many of the catches are sold at the Boston Fish Exchange before they are processed and shipped to all parts of the country. The Boston Fish Exchange Auction has been held in an old building at the end of the Boston Fish Pier since 1929. Fish are brought to the auction by local fishing fleets, as well as by large trucks from other New England ports. The auction begins at 6 a.m. six days a week and is limited to the selling of the same 20 species handled here for more than 25 years. Bidding gets tough, since the buyer can bid on all or part of a catch. The buyers never see the fish they are bidding on, because the catches are still outside in the boats or trucks. The auction is hectic, with as much as 50,000 pounds of fish sold daily in as few as 15 minutes.

New Bedford, Massachusetts, also has a fish auction, although of a different nature than Boston's. Flounder is usually the star of the show. A buyer must purchase the entire boat's catch, making it imperative that he knows he can sell the fish. Usually the auction lasts about 25 minutes, since the buyers carefully inspect the catch.

artichoke for use in their stews and soups. Champlain took some back to France, where they became popular. There, the tubers were called *girasoles,* a word the English tongue turned into Jerusalem. Jerusalem artichokes are still grown in Massachusetts and sold as a specialty food.

The early colonists brought apple seeds and seedlings to Massachusetts in 1629. In the early 1800s John Chapman, better known as Johnny Appleseed, traveled from Massachusetts with an axe and a short-handled hoe to plant apple

orchards throughout the Ohio River Valley.

Many of the fruits and vegetables we use today are tied historically to Massachusetts. Diederick Leertower of Worcester County brought the first asparagus to Massachusetts from Holland in the eighteenth century. In 1843 Ephraim Ball, after years of patient experimentation, developed a seedling grape destined to become the most popular and useful grape in America. He named the grape after his home town—Concord.

NEW HAMPSHIRE

NEW HAMPSHIRE is a small state, only 90 miles wide at its widest point and 168 miles long. It has a diverse topography and climate, however, with lowland meadows, farmland along the Connecticut River, and upland pastures with scattered rocks. One of New Hampshire's most valuable assets has always been the 18-mile strip along the sea. This is where the first settlers landed in 1623. Towns quickly developed around the ports where fishermen and merchants plied their trades.

The first New Hampshire colonists were two small groups sent by the Laconia Company, an investment company sanctioned by King James I of England to establish settlements in the New World. One of the groups was headed by David Thomson, the other by Edward and William Hilton. All three were fishmongers from London.

The first colonists built homes, started fisheries, and traded with the Indians for furs. These settlers had no agricultural experience and found it hard to adapt to the new surroundings. Although familiar with saltwater fishing, they still depended on England for most of their food supplies. Wild game and turkey were plentiful, but the early settlers did not know how to catch them, and ammunition was in short supply.

Colonists who did start to farm found it to be a tremendous undertaking. The land was covered with trees and rocks. Before seeds could be planted, trees had to be cut and burned. After a spring rain when the ground was soft, seeds were placed in crevices among the rocks. Plowing was impossible until the rocks and stones had been dug out by hand, which usually took at least three years.

During the summer the settlers learned to gather wild black currants, raspberries, and strawberries. They started importing seedlings and cuttings of fruit trees from England, and soon almost every farm (called plantation) had an orchard. Vegetable gardens could not be relied upon as a steady supply of food, however, due to the short growing season and sudden changes in the weather.

While the men farmed, the women cooked the meals, kept clothes and home clean, tended the gardens, processed the food, cleaned sheep's wool, spun the wool, and wove it into cloth. They also helped with farm chores. Women earned extra money making butter, which they stored in cold cellars. Once a year these New Hampshire farm women rode 60 miles or more to Boston to sell their butter, which they transported in two 50-pound tubs slung in bags over a horse's back. Many women later used this butter money to pay for their sons' tuitions at schools such as Amherst, Dartmouth, or Harvard.

Bartering

Bartering became a way of life in seventeenth- and eighteenth-century New Hampshire. There was little British currency in circulation and few stores in which to spend it. A farmer, for example, would take six bushels of turnips, five calves, and three pounds (sterling) to a neighbor. The neighbor would kill and dress the calves and keep the money and the turnips. He would return the dressed meat and four skins, keeping one. The farmer would then take the skins to another neighbor who would tan them for a pound plus a half a bushel of wheat.

Sometime later another man would come to the farmer's house for three days and make five pairs of shoes and a pair of pumps out of the calf skins.

If a man wanted a house built in the late-eighteenth century, he would supply the materials and room, but not board, to the man and his two boys who were building the house. House-building usually took from November until June. In June the builder would receive 100 dollars and a two-year-old heifer. When the house was completed, there was usually a feast of cooked beef, "flour bread" (instead of the usual corn bread), and Chinese tea.

Early Farm Life

In 1719 five shiploads of Scotch-Irish families arrived and settled near the Merrimack Valley in New Hampshire, establishing the town of Londonderry. These settlers brought potatoes with them, although most Europeans at the time considered potatoes food only for pigs. The Scotch-Irish settlers planted enough of the seed cuttings to feed their families for an entire winter. News of this tuber spread, and soon other colonists in New Hampshire and throughout New England were also planting potatoes. Within two decades potatoes became an important crop in New England. The English, who also settled in New Hampshire, introduced another root vegetable, the turnip, to New England.

The Revolutionary War drained New Hampshire financially, but it also brought new vitality to the colony. Unable to obtain food from Britain, the inhabitants had to become self-sufficient. They developed more agricultural land

GORHAM, NEW HAMPSHIRE by Sanford Robinson Gifford, oil, 10 ¹/8 x 16 ³/8 inches, courtesy of Richard York Gallery, New York, New York.

and started a lumber industry in the northern part of the state. The lumber was brought overland to the coast and used to build trade and fishing vessels. Portsmouth became one of the ship-building centers of New England.

Corn huskings, quilting bees, and house raisings became the social events of the farm communities. County fairs, where farmers exhibited their produce, were exciting celebrations of what had been accomplished during the year.

Whose apples were the reddest and whose strawberry jam was the sweetest were important topics of the day.

Church suppers, also important social events, were served country style, with a variety of dishes on the buffet table. There was baked ham, traditional New England baked beans, pineapple-cabbage coleslaw, pickles, relishes, hot corn bread, various fruit pies, and cakes.

By 1840 more than half of the land in New Hampshire was farmed. Thirty

years later this figure had declined to less than 40 percent due to westward migrations and the expansion of industry in New Hampshire. The rocky soil had proven to be too difficult to farm compared to the rich soil of the Midwest.

A Board of Agriculture was established in 1870 by the State of New Hampshire to put farmers in touch with modern methods of cultivation, feeding, and fertilizing. Soon thereafter, the state's first chapter of the Patrons of

Husbandry—the Grange—was started in Exeter. This organization exerted considerable influence over agricultural, social, and political developments throughout the state.

In addition to the English and Scotch-Irish, there was also a large influx of French-Canadian settlers in New Hampshire. They brought with them recipes for roast pork, pea soup, pickled beets, and salmon pie made with mashed potatoes, onions, milk, and seasonings. These French settlers served *La Tourtiere,* a special pork pie accompanied by applesauce or apple rings fried in butter, at Christmas or on New Year's Eve. Crusty French bread was made by French-Canadian bakers. These new immigrants learned to use local meat and fish but cooked them according to French recipes.

Apples and Apple Butter

Almost since the first apple orchards were planted by the early settlers, New Hampshire's primary agricultural product has been apples—McIntosh, Cortland, Baldwin, and 50 other varieties. They are grown in rows on hillsides in the Connecticut Valley and in the southern portion of the state. Pumpkins are also grown in the apple orchards and are harvested after the apples have been picked.

Apple butter has been made in New Hampshire since colonial times and is produced in almost the same fashion today. The early farmers collected the apples in their horse-drawn wagons a few days before the apple butter was to be made. Neighbors, friends, and relatives gathered in the farm kitchen on the evening before the apples were to be cooked. The women peeled, cored, and

quartered the apples, filling several tubs. The men swapped stories, and the children played. Usually someone would strike up a musical instrument so everyone could sing. After the apples were peeled, refreshments of homemade ice cream, cake, and pie were served.

The next morning the apples were placed in large copper kettles, sweet cider was added, and the mixture was cooked for most of the day. Sugar and spices were added toward the end of the cooking period. When the mixture was thick, it was ladled into earthenware crocks. A thin layer of paraffin was poured on top of the crocks to seal them, and they were stored for winter use. Apple butter was served on slices of home-baked bread, on buckwheat pancakes, or with cottage cheese.

Today New Hampshire grows a diversity of fruits and vegetables, primarily for local consumption. Even with its short coastline, New Hampshire continues to have a viable fishing industry.

TURNIP SOUP

When the English settled in New Hampshire in the 1720s, they brought turnips with them from their homeland. Turnips were used in stews and as a meat accompaniment. They also became the basis of a soup, which was frequently enriched by spices from the Orient brought by New England trading ships. This modern version of turnip soup is spiced with fresh ginger.

Serves 6

4 tablespoons butter

1 1/2 pounds small turnips, peeled and diced

3 tablespoons finely chopped fresh ginger

1 medium onion, chopped

Dash of garlic powder

5 cups chicken broth

Salt and pepper, to taste

1/3 cup whipping cream

Heat the butter in a large saucepan over medium heat. Add the turnips, ginger, and onion. Cover and cook over very low heat until the vegetables start to become tender, about 10 minutes. Do not let the mixture brown. Add the garlic powder and chicken broth. Simmer, covered, until the vegetables are tender, about 35 to 40 minutes.

Place the solids from the simmered mixture in the bowl of a food processor and purée until smooth. This may have to be done in several batches. Return the purée to the saucepan and season to taste with salt and pepper. Add the cream and heat the soup without letting it boil. Serve at once.

27

RHODE ISLAND

RHODE ISLAND is one of the original 13 states and the smallest state in the Union. It declared its independence from Great Britain two months before the signing of the Declaration of Independence on July 4, 1776. Rhode Islanders were strong anti-loyalists, because British trade restrictions had struck particularly hard at the economic foundation of Rhode Island.

Founded in 1636 by Roger Williams, who had fled the oppressive Puritanism of the Massachusetts Bay Colony, Rhode Island became a society of free-thinkers who tolerated all forms of religion. The dissident settlers from the Massachusetts Bay Colony were soon joined by English, Irish, and French-Canadian immigrants. They were closely followed by Portuguese immigrants, who became fishermen, dairymen, and vegetable growers in the eastern part of the state. In the 1820s Italians, Poles, and other Eastern Europeans came to work in the textile mills.

Tillable land was scarce in Rhode Island, and agricultural products were highly valued. In 1687 the colonial government authorized that taxes could be paid with certain designated farm products. Gradually Rhode Island became self-sufficient in food production and even yielded a surplus in the 1700s, which was exported to England and the West Indies.

Most early Rhode Island farmers produced only for their family's needs. They marketed any excess produce in Newport and Providence. Farmers brought their milk to various fishing ports around Narragansett Bay to be taken by steamboat to Providence and sold. On occasion farmers shipped their excess

STILL LIFE WITH FISH by Walt Kuhn, oil, 12 x 15 inches, courtesy of Midtown Payson Galleries, New York, New York.

cream by boat to a creamery in Fall River, Massachusetts, where it was made into ice cream. The farmers considered water transportation better for milk and cream than a buggy ride on rocky roads. Water transport was faster, and the cool water kept the dairy products from spoiling.

One of the oldest farms in America is still owned by the same family in Rhode Island. The Fry Farm, near the town of East Greenwich, is now on the National Register of Historic Places and is much the same as when it was settled in 1677 by Thomas Fry and his family. While he acquired several other land-holdings, Thomas Fry was primarily a merchant and owned a fleet of trading

vessels that sailed throughout the world. Today, Dorothy and Marion Fry are the ninth generation to live on the farm.

Account books dating from 1719 to 1830 tell about life on the Fry farm. The farm was primarily a dairy farm, although flax and other crops were also grown. The flax was spun on the farm for clothing. The Frys frequently bartered for items they could not produce. Entries in the books showed that butter, cheese, wood, and meat were sold to buy tea, coffee, and spices. Potatoes were once grown, and an apple orchard once produced enough fruit to pay two college tuitions.

Despite the fact that early New England settlers were somber and conservative people, it was common practice in the colonies for everyone in the family, including women and children, to start the day with a mug of beer or ale. The colonists had brought barley seeds with them from England for the specific purpose of growing barley to brew beer. The first breweries in Rhode Island were established and licensed by 1640. They were also among the first in America.

As soon as apple orchards began to bear enough fruit, apple cider became a popular drink at breakfast as well as throughout the day in Rhode Island. The cider was not the sweet, bland juice we know today, but a hard cider that varied in strength from mild to quite strong depending on how long it had fermented.

The first apple orchard was established in Rhode Island by William Blackstone in 1635. He was one of the early refugees from Puritanism in Massachusetts. It is believed that Blackstone originated the Yellow Sweeting variety. Rhode Island Greening, a greenish-skinned apple, is another of the state's apple varieties. It became famous as the ingredient for New England's green-apple pie. One type of green-apple pie was made with stewed apples flavored with nutmeg; another, with applesauce spiced with caraway seeds.

Rhode Islanders faced the same food-preparation challenges encountered by other New England colonists. White flour was scarce and expensive, so Rhode Islanders mainly used cornmeal for their breads and cakes. Fried corn bread, given the name "Jonnycake" (and its spelling) by Rhode Islanders, was first made by Pilgrim women and dates back to 1621.

It was made from a batter composed of cornmeal, hot water, and salt and poured onto a hot stone or iron griddle for cooking. The recipe for these fried corn cakes traveled with the first settlers to Rhode Island, where they were called "journey cakes" because they were small and hard and could be tucked into a travel bag. Over the years the original recipe has been varied with such ingredients as sugar, milk, butter, chopped suet, baking powder, and molasses.

In Rhode Island Jonnycake was made with a finely ground meal made from whitecap flint corn. Connoisseurs of Jonnycake claim that for best results white corn should be ground by a waterwheel-driven mill. During World War II the Rhode Island legislature, after a hundred years of dispute over the spelling, the ingredients, and the method of preparation, designated "Jonnycake" the official spelling and whitecap flint cornmeal the official ingredient. The type of mill used to grind the corn was not specified.

Many of the European settlers brought their food traditions with them, some of which are being practiced today. French Huguenots, who came to Rhode Island in the seventeenth century seeking political freedom, continued to make Boudin Blanc in their new homes. Boudin Blanc was a white sausage consisting of pork, sweetbreads, chicken, and spices. These sausages, which were first steamed in chicken broth and then sautéed until lightly browned, were served with fried potatoes and red cabbage.

In addition to new foods brought to Rhode Island by various ethnic groups, there were also attempts to improve the quality of available ingredients. In 1854 Captain William Tripp of Rhode Island and John Macomber of Massachusetts began breeding experiments to produce a meaty chicken suitable for all types of cooking. The resulting Rhode Island Red was adopted as the state's official bird a hundred years later and has become popular all over the world. Rhode Island Reds lay brown eggs, which for years were preferred by Bostonians. Adamsville, Rhode Island, is the site of the Rhode Island Red Commemorative Monument, probably the world's only memorial to a chicken.

Rhode Island Seafood

Having a limited amount of land for agriculture, Rhode Islanders turned to the sea for food and trade. Rhode Island ships became heavily involved in trade with the Orient and the West Indies, bringing back spices from the former and molasses from the latter. Initially molasses was used as an inexpensive sweetener. As the number of distilleries in Rhode Island grew, however, molasses was used primarily to make rum.

Rhode Island's prime harvests from the sea were quahog and cherrystone clams, both of which are still harvested. These clams became the basis of Rhode Island clam chowders. The controversy of tomatoes versus no tomatoes in clam chowder probably started in Rhode Island. The tomato-based chowder, now known as Manhattan clam chowder, actually originated in Rhode Island and become the variety most commonly served in the state.

COD FILLETS IN PUFF PASTRY

Cod was and still is one of the prime harvests off the New England coast. The tarragon, sherry, and tomatoes used in this cod recipe are derived from the early cod cookery of the Portuguese fishermen who settled along the coast of Rhode Island and southern Massachusetts.

Serves 4 to 6

1 tablespoon butter or margarine

1 tablespoon olive oil

1 medium onion, chopped

1 clove garlic

4 medium shiitake mushrooms, sliced

4 large white domestic mushrooms, coarsely chopped

2 ounces ham, chopped

2 Roma tomatoes, peeled, seeded, and chopped

1/4 cup dry sherry

1/4 cup chopped fresh parsley

2 tablespoons fresh tarragon leaves

2 skinless cod fillets (about 1 1/2 pounds)

1 package (17 1/4 ounces) frozen puff pastry sheets, thawed

1 egg, beaten

■

Melt the butter and olive oil in a medium-size skillet over moderate heat. Add the onion and garlic and sauté until soft, but not browned, about 4 minutes. Add the mushrooms and the ham and cook, stirring often, until the mushroom liquid has evaporated. Stir in the toma-toes, sherry, and parsley and continue cooking over medium heat for about 5 minutes until the juices are reduced to 1/4 cup. Remove from heat and mix in the tarragon leaves.

Flatten one of the puff-pastry sheets on a non-stick cookie sheet. Place the cod fillets on the pastry to within 1 inch of the edges. Trim fish as necessary. Spread the mushroom mixture evenly on the fish. Brush the uncovered part of the pastry with some of the beaten egg. Top with the second puff-pastry sheet and seal it all the way around. Using the blunt-sided tip of a knife, pull the pastry edge in about 1/2 inch at 1-inch intervals to create a scalloped edge all the way around.

Cut a 1/2-inch hole in the center of the pastry top and using the point of a knife, make a pattern of spiral lines from the center to the edges, barely cutting into the dough. Do not cut through the dough. Brush the top of the pastry with the beaten egg. Refrigerate the fish tart for 30 to 45 minutes. (May be refrigerated up to 4 hours before baking.) Bake in a preheated 375° F. oven for 30 minutes or until the tart is nicely browned.

Oysters were so popular in the nineteenth century that taverns and eating establishments featured oyster suppers in the winter months. In late autumn Rhode Islanders buried oysters and clams dampened with seawater and mixed with cornmeal to preserve them for later use. Watered twice a week, the beds provided plump, fresh oysters for succulent pies on cold winter evenings. At fashionable parties in the mid-1800s, these pies and oyster patties were midnight favorites. Creamed and curried oysters were served in patty shells. Pickled oysters were enjoyed with eggnog on New Year's Eve.

Even in colonial times, oysters were shipped far inland. At first they were piled in saddlebags and carried on horseback. Later they were packed in kegs and flour barrels and transported by wagon from Rhode Island into northern New York and Vermont.

In the 1850s Rhode Island began developing oyster beds in Narragansett Bay with oysters from the Chesapeake region. Oyster farming grew steadily until a disease brought by the 1938 hurricane destroyed the majority of the beds. Clams, lobsters, and finfish, however, are still harvested in large quantities off the coast of Rhode Island.

VERMONT

VERMONTERS are a very independent people. It took a brave soul to settle in an isolated mountainous area with no access to the sea. Since no seafood was available, the settlers of Vermont had to carve farms out of the rocky mountainsides and valleys and rely on the land for food. Early settlers had to brave not only the bitterly cold winters but also frequent Indian raids which destroyed homes, crops, and often lives.

Most of the Indian raids stopped at the conclusion of the French and Indian Wars in 1763, and gradually more settlers, initially from other New England colonies, moved into the area. First came the men, who cleared land and built primitive shelters. The next spring they brought their families, a team of oxen, and a few household furnishings to their new, rustic homesteads. The settlers were able to plant just enough food for themselves and their livestock for the following winter.

In colonial days both New York and New Hampshire claimed the territory of Vermont, but the inhabitants wanted to maintain their autonomy. For 14 years starting in 1777, Vermont was an independent republic with its own post office, a mint for coining money, and powers to naturalize citizens. Vermonters considered immigrants from the United States and particularly the Commonwealth of Massachusetts to be foreigners. Finally, in 1791 Vermont ratified the Constitution and became the nation's 14th state.

Vermont was settled primarily by the English, Irish, Scots, and French Canadians. Most of these settlers farmed, since there was little other employment except granite quarrying. Farmers used hand tools to seed, cultivate, and harvest their grain and continued doing so even long after the introduction of the McCormick reaper in the 1840s.

Farming was not an easy task in the hilly, rocky soil of Vermont. Meals were served in the field during daylight hours so that the farmers could make use of every minute of available light. The lunch break at midday was always a welcome repast. It was usually simple fare and often included a drink called *switchel*—a combination of spring water, molasses, ginger, and vinegar. A handful of oatmeal thrown on top was thought to prevent heat prostration.

Maple Sugar

Native Vermonters will tell you that there are five seasons in Vermont— spring, summer, fall, winter, and mud. Mud begins when the first robin appears in the Green Mountain State and the cold blasts of wind and snow give way to the first March thaw. That is the time Vermont sugar makers climb the mountains to drill new tap holes into the hard-rock maples. Only mature trees—at least 40 years old, a "foot through," and some 60 feet tall—are selected. At that time of year, the weather is variable, from warm days to freezing nights, all of which affect the sap run. Consequently, the sugar maker must check his trees several times a week.

Sugar making is a tedious and laborious process. Each tree produces, drip by drip, about 40 quarts of sap. These 40 quarts produce only one quart of maple syrup. The rest is water, which must be boiled away.

Long before the first settlers arrived from Europe, native Indians had been gathering maple sap in Vermont. The Indians cut a gouge in the tree to start the sap flowing and attached buckskin bags to catch the flow. After the bags were collected, they dropped hot coals into them to evaporate the water and reduce the sap to syrup. The Indians also placed the sap in small dishes and let them stand overnight, then in the morning removed the ice that had formed on top. The early settlers improved on the Indian method of gathering sap by attaching wooden buckets to the trees and boiling the sap in large iron kettles to evaporate the water.

Until 1870 all sap boiling was done outdoors near the stand of maple trees. Gradually, small houses were built to enclose the boiling kettles in order to reduce the amount of fuel required. Today, during maple sugaring time one can see many small houses on the hillsides with immense clouds of steam pouring out of them. Modern sugar makers, however, no longer need to transport buckets of sap from the individual trees to the sugaring house. Instead a network of tubing brings the sap from the trees directly to the kettles. One pipeline can handle 30 trees.

Traditionally, after the first night of the "boiling," the sugar maker's family sat down at the kitchen table to sample the results. The hard work, the sap that had frozen, the new pipeline that had been chewed by deer —all problems were forgotten as they tasted the new syrup. If there was still snow on the ground, there was a "sugaring-off" party. Hot maple

INDIAN PUDDING

The Indians taught the early settlers to make cornmeal mush, which they later evolved into Indian Pudding. This pudding was served as a main course or as a dessert, depending on how much cornmeal was used. It was a favorite New England Saturday night dessert, which shared the fireplace oven with the beans in their last hours of baking. Indian Pudding was prepared with milk, molasses, and spices, such as cinnamon and nutmeg, and in rare cases an egg or two. Raisins were often added, and, occasionally, diced apples. The pudding was served with rich cream.

This version of Indian Pudding is made with both molasses and maple syrup and includes eggs, as well as raisins and dates.

Serves 8

4 cups milk

1/3 cup yellow cornmeal

3 tablespoons butter

1/8 teaspoon salt

1/3 cup molasses

1/2 cup maple syrup

3/4 teaspoon ginger

1/2 teaspoon cinnamon

1/2 teaspoon nutmeg

2 eggs, well beaten

1/3 cup raisins

1/3 cup chopped dates

■

Bring the milk almost to a boil in a large saucepan. Pour in the cornmeal in a steady stream, stirring constantly. Continue cooking over medium-low heat, stirring constantly, until the mixture thickens. Add the butter, salt, molasses, maple syrup, and the spices, blending well. Remove the mixture from the heat and whisk in the eggs. Then fold in the raisins and dates. Pour the pudding into a buttered 1 1/2- to 2-quart baking dish and bake in a preheated 325° F. oven for 1 1/2 hours until firm. Serve pudding at room temperature with whipped cream or ice cream.

While annual production of maple sugar is only a fraction of that in the 1800s, Vermont still produces more maple sugar than any other state.

An outgrowth of the Vermont maple-sugar industry is the manufacturing of maple candies. One such operation, Maple Grove Candies, was started in 1915 by Katharine Ide Gray and her daughter, Helen, a student of home economics at Columbia University. That summer Helen and her friend Ethel McLaren experimented with maple syrup to make candies from recipes they had developed as a result of their studies. They began to sell the candies and soon outgrew the Grays' kitchen.

In 1920 the Grays purchased the Fairbanks mansion in St. Johnsbury, Vermont, for their candy operation. They opened a tearoom and inn in the front of the old mansion and named the establishment Maple Grove Inn. As the business grew from pale bonbons to 70 kinds of maple and chocolate candies, another building was purchased. At that time sap was bought directly from the farmers, and the commercial production of maple syrup under the Maple Grove label was added to the candy business. Maple Grove Products of Vermont has now become one of the largest maple candy and syrup manufacturers in the country.

Vermont Meat

In colonial times Vermonters primarily ate beef and pork. Beef was usually cooked in stews and roasts or preserved as corned beef. Hogs were slaughtered in the fall, and the pork was salt cured or cured and smoked to preserve it for winter use. In the fall, fresh pork chops were often cooked with

syrup was poured onto platters of clean snow, which turned the mixture into a tasty candy. This tradition still occurs among many sugar-making families. Vermonters eat this candy with freshly baked doughnuts and tangy pickles that cut the sweetness.

Sugar production in Vermont reached its peak in the 1880s. Maple sugar has long since become a luxury food. Until the turn of the century, maple syrup was less expensive than white sugar, and Vermonters used it to sweeten and flavor almost everything.

apples. Salt pork was cooked with vegetables and served with a cream gravy, and the smoked hams were baked with a raisin sauce.

Beef was also slaughtered in the fall, when the pastureland ceased to yield food for the cattle and the weather was cold enough to freeze the meat. When it was very cold, meat could be hung in the kitchen away from the fire without thawing. Cattle that the family did not slaughter in the late fall were driven to market in Boston by the "Green Mountain cowboys," who usually made the journey barefooted.

Vermonters also preserved beef by making it into corned beef. New England farm wives made corned beef in large stone crocks using a brine of salt, sugar, and saltpeter. In colonial days saltpeter was available in grains, called corns—thus the name, corned beef. Since early Vermonters could not obtain seafood, they were forced to depend more on meat than other New England settlers. Vermont corned beef became the basis of a boiled dinner, which included potatoes, cabbage, turnips, carrots, and parsnips. Beets were also served but cooked separately so as not to discolor the meat or vegetables. This dish later became known as a New England boiled dinner. The leftovers were chopped and pan-fried as red-flannel hash, with the redness coming from the beets.

In 1811 William Jarvis, the U.S. consul to Lisbon, Portugal, brought a flock of 400 Spanish merino sheep to his farm at Weathersfield Bow on the Connecticut River. This started the sheep industry in Vermont, which supplied wool for the New England mills and additional meat for local tables. By 1840 there were six sheep to every person in Vermont. After the Civil War, when railroad transportation and better grazing lands became available in the Midwest and mountain states, sheep-raising moved west. Recently, however, there has been a revival of the sheep industry in Vermont. More lamb is now being raised than at any time since the nineteenth-century wool boom. Today's lamb, however, is being raised for meat, not wool.

Vermont Cheese

With the decline of sheep-raising in Vermont, the farmers started raising herds of dairy cows. The dairy industry would also have languished if the railroads had not come to New England. Although Vermont was too far from major markets to develop a milk industry, accessible railroad transportation helped expand the market for Vermont's butter and cheese.

WINTER IN THE COUNTRY. GETTING ICE, by George H. Durrie, lithographic print 16 1/2 x 22 inches, published by Currier and Ives, 1864, courtesy of Gilcrease Museum, Tulsa, Oklahoma.

Cheese-making has long been an important part of Vermont history, since farm families have always made cheese and butter for their own use. Cheese was made in the summer when milk was plentiful and would spoil quickly if not used.

Vermonters are reputed to have made almost nine million pounds of cheese in their farm kitchens in 1849—a quantity not matched by commercial cheese factories until a century later. The first Vermont cheese factories were opened in the late 1800s. Although Vermont is well-known for its cheeses, there are only six major producers in the state, including a large cooperative, Cabot Cheese. Today, Vermont produces about 100 million pounds of cheese a year.

Cabot Cheese, the largest cheese manufacturer in Vermont, is a cooperative composed of 500 members. Cabot began in 1919 under the name The Cabot Farmers' Cooperative Creamery when a group of 94 local farmers joined together to market their milk. The milk cooperative did not expand into making cheese until 1930, when they were faced with a surplus of milk.

About four thousand gallons of milk arrive at the Cabot plant each morning and are processed into Cheddar, Monterey Jack, Mozzarella, and a low fat cheese called Vitalait. Cabot also produces cottage cheese, yogurt, and sour cream for local consumption.

Although the Cabot Cheese plant is fully automated, it still uses the same cheesemaking principles as were used a hundred years ago. To make Cheddar, cheese milk is heated, and a culture is added to curdle the milk. A small amount of grated carrots is added to give the Cheddar cheese its color. This practice started with the home cheesemakers in the 1800s. After the milk has set up, auto-matic stirring devices sweep slowly through the vat of milk as the curds and whey separate. The whey gradually drains off, leaving behind the curds, which become firm enough to be turned without breaking.

At that time the large pieces of curd are "Cheddared" or cut into smaller slabs and hand flipped, causing more liquid to run off. These slabs are later pressed into hoops to form a large wheel of cheese, which is aged for a number of months. The aging time depends on whether mild, medium, or sharp Cheddar cheese is desired.

The oldest continuously operated cheese factory in the United States is the Crowley Cheese Company located in the tiny town of Healdville, Vermont, 2,000 feet up in the Green Mountains. Little has changed in this rural community of 71 people since 1822, when the Crowley family started making cheese in their farmhouse kitchen. The kitchen eventually became too small, and the operation was moved to a factory building in 1824. Sixty years later, Winfield Crowley, grandson of the founder, built the present factory, where cheese is still made by hand, as it was in 1822. The Randolph Smith family purchased the Crowley Cheese Company in 1967 and has kept it as a family business. Today, Crowley produces mostly Colby cheese—technically a first cousin to Cheddar, but softer, moister, and less acidic.

In recent years Vermont cheesemakers have broadened their output into a variety of cheeses. The International Cheese Company in Hinesburg produces European types of cheese. The company is the largest producer of Feta cheese in the country. The Guilford Cheese Company, a family business started in 1984 by the Dixons on their farm near Guilford, produces Brie and Camembert according to traditional French methods.

Vermont Apples

Since colonial days each farm in Vermont has had at least a few apple trees. In the late nineteenth century there were more than 40 varieties of apples grown in Vermont, such as Spitzenburg, Snow Apple, Sheepnose, Yellow Transparent, and Duchess of Oldenburg.

Warm sunny days and crisp cool nights in the Green Mountains provide excellent growing conditions for apples, particularly the McIntosh. This apple variety came to Vermont from Ontario, Canada, where it had been developed from seedlings found by chance on the farm of John McIntosh, an American-born son of Scottish immigrants. Now the most widely planted apple in the northeastern United States, the McIntosh comprises 80 percent of Vermont's apple production.

Apple cider, the favorite family beverage in early New England, was made with freshly pressed apple juice, which was boiled down in a copper kettle to half its original volume. Then pared and cored apples were added, and the mixture was further boiled down until it developed the consistency of mush. Frequent stirring kept the mixture from sticking to the kettle. Cinnamon and other spices were added toward the end of cooking. After being filtered, the cider was stored in jugs, and the remaining pomace was fermented into apple brandy. Sometimes water was added to the pomace, and the mixture was pressed again for a weak drink for children called "cider-kins."

Turkeys

Wild turkeys were once plentiful in Vermont, but they became virtually extinct due to over-hunting. In the early 1800s turkeys were domesticated and through hybridization developed into the broad-breasted Vermont turkey of today.

In order to sell their turkeys in the early 1800s, Vermont farmers literally had to walk their birds to the Boston fowl market, because turkeys were too bulky and perishable to cram into wagons. The birds were driven to market, 10,000 at a time, by a team of 100 drovers, who kept them together on the 200-mile journey. That may have been the original turkey trot!

Vermont turkeys are plumper than other turkeys because they are grown for an extra four to five weeks beyond the usual 17-week period. The cool fall weather encourages them to eat more.

In the early part of this century, more than 200,000 Vermont turkeys were sold annually in an area from Canada to Pennsylvania. The advent of strict interstate-shipping regulations for fresh meat made it uneconomical for Vermont producers to raise, process, and ship turkeys in large numbers. By 1980 the industry had dwindled to just a few thousand birds. Nevertheless, the image of Vermont turkeys as an extra special bird has persisted. Fine restaurants all over the country still feature "Vermont turkeys," although no birds have left the state in years.

Turkeys are only a part of the culinary heritage of Vermont. The cooking of the state takes the essentials of New England cooking and enhances them with the addition of maple sugar, cream, and other dairy products.

Additionally, the diverse ethnic

SPICY LAMB STEW

When sheep were first brought to Vermont in 1811, they were raised primarily for wool. Since only the older animals were slaughtered, the meat was tough and used in stews, which were well-seasoned to mask the tangy flavor of mutton. Sheep raising in Vermont declined in the mid-1800s and was not revived until the latter part of this century. Today, Vermont produces more than 10,000 young meat lambs annually.

Spices and citrus fruits brought back from the Orient, West Indies, and the Mediterranean were frequently used in New England cuisine. Cinnamon, cloves, and coriander enhance this modern lamb stew, which also has a hint of citrus flavorings.

Serves 4

■

2 tablespoons olive oil

2 pounds lamb stew, carefully trimmed
    and cut into 1 1/2-inch cubes

1 medium onion, chopped

1 clove garlic, minced

1/2 cup diced carrots

1 cup thickly sliced mushrooms

1/2 small orange, seeded and cut into
    8 pieces

1 large strip lemon peel, cut in 4 pieces

1 cup red wine

1 cup tomato juice

1/2 teaspoon ground cloves

1/2 teaspoon ground cinnamon

1 teaspoon powdered coriander

Flour and water, for thickening, optional

Heat the olive oil in a medium-size Dutch oven over medium-high heat. Add the lamb and brown it. Add the onions, garlic, and carrots and sauté briefly. Then add the remaining ingredients. Cover and bake in a preheated 325° F. oven for 1 1/2 to 2 hours or until the meat is tender. Check occasionally to see if more liquid is needed; if so, add equal parts of wine and tomato juice. Remove any fat that may have accumulated on top of the stew and thicken with flour and water, if desired.

heritage of Vermont's population has created a variety of unique dishes, including vegetables and potatoes served with milk, apple pie served with Cheddar cheese, rhubarb and apple crisps, deep-fried pies made with cinnamon-flavored applesauce, and mincemeat pies. Meat pies originated with the Welsh miners who settled in western Vermont to mine its slate. Baked beans, a favorite dish of New England, has always been flavored in Vermont with maple syrup, even while other parts of New England preferred to use molasses.

An Indian summer view of the Farm & Stock of JAMES C. CORNELL of Northampton Bucks county Pennsylvania. That took the Premium in the Agricultural society, october the 12. 1848

THE CORNELL FARM by Edward Hicks, oil, 36 ³/4 x 49 inches, courtesy of National Gallery of Art, Washington, D. C.

MIDDLE ATLANTIC

THE MIDDLE ATLANTIC region, which today includes the states of New York, New Jersey, Pennsylvania, Maryland, and Delaware, became prosperous due to the relatively mild climate and abundant resources. An irregular coastline provides inlets and bays, which are rich in seafood and make natural harbors. The most famous of these is the Chesapeake Bay.

Inland from the seashore are pleasant rolling hills and fertile valleys, which became the basis of agriculture for the region. At one time the western part of New York State supplied the wheat for the Northeast. Even the more southern state of Maryland grew sufficient wheat to meet the demands of its settlers and for export.

Before white settlers arrived the Middle Atlantic region was primarily occupied by the Algonquian and Iroquois Indians. Like the other tribes in North America, these Indians grew corn, beans, and squash and hunted wild game. The Indians living near the seashore used seashells to skin the wild game. Passenger pigeons were so numerous that the Indians downed them by throwing rocks. Around Lake Erie, the Iroquois hunted buffalo for meat and hides.

Indians along the seashore had an ample supply of shellfish—clams, oysters, and crabs—as well as migratory geese, ducks, and other waterfowl. In what is today New York Harbor, the Indians harvested enormous oysters and six-foot-long lobsters. Snapping turtles were caught along the shoreline by the Indians, a practice later adopted by the settlers.

In northern New York State, the Iroquois made maple syrup, just as their Algonquian neighbors did in Vermont. Early French travelers passing through the area wrote that they were served dried popcorn by the Indians with maple syrup poured over it.

The Middle Atlantic states, particularly New Jersey, New York, and Pennsylvania, shared a culinary tradition. The origins of much of the area's cooking lie in the cuisines of the primary settlers of the region—the English, the Germans, and the Dutch. Pork and ham, yeast breads, coffee cakes, and pies, along with jams, jellies, pickles, and preserves were the staple foods of many Mid-Atlantic households. The melding of these cuisines later became part of the cooking of the Great Lakes region and the Midwest as eastern settlers moved west.

The early settlers of the Middle Atlantic area were primarily farmers, quite a few of whom had been the wealthy second sons of English nobility, who had been denied estate inheritance in England. They soon established large plantations in Delaware and Maryland and grew tobacco. They raised their own fruits and vegetables as they had been accustomed to do in England. Thus the cooking of this area was more sophisticated than that of their New England neighbors, who were typically tradesmen with little farming experience.

The Pennsylvania Dutch, who were actually Germans (the colonists routinely mispronounced the word "Deutsch"), followed William Penn into the wilderness and settled on the rich farmland of Penn's land grant. They cleared the fields, built homes, and hung their cast-iron pots in their fireplaces to create a cuisine that is still being cooked. Their cooking was based on old German recipes modified by local ingredients.

Most of the Middle Atlantic settlers grew a great variety of vegetables, including cabbages, potatoes, yams, carrots, and corn, in their kitchen gardens. The orchards provided fruit, and there was also a variety of berries. Root vegetables were stored in the root cellar for winter use.

Due to the proximity of the Chesapeake Bay and the Atlantic coastline to the Middle Atlantic region, seafood played a dominant role in much of the cooking. Venison and other game, as well as pork, were also used as ingredients in main dishes.

Oyster roasts became the Chesapeake's version of the New England clambake. They remain a popular reminder of the days when barrels of oysters, spread out to roast, were only an introduction to the enormous meals served at the plantations along the Chesapeake Bay. Oyster vendors used to frequent almost every corner of the cities along the Chesapeake Bay, and oyster saloons were just as common.

Oysters were so plentiful in the New York Harbor area when the Dutch established their colony in 1625 that they became regular fare at breakfast, lunch, and dinner. The abundance continued for many years, and by the late 1700s oyster parlors and oyster saloons were everywhere. Even in the late 1800s, one could eat an unlimited amount of oysters for ten cents.

The many immigrants who settled the Middle Atlantic states contributed a great variety of cuisines to the region. For example, pastrami, the dry-cured spicy beef of Romanian origin, is still served in Jewish delicatessens throughout New York City. Pizza has become a way of life in many of the large cities of the region. Corned beef and cabbage, the hot dog, baked lasagne, and lox and bagels all originated somewhere else, but they, along with Long Island scallops, Maryland crab, and Philadelphia scrapple, have melded into a Middle Atlantic cuisine.

DELAWARE

BOTH HOLLAND AND SWEDEN established settlements in Delaware in the 1630s. The Swedish settlers, including several Finnish families, purchased land from the Indians and founded Fort Christina as their headquarters in New Sweden. They began farming and started trading for furs with the Indians.

When England took over the Dutch and Swedish settlements in 1664, Delaware became an English territory. In 1682 the land was transferred to William Penn, who allowed the Delaware colony to establish a separate legislature in 1704.

The settlers found an ample supply of food in Delaware, including oysters, venison, wild fruits, and berries. They planted gardens and raised many of the vegetables and herbs familiar to them from their homelands. Peaches, a new fruit for the Swedes and Finns, were grown in orchards, along with cherries and wild plums. By the late 1600s Delaware was growing sufficient corn to be able to sell the surplus to neighboring colonies.

Agricultural Fairs

One of the country's first agricultural fairs was held in Delaware on October 12 and 13, 1763. The purpose of this, as well as other early fairs, was to buy and sell horses, cattle, and all types of farm merchandise. At the fair there was also a special section that exhibited "Ladies Work," which included quilts, samplers, and crafts made from shells and leather. The women exhibited their best pies, jellies, jams, and cakes. Other exhibits featured new household products, some new inventions, horticulture, and farm implements.

Poultry products were seldom found at these agricultural fairs. Prior to the late nineteenth century, production of butter and eggs was a family affair in Delaware. There were essentially no commercial dairies or egg farms. Most Delaware farmers kept milk from the family cow in spring houses or wells and butter making was almost a daily task for the housewife and the children. If there was a surplus of butter, farmer's wives took it, along with eggs, to the community general store to be sold or bartered for other goods.

The Broiler Industry

Delaware's broiler industry began to take shape in the second half of the nineteenth century. Following the Civil War, farmers became interested in breeding better chickens for egg produc-

POULTRY MARKET by Lee Jackson, oil, 30 x 40 inches, courtesy of Midtown Payson Galleries, New York, New York.

tion and began to house chickens in laying-houses. Until that time chickens had fended for themselves in the farmyard. Farmers built clean, ventilated chicken houses with windows covered by chicken wire and cotton curtains. Oyster shells, rich in calcium, were crushed for feed, and crooks held drinking water. The laying-houses were built close to the farmer's house so that the housewife could take care of the chickens and the eggs.

The modern poultry (or broiler) industry, which started in Delaware in the 1920s and '30s, is today the state's biggest agricultural commodity. This includes both poultry and eggs. Poultry became so important for the state that in 1939 the state legislature designated the "Blue Hen Chicken" to be the official state bird.

Delaware's broiler industry was started by accident in 1923 by Cecil Steele of Ocean View. She had ordered 50 chicks to provide eggs and meat for her family. Due to a mix-up, 500 chicks arrived, and she proceeded to build a chicken house for them.

Mrs. Steele decided to market her chickens at age 16 weeks, when they weighed approximately two and a half pounds. This was a younger age than customary and eliminated any diseases older chickens tended to have at that time. (Today, broilers reach maturity at 7 weeks and weigh up to four pounds.) Mrs. Steele called these young chickens "broilers," because they could be cooked quickly. The Cecil Steele chicken house is on the National Register of Historic Places in recognition of her pioneering efforts.

By 1935 the broiler industry was

FRIED CHICKEN

The development in Delaware of the broiler or small chicken in the 1920s further popularized fried chicken. There are many versions of fried chicken. Some cooks only flour the chicken; others use a combination of flour and cornmeal, while others dip the chicken pieces in milk or cream before breading. Maryland cooks either make a cream gravy with the drippings or serve the fried chicken plain.

This version of fried chicken uses a gravy and includes some spices for extra flavoring.

Serves 4

1 chicken (3 1/2 to 4 pounds), cut into
   serving pieces

1 can (6 ounces) evaporated milk

1/3 cup all-purpose flour

1/3 cup cornmeal

1/2 cup cornflake crumbs

1/4 teaspoon salt

1/4 teaspoon pepper

1/4 teaspoon garlic powder

3/4 teaspoon dried thyme

Paprika

2 tablespoons margarine

3 tablespoons solid vegetable shortening

■

Rinse the chicken pieces and dry them. Place the evaporated milk in a bowl or soup plate. Combine the flour, cornmeal, cornflake crumbs, salt, pepper, garlic powder, and thyme on a piece of waxed paper. Dip each piece of chicken in the milk and then roll it in the flour combination, coating it well on all sides. Then sprinkle each piece with paprika.

Melt the shortening and butter in a large skillet over medium heat. Add the chicken pieces, paprika side down, and brown them, about 8 minutes. Sprinkle the top side with paprika, turn, and brown the other side. Cover the skillet and continue cooking over medium-low heat for 15 minutes. Turn the chicken and cook another 20 minutes, or until done, turning the chicken once. Serve chicken with the following gravy, if desired.

Gravy

2 tablespoons all-purpose flour

1 1/2 cups half-and-half

Salt and pepper, to taste

■

Pour off all except 3 tablespoons of the fat in the frying pan. Stir in the flour and cook for a few minutes. Pour in the half-and-half and cook, stirring constantly, until the sauce is smooth and thick. Season to taste with salt and pepper. Serve with the chicken.

firmly established in Delaware. Associated industries, such as feed manufacturers, hatcheries, poultry processors, and shippers, also developed.

In 1938 Jacob Udell of Frankfort, Delaware, started the first large poultry-dressing plant. Prior to this time, farm families who wanted chicken for dinner had to slaughter their own. Even city dwellers had to buy live chickens. The slaughtering and plucking was usually done by the female of the family, who chopped off the head of the chicken, plucked its feathers, and then cleaned and prepared it for cooking.

Delaware now ranks eighth nationally in broiler production, but no U.S. county grows more chickens than Sussex County, Delaware. Almost all of Delaware's 1,200 growers are under contract to one of the nine local poultry companies. They provide the chicks and the feed, then process and market the birds. The growers provide the chicken house and pay the electric bill. The lights remain on constantly in the chicken house to encourage the chickens to eat from automatically refilled feed pans.

Milling of Flour

Oliver Evans, originally a Delaware farmer, automated flour milling with the invention of a continuous conveyor belt. Caught up in the spirit of the Industrial Revolution, Evans experimented with his inventions at a mill he built on Red Clay Creek in Delaware in 1785 and obtained a patent for his process in 1787.

The basic function of using millstones powered by waterwheels was not altered in the Evans mill. His changes involved the use of machines to replace human labor. Evans' automated mill reduced the manpower from four men and a boy to two men, who basically set the waterwheel in motion, supervised certain aspects of the operation, and stored the filled barrels of flour.

Evans' conveyor belt transported the wheat from the wagon or boat at the dockside to the top floor of the mill. This was accomplished with a set of small buckets attached to an endless leather belt, which made it possible to move the grain vertically.

The "hopper boy" was also an Evans invention. So named because it took the place of a boy who had previously performed this mill function, the hopper boy mechanically raked out freshly ground flour to cool and dry. The machine then raked the flour into a hole in the center of a hopper, from which it was taken to the next operation.

Many millers were skeptical of the Evans mill and did not readily accept it. By 1792, however, his inventions had been licensed to more than a hundred mills. The use of the Evans-mill improvements was limited to the then wheat-producing states—Delaware, Maryland, Virginia, Pennsylvania, New York, and New Jersey.

At that time large quantities of milled wheat were shipped overseas, and many mills ceased grinding small amounts of grain for local families, claiming it was uneconomical. Delaware citizens, however, succeeded in getting the state legislature to enact a law requiring that mills set aside a certain period of time each week to grind wheat for local farmers.

Delaware Foods

The foods of Delaware are primarily English with some German influences. The Germans who settled Pennsylvania also settled in the northern part of Delaware and continued to prepare their traditional German dishes, which eventually intermingled with those of Delaware.

After the broiler industry started, broiled chicken with sour-milk biscuits became a favorite. Shrimp steamed over a pan of spiced vinegar and served with tartar sauce was a traditional seafood dish. Cooks prepared cauliflower with a custard sauce and creamed-corn pudding as accompaniments to meat dishes. There was also a fish stew, called Muddle, which included fin and shellfish and was cooked in a Dutch oven. Lemon butter and lemon jelly were used as sandwich fillings. Steamed crabs were cooked at beach picnics. Ham smoked to a rich brown, almost the shade of mahogany, and aged at least a year has been a Delaware specialty.

Delaware has also contributed to the cooking and packaging of food. Cellophane was invented by the E.I. Du Pont de Nemours Company of Wilmington.

MARYLAND

SEAFOOD is a prime ingredient in Maryland's cuisine and is also the state's primary food product. The Chesapeake Bay, the largest estuary in the United States, has provided a livelihood for watermen since colonial days. The term "waterman" is an old English word referring to anyone who earned his living on water—fisherman, trader, or smuggler. Today, on the Chesapeake Bay it refers to the men and women who work the seasonal round of seafood.

Harvesting seafood in the Chesapeake Bay dates back to the Indians, who fished with spears or bush weirs and used their surplus catch to barter with nearby tribes for other necessities. Many of the Indians preserved their catches for winter by salting or smoking them.

Prior to the nineteenth century, the economy of Maryland was based on agriculture. As refrigeration and transportation became available, commercial seafood began to take over in importance.

Today, the Chesapeake Bay seafood harvests total about 400 million pounds annually. The Chesapeake yields more oysters, blue crabs, and soft-shell clams than any other body of water in the world. Almost 20,000 watermen make their living from the Bay, and several thousand more people are employed in related industries.

Oysters

Chesapeake Bay oysters have been eaten for centuries. The first English settlers originally thought them starvation food but soon learned from the shell piles left by the Indians that oysters were one of their basic foods. In the early twentieth century, some Bay communities had a saying, "The only thing anyone steals here is whiskey and oysters." So valued were the succulent mollusks that oystermen once fought shooting wars over them.

OYSTER STEW

At one time oysters were so plentiful in the Chesapeake Bay area that they were served at every meal. Shooting wars were once fought by fishermen over territorial rights to oyster beds. Oysters have been served in the Middle Atlantic states for centuries, either on the half-shell, broiled, scalloped, baked, or stewed.

Serves 6

1 quart shucked oysters with liquor

8 tablespoons (1 stick) butter or margarine

1/2 teaspoon salt

1/4 teaspoon freshly ground pepper

3 cups milk

2 cups half-and-half

1 cup whipping cream

2 tablespoons chopped fresh parsley,
   for garnish

■

Pick over the oysters to remove any shells, drain them, and reserve the liquor.

Melt 6 tablespoons of the butter in a large saucepan over medium-low heat. Add the oyster liquor, salt, and pepper and stir to blend well. Cook until heated through. Add the oysters and cook until their edges begin to curl. Do not overcook them or they will get tough.

Stir in the milk, half-and-half, and whipping cream and heat until the mixture comes almost to a boil, but do not let it boil. Serve the stew in hot bowls and top each serving with a dab of the remaining butter and a sprinkling of the parsley.

The Patuxent River, which flows southeast through Maryland, has been an important source of Maryland oysters. Since 1867, when Isaac Solomon opened the first cannery on the river, dozens of packing houses were established to buy, pack, and ship Patuxent River oysters.

OYSTER PARTY by Lucille Corcos, tempera, 18 1/4 x 22 inches, courtesy of Babcock Galleries, New York, New York.

They were packed in paraffin-lined barrels with a block of ice for coolant and shipped to many of the eastern cities.

Patuxent oystermen invented new gear to suit the special characteristics of the river. In 1887 Charles L. Marsh, a Solomons, Maryland, blacksmith, patented his design for deep-water oyster tongs. Seventy years later, another blacksmith, T. Rayner Wilson, and oysterman Edward Barrett developed an oyster-tong rig powered by hydraulics.

These two inventions revolutionized the Chesapeake oyster industry by allowing rapid harvest of oysters lying in deep water.

Today, Maryland watermen go out in skipjacks hoping to dredge up good harvests. By law they work three days under sail and the remaining two days per week assisted by power boats. Maryland watermen also go out in power boats with hand tongs to public "rock," which are state-owned oyster beds. Both Maryland and Virginia strictly regulate oystering in the Chesapeake Bay to prevent over-harvesting.

Oysters spawn between late May and October, when the water is 68 degrees. Each female produces about five million eggs, but only 15 actually reach maturity. Oysters grow rapidly for the first five years of their life.

Oyster harvests have declined considerably since 1885, when Maryland watermen harvested 15 million bushels of oysters. Pollution and disease have eliminated many oyster beds. Today, only about three million bushels are harvested annually, conservation and the cleaning-up of the Bay are steadily increasing the oyster supply. Maryland oystermen still harvest about 30 percent of the nation's catch.

The Chesapeake oyster, which is harvested in the winter months, is that season's prized food. Maryland oyster chowder and fried oysters have became famous. At one time oysters were so plentiful that they accompanied almost any food—meats, cheeses, and even pretzels. They also became a featured item on the free-lunch counters of the bars in Baltimore.

Blue Crabs

The Chesapeake Bay commercial crabbing industry began in the mid-nineteenth century with the advent of refrigeration and regular steamboat and rail transportation. Until then the highly perishable crabs could not survive ship-ments to markets outside the local area.

Chesapeake Bay's blue crabs are highly prized and have some special characteristics. The blue refers to the color on the underside of the large claws. Most of the crab's life is spent on the floor of the Bay. Each female blue crab produces about two million eggs, but only about 50 reach maturity. Eggs, which are hatched in June, mature in July or August of the following year.

The blue crab may shed its shell as many as 23 times during its natural life span of three years. Each molt increases the crab's size by one-third. Before molting the crab develops a soft, new internal shell. The old shell then cracks, and the crab wiggles out. This fresh "soft crab" draws in water to expand its wrinkled shell, and after two days the shell hardens. As the crab ages, molts are less frequent. There is only a 24-hour

CRAB CAKES

Blue fin crabs are found predominantly in the Chesapeake Bay region of Maryland and Virginia. They are used in crab cakes, crab soups, Crab Imperial, and crab salads.

The addition of baking powder to this crab mixture results in a light and fluffy crab cake.

Serves 8

1 pound crab meat

1 egg, beaten

2/3 cup finely crushed saltine cracker crumbs

1 1/2 teaspoons Old Bay Seasoning

3 dashes Tabasco sauce

1/2 teaspoon dry mustard

1 teaspoon Worcestershire sauce

1 teaspoon baking powder

1 tablespoon lemon juice

3 tablespoons chopped fresh parsley

3 to 4 tablespoons mayonnaise

Butter or margarine for frying

■

Pick over the crab meat, removing any loose shells. Place in a bowl and add all of the ingredients except the mayonnaise. Gently fold to mix, being careful not to break up the crabmeat. Fold in enough mayonnaise to hold the mixture together. Shape the crabmeat mixture into 8 three-quarter-inch patties.

Melt enough butter in a large skillet over medium heat to cover the bottom of the skillet. Add the crabmeat cakes and fry until brown on one side, about 3 to 4 minutes, then turn and brown the other side, also about 3 to 4 minutes. Serve at once.

period when the shell is soft enough so that the whole body of the crab can be eaten.

With each summer dawn a Chesapeake Bay crabber loads his workboat with barrels, baskets, and frozen bait and heads out for the creek mouths or the open, choppy Bay. On a bright day he can easily spot the lines of floats that mark his line of crab pots. At the start of each line, he idles his engine, reaches over the side with a hooked pole, and catches the line under the first float. In rapid succession he raises the pot, dumps the catch into a basket, slashes a new piece of fresh bait and puts it into the pot's funnel neck, closes the pot, and drops it back. He may do this 20 times or hundreds, depending on the weather, the market, and the size of his operation. Heavy gloves save his hands from the snapping crab claws.

One crab pot can trap up to 50 crabs. The Atlantic blue crab that ventures into the crab pot averages five to seven inches across the back of the shell. Crab potters will keep almost all forms of legal size crabs, although they prefer the crab with the hard shell. "Jimmy" crabs, or males, are the fattest and meatiest. Egg-bearing females are not harvested commercially and are thrown back. According to state law, on the Bay tributaries, trotlines, which are baited every four to six feet, must be used.

As baskets or barrels are filled, the waterman keeps his wooden sizing gauge at hand to make sure the crab is more than the five inch minimum legal size. Then he heads to the picking house, where his baskets and barrels are weighed and their struggling contents are sent to be steamed, picked, graded, and packed.

Crab pickers are paid by the pound. It takes 12 to 20 seconds to pick one crab, and they are never picked by machine. Professional crab pickers use a small sharp knife and their hands to break the crab into manageable pieces.

Soft-shell crabs are "peeler" crabs in a molting phase that have shed their shells. Crabs, intended for market as soft-shell crabs, are often held in raft-like floats in creeks or in concrete tanks ashore until they shed their hard shells. As soon they shed and while their new shell is still soft and edible, they are quickly removed and packed in ice and eel grass on flat trays for shipment.

Blue crabs are the basis of Maryland crab cakes, cream of crab soup, and deviled crab. Soft-shell crabs are usually served fried.

Clams

Shellfish in the Chesapeake Bay are not limited to oysters and crabs, but include both hard- and soft-shelled clams. They are still so abundant that much of the harvest is shipped to New England.

Clams have always existed in the Bay in large numbers, but they only became a commercial harvest when the clam beds in New England declined in the 1950s. About the same time, Fletcher Hanks of Oxford, Maryland, developed the hydraulic clam dredge, and within six years, harvesting clams became a million-dollar-a-year business.

Life and Food in Early Maryland

The first settlements in what is today Maryland were founded by Englishmen on the shores of the Chesapeake Bay in 1634 under a land grant by King Charles I to Cecil Calvert, Lord Baltimore. One hundred and forty Englishmen were recruited to come to the New World by Lord Baltimore. The group included 17 "gentlemen adventurers" (who had invested in the colony), their indentured servants, and three Jesuit priests.

Despite the hazardous voyage, the settlers were attracted by Lord Baltimore's offer of 100 acres to anyone who would transport himself to the colony, with an additional 100 acres for each servant he brought along. If not able to pay the passage, settlers could indenture themselves to a landowner for a specific period of years and then be entitled to land.

The first settlers who came to the Maryland shores were wealthy men, most of them Catholic, who built grand manor houses and imported slaves to work the tobacco fields. They soon established the lavish social life they had been used to in England.

Just as lavish was the cuisine that was served by these gentry. Typical English foods were combined with the Negro cooking skills and the natural ingredients available. Wild turkey and venison were served with sweet potatoes. Oyster stuffing for roasted wild turkey became a speciality of Maryland cuisine, since there was an abundant supply of oysters in the Bay. Wild strawberries and steamed English puddings were favorite desserts.

Life in the eastern part of Maryland closely resembled that of the plantations of Virginia. The western or Piedmont area, however, was settled in the 1730s by Pennsylvania Germans, who came across the northern border. Thus Maryland developed two entirely different cuisines, one southern and the other influenced by Pennsylvania German cookery.

Although wild game was the main source of meat in colonial days, those who could afford beef and lamb added them to their cooking. Almost everyone raised pigs, and pork became the staple of the region. In the nineteenth century veal and lamb became popular due in part to affordable pricing. Veal was often roasted with herbs or paired with sweetbreads. Lamb was stewed with exotic spices from the Far East, and curry powder became a favorite mixture of spices for lamb. Since terrapins abounded near the Maryland shores, terrapin stew became a well-known dish.

Hams were cured in various fashions: in brine, cold smoked, or sugar and salt-cured. According to legend, many cooks in Maryland regarded "The making of a ham dinner, like the making of a gentleman.... both start a long, long time before the event."

Spices were brought to Baltimore in trading ships and became part of Maryland cooking. Ginger, cloves, allspice, and mace were often used in meat cookery. Kitchen gardens provided such herbs as thyme, savory, and marjoram.

Along with herbs grown in kitchen gardens, the early settlers also grew greens, such as dandelion, sorrel, and salad leaves (lettuce) for salads. The flowers and tender leaves of herbs, nasturtiums, violets, and rose petals were also used in salads. The tender shoots of a wild plant called pokeweed, however, had to be picked carefully, since the roots were poisonous.

Cooked salads, called pot salads, a traditional English dish, were popular in colonial Maryland. Hot salads at the time consisted of greens that were cooked and then served with a dressing. Potato salad also became a mainstay of Maryland cuisine.

BEATEN BISCUITS

Beaten biscuits originated in Maryland more than 200 years ago, when a mixture of soda and cream of tartar was used as the leavening. The dough was beaten to make it light and airy. These biscuits became such a necessity that a machine similar to a wringer was invented to manipulate the dough. Even in modern times, this type of biscuit dough is still beaten. By tradition the dough is beaten with a hammer, a mallet, or an ax for about 30 minutes. Lard was originally used in the biscuit dough, but today either solid vegetable shortening, margarine, or butter is often substituted.

Makes 3 ½ to 4 dozen biscuits

4 cups all-purpose flour
1 teaspoon baking powder
1/2 teaspoon salt
1 teaspoon sugar
1/2 cup lard, solid vegetable shortening, margarine, or butter
1/3 cup milk combined with 1/3 cup water

■

Combine the flour, baking powder, salt, and sugar in a bowl. Cut in the shortening until it resembles coarse meal. Add just enough of the liquid, a little at a time, to make a stiff dough. Knead the dough several times in the bowl and then turn it out on a lightly floured board. Beat the dough for about 30 minutes, turning it several times until it pops and is smooth and elastic. Shape the dough into small balls by hand. Place on a cookie sheet and prick each biscuit with a fork, making 3 rows of holes. Bake in a preheated 400° F. oven for 20 to 25 minutes, or until light brown.

Negro cooks added their own touches to local ingredients. Black bean soup was cooked with veal and seasoned with sherry and allspice. Consommé was flavored with sherry and caramelized sugar.

Wheat Growing In Maryland

Although tobacco was the mainstay of Maryland's economy in the seventeenth and eighteenth centuries, wheat became an important crop as more overseas markets developed.

In the 1750s John Stevenson, an Irish immigrant, sent the first cargo of wheat to Ireland and began trading in that commodity. The Baltimore economy soon centered around the wheat trade with Great Britain, the West Indies, and southern Europe. Water provided the necessary power for milling the grain grown in northern and western Maryland. In 1804 there were 50 mills within 18 miles of Baltimore. Isaac McKim built the first steam-operated flour mill in 1822.

In the 1760s a group of Scotch-Irish

Presbyterian flour merchants from Lancaster County, Pennsylvania, moved to Baltimore so that they could ship wheat flour and other products directly from the port. They were soon joined by others. These merchants built wharfs and countinghouses to handle the tremendous orders for flour in the 1780s. Roads were built to Frederick in the hinterland to obtain the flour.

City Markets

The city markets of Baltimore have been famous for centuries. Lexington Market, founded in 1782, is one of the oldest continuously operated markets in the United States. There are stalls selling fresh produce, meats, and seafood. Since the market is near the downtown business area, it is a favorite place for lunch, with both lunch stands and sit-down restaurants.

Broadway Market, founded in 1785, is a popular market located in the historic harbor-side neighborhood. There are five other such markets in Baltimore. In addition to their customer loyalty, which has remained for generations, these markets have survived due to the wonderful freshness and diversity of their foods.

Maryland Foods

Although Maryland cookery began with the Indians' food of corn, beans, and wild game, it was soon changed by Lord Baltimore and his gentry, whose orchards and vegetable gardens provided lavish foods.

Germans settled in western Maryland, where they tilled the soil and raised crops, including wheat. Western Maryland became known as the breadbasket for the Chesapeake. These German settlers baked wholesome breads, such as pumpernickel, rye bread, and Kaiser rolls—all a welcome change from the quick breads of the early settlers.

Soups and chowders have always been an important part of Maryland cuisine. For the more affluent, soups were the start of a meal, but for the poor a hearty soup was often the entire meal. Bones, scraps of meat, and vegetables were saved for the soup pot. Dumplings were often added to the top of a vegetable soup. Maryland crab soup, with a beef base and bacon flavoring, became a staple of Maryland cookery. She-crab soup, a more delicate cream soup containing crab eggs, was served in the days before crab harvesting was regulated and she-crabs could still be taken.

Early Maryland cooks combined chicken, vegetables, and seafood in a chowder. Some of these chowders contained clams; others crabmeat or rock fish. Corn, potatoes, peas, and celery were added to purely fish chowders.

Maryland fried chicken and corn bread made with white cornmeal became a staple dinner, as did Maryland fried chicken with cream gravy and beaten biscuits. Depending on the cook, the chicken was first dipped in milk or buttermilk, then coated with cornmeal or flour and fried to a golden brown. Lard was the preferred shortening.

Stuffed ham was and still is popular in Maryland. The ham was a fresh one or one that had been only lightly cured. Before stuffing, the ham was partially boiled, then removed from the water, and slits were cut in the ham. A stuffing mixture of greens, such as watercress, kale or cabbage, celery, pepper, and mustard seeds was moistened with some of the cooking liquid and then stuffed into the slits. The whole ham was then put into a cloth bag and returned to the boiling liquid to finish cooking. When sliced the ham was colorful, and the stuffing added additional flavor.

Beaten biscuits, popular on the eastern shore, were made by beating the dough for at least a half an hour until the dough was full of air. These light and fluffy biscuits accompanied ham, crabmeat, and chicken dishes.

Maryland clams are often served deviled with a mustard sauce. They are also fried in cornmeal or pancake batter and can be chopped as an ingredient for fritters.

Well into the present century, baking was a matter of necessity as well as tradition in Maryland. The women did all of the baking—breads, biscuits, cakes, pies, and cookies—although the men often helped beat the biscuits. Loaf breads were not prevalent, but biscuits, corn bread, or yeast rolls were the norm at dinner.

NEW JERSEY

NEW JERSEY is called the Garden State for good reason. Although many think of New Jersey as a concentrated industrial area, it is still one of the garden baskets of the country. Away from the noise and activity of freeways, the state's agricultural areas produce more than 150 crops. New Jersey has a ready-made market for its produce in the New York City area.

The variety of soils in New Jersey has contributed to the state's successful agriculture. Sandy soil near the seashore yields large juicy blueberries, luscious strawberries, and asparagus. Green vegetables are grown in the black, fertile soil of the state's higher valleys. Root vegetables are also an integral part of New Jersey's agriculture, and the cultivation of parsnips dates back to the English heritage of some of the early settlers.

In the late 1800s railroads ran a special train from New Jersey's agricultural regions to New York City. The train, known as the "Pea Line," provided city dwellers with large quantities of fresh produce at low prices.

Agricultural and Food Research

For more than two centuries, New Jersey has been a leader in agricultural research. In 1797 Charles Newbold obtained the first patent for a plow with a wrought-iron plowshare. Until that time plowshares were made of wood and reinforced with strips of steel.

Tomatoes were considered poisonous in the late-eighteenth and early-nineteenth centuries. Robert Gibbon Johnson of Salem County, New Jersey, stood in front of the county courthouse in 1830 and demonstrated to the public that the tomato was not poisonous by eating one of the feared ornamental fruits.

A food experiment conducted in 1897 by John T. Dorrance has affected almost every American ever since. Dorrance, a chemist, went to work for $7.50 a week in a small Camden factory owned by Joseph Campbell and Abraham Anderson. He came up with the idea of condensing and canning soups. When he died, Dorrance was worth $117 million, and Campbell Soups have become household staple.

A great deal of agricultural research was performed at state and university

GRILLED MONKFISH

New Jersey has a long history of fishing, both commercial and sport fishing. George Washington is the first person known to have chartered a fishing boat in New Jersey. He was probably fishing for gray sea trout. Washington and the Marquis de Lafayette both cooked seafood when they were members of the Schyullkill Fish and Game Club.

Monkfish are among the many fish harvested off the coast of New Jersey. Although a rather ugly fish, it has often been called "poor man's lobster" because of its firm flesh. Monkfish is ideal for grilling.

Serves 3

2/3 cup olive oil

3 tablespoons lemon juice

1 tablespoon chopped fresh parsley

1 tablespoon chopped fresh basil

1 clove garlic, minced

1/4 teaspoon salt

1/4 teaspoon pepper

2 pounds monkfish, cut into 1 1/2-inch cubes

1/2 green pepper, cut into 1 1/2-inch cubes

1/2 red pepper, cut into 1 1/2-inch cubes

16 cherry tomatoes

■

Combine the olive oil, lemon juice, parsley, basil, garlic, salt, and pepper in a shallow dish. Add the fish, cover, and marinade in the refrigerator for 5 hours or overnight.

Thread the fish alternately with the pepper pieces and tomatoes onto 8 water-soaked bamboo skewers. Grill 4 inches above hot coals for about 3 minutes on each side, brushing with the marinade occasionally. Serve with rice.

experimental stations. One of the New Jersey Agricultural Experimental Stations developed the Golden Jubilee and Cumberland peaches in the early 1900s. This involved pollinating 30,000 peach trees by hand. The same experimental station also developed strawberries so large that 15 of them made a pound—three times larger than the normal commercial strawberries at the time! The Rutgers University Agricultural Experiment Station developed a new tomato; perfected a compound which produces juicier, shinier, and better-tasting apples; and developed a new sweet potato, the Jersey Orange.

In the 1950s Seabrooke Farms spanned 90,000 acres in the southern part of New Jersey and two adjoining states. It was the largest vegetable farm in the country. Most of the produce grown on the farm went immediately to a frozen-food plant. Radio communications in the fields advised the plant almost hourly as to what was being picked so that the produce could be frozen at optimum freshness. Seabrooke Bros. & Sons, Inc., has smaller acreage today, but it still grows produce and flash-freezes it.

Early New Jersey

New Jersey has a rather strange history, because it began as two separate colonies—East Jersey and West Jersey. East Jersey, across the Hudson River from New Amsterdam, was settled by the Dutch and later by English, Scots, and French Huguenots. West Jersey began as a Quaker settlement on the banks of the Delaware River in 1674, seven years before William Penn obtained the land grant that later became Pennsylvania.

Between the two settlements lay a swampy wasteland, which greatly hin-dered communications between them. Even after the two colonies were united in 1702, the middle area was neglected. Also, New Jersey's seacoast was not conducive to settlement because of dangerous shoals and treacherous harbors. Jersey settlements continued to concentrate along the Hudson and Delaware Rivers, with the farming areas providing wheat for New York City and Philadelphia. Over the years, however, the coastal plain, which was not suited to wheat farming, proved to have very fertile soil ideal for vegetables, and it became part of New Jersey's "Garden Basket."

Quartering of Troops

After the French and Indian War in 1765, British troops remained in the colonies. They were quartered in private homes, whose owners had to provide candles, vinegar, salt, and no more than five pints of beer or cider or a half pint of rum mixed with water to each British soldier every day. Although the homeowners were not required to provide meals, the soldiers were allowed to use the fireplace and its utensils to cook their food. Later, firewood was added to the list of required provisions. Innkeepers and homeowners were to be reimbursed for their expenses but probably never were.

During the Revolutionary War many of the American troops were quartered in New Jersey homes. They were welcome guests and were frequently invited to partake of the family's meals. A typical meal at the time might have consisted of potato soup made with a generous amount of onions, wild turkey with corn-bread stuffing, and mashed potatoes. Depending on the time of year, a green or root vegetable accompanied the turkey, and rice pudding topped with currant jelly was served for dessert.

Applejack

Apple cider was a common drink in the colonies, and one of the earliest types was developed in New Jersey. The apples for the cider came from trees planted in the early 1630s. A century later a leading world botanist, Peter Kalm of Sweden, pronounced New Jersey cider to be one of the best he had ever tasted. This was probably the first European recognition of an American food product.

The New Jerseyites were not content with simple cider. At the end of the 1600s, William Laird began to distill the cider, producing apple brandy, now better known as applejack. This distilling process is the final step in transforming apple juice into an alcoholic beverage. The mid-point of this fermentation results in hard cider. This type of cider, with an eight-percent alcohol content, was the prevalent drink in the colonies.

To make applejack, the cider is allowed to ferment to 12-percent alcohol and then distilled to an 80- or 100-proof brandy. In 1780 one of Laird's descendants began commercial production of apple brandy under the firm name of Laird & Co. in Scobeyville, New Jersey.

Milk Inspection

The first system of efficient milk marketing and inspection took place in New Jersey in the late 1880s. Until that time, milk was sold in grocery stores and was ladled out of an open can into the customers' containers. In 1885 the Borden Company began delivering milk in closed bottles, and in 1892 the company instituted bacterial counts of the milk, which helped assure its freshness. Until that time most of the commercial milk consumed by the American public had to be boiled before usage. In 1904 at the Walker-Gordon farm near Princeton, the first quart of certified pasteurized milk was produced.

From Tea to Soups

Sir Thomas Lipton, a frequent visitor to the United States, greatly admired this country and often referred to it as his second home. In 1890 on one of his trips, the millionaire Scottish grocer decided to give the American tea business a try. Lipton reportedly got the idea when he ordered tea in a Chicago hotel, only to find that the waiter returned with a cup of coffee.

Prior to Lipton's entry into the American tea business, most of the tea retailed in America was green tea and of an inferior quality—hardly a brew that would return Americans to their tea-loving ways that had existed before the Revolution.

In the late 1880s Lipton had purchased several tea plantations in Ceylon. He had already changed the merchandising of tea in the British Isles by packaging tea in one-pound, half-pound, and quarter-pound packages to assure freshness and exact weight.

In 1891 Lipton established a chain of agents to sell his robust blend of black Ceylon and Indian teas to the hotel and restaurant trades in America. By 1910 his American tea business and other food enterprises had grown to a size that warranted the opening of a combination plant and corporate headquarters in Hoboken, New Jersey.

Although Lipton did not invent the

STILL LIFE: BASKET OF STRAWBERRIES, Severin Roesen, oil, 25 x 21 1/4 inches, courtesy of Richard York Gallery, New York, New York.

BERRIES AND CREAM

New Jersey, the Garden State, has long been known for the great variety of vegetables and fruit it produces. Strawberries, blackberries, raspberries, and blueberries are cultivated in the sandy soil near the seashore.

These berries are combined with a light cream for a refreshing summer dessert.

Serves 4 to 6

3/4 cup sugar

1 envelope unflavored gelatin

1 1/2 cups water

1 cup sour cream

1 1/2 teaspoons vanilla extract

1 1/4 cups whipping cream

1 cup blueberries

1 cup raspberries or blackberries

1 cup sliced strawberries

■

Mix the sugar and gelatin in a small saucepan. Add the water and stir over low heat to dissolve the sugar and gelatin. Remove from heat, pour into a bowl, and blend in the sour cream and vanilla. Chill until slightly thickened. Whip the cream until thick and fold it into the sour cream mixture. Pour into a 1-quart mold and chill until firm, about 3 hours. Unmold the cream onto a plate and pour the fresh fruit over it.

tea bag, he became the first to recognize its marketing possibilities. Since the production of tea bags was labor intensive, it was limited at first, but consumers were willing to pay 25 cents for 15 tea bags that came in an attractive gold tin. By 1932 the price had increased and the gold tin had been replaced by a red and gold cardboard carton bearing on its side a small vignette of Sir Thomas, who had died in 1931 at the age of eighty-one. Over the years the Lipton Tea Company

has continued to improve the tea bag and has added instant tea and instant iced tea to its product line.

The Lipton Company has also continued Sir Thomas's philosophy of growth through new products. In 1940 Lipton purchased Continental Foods of Chicago, a soup manufacturer. Two years later, the Lipton Company purchased a dehydrated food plant that produced tomatoes and other wartime food needs. With these two acquisitions,

dried soup mixes became a part of the Lipton Company. Today, the corporate Lipton umbrella includes the Wish-Bone Company, Good Humor Ice Cream, Knox Gelatin, and Lawry's Foods.

New Jersey Seafood

New Jersey's commercial fishing history dates back to the first half of the nineteenth century, when the catches were sold in New York, Philadelphia, and New Jersey's inland cities. By the 1950s New Jersey fishermen were catching millions of pounds of fish each year.

New Jersey has six modern fishing ports, with thousands of fishermen, as well as processing plants. Butterfish, monkfish, tilefish, mackerel, red and silver hake, sea bass, crabs, oysters, and scallops are some of the seafood harvested off the coast of New Jersey.

Squid and tuna have become important catches for New Jersey fishermen. Until recently squid have been a "by-catch" of commercial fishermen, but the demand for squid has grown rapidly, and fishermen now fish specifically for them. Squid prefer the deep waters beyond the continental shelf and are usually caught offshore during the summer and fall. The demand for tuna has also increased. During the summer and early fall, boats leave Cape May to fish tuna off the New Jersey shore.

NEW YORK

IT WAS HARD TO RECRUIT Dutch settlers for the New World since there was prosperity and religious tolerance in Holland. Those Dutch settlers who did come to the New World preferred fur trading to farming. As the number of settlers who brought livestock and farm implements increased, farming became a full-time livelihood. In 1626 Peter Minuit purchased Manhattan Island from the Indians, and the permanent settlements of the New Netherlands colony were firmly established. Manhattan Island was renamed New Amsterdam and became the capital of the Dutch colony. Although the Dutch only governed their domain in America for about 40 years, their influence on American cuisine has been lasting.

Probably the most important contribution the Dutch made to the New World was the introduction of grain. Their principal crop was wheat, although they also raised barley, rye, and buckwheat. Wheat became an important commodity in New Netherlands and was sold to both the New England and Southern colonies. It continued to be a major source of income after New Netherlands was taken over by the British. In the late 1700s New York was growing so much wheat that the colony became known as the "granary of the Revolution."

The Dutch loved cakes, pastries, and breads. Dumplings, pancakes, and waffles, which the Dutch introduced to American cuisine, figured prominently in their daily menus. Settlers brought long-handled waffle irons from Holland and used them in the fireplaces of their colonial homes.

MADAM LACHET by Warren Baumgarten, watercolor, 16 x 20 inches, courtesy of Hastings Art, Ltd., New Canaan, Connecticut.

The Dutch quickly adopted Indian corn, which they called "Turkey wheat," and made it into a porridge. The cornmeal was boiled in milk and became known as *Suppawn*. The pounding of dry corn into meal with a mortar in the Indian fashion soon became a tiresome job for the Dutch settlers. Consequently, they built Dutch-style windmills to grind their corn, as well as their wheat and rye.

The Dutch, who enjoyed baked goods, started the first public bakeries in America in 1656. Until that time all baking was done at home. Laws were passed by the Dutch that cookies and other sweet cakes could not be sold by the bakery unless they also sold bread. It was also stipulated that the bread selection had to consist of both white loaves and coarse-grain loaves, and the price was set by law.

Dutch Food

Since the Dutch settlers were used to dairy products, they brought dairy cattle with them from Holland and produced milk, butter, and cheese. The Dutch settlers loved to coat their bread with a thick layer of butter, and they

SHAKER BEEF STEW WITH DUMPLINGS

Meat was an important part of the Shaker diet at both breakfast and dinner. In the early days of their settlement in New York in the late 1700s, they butchered surplus stock in the fall and ate it as soon as possible. Some of the meat was stored in cold cellars or corned in brine.

The Shakers prepared food efficiently, nutritiously, and as tasty as possible. They believed that meals should create joy and contentment. Herbs played a large part in making their food tasty and were used in meat cookery, as well as in vegetable and dumpling preparations.

Serves 6

3 pounds beef stew meat, cut into
    1 1/2-inch cubes
Salt and pepper, to taste
All-purpose flour
2 tablespoons butter
3 cups beef broth
2 cups water
3 medium onions, sliced
1 1/2 cups carrots, cut into large cubes
1 1/2 cups turnips, cut into large cubes
2 stalks celery, sliced

■

Season the meat with salt and pepper and dredge it in flour. Melt the butter in a large heavy iron pot and sear the meat. Add the broth and water. Bring to a boil and simmer for 2 1/2 hours. Add the vegetables and cook over low heat for 30 minutes or until the vegetables are tender.

While the vegetables are cooking, prepare the dumpling mixture. Drop the dumpling batter by heaping tablespoons onto the stew. Cover the pot tightly and cook for 12 more minutes.

Dumplings

2 cups all-purpose flour
6 teaspoons baking powder
1/2 teaspoon salt
1 tablespoon chopped fresh parsley
1/2 tablespoon chopped fresh thyme
1/2 tablespoon chopped fresh chives
2 eggs
3/4 cup milk

■

Combine the flour, baking powder, and salt in a bowl. Add the herbs. Beat the milk and eggs together in another bowl and mix into the dry ingredients.

featured hearty food. A favorite dish was a derivation of the Dutch *Hutspot* (meaning hodgepodge), which consisted of cornmeal porridge cooked with chunks of corned beef and root vegetables. This dish was often cooked for three days until it formed a thick crust on top. Another favorite dish was split-pea soup made with a ham hock and served with *Koolslaa,* coleslaw.

Roast duck with dumplings, pork with cabbage, or roast goose were served on holidays. Almost every Dutch housewife had a flock of geese waddling in the garden and near the ponds to provide holiday eating and feathers for the beds. The settlers also supplemented their holiday meals by obtaining venison, wild turkey, partridge, and passenger pigeons from the Indians.

For dessert, *Oliekocken* were often served. These pastries, made with a raised yeast dough, shaped into small balls, and fried in hot lard until golden brown, were named "doughnuts" by Washington Irving in his *History of New York.* After frying, the doughnuts were rolled in sifted sugar and served warm. The hole in the doughnut came later, when Dutch bakers decided to eliminate the often-soggy center and give more crispness to the edges.

The early Dutch settlers served *Doed-koeckje* with Madeira wine at funerals. These were thick round cookies made with caraway seeds that had the initials of the deceased on top. Many of the cookies were taken home by the mourners and kept as a remembrance for years. These cookies were home-baked, except in the Albany area where a bakery specialized in *Doed-koeckje.* The word "koeckje" was later anglicized into "cookies."

Tea, sugar, spices, chocolate, wines,

often served slices of firm cheese for breakfast along with a glass of buttermilk.

In the Dutch colony a typical day began with a breakfast of *Suppawn,* rye bread, headcheese, and a draft of beer for the adults. Headcheese was a type of

sausage made from pieces of cooked meat from the head and feet of the hog and combined with vinegar and spices. The mixture was then pressed into a ball the shape of a cheese.

Dinner in the middle of the day

and brandies were all readily available in the Dutch colony. Ships from Holland traded in ports all over the world and came to New Netherlands to obtain furs, lumber, and grain in exchange for these culinary luxuries. One of the great luxuries at the time was sugar. In Dutch homes both granulated and small lump sugar were offered to visitors at tea time in compartmentalized, little silver boxes. Sweet cakes, cookies, waffles, *Oliekocken,* or Dutch apple cake were served with tea. The apple cake consisted of a yeast dough topped with apple slices and sprinkled with sugar and cinnamon.

Shaker Influence

The Shakers were another group of settlers who had a profound influence on the food of New York. The first Shakers arrived in America from England in 1774 with their leader Mother Ann Lee, who had seceded from the Quakers. They received their name from their manner of worship, which included dancing, shaking, falling into a trance, and experiencing religious visions. They believed in communal living and the common ownership of goods and property. The Shakers settled in New Lebanon, near Albany, and eventually established other communities in Ohio.

The Shaker communities were organized into families of 30 to 100 members, each supervised by an elder, who directed his family's activities in farming, building, preparing food, and furniture making.

Meals were eaten at long tables in a common dining room, where silence reigned at each meal. Jugs of milk or cider and large baskets of bread were placed on each table to accompany fish, poultry, and vegetables. The Shakers

leaned toward a vegetarian diet.

As the communities grew, the Shakers learned large-scale cooking and set up three kitchens in each community—one for cooking, the second for baking, and the third for canning. They invented many gadgets to speed up their kitchen work, such as one for paring, coring, and quartering apples; another for shelling peas; a cheese press; and a water-powered butter churn. They also invented the clothespin.

The Shakers were some of the first people to write down recipes using exact units of measurement. They can be credited with developing a basic baking mix by combining flour, baking powder, salt, and shortening. With the addition of liquid, the mixture could be turned into biscuits, pancakes, or muffins.

Shaker cooks used a wide range of spices in their cooking—rosemary, savory, basil, chives, chervil, and thyme. They packaged the herbs they grew and sold them with pamphlets instructing the purchaser in their use. Typically, there were several buildings in the Shaker community devoted to the drying, grinding, and packaging of herbs.

New species of fruits and vegetables were developed by the Shakers, and they established plant nurseries, where they developed seeds. Their seed catalogs offered tremendous varieties in many vegetables and fruits, such as eight types of beans, four kinds of squash, and six varieties of carrots and beets.

The Shakers also were among the first to advocate that the entire wheat kernel be ground into flour, thus creating whole-wheat flour. One of the greatest believers in the excellent properties of whole wheat was food evangelist, Sylvester Graham, who spent most of his life telling people about the good proper-

ties of grains and healthy diets in general. He did not want man "to put asunder what God joined together"—bran and wheat flour. He developed Graham bread and the Graham cracker in the late 1830s.

A New Cereal Is Born

A little more than a half century later, another advocate of wheat in the diet was Henry Perky, a Denver lawyer. Perky found he preferred inventing to pleading cases in court, and at the age of forty-seven, he started searching for a method of processing corn so that it would remain edible after being dehydrated. In 1892, he came east to Watertown, New York, where he developed a machine that could press wheat into shred-like strips. When baked, these strips became delicious biscuits, which Perky named "Shredded Wheat." Demand for the new biscuits was so great that Perky built a bakery equipped with several ovens and 11 wheat-shredding machines in Roxbury, Massachusetts, in 1895.

Since this facility was also not sufficient to meet national demands for Shredded Wheat, Perky decided to build one huge bakery rather than many small ones. He bought a ten-acre site in Niagara Falls, New York, where he erected a two-million-dollar, air-conditioned plant of marble, tile, and glass, which he called the "Palace of Light." In May 1901 the plant turned out its first Shredded Wheat within sight of the mighty falls. A picture of Niagara Falls adorned each package of shredded wheat for many years. The Shredded Wheat Company was acquired by Nabisco Brands in 1928.

HEBREW DINNER TABLE by Tibor "Stibor" Silberhorn, oil, 36 x 24 inches, courtesy of Kertesz Fine Art Galleries, San Francisco, California.

with almonds, is often served after the Greek or Russian Orthodox Easter service along with hot tea poured from samovars.

French Canadians came south across the border and helped settle northern New York State. They brought their *Cassoulet,* an oven dish of white beans cooked with bits of roast goose and pork. Onion soup with onions that had been simmered in butter, yellow split-pea soup, and venison meatballs served with a tomato and sour cream sauce were some of the other dishes prepared by the French Canadians.

Italians came to New York City's East Side by the thousands around the turn of the century. They primarily came from southern Italy and brought their region's cooking with its liberal use of tomatoes and olive oil. Italian spaghetti with meat sauce and pizza, as well as salads with oil and vinegar dressings, have become classics of American cookery.

Jewish Food Influence

The first Jews came to the Dutch colony in 1654, when they were rescued from their capsized boat off the coast of Jamaica by a French sea captain. He brought the 23 Jews, who were some of the last to be expelled from the Iberian Peninsula, to New Amsterdam.

From then until the 1820s only a few thousand additional Jews came to America, after which Jewish immigration increased rapidly. Frequently whole European Jewish communities packed up and came to this country. Many Jewish immigrants remained in New York City.

Their cooking was not based on that of their native lands, but on the Jewish dietary laws as enumerated in the Bible. The Bible prohibits devout Jews from eating hornless, cloven-hoofed animals,

Other Ethnic Food Influences

Since New York was a major embarkation port for European immigrants, the state has a large variety of ethnic foods. The Germans, for example, who settled in the Mohawk Valley in 1735, used the wild gooseberries they found to bake their favorite tarts. Sugar was sifted over the berries and raisins

were added to the mixture before placing it in the tart shell for baking.

Poles and other Eastern Europeans settled in the Buffalo area. Many traditional foods are still served there during the holidays and at weddings. The Polish community prepares *Pierogi,* a boiled dumpling made with potato dough, filled with plum jam, and served with a spiced cream sauce. *Kulich,* a rich yeast cake thus all pork is forbidden. It further prohibits the eating of fish without fins and scales, thus no shellfish is eaten. Another religious statute prohibits the serving of meat and dairy dishes at the same meal. Fortunately, there is a third category of food, called *pareve* or neutral, which includes eggs, fish, vegetables, fruits, and grains that can be served with either meat or dairy meals. Today, many Jews dismiss these kosher dietary laws as being obsolete, while others observe parts or all of them.

In the late nineteenth century in New York, meat was slaughtered according to kosher laws and was usually stewed or braised. Jewish housewives baked cakes and breads sprinkled with poppy seeds and bought pickles, smoked fish, and pastrami at the delicatessens. They made chicken soup with matzoh balls, and *Kugel,* noodle pudding, was often served for dessert. *Challah,* the traditional braided egg bread, was baked for holidays, and matzoh, unleavened bread, was commercially baked for Passover. *Latkes,* or potato pancakes, were served at Hanukkah.

Friday night Sabbath dinner was always a hallowed occasion in Jewish homes. The women of the house had scrubbed the kitchen clean, and mother lit the Sabbath candles and intoned a prayer over them. Then the most substantial meal of the week was served featuring some of the highlights of Jewish cuisine. Gefilte fish, chopped liver, and chicken soup started the meal. For the main course there was either chicken or beef with *Tsimmes,* a pudding of dried fruits, potatoes or carrots, and onions; a *Kugel*; and *Challah.* A sponge or honey cake was served with fruit for dessert.

Eating Establishments

In the late 1700s taverns were the eating and drinking establishments of the day. One of the most successful of these was founded by Samuel Fraunces in 1763 on the corner of Pearl and Broad Streets in Lower Manhattan. Fraunces Tavern was an elegant place, with five guest rooms, an ale room, and an eating room seating 75 diners. Fraunces also did catering and had a take-out service of pastries and desserts or of whole meals for sea captains and their passengers. He even exported pickled oysters and lobsters.

Although during the American Revolution many taverns remained loyal to the British, Fraunces Tavern hosted several American rallies, including a protest to the tea tax. It was only appropriate that George Washington chose the Fraunces Tavern as a place to say farewell to his troops.

By the beginning of the nineteenth century, New York City had several types of eating establishments, including coffeehouses, oyster houses, a tea garden, a cookshop, and more than forty combination taverns and boardinghouses. There hearty meals were the norm for the

NOODLE KUGEL

Kugels are traditionally served on the Jewish Sabbath. They are baked puddings usually made with noodles or potatoes. The non-sweet versions are served as meat accompaniments, and the sweet versions, as dessert. Noodle Kugels, which are sweet and contain spices, are usually served for dessert.

Serves 6

5 ounces medium-wide egg noodles

3 eggs

1/2 cup milk

1 package (3 ounces) cream cheese, at
    room temperature

3/4 cup large curd, cream-style cottage
    cheese

2 tablespoons sugar

3/4 teaspoon vanilla extract

1/4 teaspoon ground cinnamon

1/4 teaspoon ground nutmeg

1/2 cup golden raisins

2 tablespoons melted butter

■

Cook the noodles until they are tender, then drain them, and place them in a mixing bowl.

In another bowl beat together the eggs, milk, and cream cheese. Fold in the cottage cheese, sugar, vanilla, and spices. Add the egg mixture to the noodles, mixing well. Then add the raisins.

Pour the noodle mixture into a well-greased 8-inch square baking dish. Drizzle the melted butter on top. Bake in a preheated 325° F. oven for 30 to 35 minutes, or until a knife inserted in the center comes out clean. Serve warm as a dessert.

workers, merchants, and immigrants who did not have a permanent place of residence.

The concept of eating houses changed in New York with the establishment of a pastry shop by Swiss-born Giovanni Del-Monico. John Delmonico, as he became known, was an ex-sea captain who had opened a wine shop on the Battery in Lower Manhattan in 1825. He started observing that his customers were buying the more expensive items and decided that the city needed a pastry shop. Delmonico went back to Switzerland and convinced his brother, Pietro, a confectioner, to join in his venture. They opened a pastry shop, selling European-style desserts, on Williams Street in 1827. Four years later, the two brothers bought the building next door and started serving hot lunches to businessmen. The food was prepared by a French chef, and it quickly en-

chanted the New York public, who made lunch a dining experience. At Delmonico's they were able to enjoy such unknown delicacies as endive and eggplant.

A second Delmonico restaurant was opened on Broad Street in 1832. When the first restaurant was destroyed by fire, it was replaced by a much more elaborate one that served multi-course, sophisticated French meals. Over the next 50 years, the restaurant moved to several locations in New York City and became one of the most fashionable places to eat in the world. As the population of New York City moved uptown so did Delmonico's. The family opened another restaurant at the corner of Fifth Avenue and Forty-Fourth Street in 1897.

The early Delmonico menus were printed in both English and German, a format that was popular with many restaurants in the mid-1800s. The restaurant's name became attached to a special steak, a

dish of potatoes, and an elegant veal hash served in a chafing dish. The latter was so popular that for many years chafing dishes became necessary pieces of equipment in fine restaurants and many affluent homes. Baked Alaska, an ice-cream dessert covered with meringue and then baked, was created by Delmonico's to commemorate the purchase of Alaska.

A direct competitor of the Delmonico's restaurants was Louis Sherry, a Vermonter, who catered to the eating whims of the affluent. One of the most famous evenings at Sherry's restaurant, which he opened in 1882 at Fifth Avenue and Forty-Fourth Street (across from Delmonico's), was the 1903 Horse Dinner of the New York Riding Club. Horses were brought to the fourth-floor ballroom in the freight elevator and tied to a large dining table, where they fed on oats while their owners sipped champagne from bottles displayed in saddle bags and enjoyed a 14-course dinner.

Waldorf Salad, probably the most famous dish of the late 1800s, was conceived by Oscar Tschirky, maître d'hôtel of the Waldorf Astoria Hotel, to celebrate the opening of the hotel in 1893. The basic salad was a mixture of apples and celery with mayonnaise served in lettuce cups. Later, chopped walnuts were added and more modern versions include raisins and crushed pineapple.

New York's most famous German restaurant for many years was Lüchow's on Fourteenth Street. August Lüchow started in the restaurant business in 1882 by running a beer hall. In order to attract crowds, he opened a menagerie next door, and one night a lion escaped, scaring the diners. The restaurant always had a joyous atmosphere, and over the years Lüchow's continued to serve traditional German food until it closed in the mid-1970s.

WALDORF SALAD

Waldorf Salad was created by Oscar Tschirkey, maître d'hôtel of the Waldorf Astoria for the opening of the hotel in 1893. Originally the salad consisted of apples, celery, and mayonnaise. Over the years other ingredients have been added.

Serves 4 to 6

2 cups diced tart apples

1 teaspoon sugar

1/2 teaspoon lemon juice

1/4 cup semi-dry white wine

1/2 cup diced celery

1/2 cup broken walnuts

1/2 cup miniature marshmallows

1/3 cup seedless raisins

1/4 cup mayonnaise

1/2 cup whipping cream, whipped

■

Combine the apples, sugar, lemon juice, wine, celery, walnuts, marshmallows, and raisins in a bowl. In another bowl fold the mayonnaise into the whipped cream and gently fold the combination into the apple mixture. Chill and serve on lettuce leaves.

NEW WINE by Warren Baumgarten, watercolor, 17 x 22 1/4 inches, courtesy of Hastings Art, Ltd., New Canaan, Connecticut.

Another phenomenon of New York eateries was the New York delicatessen. Established in the late 1880s to serve the Jewish settlers in New York, most of whom came from Eastern Europe, these delicatessens served Polish, Rumanian, Hungarian, and Russian foods, as well as some German dishes. Bagels, lox, pastrami, *Latkes,* cheesecakes, and gefilte fish became the fare of these informal restaurants and also became popular with non-Jewish New Yorkers. The deli-sandwich with its layers of pastrami, corned beef, smoked tongue, and special slaw on rye or pumpernickel became a New York City institution. Kosher pickles and fried potatoes were served on the side. Blintzes with sour cream evolved into a famous Sunday brunch specialty.

New York Agriculture

Agriculture is a major industry in New York State, with more than eight and a half million acres under cultivation on 40,000 farms. New York's leading agricultural products are dairy products, veal, apples, grapes, tart cherries, cabbage, and cauliflower.

New York is second only to Washington in apple production. Most of the apples are grown along the southern shore of Lake Ontario in the Hudson and Lake Champlain Valleys. They include such varieties as Baldwin, Cortland, Northern Spy, Rome Beauty, and Winesap.

The Hudson Valley has had apple orchards almost from the time of the first settlers. Peter Stuyvesant, governor of New Netherlands, is said to have brought the first grafted apple trees to New York in 1647. The Newton Pippin was developed by Gershom Moore in 1759 on Long Island. This new apple was so flavorful that Benjamin Franklin took a basketful of them to the King of England.

With the exception of California, New York produces more wine than any other state in the country. There are four major grape-producing regions in the state—Lake Erie, Finger Lakes, Hudson Valley, and Long Island. Each region has unique growing conditions, but all have nearby bodies of water which moderate the temperature year-round.

The Finger Lakes region has been producing wines and champagnes since the middle of the 1800s. After the Civil War the Finger Lakes wine industry expanded rapidly, with the Taylor Wine Company and Gold Seal Vineyards being two of the largest wineries. Smaller wineries, owned primarily by German and Swiss immigrants, sprang up along the shores of the Finger Lakes.

It was soon realized that the area had great similarities in soil and climate with the Champagne region of France. Thus champagne production in the traditional French style of *méthode champenoise* became an integral part of the wine production of the Finger Lakes.

Hudson River Valley

The Hudson River Valley has become a veritable cornucopia of gourmet produce. Broccoli raab (a non-heading variety of broccoli), radicchio, and white eggplant are examples of these unusual crops. Other new and exotic items being grown in the Hudson Valley include edible flowers, such as nasturtiums, borrage, squash blossoms, and pansies. Another specialty is miniature produce such as baby zucchini and baby yellow pattypan squash.

Since these types of produce are too specialized to sell through traditional channels and need to be moved quickly, specialized markets have come into being. Most of these specialty produce items are sold to restaurants in the New York City area, and many of the growers

participate in the Greenmarket on New York's Union Square. This twice weekly market is open to the public. In 1987 the Hudson Valley Growers formed a cooperative that sells specialized vegetables to outlets in Manhattan, executive dining rooms, and produce stands.

The Hudson Valley climate, which is moderated by the air flow along the river, has also proven to be favorable for fruit growing. One of the farms in the Hudson Valley, Breezy Hill owned by Elizabeth Ryan and her husband Peter Zimmerman, grows 35 apple varieties. Some of the varieties are considered "antique," reflecting the marvelous range of apples that was available in the nineteenth century.

Originated in New York

In the mid-1800s a cook in one of the fabulous mansions in Saratoga Springs over-cooked her round-sliced, French-fried potatoes one day but decided to serve them anyway. Almost overnight these thin, delicate potato slices, which were served with cocktails, became a sensation with Saratoga Society. They were the ancestor of potato chips and became known as Saratoga chips.

Contrary to its name, Philadelphia Brand cream cheese was invented by a New Yorker, a Mr. Lawrence, in 1872. It was first produced in 1880 by the Empire Cheese Company of South Edmeston, New York, who named the product "Philadelphia," because at the time the first capital of America was associated with purity and freshness in food. Today Philadelphia cream cheese is part of Kraft Foods.

The history of gelatin desserts is another New York State story. It starts in 1845 when Peter Cooper, who

invented the famous locomotive "Tom Thumb" and was a patron of the arts and sciences, obtained the first patent for a gelatin dessert. In obtaining the patent he described his dessert as a transparent, concentrated substance, which when dissolved with hot water could be poured into molds and solidified when cold. However, Cooper did nothing about his patent and neither did anyone else for half a century.

In 1895 P.B. Wait, a manufacturer of cough medicine in LeRoy, New York, decided to enter the newly created packaged-food business. Looking for a product, he found Mr. Cooper's gelatin dessert. Wait improved on the process, and his wife, May Davis Wait, coined the name "Jell-O." Early in 1897, they began production of Jello®.

Charles B. Knox was another New Yorker who created a dessert ingredient. In 1889 Knox founded the Knox Gelatine Company in Johnstown, New York. He was convinced that there was a market for a commercially produced and packaged granulated gelatine. At that time gelatine was being sold in sheets, which the consumer had to soak in water before using.

Knox successfully marketed his granulated gelatine, and by the time of his death in 1908, he was the largest manufacturer of unflavored gelatine in the world. One method of marketing the company used was to publish pamphlets and cookbooks on the use of Knox gelatine. After his death, the company was managed for more than 40 years by his widow, Rose Knox. In 1972 the Knox Gelatine Company was acquired by Thomas J. Lipton, Inc., which today manufactures Knox gelatine in its Sioux City, Iowa, plant.

New York Seafood

Soon after the Dutch had purchased Manhattan from the Indians for $24, they stopped buying seafood from them and began to fish on their own in locally built small craft. Finfish and oysters were so abundant that they did not have to venture beyond the safety of the bay. During the spring shad run, the fish were supposedly so dense that one could walk across the Hudson on their backs.

Commercial fishing began on Long Island in the early 1800s. The earliest commercial fishing was for oysters and clams, which were shipped to New York City. Finfish were harvested with primitive weirs, hoop nets, and baited hooks. With the exception of whaling, commercial fishing remained a part-time industry in New York.

The Civil War created a heavy demand for fish and fish products, especially fish oils. Steam power, introduced in 1890, and the outer trawl, introduced in 1905, greatly improved the efficiency and harvest capacity of New York's offshore fishing fleet.

By the 1920s trawling was the accepted method of harvesting cod, haddock, and flounder. During World War II the large demand for seafood brought more vessels into New York's fishing fleet, but after the war the demand for fish declined. Since 1976 commercial fishing has been on the increase, and environmental conditions have improved for both offshore and inshore finfishing.

The Fulton Fish Market

As the population of Manhattan grew, so did the need for markets. By 1638, with the establishment of ferry

FULTON FISH MARKET by Max A. Cohn, oil, 22 x 28 inches, courtesy of Michael Rosenfeld Gallery, New York, New York.

service to Brooklyn and Long Island, farmers could bring their produce to the general markets at the foot of Maiden Lane (Lower Manhattan). Even though smaller fish markets existed, a centralized one did not come into being until the mid-1700s, when the Beekman landfill near the East River was completed. It became known as the Fulton Fish Market when in 1807 one of the streets adjacent to the market was named Fulton in honor of Robert Fulton, the inventor of the steamboat.

The area of the Fulton Fish Market continued to prosper with eateries and oyster houses. Dorlan's and Sweet's, across the street from each other, were two well-known fish restaurants at the time. Oysters, some as big as dessert plates, were served pan fried, stewed, or on the half shell.

When the Fulton Fish Market was created in the early nineteenth century, in pre-refrigeration days, all of the seafood was handled live. Boats were constructed in such a manner that it was possible to keep the catch in the water all the way to the market. The fish were transferred from the boats to floating wooden holding pens, which were tied up in the East River behind the Fish Market. As needed, the fish were removed to woven hampers and carried by "basket boys" to the back of the Market. There, pulleys hoisted the basket up to the selling floor. At the time it was quite an event to see one of the fishmongers wrestle a 200-pound green sea turtle out of the basket. Eventually iced deliveries began to replace the baskets, and fish were no longer held live in the river.

PENNSYLVANIA

IN 1681 WILLIAM PENN, a Quaker and an influential man at the English court, obtained a land grant in America from King Charles II as payment of a debt to his family. The tract of land was almost as large as England and Wales and contained rich farmland with abundant rivers and streams. Penn named the new land Pennsylvania and encouraged the Quakers, who had been persecuted for their religion, to settle there. The Quakers established the first settlements in and around Philadelphia in 1682, and three years later it was a bustling city.

Most of the Quakers were people of means, so they brought with them ample supplies of food and tools. They got along well with the Indians and learned from them how to use corn and wild game in their cooking.

At the invitation of William Penn, many Germans also immigrated to Pennsylvania. They were of numerous religious affiliations, the largest of which were the Mennonites and Amish. Most of the German settlers opted to move out into the wilderness to farm rather than live in Philadelphia.

Pennsylvania was a very open and tolerant colony and soon attracted settlers of various religious sects and nationalities, including Welsh, Scots, Irish, and even English, many of whom had been violently opposed to the Quakers back in England. Swedish settlers who had inhabited the area along the Delaware River in Pennsylvania were absorbed into the colony. Thus Pennsylvania quickly developed a blend of ethnic heritages, although it remained primarily English and German. In the 1800s Eastern Europeans and Italians came to Pennsylvania to work in the coal mines and steel mills and thus added other cultures to the ethnic mix.

Some Pennsylvania Specialties

Pennsylvania developed many culinary specialties, one of the earliest being peach pies and tarts baked by the first Quaker housewives in Philadelphia. Apparently the peach trees left by the Spanish in Florida in the 1500s had been carried north by the Indians, as the Quakers found peach trees in Pennsylvania when they arrived.

Soups and stews provided hearty meals for the early colonists. One of the most famous was Philadelphia Snapper Soup, made from the snapping turtle found in the Delaware River. The turtle also became the main ingredient in snapper-oyster stew.

Philadelphia Pepper Pot, another thick stew-like soup, was created by the chef of the Revolutionary army at Valley Forge on the order of General George Washington. The general wanted a dish to raise the morale of his starving soldiers. The chef had only two ingredients with which to create anything—a few hundred pounds of tripe, a gift of a nearby butcher, and some peppercorns from a man in Germantown. He scrubbed the tripe and simmered it with the crushed peppercorns and a few other hastily procured ingredients to create this new stew, which the chef named Philadelphia Pepper Pot. Even today Philadelphia Pepper Pot is made with tripe, onions, potatoes, and other vegetables. Crushed peppercorns give the soup its zesty bite.

Among several poultry specialties of the Quakers was a dish consisting of a young chicken cooked in a skillet with green pepper and bread crumbs. Another poultry specialty featured tiny wild birds baked with oysters. There was also an abundance of wild turkey which was cooked with a variety of stuffings.

Philadelphia considers itself the birthplace of ice cream in the United States. In 1851 Jacob Fussell became the first wholesale manufacturer of ice cream, while Robert N. Green, another Philadelphian, originated the ice-cream soda. Green had come to the Franklin Institute Exposition in 1874 to demonstrate soda fountains. He served a concoction of sweet cream, syrup, and carbonated water. One day, however, he ran out of cream and substituted vanilla ice cream, which he ladled into a glass with the syrup and soda. Thus the first ice-cream soda was born.

Sticky buns are another Philadelphia specialty. They were probably descendants of German *Schnecken,* which are similar to cinnamon rolls. The recipe for *Schnecken* ("snails") was brought by the Germans who settled Germantown (now a part of Philadelphia) in the early 1680s. Sticky buns were made with a yeast dough that was rolled out into a rectangle and sprinkled with cinnamon, sugar, raisins, and chopped nuts. The dough was then rolled up, sliced, and put on a cookie sheet and baked. When the sticky buns were removed from the oven, they were brushed with a mixture of brown sugar and honey or syrup, making them very sticky.

Scrapple can be traced to German immigrants and was usually prepared at hog-killing time. It was made of pork scraps and spices to which cornmeal was added. The mixture was simmered for hours until it was a thick mush. It was then cooled and cut into pieces, which were fried for breakfast. Scrapple was served with fried eggs, applesauce, and syrup. Today, in some areas of Pennsylvania, scrapple is sold in cans.

Pennsylvania Dutch

Pennsylvania Dutch cooking has remained almost unaltered for 200 years. Knit together by strong family and religious ties, the Pennsylvania Dutch have preserved their own regional cooking.

The Pennsylvania Dutch came from Germany in the early eighteenth century and were primarily Moravians, Dunkards, Mennonites, Schwenkfelders, and Amish. All had a tradition of thrift, and many were highly productive farmers, since they had come from some of the best farmland in Europe. In Pennsylvania these immigrants found similar rich, fertile soil interlaced with rivers and streams.

The Mennonites and Amish, in particular, have retained many of their traditions and continue to live in close-knit communities. The Amish, for example, attend two lengthy church services each Sunday. Services are held in church members' homes on a rotating basis, since the Amish have no church buildings. Between the services Preaching Soup is served to "stay the stomach." It is a hearty soup of ham and beans. Little half-moon pastries called Preaching Pies are fed to the children during the services to help keep them quiet.

"Eat yourself full," describes Pennsylvania Dutch food. It is good peasant food, unadorned, and filling. The favorite meat of the Pennsylvania Dutch is pork—smoked hams, roasts, spareribs, chops, and sausage. Every part of the pig is used; even the pig's feet are pickled or become an ingredient for souse, which is a jellied loaf of cubed meat, vegetables, and spices served cold. The ears and snout of the pig go into headcheese.

German immigrants brought recipes for stews and pot-roasted meats with them from the farms and small villages of Germany. Sauerbraten, a sweet and sour pot roast; *Boova Shenkel,* a beef stew with potato dumplings; *Hinkel Bot Boi,* a chicken potpie; and pig's knuckles with sauerkraut have remained Pennsylvania Dutch favorites. The *Hinkel Bot Boi* consists of chunks of tender chicken and very broad noodles in a golden creamy sauce, topped with a flaky brown pie crust.

THE AROMA OF FALL *by Mary Ann Vessey, acrylic, 24 x 36 inches, courtesy of the artist, Staunton, Virginia.*

GOLDEN JOY by Patricia Buckley Moss, watercolor, 41 x 32 inches, courtesy of P. Buckley Moss Museum, Waynesboro, Virginia.

Pennsylvania Dutch cookery is noted for its "sweets and sours." There is a superstition that each meal must have seven sweets and seven sours. The seven sweets and seven sours were probably originally served to counteract the bland food and bring out the heartiness of the ingredients of the main part of the meal. The sweets might include apple butter, spiced pears, lemon honey, sweet pickles, spiced peaches or pears, jams, and jellies. Desserts count as sweets. The sours include corn relish, green-pepper relish, mustard beans, pickled beets, dill pickles, ketchup, and marinated vegetables. The famous Pennsylvania Dutch Pepper Relish is a combination of red and green peppers mixed with shredded cabbage, diced celery, and onions, and pickled with vinegar, brown sugar, and spices.

Although a relish, it is served as a salad.

Even though many of the dishes are plain and hearty, spices are used in Pennsylvania Dutch cooking. Coriander and sage enhance the flavor of sausages, while cloves are used in scrapple. Saffron, the most frequently used spice, flavors many chicken dishes, soups, homemade noodles, and pastries. Although saffron is a very expensive spice, it is not used sparingly, but to provide ample flavoring. Saffron has traditionally been part of German cooking since the early fifteenth century, when the crocus plants from which the saffron comes were grown in Germany.

Traditional Pennsylvania Dutch meals are huge, and all of the dishes are served at the same time. There was a tradition that each meat dish had to have a corresponding pie. Thus 20 or 30 dishes might have been crowded onto the table, and even today there are often a dozen.

Dumplings and noodles are the mainstay of Pennsylvania Dutch cooking. Rival Soup uses another form of dumplings. *Rivals* are tiny pieces of egg dough, which are crumbled into chicken or beef broth and look like rice when cooked.

Dumplings are one of the main ingredients in Pennsylvania Dutch *Schnitz un Knepp,* a dish of sliced (schnitzed) dried apples and dumplings. It consists of a thick slice of ham that has been gently boiled in water for two hours and then topped with dried apple slices and brown sugar. After boiling for another hour, a dumpling batter is dropped by spoonfuls on top of the simmering liquid. The resulting dish consists of tender smoked ham, plump apple slices, and feathery light dumplings.

Huge outdoor ovens were used to dry apples and pears, as well as to bake breads and pastries, and many families shared one oven. The interiors of these ovens were six to seven feet wide, just as

they had been in Germany. They could accommodate five to six loaves of bread, in addition to eight pies, a half-dozen cakes, and several batches of cookies. A six-foot baker's shovel was used to insert and remove the baked goods. Most women continued to bake in outdoor ovens even after cookstoves were introduced around the middle of the nineteenth century.

Baking bread was a weekly occurrence in many Pennsylvania Dutch homes. After mixing the dough in a wooden bowl and kneading it, the dough was placed in a dough box to rise. For the final rising dough was usually placed in a round coiled basket of rye straw, resulting in round loaves of bread.

Pies became a favorite of Pennsylvania Dutch cooks, and it was not unusual for a housewife to bake 20 pies at a time in the large outdoor oven. There would be *Schnitz* pie made with cooked dried apple slices, raisin pie, and shoo-fly pie. Raisin pie, also known as funeral pie, was traditionally served with a meal to the mourners after the funeral.

Shoo-fly pie is an invention of pioneer days, when the settlers had to make do with ingredients on hand. The pie's origin can probably be traced to German crumb cake. The crumb-cake mixture, sweetened with molasses, was then turned into a pie shell and baked. The filling used no eggs, milk, cheese, or fruit, since its main ingredients were flour and molasses. This pie was a favorite in late winter, when there were no fresh fruits and the dried ones had been used. After baking, the pie was set on the window ledge to cool, and the patches of molasses not covered by crumbs on the pie were always an enticement for flies, which were shooed away. Thus shoo-fly pie.

Christmas dinner was the highlight

of Pennsylvania cooking. Roast duck or goose with sauerkraut was preceded by Rival Soup. Potato pancakes or hot potato salad was served along with the seven sweets and seven sours. Desserts usually included two types of pies, an assortment of Christmas cookies, and *Pfefferneusse,* spiced round cookies, or *Lebkuchen,* a fancy spice cookie covered with a sugar glaze.

Many of the Mennonites served homemade wine, beer, or punch, because they believed that the water was not safe for drinking. The wine was made from any fermented fruit leftover after canning and pickling, although blackberry wine was the favorite. Wine was also made from dandelions, while beer was brewed from sarsaparilla roots and ginger. Vinegar Punch (vinegar, sugar, nutmeg, and water) and Ginger Water (ginger, sugar, and water) were favorite hot-weather drinks.

Lebanon Bologna

Lebanon bologna is the famous smoked beef sausage of the Pennsylvania Dutch country. Although originally made by the farmers of Lebanon County at beef-killing time for local consumption, it is now sold commercially. The flavor and the long-keeping quality of Lebanon bologna comes from its spices and the long, slow smoking process over a fire of hickory wood.

Today, Seltzer's Lebanon Bologna Company, a family-owned business in Palmyra, Pennsylvania, is the largest producer of the famous Pennsylvania sausage. The plant is the oldest meat-processing plant in the state and was founded in 1902 by Harvey Seltzer, a butcher of German heritage. The plant is now operated by his son and grandson, Jack and Craig Seltzer, respectively.

The precise formula for the bologna is a well-guarded secret. More than 60 tons of fresh, lean beef are coarsely ground every week and mixed with salt, sugar, spices, and potassium nitrate. The mixture is then aged in special coolers, and each day 400 tubes or casings are stuffed by machine, resulting in one- or two-pound sausages.

The sausages are then taken to specially designed wooden smokehouses. They are smoked for three to four days over hickory wood and moistened sawdust, called a wet-smoke process. A sprinkler system periodically wets the sawdust. The nine smokehouses are very

SWEET AND SOUR PARSNIPS

Sweet and sour dishes are still served with Pennsylvania Dutch meals. The traditional rule was that seven sweets and seven sours should be served at every meal. This provided enough sweets and sours to give a palatable balance to the meal. In Pennsylvania Dutch language, this dish would be referred to as a *schnittle,* meaning "cut-up."

In this recipe the term refers to the julienne strips of parsnips; hence it would be known as *Parsnip Schnittels.*

Serves 4

4 medium parsnips

4 slices bacon, cut into 1-inch pieces

1 small onion, chopped

1 tablespoon flour

2 tablespoons white wine vinegar

1 teaspoon honey

1/4 teaspoon nutmeg

Salt and pepper, to taste

■

Peel the parsnips and cut them into julienne strips, about 1/4 x 2 1/2 inches. Cook the parsnips in a medium saucepan in boiling water until tender, about 10 minutes. Drain and reserve 1 cup of the cooking liquid.

Cook the bacon in a large skillet over medium heat, stirring often, until browned. Remove bacon pieces to paper towels to drain. Leave 1 1/2 tablespoons of the fat in the skillet. Add the onion and sauté until softened. Add the flour and cook over low heat until combined. Then add the cup of parsnip water and stir with a wire whisk until smooth. Bring to a boil and simmer for 5 minutes. Stir in the vinegar, honey, and nutmeg. Taste for tartness and sweetness and add a little more vinegar or honey, if desired. Add the parsnips and heat through. Stir in the bacon and season with salt and pepper to taste.

SHOO-FLY PIE

There are three kinds of Pennsylvania Dutch shoo-fly pies—dry, moist, and in-between. The dry kind resembles a crumb cake, and the Pennsylvania Dutch traditionally dunked it in their coffee. The moist pie contains a filling layer topped with crumbs. The in-between type is the most common and can either have the liquid and the crumbs combined or put into the pie shell in alternating layers, as in this recipe. All shoo-fly pies contain molasses, which is probably responsible for the name, since flies are partial to molasses and have to be chased away while the pie is being made and after it has been baked and set out.

Serves 6 to 8

1 1/3 cups flour

2/3 cup dark brown sugar

1 teaspoon cinnamon

6 tablespoons butter or margarine

3/4 cup dark molasses

3/4 cup boiling water

3/4 teaspoon baking soda

1 unbaked 9-inch pie shell (recipe
    follows)

■

Combine the flour, sugar, and cinnamon in a bowl. Cut in the butter until the mixture resembles fine crumbs.

In a small bowl combine the molasses, water, and soda and mix well.

Roll out the pie dough 1 inch larger than the top of the pie plate. Place the dough in the pie pan and crimp the edges.

Pour one-third of the molasses mixture into the pie shell and sprinkle with one-third of the flour mixture. Continue alternating layers, ending with the flour mixture. Bake in a preheated 375° F. oven for 35 to 40 minutes, or until the filling is set and the crumbs are golden brown.

Pie Shell

1 cup all-purpose flour

3 tablespoons butter or margarine

3 tablespoons solid vegetable shortening

4 to 5 tablespoons ice water

■

Place the flour in a bowl. With a pastry blender, cut in the butter and shortening until the solids are the size of very small peas. Fluff the mixture with a fork. Add the ice water, one tablespoon at a time, tossing the mixture with the fork until the dough sticks together and forms a ball. Wrap the dough in plastic wrap and refrigerate for at least 1 hour.

narrow, 30 feet tall, and maintain a temperature of about 100 degrees Fahrenheit.

Farmer's Market

An institution of Pennsylvania Dutch country has been the Farmer's Market in Lancaster. The market, which was established by a decree of George II in 1742, has been in continuous operation ever since. Market day occurs twice a week, opening very early in the morning. Most of the stalls belong to Amish or Mennonite farmers, who sell their produce, processed meat, and baked goods. There are a number of long-established farmer's markets throughout Pennsylvania Dutch country.

At the Lancaster market the scent of smoked hams, Lebanon sausages, dill pickles, and freshly baked pastries fills the air. The produce and fruits are freshly picked. Shoppers patronize favorite stalls just as they would favorite shops, attesting that one farmer's sausage is better than the others. There are also stalls that sell freshly baked bread, which came out of the oven just before the stall-keeper's buggy departed for the market. One stall sells only grated horseradish; one headcheese; and another an array of soft and hard cheeses.

Pretzels

Pretzels, large and small, abound in Pennsylvania Dutch country, and today, most of this country's pretzels are manufactured in Pennsylvania. In 1861 two cents would buy a hundred pretzels. They became so popular that there was even a Pretzel Soup. It consists of hot milk and a dab of butter with crumbled pretzels added to absorb some of the milk.

The history of pretzels is a long and varied one. It goes back to the time of the Crusades. The shape of the pretzel is said to symbolize crossed arms in prayer, and many believe that the three holes signify the Father, the Son, and the Holy Ghost. The name originated in a monastery in France where *Pretzeola,* meaning three holes, were given as a reward to children.

The Germans brought the art of pretzel making to America. The first pretzel bakery was founded by Joseph Sturgis in Lititz, Pennsylvania, in 1861. In the early 1860s when Sturgis started making pretzels, he also established a delivery route covering the radius of one-day's driving distance by horse and buggy from the bakery. The demand was great enough that eventually three drivers with horses and wagons were retained to deliver pretzels to local stores.

Pretzels then and now are made with a kneaded yeast dough. Then small chunks of the dough were pulled off and rolled into a thin, long pencil shape and left to rise for about an hour. After rising the pretzel twister would form each long piece of dough into a pretzel. In the 1800s all commercial pretzels were twisted by hand, and each twister received two cents for a tray of a 100 pretzels.

After the pretzels were twisted, they were left to rise a second time. They were then cooked like a doughnut, except that they were cooked in straw water instead of oil. The straw water gave the pretzel its sheen and rubber-like firmness. It took about ten seconds to cook each pretzel, which was then placed on a long-handled wooden board called a peel. The wet pretzels were salted and then baked in a very hot oven for about ten minutes until brown. The result was a soft pretzel. Hard pretzels were kiln-dried (baked in a slow oven) for about two and a half hours.

Both hard and soft pretzels are now made from soft winter-wheat flour, barley malt, yeast, and water. Soft pretzels are still made by hand, while hard pretzels are now made by a machine that extrudes the dough in the shape of a pretzel. Most large pretzels are now baked for ten minutes in a 500 degree Fahrenheit oven; then the temperature is lowered to 200 degrees Fahrenheit, and the pretzels are baked for another two hours.

The tradition of eating pretzels with mustard started at the turn of the century

at baseball games. Hot dogs were covered with mustard, why not pretzels? Some Pennsylvanians eat their pretzels with a dish of vanilla ice cream. Pretzels have always been enjoyed with a mug of lager beer.

The Peanut Vendor

As a new American in Scranton, Pennsylvania, teenaged Amedeo Obici, an Italian immigrant, led a double life. He tried to finish his education, and during his spare time he worked long hours at his uncle's fruit stand. He unloaded crates, sold fruit, and made deliveries. After a year Obici quit school and went to work for several fruit merchants in Pittston and Wilkes-Barre.

In 1896, at the age of nineteen, Obici opened his own fruit stand in Wilkes-Barre. His stand was different than others, because it had a peanut roaster, which Obici had purchased for $4.50. He discovered that the peanut roaster had to be constantly turned by hand so that the peanuts would not burn while roasting. Obici spent a year developing a device with pulleys that would turn the roaster automatically.

He also conceived the idea of salting the peanuts to enhance their flavor. Once the automatic roaster was installed and the salting process perfected, he put up a sign saying "Obici, the Peanut Specialist." Customers came from miles around to buy unscorched, salted peanuts. As an added attraction Obici later started selling chocolate-coated peanuts.

Obici devoted more time to the peanuts than to his fruits, and in 1906 he gave up the fruit stand. He formed a partnership with a fellow immigrant, Mario Peruzzi, and they decided to call their new venture, Planters Nut & Chocolate Co.

H.J. Heinz "57" Varieties

As a young boy Henry Heinz of Sharpsburg, Pennsylvania, cultivated a vegetable garden next to his family's home. He was soon growing more than the family needed and started selling the surplus to his neighbors. By the time he was sixteen, young Heinz had progressed from distributing his produce by basket and wheelbarrow to selling it to grocers in Pittsburgh, five miles downriver, by horse-drawn wagon.

In 1869 at the age of twenty-five, Henry Heinz started his first food-processing plant. His first product was horseradish, a preparation which was popular with the Eastern European immigrants at that time. Housewives did not like to prepare horseradish, since it involved a great deal of scraping using primitive tin scrapers. Henry Heinz packed his horseradish in clear glass bottles to show that he had not used turnip filler. By using a glass bottle, he helped establish a reputation for convenience, quality, and truth in advertising.

Historians have described Heinz as a genius in the fields of advertising and marketing. He hit on the magic "57" because of its rhythmic appeal, although he was selling more than 57 products. Heinz created New York's first electric sign—a six-story, 1,200-light display that advertised "good things for the table" from Heinz.

Heinz Ketchup was first introduced in 1876. Mr. Heinz created the name "ketchup" from a Malay word *kechap* which means a spiced fish sauce. For centuries the word "catsup," another derivation of the Malay word, had been used in England for a sauce in which the main ingredient was salted, spiced mushrooms. In England other catsups

CHOCOLATE KUMQUAT PIE WITH WALNUTS

John Hershey only produced the well-known Hershey bar when he first established his plant in Derry Church, Pennsylvania, in the early 1900s. The Hershey Food Corporation has become one of Pennyslvania's most famous companies and now produces a wide variety of chocolate products for cooking and baking.

In this pie both unsweetened and semi-sweet chocolate are accented with orange flavoring.

Serves 6 to 8

6 kumquats

3 tablespoons Grand Marnier or other
    orange-flavored liqueur

6 ounces semi-sweet chocolate

2 ounces unsweetened chocolate

2 tablespoons milk

4 eggs, separated

1/3 cup coarsely chopped walnuts

1/3 cup very cold whipping cream

1 baked 9-inch pie shell (recipe follows)

Walnut halves or quarters, for garnish

■

Finely dice three of the kumquats to yield 3 tablespoons of chopped fruit. Place this in a small bowl and add the Grand Marnier, stirring to make sure that the fruit is coated with the liqueur.

Place the chocolates and milk in the top of a double boiler over boiling water and melt the chocolates, stirring occasionally. Remove from heat and add one egg yolk at a time, beating well after each addition. Cool mixture to room temperature. Fold in the chopped kumquats and walnuts. Transfer the mixture to a larger bowl, if necessary.

Beat the egg whites until they hold stiff peaks and fold them into the chocolate mixture. Then beat the whipping cream until it holds stiff peaks and fold it into the chocolate. Gently pour the filling into the baked pie shell and refrigerate at

least 3 hours before serving.

Just before serving, thinly slice the remaining kumquats and place the slices around the outer edge of the pie filling. Arrange some walnut halves or quarters in the center.

Pie Shell

1 cup all-purpose flour

3 tablespoons butter or margarine

3 tablespoons solid vegetable shortening

4 to 5 tablespoons ice water

■

Place the flour in a bowl. With a pastry blender, cut in the butter and shortening until the solids are the size of very small peas. Fluff the mixture with a fork. Add the ice water, one tablespoon at a time, tossing the mixture with the fork until the dough sticks together and forms a ball. Wrap the dough in plastic wrap and refrigerate for at least 1 hour.

Remove dough from refrigerator, place on floured board, and roll 1 inch larger in diameter than the top surface of the pie pan. Place dough in pie pan, crimp the edges, and prick the bottom and sides with a fork. Cover the bottom of the crust with aluminum foil, shiny side down, and weight with either pie weights or beans. Bake in a preheated 425° F. oven for 10 to 12 minutes, or until lightly browned. Remove the pie weights and foil and cool before filling.

were made from tomato, cucumber, or walnuts.

In 1892 Heinz established a second plant near Muscatine, Iowa. It, like many other subsequent plants, was chosen for its accessibility to fertile farmlands, thus minimizing the time between harvest and processing. Heinz pickles are produced in Michigan, since it is one of the leading growers of cucumbers.

Today, nearly 75 percent of all tomatoes used in Heinz products are processed at Heinz plants in Tracy and Stockton, California. During the harvest season tomato paste is shipped in bulk from these factories to Heinz facilities in the Midwest and East for production of condiments, soups, and sauces later in the year. The Tracy plant and the Muscatine, Iowa, plant are the main producers of ketchup.

Early in the twentieth century, Heinz and his son, Howard, urged Congress to pass the Pure Food Law of 1906. With the passage of this law, they felt that consumers would gain confidence in products that were prepared in places other than in their own kitchens. Three years before Henry Heinz's death in 1919, the company instituted the first formal agricultural research program in America.

Over the years the H.J. Heinz Company has acquired Weight Watchers, Star-Kist with its fleet of fishing boats, Ore-Ida, and 9-Lives. Heinz is now a multi-national company with subsidiaries throughout the world.

Hershey Chocolate

Milton Hershey was born in Derry Church, Pennsylvania, in 1857 and spent his early years there until his family moved to nearby Lancaster County. As an adolescent Hershey was apprenticed to candy maker Joe Royer in Lancaster.

At nineteen, impatient to be his own boss, Hershey left his apprenticeship and opened his own business in Philadelphia. There he produced a variety of confections, including cough drops. Even with help from his parents, aunt, and other relatives, his business was not a great success. When he could no longer obtain the needed sugar for candy making on credit, he closed his shop.

Milton Hershey's father had moved to Denver to strike it rich in a silver mine, and after the close of his shop, Milton followed. While there he worked with another candy maker and learned to make caramels with a special recipe using fresh milk, which made the confections tastier, chewier, and longer lasting.

From Denver, Hershey went to Chicago, New Orleans, and New York without much success. He returned to Lancaster penniless and was not welcomed with open arms by his relatives. However, Hershey did manage to raise a little capital and open his caramel making business again. This time he was successful, since an abundant supply of fresh milk was available from the dairy farms around Lancaster. Production expanded, and at the age of thirty-five, Milton Hershey was one of Lancaster County's most prosperous citizens.

On a trip to the Chicago Exposition in 1893, Hershey became fascinated with the chocolate-making equipment displayed there. Shortly thereafter, he purchased several pieces of German chocolate-manufacturing equipment and developed his own formula for making a chocolate bar. "Chocolate is a food as well as a confection," he said and felt it to be the basis of a new industry. In 1903,

deciding that caramels were only a fad, Hershey sold his caramel factory for $1 million while retaining the chocolate-making equipment.

The chocolate business grew, and soon Hershey needed additional space. Instead of building a factory in Lancaster, he chose to build in Derry Church, in the countryside where he was born. There he found a plentiful supply of fresh milk, a commodity most important to his production of milk chocolate.

Hershey decided to mass produce a single product—the Hershey chocolate bar—rather than follow the competition by producing a variety of chocolate novelties. This enabled him to beat the competition by selling at a low price. The decision was a wise one, and the business grew by leaps and bounds. The town of Hershey sprang up around the factory to house the employees.

Today, the Hershey Food Corporation produces many more products than the nickle chocolate bar—cocoa, chocolate morsels, candy kisses, chocolate bars with almonds, and Reese's peanut butter cups, to mention a few. The Reese Chocolate Company was acquired in 1963. The most recent Hershey acquisition is the Peter Paul/Cadbury Candy Company. Also included under the Hershey corporate umbrella today are the San Giorgio pasta products.

Mushroom Growing

In the early 1900s mushroom nurseries were established in the southeast corner of Pennsylvania. Today, the region grows about three-fourths of all of the mushrooms used in this country.

Within a ten-mile area of Kennett Square, more mushrooms are grown than anywhere else in the world. There are

no special climatic or soil conditions in the area that make the cultivation of mushrooms attractive. However, in the 1930s mushroom farmers developed many of the techniques used in mushroom cultivation today. William W. Phillips, for example, experimented with temperature control, using ice to moderate summer heat so that mushrooms could be grown year-round.

Mushrooms are now grown in specially built, windowless and air-conditioned buildings. The inside walls of each "mushroom house" are lined with tiers of mushroom beds about six feet wide. Before each planting the house is subjected to steam for several hours to sterilize the inside of the house.

Compost is prepared by allowing it to ferment at temperatures of up to 170 degrees Fahrenheit. After the compost has reached the proper stage, it is spread in the beds in the mushroom houses. The doors are kept closed for ten days during which time the temperature rises to 140 degrees Fahrenheit and then subsides to 75 degrees. The spawn is then spread on the beds and topped with a light covering of soil.

Three weeks later, thousands of mushrooms appear, and the picking process begins. The pickers wear miner's lamps. They have been trained to select the mature mushrooms by shape and formation. Size has nothing to do with the maturity of the mushroom, but its firmness and shape do. Pickers go over the beds every day for about two months, as the crop continues to produce. After all of the crop is harvested, the house is sterilized and the process starts over.

GATHERING CORN IN VIRGINIA by Felix O. C. Darley, watercolor, 17 x 24 inches, courtesy of Taggart & Jorgensen Gallery, Washington, D.C.

UPPER SOUTH

THE UPPER SOUTH encompasses Virginia, West Virginia, Kentucky, Tennessee, and North Carolina. It has a distinctly different climate and topography from the Deep South. Although the economies of both regions were agrarian, the Upper South was settled first and developed a more sophisticated society.

The westward movement began from the coastal regions of Virginia within a decade after the establishment of Jamestown in 1607. By the 1650s the growth in population and the depletion of nutrients in the soil of the Tidewater region from tobacco cultivation had accelerated the movement toward the Piedmont.

Westward-moving pioneers reached the crest of the Blue Ridge Mountains in 1670. From there they could see a great stretch of land, the Shenandoah Valley, and the mountains of what is now West Virginia beyond. The first white settlers in the Shenandoah Valley, however, were Pennsylvania Germans who had come south from Pennsylvania to find farmland.

At about the same time, Scotch-Irish immigrants came to the Upper South seeking religious freedom. The Scotch-Irish were Scots who had originally emigrated to Ireland because of religious persecution. In Ireland they worked mainly as cloth weavers, but English laws had put high tariffs on their goods and generally made life miserable, so they came to America. A great many of these immigrants settled in the hilly frontier country of Virginia, western North Carolina, Tennessee, and Kentucky. Welsh and English immigrants also settled in this same territory. By the start of the Revolutionary War, westward settlement had reached the Appalachian

Mountains in what is now West Virginia, although at the time it was still part of the Virginia colony.

The area of the Upper South has a diverse terrain. In Virginia the coastal plain is known as the Tidewater. In North Carolina this coastal plain is buffered from the rough seas by the Outer Banks. Both areas have ready access to seafood. The Tidewater area of Virginia and the coastal plain of North Carolina contain good agricultural land. The western sections of Virginia and North Carolina are bordered by the southern Appalachian mountains, which in colonial times were rich in game. The mountains of Kentucky, West Virginia, and Tennessee at that time contained small farms, while central Kentucky had a huge meadow which eventually became Bluegrass country.

In eastern Virginia the Powhatan Indians, a tribe of the Algonquian family, were the first to greet the settlers at Jamestown. The Cherokee, an isolated tribe of the Iroquois family, lived in the interior, having fled from the white man to the mountains of Tennessee and North Carolina. The Creek Indians dwelt primarily in Tennessee.

The warmer but moderate climate of the Upper South permitted the Indians to cultivate a variety of crops in addition to their staples of corn, beans, pumpkins, and squash. They also grew sweet potatoes and melons. Some Indians cultivated sunflowers both as a food and for the oil. Others extracted oil from hickory, pecan, and other nuts that grew wild.

Wild strawberries and blackberries grew abundantly. The Scuppernong grape grew wild in North Carolina and later became the basis of jams and jellies,

as well as wine for the colonists. The persimmon, when left to ripen until the first frost, was used as a fruit by the Indians and later by the settlers.

In addition to bear, deer, squirrels, and rabbits, the Indians also hunted opossum. The Virginia opossum was especially prized for its fattiness and tasty white meat. Opossum were hunted mostly during the autumn and winter months, when the animal had a thick layer of fat under the skin. The colonists learned to eat opossum from the Indians and most often followed the Indian practice of baking it whole. It was served with sweet potatoes and became known as "possum 'n taters." Wild turkey, grouse, quail, ducks, and geese were also Indian foods, which the settlers adopted. The Indians living near the bays and the ocean fished for crabs, clams, and oysters and taught the settlers how to harvest them.

The settlers of the Upper South embellished the native ingredients with European foods. They brought seeds and cuttings for the fruits and vegetables from their homelands and imported spices from abroad. The blacks who came as slaves and became the plantation cooks added peanuts, okra, and sesame seeds to the cuisine of the Upper South.

Much of the cooking in early colonial days in the coastal regions centered around corn, pork, fish, and fowl. The settlers found pigs easier to raise than cattle or sheep, and the result was that the cuisine was heavily laced with cured hams, spareribs, crackling, fatback, and chitterlings. Country-cured ham became a speciality of the Upper South. Corn and cornmeal were used in a wide variety of dishes.

The cooking of the region near the

BRUNSWICK STEW

Although Brunswick County, Virginia, is supposed to be the birthplace of Brunswick Stew, almost every place named Brunswick from Georgia northward has claimed the origin of this dish. The stew was originally cooked all day in a big iron pot over the hearth. Brunswick Stew became a tavern favorite and is still frequently served at political functions. During colonial times squirrel was used to make the stew, but chicken has been substituted in modern times. Some Brunswick stews include beef and pork along with the chicken.

Serves 4

1 chicken (3 to 3 1/2 pounds), cut-up

1 can (1 pound) tomatoes, chopped

1 large onion, sliced

1 cup okra pieces

1 cup lima beans

2 medium potatoes, peeled and diced

2 cups fresh or canned corn kernels

1 stalk celery, diced

3/4 teaspoon salt

1/2 teaspoon pepper

1/8 teaspoon oregano

1/8 teaspoon thyme

■

Simmer the chicken in 4 cups of water, which has been lightly salted, for 1 hour or until the meat can easily be removed from the bones. Remove the chicken from the broth. Add the tomatoes and their juice, the vegetables, and seasonings to the broth and simmer until the beans and potatoes are tender, about 25 to 30 minutes. Stir occasionally to prevent the vegetables from sticking.

In the meantime, remove the skin and chicken meat from the bones and cut the meat into bite-size pieces. When the vegetables are tender, add the chicken pieces, heat through, and serve.

Since long cooking improves the flavor of Brunswick stew, many cooks prefer to cook the stew one day and then slowly reheat and serve it the next day.

Chesapeake Bay took full advantage of the abundant seafood. Oyster roasts, the Southern version of the New England clambake; Fish Muddle, a stew of various kinds of fish with onions, potatoes, and pepper; and She-Crab Soup were all specialties of the coastal regions.

Frontier Food

In the 1770s the first white settlements were established beyond the Appalachian Mountains. Most of the settlers were of English and German heritage and came from Maryland, Virginia, North Carolina, and Tennessee.

After the supply of wild game had diminished on the western frontier, pork became the principal meat. It could be preserved for winter use by smoking. Salting and sugar curing did not become generally popular until the early 1800s, since before that time salt was very expensive. Salted or corned beef was never popular in the Upper South.

If a cow was slaughtered, the meat was usually divided among the neighbors who were within a reasonable distance. Other neighbors would do the same, and some fresh beef was available throughout the year.

Watermelons grew in the corn patch, and wild berries were abundant, but tree fruits were not cultivated at first on the western frontier. Wild honey was the primary sweetener, since molasses from the the West Indies was difficult to obtain during the Revolutionary War, and sugar was too expensive. Consequently, hot corn bread with butter was topped with honey or sorghum molasses.

Beverages were limited on the western frontier. Cider was scarce since very few apple trees had been planted. Rum was not available during the Revolutionary War and barley and other grains for beer grew poorly in the soil of the frontier. As a result, the settlers turned to making corn whiskey. Many frontier cabins had a small still in the backyard. Corn whiskey was often drunk at breakfast, which was considered a hearty meal.

All of the frontier meals were very substantial. Mountain cooking was often based on what could be shot, hooked out of a mountain stream, or grown in the stubborn hillside soil. Breakfast consisted of eggs, grits, corn bread, and several meats, such as ham, bacon, sausage, fried squirrel, or wild game. Dinner, at midday, included many of the same meats, with chicken or grouse added. Cooked vegetables, including greens, and sweet potatoes were served along with the meats. Cornmeal mush was a favorite of the children at supper, while the adults had more of the same meats.

Hot breads accompanied almost every meal. Corn bread, in particular, tasted better served hot. Since the fire was kept going all day in the fireplace, it was easy to bake hoecakes, plain biscuits, or corn bread in a Dutch oven. Spoon bread and beaten biscuits were reserved for special occasions, since they were too time consuming for the frontier women who always had numerous chores to do.

By the time of the Revolutionary War, the cooking of the Upper South consisted of English, Scotch-Irish, and some German recipes, modified by the native cooking of African slaves. Thomas Jefferson, who had served as ambassador to France in the 1780s, brought back French and Italian food plants and cooking techniques when he returned. He subsequently promoted French cooking among the leaders of the new nation and installed a French cook in the White House, when he became president in 1803. Thus, Jefferson became known as America's first gourmet.

The Upper South has maintained many of its culinary traditions. Hams are still cured as they were a hundred years ago, a wine industry is flourishing in the region, and some of Thomas Jefferson's culinary influences and agricultural practices still prevail.

PUMPKIN PATCH by William F. Reese, watercolor, 10 x 10 ¹/2 inches, courtesy of Thomas Nygard, Inc., Bozeman, Montana.

71

KENTUCKY

THE KENTUCKY REGION formed the western part of the wilderness granted to Virginia under the royal charter of 1609. By 1729 hunters began to visit the thick forests of what is now eastern Kentucky. These early explorers were known as "long hunters," either because they stayed away months at a time or because of the long rifles they carried.

In the late 1700s explorers touched off a land rush to the Great Meadow, a vast grassy plain that was teeming with buffalo and deer. Over the years this Great Meadow has become known as the famous Bluegrass Region of Kentucky. The rich land, nurtured by underground water flowing through limestone, has provided a breeding ground for some of the finest horses in the world.

When the Cumberland Gap, a pass through the Appalachian mountains, was discovered in 1750, it opened the area of Kentucky for exploration and settlement. Daniel Boone passed through the Gap in 1769 and spent almost two years exploring Kentucky. He blazed what is now called the Wilderness Road and opened the Kentucky frontier for settlement. More than 300,000 pioneers came westward through the Cumberland Gap in the late 1700s.

There were also many hunters in Kentucky at the time who had come to trap wild game for furs and hides. One of the earliest dishes of Kentucky was a hunter's stew. It was made without a recipe and consisted of whatever choice pieces of meat from freshly killed game were available. The meat—deer, elk, bear, or wild turkey—was cooked in an open kettle over a fire. Dried sage and pepper were added to give the stew an English flavor.

At the end of a long hunt, the supply of cornmeal was usually exhausted, and the hunters relied solely on meat for subsistence. Since the breast of the wild turkey had a bland taste and grainy texture, it became the hunter's bread. Roasted kidney or stewed bear's liver was served on the "bread" and provided a contrast of flavors as well as textures.

Colonists from Pennsylvania, Virginia, Maryland, North Carolina and eastern Tennessee—mostly of English, Scotch-Irish, or German extraction—established the first white settlements in Kentucky in 1774. They brought basic supplies such as cornmeal, salt, smoked ham and bacon, and hard-to-get wheat flour. As soon as land was cleared, the settlers planted corn, which provided food for themselves and their livestock. They also used corn to make distilled whiskey.

These early settlers brought with them recipes for the dishes served in New England, Pennsylvania, and the tidewaters of Virginia, Maryland, and the Carolinas. French cooking also influenced that of Kentucky. It came from the French-style dishes served in the larger eastern cities and from the French cooking practiced along the rivers extending down to New Orleans. Later Kentuckians claimed these French recipes as their own.

Early Kentucky Foods

Wheat did not grow well in the Kentucky soil, and corn proved to be a hardier crop. The little bit of wheat flour the settlers could obtain, at about four times the price of cornmeal, was saved for special uses, such as biscuits for company, a pie crust, or gingerbread. Cornmeal was used for most breads and for mush.

The settlers planted some of the vegetables to which they had become accustomed in their previous eastern homes. These included Irish and sweet potatoes, carrots, green beans, and okra. Green beans simmered all day with bacon was a favorite dish. By serving time the beans had almost turned to mush, but the smoky flavor of the bacon was delicious. Sometimes cut-up Irish potatoes, okra, and chunks of corn were added to the bean dish, making it a vegetable stew.

Almost as soon as the first green sprouts appeared above ground in the spring, the women gathered wild greens while the men plowed the fields for planting. The greens were cooked with smoked ham hocks, hog jowl, bacon, or "pot likker" (juice that had been saved from greens previously cooked with cured or smoked meats). "A mess of greens" was a welcome treat after having only root and dried vegetables over the winter. During the first years on the Kentucky frontier, women followed the cows into the fields and picked only the greens the cows ate. This helped assure them that the plants were not poisonous.

Since many of the settlers were of English origin, they had retained the English love of meat and ate it almost three times a day. In the hills of Kentucky, bear was the common game and was treated similar to pork by smoking the bear hams and bear bacon. Bear cubs were regarded as a delicacy, and bear bacon and grease were used to lard wild turkeys before spit-roasting them. When wild game became scarce, pork was

MAKING APPLE CIDER by Queena Stovall, oil, 16 x 20 inches, courtesy of Virginia Arts, Lynchburg, Virginia.

substituted as the primary meat, because it could be smoked and cured to preserve it for the winter months.

Burgoo Stew

Burgoo Stew is probably the most famous Kentucky dish. Its recipe has been handed down through the genera-tions. No two burgoo stews are alike, however, and no one really knows where the name came from. Some say it is a mispronunciation of barbecue, while others say that it is a slurred word for bird stew.

In frontier days it was a hunter's stew made from available meats or game. Most burgoo recipes combined one kind of fowl with a red meat. They all had a variety of vegetables, of which the most common were tomatoes, lima beans, corn, onions, and potatoes. The stew was slowly simmered for many hours and seasoned with peppers, curry powder, filé powder, bourbon, spices, and herbs. The type and amount of seasonings were up to the cook.

Sweet Potatoes with Bourbon

Sweet potatoes were traditionally served with ham in the Upper South. The sweetness of the potatoes acted as a balance to the saltiness of the ham.

Serves 6 to 8

3 pounds large sweet potatoes

4 tablespoons butter or margarine

1 unpeeled orange, cut into 2-inch pieces

12 dates, cut in half

1/8 teaspoon pepper

1 tablespoon sugar

1/3 cup bourbon

■

Place the potatoes in a large pot, add cold water, and bring to a boil. Reduce heat to medium and cook until the potatoes are tender around the edges, but firm in the center, about 15 minutes. When the potatoes are cool enough to handle, peel them and cut into 1/2-inch rounds.

Butter a round or oval gratin dish with 1 tablespoon of the butter. Arrange the potato slices, overlapping them slightly, in rows in the dish. Tuck orange and date pieces in among the potatoes. Flake the remaining butter over the potatoes. Sprinkle with the pepper and sugar. (The potatoes may be prepared to this point and set aside at room temperature for 2 hours or refrigerated up to 10 hours. Return the dish to room temperature before baking.)

Bake the potatoes in a preheated 375° F. oven for 30 minutes. Remove from oven. Pour the bourbon into a small saucepan and warm over low heat for about 1/2 minute until hot. Pour the bourbon in a small stream over the sweet potatoes. Serve at once.

Legend has it that General John Morgan's cavalry troops were short on rations during the Civil War. To help feed them a Lexington chef named Gus Jaubert shot some blackbirds, gathered up all the meat and vegetables he could find, and dumped them into a large kettle, thus creating the first burgoo. The chef later showed his impartiality by preparing 6,000 gallons of the stew for a reunion of the Grand Army of the Republic in Lexington in 1895.

The modern version of burgoo includes a myriad of vegetables, such as okra, cabbage, and potatoes. Chicken is always used, in addition to some lamb, pork, or beef, and red pepper is the primary seasoning. Burgoo takes several hours to cook, and this is usually done outdoors in big iron kettles. If the crowd is large, burgoo is served in tin cups. Recipes for burgoo vary from those serving a dozen people to those making more than a thousand gallons of the stew. It is now served in Kentucky on Derby Day and at other sporting events, as well as political rallies.

Kentucky Bourbon

Although whiskey was made in early colonial times from rye, by the 1780s corn whiskey had become popular. Corn whiskey was first made by gristmill owners and some of the Irish and Scotch settlers in Pennsylvania and Maryland. Gradually, whiskey making from corn drifted into Virginia, particularly into its western mountain regions.

The hill regions of western Virginia (later Kentucky) were better suited for growing corn than other grains. Farmers soon found it more profitable to transport corn whiskey rather than corn out of the hill country to eastern markets.

Records show that Evan Williams started the first distillery in Kentucky in 1783. But it was the Reverend Elijah Craig of Bourbon County, Kentucky, who accidentally discovered one of the secrets of making bourbon. One day while heating staves of white oak over a fire to make aging barrels, the Reverend was called away. When he returned, he found the staves charred, but decided to use them anyway. He later found that the whiskey stored in those charred barrels was far superior to that from his other barrels.

Another incident that contributed to the quality of Kentucky bourbon was the discovery of aging whiskey. Whiskey makers used to ship their barrels of whiskey down the rivers to the Mississippi and on to New Orleans. Since the shipments had to wait for the rivers to rise in the spring, it was discovered that the whiskey that sat the longest awaiting shipment tasted best.

Today, corn whiskey and bourbon whiskey do not mean the same thing. Corn whiskey, frequently called "white lightning," now refers to moonshine made in a homemade still. Its alcohol content is not specified. To be classed as bourbon, the whiskey must not exceed 160 proof, must be aged in new charred barrels for at least four years, and its mash must be at least 51-percent corn. Most bourbons are 80 to 100 proof, aged six years, and contain up to 80-percent corn mash, with the rest being rye, wheat, or other grains.

Bourbon is made by cooking the corn and other grains with some water to convert the grain starch to sugar. The resulting mixture is called mash. After cooking it is cooled to 70 degrees Fahrenheit and injected with yeast. As the warm mixture ferments, the sugars are converted into alcohol. The liquid from the mash is then distilled, and the resulting condensed liquid becomes known as "new whiskey," which is clear and sweet.

After aging for at least two years in new charred white-oak barrels, the bourbon is mixed with pure distilled water to lower the proof for bottling. It is then filtered as much as 35 times to ensure purity.

The early distillers of whiskey in Kentucky found that the limestone and iron-free water in the area improved their product. In the days before mechanical pumps, distilleries were always built at the foot of a hill where there was a natural spring. Today about 90 percent of all whiskey produced in the United States is made in Kentucky, although the water is no longer obtained from underground springs.

Mint Juleps and the Derby

The most famous use of bourbon in Kentucky is the mint julep, which is the unofficial drink of the Kentucky Derby. Many aficionados recommend that a proper mint julep be prepared in a silver goblet filled with shaved ice. Fresh mint leaves are then gently crushed between the thumb and forefinger and added to the goblet. Kentucky bourbon is then poured into the goblet almost to the top, and the mixture is stirred with a long spoon. Others like to add a bit of confectionery sugar to the crushed mint before adding the bourbon, while still others advocate letting the silver cup stand with shaved ice for at least half an hour to frost the cup. Regardless of how the julep is made, the sterling silver cup has been the vessel of preference since the early 1800s.

The Kentucky Derby is not only a horse race of a few minutes but a week-long celebration in anticipation of the event. There are luncheons, picnics, and balls. The Derby Day buffet features mint juleps, accompanied by tiny sandwiches and hot-sausage balls. Burgoo is served in the empty julep cups. This is followed by creamed chicken on waffles and bourbon-glazed country ham. Beaten biscuits and Sally Lunn are traditional accompaniments. Hickory Nut Whiskey Cake, Racing Silks Chocolate Pie, Lemon Squares, and Strawberry Fluff are some of the desserts served on Derby Day.

Fox hunting, another favorite sport in Kentucky, is enjoyed in the fall. The hunt is usually preceded by a breakfast, which is an elaborate meal featuring fried country ham, eggs, buttermilk biscuits, and a coffee cake. After the hunt there is a cold buffet with various salads, cold meats, and a variety of desserts, including Pecan Tarts and Bourbon Pound Cake. In the 1800s the hunt day's activities concluded with a ball, where even more elaborate food was served.

Kentucky Fried Chicken

"My mug is my trademark," was an often-used remark of Colonel Harland Sanders, the creator of Kentucky Fried Chicken. Born in Henryville, Indiana, in 1890, Sanders became the family cook at the age of six, when his widowed mother had to go to work to provide for the three children. By the age of seven, he was excellent at breadmaking and vegetable cookery and was learning to cook meats.

Sanders' mother remarried when Harland was twelve. Since his stepfather did not like children, Sanders and his brother and sister were sent away. Harland worked as a farmhand near Greenwood, Indiana, for $15 a month and room and board until he was fifteen. From then on he had a 25-year career of poorly paying jobs, such as buggy painter, streetcar conductor, plowman, ferryboat operator, insurance salesman, and "ash doodler" on various railroads. He also spent a year in the U.S. army in Cuba. While working on the railroad Sanders took a correspondence course, which eventually earned him a Doctor of Law degree. (His military title is an honorary one, granted to him in 1936 by the governor of Kentucky.)

During his various jobs Sanders had no thoughts of turning his culinary talents to profit. In 1929 when he opened a filling station in Corbin, Kentucky, Sanders cooked for his family in the back room of the station and also fed occasional hungry travelers. His specialties were Southern dishes, such as pan-fried chicken, country ham, fresh vegetables, and homemade biscuits. Slowly, the good food at the Sanders' place gained a reputation, and finally the demand for his cooking became so great that he closed the gas station and opened a restaurant called Sanders' Cafe.

In the late 1930s Sanders' Cafe was endorsed by Duncan Hines in his *Adventures of Good Eating*, and Sanders enlarged the establishment to seat 150 people. He also went to Cornell University and took an eight-week course in restaurant and hotel management.

Fried chicken was Harland Sanders' specialty, but frying chicken for a large restaurant presented problems. Pan-frying was too slow, and Sanders felt that deep-fat frying made the chicken too greasy. When the pressure cooker was invented in 1939, Sanders discovered it was ideal for cooking chicken. In just eight or nine minutes, the pressure cooker produced chicken with all of the flavor and moisture retained and with a tasty finish, not oily or crusty. By that time Sanders had perfected a blend of 11 common herbs and spices that is still used to make Kentucky Fried Chicken.

By 1953 Sanders' Cafe was valued at $165,000. Unfortunately, a new interstate highway bypassed Corbin and caused business to decline. This forced Sanders to sell his restaurant at auction for $75,000, which was barely enough to cover his debts.

Sanders remembered that in 1952

he had sold his chicken recipe to a Utah restaurant, which had done well with it. Impressed with that success, a few other restaurant owners agreed to pay Sanders four cents for every chicken they cooked with his process. He thought that additional restaurants might possibly be interested in such an arrangement.

At the age of sixty-six, Colonel Harland Sanders set out in a 1946 Ford with his pressure cooker and his blend of seasonings to establish a franchise business. He would drive up to a restaurant and offer to cook his chicken for the manager and employees. If they liked it, he would stay for a few days cooking chicken for the customers. If they, too, liked it, he would enter into an agreement with the restaurant's owners to receive four cents for every chicken they cooked by his method. During those demonstration days, Sanders adopted his famous attire—white suit, white shirt, black string tie, black shoes, and cane. This look was designed to conjure up an image of gracious living in the South and, by extension, an image of fine food.

In the first two years of travel, Sanders only collected five franchises. "When you tell a restaurant man that his chicken isn't good, it insults him," Sanders complained at the time. Good cooking prevailed, however, and by 1960 there were 200 outlets in the United States and Canada serving Kentucky Fried Chicken. The Colonel stopped traveling, did his own bookkeeping, and he and his wife Claudia mixed and mailed out the secret mixture of spices.

By 1963 there were more than 600 outlets, and Sanders was showing a profit of $300,000 before taxes. Sanders had

turned down a number of offers to sell the business, worried that others would run it into the ground. In 1964, however, Sanders sold his Kentucky Fried Chicken business to John Y. Brown, Jr., a bright young man who saw the growth potential of the operation using modern sales and management techniques. Sanders received $2 million, plus a lifetime annual salary of $40,000 (later increased to $75,000) for advisory and publicity work.

Brown transformed the healthy growth rate of the company into a miraculous one and went on to become governor of Kentucky in the 1980s. In 1971 Heublein, Inc., acquired Kentucky Fried Chicken from Brown, and in the mid-1980s Heublein sold it to PepsiCo, Inc. Colonel Sanders died in December 1980 at the age of ninety, but his genius and hard work live on in the Kentucky Fried Chicken franchises located around the world.

Another aspect of the Kentucky chicken story is a relatively new product called Chicken By George. It is the brainchild of Phyllis George, a former Miss America and television sportscaster, who married John Y. Brown, Jr., in the early 1980s. Chicken By George features a variety of marinated chicken breasts and turkey slices ready for cooking and is sold in supermarket meat departments.

NORTH CAROLINA

MORE THAN 400 YEARS AGO two English gentlemen, Philip Amadas and Arthur Barlowe, stood on the banks of the Scuppernong River tasting white, honey-sweet grapes. They liked the taste, so they dug up several vines and carried them to a pleasant island they had spotted earlier in the day. After planting the vine, they named the island Manteo for the handsome Indian they were taking back to England with them. The year was 1584, and the island was later to become famous as Roanoke Island.

Amadas and Barlowe had been employed by Sir Walter Raleigh to find a suitable sight for an English colony for which he had received a charter from Queen Elizabeth I. When Amadas and Barlowe returned to England, they told the queen and Raleigh that they had found suitable land for the colony with plentiful game, fish, and vegetation.

The first expedition to establish a colony on Roanoke Island was sent in 1585. It failed, however, and the colonists returned to England. A second colony of 100 settlers, including 17 women and 9 children, was established on Roanoke Island in April of 1587. Governor White returned to England in August for more supplies, but when he returned three years later, he found no one. The only evidence that the colony ever existed was the word "cro" on a tree and the word "croatan" on a post. The fate of the colony has never been established.

Today, Roanoke Island still has Scuppernong vines, and the local residents make jellies and pies from the grapes. They also make hominy in the same way the Indians did at the time the two English gentlemen first visited the island.

The first permanent settlements in North Carolina were made by Virginians of English, Scotch, and Irish descent in about 1650. In 1663 King Charles II of England granted a charter to eight of his trusted and well-loved supporters to settle the region of the Carolinas. The charter was an ambitious one, as the king defined the region as embracing all lands from Virginia to Spanish Florida and westward to the Pacific. The charter guaranteed "all liberties, franchises, and privileges in this our kingdom of England."

German and Swiss colonists settled the coastal town of New Bern in 1710. Rough shoreline and inadequate roads kept the northern part of the Carolina territory sparsely settled for many years. North Carolina settlements increased sufficiently, however, by 1729 to bring about a separation from South Carolina. Most of the population farmed and was basically self-sufficient.

There are three distinct geographical regions in North Carolina—the eastern coastal plain, the central Piedmont, and the western mountains. Each has its own climate, vegetation, and lifestyle. The flat coastal plain, with its irregular coastline, is protected by a 175-mile-long string of islands, the Outer Banks. These hurricane-swept shoals are surrounded by treacherous waters, and many of the inhabitants of North Carolina trace their ancestry to the seventeenth- and eighteenth-century shipwreck victims who were washed ashore.

The central Piedmont, with rolling,

STEWED TOMATOES

Tomatoes were considered to be poisonous well into the eighteenth century. They had originated in the Americas, were taken to Europe, and then returned to this country in the late 1700s. Thomas Jefferson was one of the first to grow and serve tomatoes. Slightly stale biscuits were used as an ingredient in stewed tomatoes to absorb the juices and give body to the dish.

Serves 6

4 cups peeled and quartered tomatoes

3 tablespoons butter, melted

1/3 cup sugar

1/2 teaspoon salt

6 large biscuits

■

Mix the tomatoes, butter, sugar, and salt together in a bowl. Crumble the biscuits and add them to the tomato mixture. Transfer to a flat baking dish and bake in a 350° F. oven for 20 minutes.

UNCLE ELMO'S FRUIT STAND by Mary Ann Vessey, acrylic, 18 x 24 inches, courtesy of the artist, Staunton, Virginia.

wooded hills, is an area of large farms that still grow tobacco primarily. The forests of pine are the source of tar, turpentine, and pitch that gave North Carolinians their nickname of Tar Heels. The western mountain region of the state is dotted with small farms.

These three areas provide a diverse number of ingredients for North Carolina's cuisine. The coastal areas along the Outer Banks are a fisherman's paradise and the source of a great variety of fresh seafood, including crab and shrimp. The Scuppernong grape, which makes delicious jams and preserves, is native to the eastern and central part of the state. It was also used in early winemaking. The fertile soils of the coastal plain are conducive to a variety of vegetable cultivation, including sweet potatoes, beans, blueberries, and peanuts. The Piedmont and the mountain region of the west provide fresh river fish, wild game, and some produce.

Culinary Influences

Inland North Carolina was an area of small farms and mountain communities settled primarily by indentured English servants, Scots, and Scotch-Irish refugees who had been forced to leave Ireland. Their foods were obtained from the land. Wild game birds and animals, fish, and the small amount of vegetables they could grow provided daily fare. Stews and corn breads often appeared at their tables, and their meals were simple and included such dishes as fried squirrel and grits.

During colonial times and early statehood, North Carolina was a rather rough area. Members of the 1668 legislature had to be told that they must wear shoes, if not stockings, and that they "must not throw chicken bones on the floor."

The colonial kitchen centered around the fireplace. Cooking was done in the open hearth. Pewter plates were warmed on iron stands near the fireplace. A coffee roaster made in Salem around 1700 produced better coffee than the traditional method of roasting beans in an iron pot.

North Carolina cuisine reflects the food preferences of its settlers. Many of the seafood and game dishes use the same seasonings of peppers, onions, and garlic as the dishes in neighboring states. North Carolinians eat their share of cornmeal mush, black-eyed peas, and biscuits. Hoppin' John made with dried peas, salt pork or ham hocks, and rice is also a favorite dish in North Carolina. The North Carolina version of fish stew, called Fish Muddle, began in colonial days when a cook, who was trying to save herself some work, combined all of the fish from the day's catch in a big kettle with onions, potatoes, and salt pork.

Cream, butter, and eggs enrich many dishes, including desserts. Even simple fruit-based desserts are embellished with rich, sweet sauces and are accompanied by feather-light cakes.

Breakfast for the lower-income families usually consisted of biscuits and ham, topped with cream gravy made with salt pork drippings, and some coffee. There might also be cornmeal mush or grits.

The more affluent would serve eggs and country ham, sausage, or bacon. Fresh or saltwater fish, fried apples or tomatoes (in season), hominy, grits, buckwheat or batter cakes, waffles, hot biscuits, and a wide variety of jams and jellies were additional choices for breakfast. In the spring and summer, fresh berries were served with pitchers of heavy cream, along with fresh sliced peaches, cantaloupe, or muskmelon.

Dinner was eaten in the middle of the day. For a typical farm family, it might consist of only pinto beans cooked with salt pork or some other meat, biscuits, and sorghum molasses. Greens such as turnip tops, mustard, cabbage, or watercress were added when available. In the summer with the arrival of fresh garden produce, there was more variety of food.

It is hard to describe the quantity of beans used during "hard times." Many families bought beans in 100-pound bags, and rarely a day passed when there was not a pot of beans simmering on the back of the stove.

Fried chicken with cream gravy, country-fried ham, breaded pork chops, or beef stew was usually served for dinner in the plantation homes. Those living on the seacoast often prepared some type of seafood. In the winter the vegetables were limited to dried beans, potatoes, onions, cabbage, and turnips. Canned or pickled vegetables, such as corn, okra, string beans, peas, and beets added variety. Often, Irish and sweet potatoes were served at the same meal. Some form of corn bread, either sticks, squares, or on occasion spoon bread, accompanied the midday meal.

Supper was often a "set out" of leftovers from dinner. In the summer the "set outs" would be served cold, while in

the winter they would be warmed. A fresh pan of biscuits was added, and in the winter soup or oyster stew might also be served. If there was company there might be fried chicken or pork at dinner, as well as at supper.

The Germans and Moravians

In the early 1700s Germans moved into North Carolina. They represented three branches of Protestantism—Lutheran, German Reformed, and Moravian. Many of these Germans had left their country for England because of a series of wars, agricultural failures due to extremely cold weather, and religious persecution from the Roman Catholic Church. Queen Anne of England provided transportation for some of these Germans to Pennsylvania. Upon finding that most of the land was already taken, they moved south into North Carolina and established their own communities, building large stone houses and barns. They spoke only German, had their own newspaper, and continued cooking traditional German dishes.

In 1752 the first group of Moravians arrived in North Carolina from Bethlehem, Pennsylvania, to occupy a large tract of land they had purchased from the Earl of Granville. The Earl was head of the Carteret family, one of the original eight recipients of Carolina charters from King Charles II.

The Moravians developed a highly centralized church-business community near Salem. They pioneered an intricate water system, which used wooden pipes to supply water to the buildings in Salem. They developed a wholesale produce business, buying from local growers and selling to markets as far away as Philadelphia.

The Moravians had many food

traditions, including their paper-thin ginger cookies, citron pie, sugar cakes, and light cream cakes. On November 17th the Moravians of Salem traditionally served wine and cakes topped with a cream nut frosting to commemorate the first Carolina Love Feast. This feast celebrated the Moravians finding shelter and safety in North Carolina. Any special occasion such as Christmas Eve can also be celebrated by a Love Feast. At Easter loaves of yeast bread studded with raisins are served for breakfast.

One of the first business establishments in the Moravian community of Salem was Winkler's Bakery. The yeasty aroma of bread baking beckoned the housewives to buy a supply. In addition to bread and Moravian sugar cakes, Winkler also baked a variety of cookies. Little children used to wander in and out of the shop eying the cookies and exchanging their hard-saved pennies for a bag full.

Today, the Winkler Bakery still exists and has a crew of seven who bake 125 loaves of assorted breads, 20 pounds of Moravian cookies, and 25 trays of sticky brown Moravian sugar cakes daily, except Sundays. Each morning an oak and hickory fire is built in the 200-year-old oven. When the heat in the oven reaches 440 degrees Fahrenheit, the coals are raked out, and the baking proceeds in descending order of temperature needs— breads first, then cakes, and lastly cookies. The output of the bakery seldom meets the demand for its products.

Moravian cooking has a German heritage and retains some of the characteristics of the cuisine, although some of the German words have been altered as to their meaning. For example, in German the word *Kuchen* refers to cake, but in the Moravian usage it refers to any

sort of cookie, sweetened yeast breads, and coffee cakes, as well as regular cakes made with baking powder.

One of the more famous cakes of the Moravian community is the Magnolia Cake, which has black walnuts in the dough instead of in the frosting as in other similar cakes. Nut cakes were common, since nuts were available year around.

The crisp, paper-thin Moravian Christmas ginger cakes (cookies) have become world famous. Although many cooks considered making these cookies a tedious chore, the making of the dough was simple. The rolling and baking of the cookies took the time. The custom was to make the dough the night before baking the cookies. In winter some cooks made extra dough and stored it on the back porch so that they could "bake off it" for four to six weeks. They claimed that the spices had a better chance to meld with the dough ingredients when stored over a longer period of time. If the cook wanted a "bite" to the cookies, she added more ground ginger.

The famous Moravian citron tarts and pies were not made with candied citron but with a lemon custard filling (the German word for lemon is *citrone*). The secret of this filling, according to old Moravian cooks, was that the butter and sugar was cut into the egg yolks and not stirred in.

North Carolina Seafood

Fishing for mullet has been popular in North Carolina since colonial days. By the early 1800s mullet was one of the main cash crops from the Outer Banks. During the fall mullet runs, Outer Banks fishermen built temporary camps of small thatched huts near the beach. Lookouts

kept watch on the waters for the dark mass that indicated a large school of mullet.

With one end of a seine net secured on the beach, part of the fishing crew would row into the surf and position the other end of the net in front of the approaching fish. As the mullet filled the net, the boat slowly circled toward the shore. The fishermen then cleaned, salted, and packed the mullet in barrels for shipment.

Since the 1920s shrimp have been a major seafood harvest off the North Carolina coast. Until that time shrimp were thought to be pests that clogged the nets. Besides, the fishermen received only three cents a pound for shrimp.

Shrimping is now a valuable enterprise. Special boats have been developed for harvesting the shrimp. These large trawlers are rigged with either one or two huge nets that are pulled along the bottom to scoop up the shrimp. As the large, funnel-shaped net is pulled along, shrimp, plus fish, crabs, and some grass are scooped up into the net. A shrimping "tow" usually lasts about two hours. By then the net is full and is slowing the progress of the boat. Once the catch is hauled on deck, there is always excitement to see what it contains. The net goes back in the water immediately, and the men sort through the pile of seafood on the deck. Grass, fish, crabs, and jellyfish get tossed back, and then the shrimp are iced down in baskets and stored below deck. Just as that catch is sorted another full net is brought up.

North Carolina fishermen harvest approximately two and a half million pounds of finfish and 11 million pounds of shellfish annually. Wilmington, the largest seaport on the North Carolina coast, ships oysters, blue crabs, clams, and other fish throughout the country.

North Carolina Cornmeal

Grinding corn into meal is one of the oldest industries in the state. At the beginning of the twentieth century, corn mills were located in nearly every community.

Corn was easier to grow than wheat, and it was also easier to grind with the often crude machinery that was used in the mills at the time. For the cook it was easier and faster to make corn bread than it was to make a bread using flour. Historians have estimated that as late as the 1930s, the average southern family consumed 500 pounds of cornmeal a year, as compared with about 100 pounds in the rest of the country.

Cash was not used in the early corn mills, but rather a toll was extracted from each customer. The toll was one-eighth bushel of corn, which was measured into a metal or wooden container, called a "toll dish." The miller would "strike the toll" by using a stick to level the dried corn in the toll dish. He always took his toll first and then would do the grinding. In later years the toll increased to one-fourth bushel, and then finally it was replaced by cash.

One of the most famous cornmeal dishes along the North Carolina coast is corn dumplings. Each cook has a different recipe for them and claims his or hers is the best. Some use all cornmeal, while others prefer a mixture of half cornmeal and half plain flour. Some add water, and others add broth from their stew or chowder. The dumplings can be fat and fluffy or thin and flat. Whatever the choice, corn dumplings usually top pots of chowders, soups, or stews.

BAKED SCALLOPS IN WINE SAUCE

Sea scallops are harvested off the coast of Virginia and North Carolina year-round and have been cooked by coastal residents since the first settlers arrived. Today, with rapid means of transportation, fresh scallops are available inland. This recipe combines sea scallops with vegetables in a creamy wine sauce.

Serves 4

1 sheet puff pastry from 1 package
   (17 1/4 ounces) frozen puff pastry sheets
2 tablespoons butter or margarine
2 medium zucchini, thinly sliced
   (about 2 cups)
1 carrot, cut into 1-inch julienne strips
5 large mushrooms, sliced
1/4 cup chopped red pepper
2 tablespoons flour
1/2 cup whipping cream
1/4 cup milk
1 pound scallops
2 tablespoons freshly grated Parmesan
   cheese
1/4 teaspoon dried thyme
1/8 teaspoon pepper
3 tablespoons dry white wine
1 egg white, beaten
Freshly grated Parmesan cheese, for garnish

■

Thaw the sheet of puff pastry and, with a glass or cookie cutter, cut it into 2-inch rounds. Refrigerate the puff pastry rounds while preparing the scallops.

Melt the butter in a large skillet over medium heat. Add the zucchini, carrots, mushrooms, and red pepper and sauté for 3 to 4 minutes, until the vegetables are crisp-tender. Sprinkle the flour over the vegetables and stir gently to combine. Add the cream and milk and cook for 1 minute, stirring constantly. The mixture will be very thick. Add the scallops, Parmesan cheese, thyme, and pepper and cook over medium heat until the mixture comes to a boil. Remove from heat and stir in the wine.

Spoon the scallop mixture into an ungreased, 9-inch quiche pan. Place circles of puff pastry around the edges of the dish, leaving the center exposed. Lightly brush each pastry circle with beaten egg white and sprinkle with some Parmesan cheese. Bake in a preheated 375° F. oven for 25 to 30 minutes, until the pastry is golden brown and the scallop mixture is bubbling.

TENNESSEE

WESTERN TENNESSEE along the Mississippi River was first explored by Hernando de Soto in 1541 and by Jacques Marquette and Louis Joliet, the French explorers from Canada, in 1673. Despite the early Spanish and French claims to what is today Tennessee, the first permanent settlements were made by the English in eastern Tennessee in 1679.

Tennessee was once a part of the Virginia Territory and was considered the western frontier of the American colonies in the 1700s. It was the home of the Cherokee and Creek tribes, who strongly resisted any settlement by the white man.

The majority of the first white settlers in Tennessee were from Virginia and the Carolinas and were of English, Scotch-Irish, or French Huguenot descent. These were followed by immigrants from Scotland, Ireland, and Germany, who reached Tennessee via Pennsylvania and Maryland. The early settlers established homes on the sides of the mountains, in the hollows, and then later on the prairie lands.

The pioneers grew corn, potatoes, some vegetables, and a little fruit. Most settlers had at least one apple tree. In the mountains and hollows, deer and wild turkey were plentiful. Raccoon, whose lard was considered choice, abounded. So did bear, squirrel, and rabbit. A hog or two provided meat for winter. The women learned to make stews of opossum and squirrel, and stews have remained a part of Tennessee cooking.

The movement westward was aided by two factors. The first was the scarcity of land around Philadelphia, where many Scottish, Irish, and German immigrants had landed. They were attracted by the promise of new land in the west. For the most part the immigrants were peasants, who were accustomed to hard work. They came through the Shenandoah Valley looking for virgin land to cultivate. Some went west to Kentucky, but the more adventuresome turned south into Tennessee.

The second factor which aided the settlement of Tennessee was the American Revolution. Many people, eager to save their families, moved westward to avoid the turmoils of war.

Tennessee can be divided into three distinct areas—the east Tennessee hill country, the middle Tennessee plains, and western Tennessee, which encompasses the Mississippi Valley lowlands. Two different kinds of people and lifestyles emerged from the settlements in Tennessee. One was the informal mountain folk, with their picturesque pattern of speech, songs, customs, and foods. The other group was the sophisticated plantation owners, who raised tobacco, cotton, and horses in the fertile western prairie regions. A slave market was established in Memphis in the early 1800s to provide a labor force for the western plantations, a way of life that was foreign to the eastern mountain folk.

Tennessee Foods

The cuisine of Tennessee followed the terrain. In the hill country the main dishes were basically stews and roasted meats. This food had more in common with the mountain folk of Kentucky and West Virginia than that of the western part of the state. The food of western Tennessee, with its more luxurious plantation life, had more formal meals with multiple dishes. Plantation cooking was similar to that of Tidewater Virginia and the Carolina low country. There was also a French influence, which had come up the river from New Orleans.

Two foods that were common to both groups were corn and ham, especially country cured ham. Each small settlement had its own flavor of country ham, and travelers claimed they could travel hundreds of miles without tasting the same ham twice. Corn was not only served as a vegetable but was used in different breads. Greens, which were frequently cooked with some ham, pork, or "fat back" for flavoring, were also eaten by both cultures in Tennessee.

The mountain people had a folklore of their own. They believed that you should not say "thank you" for a gift of seeds lest they perish in the ground. Onions had to be planted at a respectable distance from the potatoes, so that the potatoes would not have their eyes burned out. Another piece of folklore was that a man should not plant peppers when his wife was angry.

Food was so important to the mountain people that it was often honored with songs such as "Jimmy Cracked Corn," "Chicken in the Bread Tray," and "Possum Pie." Cheatham County was so famous for its chitterlings that a song was created called "When It's Chitlin' Time in Cheatham County."

Ramps, called wild leeks outside of Tennessee mountain country, still grow abundantly in the mountains of Tennessee. Both the leaves, which are wider than those of scallions, and the bulbs are used in soups and as a vegetable by

MAKING SORGHUM MOLASSES by Queena Stovall, oil, 20 x 30 inches, courtesy of Virginia Arts, Lynchburg, Virginia.

Tennessee mountain folk. Today, because of their rarity, foraging for ramps has become a challenge. Each spring, Cosby, Tennessee, has a ramp festival with country music and various dishes prepared with ramps.

Tennessee Hams

Home-cured country hams became well-known in Tennessee and often rival those of Virginia. Tennessee hams are known as "country hams" and are substantially different from the Smithfield hams of Virginia. The hog is fed corn and other grains, rather than peanuts. The cut of meat is also different in that the country ham uses the full butt, and the shank bone is removed before packing.

Tennessee hams are mahogany in color, highly salted, and fairly dry due to long smoking. These hams are still cured in old-fashioned smokehouses, just as they have been for more than 200 years. They are first liberally rubbed with a mixture of salt, sugar, and nitrate and cured for a month. Then the hams are smoked over a hickory fire to a deep mahogany red.

Ham and red-eye gravy have become a traditional Tennessee dish. Red-eye gravy starts with the drippings in a pan, in which slices of ham were fried. To this is added some water and a little black coffee. The gravy is then poured over the ham slice and served with grits or biscuits. Both the grits and biscuits are bland enough to contrast the ham and dry enough to absorb the gravy. Fried ham slices are also served with creamed potatoes and wilted lettuce.

"Lassie-making" Time

Most hill farms in East Tennessee had a few rows of molasses-producing sorghum planted along the edge of the vegetable garden. Sorghum looks similar to corn stalks but without the corn husks. Lassie-making refers to the process of converting sorghum stalks into molasses.

Lassie-making time was in the fall. The sorghum stalks were cut and trimmed to remove the leaves and top tassels, which contain seeds. Then the cane was hauled to the mill and the cooker. Usually one family in the neighborhood had a mill or grinding devices for the cane and a cooker for the syrup. The mill consisted of heavy rollers similar to a clothes wringer.

The cane mill was operated by a mule or a horse hooked to a long pole.

The animal walked in endless circles moving the grinding stones that pulverized the cane stalks. As the cane was crushed, a green juice ran out the bottom of the mill into a pan. This juice was poured into the cooker, which held 60 to 80 gallons of syrup at a time, and brought to a low boil. As the mixture cooked it was stirred constantly. After five to six hours of boiling, a rich brown syrup remained, which was funneled into jars. It took 60 gallons of juice to make six to eight gallons of syrup. This sorghum molasses was used on corn bread, waffles, pancakes, and in coffee as a sugar substitute.

Tennessee Whiskey

Tennessee whiskey is different from other corn-based whiskeys. To be labeled Tennessee whiskey it must be made by a specific process. All corn-based whiskeys are made by cooking a mash of corn, barley, and wheat or rye and then distilling the liquid. In Tennessee whiskey the resulting liquid is filtered through charcoal made from maple logs and then aged in charred white-oak barrels. The charcoal filtering gives Tennessee whiskey its unique taste.

Jack Daniel, whose name has become synonymous with Tennessee whiskey, was one of the first to use this process. He was born in 1850 and left home at the age of thirteen to live with Dan Call, a Lutheran preacher who owned a country store. Call had a still behind the store where he made whiskey and taught Daniel how to make it. Three years later Call had a pang of conscience, when a traveling lady evangelist extolled the evils of whiskey. He sold the still to Jack Daniel, and the Jack Daniel Distillery became the first whiskey distillery to be registered by the government in 1866.

When Jack Daniel, a life-long bachelor, died in 1911, he left his distillery to his nephew, Lem Motlow. The distillery then passed on to Motlow's four sons, who sold it in 1956 to Brown-Forman Beverage Company of Louisville, Kentucky.

Summer Squash Bake

Pudding-like vegetable dishes were often served by the early settlers, because they could be baked in the fireplace oven along with meats. They frequently had a bread topping in order to stretch the dish and make use of stale bread.

Serves 6 to 8

2 1/2 pounds yellow crookneck squash, trimmed and cut into 1 1/2-inch pieces

4 tablespoons butter

1 tablespoon sugar

1 extra large egg, lightly beaten

Salt and pepper, to taste

1 1/2 cups stale white bread crumbs

3 tablespoons melted butter

■

Place the squash in a large saucepan and barely cover with water. Bring to a boil, reduce heat to medium, and cook the squash until very tender, about 15 minutes. Drain the squash thoroughly and put it in the bowl of a food processor. Add the butter and sugar and purée the mixture. Place the squash in a bowl, add the egg, and salt and pepper, to taste.

Combine the bread crumbs and melted butter in a small bowl. Transfer the squash to a 1 1/2-quart casserole and sprinkle with the bread crumbs. Bake in a preheated 350° F. oven for 30 minutes, or until the squash mixture is set and the crumbs are golden brown.

Hog-Killing Time and Sausage

For many Tennessee mountain people, hog-killing time rated next in importance to Christmas. It occurred in late fall, just before the onset of winter. The children of the family were kept out of school that day so that they could help wherever needed. Neighbors "swapped work" to help each other with the butchering, for it took many strong backs to lift a 500-pound hog.

Hog killing was usually done near the stream, if the farm had one, or near the spring house. A big kettle filled with water from the stream was put on to boil over an outdoor fire pit. The boiling water was used to scald the hog so that the hair could be scraped off. Each neighbor who helped with the butchering brought his own knife, which was handmade and razor sharp. The women provided hot coffee, biscuits, and fried pork, which had been cooked over some of the coals taken from under the kettle.

After the hog had been cut in the traditional pieces, it was usually put in a vacant building on the farm to chill overnight. The next day the meat would be trimmed. Trimming a ham was a work of art. The meat was then hand-rubbed with salt and put into the salt-covered bottom of the meat box. Each layer of meat was covered with more salt, and the box was covered and stored in a cool place for three to six weeks.

After that time the meat was ready for further processing. It was removed from the salt and thoroughly rinsed. The hams were hung in the smokehouse for smoking and aging. Green hickory wood was used to provide a slow, smoldering smoke. The fire was kept going for six weeks until the hams turned a deep mahogany red. Some of the cured meat, which was not destined for the smokehouse, was put in cloth bags and hung in a cool place to age.

The day after hog killing, all of the hog fat was cut into small pieces and placed in a large cast-iron kettle and cooked over an outdoor fire. When the pieces of fat turned to brown cracklings, the lard was ready, and it was carefully ladled into 50-pound tins. The crack-lings were saved and became a much sought after ingredient in corn bread.

An essential part of hog killing and meat preservation was the making of sausage. All of the lean trimmings, along with some fat, were saved for sausage. Each family had its own special favorite blend of seasonings, which commonly included pepper and sage. Sausage was kept cool in the spring or ice house for winter use. Many families also put sausage into cloth bags and smoked them for a week to ten days in the smokehouse.

One of the most famous sausages in

TENNESSEE BARBECUED RIBS

"A mess of barbecued ribs" was a meal always eagerly anticipated after hog butchering. Cooked over a hickory fire, the ribs were often basted with a tomato sauce to which bourbon had been added.

Serves 4

1 side pork ribs (about 4 pounds)

Sauce

1/2 cup ketchup

1/3 cup light molasses

1 tablespoon light brown sugar

2 tablespoons orange juice

1 teaspoon grated orange zest

2 tablespoons vegetable oil

1 medium onion, finely chopped

1 clove garlic, minced

1 teaspoon prepared mustard

1 teaspoon Worcestershire sauce

1/8 teaspoon red pepper flakes

1/4 cup bourbon

■

Place the side of ribs in a pan and bake in a preheated 350° F. oven for 45 minutes. Remove the ribs and discard the accu-mulated fat.

In the meantime combine all of the sauce ingredients in a saucepan. Bring the mixture to a slow boil and simmer for 15 minutes.

Place the ribs on the grill of a barbecue over slow coals, preferably hickory chips. Baste with the sauce and grill for about 45 minutes, or until done. Turn the ribs every 15 minutes and baste with the sauce. Cut the ribs into serving pieces and pass any leftover heated sauce.

the country is Odom's Tennessee Pride Sausage of Madison, Tennessee. Raised in the meat business as a child, Douglas Odom, Sr.,was well versed in sausage making. In 1943 he began a business blending the best cuts of the hog—tenderloins, loins, and hams—into sausage and added his family's secret spices. Soon he was selling his product to local markets and to grocery stores in Nashville.

In the early days the entire Odom family worked in the business. Mrs. Odom sewed the cloth bags for the sausage, and the two sons, Richard and Doug, stuffed them. Then they pulled

out the back seat of their old car, filled it with a 100-pound tub of sausage, packed it with ice, and proceeded to make deliveries. The famous logo, the little animated country farm boy, was drawn by Odom's daughter Judy.

Time has changed, and there are now refrigerated trucks crisscrossing the country with Tennessee Pride Sausage, and additional plants have been built in Adairville, Kentucky, and Little Rock, Arkansas. The Odom Sausage Company is still a family-owned-and-operated business under the management of the third generation of Odoms.

VIRGINIA

THE ADVENTURESOME MEN who arrived at Jamestown under the leadership of Captain John Smith in 1607 expected to find gold and silver in Virginia. They were so certain that the new land contained these valuable metals that in their land-grant contract, they agreed to give one-fifth of their findings to the British Crown. Since the men did not intend to establish a permanent settlement, they brought no women and insufficient supplies for a permanent settlement. During the first winter more than half of them died.

In 1609 the first women arrived in Jamestown to become the brides of the male settlers. That same year John Smith, who had been seriously wounded, returned to England. Without their leader, the colonists fared even worse than the previous winter. They ate snakes and some even turned to cannibalism. By 1610 nine-tenths of the colonists had died of starvation or disease. The remaining settlers decided to abandon Jamestown and might well have disappeared if the relief fleet under Thomas West, Lord Delaware, newly appointed governor of Virginia, had not arrived.

The years that followed saw the successful experimentation of tobacco growing by John Rolfe. Little by little tobacco plantations were established along the James River. Additional manpower, however, was needed to tend the tobacco fields. This need was met when a Dutch ship sailed into the harbor at Jamestown in 1619 with a cargo of Negro slaves. The tobacco economy became firmly established, and with it slavery was introduced into Southern plantation life.

Life on Virginia tobacco plantations and among the upper class in the capital, Williamsburg, was luxurious. An enormous number of slaves was required to provide the lavish rural living the plantation owners enjoyed. Distances between plantations were great, and when people came to visit, they stayed for a week or even a month. Virginia hospitality meant that neighbors, friends, and relatives were entertained with an abundance of elegant food.

The kitchens of plantation manor houses were located in separate buildings, usually to the side or in back of the main house. Sometimes a covered walkway connected the kitchen to the main house. This separation was done to protect the main house from fires, which frequently erupted in the kitchen. It also kept the heat from cooking away from the main house in the summer months. Once the food was brought to the house, it was kept hot in front of the fireplace in the warming room or in a small pantry.

The kitchen building of the Virginia plantation was usually the largest of the outbuildings. Frequently, it had been the original dwelling of the owner, who had prospered and built a larger house.

Kitchen fireplaces were often six feet high and ten feet wide. They were equipped with a lug pole, swinging cranes, and an assortment of iron and copper cooking utensils. Vegetables and herbs hung from the rafters to dry, and small pots of fresh herbs sat near the windows. Flour, meal, sugar, and other staples were stored in crocks or tins on shelves. Since most plantation kitchens were large and well-staffed, many dishes could be prepared at the same time. One of the cooks might be turning the spit on which a wild turkey was roasting, while another might be making fruit pies, and a third beating biscuit dough.

Cooking was done in brick ovens, on spits over open fires, in heavy iron pots suspended above the embers, in Dutch ovens, or in three-legged skillets called "spiders." Kitchen equipment included pots, kettles, waffle irons, swinging cranes, tin bake ovens, scales, and various wooden and pottery mixing bowls.

There were other adjacent buildings that were necessary for food preparation in colonial days. Icehouses were usually built near the river bank and were often reached by an underground passageway. Ice was cut from nearby ponds in the wintertime or was brought by ship from New England. Layers of straw kept the ice from melting. On the larger plantations the icehouses had enough room to store 20 tons of ice. Thus the plantation owner and his guests could enjoy cold drinks, ice cream, and other frozen desserts all summer.

The springhouse was built over a rippling spring and was the storage area for butter, milk, and cream, which were kept in crocks halfway submerged in the cool flowing water.

Cellars were stocked with jars and crocks containing jams, preserves, jellies of wild berries and tree fruits, and pickled vegetables. The fragrance of nutmeg, thyme, and pickling spices scented these cool cellars. Cabbages, okra, carrots, turnips, yams, potatoes, and onions were preserved in loose earth in one corner of the cellar for winter use.

Hams, which had first been soaked in a brine solution or rubbed with a sugar and salt mixture, were smoked in the smokehouse. The hams were suspended from hooks in the ceiling over a smoky fire of green logs. Hickory chips were added for flavor and corncobs for additional fire.

If it was summer and the kitchen was hot, the cook making the biscuits might take the dough outdoors and beat it on a smooth tree stump with a flat iron or the side of a hatchet. Biscuit dough was beaten to incorporate air into it, causing the biscuits to rise during baking. (This was before the advent of baking powder in the 1870s.) Biscuits for everyday use were given 300 whacks, but those for company had to have 500 wacks. When the dough was smooth and satiny, it was rolled out and cut into rounds with a biscuit cutter. The tops of the biscuits were pierced with a fork and baked until light brown. They were always brought to the table piping hot and served with ham and chicken and plenty of gravy.

PARTY AT SUPPER from Sketchbook of Landscapes in the State of Virginia by Lewis Miller, courtesy of Abby Aldrich Rockefeller Folk Art Center, Williamsburg, Virginia.

Early Virginia Foods

Virginia is credited with many "food-firsts" in America. In 1607 the first settlers brought chickens and eggs to the New World, which they purchased in the Caribbean Islands en route. Chickens were easy to feed and maintain and became a mainstay of most colonial farms. Eggs became an important source of farm income and were used to barter for other goods.

In 1611 Sir Thomas Dale, Jamestown's colonial administrator, arrived with 100 cattle and 200 hogs. The Indians were impressed with the milk they were given but not with the meat, since they were used to eating wild game. At first the cattle were allowed to roam free, but the winter climate dictated that they be confined during harsh weather. Dale built the first cattle barn in America. As the population grew and wild game became scarce, hogs, poultry, and beef cattle were imported from England.

The first sophisticated cooking in Virginia was done by the women who came in 1609. They are responsible for the first corn puddings and pumpkin fritters. Once the early settlers were able to fight off starvation, Virginians began to combine the Native Indians' ingredients with English food.

Sturgeon as long as 12 feet came from Virginia waters. They were usually cut in pieces and baked with parsley and sage in a wild mushroom and wine sauce.

Trout were so plentiful that the housewife took a large frying pan to the river and scooped up enough fish for dinner.

Spoon bread originated in Virginia. It is made with cornmeal, eggs, and milk and baked slowly in a deep dish so that the fluffy mixture under the golden-crisp crust is so soft that it must be spooned onto a plate. In colonial days, children of the household servants formed a brigade of runners to whisk the hot spoon bread from the outside kitchen oven to the dining room.

Sally Lunn, another favorite Virginia hot bread, was reportedly named after an English girl, who went through the streets of her hometown of Bath, England, selling her hot homemade buns. These delicate rich buns were made with

COLONIAL PASTRIES

Dates, raisins, currants, figs, and citrus fruits from the Mediterranean countries were popular ingredients for cooking and baking during colonial times in the Upper South. Dried fruits were used in baked goods and steamed puddings during the winter months. This adaptation of an early Virginian recipe is a free-form pastry filled with chopped lemon, dates, and currants.

Makes 10 to 12 pastries

Pastry Crust

1 1/2 cups all-purpose flour

1/8 teaspoon salt

5 tablespoons butter

4 tablespoons solid vegetable shortening

4 to 5 tablespoons ice water

1 egg

1/4 cup sugar

3/4 teaspoon cinnamon

■

Mix the flour and salt in a bowl. Cut in the butter and shortening with a pastry blender until the mixture resembles fine crumbs. Add the water, a tablespoon at a time, stirring until the mixture forms a ball. Wrap the dough in plastic wrap and refrigerate for 1 hour before preparing the filling.

Filling

1 large lemon

3/4 cup pitted dates

3/4 cup dried currants

■

Cut the lemon into large pieces and remove the seeds. Place the lemon, dates, and currants in the bowl of a food processor and pulse to a coarse texture. Beat together the egg, sugar, and cinnamon and add the date mixture.

Roll out the pastry thinly and cut into 4-inch squares. There will be 10 to 12 squares. Place 1 heaping tablespoon of filling in the center of each square. Lightly brush the corners of each square with cold water and draw up the corners toward the center, pinching them together to seal them. The pastries should resemble little packets. Place the pastries on an ungreased cookie sheet and bake in a preheated 425° F. oven for 20 to 25 minutes, or until lightly browned.

a leavening, eggs, milk, flour, sugar, and butter and were so well liked that the colonists brought the recipe with them to Virginia. In the colonies, however, the buns became a bread baked in a shallow pan, then cut into squares and served hot with butter. Eventually Sally Lunn bread evolved into a loaf bread made with yeast.

Sugar, which was very expensive in colonial days, was used only by wealthy plantation families. The mistress of the household kept the cone of sugar in a locked cupboard, and when it was needed, she cut off some from the cone with special shears.

Some of the dinner entrées on early Virginia plantation dining tables included fricassee of lamb with shallots and wine; Virginia oysters in brown butter; and Mutton `a la Royal, which was a roast prepared with bacon, sweet herbs, and an onion stuck with cloves. Breads were a part of eighteenth-century Virginia meals.

Almost every Virginia recipe of the 1700s had two versions—one plain and the other for company. Company recipes increased the eggs, butter, and cream twofold, particularly in desserts.

Gingerbread was a popular dessert and was baked in nearly every home of the colony. There were almost as many recipes for gingerbread as there were families—one of the most famous being that of Mary Ball Washington, mother of the first U.S. President. Several years ago her recipe became the basis of a modern gingerbread mix, which was sold to help finance the reconstruction of Mary Washington's home in Fredericksburg.

In early Virginia recipes were handed down from mother to daughter by word of mouth. The slaves who did the cooking were instructed verbally by the mistress of the house. These cooks could neither read nor write, and consequently, many of their own recipes were never recorded.

The first cookbooks used in this country were English. One of the most popular in colonial Virginia was Hannah Glasse's *The Art of Cookery Made Plain and Easy,* published in London in 1747. The first cookbook actually printed in America was Eliza Smith's *The Compleat Housewife,* published originally in 1727 in England and then reissued in America in 1742 by a public printer in Williamsburg. The American version excluded recipes whose ingredients were not available in the colonies. Eliza Smith's book was unique, because it was the first to include distinctive New World ingredients in the recipes. Five of the recipes called for cornmeal. The book also included recipes for cranberry tarts, Jerusalem artichokes, "Pompkin" pie, and "water-melon-on-rind" pickles.

In contrast to the elegant meals and entertaining of the Tidewater region, life on the Virginia frontier was primitive. Many wives had to cook for their numerous children and husband over an open fire with few ingredients. The men were often away from home fighting Indians up and down the border region. A simple meal might consist of wild garlic served in a stew with vinegar. Small game birds, which one of the sons might have shot, were cooked in a potpie with a cornmeal crust. Black-eyed peas, wild persimmons, and corn supplemented the daily fare. If there was enough molasses, spicy cookies, called Cry Babies, were baked to keep the youngsters from crying.

Dining in Colonial Williamsburg

By the middle of the eighteenth century in Virginia, elegant two-course dinners became common among the Virginia well-to-do. The typical family in Williamsburg ate dinner, the main meal of the day, between two and three o'clock in the afternoon. The meal generally lasted for several hours. The more affluent gentry ate later in the afternoon.

The mistress of the house invited her guests into the dining room when all of the dishes to be served with the first course had been placed on the table. The mixture of aromas from the various dishes held promises of an enjoyable, leisurely meal. The more dishes on the table, particularly meat, the more affluent the household was thought to be. A wealthy family might serve five meat dishes, with one being a large turkey or roast.

Food during the winter months was considerably different than in the summer, because fresh vegetables were available from the kitchen gardens. Winter vegetables tended to be root vegetables that had remained in the garden or had been stored in the root cellar under the house. Game and domesticated meats were more prevalent in the winter, since some slaughtered meat could be kept in a cold room.

In addition to root vegetables, which were frequently prepared in the form of pies or puddings, vegetable fritters and puffs were cooked in melted lard in deep pots, called Dutch ovens. Pickled vegetables were also set out on the table and rolls were placed on each napkin and served without butter.

Winter dinners began with soup, often an onion, split pea, or pumpkin soup. After the soup bowls were cleared away, the soup tureen was replaced by a "remove," a dish of meat or fish. This dish was often a fricassee that had the same light feeling as the soup. Symmetrical balance of dishes was most important on the upper-class colonial Virginia dinner table.

Ham, a popular dish at the head of the table, was often balanced at the foot by roast beef, veal, venison, or a leg of lamb. Fish, seafood, and game birds, including wild turkeys, were popular seasonal foods. Domestic fowl, including chickens, ducks, geese, and turkeys, supplemented the meat dishes. Boiled turkey was often served with a white oyster sauce. Fricassees of chicken and other fowl were winter and holiday dishes.

One of the most popular fowl dishes at Christmas was a Yorkshire Christmas Pie. The pastry for this seasonal concoction was a very dense and heavy bread-like dough, similar to that used for sculptured dough pieces today. It was not to be eaten but merely encased two to five kinds of fowl. The dough contained a boned turkey, inside of which was a boned chicken, inside of that a boned pheasant or partridge, and inside of that a boned squab, dove, or pigeon. All of the fowl were generously seasoned and then baked in the pastry wrapping. At serving time the dough was broken, the fowl removed, and succulent slices offered to the diners.

At the conclusion of the first course, the table was cleared and the tablecloth removed. There was always another tablecloth underneath, ready for the dessert course. This course also had a multitude of dishes. Three or four pies, tarts, custards, creams, jellies, syllabubs, cheesecakes, sweet puddings, and cakes made up the selection. Jellies were served in very small individual glasses.

The typical winter dessert course might feature Indian meal pudding, syllabubs, a pyramid of sugar cakes, dried apricots, almonds, pineapple, and brandied cherries. At Christmas plum puddings, a rich fruitcake, pound cake or seed cake, as well as small tarts filled with cranberries from New England were popular. Pyramids of cakes, which we would call cookies today, were attractively arranged on serving plates. These cookies were made by rolling the dough into a ball and then slicing it. This resulted in baked slices of different sizes that could then be arranged in a pyramid fashion.

One of the most popular holiday desserts was called a hedgehog, made of almond paste with sugar, eggs, and cream. The hedgehog, decorated with slivered almonds to resemble the spines of the animal, had the consistency of fudge so that it could be easily sliced. Another popular winter dessert was a Blanc Mange, similar to a present day mousse. The gelatin for this dessert was obtained from calves' or pigs' feet or the bladders of sturgeons. In the summer fruit ices and ice cream were popular.

After the dessert course the tablecloth was removed, leaving a bare table. Dishes of nut meats, sweetmeats, preserved fruits, and bottles of dessert wine were placed on the bare table. Toasts were drunk to the ladies, who then retired to the parlor after one or two rounds of drinks and left the gentlemen to smoke and discuss the events of the day. At the conclusion of the meal, the table was cleared. A crumb cloth, which had been placed on the floor around the edge of the table to catch any spills and crumbs, was also removed. In those days there were no vacuum cleaners to quickly clean the carpets.

America's First Gourmet

One of the most famous Virginians, Thomas Jefferson, has often been described as this country's first gourmet. He was hospitable and loved to entertain with excellent foods and wines. The rather frugal New Englander, John Adams, who preceded Jefferson as U.S. president remarked about Jefferson's entertaining in the White House: "I dined a large company once or twice a week. Jefferson dined a dozen every day. I held levees [receptions] once a week. Jefferson's whole eight years was a levee!"

Jefferson developed a great interest in French food while he served as ambassador in France in 1785. He brought back French recipes and cooking techniques, as well as seeds and seedlings to grow the European vegetables and fruits he had grown to like.

At his home, Monticello, Jefferson tried to grow almost every possible fruit and vegetable known to man. He kept detailed records of his gardens and had a precise planting schedule for his vegetables. He grew broccoli and endive, two delicacies unknown to America at the time. He also grew and ate tomatoes at a time when the majority of the country considered the fruit poisonous. Jefferson favored the Spanish variety of tomato, which is similar to today's beefsteak tomato. He tried to grow figs and olives as well as capers, but the Virginia climate proved to be too harsh.

While traveling in France, Jefferson became acquainted with olive oil in Provence. He sent cuttings of the trees to North Carolina, where he hoped they might grow. They did not. Jefferson became an avid user of olive oil and attributed his long life to a diet largely of vegetables and salads dressed with olive oil. He was primarily a vegetarian.

Jefferson is credited with the introduction of pasta in this country. He brought back a macaroni machine from Italy. His daughter, Mary Randolph, who acted as his hostess after Jefferson's wife died, created a new dish with

PEANUT SOUP

In 1794 Thomas Jefferson's garden contained 65 peanut hills. Generally, however, the nuts were considered a novelty until after the Civil War. They were used principally by the Negro slave cooks when cooking for themselves, although occasionally in dishes for their masters. Peanut Soup, a Virginia specialty, was one of the few peanut-based dishes enjoyed by the colonists.

Serves 4 to 6

4 tablespoons ($1/2$ stick) butter or
   margarine

$1/3$ cup very finely minced onion

$1/3$ cup very finely minced celery

1 $1/2$ tablespoons flour

1 cup smooth peanut butter

4 cups chicken broth

$1/2$ cup half-and-half

Salt and pepper, to taste

$1/4$ cup chopped peanuts, for garnish

■

Melt the butter in a large saucepan over medium-low heat. Add the onions and celery and sauté until soft, but not brown. Stir in the flour and blend until smooth. Lower heat to simmer and stir in the peanut butter. Slowly add the chicken broth, bring to a slow boil, and simmer the soup for 20 minutes. Add the half-and-half and heat the soup just to the boiling point. Add salt and pepper, to taste. Ladle the soup into bowls and garnish each serving with some chopped peanuts.

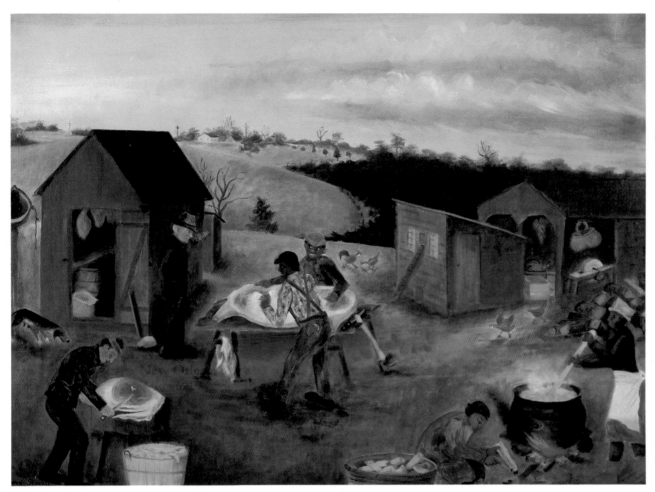

CUTTING OUT THE MEAT by Queena Stovall, oil, 18 x 24 inches, courtesy of Virginia Arts, Lynchburg, Virginia.

macaroni and Parmesan cheese. Later, a version of this dish using macaroni and Cheddar cheese became a staple of the American diet.

The style of cooking in Jefferson's kitchen was both Virginian and French. When he was President he employed the first French chef in the White House and brought 11 of his servants from Monticello to the White House to learn French cooking. Jefferson and his steward, a Frenchman named Lamar, would go early in the morning to the market in Georgetown. "It often took

50 dollars to pay for the marketing that would be used in a day. Mr. Jefferson's salary did not support him while he was President," observed Edmund Bacon, Jefferson's Monticello overseer.

Through Jefferson's influence, many French dishes were added to American cuisine. Very thin French crêpes became a popular dessert item at Jefferson's dinner table. They were made one at a time, stacked one on top of the other, sprinkled with maple sugar, and then cut into wedges. These wedges were served with a fruit sauce, or sometimes pieces of

fruit were folded into the batter before cooking. A lacy effect for the pancakes was achieved when rice was folded into the batter. Pink pancakes became very chic during Jefferson's time and were made with tiny slivers of beets added to the batter.

Wine was an important part of the meal for Jefferson, who was well versed in the wines of France, Spain, Germany, and Italy. Numerous notes and meticulous calculations enabled Jefferson to perceive how many bottles of wine to serve at each dinner party. He figured that a bottle of champagne would serve three and one-seventh guests. His White House wine cellar numbered close to a thousand bottles, and he spent $3,000 on wine his first year as President, exceeding the wine budget by many times over.

Jefferson's interest in wine prompted him to have vine cuttings sent to Virginia, where he attempted to grow the European wine grapes. Even after he brought over an Italian viticulturist, his attempts to grow *vitis vinifera* grapes in Virginia were not successful. It would be another 200 years before the popular European wine grapes such as Chardonnay, Riesling, and Cabernet Sauvignon would be successfully cultivated and a substantial wine industry established in Virginia.

Upon his return to Monticello, Jefferson still continued to entertain constantly and lavishly. There were usually eight for dinner, which was served promptly at four o'clock. "He was never a great eater, but what he did eat he wanted to be very choice," recounted Bacon. "He never ate much hog meat." Jefferson really never ate much meat at all. He regarded meat as condiments for vegetables.

In his later years Jefferson continued to experiment with plants and livestock. Many of his practices are still in use today. His numerous inventions included the first American plow.

BAKED HAM

Smithfield and country hams are rarely served as a main course because of their saltiness. Instead, they are sliced paper thin and served as an hors d'oeuvre with biscuits or as an accompaniment to chicken or other fowl. Smithfield or country ham is also used with crabmeat as a stuffing for chicken breasts. Sometimes thicker slices of these types of ham are fried and served with red-eye gravy, primarily with eggs for breakfast.

Both Smithfield and country hams should be soaked at least overnight before cooking. The following is an old Virginia recipe for ham, which has been handed down for several generations. The addition of sugar and vinegar to the boiling water both sweetens and tenderizes the ham.

1 Smithfield or country ham (12 to
     14 pounds)
1 cup brown sugar
1/2 cup vinegar

■

Scrub the ham with a stiff brush to remove any mold and the coating of seasonings. Place the ham in a large kettle, completely cover with cold water, and soak for 24 hours.

The next day drain the water and scrub the ham again, if necessary. Place it in a large kettle. Cover the ham with water to which the sugar and vinegar have been added. Bring to a boil, reduce heat to low, and cook for 25 minutes per pound.

When done, allow the ham to cool in the cooking water. Then remove the rind and score the fat. Place the ham, fat side up, in a large baking dish and cover the fat with the following mixture:

1/4 cup light brown sugar
2 tablespoons bread crumbs
3/4 teaspoon ground cloves
1/4 teaspoon black pepper
4 teaspoons semi-sweet sherry

■

After combining the sugar, bread crumbs, cloves, and black pepper, press the mixture onto the fat and pack it down well. Bake in a preheated 375° F. oven for 15 minutes, or until the topping starts to melt. Drizzle the sherry over the ham and continue to bake for another 10 to 15 minutes, until nicely browned. The ham may be served warm or cold.

Smithfield Hams

The curing of hams is part of Virginia's culinary tradition. In 1608 the Indians taught the Jamestown colonists how to cure meat. Their method of salting, smoking, and aging venison was adopted by the settlers to preserve the meat of the plentiful razorback hog. This hog, which was brought by the Spanish to Florida, had migrated to Virginia. Hams from domesticated pigs date from the 1620s.

By the mid-1600s the meat from the pigs of English origin had acquired a unique flavor. It seems that the pigs were allowed to roam loose and ate primarily peanuts. In addition they were fed peaches, Jerusalem artichokes, and corn.

In Virginia there are two processes for curing ham. One is known as country cure and the other as Smithfield. The country-ham curing process varies from area to area but basically uses salt, sugar and nitrate (saltpeter). The process may or may not include smoking. The aging time of the hams depends on the individual producer. Country-cured hams are usually not as rich or as salty as the Smithfield type.

As the hogs brought from England multiplied and more peanut fields were planted, hogs began to feed on peanuts. Eventually a special curing and aging process was developed to bring out the rich flavor of these hams.

To produce a Smithfield ham, the meat is rubbed with a combination of salt, sugar, and saltpeter. The hams are allowed to cure from 30 to 90 days and are then smoked over hickory, apple, and oak coals for three to five days. After the hams are smoked, they are rubbed with black pepper, put into a porous bag, and then air-cured for a least six months but frequently up to two years. The longer the curing time, the stronger the taste. This is due to the steady evaporation of moisture in the ham as it cures.

The town of Smithfield, in the center of Virginia's peanut-growing and hog-raising region, became the headquarters for the ham that bears its name. In order to be a Smithfield ham, according to a 1968 Virginia law, it must have been produced within the city limits of the town of Smithfield. In practice, however, the name applies to hams from the five counties surrounding Smithfield. While hogs today are still turned loose in harvested fields to forage out the remaining peanuts, producers of Smithfield hams say that it is primarily the curing process, not the feed, that produces the famous hams.

Smithfield hams are always sliced wafer thin and served as a side entrée or

FRUIT TRIFLE

Early English settlers of Virginia brought many of their recipes with them from their homeland. One of these was Trifle which became a favorite in colonial Williamsburg. This modern version uses a packaged pudding mix for a quicker and easier preparation.

Serves 10

■

3 packages of lady fingers or 1 pound cake

1/3 cup sherry

1/3 cup orange-flavored liqueur

1/2 cup raspberry preserves

2 packages (3 and 3/4 ounces each) vanilla instant pudding

2 1/4 cups milk

2 1/2 cups whipping cream

1 box of fresh raspberries or 1 package (10 ounces) frozen raspberries, thawed and drained

1/2 cup sliced fresh or frozen strawberries

1 small can (8 ounces) sliced peaches, drained

2 tablespoons confectioners sugar

2 kiwis, peeled and sliced

1/2 cup toasted almond slivers

Separate the lady fingers or slice the pound cake 1-inch thick. Line the bottom and sides of a 2-quart glass bowl with the lady fingers, rounded side out, or with slices of pound cake. Combine the sherry and orange liqueur and brush over the exposed sides of the lady fingers or cake. Lightly spread the raspberry preserves on the ladyfingers or cake in the bottom of the bowl.

Prepare the instant pudding with milk and 1 1/2 cups of the cream. Whip 1/2 cup of the cream until stiff and fold it into the pudding. Spoon one-third of the pudding into the trifle dish. Top with half of the fruit and another third of the pudding. Add the remaining fruit and top with the rest of the pudding.

Just before serving, whip the remaining 1/2 cup of cream with the confectioners sugar until stiff and spoon it into a pastry bag fitted with a star. Pipe the cream around the top of the custard. Garnish the top of the custard with the kiwi slices and the toasted almonds.

used as a cooking ingredient. More neutral-tasting meats such as chicken are enhanced by the sharper flavor of Smithfield ham. Today, more than 50 percent of the hams are sold between October and December for holiday meals.

Two of the leading producers of

Smithfield hams are the V.W. Joyner Company of Smithfield and S. Wallace Edwards and Sons in Surry. The Joyner Company operates the oldest commercial smokehouse in the nation and uses the same smoking and curing methods that its founder, V.W. Joyner, perfected when he founded the company in 1889. Part of the original smokehouse still stands.

S. Wallace Edwards and Sons is a family business that was started in 1926 by Captain S. Wallace Edwards, Sr., an enterprising young pilot for the Jamestown-Surry ferryboat. As a sideline he started selling ham sandwiches, made with his own hams, to his passengers. His sandwiches became so popular that he soon gave up river piloting and began curing hams on a full-time basis. Edwards claimed that he used an old recipe, which has its origins in the methods the Indians taught the settlers at Jamestown.

Traditional Virginia Foods

Traditional Virginia foods can be divided into three distinct categories—native foods of the Indians, food styles of the early English settlers in the Tidewater region, and food eaten by the farmers in the mountainous regions of Virginia. The Indians used corn and cured game meat. Their foods were forerunners of the colonists' various corn breads and corn puddings, as well as the basis for curing hams. Tidewater Virginia was characterized by mostly English foods, such as Roast Beef and Yorkshire Pudding, Sally Lunn, and Orange-Wine Cake. Further west in the Shenandoah Valley and the mountains, country-cured ham, Brunswick Stew, and corn bread were popular.

In addition to its typically English foods, the Tidewater region was known for its rich desserts made from English recipes and with ingredients imported from England. Steamed puddings made with raisins, currants, citron, spices, and brandy were popular at Christmas. Trifle, a concoction of cake slices soaked in rum or sherry and layered with jam and a rich custard, had several variations. One version omitted the jam but used the rich custard in the center and on the outside of the cake. It was then frosted with sherry flavored whipped cream. The cake was known as "Tipsy Parson" because of its alcoholic content.

Probably the most famous of all Tidewater Virginia cakes was the pound cake. Taken from an old English recipe, it was made with a pound each of butter, sugar, flour, and eggs and flavored with brandy and mace. Since pound cakes were made before the invention of baking powder, the batter had to be beaten for at least an hour to incorporate enough air into it to make the cake light. Some recipes said that the eggs should be beaten for five hours.

Virginia Apples

Apples were one of the early ingredients used in Virginia cooking, particularly in pies and cakes. Since the state's first settlement, apples have played an important role in the agricultural development of Virginia. In 1622 early settlers at Jamestown grafted cuttings of English apple trees onto wild crab-apple rootstocks. Some of these cuttings were sent by the London Company to start the first Virginia apple orchards. As more settlers came to Virginia, they brought branches of their favorite apple trees with them and also grafted them onto the wild crab-apple rootstocks. Apple trees reminded the early settlers of home and helped relieve the homesickness. In colonial days each farm had at least one or two apple trees.

There were a great variety of apples grown in Virginia. The Winchester area of the Shenandoah Valley along with Albemarle County in central Virginia became known as "apple country." Albemarle Pippins became so well known for their crispness, tartness, and long storage capabilities that they were being shipped to England by the 1750s.

Today, commercial Virginia apple growers principally grow Golden Delicious, Black Twig, Stayman, Red Delicious, Romes, Winesaps, and Summer Rambo. They are also experimenting with some of the older varieties, such as Black Amish and Thomas Jefferson's favorite, Esopus Spitzenburg. Colonial period apples are more disease resistant than modern varieties but not as attractive.

The Chesapeake Bay

When the English arrived at the Chesapeake in 1607, they knew little about hunting, farming, or harvesting food from the waters of the Bay. Fortunately for the English, the Indians taught them their techniques of fishing and hunting. Although the Powhatans did not use sails, their dugout canoes proved to be very serviceable, and the colonists copied them, as well as some of their fishing tools.

The shoreline of the Chesapeake Bay was explored by Captain John Smith when the first settlers landed in Virginia. He found the waters teeming with fish. Captain Smith wrote that the fish were so abundant and thick in the Chesapeake Bay that they could be scooped up with a frying pan. He also speared skates with his sword. "We tooke more in owne hour than we could eate in a day," he wrote.

The Bay still provides clams, crabs, oysters, and finfish for the fishermen of Virginia. Sea bass, blue fish, and shad are the most popular fish commercially harvested from the Bay. The shad, which is a highly perishable fish and is seldom sold outside the region, is prized for its roe. The traditional method of preparing the roe involves frying bacon to crispness, then gently adding the roe to the bacon fat and carefully sautéing it. The bacon is then served with the roe.

Crab feasts and seafood dinners are still popular fare with Chesapeake Bay residents. Roasted corn, potato salad, biscuits or corn bread, and fruit cobblers often accompany these seafood dinners. Oyster chowder, steamed clams, sautéed soft-shelled crabs, crab cakes, crab imperial, and crab salad are some other Chesapeake Bay as well as Virginia favorites.

Virginia Wines

After Jefferson's failure at *vinifera* grape growing and winemaking, various Virginians continued to make wine from native grapes, although the wine had a strong and wild or foxy flavor. Around 1800 considerable acreage of the Alexander grape, one of the first American-bred wine grapes, was grown in Virginia. The Alexander grape had been developed in Pennsylvania by James Alexander, gardener to the son of Governor William Penn. Jefferson also grew this grape as a replacement for his defunct European varietals.

In the 1830s Dr. D.N. Norton of Richmond domesticated an American hybrid grape called the Virginia Norton. Many considered this red wine grape to be one of the best of the American hybrids. The wine from this grape became famous as Virginia Claret and won awards on both sides of the Atlantic in the 1870s and 1880s.

Virginia reached its peak wine production in the 1850s, just prior to the Civil War. Many of the vineyards were

BAKED FILLET OF FLOUNDER

When the first settlers came to Jamestown, flounder were so abundant that they could be scooped up by hand. They found them to be similar to the European sole.

Serves 6

4 tablespoons butter or margarine

1/4 cup chopped red onion

6 flounder fillets (about 2 pounds)

2 tablespoons tarragon mustard

3 1/2 tablespoons dry white wine

1/2 cup freshly grated Parmesan cheese

1/2 cup bread crumbs

■

Melt 2 tablespoons of the butter and coat a flat baking dish large enough to hold the fish in a single layer. Distribute the chopped onion evenly over the bottom of the dish. Place the fish on top of the onion.

In a small dish combine the mustard with the wine. Then brush each fillet with the mustard mixture. Sprinkle with the Parmesan cheese and bread crumbs. Dot with the remaining 2 tablespoons of butter. Bake in a preheated 425° F. oven for 5 to 8 minutes, or until the fish is barely done. Place the fish under the broiler for a minute or two, until lightly browned. Serve immediately.

destroyed during the Civil War, since a number of battles were fought in and around Virginia vineyard lands. In addition winery hands became scarce as they left to join the Confederate army. The South fought hard to maintain control of the Shenandoah Valley, not for the wine it produced, but because it was the "bread basket" of the Confederacy.

Prohibition, which was enacted in Virginia in 1914, successfully killed the Virginia wine industry for the next 50 years. It was not until the early 1970s that wine-grape vineyards again flourished in Virginia.

Today, there are 40 wineries in the state producing primarily Riesling, Chardonnay, and Cabernet Sauvignon. The winemakers are of a varied background—French, Belgian, and Italian. Many are enology graduates of the leading universities in California and Europe. Others are self-taught winemakers. Virginia wines are now winning medals in state, regional, national, and international competitions. After 350 years wine is again being made in Williamsburg, and there is a successful winery adjacent to Monticello, home of Thomas Jefferson.

WEST VIRGINIA

TAKING GRANDPA TO SEE THE COWS by Mary Ann Vessey, acrylic, 24 x 18 inches, courtesy of the artist, Staunton, Virginia.

AT THE TIME OF THE CIVIL WAR, the western part of Virginia opposed the state's secession from the Union and in 1861 organized a separate government. This break brought about the creation of the state of West Virginia. The development of West Virginia's coal industry after the Civil War attracted Italian, German, Polish, and Hungarian immigrants and gave the state a contrast of people and lifestyles.

West Virginia is a mountainous state with only the "Panhandle" in the northeast providing sufficient flatland for large-scale farming. The mountain regions still contain isolated cabins, whose inhabitants make a meager living on their small plots of cleared land. Today, in order to survive much of the state's population is engaged in manufacturing and coal production.

Buckwheat, peaches, and apples are the most important agricultural food products of the state. The Golden Delicious apple, which was developed from a stray seedling by A.H. Mullins in Clay County, West Virginia, in 1890, is now grown throughout the country and is known for its mellow flavor and lovely pale-yellow skin.

At one time, when Virginia was still an English colony, King George II decreed that West Virginia (then a part of Virginia) was to be a forbidden territory for settlers. The German and Scottish settlers ignored his decree and settled there anyway. The Germans claimed they could not read English, and the Scottish settlers merely ignored the edict. One story is that the Scots settled on land so steep that they had to use ladders to climb up to their orchards.

One of the main meals of the early

frontier families was stewed squirrel cooked with onion, garlic, thyme, and bacon. Bear meat was also prized. Wild greens were the early vegetables of the settlers until they planted corn, beans, and potatoes. Most pioneer families maintained a few pigs to supplement their diet of wild game meat.

Lumbering became one of the early industries of West Virginia. Some West Virginians claim that peanut brittle accidentally came into existence when a logger named Tony Beaver cooked up an extra supply of maple syrup and threw in some peanuts. He emptied the unwanted mixture onto a log, and after it had cooled he tasted a piece. Beaver and his fellow loggers liked it and named it peanut brittle.

One of the first cartels (now illegal) formed in the United States was in West Virginia. In 1817 the price of salt dropped from ten cents a pound to four cents in a very short time. To avoid this happening in the future, the West Virginia salt men agreed to fix the price of salt. By so doing they were able to control the salt market in Ohio, Indiana, Illinois, and Kentucky for many years.

Moonshine

During the 1800s moonshine whiskey was one of the most famous products of West Virginia's underground agriculture. It continued to be made until well after World War II. In fact illegal moonshine is still made today in some very remote areas of West Virginia.

The issue of illegal whiskey arose in 1791, when a federal law was passed taxing whiskey. The whiskey tax led to a number of political protests throughout

West Virginia and culminated in the Whiskey Rebellion of 1794. While the rebellion was quickly put down, it took the federal "revenooers" more than 150 years to stamp out moonshining in the mountains of West Virginia.

SALLY LUNN

Sally Lunn was originally a bun sold in Bath, England. When the recipe came to Virginia with the English colonists, it became a beaten bread, which was baked in a shallow pan. By the nineteenth century the recipe had evolved into a rich loaf bread that was baked in a Turk's-head mold and served with tea. If a Turk's-head mold is not available, Sally Lunn may be baked in a tube pan.

Makes 1 loaf

1 package dry yeast

1/4 cup lukewarm water (110° to 115° F.)

3 tablespoons sugar

2 large eggs, lightly beaten

3/4 cup milk, scalded and cooled to lukewarm

3 1/2 cups all-purpose flour

1/2 cup melted margarine or shortening

1 teaspoon salt

■

Combine the yeast with 1 tablespoon of the sugar and sprinkle over the lukewarm water in a large bowl. Let stand for several minutes and then stir until dissolved. Add the remaining sugar and beat in the eggs; then add the lukewarm milk. Stir in half of the flour, a little at a time, and beat the dough well. Beat in the melted shortening and salt. Gradually beat in the remaining flour to form a medium-thick dough. Scrape down the sides of the bowl to incorporate all of the ingredients. Grease the top of the dough, cover the bowl, and let the dough rise in a warm place until doubled in size, about 1 hour.

Punch down the dough, re-cover it, and let it rest for 10 minutes. Put the dough in a greased Turk's-head mold, 8 1/2-cup baking mold, or 10-inch tube pan. Cover and let rise in a warm place until double in bulk, about 45 minutes. Bake in a preheated 350° F. oven for 50 minutes to 1 hour, or until nicely browned.

The nature of the land almost dictated and certainly encouraged moonshining. The small farms on the ridges of the mountains or up in the steep hollows were virtually inaccessible to outsiders. Most farmers had only a small plot of cleared land, and the only crop they could raise was corn. Since the area was too remote to ship the corn to market, it made more economic sense for the farmers to convert their corn into whiskey and sell it locally.

Prior to World War II most mountain farmers could sell a bushel of corn for $2 to $3. By comparison, one-fourth of a bushel of corn would make a run of moonshine that would sell for about $100. It normally took a peck (8 quarts) of shelled corn, 25 pounds of cornmeal, and 25 pounds of sugar to produce a proper sour mash for making whiskey. Fermentation was induced by adding yeast.

Moonshine stills were homemade, and the quality of materials used, particularly the copper piping, gave still whiskey its unusual taste. Most stills consisted of three main parts—the cooker, the coils, and the container. The cooker evaporated the liquid in the fermented mash, which condensed in the coil, and the resulting moonshine was collected in the container.

FLUFFY SPOON BREAD

Spoon bread, so named because of its light, fluffy, custard-like texture, is served with a spoon. The addition of cream in this recipe gives the spoon bread a richer consistency.

Serves 6 to 8

1 2/3 cups milk

1/4 cup whipping cream

1 cup stone-ground white cornmeal

2/3 cup water

3 tablespoons soft butter

1 tablespoon sugar

Dash of salt

4 extra-large eggs, separated

2 teaspoons baking powder

■

Combine the milk, cream, cornmeal, water, butter, sugar, and salt in a medium-size saucepan. Bring to a slow boil over medium-low heat and then simmer for 2 minutes, stirring vigorously. Remove from heat and turn the mixture into a large bowl. Let it cool slightly.

Beat the egg whites until they hold stiff peaks. Beat the egg yolks with the baking powder until the yolks are light and lemon-colored. Stir the egg yolks into the cornmeal mixture quickly. Fold in a quarter of the egg whites and then fold in the remaining egg whites. Gently pour the batter into a greased 3-quart soufflé dish and bake in a preheated 375° F. oven for 35 minutes, or until the top is lightly browned and a knife inserted in the center comes out clean. The center should still be creamy and soft. Spoon out individual servings at once and top with butter.

West Virginia Food Festivals

The area of White Sulphur Springs, West Virginia, is famous for the Greenbrier resort complex, which annually hosts a series of cooking classes conducted by renowned chefs. The region is also known for what botanists believe is one of the world's oldest living plants, the huckleberry. These huckleberries were first picked by the Indians and later by the settlers. For centuries the berries have been used to make muffins, pies, and cakes.

Early get-togethers in West Virginia frequently centered around church and civic organizations. These meetings were called "Soups," because each member contributed some corn, onions, potatoes, vegetables, and meats to a gigantic soup kettle. Soup was served with homemade bread, and ice cream and cake were usually provided for dessert. Chicken-corn soup was a favorite.

Different seasons of the year highlight various food events in West Virginia. There is maple sugaring in the state, and each spring there are various maple-sugar festivals. In the fall pumpkins are the subject of festivals and are used in many baked goods. Pumpkins have been a special part of the culinary history of West Virginia since 1753. In that year the Potomac River flooded its banks near Harper's Ferry, and its waters swept a flood of pumpkins onto the land. The local citizens interpreted this as a good omen, and ever since there has been a tradition of using pumpkins in the fall to make pumpkin pies, pumpkin butter, and even drying the pumpkin pulp for later use.

PUMPKIN PIE

Pumpkin pie was strictly an American invention. While the English had long been making pastry for their meat pies and the American Indians had stewed pumpkin, it took the settlers to combine the two. In colonial days the settlers served pumpkin pie both as a vegetable to accompany meats and as a dessert.

This lighter version of pumpkin pie includes the traditional spices brought to colonial America by the trading ships. The nuts are added for additional flavor and texture interest.

Serves 8

Filling

1 3/4 cups canned pumpkin

3 eggs

1 1/2 teaspoons ground ginger

1 teaspoon nutmeg

1 teaspoon cinnamon

1/3 cup molasses

1 tablespoon light brown sugar

1/2 cup whipping cream

1 cup sour cream

3/4 cup small walnut pieces

Pastry for single crust pie (recipe follows)

■

Combine the pumpkin, eggs, ginger, nutmeg, and cinnamon into a smooth texture in a medium-size bowl. Add the molasses, sugar, whipping cream, sour cream, and nuts and blend well.

Roll out the pastry dough to fit a 9-inch pie pan. Fit the dough into the pan and flute the edges. Pour the pumpkin filling into the pie shell and bake in a preheated 350° F. oven for 50 to 55 minutes or until the filling is set and a knife inserted toward the center comes out clean. Cool before serving.

Pastry

1 cup all-purpose flour

3 tablespoons butter or margarine

2 tablespoons solid vegetable shortening

3 to 4 tablespoons ice water

■

Place the flour in a bowl and cut in the butter and shortening until the mixture resembles coarse crumbs. Add the water, a tablespoon at a time, and stir with a fork until the dough can be formed into a ball. Wrap the dough in plastic wrap and chill for at least 1 hour.

JULY SETTING by Jose Trinidad, oil, 30 x 40 inches, courtesy of Miner's Gallery Americana, Carmel, California.

DEEP SOUTH

THE DEEP SOUTH was settled initially by the Spanish, French, and English. The earliest settlers were the Spanish, who established St. Augustine in 1565. They were followed by French settlers, primarily soldiers who had remained on the Gulf Coast after their expeditions of the seventeenth century. Later, at the end of the eighteenth century, refugees from the French Revolution settled in what is today Louisiana. Still another strain of French immigrants to Louisiana came from the Acadia provinces of Canada. At about the same time, English and Anglo-American settlers came to the Deep South from England or from the more northerly American colonies.

The leisurely lifestyle in the southern cities of New Orleans, Savannah, and Charleston was a mingling of the aristocratic life of the French and English upper-class settlers. This life extended into the rural areas of the Deep South where the wealthy upper class established plantations along navigable rivers that stretched well into the interior. Plantation crops were mostly tobacco, cotton, and rice, which were traded locally for needed supplies or sold in England through brokers.

A southern plantation was a self-contained society. Plantation blacksmiths made all the necessary farm tools and the ornate ironwork on the plantation houses. Cattle provided meat and hides for shoes and saddles. Sheep furnished wool and the fields provided cotton for clothing. Slaves prepared the meals under the direction of the mistress of the house. The cooking chore was a heavy one since gracious hospitality with abundant food was the norm on southern plantations.

Almost from the start, southern hospitality was a custom among the white settlers, both the wealthy and poor. Friend and stranger alike were invited to dine and stay for the night or for a few weeks. Parties, musicals, and balls brought people from far and near. Picnics, barbecues, and seafood feasts were regular summer activities on the plantations. The less affluent people of the remote Piedmont region eagerly shared a meal with strangers in return for news of the outside world.

Life on the hilly Piedmont plateau was much more primitive than in the lowlands. Farmers cleared the land of trees and rocks and planted enough crops to provide food for the family. Meals featured wild game, and there were many versions of Brunswick Stew. Some contained rabbit; others, squirrel or venison.

All of the early settlers contributed to the cuisine of the Deep South. The Spanish brought citrus to Florida, while the French introduced Creole and Cajun cooking to the Gulf states near New Orleans.

On the Atlantic seaboard, the cuisine of the French Huguenots, who settled the low country around Charleston, South Carolina, combined with that of the English settlers to produce a unique variety of dishes. African slaves of the rice plantations added their foods to low country cooking, while sea captains contributed spices from the Orient and the Caribbean Islands. Anglo-American settlers from parts of Virginia and the upper Carolinas blended their American-ized cuisine with that of the earlier settlers along the Atlantic seaboard.

After America's alliance with France in 1778 during the War of Independence, many southern aristocrats adopted the fashionable French cuisine. French soups, salads, bonbons, and fricassees became regular dishes at southern dinner tables. French cuisine had an important influence in the Deep South that has continued into the twentieth century.

Since all of the states of the Deep South have a coastline bordering either on the Atlantic Ocean or the Gulf of Mexico, seafood has played a significant role in the cuisine of the region. Shrimp, crabs, oysters, crayfish, and finfish have all become primary ingredients in a wide variety of dishes typical of the Deep South.

Corn breads were the most popular hot breads in the Deep South, since very little wheat flour was available. Southern corn bread, made with local white cornmeal, was baked in shallow pans, then cut in squares and served hot with butter. No sugar was added to southern corn bread, which was a sharp contrast to the northern variety made from yellow cornmeal. Corn breads such as hoecake, ashcake, corn pone, and corn sticks were baked as individual servings and eaten primarily by slaves or poorer farm families.

Pork was a favorite meat in the Deep South since hogs were easy to raise. At hog-killing time every part of the animal was used. The small intestines of the hog, known as chitterlings, were often given to the slaves to eat. They cooked them in boiling water with a few spices until tender. Then the chitterlings

HOPPIN' JOHN

Traditionally served on New Year's for good luck, Hoppin' John is said to have been created during the plantation era by a lame black cook who hopped on one leg while preparing the dish.

Hoppin' John is usually a very bland dish. Spices and chopped tomato have been added to this version to give it more flavor.

Serves 6

1 cup dried black-eyed peas

1 clove garlic, chopped

3/4 cup chopped celery

3/4 cup chopped onion

1/3 cup chopped green pepper

3/4 pound smoked ham, chopped

1/2 teaspoon dried thyme

1/4 teaspoon dried sage

2 tablespoons white wine vinegar

3 tablespoons olive oil

1/4 cup chopped fresh parsley

1 medium tomato, peeled, seeded,
   and finely chopped

1 cup regular rice

Dash of Tabasco sauce, to taste

■

Rinse and pick over the peas. Soak them in water overnight and drain well.

Combine the peas, garlic, celery, onion, green pepper, ham, thyme, and sage in a medium sauce pan. Add enough water to cover, bring to a boil, and simmer, covered, for 35 to 40 minutes, or until the peas are tender but not too soft.

In the meantime combine the vinegar, olive oil, and parsley in a small bowl. When the peas are tender, drain them, reserving the liquid. Add the oil mixture and the tomato to the peas in the saucepan.

Add the rice to another saucepan. Combine the drained cooking liquid with enough water to measure 2 cups and add to the rice. Bring to a boil, then cook, covered, over low heat for 18 to 20 minutes, or until the rice is done. Add the peas to the rice and warm, just to heat through. Season with a dash of Tabasco sauce.

There is an old saying that if you eat black-eyed peas on New Year's Day you will have good luck the rest of the year. That is why Hoppin' John, whose main ingredient is dried black-eyed peas, traditionally is served on New Year's Day in the South. Other ingredients of the dish include rice and a ham bone, hog jowl, salt pork, or bacon. The meat and peas are simmered overnight; then the rice is added, and the mixture is cooked until the rice is tender. Hoppin' John is served with corn bread.

For years there has been a controversy as to where pecan pie originated. Georgia, Texas, Mississippi, and Alabama all claim the honor because they all grow pecans. Pecan pie could also have been developed in Louisiana since cane sugar, another ingredient of the pie, was readily available there. Over the years many variations of the rich butter, egg, sugar, syrup, and pecan combination have come into existence. Some cooks use light syrup, others dark; some add bourbon, and others add chocolate.

The coastal areas of Georgia and South Carolina were rice-growing country until the abolition of slavery; however, the tradition of cooking with rice has prevailed throughout the South. Combined with seafood, rice enhances such dishes as pilafs in the Carolinas and Georgia and gumbos and jambalayas in Louisiana.

For more than two centuries, "soul food," the food eaten by the slaves and poorer hill farmers, has been a part of Deep South cooking. It is based on such staples as pork, black-eyed peas, grits, fried yams, and sweet potato puddings and pies. Soul food's natural, unpretentious approach to good eating has been quite popular from the Carolinas to the Gulf.

were cut into small pieces, dipped in cornmeal, and fried in hot lard until golden brown. Hog jowl was cooked with turnip greens or black-eyed peas.

Bacon was used to flavor string beans, black-eyed peas, and greens of all types. Juice left in the pot after the vegetables had been removed was called "pot likker" and was supposed to have nutritive values. Many southern politicians, including Huey Long of Louisiana,

talked about the virtues of corn pone and pot likker.

Southern Fried Chicken, for which the South is famous, has many versions. Most southern cooks agree, however, that it should be served with biscuits and cream gravy. Some cooks dip the chicken pieces in beaten egg before coating them with flour or cornmeal for frying, while others dip the pieces in milk or a combination of eggs and milk.

ALABAMA

THE FIRST EUROPEANS to visit Alabama were Spanish seamen in 1505. Upon returning to Spain they reported that "the natives wore hats of solid gold and that life on the new continent was luxurious." In 1540, Hernando de Soto explored the interior of what is now Alabama looking for gold. Twenty years later, Tristan de Luna and 1,500 Spanish settlers unsuccessfully attempted to establish a Spanish colony on Mobile Bay. After returning to Spain they reported that the Indians feasted on wild turkey, game, fish, melons, and squash.

Around 1700, two French brothers, Pierre and Jean Baptiste Lemoyne established an all-male settlement at Biloxi, Mississippi, and later one at Mobile, Alabama. Two years after the founding of Mobile, a ship called the *Pelican* brought 23 girls from France, who had agreed to come to the New World to marry the French settlers. The girls were known as *filles du roi,* or daughters of the king. Louis XIV had sponsored their trip and provided each girl with a trunk, or *cassette,* containing her dowry, which included a rosary and a needlework box.

Although the girls were not necessarily adept at needlework, they loved to cook. Consequently, soon after arriving, the young women staged a petticoat rebellion against the crude food of the settlement, which mainly consisted of game, fish, wild plants, and berries. Their persistence prompted their husbands to clear the land and plant a variety of food crops, thus greatly improving the cuisine of Mobile Bay. In 1719 slaves came to the Mobile Bay settlement and added African cooking techniques, seasonings, and sauces to their owners' recipes.

By the middle of the 1700s, Mobile had become well-established, and exotic foods and drinks were gracing the dinner tables. Pale wine made from native grapes and oranges; peaches baked in sugar-crusted tarts; baked, stuffed Gulf snapper; and an endless variety of aromatic soups and sauces were being served. Native squash was baked and candied, and Gulf shrimp were used in bisques and jambalayas.

American settlers who came to northern Alabama, then the nation's frontier, had a more meager existence. The new frontier consisted of 20 million acres forcibly ceded from the Creeks to the United States. Among the first Americans to claim land in this "new Southwest" were Indian fighters who had served as privates in Andrew Jackson's militia.

Most of the settlers came in the late 1700s and early 1800s and were second- and third- generation Americans from the Carolinas, Georgia, and Virginia. They cleared the virgin land in hopes that it would yield profitable crops similar to those in more settled areas in the North and East.

Year-round, the Alabama hills reverberated with the thump of axes felling trees to clear pastureland or construct cabins. Many of the cabins were crude huts about 15 feet square with dirt floors, and a single window. The beds, which were known as "Alabama bedsteads," consisted of rough frames with pallets of broom sage, crabgrass, or corn shucks. A fireplace of bricks or wooden slats plastered with mud was used for cooking and heating.

Alabama soon evolved into a new and gracious society, which, until the Civil War, was based primarily on a cotton economy. Hospitality dominated plantation life, and it was not unusual for guests to visit for long periods of time, even up to a year. Balls, parties, and barbecues were held year-round to entertain visitors and neighbors. By the mid-1800s, however, ore and coal had been discovered in the hills of Alabama, and the state transformed into an industrial economy.

Alabama Foods

The culinary influence of the early French settlers was most prevalent along the Gulf Coast, where fish and seafood dishes continue to have a strong French accent. The French influence was also evident in the early attempts to grow wine grapes and make wine. Until Prohibition there was a considerable wine industry in Alabama based on the domestication of local wild grapes, such as Scuppernongs, Magnolias, and Higgins.

Away from the coast, southern cooking with fried chicken, green beans, yellow squash, okra, and biscuits became the staple food. There were many types of biscuits, ranging from thin baking-powder biscuits to thick fluffy ones, which are split and served with fruit and whipped cream for dessert. Some biscuits are enriched with mashed potatoes or cheese, but the trickiest ones to make were beaten biscuits, which originated in Maryland but became popular throughout the South. No leavening agent was used in these biscuits, and their fluffiness depended on the long beating of the dough. In plantation kitchens the cooks

THE FIRST CUT by Robert Spear Dunning, oil, 12 ¹/2 x 17 ¹/4 inches, courtesy of Richard York Gallery, New York, New York.

gave the dough 200 "licks" for the home folks and 500 if company was expected.

Fried pies are said to have originated in Alabama. To make a fried pie, a small amount of filling was heaped on a round piece of rolled-out pie dough. Then the pastry was closed in the shape of a half moon, sealed at the edges, and fried in deep fat. The pies were dusted with powdered sugar and eaten hot. Fillings for these delicate half-moon pastries were usually fruit, which varied with the locality. In Alabama fried pies were filled with peaches or peach butter.

Mobile used to be famous for its oyster bars. The succulent Bon Secour oysters from the bay were sold by the dozen and were opened just before they were served on trays of cracked ice. The first nine oysters were eaten with a squeeze of lemon and the last three with some horseradish. This custom was repeated with the next dozen. Unfortunately, Mobile Bay is no longer a source of oysters, as the oyster beds have been destroyed by pollution from industrial waste.

Seafood harvested off the coast of Alabama continues to play an important part in the cuisine of the state. Today, crab salad and pompano baked in parchment are two popular dishes served in towns along the Gulf. Gulf shrimp are served in various ways, including fried, in salads, and in Creole dishes.

To satisfy the large demand for shrimp in the South, fleets of trawlers from ports such as Bayou La Batre, range out into the Gulf of Mexico as far as the Yucatan Peninsula to harvest tons of shrimp. Tropical storms make it a risky livelihood. One shrimper describes the coast as "God's blackboard" since the coastline is changed every 10 to 15 years by a major hurricane.

Alabama Celebrations

Barbecues and politics have been inseparable in Alabama. George Steele, a famous nineteenth-century plantation owner, announced that he would barbecue an ox on election night if Martin Van Buren was elected president. Van Buren was defeated, and the ox was put out to pasture to fatten up for the next election. Van Buren won the next time around, and 4,000 enthusiastic guests partook of a delicious barbecue in November 1840.

There have been many memorable parties in Alabama, among which was the one given for a cow. Lily Flag, a droopy-eyed Jersey beauty owned by Samuel B. Moore, won first prize in the butter-producing category at the 1893 Chicago Fair. When cow and owner returned home to the Moore plantation in Huntsville, Moore decided to honor his cow with a ball in his handsome

WATERMELON SOUP

Watermelon is one of the most popular melons of the Deep South. In this recipe watermelon is combined with buttermilk for a refreshing cold soup.

Serves 10

1 medium elongated watermelon

■

Cut the top third off the watermelon. Scoop out the pulp of both sections, removing the seeds. Purée the pulp in a food processor. It will become quite watery. When 9 cups of puréed pulp have been achieved, save the extra pieces of watermelon flesh for other uses, such as fruit salad.

Cut zigzags in the top of the larger piece of scooped-out watermelon shell. Refrigerate until ready to serve.

Soup

9 cups watermelon pulp

1 1/2 cups buttermilk

2 tablespoons chopped fresh mint leaves

Mint leaves, for garnish

■

Combine the watermelon pulp, buttermilk, and chopped mint leaves in a large bowl. Refrigerate for 4 hours before serving.

To serve, pour the soup into the cold watermelon shell and garnish with mint leaves.

Georgian brick mansion. Formal invitations to the ball were sent to Moore's friends all over the country. On the night of the ball, Lily Flag stood under an arch of roses with a garland of flowers around her neck. She was toasted with champagne, the guests danced to the music of an imported European orchestra, and an elegant midnight supper was served.

Today, Alabama hostesses continue to offer gracious southern hospitality

melded with casual entertaining. Seafood and many southern dishes still predominate. Just as there is a mix of food traditions—French, Spanish, Caribbean, and American—in Alabama, there is also a diversity of food products. Beef and dairy cattle graze throughout the state, and major crops include corn, peanuts, pecans, watermelons, and peaches. Commercial fishermen provide red snapper, flounder, mullet, shrimp, crabs, and oysters for the tables of Alabama.

ARKANSAS

EXPLORED BY THE SPANISH in the 1500s and the French in the 1600s, Arkansas remained very sparsely settled until after the Louisiana Purchase in 1803. It did not become a state until 1836. The earliest Arkansas pioneers were of English and Scotch-Irish ancestry who came primarily from Tennessee and Kentucky. Some cotton planters from Mississippi also settled in the area.

Most of the early pioneers who moved west bypassed what is now Arkansas and its Ozark Mountains because of the rocky landscape and poor soil. In the late 1700s and early 1800s, however, hard-working farmers from Kentucky, Illinois, and Tennessee, who were used to farming under difficult conditions, settled in Arkansas. They brought their recipes for curing hams, roasting pork ribs over open fires, and baking soda biscuits and molasses cakes.

Although many people have an image of mountain folk when they think of Arkansas, the Ozark mountains cover only about a quarter of the state. The Mississippi River forms the eastern border with flat, fertile farmland in the surrounding plains. Cattle ranches and oil rigs dominate the southwestern part of Arkansas. The Arkansas River, which cuts through the state and drains into the Mississippi, has made the capital of Little Rock a bustling inland port.

Arkansas consists of several distinct regions. In the south, bordering Louisiana, there are cotton plantations where mechanized farming has replaced human labor. The west is dotted with cattle ranches, while the northern area is reminiscent of the Midwest with its wheat fields and apple orchards. In the

THE SOWER
by James B. Turnbull,
watercolor, 22 x 15
inches, courtesy of
Michael Rosenfeld
Gallery, New York,
New York.

Ozark mountains and in the north of the state, fruits and vegetables are grown on small farms.

Arkansas Cuisine

Since Arkansas borders the South, the Southwest, and the Midwest, it has a mixture of cuisines. Plantation cookery of the Mississippi Valley, the hill cooking of the Ozarks, and the Mexican influences of Texas and Oklahoma all combine to make a unique style of food. Nevertheless, most of Arkansas' cuisine resembles that of the South, drawing upon southern traditions and ingredients.

There is a great emphasis on real "down-home" flavors. Fried pork chops with a light-brown cream gravy to which bits of sausage have been added have remained a favorite dish. Sausage is also used in poultry stuffings, along with cooked rice. Arkansas-style chicken is prepared by first simmering the chicken pieces in a skillet and then baking them in the oven with a Creole sauce.

Each region of Arkansas has its own unique food. In the southern bayou country, roast duck, candied yams, fried chicken, fluffy biscuits and peach cobblers are often served. Around Texarkana, pinto beans and barbecued beef of the Southwest are typical fare. Along the Mississippi River, catfish are popular in stews and fried.

Catfish stews include onions, tomatoes, and red pepper sauce. Fried catfish is coated with cornmeal, then fried until crisp and served with hot corn bread, baked potatoes, and turnip greens. Cornmeal is also used to coat okra, which is fried and eaten as a snack or as an accompaniment to meat and poultry dishes.

In the hill country of the Ozarks, dishes such as bacon with cracklin' corn bread, baked beans, wilted lettuce with bacon and vinegar, bread and apple jelly, and gingerbread for dessert are traditional everyday fare. Wild honey and sorghum have long been used as sweeteners in the mountains. Store-bought sugar was saved for Christmas cakes and candies. Many of the meals in the Ozarks ended with hot black coffee sweetened with wild honey and fried pies made with dried apples or peaches encased in a lard pastry.

Roasted raccoon, roasted beaver-tail, and baked opossum are Arkansas soul food. Baked possum has become such a famous regional dish that an annual festival is held at which possums are baked with red peppers and served with baked sweet potatoes.

Arkansans prefer hot bread with their meals and barely tolerate cold white bread. They like steaming-hot corn breads, hot biscuits, or fresh-out-of-the-oven rolls.

Strawberry shortcake is a favorite dessert of Arkansans. Recipes for the shortcake date back to the 1600s, when the first settlers in the East were introduced to wild strawberries by the Indians. The Arkansas version of the shortcake uses a crisp, buttery biscuit, which is split in half, soaked in strawberry juice, and then topped with a mound of whipped cream and fresh strawberries.

Early Barbecue, Arkansas Style

In its early statehood Arkansas produced memorable feasts when cel-

OLD-FASHIONED CORN BREAD

Over the years corn bread has had many variations. Bits of bacon, or cracklings, corn kernels, chili peppers, cheese, or onions have all been added to corn bread batter at one time or another.

This corn bread can be baked either in an iron skillet, similar to the Dutch ovens the early settlers used, or in an 8-inch square baking pan. The sugar used in this recipe is traditional in southern corn bread.

Serves 6 to 8

1 1/2 cups cornmeal

1/3 cup all-purpose flour

1 teaspoon sugar

1/2 teaspoon salt

2 1/2 teaspoons baking powder

1/2 teaspoon baking soda

1 1/2 cups buttermilk

2 eggs, lightly beaten

4 tablespoons melted butter, margarine,

   or bacon drippings

■

Combine the dry ingredients in a bowl. Stir in the buttermilk, eggs, and 3 tablespoons of the melted butter. Mix well.

Brush a 10-inch iron skillet with the remaining tablespoon of melted butter. Pour the batter into the skillet and bake in a preheated 425° F. oven for 25 to 30 minutes. Serve warm.

Spinach Salad with Tomato Aspic

Molded salads were at the height of their popularity in the 1950s and '60s. This molded salad combines a spinach layer with tomato aspic, a popular meat accompaniment in the South. Each salad may also be prepared separately.

Serves 8 to 10

Spinach Layer

1 package (3 ounces) lime gelatin

1 cup hot water

3/4 cup mayonnaise

3/4 cup small curd cottage cheese

1/4 cup minced red pepper

1/4 cup minced scallions

1/4 cup shredded carrot

2 cups finely chopped raw spinach

■

Dissolve the gelatin in hot water and cool to room temperature. Add the mayonnaise and cottage cheese and mix well. Fold in the remaining ingredients. Pour into an oiled 8-cup ring mold and refrigerate until set. After the spinach layer has set, prepare the tomato layer.

Tomato Aspic Layer

3 2/3 cups tomato juice

1 stalk celery, cut in pieces

1 small onion, quartered

1 small bay leaf

1/8 teaspoon pepper

2 envelopes unflavored gelatin

1/4 cup white vinegar

1/3 cup finely chopped green pepper

1/3 cup finely chopped celery

Lettuce leaves, for garnish

■

Combine 3 cups of the tomato juice, the celery pieces, onion, bay leaf, and pepper in a medium-size saucepan. Bring to a boil; then simmer for 10 minutes. Strain the mixture into a bowl.

While the tomato juice is simmering, soften the gelatin in the remaining 2/3 cup of tomato juice. Add softened gelatin to the strained tomato juice along with the vinegar. Stir until the gelatin is completely dissolved. Fold in the green pepper and celery and gently pour on top of the spinach layer. Refrigerate for 3 to 4 hours before serving. Unmold on lettuce leaves.

ebrating the Fourth of July. Friedrich Gerstacker, a German newspaper journalist, reported on his attendance at Little Rock's annual celebration on July 4, 1843.

According to Gerstacker, the barbecue was held in an open space where two tremendous ditches at least 20-feet long had been dug. Each trench was filled half-a-foot deep with glowing coals over which strong wooden poles were laid to serve as grates.

The first trench contained two halves of big, fat oxen; about a dozen sheep, calves, pigs, and deer; and a skinned bear. The second trench held four or five pieces of red deer, about 30 wild turkeys, opossums, raccoons, a young bear, squirrels, chickens, geese, ducks, prairie chickens, and partridges.

The men tending to the cooking used large pokers to stir up the coals under the biggest and thickest pieces, so that they were penetrated all the way through by the heat. Two of the men, one standing on each side of the trench, used strong poles with iron hooks to turn the meat.

Someone blew a great metal horn, which apparently resounded all over the town, when the meal was ready. People came running from everywhere to take part in the barbecue. Nothing resembling a table, tablecloth, or cutlery, much less dishes, was to be seen. People ate with their hands, and men used their pocket knives to cut the meat.

Gerstacker said he headed for the young bear and worked out a fine rib chop with his knife. For "bread" he used the whole breast of a turkey on which he put the bear meat. The taste of the roast game was apparently excellent as he enjoyed a roast duck for dessert. The barbecue lasted well into the night.

Arkansas Agriculture

Over the past 50 years, Arkansas has become an important poultry-producing state, as well as a major producer of fruits, vegetables, rice, and soybeans.

In the 1840s Arkansas farmers began experimenting with orchards. Their apples soon won first prizes at big-city exhibitions. Eventually apple orchards spread over much of the northwestern part of the state between Bentonville and Fayetteville. Women developed recipes for deep-dish apple pies, cinnamon-apple tarts, and apple jelly. A special applesauce flavored with lemon peel, cinnamon, and nutmeg was made.

Peaches also became an important Arkansas fruit crop. The Cherokee Indians, who had been forced to leave their homes further south and east and relocate in Arkansas, brought cuttings of peach trees that had been originally planted by Spanish settlers. Peaches, however, did not become a commercial crop until the hardy Elberta variety was introduced in the state in the late 1800s.

At the turn of this century, the Grand Prairie, in the northwestern corner of the state, was discovered to be a natural paddy for rice. The Rock Island Railroad, which owned the land, advertised this fact when they put the property up for sale. German-American farmers from Illinois and Iowa purchased the majority of the land and began to grow rice. Today, huge grain elevators outside of Stuttgart, Arkansas, store the rice, which ultimately goes to Campbell Soup, Quaker Puffed Rice, and is also exported to the Soviet Union and the Middle East. In the non-rice growing season, catfish swim in the paddies. Arkansas is second only to Mississippi in catfish production.

Catfish are to Arkansas and the South what salmon are to the Pacific Northwest. One of the pioneer catfish farmers was Edgar (Chip) Farmer of Dumas, Arkansas, near the junction of the Mississippi and Arkansas rivers. He began in the late 1950s by raising catfish in ponds he had created in his rice fields. Farmer made $55,000 the first year selling ready-to-eat catfish to restaurants in the South. He also sold fingerlings to stock freshwater lakes in Missouri and other parts of the country. Farmer's original dozen catfish became the brood stock for several large aquaculture farms in the United States.

Tyson's Chickens

In the depths of the Great Depression of the 1930s, John Tyson became a pioneer in marketing chickens, particularly broilers. With an old truck and a seemingly impossible idea, Tyson founded what is today one of the world's largest poultry-processing companies.

John Tyson was a produce buyer and trucker when he moved with his wife and young son, Don, from Missouri to Springdale, Arkansas, in 1931. He started looking for loads of produce to haul to market and by 1935 was making frequent trips to Kansas City and St. Louis.

At that time some farmers were raising as many as 500 "spring (young) chickens" at a time. Growing them was one thing, the farmers told John; selling them for a fair price was another. Encouraged by a newspaper report that chickens were selling for a higher price in Chicago than in markets closer to Arkansas, John Tyson decided to make the long trip.

He and a partner bought a load of Arkansas "springs," and John took them north in a battered truck. At the end of his first day in Chicago, he had sold the chickens for a good price. When everything was settled, Tyson cleared $235. He wired the original investment and $220 of the profit back to his partner with instructions to buy more chickens. Tyson kept $15 to pay for his hotel room and his expenses back to Arkansas, 700 miles away.

That journey marked the beginning of the Tyson family's involvement in the broiler business. Soon after that first big sale, John Tyson bought more trucks and started shipping chickens not only to Chicago, but also to Cleveland and Detroit. In 1940 he bought a small hatchery to supply chicks to local growers. Then he started mixing his own feeds. Five years later, Tyson bought his own meat-type breeding stock, which enabled him to control the quality of the chickens.

In 1952 at the age of twenty-two, Don Tyson joined his father in the business as general manager. By 1958 it became apparent that the company had to expand in order to survive. The Tysons built their first processing plant in Springdale. Since then Tyson's has added 29 other processing plants and hatcheries to become one of the largest poultry processors and marketers in the world. A major contribution to this growth was the acquisition of Holly Farms in 1989. Tyson is also the largest swine producer in the nation. Unfortunately, John Tyson did not live to see the full potential of his company realized; he was killed in a tragic auto-train collision in 1967.

FLORIDA

SPANIARDS were the first people to discover the riches of Florida. Ponce de León, Hernando de Soto, and Pánfilo de Nárvaez explored the Florida peninsula during the first half of the 1500s. They brought seeds for oranges, lemons, and other tropical fruits but were too busy searching for gold to care for them. Consequently, the trees grew wild.

Ponce de León gave Florida its name when he landed on its shores on Easter Sunday in 1513. The name "Florida" is taken from the Spanish *Pascua Florida,* or the Easter Feast of flowers. Under the leadership of Pedro Menéndez de Avilés, Spain established the first permanent settlement in North America at St. Augustine, Florida, in 1565—42 years before the English landed at Jamestown.

During the 1600s Spain continued to establish small settlements along the Florida coast. In 1763 Spain ceded Florida to the British in order to repossess recently captured Havana. At the end of the Revolutionary War, Spain regained Florida but finally gave it up to the United States in 1819.

The first large group of permanent settlers in Florida were not English or American, but Minorcans, Greeks, and Italians. They were recruited in 1764 by an Englishman to immigrate to Florida and grow indigo. Settling 60 miles south of St. Augustine, they established the community of New Smyrna. For a while the colonists grew indigo but turned to fishing when they found that the sea was laden with shrimp and fish similar to those of their homeland. They also discovered that lemons, eggplant, and olives—all staples of their native diets—

STILL LIFE by William Michael Harnett, oil, 12 1/8 x 8 inches, courtesy of Richard York Gallery, New York, New York.

grew well on the land. Eventually, the growing of indigo was replaced by food agriculture.

In the mid–1760s English colonists to the north began to expand into Florida. The Carolinas and Georgia were becoming crowded, and land for plantations had become scarce. Also, England feared French expansion into the Florida panhandle and, therefore, encouraged their colonists to establish tobacco and

cotton plantations in the region.

Unfortunately for these settlers, Florida soil proved unsuitable for growing cotton or tobacco. American settlers who tried to establish cotton plantations in the inland regions of Florida found that the free-growing groves of citrus established by the Spanish provided an easier livelihood. Thus, small citrus farms were started by families from Georgia, Alabama, and the Carolinas in the late 1760s.

Culinary History

Although the Spanish first settled Florida, their culinary influence was minimal. The Spanish conquistadors, however, did bring some Caribbean fruits and vegetables to Florida. They also introduced black beans.

A typical dish of the Spanish settlers at St. Augustine was *Garbanzo* Soup, which was prepared with dried chick peas and other vegetables. The soup also contained *chorizo,* a Spanish sausage, plus a pinch of saffron for color and flavor.

The first permanent culinary influence in Florida came from the American settlers who established citrus farms in the late 1760s. They brought with them a fairly developed Southern cuisine, which was enhanced in Florida by salads and substantial quantities of citrus. Southern Ambrosia, a mixture of coconut and citrus fruits, became an integral part of Christmas dinners from Florida northward to Maryland. Traditional southern dishes of ham, chicken, seafood, and greens were enhanced with spices from the Caribbean Islands.

Recently, Spanish food heritage has been reinvigorated in Florida by the influx of Cuban immigrants. Cuban sandwiches filled with ham, roasted pork, or sausage, cheese, and pickles have become popular. Street vendors sell heavily spiced deviled crabs. Two other popular Cuban dishes are *Verzada,* a thick vegetable soup with beans, potatoes, and pork and *Bollitos,* little, deep-fried balls of black-eyed peas and garlic.

Arroz Con Pollo, a chicken and rice dish, is served in many Cuban-American homes. Depending on the region of Florida, *Arroz Con Pollo* is enhanced with olives, capers, tomatoes, and various kinds of chilies. *Paella,* another Spanish-Cuban favorite, features Florida seafood. A traditional dessert is *Flan,* a caramelized baked custard.

Key West, with its proximity to Cuba, has had an almost continual Spanish-Cuban influence on its regional cooking. Such specialities as *Bolichi,* roast beef stuffed with hard-boiled eggs; *Alcoporade,* a beef stew made with peppers, herbs, raisins and olives; and a rich Cuban bean soup have became standard dishes of the area.

Orange Glazed Pork Chops with Carambola

Pigs were brought to Florida by the Spanish conquistadors and were abandoned to run wild when they left. The Spanish also brought seeds for growing citrus.

This recipe combines pork and oranges with a relatively new fruit being cultivated in Florida — the carambola.

Serves 6

1 1/2 tablespoons vegetable oil

6 well-trimmed pork chops, 3/4-inch

    thick

Salt and pepper, to taste

1/2 cup orange juice

4 tablespoons sugar

2 teaspoons cornstarch

1/4 teaspoon ground cinnamon

1/8 teaspoon ground cloves

3 teaspoons grated orange zest

6 orange slices, peel removed

1 large carambola, sliced

■

Heat the oil in a large skillet over medium heat. Season the pork chops and add them to the skillet, browning the chops well on both sides. Add 2 tablespoons of the orange juice, cover the skillet, and simmer the pork chops for 45 minutes, or until tender.

In the meantime combine the sugar, cornstarch, cinnamon, cloves, and grated orange zest in a small saucepan. Stir in the remaining orange juice. Cook over low heat, stirring constantly, until blended and smooth. Add the orange and carambola slices and simmer for 2 minutes. Drain the pork chops and top each with some glaze and fruit slices.

Tart Lime Tart

Florida lime juice is the main ingredient in this delicate soufflé, which is baked in a traditional tart shell.

Serves 6 to 8

Tart Shell

1 cup all-purpose flour

3 tablespoons sugar

6 tablespoons ($3/4$ stick) butter or

  margarine

3 to 4 tablespoons ice water

■

Combine the flour and sugar in a bowl. Cut the butter into small pieces and then cut it into the flour until the mixture resembles small bread crumbs. Sprinkle the ice water into the flour mixture, a tablespoon at a time, and combine it until the dough forms a ball. Sprinkle a little flour onto a pastry board and quickly, but gently, knead the dough four or five times to distribute the butter. Wrap the dough in plastic wrap and refrigerate it for at least one hour.

Roll the dough on a floured board to fit a 9-inch tart pan, allowing for a $1/2$-inch overhang. Press the dough into the tart pan and fold the overhang back under the dough, pressing it into the side of the pan to form a fluted edge. Prick the bottom of the tart shell, line it with aluminum foil shiny side down, and fill the bottom with dried beans or pie weights. Bake the shell in a preheated 400° F. oven for 8 minutes. Carefully remove the beans or pie weights and the foil and continue baking the tart shell for another 10 to 12 minutes, or until lightly browned. Cool on a rack before filling.

Lime Filling

3 large eggs, separated

$1/4$ cup plus 3 tablespoons sugar

2 tablespoons lime zest

$1/2$ cup fresh lime juice

■

In a bowl beat the egg yolks with the $1/4$ cup of sugar until the mixture is thick and pale in color. Beat in the lime juice and lime zest. Transfer the mixture to a small saucepan and cook over medium-low heat, stirring constantly with a wooden spoon, until the mixture begins to coat the spoon and starts to thicken. Do not let the mixture boil. Cook for another two minutes. Transfer the lime mixture to a bowl and let it cool to room temperature.

In another bowl beat the egg whites until they hold soft peaks. Sprinkle in the remaining 3 tablespoons of sugar, a tablespoon at a time, beating well after each addition. Beat the meringue until it holds stiff peaks. Fold one-fourth of the meringue into the lime mixture and then fold in the remainder of the meringue. Gently transfer the lime soufflé into the tart shell, mounding the soufflé slightly in the center. Bake in a preheated 400° F. oven for 10 to 12 minutes or until the top is puffed and golden brown.

Foods of Florida

The Spanish first encountered American foods such as beans, corn, and squash in Florida. Many of the native foods of Florida came originally from either Central or South America by way of the West Indies and became staples of the Indians' diet. Other foods that are associated with Florida were brought there or came by accident. For example, coconuts were not growing in Florida at the time of the Spanish arrival. They came from the West Indies aboard the ship *Providence* when it wrecked off the coast of Florida in 1879. Reportedly, the nuts floated to shore and took root.

The settlers soon learned to use the fruits of the seas around Florida. Red snapper, pompano, and mullet were some of the native fish used by Indians and early settlers alike. Huge sea turtles were caught off the Florida Keys, and their flesh was stewed, baked, or grilled. Tiny clams became the basis of a broth known as *Coquina* Soup.

One of the unique dishes of Key West in southern Florida is Conch Chowder made from the mollusk that is prevalent in the nearby coral reefs. The British who first came to the Florida Keys in the late 1700s took a liking to conch, which has a taste similar to clams. This fondness for conch eventually earned these British settlers their nickname, "the conchas." Today conch is still cooked as it was centuries ago. Since the meat is tough and strong, it is first pounded and then marinated in Key lime juice.

Two of the most popular fish used in Florida cooking are the red snapper and the pompano. Since many red snappers are large, they are typically cut into steaks or fillets. These are baked with either orange juice and grated orange rind or tomato sauce. Red snapper is also served broiled. Pompano is usually cooked in a paper bag, known as *en papillote*, with herbs and other seasonings. The fish can also be stuffed with Gulf shrimp and baked.

Black beans, one of the staple foods the Spanish brought to Florida, are often simmered with rice and a ham hock or used as a soup ingredient. In southern Florida black beans are often combined with chili powder, tomato sauce, and cheese to make a cocktail spread.

Florida Oranges and Other Citrus

The Spanish planted the first orange trees in the early 1500s. Lemon and grapefruit were not introduced into Florida until 300 years later. Tiny limes, however, grew wild in the southern Florida Keys.

Florida has been called the "Orange State." The first orange grower of any magnitude is said to have been Jesse Fish, who in 1776 shipped 65,000 oranges and two casks of orange juice to England. The English particularly liked the oranges from the colonies because they were juicier than the Spanish varieties.

Even with this great beginning, Florida orange cultivation did not become significant until the United States acquired Florida in 1819. Although Florida oranges were shipped north on fast sailing ships, North Americans unfortunately continued to prefer Mediterranean oranges. These oranges fared better in transport since the transatlantic clipper ships from Spain passed through cooler waters, which made the fruit less susceptible to rotting.

Frost has been the biggest problem for orange growers. Over the years new and hardier varieties of oranges have been developed to minimize losses to frost. The Indian River orange, a frost-hardy variety (grown near the Indian River in central Florida), has become the father of most Florida orange groves. This variety first proved its worth during the February 1835 freeze that killed most of the orange buds except those in the groves of Douglas Dummett. Buds from the Dummett trees subsequently rejuvenated many of the damaged groves.

In addition to its hardiness, the Indian River orange has become recognized over the years for its taste and juiciness. Russian ships used to come periodically to Florida to procure Indian River oranges for the Czar. Florida laws protect these oranges and only permit those of the Indian River variety grown in that area to be stamped "Indian River."

It was not until the end of the nineteenth century that Florida oranges became more accessible. Insulated ships and rail cars provided a faster and more efficient means of shipping the fruit to market. Oranges, however, did not become an everyday item in American cities until after World War I, when refrigerated cars began transporting oranges all over the country. By the mid-1930s Florida was growing a wide range of oranges and other citrus, producing about two-thirds of the nation's needs.

After World War II frozen and refrigerated orange juice became available, and demand for fresh oranges declined. Since Florida oranges have a higher sugar content than those of California, most of the nation's orange juice is produced in Florida.

Florida is also credited with the development of the modern grapefruit. The ancestor of the grapefruit, the pomelo, was brought from the East Indies to Barbados and other Caribbean Islands in the late 1600s. The grapefruit was introduced into Florida by a French doctor, Odet Phillippe, who in 1823 established a grapefruit orchard near Tampa. Originally pear-shaped, thick-skinned, pulpy, and with little juice, the fruit was developed into its present white and pink varieties in Florida.

Although California grows 80 percent of the lemons in the United States, Florida produces the majority of the limes. A unique lime is the Key lime, which grows in the southern extremity of Florida and is the prime ingredient in Key Lime Pie. Unlike other limes, the Key lime is yellow on the outside with a green-tinged pulp. It is also juicier and more acidic in flavor.

The origin of the Key lime is unknown. It is believed that Columbus brought this variety of lime seeds with him from the Mediterranean area to Haiti in 1493. In Florida Key limes were initially grown in home gardens. Their cultivation became a commercial venture in 1906, when a hurricane forced the abandonment of commercial pineapple cultivation. Key limes remained a crop for only 20 years; then a hurricane destroyed the lime groves. Today, they are again being grown in small home gardens. The Tahiti lime, a larger, thicker-skinned fruit, has taken the place of the Key lime as a commercial fruit, because it is more conducive to machine handling and truck transportation.

Other Florida Produce

Florida has been a pioneer in the cultivation of exotic fruits such as mangoes, papayas, kumquats, and carambola (otherwise known as star fruit). The first mangoes were grown in the state in 1889, and today there are more than 50 varieties available from Florida growers. Papayas are grown for their fruit, as well as for use as an ingredient in meat tenderizers.

Carambola, which is a tree fruit, has been cultivated in Asia and the Middle East since the twelfth century. It was almost a hundred years ago when the first carambola trees were transplanted from the Hawaiian Islands to Florida, but the fruit has only been marketed commercially for the last few years.

The common name "star fruit" was given to carambola because of its five deep longitudinal ribs, or wings, that form star shapes when the fruit is sliced. It varies in length from two to five inches. The flesh of the fruit is firm, crisp, and very juicy.

The palmetto palm, the official state tree of Florida, is the source of palm hearts, which have become a luxury salad ingredient. The heart of the palm is the bud of the tree, and the entire tree has to be cut down to harvest the heart. Fortunately, this small palm grows in abundance in Florida so that harvesting does not threaten extinction of the trees. Before the heart can be sliced, the fronds are stripped away, and the heart trimmed until a smooth, slim stalk remains. Fresh hearts of palm have a delicate flavor reminiscent of asparagus.

Florida Seafood

The state's coastal and inland waters have provided food for the area since pre-Columbian times. Spanish fishing boats from Cuba and the West Indies made regular forays to the waters off the Gulf Coast of Florida during pre-colonial days to harvest finfish and green turtles. Fishing has remained an integral part of Florida's cuisine and economy.

Stone crabs are a much-prized Florida seafood and are harvested along the Florida Keys and the Gulf coast for their exceptionally large claws. The body of the crab is not eaten, only its claws. When a crab is harvested, one of its large claws is broken off, and the crab is returned to the sea, as Florida law prohibits the taking of whole stone crabs. It takes approximately 18 months for a new claw to be grown to legal size. During the life of a stone crab, the same appendage may be regenerated three or four times.

The spiny lobster is another favorite seafood in Florida. It is different from the New England lobster because it prefers warm water and has no claws but five pairs of legs. The tail portion provides the meat, which is coarser in texture than the New England lobsters. In Florida spiny lobsters are most commonly prepared by stuffing the tail section with other seafood.

Rock shrimp, a deep-water cousin of the brown and white shrimp, is harvested off the Atlantic and Gulf coasts of Florida. Since these shrimp have a very hard shell, they were discarded by commercial fisherman until recently. Special equipment has been developed to remove the shells and the sand vein of these shrimp. They are now harvested commercially and are available already shelled. Rock shrimp taste like a cross between shrimp and lobster.

Red snapper and pompano are the principal finfish caught off the coast of Florida. It is not unusual for a red snapper to weigh 50 pounds. The name "pompano" comes from the Spanish word meaning grape leaf and refers to the shape of the fish. Since pompano do not migrate, most of the species are harvested in Florida waters, primarily in the Gulf of Mexico.

Other specialized food products of Florida include frog legs and alligator meat. Both creatures are found in the swamps of the Everglades. Alligators are now being grown commercially, although principally for hides. Alligator meat has a mild taste and adapts to recipes developed for chicken, veal, and most seafoods. The choicest cuts are the tail and jaw. Alligator meat is usually available frozen and alligator paté is marketed canned.

GEORGIA

GEORGIA WAS SETTLED in 1733 by the English under the leadership of James Oglethorpe ostensibly as a home for jailed debtors and paupers. An aristocrat and idealist, he envisioned a land where the unemployed and imprisoned English debtors could begin life anew. The real purpose of settling this area, however, was to keep the Spanish from moving northward from Florida into the Carolinas and Virginia. The region had previously been explored by Hernando de Soto in 1540, and the Spanish had established a series of missions along the Atlantic coast.

Oglethorpe and his followers landed in Savannah in 1733 with the intent of building an ideal city and economy based on wine growing and the raising of silk worms. The colony prospered, but not in the manner Oglethorpe had envisioned. Most of the English settlers did not want to work. In order to preserve his dream colony, Oglethorpe brought over a group of 135 Scotch Highland political refugees, who, complete with kilts and plumes, settled New Inverness, Georgia, and became farmers.

In the mid-1700s Savannah became a haven for other immigrants, including large groups of Spanish and Portuguese Jews. Possessing an excellent port, the city became an important export and trade center. When Oglethorpe had planned the city, he had designated a ten-acre plot as a garden where all types of fruit trees, including oranges, palms, and coffee were successfully cultivated. Orange trees became so popular that they lined the garden walks. Large quantities of Georgia orange juice were shipped to England in the 1760s.

Oglethorpe's dream of a utopian colony with diverse agriculture was doomed when slavery came to Georgia. Set up originally as a free colony, the planters of Georgia soon found that it was easier and more profitable to grow cotton using slave labor than food crops. Tobacco, indigo, and rice also became the leading crops of the Georgia coastal lowlands. As the planters gained wealth they moved out of their wooden cabins and built magnificent mansions where hospitality reigned.

The Cuisine of Georgia

Food historians allege that the first pork dinner eaten in America was probably consumed in 1540 in what is now Georgia. That year de Soto herded pigs from the Everglades to the Ozarks on his exploration of the southern interior. The pigs provided food for the half-starved, foot-sore conquistadors when they could no longer get food from the Indians.

The de Soto expedition left behind the nucleus of herds of hogs and cattle when it returned to Spain. By the time the white settlers arrived, two centuries later, they found that the Indians had learned to butcher both cattle and hogs and how to preserve the meat for later use. They had developed a type of cure for hams.

In the years between the first settlement of Georgia and the American Revolution, various ethnic settlers contributed their native cuisine to the colony. Many French Huguenots arrived directly from France or via South Carolina and found the city of Savannah to their liking. To this day foods served in Savannah have

a distinctly French style. German immigrants settled further up the Savannah River. The cookery of this region included sauerkraut, Pepper Pot Soup, and other German dishes. Some of the Scottish Highland families added recipes for scones and haggis, a stew made with sheep or calf innards, to this melange.

Southern cuisine, which had been developing for almost a hundred years when Georgia was settled, dominated Georgia cooking during the early years of settlement. Georgia Squirrel Stew, for instance, is closely related to the Brunswick Stew popular in other parts of the South. Hoecakes, small cornmeal cakes originally baked on a hoe in the family fireplace, remained a Georgia-type of corn bread. In later years they were baked in an oven. Okra, which was brought to the South by African slaves, was stewed with tomatoes for a tasty accompaniment to meats.

"Plain but plentiful" food typified the cuisine of the early Georgian homes. Fish, a prime ingredient in cooking, was plentiful, since almost every farm or plantation was located on a river or its tributaries. Shellfish predominated the cooking along the coast.

Some of the other staple foods of Georgia included rice grown in the coastal marshes and hot breads or biscuits spread thick with homemade preserves. Chicken and ham were the main meat dishes. In-season vegetables from the garden accompanied the main course. Cake, pie, or other rich desserts finished the meal. Georgia housewives prided themselves on their light-textured pound cakes, which used a pound each of butter, sugar, and eggs.

COUNTRY CAPTAIN CHICKEN

The recipe for Country Captain Chicken was brought to Savannah in the 1700s by a sea captain who was involved in the spice trade. There have been many variations of the dish since then. Some cooks use a stewing hen and let it cook for several hours.

Serves 4

1/2 cup flour

3/4 teaspoon salt

1/2 teaspoon black pepper

1/2 teaspoon paprika

2 tablespoons butter or margarine

2 tablespoons vegetable oil

1 chicken (3 to 3 1/2 pounds), cut-up

1 large onion, chopped

1 green pepper, chopped

2 small cloves garlic, minced

3 tablespoons chopped fresh parsley

1 tablespoon curry powder

1/4 teaspoon dried thyme

1 can (16 ounces) tomatoes

1 teaspoon Tabasco sauce or 1 small

   jalapeño pepper, seeded and chopped

1/2 cup dried currants

3/4 cup slivered almonds, toasted

■

Combine the flour, salt, pepper, and paprika and dredge the chicken pieces in the seasoned flour. Heat the butter and oil in a large, heavy skillet over medium-high heat. Sauté the chicken pieces until golden brown and then remove them to a plate.

Discard all but 2 tablespoons of the drippings from the skillet. Add the onions, pepper, and garlic and sauté over medium-low heat until the vegetables start to soften, about 5 minutes. Add the parsley, curry powder, thyme, tomatoes, and Tabasco sauce. Return the chicken to the pan and spoon some sauce over it. Cover and cook on low heat for 30 minutes. Add the currants, re-cover, and cook for another 30 minutes, or until the chicken is tender. Sprinkle the chicken with the toasted almonds and serve with boiled rice.

early 1800s, described a dinner in Augusta. The meal consisted of "turtle soup followed by brook trout fried in butter, then baked sweet potatoes and roast ham, wild turkey stuffed with walnuts and cornmeal, accompanied by dishes of rice, asparagus, and green beans, with a cooling orange sherbet to give the guests a breather before they tackled the cold venison, stewed corn and cheese, and the dessert of corn fritters with syrup and sweet potato pie. Madeira wine, beer, and milk were the beverages."

Oyster suppers, popular at the plantations around Savannah, were often held outdoors by the light of the moon. A large sheet of tin covered a crackling fire, and the master of ceremonies, using a rake, spread small, delicately flavored oysters on the hot tin to cook. When cooked, the oysters were served with individual cups of melted butter that had been mixed with lemon juice or Worcestershire sauce. Hoppin' John (black-eyed peas with rice) and a green salad completed the informal feast.

Other Savannah dishes included crab soufflés seasoned with nutmeg and sherry, chicken pies with hard cooked eggs and tiny mushrooms, creamy corn puddings, and fried Georgia peach pies. The use of "bird's-eye" pepper, a small red pepper pod that grew on potted plants on many Savannah porches, became a ritual when eating soup. These peppers were crushed in the bottom of a bowl before adding the soup. Some cooks put scalded peppers in the bottom of a cruet, filled it with sherry, and let the mixture stand for 24 hours. The liquid was then used to flavor soups and other dishes. Many gentlemen in Savannah carried small silver boxes full of bird's-eye peppers to add to whatever they were eating.

Negro cooks prepared the meals on Georgia plantations for the family and their ever-present guests. Some of the most innovative dishes were created by these slaves. Whole hams were boiled in large tubs with tea and molasses over an outdoor fire. For the final stage of cooking, the hams were basted with beer, then coated with catsup, mustard, and brown sugar and baked for a half an hour in the oven.

These same cooks burned sugar for a dessert called Burnt Cream, which came to the table heaped with whipped cream and toasted almonds. Another dessert, Serene Pudding, was rich with eggs and cream.

W. E. Woodward, a historian of the

The food served on the small family farms of the Piedmont area differed from that of the coastal lowlands. Corn bread was served at almost every meal, while rice was seldom seen. Dairy products from the family cow—butter, cheese, milk, and cream—were prevalent in the cooking. Just as in the lowlands, ham and chicken were the main meats, but venison and small game were also common, especially in the local version of Brunswick Stew.

Georgia Specialties

Passenger pigeons were numerous in the 1800s and migrated from the north into the Carolinas and Georgia. Hunters regularly followed the flocks into Georgia and slaughtered the pigeons by the thousands. They were then salted and shipped to northern cities and sold for as little as 20 cents a dozen. Passenger pigeons were also exported to Europe, where they were called squabs. The passenger pigeon finally became extinct when the great white pine forests in Georgia were cut in the late 1800s.

Although most of Georgia's territory is inland, the state has more than 100 miles of coastline, home to fishermen and sea captains who traded in the Far East. The sea captains brought back exotic spices from the East Indies that were used in Georgian and Southern cooking. One such dish that originated in Georgia was Country Captain Chicken.

The recipe for Country Captain Chicken is said to have been created by a Georgia sea captain in the 1700s. Since long voyages to and from the East Indies meant months at sea, live fowl were kept aboard ship for eggs and eating. The daily fare became boring, so to relieve the monotony spices were added to the food.

PEACHES ARE IN by Queena Stovall, oil, 18 x 24 inches, courtesy of Virginia Arts, Lynchburg, Virginia.

When the sea captain dropped anchor at Savannah with his precious cargo of spices, he asked his friends ashore to join him for a taste of his curried chicken. They ate the dish, liked it, and named it Captain's Chicken. Soon it was served at the finest tables in Savannah and at surrounding plantations. The dish later became known as Country Captain and has been modified over the years to include tomatoes, green peppers, and parsley. It always contains curry powder and is usually served with rice.

Georgia Peaches and Other Crops

Peaches were introduced to the New World by the Spanish when they established a settlement at St. Augustine, Florida, in 1565. Eventually peach orchards spread northward to Georgia, where the warm climate was favorable for peach cultivation.

The peach industry began to flourish in Georgia in the mid-1800s and was further expanded with the advent of refrigerated railroad cars to transport the crop out-of-state. The Elberta peach, which was developed in Georgia, also helped establish peach cultivation in the state.

The story of the famous Elberta peach began at the Rumph plantation near Marshallville, Georgia, in 1857. A gentleman living in Delaware sent an assortment of peach-tree buddings to his friend Samuel Rumph. The trees flourished and in a few years produced

PEACH SOUP

Traditionally, peaches are baked in pies and cobblers or used to make preserves. In this recipe peaches are the main ingredient in a refreshing summer soup.

Serves 6

3 cups fresh peaches, peeled and sliced

1 tablespoon lemon juice

1/4 to 1/3 cup sugar, depending on
    tartness of peaches

1 1/2 cups dry white wine

2/3 cup whipping cream

Fresh mint leaves, for garnish

■

Immediately after slicing the peaches, sprinkle them with lemon juice. Place the peaches, sugar, and wine in a medium-size saucepan. Slowly bring the mixture to a boil and simmer for 6 to 8 minutes, or until the peaches start to soften. Add the cream and continue to simmer slowly for another 10 minutes. Place the mixture in a food processor and process until smooth. Chill. Garnish each serving with a mint leaf.

fruit. Mrs. Rumph had a habit of eating peaches while sewing and would occasionally drop a peach seed into her sewing basket. More than ten years later, her grandson, also named Samuel, decided to start his own orchard. Mrs. Rumph dug out her dry old seeds, and for fun Samuel planted them.

An accidental cross-pollination fostered by the wind and bees took place. When the first trees bore fruit in 1870,

they produced great golden peaches—a species new to the fruit world. Samuel named the peach Elberta for his wife. He was one of the first fruit growers to package fruit attractively and to ship it by sea in refrigerated containers to the Northeast. By 1889 there were 3,000 acres of peach orchards in Georgia.

Today, almost every Georgia cook has his or her own version of peach pie. Some make it with a custard filling, others prefer deep-fried peach pies, while still others like a double-crusted peach pie.

When Columbus reached the New World, he took pimientos back with him to Spain, where they became very popular. About 400 years later an enterprising Georgia farmer brought a packet of pimiento seeds back from Spain and began growing the mild pepper. Today, the country's supply of pimientos, the majority of which are canned, comes from Georgia and the southeastern part of the United States.

In the late spring of 1931, Moses Coleman discovered that the onions he had planted on his south-Georgia farm had a most unusual flavor. They were so sweet that one could enjoy eating them raw. Scientists concluded that these onions were a result of the mild climate and unique soil of southeast Georgia. Vidalia Onions have today become a $30-million business in Georgia. However, they are only available for a short time each year—from the first of May to the middle of June.

Peanuts

Peanuts are an important part of the agriculture of Georgia, where almost two billion pounds are harvested annually.

It is believed that peanuts originated in Brazil, where pottery jars in the shape

of peanuts have been found that date back 3,500 years. Drawings of peanuts decorated these ancient jars, and containers of the nuts have also been found in ancient Inca graves.

By the time the Spanish began their explorations of the New World, peanuts were grown as far north as Mexico. The explorers took the nuts back to Spain. From there traders and explorers carried them to Africa and Asia. In Africa the peanut became almost a sacred symbol to the natives, who believed it to possess a soul.

When the Africans were brought to Georgia as slaves, they brought peanuts with them. Peanuts, however, had already migrated into North America from South America. The settlers of Jamestown found the local Indians growing them and regarded peanuts only as food for pigs.

Large-scale peanut production is credited to the research done by the famous botanist, Dr. George Washington Carver, at Tuskegee Institute in Alabama. In order to encourage peanut production, he invented 300 uses for the nut, from oils to soups to ice cream. In addition peanuts are used in candy, peanut butter, and as a snack food.

The peanut is an unusual plant because it flowers above ground, but the fruits develop below ground. A peanut seed grows into a small green bush about 18 inches tall that develops delicate yellow flowers. As the flowers begin to lose their petals, "pegs" begin to form and eventually drop down and enter the soil. These pegs or embryos mature into peanuts in about four months. Since peanuts grow underground, they have also been called "ground" nuts.

Today, peanuts are planted and harvested with special machinery. The peanut seeds are planted in rows in sandy soil. When the plant has matured and the peanuts are ready for harvest, a mechanical digger cuts the tap root, lifts the plant from the soil, shakes the dirt from the nuts, and then lays the plant back down in rows, peanuts up. The peanuts are left on top of the rows for at least two days to dry. A combine then gathers the nuts.

Coca-Cola

The first of the famous cola drinks was concocted in 1886 by John S. Pemberton, a druggist in Atlanta. He did not envision its ultimate popularity, since he had mixed the ingredients as a remedy for headaches and hangovers. According to various accounts of the event, the first batch of coca cola was made from extracts of coca leaves and cola nuts. It was concocted in Pemberton's backyard in a big iron kettle and stirred with an oar. The first year he sold enough of this headache and hangover remedy, which he named Coca-Cola, to warrant the making of 25 gallons of the syrup. At the end of the first year, Pemberton made a profit of $50.

Pemberton then began to peddle his Coca-Cola syrup to other druggists. The next step in the development of America's favorite drink was purely an accident. Another Atlanta druggist spilled some soda water into his Coca-Cola syrup and found that it gave the drink more pep than water did. Then a third druggist, Asa G. Candler, purchased Pemberton's Coca-Cola formula and all of its manufacturing rights for $2,000. One hundred years later, the formula is now valued at more than a hundred million dollars.

ONIONS AND COPPER POT by Harl Nobles, oil, 12 x 16 inches, courtesy of Miner's Gallery Americana, Carmel, California.

STEAK SALAD WITH VIDALIA ONIONS

Georgia's Vidalia Onions are very sweet and have no aftertaste. Consequently, they are often eaten raw, as in this steak and onion salad. Serve the meat either at room temperature or cold.

Serves 4

1 large Vidalia Onion, sliced thin

1 pound lean broiled steak, sliced into
   1-inch strips

1/2 cup chopped celery

3/4 cup sliced mushrooms

Lettuce leaves

1 cup crumbled blue cheese

■

Combine the onion, steak, celery, and mushrooms in a bowl. Pour the dressing over the mixture and toss lightly. Line a salad bowl with lettuce leaves. Spoon the steak mixture into the bowl and top with the crumbled cheese.

Dressing

2 tablespoons red wine vinegar

2 tablespoons water

1/2 teaspoon Dijon mustard

1 tablespoon chopped fresh parsley

4 tablespoons olive oil

■

Combine the vinegar, water, mustard, and parsley in a small bowl. Whisk in the olive oil.

LOUISIANA

VARIOUS NATIONS have flown their flags over what is now the state of Louisiana. The region was first claimed for Spain by the explorer Hernando de Soto in 1541, when he crossed the Mississippi River. From then until Louisiana became part of the United States with the Louisiana Purchase in 1803, it was at various times under the control of France, Spain, Britain, and the West Florida Republic.

The Louisiana Delta and what was to become New Orleans were first discovered in 1682 by the French explorer, Sieur Robert Cavelier de la Salle, when he floated down the Mississippi River. He claimed the area for King Louis XIV of France. The first French settlers—all men—began to arrive in 1699. At the time much of Louisiana was a decaying, insect-infested swamp, and the food of the settlers consisted primarily of smoked meat, stewed alligators, and some native root vegetables.

The quality of Louisiana food improved greatly when French girls who were to wed the French settlers arrived in 1706. Many of these girls were poor but respectable orphans who were chaperoned on the long voyage by nuns. The French government provided these orphans with a chest or casket containing some clothing and household articles similar to a trousseau. The girls became known as *filles 'a la cassette,* or casket girls.

Although their first homes were crude huts built of clay held together with Spanish moss, the casket girls brought a touch of elegance to New Orleans in their manner of dress, their personal belongings, and their French cooking. They quickly found that the traditional ingredients to which they were accustomed—spices, herbs, vegetables, and meats—were not available. Their chief dislike was cornmeal, which they did not consider to be a substitute for the fine white wheat flour they had known in France. The French women, however, learned to use Indian herbs and native ingredients, primarily seafood, and combined them with French cooking skills.

Creole Cuisine

In 1762 France ceded her Louisiana territory to Spain, and this brought wealthy Spaniards to New Orleans. In spite of Spanish ownership, however, a number of French aristocrats fled to Louisiana during the French Revolution, bringing their chefs with them.

The intermarriage of French and Spanish settlers produced a people known as Creoles, as well as a distinct style of cooking that has interspersed sophisticated French cuisine with Spanish spicy seasonings and the lavish use of tomatoes. Many wealthy French and Spanish settlers used black slaves as cooks who added still another dimension to Creole cooking.

The *grande cuisine* of the rich Louisiana planters featured delicate and subtle blends of flavorings in their entrées, which were served with separate sauces. To enhance their cuisine they obtained spices, bananas, sweet potatoes, vanilla, and chocolate from the Caribbean Islands and Central America.

The black slaves from Africa brought with them seeds for okra, a pod-like vegetable, which they called "gumbo." Later the name gumbo was used to refer to a stew made with this vegetable. Okra has a mucilaginous quality and therefore can be used to thicken a stew or soup.

Filé powder was probably the most important contribution of the Choctaw Indians to Louisiana cooking. They made it by drying and pulverizing the leaves of the sassafras trees that grow wild along the Gulf Coast. The Choctaws used filé powder for medicinal purposes, but the Negro and Creole cooks adapted it as a thickener for gumbos, since it had a mucilaginous quality similar to okra. Thus Creole cuisine became a blend of traditional French cooking with Spanish, African, and Indian influences.

Cajun Cuisine

The Cajuns made the other major contribution to Louisiana cuisine. Originally French settlers living in Acadia (now Nova Scotia), Canada, the Acadians were hardy people who lived off the land and the sea. They kept their own language and their Catholic religion and refused to swear allegiance to Great Britain when that country took over Canada. In 1755 the English became suspicious of these aliens and routed them out, separating the women and children from the men. They deported the entire settlement, sending them off in different directions with total disregard to family ties.

For more than ten years, the Acadians wandered, searching for each other and for a new home. Many of the survivors came down the Mississippi River and were welcomed by the French and Spanish Catholics who had settled in southern Louisiana. The locals could not pronounce Acadian and called them "Cajuns."

The Cajuns were accustomed to a rugged life and made the swamps and bayous of southern Louisiana their home. They continued to cook plain, hearty country food, reminiscent of cooking in the southern and western regions of France. The Cajuns adapted their cooking to the new game and seafood they found in the bayous. Inland lakes yielded crawfish by the millions. Vegetables such as okra were included in their one-pot dishes. Often ingredients were cooked together in the same pot with the spices and hot peppers of their new homeland. These spicy concoctions were served over bland rice, the staple grain of southern Louisiana.

When the Acadians settled around the inlets and bayous near New Orleans, they learned about native foods from the Choctaw and Chickasaw Indians. The black bear was a primary food source for the Indians, and the Cajuns also began eating bear. Today, Louisiana black bear is considered a great delicacy, although it is not readily available.

Wild boar was also a source of meat for the Cajuns. Boars were not native to the Mississippi Delta, but were descendants of the 13 European pigs that had been brought to America by the Spanish explorer Hernando de Soto.

Cajun cooking was regarded as an art and a secret to be kept by the cook. Recipes were handed down from one generation to the next by word of mouth. Often key ingredients were left out in the telling. Consequently, basic

BAKED FRENCH TOAST

Pain Perdu, or French toast, was a popular breakfast dish in New Orleans. It is now served throughout the country.

This version of French toast is prepared the night before so that the bread will soak up as much of the liquid as possible. All that is necessary the next morning is to place the dish in the oven and bake it.

Serves 4 to 6

3/4 cup dark brown sugar

8 tablespoons (1 stick) butter

2 tablespoons light corn syrup

1 loaf French bread, cut into 1-inch slices

5 eggs

1 1/2 cups milk

1 teaspoon vanilla extract

■

Spray a 13 x 9-inch glass baking dish with a non-stick cooking spray.

Combine the sugar, butter, and corn syrup in a saucepan. Cook over medium heat until the mixture is melted and blended, being careful not to let it caramelize.

Pour the butter mixture into the prepared pan and arrange the bread slices in one layer in the syrup. Beat the eggs with the milk and vanilla. Carefully pour the egg mixture over the bread slices, covering them well. Use all of the egg mixture, as the excess will be absorbed by the bread slices. Cover the baking dish and refrigerate overnight.

The next morning, uncover the dish and bake in a preheated 350° F. oven for 30 minutes. Serve directly from the baking dish. Butter and syrup are not needed with this French toast.

dishes varied greatly. What developed along the Bayou was a home-style Cajun cooking with no hard, fast rules for gumbo, jambalaya, or other Cajun delicacies.

Louisiana Cuisine

Louisiana had been described as a state divided into north and south. The north was settled by Anglo-Saxons, Germans, and other northern Europeans. The south is home to descendants of the French and early Spanish settlers as well as Africans. Italians settled around New Orleans in the mid-1800s and became truck farmers, raising much of the produce used in that city. The north and south divisions in cookery still prevail. Typical Southern cooking is prevalent in the northern area, while Creole and Cajun dishes predominate in the southern area. For instance, the northern parishes preferred cornmeal for various corn breads, while the southern parishes used wheat flour, which they first imported from Europe and later obtained from the northern states.

Gradually Creole and Cajun cooking merged into one, and a cuisine called southern Louisiana developed. The evolution of bouillabaisse is an example of this development. The recipe for bouillabaisse came with the first French settlers. Upon finding that French types of fish were unavailable, they started making their bouillabaisse with crabs from Lake Pontchartrain and red snapper, pompano, shrimp, and oysters from the Gulf.

Later the Cajuns showed the Creoles that they did not need fish for their stew since crabs and shrimp would do just as well. The Spanish settlers contributed red peppers to the stew. The African slaves added okra, and the native Indians taught the settlers how to use filé powder. After about a century of various additions, the stew was no longer French bouillabaisse but became Cajun gumbo.

Louisianians, whether Creole or Cajun, have always enjoyed hot and spicy food. There are probably more peppers grown and used in Louisiana than in any other region of the United States. The famous red and green tabasco peppers are the ingredient of the sauce by that name. The state also grows sweet peppers, which are the basis of paprika.

The age-old French technique of making a roux to provide added flavor and richness is also found in both Creole and Cajun dishes. A roux is basically flour and fat cooked together slowly. Cajun cooks use dark reddish-brown roux with light meats, chicken, rabbit, fish, and seafood and golden or pale roux to balance the intense flavors of beef, venison, and other game. Roux is also the basis of Creole and Cajun gumbos and is used in the Creole version of bouillabaisse in which the spices and herbs are cooked in a light roux. The Creole roux is made with butter and flour, while the Cajun version uses oil and flour.

Many other ingredients appear in both Creole and Cajun cooking. Rice is the staple ingredient of both cuisines. It is used in gumbos, jambalayas, and other Louisiana dishes as well as in rice cakes for dessert. Other ingredients used in both cuisines are homemade sausages, beans, tomatoes, yams, pecans, and oranges. At one time, Louisianians served rice three times a day.

Gumbo and Other Specialties

It has been said that if a true Louisianian died and went to heaven and found no gumbo there, he would come right back. Gumbo is one of the unique contributions of New Orleans to American cuisine.

A noted society banquet held in 1803 featured 24 different kinds of gumbo. One of the more interesting was Gumbo Z'herbs, a Lenten dish traditionally served on Good Friday. Legend says that you would make as many friends as the number of different greens used in this gumbo—seven greens would result in seven friends. Gumbo Z'herbs, a light gumbo, did not contain a roux, okra, or filé powder. It is still being served, but as a first course.

Today, the most common gumbo ingredients are crabs, shrimp, chicken, sausage, and game. Crab gumbo was and still is probably the most popular in Louisiana, although chicken, shrimp, and oysters are often used, alone or in combination. Okra, green peppers, and onions are the principal vegetables included. Often if okra is omitted, filé powder is used liberally. The powder is never cooked but is added to the gumbo just before serving. Rice is served as a base for the gumbo but is always cooked separately.

Jambalaya also uses rice as a base for seafood and meat. It is a stew of rice and other ingredients such as ham, crabmeat, oysters, shrimp, chicken, and sausage, or combinations thereof. Tomatoes and their juice provide the liquid for the raw rice which is cooked with the main ingredients and seasonings. Many believe that the dish was brought here by the Spaniards, since it is very similar to the Spanish *Paella*. Jambalaya was traditionally cooked out of doors in big iron pots.

Oysters have always been abundant in the waters around New Orleans. Since the salt water of the Gulf of Mexico mingles with that of the lakes and rivers surrounding the city, oysters have a special taste that the natives call salty. These oysters were so plentiful in the mid-nineteenth century that city directories listed ten restaurants that specialized in oyster dishes and three pages of oyster houses and bars. Many French restaurants in the city substituted oysters for snails in their recipes.

Rice, which has been grown in Louisiana since the early 1700s, was the basis of many dishes including a deep-fried rice fritter called *Calas*. The name *Calas* is thought to have come from the African word for rice. Negro women sold hot *Calas* on the streets of the French Quarter of New Orleans, calling *"Belle Cala, tout chaud."* It was the custom for churchgoers to buy the hot *Calas* and take them home for breakfast with *Café au Lait.*

Café au Lait became a New Orleans tradition and was served not only in the coffeehouses in the French Quarter but also at home. Chicory was added to make New Orleans coffee stronger and thicker but gave it a bitter flavor. It was first used in New Orleans during the Civil War when coffee was hard to obtain. Even today, New Orleans coffee is a much darker roast than normal and is served with equal parts milk.

Another deep-fried pastry often eaten with *Café au Lait* was *Beignet,* a rectangular doughnut, heavily powdered with confectionery sugar, that was served in the French Quarter coffeehouses. The doughnuts were made with canned evaporated milk to give them a rich flavor. Many older New Orleanians consider evaporated milk a great delicacy and refer to it as "pet cream."

Pain Perdu, meaning lost bread, was a popular breakfast dish of French origin. It was a way of reviving stale bread by dipping it in a sweetened egg and milk mixture and then frying it in butter. Served with jelly, syrup, or honey, it quickly became known as French Toast.

Bread Pudding With Whiskey Sauce, a popular New Orleans dessert, also made use of stale French bread. The dessert was so popular that the making of a perfect bread pudding became a local art, and it was an on-going contest to determine who in the area made the best.

Louis Armstrong, the famous New Orleans jazz trumpeter, used to sign his letters "Red beans and ricely yours," which expresses his attachment to one of Louisiana's favorite dishes. Originally cooked in big iron pots over open fires, red beans have been a traditional part of Louisiana cooking. The *Picayune Creole Cookbook* of 1900 notes that red beans

ZUCCHINI SOUFFLÉ

The first Italians to come to the Deep South settled near New Orleans, where they became produce growers. They were the first to cultivate zucchini. In the South zucchini is still known as "green squash." Recipes for soufflés came to Louisiana with the French settlers. This light soufflé may also be made with 2 cups of freshly cut corn for a more traditional southern dish.

Serves 6

1 1/2 pounds small zucchini, cut into
  2-inch pieces

3 eggs

1/2 cup whipping cream

1 1/2 tablespoons cornstarch

1/4 teaspoon pepper

1/2 teaspoon nutmeg

4 ounces shredded Gruyère cheese

■

Cook the zucchini in lightly salted water until barely tender, about 6 minutes.

Drain the zucchini pieces very well and then place in the bowl of a food processor and lightly process. The resulting purée should have some small shredded pieces of zucchini in it.

Separate the eggs and beat the yolks with half of the cream. Add the cornstarch and the remaining cream, pepper, and nutmeg to the beaten eggs. Lightly fold in the puréed zucchini and the cheese. Beat the egg whites until stiff and fold them into the zucchini mixture. Gently pour the soufflé into a buttered, 6-cup soufflé dish and bake in a preheated 375° F. oven for 40 minutes. Serve immediately.

and rice were served several times a week in schools and colleges so that the young people would become strong and useful individuals.

Red beans were traditionally cooked all day on Monday while the wash was drying on the line. The beans, which had been soaked overnight, were cooked with the ham bone left over from Sunday dinner. To give the beans their subtle, smooth flavor, the ham bone was cracked open at one end. The cooked

beans were served over boiled rice, sprinkled with chopped green onions, and accompanied by a green salad.

An oyster loaf was often brought home by husbands when they needed to placate their angry wives. It was called the "peacemaker" because the men were certain that such a treat would settle any quarrel. The classic oyster loaf consisted of a loaf of French bread split open and filled with fried oysters.

Pralines, the famous candy of New

JAMBALAYA

This version of Creole Jambalaya incorporates many of the ingredients of Creole cookery. The type of ingredients in a jambalaya can vary, but must always include rice.

The use of diced chicken breasts instead of chicken pieces in this recipe reduces the cooking time. More readily available mild Italian sausage is used in this recipe, although *Andouille* sausage would give this jambalaya a sweeter flavor.

Serves 4

1 tablespoon butter

6 ounces sweet Italian sausages, cut into 1-inch pieces

12 ounces boned and skinned chicken breasts, cut into 1-inch pieces

1/4 cup chopped red pepper

1/4 cup chopped green pepper

1 jalapeño pepper, seeded and chopped

1 medium onion, chopped

1 clove garlic, chopped

2 large tomatoes, peeled, seeded, and chopped

8 large okra, cut into 1-inch pieces

1 cup medium-grain rice

1 1/2 cups chicken broth

1 1/2 cups water

1/4 teaspoon dried thyme

1/4 bay leaf

1/8 teaspoon ground cloves

A pinch of red pepper flakes

1 teaspoon paprika

6 ounces boiled ham, cut into 1-inch pieces

1/3 cup chopped fresh parsley

■

Melt the butter in a large, deep skillet over medium heat. Add the sausage and lightly brown the pieces on both sides. Remove the sausage and add the chicken pieces and lightly brown them; then remove. Add the peppers, onions, and garlic, and sauté until the vegetables are no longer crisp, 3 to 5 minutes. Add the tomato, okra, rice, chicken broth, water, and seasonings. Bring to a boil, reduce heat, cover, and cook over low heat for 18 to 20 minutes, or until the rice is barely done. Return the chicken and sausage to the pan along with the ham and parsley. Continue cooking for 5 to 7 minutes, or until the chicken is done and the ingredients are heated through.

Orleans, were named for a French butler, Praslin. As a precaution against indigestion, Praslin prepared a candy of almonds coated with sugar. How useful this remedy was, no one knows.

In Louisiana early French housewives, homesick for Paris almond candy, made do with the pecans they found locally, and concocted the brown-sugar confection called pralines. The addition

of butter and cream gave the pralines a fudge-like texture and a rich flavor.

Sugarcane and Rice

Sugarcane and rice became two early crops of Louisiana. In 1742 the Jesuits in New Orleans imported a quantity of sugarcane from Santo Domingo and arranged to have it planted on local plantations. Negro slaves were brought in to work the cane fields. By 1795 a method of refining sugar commercially had been perfected and sugarcane has been grown in the delta of the Mississippi River ever since.

In plantation days sugarcane syrup was cooked in an open kettle into a taffy-like consistency. It was a popular confection, since varieties of candy did not exist. Children would wrap the taffy around a stick, dip it into chopped pecans, and eat it like a lollipop. The first pale, boil-off syrup of the sugarcane was a traditional topper for rice griddle cakes and waffles.

The early settlers learned rice cultivation from the Indians, who grew a similar wild grain in the bayous of the Mississippi Delta. Later, rice became the staple grain of southern Louisiana and the principal crop of many of the plantations in the area. Today, rice fields flourish around the small towns of southern Louisiana that dot the intercoastal waterway, where the rice fields can be flooded periodically.

Crawfish and *Les Crevettes*

Flooded rice fields also make excellent crawfish farms. Louisiana produces almost 100-million pounds of crawfish annually, both in natural bayous and man-made ponds. Crawfish are harvested in the wild from November through June. Rice farmers around Breaux Bridge, the Crawfish Capital of the World, flood their fields in the fall and harvest crawfish in the off-season before planting rice again.

During crawfish season thousands of trappers drop chicken-wire cages shaped like puffed, hollow pillows to the bottoms of ponds, lakes, and swamps. The traps, which have holes in one end that allow the crawfish to enter the traps but not to leave them, are baited with small pieces of meat.

The majority of Louisiana's crawfish, however, are now raised in man-made ponds or plastic tanks. There are more than 300 crawfish farms in Louisiana, which produce more than 70 million pounds of crawfish annually. Crawfish resemble small lobsters and can vary in size from little more than an inch to the more usual three to five inches.

Crawfish "boils" or feasts, like oyster roasts in other parts of the South, are informal gatherings where newspapers are spread on tables outdoors, and the boiled crawfish are dumped on top for all to enjoy. They are also served fried, stuffed, in bisques, jambalayas, salads, and étoufées, a dish in which the crawfish are covered with a rich sauce. Crawfish balls, made by combining the meat with rice and finely chopped vegetables, are deep-fried. A delicacy of the bayou is crawfish pie. The flaky pie crust conceals shelled crawfish tails baked with onions, parsley, and celery.

Although crawfish are a speciality of Louisiana, the harvesting of shrimp is the state's main seafood industry. *Les crevettes,* the French term for shrimp, have been an important ingredient in Cajun and Creole cooking for more than two centuries. Even before the Acadians settled in Louisiana, the Indians used to dip shrimp out of the bayou and dry them in the sun. After the Cajuns came, these dried shrimp became known as Cajun peanuts. Only the Cajuns and the Indians consumed the local shrimp until after the Civil War, when canning made commercial production possible. Using modern transportation and refrigeration, fresh and frozen Louisiana shrimp are now marketed throughout the country.

Louisiana Sausages

Years ago hog butcherings, known as *boucheries,* were held everywhere in Cajun country when the cool fall weather arrived. Usually the entire family was involved in the butchering, from which the women made headcheese, white sausage, blood sausage, and cracklings. The day ended with a large feast, including pork stew, rice, yams, and salad.

Cajun sausage has gained national popularity, thanks to the efforts of Paul Prudhomme's popularization of Cajun cooking. The two principal types of sausage are *boudin* and *andouille.* They are produced both at home and commercially. Most Louisiana sausage is made with finely cubed meat, as it was originally made in France.

There are basic differences in the two types of sausages. *Boudin blanc* is a Cajun white sausage made with rice, ground pork, chicken, and vegetables. When it is cooked, the casing breaks open and the creamy stuffing becomes a smoky, spicy rice stew. *Andouille* sausage, a thick Cajun sausage made with lean pork, pork fat, and lots of garlic, is traditionally very hot and spicy. The Creole version of *andouille* reduces the pepperiness by basting the sausages with sugarcane syrup during smoking.

A less popular Louisiana sausage is the *chaurisse,* which is probably a version of the Spanish *chorizo.* It is a small, dark-red, hotly spiced sausage. When used in jambalaya the dish resembles the Spanish *Paella.*

Mardi Gras

The first Mardi Gras was celebrated in 1699 by the French settlers in New Orleans. They were homesick and wanted to recall some of their French customs before the onset of Lent.

Twelfth Night, January 6th, marks the beginning of carnival season, which culminates with Mardi Gras on the last Tuesday before the Lenten season begins. By the mid-eighteenth century the custom of Mardi Gras, which in French means "Fat Tuesday," was well established. It was a celebration that literally meant farewell to meat until Easter. By 1857 Mardi Gras took on its present form of celebration, parades, and balls.

In the rural areas Mardi Gras is celebrated differently than in New Orleans. Masked men ride on horseback from farm to farm gathering ingredients for a gigantic gumbo and jambalaya—a chicken from one house, a sausage from another, and rice from a third. All of these are put together in great iron pots on the town square to simmer slowly until evening, while people dance and hold contests in celebration of Mardi Gras.

King Cake, traditionally served at Mardi Gras, was originally part of the Twelfth Night celebrations at the start of the carnival season. The cake was introduced by the early French settlers, who continued a custom dating back to the Middle Ages. Similar to French *Gâteau des rois,* the cake is made with a rich yeast dough to which chopped citron has

FISHERMAN by Byron Browne, crayon on paper, 18 1/2 x 16 inches, courtesy of Michael Rosenfeld Gallery, New York, New York.

been added. It is decorated with a tinted sugar icing. A pecan, bean, or small toy is hidden in the cake, and whoever finds it is declared King or Queen of the Twelfth Night celebration.

Other Mardi Gras dishes include ham, coffee mousse, and pecan pralines. Paper thin crepes are also served with a flaming bowl of *Café Brûlot,* a hot coffee flavored with brandy, curaçao, and sugar.

Tabasco Sauce

Tabasco Sauce has been produced by the McIlhenny family since shortly after the Civil War. Before the war, Edmund McIlhenny, a New Orleans banker and founder of the McIlhenny Company, married Mary Eliza Avery, the eldest daughter of a Baton Rouge judge. The Avery family owned a 2,300-acre "island" in the swamplands of Louisiana, 120 miles west of New Orleans, on which a salt mine was located. The property, however, was not an actual island but an oversized hill, the base of which was pure salt.

The salt mine became a strategic target of the Union Army in 1863. They seized the island, flooded it, and forced the Avery family to flee. When the family returned in 1865, the only thing on the island that had survived was a small capsicum pepper plant. Edmund McIlhenny had grown the plant from seeds given to him by a friend who had brought them from Mexico.

McIlhenny took the tiny red peppers from the surviving plant and mixed them with Avery Island salt to age. Later vinegar was added, and the result was a unique pepper sauce. McIlhenny poured it into small cast-off cologne bottles and called it Tabasco Pepper Sauce, after the name of the river and town in southern Mexico from which the peppers originally came. He continued to experiment and perfect his sauce. The first year McIlhenny produced 350 tiny bottles of Tabasco Sauce.

In 1868 McIlhenny obtained a patent for his unique formula, and by 1870 he had received orders for thousands of bottles of Tabasco Sauce at the unheard-of price of one dollar per bottle. Two years later, he opened an office in London to meet the increasing demand for Tabasco Sauce in Europe. Succeeding generations of the McIlhenny family have operated the firm and supervised the production of Tabasco Sauce.

Tabasco Sauce peppers are now also grown in Mexico, Colombia, Honduras, and Venezuela—all from seeds from Avery Island plants. As the plants develop, each branch becomes almost like Joseph's coat of many colors with beautiful peppers ranging from green to yellow to orange to bright red.

Toward the end of the summer only the bright-red peppers are hand picked. This involves many pickings since the peppers do not ripen simultaneously. The freshly harvested peppers must be processed the same day to retain their flavor. They are ground with a small amount of Avery Island salt, and the fresh "mash" is put into white oak barrels for fermentation and aging.

After years of fermentation, the mash is blended with high-grain, distilled vinegar. The mixture is then gently stirred by hand periodically with wooden paddles for four weeks. The seeds and skins are removed, and the resulting sauce is bottled and labeled "Tabasco."

New Orleans Restaurants

Throughout much of the nineteenth century, New Orleans was largely a French city with French restaurants and cafes. The first eating establishment in the city was the Café des Emigrés which opened in 1791. The coming of businessmen in the early 1800s resulted in several hotels being built with elaborate dining rooms. Antoine's, New Orleans's oldest French Creole restaurant, opened in 1840 as a French boarding house, then moved in 1874 to its present location on St. Louis Street in the French Quarter.

In 1885 William H. Coleman persuaded two young New Orleans writers to compile the *Historical Sketch Book and Guide* to New Orleans. The book not only profiled the sights of the city but also many of its eating establishments in various price ranges. According to the guide, a ten-course meal at the grand St. Charles Hotel consisted of oysters, soup, two entrées, a soufflé, pastry, dessert, and coffee—all at a cost of $20. A seven-course dinner at a first class restaurant cost $6. For an ordinary dinner the *Guide* noted that a man could casually drop into a restaurant and partake of soup, some fish, an entrée of sweetbreads or a lamb chop. This then could be followed by spring chicken or roast beef, mutton, or veal with two dishes of vegetables. For dessert some fruit, cheese, and coffee would suffice. This fare, including a half bottle of claret, would cost between $1.50 and $2.50.

The three most famous restaurants, Antoine's, Galatoire's, and Brennan's owe much of their long-lived success to continuous family management. Antoine's was founded in 1840 by Antoine Alciatore, a native of Marseilles. Many of the dishes served at the restaurant were perfected by Antoine's son, Jules. The menu consists of French cuisine, including Oysters Rockefeller.

Oysters Rockefeller, one of Jules creations derived from a French recipe for snails, was to be an alternative to the popular Snails Bourguignon. The recipe for Oysters Rockefeller is a well-guarded secret and is supposed to include 18 ingredients with spinach being a must. The baked oysters are served on the half shell on a bed of hot rock salt. Each oyster is covered with a green sauce so rich that the dish was named for the richest man Alciatore could think of—John D. Rockefeller, Sr., who never set foot in Antoine's.

Another famous Antoine dish is Chicken Rochambeau. It consists of slices of chicken, which are served on a Holland rusk that has first been covered with a slice of ham. A slightly sweet sauce covers the ham, which is then topped with slices of sautéed chicken. The combination is served with a lemon béarnaise sauce.

When French balloonist Alberto Santos-Dumonty visited New Orleans in 1901, Antoine's honored him with a dish made to look like a balloon. The resulting *Pompano en Papillote* was cooked in parchment with a cream sauce richly adorned with shrimp, crabmeat, and mushrooms. As the fish cooks the parchment puffs up like a balloon. It is served while still puffed.

Galatoire's was founded in 1906 and serves such Creole specialities as trout with shrimp, mushrooms, and truffles in a hollandaise sauce. It is said that the Creole chefs at Galatoire's can transform any classic French recipe into a Creole dish by adding their own flavorings. The result is often a much lighter dish than the original French one.

The tradition of the grand New Orleans breakfast originated during the late nineteenth century in the French Market, where restaurants served a hearty, full meal at mid-morning to merchants and tradesmen who had begun their day at dawn. The most famous of these eating places was Madame Begue's, which opened in 1882. French coffeehouses, however, continued to serve lighter fare such as *Beignets,* French market doughnuts, or *Calas,* hot rice cakes.

The reputation for full-meal New Orleans breakfasts spread during the Cotton Exposition of 1884-85 and became one of the hallmarks of Creole cuisine. Sauced egg dishes and fancy omelets were the stars of these breakfasts. Eggs Sardou was created at Antoine's in 1908 in honor of the visiting French dramatist Victorien Sardou. It was the first of the elaborate egg dishes. Eggs Sardou consists of artichoke hearts on a bed of creamed spinach, topped with poached eggs and hollandaise sauce.

Breakfast at Brennan's has been a tradition since the restaurant first opened its doors in 1946. Owen Brennan, Jr., has continued his father's custom of serving the clientele gargantuan breakfasts.

There are also many casual eateries in the French Quarter. The Gumbo Shop, for example, specializes in Louisiana gumbo made with crab, shrimp, and okra. Crawfish from the bayou is the specialty of the Bon Ton Cafe, where owner Al Pierce, an Acadian descendant, has kept much of the style of cooking of his ancestors in the food he serves.

MISSISSIPPI

THE STATE OF MISSISSIPPI is dominated by the great river the Algonquian Indians called the "Father of Waters." The mighty Mississippi River was the lifeline to the outside world from the interior of the state. Paddle-wheel steamers became the principal means of transportation for Mississippians during most of the nineteenth century.

Like its neighboring state, Louisiana, Mississippi was discovered by the Spanish explorer Hernando de Soto but was first settled by the French in 1699. The French established the cities of Natchez and Vicksburg on the Mississippi River. Natchez, which was later acquired by the British, became one of the richest cities in the South, because it was a major shipping point for cotton.

Early Food

The first explorers of what is now northern Mississippi were French fur traders who set up trading posts in Indian villages. They learned to eat the same food as the Indians, primarily a mush concocted from ground brier root, fish, and wild game.

When the first permanent settlement was established along Biloxi Bay around 1700, the settlers found they could obtain chickens from the Indians in addition to fish. Historians believe that the chickens originally came from a ship wrecked offshore several years earlier.

The French brides who came to Biloxi, like those who came to New Orleans, soon learned to use native ingredients in their cooking. Redfish, green peppers, and assorted wild herbs became the basis of their fish stews.

From the earliest days, Mississippi cooks usually had available the basic ingredients for a soup or a stew—carrots, celery, onions, okra, and a sprig or two of parsley. Tomatoes were not included until well after the Revolutionary War, because many still regarded them as poisonous. In the 1870s, however, Mississippi became one of the leading producers of tomatoes when immigrants brought seeds from Italy and began cultivating them.

Natchez, after being acquired by the

PECAN PIE

In recent years some pecan pies have included a layer of chocolate or bourbon in the filling. This less sweet version of pecan pie is a traditional one. The richness of the filling is due to the use of some brown sugar.

Serves 6 to 8

4 tablespoons butter or margarine, at

    room temperature

1/4 cup sugar

1/4 cup light brown sugar

1 cup light corn syrup

3 eggs

1 1/2 cups pecan halves

Pastry for 9-inch pie (recipe follows)

■

Cream the butter and the two sugars in a medium-size bowl until light and fluffy. Add the syrup and beat well. Then add the eggs, one at a time, beating well after each addition. Fold in the pecans.

Pour the filling into the prepared pie shell and bake in a preheated 350° F. oven for 50 minutes, or until a knife inserted halfway between the center and the outside of the filling comes out clean.

Pastry

1 cup all-purpose flour

3 tablespoons butter or margarine

3 tablespoons solid vegetable shortening

3 to 4 tablespoons ice water

■

Place the flour in a bowl. With a pastry blender cut in the butter and shortening until the solids are the size of very small peas. Fluff the mixture with a fork. Add the ice water, one tablespoon at a time, tossing the mixture with the fork until the dough sticks together and can be formed into a ball. Wrap the dough in plastic wrap and place in the refrigerator for at least one hour.

Remove dough from the refrigerator, place on a floured board, and roll 1 inch larger in diameter than the top surface of the pie pan. Place dough in pie pan; crimp the edges.

INTERIOR OF THE STEAMBOAT PRINCESS by Marie Adrien Persac, gouache on paper, 22 ¹⁵/₁₆ x 17 inches, courtesy of Anglo-American Art Museum, Louisiana State University, Baton Rouge, Louisiana, gift of Mrs. Mamie Persac Lusk.

English, became known as the "four-teenth colony," since many Tories settled there. They continued their luxury-loving lifestyle by purchasing spices and wine from abroad. The town became the British equivalent of French New Orleans.

Natchez was a bustling city in the late 1700s and early 1800s. Most of the early travelers to the region arrived via the river. Beginning in 1785, rafts and flatboats floated down the Ohio and Mississippi rivers loaded with produce from the Ohio Valley. They also

brought wheat, flour, barrel pork, hides, furs, and tobacco. Shut off from markets on the Atlantic coast by the Appalachian mountains, these traders came south to sell in the markets of Natchez. They were often welcomed by an orchestra of Indians who played cane flutes and drums made from iron kettles.

Since they could not fight their way back upriver against the swift current of the Mississippi, the traders sold their crafts for lumber and returned north on foot or horseback. They were called "Kaintucks," regardless of whether they were originally from Kentucky or elsewhere. In 1806 one of the early Kaintucks to walk the Trace (from an old French word for a line of footprints) back to Kentucky was Thomas Lincoln. Twenty-two years later, his son Abe also made the trip back up the river from Mississippi but on a steamboat.

Mississippi Cuisine

The cuisine of Mississippi varied with aspects of its history. Although New Orleans remains the bastion of French-cooking influence in America, French influence was also dominant in the cuisine of the plantation mansions along the Mississippi River. Rich sauces and spectacular desserts abounded on manor-house dinner tables.

Food was presented in great splendor in ante-bellum Mississippi. The luxurious day began with hot, strong, black coffee, which was brought to houseguests before sunrise. This was followed by mint juleps before breakfast. In warm weather late breakfasts were served on shaded verandas and included three kinds of meat, an assortment of eggs, hominy grits, hot biscuits, and waffles. Some cooks also prepared fried chicken for breakfast along with muffins and quick breads.

Food for the plantation workers was much simpler. Freshly caught catfish from the Mississippi River often constituted dinner. It was accompanied by turnip greens flavored with salt pork;

corn bread; hot, spicy red beans; and rice. Baked ribs and beans baked with bell peppers accompanied by corn bread was a typical winter meal.

Chicken bread was a particular favorite among plantation workers. It consisted of a batter made with flour, cornmeal, shortening, salt, and milk, which was baked in the frying pan after the chicken had finished frying. The bread was similar to English Yorkshire Pudding.

For many years only the slaves ate corn pone (eggless corn bread which is fried or baked in small batches) and pot liquor, the juice that remains after vegetables, particularly greens, are cooked. One day a plantation mistress noticed that the black children seemed healthier than her own. She decided that their practice of dipping the corn pone into the juice left over from cooking turnip greens was the reason and adopted it for her own children. Years later it was discovered that there was sound reasoning behind this practice, as most of the vitamins and minerals remain in the water when vegetables are boiled.

John Jenkins, a far-sighted Mississippi planter, experimented with growing fruits and vegetables. He grew quince that weighed more than a pound, new varieties of peas, and an assortment of prize apples and pears. Jenkins became a forerunner of modern marketing when he shipped a basket of his pears in an icebox to New York in the 1840s. Houseguests were often astonished that he was able to keep fresh fruit in good condition until late winter and loved to partake of his juicy pears and peaches at Christmas.

During the Civil War people in the Confederacy were continually short of food staples. To compensate, Mississippi

women made pie crusts from potatoes, salad oil from sunflower seeds, and leavened breads and cakes with corncob ashes. None of these war-time foods became permanent fixtures in Mississippi's culinary heritage.

Catfish and Hush Puppies

Mississippi is catfish country, and catfish weighing from 30 to 100 pounds have been caught in the state's rivers. In the days before catfish became a commercial product, fresh-caught fish were cleaned, rolled in cornmeal, and fried over an open fire outdoors. An almost essential accompaniment to the fried fish was the hush puppy, which was made with cornmeal, milk or water, and sometimes an egg. Small lumps of this batter were fried in the same fat as the fish.

The story of how hush puppies got their name probably goes back to one of the first fish fries. The dogs who had come along on the outing began to whine as they smelled the frying fish. In order to quiet the hungry dogs, the fishermen tossed them fried bits of the cornmeal batter with the comforting words, "Hush, puppy."

Although pond cultivation of catfish began in Arkansas, Mississippi is now the number one producer of catfish in the nation, harvesting more than 250 million pounds annually. Deep in the delta region of Mississippi, acres of catfish ponds have been placed among rows of cotton and soybeans. Catfish farming flourishes in the region because of the sunny and warm climate, an abundant supply of pure well water, and a heavy clay soil that holds the water in the pond.

Delta Pride of Indianola, Mississippi, is one of the largest processors of catfish in the country. The company, a farmer-owned cooperative, was formed in 1980 by 119 catfish farmers to market their fish. They built a processing plant and have since expanded the operation to three other plants that now produce 135 million pounds of catfish annually. The members of Delta Pride control about 64,000 acres of catfish ponds, and the organization also has special breeding ponds and hatcheries.

Catfish are raised in a controlled environment. The quality and temperature of the water in the fish ponds is scientifically regulated, and the fish are fed a specially formulated diet. There is a purification system for each pond that constantly removes natural wastes from the water. Most catfish are about 18 months old when they are harvested and weigh about one and a half pounds. At harvest catfish are netted, placed in specially designed carrier tanks, and transported live to the processing plants.

Shrimp Fishing

Shrimp and oyster harvesting has always been important to Mississippi. At one time the streets of Biloxi were paved with oyster shells, and the area continues to be famous for outdoor oyster bakes.

Today, shrimp harvesting takes place at night, because the shrimp are dormant in the sand at that time. Shrimp have a two-year life cycle. They spawn in estuaries, then grow up in the Gulf, and are caught on their way back to the estuaries to spawn.

Most shrimp boats operate for two days to two weeks at a time. During shrimp harvesting the nets are kept on the sandy bottom for several hours. When the nets are brought up, the shrimp are placed in baskets similar to

FRIED CATFISH WITH PECAN SAUCE

Freshly caught catfish were fried on the riverbank in the nineteenth century and served with Hush Puppies. Today, the majority of marketed catfish are pond raised and are served either fried or baked.

A sauce with lightly toasted pecans tops these fried catfish fillets.

Serves 4 to 6

2 pounds catfish fillets

1/2 cup all-purpose flour

3/4 cup cornmeal

1/4 teaspoon salt

1/8 teaspoon pepper

Vegetable oil, for frying

Pecan sauce (recipe follows)

■

Rinse the catfish fillets and pat them dry.

Mix the flour, cornmeal, salt, and pepper on a plate or piece of waxed paper. Roll the fish in the cornmeal mixture.

Place enough oil in a heavy 10-inch iron skillet to cover the bottom by 1/4 inch. Heat the oil over medium-high heat and add the fish. Fry for 4 to 5 minutes, or

until brown. Then carefully turn the fish and fry for 4 to 5 minutes on the other side, or until the fish is done. (The frying may have to be done in two batches.) Drain the fish on paper towels.

Pecan Sauce

1/2 cup lightly toasted pecans, coarsely chopped

4 tablespoons butter, melted

1 1/2 teaspoons lemon juice

1/4 teaspoon Worcestershire sauce

A few drops of Tabasco sauce

■

Combine the sauce ingredients in a small bowl and spoon some sauce over each serving of catfish.

laundry baskets, and then iced down. Once ashore, they are processed in various plants in or near Pascagoula. The processors grade the shrimp according to size, pull off the heads, place them in a little water, and freeze them. The majority of the shrimp are shipped frozen.

Along with shrimp, the Mississippi coast fishermen also harvest oysters, butterfish, and the *geryon* or red crab, which, like lobster, lives in cold water and normally inhabits depths of 1,200 to 6,000 feet. Special traps have been developed for this crab, whose meat is similar in appearance and flavor to the king crab.

Spinach Fettuccine with Shrimp

Shrimp are harvested year-round along both the Gulf and Atlantic coasts of the Deep South. Italians, who emigrated to Mississippi in the 1870s, started growing their native tomatoes from seeds that they had brought with them. Thus Italian-style shrimp, tomatoes, and pasta were often combined in a tasty dish.

This modern version uses green pasta and tomato sauce for a colorful and light dish seasoned with basil.

Serves 4

2 tablespoons olive oil

1/2 pound mushrooms, sliced

4 green onions, sliced

1/2 cup chopped red pepper

1/2 cup chopped yellow pepper

6 large Roma tomatoes, chopped

1 cup white wine

1/8 teaspoon pepper

1/2 cup whipping cream

1/2 cup fresh chopped basil

12 ounces spinach fettuccine

3 tablespoons butter

1 pound shrimp, shelled and deveined

■

Heat the olive oil in a large deep skillet and sauté the mushrooms, onions, and red and yellow peppers for 2 to 3 minutes. Add the chopped tomatoes and continue cooking on medium-low heat until the tomatoes become soft, about 5 minutes. Add the wine and pepper and cook until the sauce begins to thicken, about 7 minutes. Then add the cream and cook to reduce to sauce consistency. Fold in the basil and beat through.

In the meantime cook the spinach fettuccine, al dente, and keep it warm.

In another skillet, melt the butter over medium-high heat. Add the shrimp and sauté until just done. Do not overcook the shrimp. Cooking time depends on the size of shrimp used.

Divide the fettuccine among 4 warm plates and top with the sauce. Then place one-fourth of the shrimp on top of each serving.

Steamboats on the Mississippi

With the arrival of the steamboats on the Mississippi River in 1811, passenger travel became a reality between New Orleans and St. Louis. Although the *New Orleans* paddle wheeler, with its 24-inch cylinder head and six-foot piston, made headlines, other boats were soon bigger and more luxurious.

The food on these steamboats for the upper-deck passengers was gourmet and was prepared and served elegantly by well-trained Negro chefs and waiters. A simple breakfast aboard the riverboat consisted of broiled steaks and waffles, plus choices from the multi-page breakfast menu. Dinner was served at noon, and the evening meal was a light supper. Biscuits, sweet breads, corn breads, pies, tarts, and éclairs were baked each morning. There were also such exotic desserts as charlottes of peach with Cognac sauce, nougats, glacés, and fancy pastries. The steerage passengers below the main decks did not fare as well.

Provisions were put on board at the beginning of the journey and were also procured along the way. Live lambs, chickens, and pigs were loaded onto the boiler deck, where they were kept in pens and slaughtered as needed. There was no refrigeration, and ice was kept only for the drinking gentry. Smoked, pickled, and preserved foods were also brought aboard in hogsheads. Wild game was picked up at the quays along the way from backwoods hunters. Giant catfish and river shellfish were either caught off the boat or purchased at the various landings.

Most of the well-known steamers, such as the *Enterprise, Robert E. Lee,* and *Sultana,* spent about $2,000 per month on food for the passengers. This was at a time when chickens were a dime each and eggs and a pound of butter cost less than a nickel. The cabin passengers ate from French Sèvres china with solid silver cutlery on white linens.

SOUTH CAROLINA

THE TERRITORY OF CARO-
LINA, which at one time included
present-day North Carolina, South
Carolina, and a part of Georgia, was a
1663 land grant from King Charles II of
Great Britain to eight proprietors. The
English explored the area and found
fertile soil and a warm climate. Settlers
soon followed who brought seeds and
root cuttings, which they envisioned
would become fields of grain, English
vegetable gardens, and orchards. England
hoped that the Carolina colony would
supply it with citrus, wines, and other
Mediterranean-type produce. Unfortunately, the hope was never realized.

In 1670 Charles Town (renamed
Charleston at the start of the Revolutionary War) was founded on the coast of
South Carolina. Charles Town was the
first significant city in the South and for
many years remained the principal
seaport and trading center for the Deep
South.

Being a seaport, Charles Town
enjoyed a variety of exotic food ingredients from its early days. Sea captains
brought spices from the Far East and the
Caribbean Islands. Bananas picked only
days before in the Caribbean were
commonplace in produce markets.
Chocolate from Central America became
a favorite dessert ingredient used in ice
creams, pies, soufflés, and cakes.

Pickles became popular in colonial
days when Charles Town sea captains
brought back mango pickles from India
and Madagascar. Recipes for mock-
mango pickles, using other types of fruit,
abounded in the low country as early as
1699. Cucumber pickles made with
turmeric or other spices were also

*CHARLESTON SQUARE by Charles J. Hamilton, oil, 36 5/8 x 38 5/8 inches, courtesy of
Abby Aldrich Rockefeller Folk Art Center, Williamsburg, Virginia.*

GREENS SOUP

This soup is English in origin and was probably brought to South Carolina by the Scots and English who settled there. A similar soup of Portuguese origin is also prepared in New England. This modern version combines collard greens with kale for a milder flavor. Serve the soup with corn bread.

Serves 6

1 cup dry small white beans

3 slices bacon, cut into 1-inch pieces

1 pound smoked sausage, such as

    Kielbasa, cut into 1-inch slices

1 medium onion, chopped

2 cups chicken broth

6 cups water

1 pound collard greens

1 pound kale

1/3 cup chopped red pepper

1 medium potato, peeled and cut into

    small cubes

Salt and pepper, to taste

∎

Place the beans in a saucepan and add 3 cups water. Bring to a boil and boil for 2 minutes. Remove the beans from the heat and cover the saucepan. Let the beans stand for 1 hour.

Cook the bacon in a large skillet over medium heat. When some of the fat has been rendered, add the sausage and onion. Sauté for 5 minutes until the onions are transparent and the sausage has started to brown.

With a slotted spoon remove the sausage, bacon, and onion to a large soup pot. Drain the beans and add them with the chicken broth and water to the soup pot. Bring to a slow boil and continue cooking over low heat for 1 hour.

In the meantime remove the center stem from the collard greens and kale. Wash the greens and shred them into bite-sized pieces. Add the greens to the soup and continue cooking over low heat for 45 minutes. Then add the red pepper and potatoes and cook another 20 minutes on medium heat, or until the potatoes are soft. Season to taste with salt and pepper.

favorites and were served with bread.

Charles Town quickly developed a French style of cuisine when a shipload of French Huguenots came in 1680, and thousands more arrived by 1685. They brought with them years of experience in producing wine, raising silkworms, and growing olives, in addition to a lifestyle that firmly established a French influence on food and etiquette. Many of these new colonists started rice plantations along the marshy lowlands of the coast.

The French South Carolinians enjoyed plantation life, but they also craved the companionship of others. Thus many plantation owners had a town house in Charles Town where they and their families lived during the social season—usually the winter months when crops did not have to be planted or harvested.

The English settlers copied the lifestyle of their French neighbors, and soon Charles Town became a thriving cosmopolitan city. An important part of the culture of the city was the elegant meals served around great tables gleaming with polished silver and candlelight. Rice, the staple crop of the area, was almost always included in the meal. Slave cooks prepared rice with vegetables, meats, or seafood, as well as traditional English and French dishes.

Although rice and indigo were the major crops of colonial South Carolina, plantation owners experimented with others. In 1755 Henry Laurens succeeded in growing olives, capers, limes, ginger, pears, strawberries, and grapes on a four-acre experimental plot. The plantations had so many peaches that they were often fed to the hogs. Other plantations grew figs, pomegranates, apricots, and oranges. In the early 1800s an unsuccessful attempt was made to establish a vineyard and make wine near Charleston.

Rice

Charles Town probably would not have achieved prominence had it not been for a storm-damaged ship that took refuge in the harbor in 1680. After the vessel was repaired, the captain, John Thurber, presented the governor of the colony with a sack of Madagascar seed rice in appreciation for the use of the harbor. Farmers found that the Madagascar rice flourished in the Carolina low country, and South Carolina began growing and exporting rice to England in the early 1680s.

The entire rice production of South Carolina was lost during the British occupation of Charleston during the American Revolutionary War. The British shipped all of the rice back to England, including the portion that should have been withheld for the next year's seeds. When Thomas Jefferson served as ambassador to France, he managed to smuggle two bags of rice out of Italy in 1787 and gave it to South Carolina to restart their rice industry. This rice from the Piedmont area of Italy was of a superior quality, and the Italians had hoped to maintain a monopoly on it.

Rice cultivation was back-breaking work in those early years. It was planted by hand in soil that oftentimes was "loosened with a kitchen spoon" and under very poor working conditions, given the hot and humid climate of the coastal region. White indentured servants, who worked to pay back their passage money, refused to work in the rice fields. Negro slaves became the answer, and the plantation system soon became established, similar to the tobacco

plantations in Virginia. A 500-acre rice field might be worked with as many as 2,000 slaves.

To prepare a rice field for the following year, the stubble remaining from the summer harvest was burned after the first killing frost of fall. Then the fields were lightly plowed and ditched. Rice seeds were sown in late March or early April, initially by hand and later by mule-drawn drills. During the growing season the rice fields were alternately flooded and dried. Rice was harvested in the late summer and threshed in the winter.

The Civil War marked the decline of rice cultivation in South Carolina, since the freed slaves no longer wanted to work in the rice fields. Immigrant Irish and Italian workers from the brickyards on the Hudson River were brought to work in the rice fields, but they proved to be unsatisfactory. Cultivation of rice declined very rapidly at the beginning of this century, and subsequent hurricanes permanently demolished many of the low-lying coastal rice fields.

In the mid-1980s Richard and Tricia Schulze reintroduced rice into South Carolina. They have successfully raised crops of Carolina Gold, a rice once favored by Chinese emperors. Grown from seeds propagated by the U.S. Department of Agriculture from a museum collection of rice seeds, Dr. Richard Schulze has steadily increased his yearly rice production at his Turnbridge plantation near the Georgia border. The crop is harvested mechanically, and the rice is milled in century-old machines. The Schulzes are raising the first substantial rice crop produced in the state in the last hundred years.

The Schulzes' experiment not withstanding, other food crops have

taken the place of rice in South Carolina. These include pecans, which are now grown in the low country on some of the defunct rice fields, and a variety of fruits and vegetables.

Tea

Tea has played an important part in this country's history, as it was partly responsible for our War of Independence. The famous Boston Tea Party was only the first of many dumpings. At the time it was unthinkable for any patriotic American to drink tea, and native roots, barks, and leaves were tried as substitutes. It was not until 1904 that ice tea became popular, when a merchant at the St. Louis World's Fair, distressed that his customers did not want hot tea on a hot and humid summer day, poured the beverage over ice.

The tea plant, which is part of the camellia family, became popular as an ornamental shrub in America in the early 1700s. Commercial tea growing in America was first attempted near Charleston, South Carolina, in the late 1700s by André Michaux, a French botanist. His efforts did not prove economically successful nor did that of others in subsequent years.

The first viable tea plantation was started near Charleston in 1890 by Dr. Charles Shepard, who continued to grow tea until his death in 1915. The Shepard tea received a special commendation for quality at the 1904 St. Louis World's Fair.

It was not until 1963 that the next serious attempt to grow tea in America occurred, when the Lipton Company started a plantation on Wadmalaw Island, a small island south of Charleston. It was created as an experiment and as a hedge against unstable foreign sources. With the stabilization of the world tea markets in the mid–1980s, however, Lipton phased out its experimental operation near Charleston. The plantation was purchased in the spring of 1987 by Mack Fleming, who had been director of research at the plantation, and William Hall, a British-trained tea taster. That fall they marketed their first harvest of American Classic Tea. Fleming and Hall pride themselves on being able to have their fresh tea on the market shelves in a matter of weeks, instead of the many months required for imported tea.

South Carolina Cuisine

South Carolina cuisine was primarily based on that of her English and French settlers. Since many settlers had business connections with the West Indies, island cuisine also influenced Charleston cooking. Cayenne pepper from the West Indies was used frequently in Charleston cooking. Rice and bean dishes in Charleston have noticeable flavors obtained from the cooking of the Caribbean Islands and Africa. Sesame seeds, which originally came from Africa, are still used in sweets and breads.

There was even a Russian influence to Charleston cuisine. Henry Middleton, who had been president of the First Continental Congress and later became ambassador to Russia, returned with his favorite dessert. He introduced *Charlotte Russe,* a custard encased in lady fingers, to Charleston, where it has been popular ever since.

A typical Sunday dinner in Charleston in the 1700s was served at three in the afternoon. It often started with a delicate shrimp soup, which was followed by fricasseed chicken served with side dishes of sweet potatoes, squash, maca-

roni, and vegetables. Fresh peach ice cream and layer cakes were served for dessert. One historian described a large meal of the 1820s that ended with the following desserts: eight pies, six bowls of syllabub, several floating islands, and six-foot-tall cakes.

Shrimp and crabs were abundant in the inlets and creeks along the South Carolina coast. "Swimpee-raw, swimpee-raw," was the cry of street vendors selling raw shrimp in the streets of Charleston. Shrimp, the basis of many dishes, were eaten hot and cold. Whole shrimp sautéed in butter was a popular breakfast dish, often accompanied by hominy grits. Shrimp and rice were a natural combination. Finely chopped shrimp were combined with cooked rice and beaten egg, then rolled into cones or balls and fried to a crusty brown in hot fat. These croquettes were the southern counterpart of New England codfish balls.

She-crab Soup was a favorite of Charlestonians. "She-crabs" were preferred over the male of the species, because the eggs of the she-crab added a special flavor to the soup. If only male crabs were available, however, Charleston cooks added crumbled hard-cooked egg yolks. To make this milk-based soup enriched with egg and sherry even richer, many cooks added a dab of whipped cream.

Frogmore Stew is to the coastal regions of South Carolina what gumbo is to Louisiana. It is a highly seasoned concoction of boiled seafood, sausage, and corn on the cob. The stew, prepared mainly in the summer when shrimp and corn are both plentiful, is usually served on a plate instead of in a soup bowl. Southern politicians have secured elections around a pot of Frogmore Stew,

and many church charities have served this delicacy. The dish gets its name from the small crossroads community of Frogmore (600 inhabitants) in Beaufort County.

Rice became the basis of many dishes in South Carolina. Often it was served boiled with a lump of butter or molded into a rice ring with vegetables or seafood in a sauce heaped in the center. Cooked rice was added to corn-bread batter and baked into a corn bread known as *philpy.* Pilaf, a popular rice dish, was a Middle Eastern stew-like dish brought to America by the African slaves. In South Carolina it included shrimp and onions, and later tomatoes were added.

When rice was plentiful in the low country, it was mixed with wheat flour to make bread. Rice flour was also produced. At one time 30 different rice breads were made in the low country. Typically, cooks mixed rice flour with grits to form a thick batter to which yeast was added.

After rice cultivation disappeared from the low country, so did the rice-birds from Charleston tables. These small bobolinks had been baked whole or split and broiled. They were served with their heads, for the brain was said to be the most succulent part of the bird.

Corn-based breads were popular in South Carolina, several of which were unique to the region. One such bread was *Awendaw,* which was made with hominy grits, cornmeal, milk, eggs, and butter. It contained no flour and was custard-like, similar to spoon bread. Carolina egg bread, another version of spoon bread, included more eggs than the typical spoon-bread recipe. The egg whites were beaten separately, making a much lighter type of spoon bread.

The African slave trade brought a

number of new food ingredients to America. One of these introduced to South Carolina was sesame seeds, which were called *benne* in Charleston. (Benne is an African word for seeds.) According to legend the Africans hastily picked the seeds and put them in their ears when they were seized in their fields and herded into slavery. These hidden seeds crossed the ocean and were planted in South Carolina soil as a reminder of their homeland. *Benne* wafers, made with brown sugar and toasted sesame seeds, became a favorite cookie of the slaves as well as their white owners. *Benne* brittle was similar to peanut brittle, with sesame seeds being substituted for the peanuts.

A popular cake in Charleston was the Huguenot Torte, a variation of a French sponge cake in which walnuts were replaced by pecans. Chopped apples were also added to the cake, and it was served with whipped cream.

The low country, which stretches from the northern part of the Sea Islands to the last of the barrier islands off the coast of South Carolina and Georgia, has contributed a great variety of fruits, vegetables, seafood, and game to the cooking of South Carolina. From the time of the early settlers, seafood, game birds, and deer provided food. Alligators, bears, and possum also were available. Freshwater turtles, called "cooters" by the local population, were used for stews. The Spanish had brought fig, pomegranate, and peach trees, which were growing wild when the English arrived. Today this area grows watermelons, peppers, and tomatoes, and it is still a significant source of seafood.

AMERICAN RATATOUILLE

Inspired by the vegetable dish of the French settlers along the Gulf Coast and in South Carolina, this Ratatouille includes several vegetables that originated in the Americas—tomatoes, corn, and peppers.

Serves 8

5 tablespoons olive oil

2 onions sliced

1 cup sliced mushrooms

1 medium red pepper, chopped

1 medium green pepper, chopped

3 small Italian eggplants, sliced 1/4-inch

   thick

1 clove garlic, chopped

Kernels from 3 ears of fresh corn

Salt and pepper, to taste

4 medium zucchini, sliced

4 to 5 medium tomatoes, sliced

1/2 teaspoon dried thyme

1/4 cup freshly ground Parmesan cheese

■

Heat 3 tablespoons of the olive oil in a large skillet over medium heat. Add the onions and sauté them until wilted. Add the mushrooms, peppers, eggplant, and garlic and continue sautéing until the eggplant begins to soften. Place the mixture into a large round or oblong casserole. Add the corn, salt, and pepper.

Arrange the zucchini slices and tomato slices in alternating, overlapping rows on top of the eggplant mixture. (May be prepared ahead to this point and refrigerated.) Just before baking, sprinkle the casserole with 1 tablespoon of the olive oil and the thyme. Bake in a preheated 350° F. oven for 35 minutes. Then drizzle the remaining tablespoon of olive oil over the vegetables and sprinkle the Parmesan cheese on top. Continue baking for another 15 minutes.

BEET THINNERS by Clyde Aspevig, oil, 9 x 12 inches, courtesy of Thomas Nygard, Inc., Bozeman, Montana.

GREAT LAKES

WHEN THE UNITED STATES won the western lands from the British as a result of the Revolutionary War, America was not really sure what or how much it had acquired. In 1787, however, Congress gave the new region a name—the Northwest Territory—and defined it as the land west of Pennsylvania, north of the Ohio River, east of the Mississippi River, and south of Lake Superior.

The Great Lakes tied the region together and moderated its temperature, making it feasible to grow fruits, berries, and vegetables. The lakes also provided an easy means of transportation for goods and people. Agricultural products and raw materials were transported from the Midwest to the East via the Great Lakes, starting in the mid-1800s. Schooners laden with grain left Lake Michigan ports for Buffalo, where it was then transported by canal or overland to the metropolitan centers of the northeast.

The Great Lakes region and the upper Mississippi Valley were first explored by the French during the late 1600s. They had come from Canada looking for the legendary Northwest Passage to the Orient but, not finding it, became fur traders with the Indians.

The territory was initially settled by American colonists moving westward. From New England, the Middle Atlantic, and Virginia, pioneer families crossed the mountains and made their way into the Northwest Territory. The first town in the new territory, Marietta, Ohio, was founded in 1788.

In many respects frontier life in the Northwest Territory was a repetition of colonial life on the Atlantic seaboard. The people who came to stay were humble folk with mundane but useful things—black iron cooking pots, wooden bread troughs, homemade quilts, and feather beds. They carried a rifle in one hand and a Bible in the other. Some came with a cow or a pig. Many brought the seeds that would transform the southern Great Lakes region and the Midwest into the major food supplier for the eastern metropolises.

The few handfuls of yellow seed corn brought west by the settlers provided the basis of farming in the region. Corn would grow almost anywhere and could be dropped into a hastily cleared patch of land. Plantings of pumpkins, squash, potatoes, beans, and cabbage soon followed the corn. The great European grain crops—wheat and oats—that needed well-tilled fields free of weeds and continuous fertilization, came later.

The pioneer farmers ground their dried corn, the staple food of the Northwest frontier, into cornmeal in a stone hand mill or grated it on a perforated tin grater nailed to a block of wood. The meal was then sieved through a deerskin punched with holes. Corn bread, including Johnnycake and hoecake, had traveled west. Cornmeal mush became a breakfast and supper dish. Often it was served as the only dish, three times a day.

Potpie was a favorite main dish. It was not a pie at all, but a stew of meat and vegetables with dumplings on top instead of the crust used in New England. These one-pot meals were easy to cook in the open hearth, easy to eat, and easy to keep as leftovers for another meal.

In the early years salt was very expensive and not readily available. Many pioneer families, therefore, dried their meat without salt over the smoke of an open fire, as the Indians had done before them. This became known as jerky and was made from either venison or beef.

The staple New England dried bean also became a staple of the Northwest, and baked beans became a standard dish. Cabbage was preserved as sauerkraut. Most farmers had at least one cow, and its milk was used for cooking, drinking, and making butter and cheese. An ersatz tea was made from spicewood and sassafras.

Fresh vegetables, berries, and fruit, such as wild persimmon, were a welcome treat to meals that consisted primarily of game and meal. Starting in the early 1800s, Ohio, Indiana, and Illinois were blessed with apples from apple trees planted by the now-legendary Johnny Appleseed.

Homes, fireplaces, and cooking utensils were crude on the frontier. The abundance of wood and the scarcity of metals and pottery led to ingenious methods of producing tableware. Porringers, small bowls used to serve most of the food, and larger mixing bowls were carved from blocks of wood. Wooden spoons and the hunting knife were the eating utensils. Most families brought with them their kitchen treasures—an iron kettle, a bake kettle with a cover (similar to a Dutch oven), a three legged iron frying pan with a lid, and maybe a gridiron for grilling meats. The frying pan was also used to bake corn bread.

Life was hard on the frontier, but special occasions such as barn raisings, house raisings, weddings, quilting bees, nutting parties, and apple cuttings were times for merriment. Many of these

POTATO PANCAKES

Raw potato pancakes are typically German and were enjoyed by the early German settlers. They were a main dish served with applesauce or accompanied by bratwurst or other sausages. Potato pancakes were also served with roasted meat. In some German homes they were served for breakfast. Potato pancakes *(Latkes)* were also enjoyed by the Jewish settlers of the Great Lakes region. They added a little grated onion to the batter.

Serves 4

6 medium potatoes

2 eggs, beaten

1/2 teaspoon salt

1/2 teaspoon baking powder

2 tablespoons all-purpose flour

Vegetable oil or solid vegetable

    shortening for frying

■

Peel and grate the potatoes, either on the large holes of a grater or in a food processor. Place the mixture in a colander to remove as much liquid as possible. Press the top of the grated potatoes with a saucer to remove excess moisture, if necessary. The mixture should be damp, not soggy, yet not too dry. Potatoes will discolor, but this will not affect the pancakes.

Combine the grated potatoes, eggs, salt, baking powder, and flour in a bowl.

Heat 1/4 inch of oil in a large frying pan. Drop the potato mixture by rounded tablespoonsful into the oil. Use two or three spoonfuls for each pancake, quickly spreading the mixture to form a flat pancake. Over medium-high heat, cook until crisp and golden brown, about 3 to 4 minutes. Turn and cook the other side. Drain the pancakes on paper towels and keep them warm in the oven until all the pancakes have been cooked.

combined work with play. Potpie was the standard dish at most frontier weddings and other community gatherings. On the Fourth of July, entire communities gathered to watch a parade and indulge in the barbecuing of a sheep or hog.

The Eastern settlers had brought with them their traditional dishes, such as baked beans, succotash, and Johnnycake from New England; fried chicken and cream gravy from the South; and sauerkraut, sausages, pickles, and relishes from New York and Pennsylvania. Eventually these cuisines intermingled. All of the pioneers adapted their foods to the resources of the region.

It was not long before these early settlers from the East were joined by European immigrants—German, Dutch, Swiss, Scandinavian, Finnish, Slavic, and Cornish. Some came seeking a better life; others came because of depressions or famines in their native lands; still others came to avoid military conscription or religious persecution in their homelands. Beginning in the 1830s the European immigrants brought about a rapid increase in the population of the Northwest Territory.

The immigrants found various employment opportunities. Many became farmers, helping to establish Wisconsin as prime dairy land, for example. Others planted grain in Minnesota or raised vegetables and fruits in Michigan. Many of the new immigrants became fishermen on the Great Lakes. The new mining industry of the Upper Great Lakes gave employment to the Cornish, Finnish, and Slavic miners who came to the area. The lumber industry also provided employment for the newcomers.

The immigrants brought with them their own culinary heritages, which they adapted to their new environment. Some of these cuisines became known as Michigan Dutch, Wisconsin German, and Minnesota Scandinavian, with a little Cornish in upper Michigan and Wisconsin. Today, ethnic feasts and festivals, such as the Great Lakes Fish Boil and Oktoberfest in Milwaukee, draw large crowds.

Fish from the Great Lakes became a main source of food for both the Eastern settlers and the European immigrants. The Scandinavians and Germans, in particular, quickly became acclimated, because they were able to prepare their traditional fish dishes.

Great Lakes cookery is as the people who settled the Northwest Territory. The first settlers from the East were only two or three generations removed from their English roots and English cooking. Those who followed from Northern Europe brought a cornucopia of different flavors. Later Eastern Europeans added their own tastes to this cuisine.

ILLINOIS

THE RECORDED HISTORY of Illinois began in 1673, when Jacques Marquette and Louis Joliet first explored the region. Although some of the early Indian tribes inhabiting Illinois were planters, raising corn, pumpkins, and beans, it was the pioneers of the late 1700s and early 1800s who first began to cultivate food crops.

Soybeans, corn, and hogs formed the cornerstones of Illinois agriculture. Decatur became known as the soybean capital of the world, since Staley Foods developed the first soybean products there in the 1930s. The state grows a wide variety of fruits and vegetables and has a significant dairy industry. Today, prize-winning blue cheeses are aged in caves near the Mississippi River in Nauvoo, as they have been for decades.

In the early 1800s two Illinois men, John Deere and Cyrus McCormick, helped revolutionize the agriculture of Illinois and the nation. John Deere perfected the steel plow, and Cyrus McCormick developed the grain reaper. At the same time Chicago started evolving as a major agricultural and industrial city.

One of the unique herbs raised in Illinois is horseradish. It is grown in an area known as the "American Bottoms," the Mississippi River basin in southern Illinois across the river from St. Louis. Sixty percent of the world's supply of this pungent root is grown here. The area's cold winters provide the required dormancy for the roots, and the long summers give the warmth needed for the roots to grow. German immigrants who settled in the area began growing horseradish in the late 1800s and passed their labor-intensive growing methods down through the generations.

COUNTRY BUTCHER by Dorothy Cogswell, oil, 33 1/2 x 28 inches, courtesy of Michael Rosenfeld Gallery, New York, New York.

The Meat Capital

In the last third of the nineteenth century, Chicago became the meat capital of America. The first great fortune in meat was made as a result of the Civil War and was a product of financial astuteness. Phillip Danford Armour became wealthy, because he foresaw the Union victory. As the war drew to an end, pork was priced at $40 a barrel. Armour realized that there would be a substantial drop in prices when the North won. He sold pork futures, so that when he had to deliver pork already paid for at the war price of $40 a barrel, he was able to buy it at $18. Armour made a profit of two million dollars (a huge fortune at the time), and the Armour meat-packing business was born.

Although Armour made his money in pork, it was beef that made Chicago the great meat center of America. Since the buffalo had almost vanished and other wild game had been practically exhausted, beef was to become the all-American meat. Beef fought a running battle with pork for top spot on the dinner menu until well into the twentieth century.

Another great name in American meat packing was Gustavus Franklin Swift, who started his career in 1853 at age fourteen as an employee in his brother's butcher shop in Sandwich, Massachusetts. While working there he saved enough money to buy a cow, which he butchered and sold. Swift continued buying beef cattle, butchering them, and then using a horse and cart to deliver fresh cuts to housewives who were too far away from a local butcher shop to go regularly. After the Civil War Swift moved westward and in 1875 set up headquarters in Chicago.

The Chicago stockyards originated before the railroads came to Chicago as a stopping off point for cattle being driven from Texas and the Midwest to slaughter in the East. Steers, which had eaten only grass on the long drives, were fattened on grain in pens for several weeks and then sent off again on cattle drives to the East. The first rail shipment of cattle from the Chicago stockyards to eastern markets occurred in 1854.

By the time of the Civil War, the majority of cattle were being slaughtered in Chicago. Butchers would purchase the cattle at the stockyards and drive them through the streets to their slaughterhouses, which were often located in residential districts of the city. Residents continually complained about the odors and health hazards of these establishments, until finally in 1873 the Supreme Court outlawed slaughterhouses near residences. This action marked the beginning of an era of improvements of health conditions in the packing industry.

Following the Civil War the refrigerated rail car was developed. It meant that cuts of meat could be sent directly from the Chicago slaughterhouses to retail butcher shops in the East.

The use of refrigerated cars for meat shipment did not originate with the railroads, however. When Chicago packers, Armour and Swift, the two men who have been called the fathers of the American meat industry, approached the railroads with the idea, they were turned down. The railroads had heavily invested in cattle cars, loading docks, and feeding facilities and did not want to see their investments become worthless.

Faced with a series of refusals by the major railroads, Swift persevered and found a small line, Grand Trunk Railway, that was willing to haul refrigerated cars if it did not have to provide them. Both Swift and Armour were informed that the freight rate would be the same as shipping live cattle in railroad-owned cattle cars. It took most of their resources to build a few dozen refrigerated cars. Eventually, the railroads discovered that there was money in owning and operating refrigerated cars.

Besides handling beef, the Chicago meat packers also began processing hogs. At first Swift and Armour only removed the hams from the hog, and the remainder of the carcass was sent to retail butchers. In the early 1900s improved methods of meat preservation were introduced, which enabled meat packers to process the whole hog. As a result sausages and hams became an integral part of Swift's and Armour's hog processing.

Another Chicago packer, J.A. Wilson, made a major contribution to the industry by inventing a metal container for canned meat. Canning meat, particularly beef, was a problem, since the meat tended to shrink in the can after processing. Precooking the meat prevented some shrinkage and made the beef more appetizing, but this improvement in canned meat packaging was not sufficient to gain its acceptance in the market. Finally, the invention of a truncated pyramid can by Wilson, enabled the can's meat contents to remain solidly in place. When opened the meat could then be easily sliced.

Processed Meats and Cheese

Illinois packers were leaders in introducing modern technology in meat processing and preservation. Their innovations made processed meats a major part of the meat industry in the last hundred years. One of the biggest segments of this processed meat market is the American hot dog. Typically, processed meat companies were started by European immigrants, who had been trained in the art of sausage making, one of the most successful being Oscar Mayer.

Oscar F. Mayer came into the meat business a little later than his competitors, Swift and Armour. Mayer came to the United States from Bavaria in 1873, when he was fourteen years old. After working as a helper in a Detroit butcher shop, he moved to Chicago in 1876, where he worked in a meat market and meat-packing plant. Mayer and his brother Gottfried, who had apprenticed in sausage making and ham curing in Germany, founded their own retail butcher shop in Chicago in 1883.

In 1919 the Mayers purchased a small farmers' meat processing cooperative in Madison, Wisconsin. The company headquarters were moved to Madison in the mid-1950s. Today, Oscar Mayer is one of the leading manufacturers of processed meats in the country and is well known for its hot dogs. The company is now a part of Kraft General Foods.

The Louis Rich Company was founded in 1921 in Rock Island, Illinois, by Louis Rich, a Russian-Jewish immigrant. He started in business buying live chickens and eggs from farmers and delivering them to local meat markets. Over the next several years, he began processing poultry, and by 1960 the company started devoting its attention to turkey processing. Louis Rich is now the largest manufacturer of processed turkey products in the country and is number two in packaged luncheon meats behind Oscar Mayer.

A young Chicago grocery clerk, J.

L. Kraft, came up with a different idea for merchandising cheese. Until that time cheese was cut to order for the customer from huge wheels of cheese that stood on the store's counter. Kraft thought that housewives would rather have smaller uniform pieces of cheese packed under more sanitary conditions. He was the first to wrap small wedges of cheese in tinfoil and pack creamier cheese in glass containers. Kraft bought a horse and buggy and sold his cheeses door to door in Chicago. That was the start of Kraft Foods. Now Kraft and General Foods have been merged and include Oscar Mayer and Louis Rich.

Hydrofarming

Historically, growing vegetables on a large commercial scale has not been economically feasible in many of the prairie and Midwestern states. In recent years, however, rising transportation costs from traditional growers in the Far West and Southwest to Eastern markets have made vegetable production in the Midwest a viable alternative. The Archer Daniels Midland Company of Decatur, Illinois, is engaged primarily in processing and merchandising agricultural commodities such as soybeans, cottonseed, sunflowers, and peanuts. In 1977 the company decided to experiment with greenhouse cultivation of vegetables.

What started as a one-acre, experimental hydroponic greenhouse in Decatur, Illinois, has grown into a ten-acre, full-production hydrofarm in Peoria, Illinois. The company harvests more than 30,000 heads of lettuce everyday, along with a wide assortment of other vegetables and herbs. Each week more than 3,000 cucumbers are harvested in one of the half-acre green-

houses. Other crops include tomatoes, basil, Belgium endives, and mushrooms. About 350,000 seedlings can be grown in a one-half acre space, and crops can be harvested every 21 days.

In the Archer Daniels Midland hydrofarm operation, waste heat from the corn sugar refining in an adjacent plant provides enough energy to reduce utility costs by 90 percent. Water at 160 degrees Fahrenheit is drawn off from a stage in the production of high-fructose corn sweetener. It is piped underground to the Archer Daniels Midland hydrofarm in a closed loop. On returning to the corn sweetener plant, the water will have cooled to 120 degrees Fahrenheit, the temperature needed for the next stage of fructose processing.

At the Archer Daniels Midland Raingarden hydrofarm, all crops are started from seed. The seedlings are pampered with full climate control and 24 hours of "sun-like" conditions provided by grow lights. After sprouting the seedlings are placed in a greenhouse environment with greater spacing. When ready for harvest, long trays of lettuce, for example, are moved by conveyor belt to the selecting area. The root blocks are removed with each head of lettuce, which is then packed in a specially designed, plastic, vacuum-sealed container. Archer Daniels Midland provides hydroponically grown fresh vegetables year-round.

Illinois Ethnic Foods

Illinois, particularly its largest city, Chicago, has a diversified culinary heritage, with Polish and Italian dishes predominating. Polish immigrants cooked local lake fish with carrots, lemon, and a garnish of hard-boiled eggs. Their beet

SPAGHETTI SAUCE

Italians, who came primarily from southern Italy and Sicily, settled in the Chicago area in the mid-1800s. They introduced tomatoes, olive oil, and all types of pasta to the cooking of the region. Pasta and pizza have been popular in the Chicago area ever since.

Serves 6

3 tablespoons olive oil

1 large onion, chopped

2 large garlic cloves, minced

1 1/2 pounds lean ground beef

2 mild Italian sausages, casings removed
    and broken into small pieces

1/2 pound mushrooms, sliced

1 medium green pepper, diced

2 cans (1 pound each) tomatoes, chopped

2 cans (8 ounces each) tomato sauce

1 can (6 ounces) tomato paste

1/2 teaspoon salt

1/2 teaspoon pepper

1/3 cup fresh chopped basil or
    2 teaspoons dried basil

3 tablespoons fresh chopped oregano
    or 1 teaspoon dried oregano

3 tablespoons fresh chopped thyme or
    1 1/2 teaspoons dried thyme

1 1/4 pounds spaghetti, cooked al dente

Freshly grated Parmesan cheese

■

Heat the olive oil in a large Dutch oven, add the onions and garlic, and sauté until limp and very lightly browned. Add the beef and sausage meat and sauté until the meat loses its pink color and is lightly browned. Mix in the mushrooms and green pepper. Then add the chopped tomatoes and their juice and the remaining ingredients, except the cooked spaghetti and grated Parmesan cheese. Thin the sauce with 1/2 cup water. Bring to a slow boil and then cook over low heat for 1 to 1 1/2 hours, stirring occasionally. Remove any accumulated fat from the top of the sauce.

To serve, place the cooked spaghetti in a warm bowl. Add the sauce and toss to coat the pasta. Serve with grated Parmesan cheese.

soup was rich with tomatoes, cabbage, apple, lima beans, and sour cream. Babka, a yeast bread filled with nuts, raisins, and candied fruit was served for dessert.

Italians, who came to Chicago from Sicily and southern Italy, helped make Illinoisans conscious of olive oil, Italian tomatoes, and all types of pasta from fettuccine and *capelli d'angelo* (angel hair pasta) to macaroni and the familiar spaghetti. The Italians also brought their cannoli, deep fried tubular pastry shells filled with sweetened whipped ricotta cheese mixed with candied fruit and nuts. Pizza, with its own deep-dish Chicago style, has become very popular.

INDIANA

THE FIRST WINTER in Indiana was hard for the pioneers who had come from North Carolina, Virginia, and Kentucky around 1800. They were forced to exist on such food as bear-meat bacon, ash cakes made from acorns, and coffee made from seeds.

Tom Lincoln was one of the early pioneers who came to the territory. Due to poor surveying practices and ill-kept land records, Tom Lincoln had lost two farms in Kentucky, so he came with his family to Indiana in 1816 to make a new start. He brought with him his wife of ten years, Nancy; their daughter, Sarah; and their son, Abraham.

Abraham Lincoln's first home in Indiana was a lean-to, which was later converted into a one-room cabin with a loft. The winter of 1816 was a harsh one, and the Lincolns lived on water from melted snow, wild game, and some borrowed corn and wheat. This primitive food was typical among the early settlers of Indiana.

By 1840 farming had become the dominant way of life in the state, with 95 percent of the population residing in rural areas. The state government had an active program to improve methods of transportation so that farm crops could reach markets in the East. One of these projects, the Wabash and Erie Canal, was a joint undertaking of Indiana, Ohio, and the federal government.

The 1850s are considered Indiana's Golden Age of Agriculture, when the state ranked high in the raising of hogs, corn, sheep, and wheat. By 1860 railroad lines crisscrossed the state, both east and west and north and south, providing markets in other states for Indiana food products.

Improved transportation also brought European immigrants to Indiana. Each nationality brought with them their culinary customs and traditions. Hungarians settled around South Bend and annually observed the ceremony of blessing the wheat seed on March 24th. They were also known for their recipes for veal paprika with tiny dumplings. Poppy-seed cake was a favorite dessert of the Hungarians.

Switzerland County is named for the Swiss immigrants who founded the town of Vevay in 1801. They grew grapes and made such excellent wine that American statesman Henry Clay used to order it from his home in Lexington, Kentucky. The Swiss settlers also made a variety of cheeses and were known for their fondues, a Swiss speciality.

The favorite Hoosier delicacy of onion pie can be traced to the Polish, Lithuanian, and Hungarian immigrants who settled in Indiana and grew onions. These immigrant farmers became known as "knee farmers" since they planted and harvested the onions on their knees.

Wild American persimmons grew in Indiana and were used in puddings each fall. The persimmons were rubbed through an enamel colander to extract their pulp. The pulp was then mixed with flour, milk, sugar, baking soda, and butter in a big wooden bowl. Finally this mixture was poured into a mold or pan, which was either steamed or baked.

Fried biscuits also became an Indiana specialty. They are made with a yeast dough, cut into rounds, and deep fried. While still hot the biscuits are split, spread with soft butter, and eaten immediately.

One of the earliest forms of baking powder was developed by two Fort Wayne, Indiana, druggists, Biddle and Hoagland, after the Civil War. They had spent several years experimenting with a chemical composition for baking powder, primarily an acid such as baking soda and a moisture-absorber such as cornstarch, and started a baking powder business in 1873. Two years later the partners moved the business to Chicago and subsequently merged it with two other baking-powder firms. The resulting product became known as Royal Baking Powder.

Pork cookery is another well-developed culinary art in Indiana. In recent years barbecued pork has become popular, although there are still regional favorites, such as pork roasts, pork chops, hams, and sausages. There is even a pork cake, which is popular in Indiana at Christmas. This moist cake contains either salt pork or sausage mixed with brown sugar, molasses, flour, citron, raisins, and spices.

"Whole-hog" sausage is made in Indiana from the lean loin and shoulder cuts. Traditionally, sausage was served for breakfast with pancakes and fried apple slices. Other Indiana breakfast favorites were fried apples with salt pork and ham with cream gravy and biscuits. Abraham Lincoln is supposed to have enjoyed both of these breakfasts.

A Covered Bridge Festival, which recreates rural life in nineteenth-century Indiana, has been held for a number of years every October in Parke County. The women, dressed in period costumes, prepare broilers (small chickens) on the grill and make wild-persimmon ice cream and other traditional foods of the times, such as fried-apple pies and corncob jelly. The latter is made by cooking red corncobs in a water and sugar mixture. Pectin is added to the delicately flavored syrup to make it congeal.

PERSIMMON PUDDING

At the beginning of the 1800s, early settlers in Indiana were supplementing their diets with plentiful, wild persimmons. They had been taught by the Indians how to use the fruit in a type of Indian bread. The Indians dried the persimmons like prunes before converting them into a dough that could be baked. The settlers soon devised their own recipes for persimmon breads, cakes, and puddings.

Serves 12

1 cup brandy

2 cups raisins, all dark or half dark and half light

1 cup sugar, or more if persimmons are not extremely ripe

2 cups all-purpose flour

1/8 teaspoon ground cloves

1/8 teaspoon nutmeg

2 teaspoons cinnamon

2 teaspoons baking soda

1/2 teaspoon salt

2 teaspoons vegetable oil

1 teaspoon vanilla extract

2 cups very ripe persimmon purée

2 cups chopped walnuts

3/4 cup milk

■

The day before you plan to make the pudding, add the brandy to the raisins, cover, and macerate for 24 hours.

Butter and flour a 9-inch angel food cake pan. (Two 8 x 4-inch loaf pans or smaller loaf pans may also be used.) Line the bottom of the pans with wax paper.

Combine all of the dry ingredients in a bowl. Combine the raisins and brandy, oil, vanilla, persimmon purée, and walnuts in another bowl. Add the dry ingredients alternately with the milk in thirds, blending well after each addition.

Pour the pudding into the prepared pan. If using smaller pans, fill only three-fourths full. Level the surface and bake in a preheated 325° F. oven for 1 1/4 to 1 1/2 hours. The pudding will bake in smaller pans for 1 to 1 1/4 hours. When done, the pudding should pull away from the sides slightly. It will be moist, but a cake tester should come out without any batter adhering to it.

Remove the pudding from the oven and cool it in the pan. Do not turn angel food cake pan upside down. When cool, remove the pudding from the pan and peel off the wax paper.

The persimmon pudding may be frozen after baking and removed from the freezer the night before serving. It can be served at room temperature or wrapped in foil and reheated in a preheated 300° F. oven for 15 minutes.

The pudding may be served with a vanilla sauce or the following topping.

Topping

1 cup whipping cream, softly whipped

1 tablespoon brandy

2 tablespoons sugar

Pinch of nutmeg

■

Combine the above ingredients and serve a spoonful on top of each slice of pudding.

PERSIMMONS AND COPPER by Joyce Pike, oil, 22 x 28 inches, courtesy of Miner's Gallery Americana, Carmel, California.

Popcorn

Indiana has been growing corn for popping since the time of the early settlers, who learned it from the Indians. By the 1930s popcorn had become so important in the state that the Indiana Agricultural Department funded the development of corn hybrids specifically for popcorn. The Indiana Agricultural Experiment Station at Purdue University became a pioneer in the development of popcorn hybrids, and the strains developed were adapted throughout the Midwest corn belt. Since then popcorn has grown into a half-billion-dollar industry nationwide.

There are now more than 30 hybrid varieties of popcorn seeds available. Hybrids are better than the natural varieties, because they produce a higher yield, and the stalks, which have superior strength, are resistant to rot. Most important, their kernels are more uniform and have better popping expansion.

Various popcorn hybrids produce different "flakes," as the popped product is called. Butterfly-like flakes are best for eating, while mushroom-like flakes are better for candy coating or flavoring. Popcorn pops because of the moisture content inside the kernel; a moisture content of 13.5 percent is standard. When heated the moisture turns to steam, and when the steam pressure is sufficient, the kernel pops.

Ducklings

Maple Leaf Farms of Milford, Indiana, is the largest producer of ducklings in the United States. Founded in 1958 on a farm two miles south of Milford, the company began producing processed ducks at the rate of 5,400 birds per week. In 1981 Maple Leaf Farms purchased its largest competitor, C & D Foods in Wisconsin.

Over the years the breeding, hatching, feeding, and growing of ducklings has become a sophisticated business. In recent years Maple Leaf Farms has bred a species of ducks from the French Muscoy duck, which is lighter in taste and leaner. They have named the breed Barbarie.

The company operates two hatcheries, which are capable of producing 270,000 ducklings per week. At one day old the little ducklings are delivered to 47 grow-out farms located in Indiana and neighboring states. The ducklings arrive at the farms weighing 2 ounces each and reach full growth in 49 days, with an average weight of five to six pounds. In order to support its feed requirements, Maple Leaf Farms owns and operates two feed mills, which produce the specified mix of feed.

Although industry became more important to Indiana's economy than agriculture after World War I, agriculture is still very vital to the state's economy. Indiana is second in the production of popcorn and spearmint, third in the harvest of corn. Spearmint and peppermint are grown in the former swamplands in the northern part of the state.

Duckling with Wild Rice Stuffing

Ducklings and geese were an intricate part of the cuisine of the European settlers of the Great Lakes region. Every farm family that had a pond raised ducks or geese, which they roasted for holiday meals. The preferred way of preparing a duck was to serve it with a crisp, crackling, brown skin. It was served with potato dumplings, and gravy was made with pan drippings.

The crisp skin of this duckling is flavored with an orange-maple glaze.

Serves 4

1 duckling (about 5 pounds)

Wild rice stuffing (recipe follows)

1/2 teaspoon salt

1/4 teaspoon pepper

1/4 teaspoon garlic powder

1/2 teaspoon onion powder

1/4 teaspoon ground marjoram

1/2 teaspoon dry rosemary leaves

1/3 cup orange juice

1/3 cup maple syrup

■

Cut the wing tips off the duckling. Rinse the bird and pat it dry. Fill the cavity with the stuffing, packing it in rather tightly. Fold the rear skin flaps over each other and secure with metal skewers.

Place the duckling in a 13 x 9-inch glass baking dish. Sprinkle with the salt, pepper, garlic powder, onion powder, and marjoram. Crush the rosemary leaves as they are being sprinkled on top of the duckling. Bake in a 325° F. oven for 2 3/4 hours. About every 45 minutes, remove the accumulated fat with a bulb baster and loosen the back of the duckling if it is sticking to the pan.

Combine the orange juice and maple syrup and generously baste the duckling. Increase oven heat to 350° F. and continue baking the bird for another 30 minutes, basting every 10 minutes (2 more bastings). Remove the duckling to a warm platter and cut into serving pieces. Serve with the wild rice stuffing.

Stuffing

3/4 cup wild rice

3/4 cup coarsely chopped mushrooms

1 small onion, chopped

1 stalk celery, chopped

1/3 cup chopped parsley

1/2 cup small fresh pineapple chunks

1/4 teaspoon pepper

1 egg, lightly beaten

■

Place the rice in a small-holed colander and then put the colander in a bowl. Pour hot water over the rice, submerging it completely. Let the rice stand for 30 minutes, then drain. Repeat this process two more times. The rice kernels should begin to open. Combine the rice with the rest of the stuffing ingredients.

MICHIGAN

THE EARLIEST EUROPEANS in the Michigan area were French explorers, traders, and missionaries in the late 1600s and early 1700s. The first big wave of immigration came nearly 100 years later, primarily from New England and New York. In the northern part of the state, settlements developed along the Great Lakes near mines on the Upper Peninsula and around sawmills located along rivers.

By 1859, twenty-two years after Michigan became a state, farm families were firmly established in Michigan's southern counties, where prairie grassland was plentiful for grazing dairy cows. Farmers grew wheat and produced milk, butter, and cheese. They raised hogs for meat, since cows were too precious to be eaten. Most farmers also had chickens and geese, and they grew their own produce. Many nineteenth-century Michigan farmers hunted wild game, and their wives tended the family vegetable gardens.

Ethnic Immigration

Michigan encouraged immigration starting in its early years of statehood. The state periodically sent promoters to Eastern cities, and even to Europe, to encourage settlement in Michigan. Mining developed on the Upper Peninsula around 1850. The mine workers came mainly from Cornwall, Ireland, Canada, Finland, and eastern Europe.

The mining families from Cornwall brought their Cornish pasties with them. This meat-and-vegetable combination encased in a pastry could easily be reheated in very cold weather on a "Cornish stove"—a shovel held over a candle down in the mine.

Many of the Cornish pasties gave the miners a complete lunch. The doughy envelope, shaped to fit into a miner's lunch pail, was filled with meat or fish at one end, vegetables in the middle, and fruit, particularly apples, at the other end. It was baked in the morning and wrapped in newspaper or a specially designed cotton pasty bag so that it would stay warm until noon. At lunchtime, the miner began eating the pasty at the meat end and worked his way through to dessert at the other end.

The pasty has now evolved into a large, half-moon of pastry filled with chopped meat and vegetables. It is sold at roadside stands on the Upper Peninsula. The 24th of May has been designated as Pasty Day in Michigan.

When the Finnish miners came to Michigan around 1900, they found the Cornish were already well established, and they adopted many of the Cornish traditions. The Finnish immigrants did bring their own recipes for pasties, however, as well as recipes for a flat rye bread called *Rieska*, and a Finnish cardamom bread. Their version of pasties was small filled pastries made of rye flour that were baked or fried and stuffed with ground meat and chopped carrots or fish fillets with vegetables. The Finnish name for these stuffed pasties is *Piirakkaa*. Today, Finnish specialities in upper Michigan include a rye-crusted fish pie called *Kalakukho*, a baked cheese called *Juustoa*, and an oven "pancake" called *Kropsua*.

In 1847 religious refugees from the Netherlands settled in Michigan in a town they named Holland. Other Dutch towns soon sprang up, patterned after the villages of their homeland, and the Dutch developed a broad belt of farmland from Grand Rapids to Lake Michigan. Long famous for their smoked and salted fish, roast goose, and other fowl, the Dutch were delighted with the fish and game birds of their new homeland.

The Dutch also found other familiar food ingredients in Michigan. The herrings of the Great Lakes were not unlike those of the North Sea. The Dutch soon began serving fresh lake herring with onion sauce or salting them away for longer keeping. They planted apple orchards, and when the apples were ripe the Dutch baked their famous *Hollandische Appel Kock*, Dutch apple cake. It had a yeast batter, which was topped with sweet apple slices and sprinkled with cinnamon and sugar. They also pickled sour cherries and served them as a relish with meats.

The Czechs and Moravians were important elements of Michigan's pioneer culture in the nineteenth century. Their weddings were festive occasions, and at the turn of the century usually entire communities were involved in the three-day celebrations. First, two women were selected to go around the neighborhood inviting guests and determining what these guests would furnish in the way of food. After the ceremony, usually in a Catholic church, there was an afternoon feast.

Soup always started the festivities. There were three or four kinds of meat, in addition to potatoes and vegetables. Baked goods and pastries such as *Vdolky, Kolache, Milosti, Baleshky,* and *Strudel* were served for dessert. *Milosti* was a delicate pastry covered with powdered sugar and often referred to as American angel wings.

Most of the pastries were of a rich dough with centers filled with fruit, jam, and nuts. Some had fruit on top of the dough.

Ukrainians came to Michigan in three main waves. The first was in the late 1800s, the second around 1922, and the third following the Second World War.

For Michigan Ukrainians, Christmas Eve is the most important time of the holiday season. The day before Christmas is a strict day of fasting—no food is eaten until *Sviat Vecheer*. This Holy Supper comprises a 12-course dinner prepared entirely without meat or dairy products. The 12 dishes symbolize the 12 Apostles at the Last Supper.

The meal starts with the appearance of the first star at sundown. At that time the head of the household leads all in prayer and a first course of *Kootya,* the symbolic Christmas dish of the Ukrainians, is served. It consists of cooked whole-grain wheat served with honey, ground poppy seeds, and chopped nuts. Each person must partake of each dish. Then 11 more foods are served, including Borscht (beet soup), *Pirohih* or *Varennikih* (cooked dumplings with a potato, sauerkraut, or plum filling), homemade twist breads, honey cake, poppy-seed cake, and *Pahmpooskih* (prune-filled cake). After dinner all present sing traditional Christmas carols and go to midnight Mass.

Soup was a mainstay of the Ukrainian diet and was served at nearly every meal throughout the year as either a hearty main course or a delicate broth. *Borscht* was a particular favorite of the Ukrainians. Mildly tart with beet flavor

CORNISH PASTIES

The Cornish families who settled in the mining regions of upper Michigan and Wisconsin brought recipes for pasties with them from their homeland. These meat-and-vegetable combinations were encased in a pastry and served as lunch for the miners. The filling included beef or pork, a potato, and any available vegetables, particularly cabbage or turnips. Some were structured so that the meat would be at one end of the dough casing, vegetables in the middle, and fruit at the other end. This gave the miner a complete meal.

The pasty has now evolved into one large or medium-size pastry filled with meat and vegetables.

Makes 8 medium pasties

Pastry

2 cups all-purpose flour

1/2 teaspoon salt

7 tablespoons lard or solid vegetable

   shortening or a combination of

   shortening and margarine

5 to 6 tablespoons cold water

■

Combine the flour and salt in a medium bowl. Cut in the shortening until the mixture resembles fine bread crumbs. Then add the water, a little at a time, until the dough can be formed into a ball. Wrap the dough in plastic wrap and refrigerate for 1 hour.

Meanwhile make the filling. Then roll out the dough very thin and cut into eight 6-inch circles. Put a heaping tablespoon of the filling on half of each

circle, fold the pastry, and seal the edges with a fork dipped in flour, pressing hard on the fork. Bake in a preheated 350° F. oven for 50 minutes to 1 hour, until the pasties are well browned.

Filling

1/2 pound lean round steak, ground

1/4 pound lean pork, ground

1/2 cup finely diced potatoes

1/2 cup finely diced turnips

1/2 cup finely shredded cabbage

1/2 teaspoon salt

1/4 teaspoon pepper

1/4 teaspoon dried thyme

1 egg beaten with 1 teaspoon water

■

Mix the filling ingredients together in a bowl.

CHERRY STRUDEL

Eastern European and German settlers of the Great Lakes region observed holidays and special occasions by baking strudels. They were not accustomed to having desserts everyday since in the old country they could not afford them. Although apple and cheese were the most popular fillings, the settlers also used Michigan blueberries and cherries.

If only one strudel is desired, use half of the dough and freeze the remainder. Also halve the filling ingredients. This thin strudel dough, traditionally stretched over a table, is merely folded over the filling, thus making preparation easier.

Makes 2 strudels or 16 servings

1 tablespoon vegetable oil

1 egg

1/3 cup warm water

1/4 teaspoon salt

1 1/2 cups all-purpose flour

6 cups pitted sweet cherries

1/4 cup sugar

1/2 cup chopped almonds

1 teaspoon almond extract

1/2 cup cherry preserves

1/3 cup melted butter or margarine

6 tablespoons fine dry bread crumbs

■

Beat together the oil, egg, water, and salt in a bowl. Gradually beat in the flour and beat until the dough pulls away from the sides of the bowl. Turn the dough onto a lightly floured board and knead several times until smooth and elastic.

Cover the dough and let it rest for 30 minutes. Cut it into two pieces.

While the dough is resting combine the cherries, sugar, almonds, almond extract, and cherry preserves in a bowl.

Roll out each piece of dough on a floured board or cloth to a 12- by 18-inch rectangle. The dough should be paper-thin. Brush each piece of dough with half of the melted butter and sprinkle evenly with half of the bread crumbs. Spread half the filling down the center of the dough lengthwise. Fold the dough over the filling on one side and then the other, carefully pinching the top together. Slide the strudel onto a greased baking sheet and brush with melted butter. Bake in a 400° F. oven for 40 to 45 minutes. Serve warm or cold, cutting the strudel into 2-inch slices.

predominating, it was made from a base of rich meat stock (except during Lent and on Christmas Eve). *Vushka,* tiny dumplings about the size of walnuts filled with meat or mushrooms, were enjoyed as an accompaniment to borsch or a plain broth.

If the Cornish immigrants had an "eye for ore," the German settlers had "eyes for the soil." Between 1890 and 1910 most of the fertile area of Michigan was settled by Germans, either from Germany or from Russia. The Germans from Russia became Michigan's prime farmers. They established fruit orchards in southwestern Michigan and also grew sugar beets, peppermint, dill, and cucumbers. The German-born Germans, who came to Michigan between 1840 and 1850, gravitated to the cities to seek business opportunities.

German farm wives were excellent cooks, especially skilled in baking cakes and pastries. In the Sebewaing area, which encompasses Huron and Tuscola Counties, a summer treat was *Hollerstreibli,* a deep-fried, pancake-like confection made from elderberry blossoms. In June and early July the larger, white blossom-heads of the elderberry plant were carefully gathered. The heads were dipped into a light batter of eggs, milk, flour, a little sugar, and a pinch of salt. Then they were deep fried until brown, drained, dusted with powdered sugar, and served with coffee as dessert.

Cereal City

Battle Creek was settled by the Seventh Day Adventists and became their headquarters. It also became known as the "Cereal City" as a result of the diet and health-care concerns of local Seventh Day Adventists.

One of its members, Ellen White, adopted the pure-food ideas of Sylvester Graham of Massachusetts (inventor of the Graham Cracker). On Christmas Day in 1865, she became convinced that the Adventists, who were frequently troubled with dyspepsia, should be treated in a sanitarium of their own. She helped establish a health facility in Battle Creek. The Seventh-Day Adventists named John Harvey Kellogg as director but first sent him to New York to receive medical training.

While studying medicine in New York, Kellogg breakfasted daily on seven graham crackers and an apple. Once a week he added a coconut to this diet and occasionally also potatoes and oatmeal. He became interested in developing healthy diets for the patients he was to eventually treat on his return to Battle Creek. While in New York he put together a workable formula for a ready-to-eat cereal and prepared his first health food, which he called Granola.

In 1876 Dr. Kellogg, having returned to the Battle Creek Health Sanitarium as director, introduced the idea of cold cereals for breakfast. In order to promote better nutrition, Dr. Kellogg invented toasted cornflakes and many other grain and nut products. He sold most of these products through mail order.

John Kellogg's theories of medical practice were ahead of his time. He conceived many of our modern ideas about nutrition, physiology, and fresh air. Thirty years after Dr. Kellogg started marketing cornflakes, his brother, W.K. Kellogg, founded the Kellogg Company. W.K. had become frustrated with patent infringements on his brother's cereals and the commercial success of rival health food producers. He formed the Kellogg

Company to mass produce and expand the market for his brother's cereals. Today Kellogg is a giant food company producing all types of ready-to-eat cereals and is still heavily promoting the original cornflakes.

Prior to the formation of Kellogg, a rival cereal company had been started by an Illinois businessman, C.W. Post. Mr. Post had come to the Battle Creek Sanitarium to recover his health. Convinced of the health benefits of Dr. Kellogg's foods, Post established his own medical facility in Battle Creek and began

the commercial marketing of his own health foods. He introduced Postum Cereal Coffee in 1895 and Grape Nuts cereal in 1898. By 1900 Post was running a million-dollar business.

Michigan Agriculture

Agriculture is Michigan's second leading industry after automobiles. With its unique geographic location, plentiful water, and diverse soil, Michigan ranks second in the nation in the diversity of its agricultural products. Four of the leading

BASKET OF CHERRIES by John F. Francis, oil, 15 x 19 inches, courtesy of Montgomery Gallery, San Francisco, California.

151

food crops of Michigan today are cranberries, grapes, blueberries, and asparagus, with cherries close behind.

Fruit growing started in Michigan in the spring of 1833, when E.D. Lay came to the area from New York to select a place for a nursery and greenhouse. In the fall of that year, he and his brother, Z.K. Lay, established a nursery at Ypsilanti with 25,000 trees they had brought with them from Rochester, New York. There were 130 varieties of apples, 75 of pears, 40 of peaches, and more than 100 varieties of other fruits, grapes, and berries.

A great variety of fruit and berry orchards now occupy about 215 miles along Lake Michigan from Benton Harbor to Traverse City. Many of these orchards originated from stock initially supplied by the Lays' nursery. They have survived and prospered, because the area is ideal for growing fruit, as the lake moderates extreme temperature fluctuations during the growing season.

The cultivation of cherries in Michigan began when early French colonists brought cherry pits from Normandy and planted them along the St. Lawrence River and throughout the Great Lakes area. Today, Michigan grows more than 75 percent of all red tart cherries raised in the United States. Almost all of the cherry trees grow within a few miles of Lake Michigan. The cool spring air off the lake prevents the budding of the cherry trees until the danger of frost is past. The densest concentration of cherry trees in the world, 22,600 in every square mile, is found on the lake's eastern shore in the area near Traverse City.

Some of the cherry crop is naturally preserved in the form of dried cherries. A special drying process preserves the flavor of fresh, tart Montmorency cherries for use year-round. Eight pounds of fresh cherries produce one pound of dried cherries. Due to the low natural sugar content of the tart cherry, a small amount of sugar is added prior to dehydration to make preserving possible.

Celery has been an important crop in Michigan for more than a hundred years. At supper one night in the 1850s, guests at the Burdick home in Kalamazoo were served a strange new green vegetable, which they were told was called celery. A few venturesome people tasted it but were not enthusiastic. James Taylor, who had grown this strange vegetable, was so disappointed in the diners' reactions that he gave up growing it. A Dutch farmer named DeBruin, who was also growing celery, was not so easily discouraged. He sent his children from door to door selling the new vegetable until the neighborhood accepted it. Today, the Kalamazoo area is nationally known for its celery.

In pioneer days dried beans were a mainstay of the Michigan diet, particularly on the Upper Peninsula. In Michigan baked beans were prepared by putting them in a pan with a topping of salt pork and baking them. When served the partially moist beans were cut in slices and served with a sauce of homemade ketchup.

Huron, Tuscola, and Saginaw Counties are the state's leading producers of dry, edible beans. The beans are planted in June and harvested from late summer to mid-fall. The dry bean varieties grown in Michigan include black turtle, cranberry, navy, and red kidney beans. Michigan beans are used in soups, casseroles, salads, and even sandwiches. Michigan-grown navy beans are the main ingredient in the famous Senate Bean Soup served at the Capitol in Washington, D.C.

Michiganians take particular pride in the state's annual crop of morels. For many decades they have picked morels in mid-May in the woods surrounding Boyne City. Morel hunting has become an annual festival, with competitions to see who can find the most. Morels camouflage themselves in leaves and underbrush and grow in the same places every year, under oak, tulip poplar, and old elms, as well as in abandoned apple orchards and burned-over fields.

The Fishing Industry

Many of the early Michigan settlers subsisted on fish from the Great Lakes during their first years. White fish, perch, and lake trout used to be plentiful, but their number have been greatly reduced by sea lamprey. In recent years the lakes have been restocked with Chinook and coho salmon. Today, Great Lakes fisheries send a large number of fish to market.

Smelt fishing in the Great Lakes has long been popular. Smelt will not budge until the water is 36 degrees Fahrenheit or below and are best caught at night when they are moving. Usually around midnight, a fishing supervisor will turn lights on along the beach, and men and women will surge into the water with nets. As soon as the fishing supervisor decides they have caught enough, the lights are turned off. If the smelt run is large, this process may be repeated again during the night and early morning. Traditionally, smelt are fried and eaten with potatoes.

MINNESOTA

WHEAT AND FLOUR have been synonymous with Minnesota since the days of the early settlers. The first flour mill in Minnesota was built near Fort Snelling in 1823 by Colonel Josiah Snelling. The 16-foot square mill was located on the Mississippi River at the Falls of St. Anthony in what is now Minneapolis.

Colonel Snelling insisted that his soldiers grow and mill their own wheat so that the fort could be self-sufficient. Unfortunately, the soldiers were not good millers. They let the wheat mold, and the bread baked from the flour was black and bitter tasting. Even with bad flour, the mill and the fort remained in existence as a frontier post until the mid-1800s.

In the 1850s most Minnesota farmers raised just enough wheat to supply their family with flour for a year. The farmer took his wheat to a nearby mill, and the millers received a portion of the flour in payment for the grinding. As more wheat was raised, farmers would trade their flour for groceries, clothing, tools, and other necessities of life.

Farmers soon found that they needed a market for their surplus wheat. Gradually middlemen, located in small farming towns, began buying wheat and selling it to eastern mills. The coming of the railroads provided storage and shipping for the wheat. Railroad companies built grain elevators alongside the tracks to store the farmers' wheat until it was shipped by rail to Minneapolis or Duluth. In these cities the grain was stored in huge terminal elevators to await shipment to mills in the East by railroad and then to Europe by boat.

Many of the men who built the first flour mills at the Falls of St. Anthony were lumbermen who wanted to provide flour for their nearby lumber camps. They soon discovered that flour milling was more profitable than lumbering.

Pillsbury

Charles Pillsbury of New Hampshire arrived in Minneapolis in 1869. With no experience in flour milling, the 26-year old Pillsbury and his relatives bought a one-third interest in the run-down Minneapolis Flour Mill on the Mississippi River at the Falls of St. Anthony.

Pillsbury used a little wooden shack as an office and dealt with each farmer individually. "The other fellows in the business rather pitied me," he recalled, "and said that another poor devil had got caught in the milling business of which he would soon get enough." To everyone's surprise the Pillsbury Mill showed a profit the first year.

Millers of that period marked the finest grades of flour with three Xs. Charles Pillsbury added a fourth X to show that his mill's flour was the best and the famous trademark "Pillsbury's BEST" was born.

On October 12, 1882, Pillsbury's giant "A" mill, the world's biggest flour mill, set a one-day production record of 5,107 barrels of flour. Five years later, Pillsbury became the world's largest flour miller.

Over the decades, Pillsbury broadened its consumer appeal. In 1900 the company held its first recipe contest, offering cash prizes of $680. Four years later, "Pillsbury's BEST" flour won three grand prizes at the St. Louis World's Fair, and the company published its first recipe collection, "Book for a Cook." By 1929 Pillsbury cooking shows were being broadcast on national radio.

In the late 1930s and early 1940s, Pillsbury diversified into flour-related convenience-food products such as Corn Meal and Cake, Pancake, Pie Crust, and Hot Roll Mixes. In 1949 Pillsbury staged the first national cooking competition at the Waldorf Astoria Hotel in New York City and called it the Grand National Recipe and Baking Contest. It was planned as a one-time event but became an American institution—"The Pillsbury Bake-Off Contest." The Streusel Spice Cake Mix is the result of the Grand Prize Winner of the 1972 Bake-Off.

Pillsbury's line of vegetable and side dishes is a result of the company's acquisition in 1979 of another Minnesota company, Green Giant. Processed vegetables started in Minnesota in 1903, when a young promoter from Baltimore met with 14 local businessmen in a harness shop in Le Sueur, Minnesota, to convince them to start a corn cannery. That first year the Minnesota Valley Canning Company packed 11,750 cases of white cream-style corn.

In 1921 Ward Cosgrove, a director of the company, returned from Europe with some green peas, an English garden variety called "Prince of Wales." He named them "Green Giant." The name stuck, and the first "Green Giant," a scowling figure wearing a bearskin, appeared on a can of peas in 1925. Several years later, Leo Burnett, a Chicago advertising man, gave him a suit of leaves and a "Ho Ho Ho." The Jolly Green Giant was born.

By 1950 the Minnesota Valley Canning Company disappeared behind the trademark it had created and officially became the Green Giant Company. The Green Giant became an animated televi-

WILD AND WHITE RICE SALAD

Wild rice is considered to be the only native American grain, although technically it is not a grain at all, but a wild grass. It grows wild in the lakes and rivers of Minnesota, upper Michigan, and Wisconsin. The early French explorers, who first experienced the nutty taste sensation of wild rice, named it "crazy oats." Today, much of Minnesota's wild rice is harvested by the Ojibwa Indians, whose harvesting methods are protected by Minnesota laws.

Serves 8

1/4 cup wild rice

1 cup long-grain white rice

2 1/2 cups water

1/4 cup diced green pepper

1/4 cup diced red pepper

1/4 cup diced celery

5 water chestnuts, finely chopped

1/4 cup sliced black olives

2 scallions, finely chopped

Salt and pepper, to taste

Sweet and Sour Creamy Dressing (recipe

   follows)

■

Place the wild rice in a small bowl and pour boiling water over it to cover by 1/2-inch. Let sit for 30 minutes. Drain the water from the wild rice and place it with the white rice in a saucepan. Add the water and bring to a boil; cover and cook on low heat until the rice is tender, about 25 minutes.

In a large bowl combine the rice with the remaining ingredients, except the dressing, stirring gently until mixed. Add enough of the Sweet and Sour Creamy Dressing to moisten the salad ingredients. If necessary season with salt and pepper. Place the rice salad in a covered container and chill for 4 hours or overnight.

Sweet and Sour Creamy Dressing

3/4 cup plain low-fat yogurt

1/4 cup buttermilk

2 tablespoons mayonnaise

1 tablespoon milk

1 tablespoon cider vinegar

1 tablespoon sugar

1 teaspoon Dijon mustard

1/2 teaspoon celery seed

Pinch of cayenne pepper

Salt and white pepper, to taste

■

Combine the dressing ingredients in a bowl and whisk until smooth. The dressing may also be prepared in a food processor or blender.

name was Lively Willoughby. He sliced and stacked unbaked biscuits, wrapped them in foil, packed them in cardboard tubes, and put them in the icebox. The compressed dough, much to the chagrin of Lively's wife, turned their kitchen into a shooting gallery. When removed from the icebox, the tubes exploded. Eventually Lively perfected the process and sold it to Ballard and Ballard Flour Company. Pillsbury obtained the process when it acquired Ballard in 1952.

In 1965 Pillsbury asked the Leo Burnett Company to create an animated character who would help inform the public about refrigerated doughs. The result was the Pillsbury Doughboy with bright blue eyes, a giggle, and a tummy made for playful poking.

During World War II American soldiers in Italy acquired a taste for an ancient concoction of dough, cheese, and tomatoes. Today, pizza is one of the most popular foods in America, and Pillsbury is the world's largest producer of frozen pizzas.

Pillsbury entered the pizza business in 1975, when it acquired Totino's Finer Foods, a regional pizza company in Minneapolis founded by Rose and Jim Totino, the children of Italian immigrants. Pillsbury produces about 300 million pizzas a year—more than one million every working day.

Grain and the Grain Exchange

Minneapolis would not have become an important milling city without the Falls of St. Anthony on the Mississippi River. They provided the power needed to run the mills. By 1890 Minneapolis had become the largest milling center in the world.

Fire had always been a hazard to the

sion character in the early 1960s with his own song ("Good Things from the Garden") and was joined by the Little Green Sprout in 1971. Today, Pillsbury, under the Green Giant trademark, is one of the largest processors of vegetables in the world.

Prepared dough is another success story of Pillsbury. It begins in 1930 with a baker in Louisville, Kentucky, whose grain business, both in the mills and in the gigantic wooden grain elevators. Near the turn of the century, Frank H. Peavey, who owned many grain elevators, decided to solve the fire problem by building cement elevators. At the time most people thought that the structure would collapse if the grain was drawn out at the bottom, and they nicknamed the cement elevators, "Peavey's Folly." In May 1899 hundreds gathered to watch the first grain flow from a cement elevator. It worked perfectly and became a model for the thousands of grain elevators throughout the country.

The Minneapolis Grain Exchange is the key marketplace where grain is sold. The Grain Exchange, formed in the 1870s, gives the buyers and sellers a place to meet.

An example of how grain is sold is that of a Crookston, Minnesota, elevator man, who has bought wheat from local farmers and wants to sell it. He ships a carload of wheat to the Minneapolis exchange. There the box car is opened by a state official, and the wheat is tested and graded according to U.S. Department of Agriculture standards. After the grain has been graded, information about the grade, ownership, and origin is written on a card and put into the sample pan at the Grain Exchange. The car of grain is now ready to be sold.

A commission man, who is a grain-marketing expert, represents the Crookston elevator man and will sell his wheat on the exchange. Commission merchants rent tables in the exchange, where they display pans containing samples of grain that is for sale. The buyers, who represent millers, cereal manufacturers, and feed manufacturers, look over the samples. They make bids, and the highest bidder receives the carload of grain.

Wild Rice

Although wheat growing and flour production is less than 200 years old in Minnesota, the gathering of another grain, wild rice, goes back thousands of years. One of the nomadic Indian tribes, the Ojibwa, settled in northern Minnesota and Wisconsin because of the abundance of a rare, wild aquatic grass they called *manomin*. We know it as wild rice, although technically it is kernels of a grass. At one time this wild rice supplied 25 percent of the Indians' food in the Minnesota lake region.

Wild rice has grown for centuries in Minnesota's shallow lakes that are now a part of the state's Indian reservations. The method used by the Indians to harvest the rice has remained unchanged over the years. Minnesota state laws now regulate every aspect of the traditional wild rice harvest on these lakes, setting an opening day for the season, protecting Indian rights over water on their reservations, and forbidding the use of any harvesting tools other than Indian-style sticks.

The Ojibwas begin their harvest in late August. Two people in a canoe glide slowly through the aquatic grass. One person poles and guides the canoe while the other, using a pair of cedar sticks called "knockers," harvests the rice. One of the sticks is used to bend the grass over the canoe and the other stick to beat the rice heads gently, shaking the kernels into the bottom of the canoe. This is done on both sides of the canoe alternately, while the canoe is moving. When the grass is released, some kernels fall into the water, becoming seeds for next year's crop.

After the rice is unloaded from the canoe, it is parched. This used to be done by spreading the kernels on birch-

bark sheets or flat rocks to dry by the heat of the sun or over smoky fires. When white settlers introduced metal pots to the Ojibwas, they began toasting the rice in caldrons set over a wood fire, stirring the grains with a canoe paddle.

The heated rice is then poured into a shallow hole that has been dug in the ground and lined with animal skins. Wearing moccasins, the Indian men literally dance on the rice to loosen the hulls. Finally, the parched rice is poured onto a blanket, so that the wind can blow away the chaff.

Commercial cultivation of wild rice in flooded fields has been in existence for about 20 years in Minnesota. At harvest time the water is drained off and the rice is harvested mechanically. Commercial yield per acre is about five times greater than the traditional pond cultivation, although the Ojibwa claim mechanically harvested wild rice lacks the delicate flavor of rice harvested in the traditional manner.

Agriculture

Minnesota's major agricultural industry is dairying, closely followed by grain. The state has been called the "bread and butter" state, because of its top ranking in butter production and its great flour-milling operations.

Minnesota encourages small dairy farmers to make cheese, believing it is one of the best ways to maintain the family farm and provide employment opportunities in rural areas. The University of Minnesota researched cheese-making in Holland and acquired a Gouda recipe, which it then passed on to a number of small dairy farmers. They all share the trademark Minnesota Farmstead Gouda.

PEELING ONIONS by Lilly Martin Spencer, oil, 36 x 29 inches, courtesy of Richard York Gallery, New York, New York.

Much of Minnesota's agriculture is concentrated in two major grain regions, the northwest part of the state and the Red River Valley, which straddles 12 counties across the Minnesota-North Dakota border. The northwestern region has a shorter growing season and is a major producer of spring wheat, as well as oats, barley, sugar beets, and sunflowers.

The Red River Valley grows primarily grain, potatoes, and sugar beets, since it has rich soil and plentiful rainfall. Settlers in the valley in the early 1800s soon established world records in grain production. Early Scandinavian, German, and Irish immigrants started growing potatoes in the Red River Valley, and today, nearly 200,000 acres in the valley produce more than 15 million tons of potatoes annually.

Sugar Beets

Farmers in the fertile Red River Valley experimented with sugar beets as early as the 1880s. By 1920 sugar beets were grown in commercial quantities and shipped to a processing plant at Chaska, Minnesota, about 300 miles away.

As farmers' enthusiasm for the potential of the sugar beet grew, so did the need for a processing facility. The Denver-based American Beet Sugar Company built the first valley sugar-processing plant in East Grand Forks, Minnesota, in 1926. In 1944 the company, which by then had changed its name to American Crystal Sugar, built a second plant in the Red River Valley with a capacity of 4,000 tons of beets per day. Over the years more plants have been added. Today, American Crystal is a cooperative owned by 16,500 beet growers, making the Red River Valley "America's Sugarbowl."

When winter snows melt and the danger of frost has passed, sugar-beet seeds are planted, and seedlings emerge in about five days. In three to five weeks, they are ready for cultivation and thinning with a machine that electronically scans the rows and removes seedlings where the stands are too thick. Some fields are "planted to stand," which eliminates the need for a thinning operation.

When full grown, some five months later, the average sugar beet is a foot-long, cream-colored root, weighing about two pounds. A cluster of eight-inch stems rises from the root's crown, bearing broad, dark-green, knee-high leaves. By harvest each root contains 15 to 16 percent sugar—14 to 15 teaspoons. Harvesting is done by specially designed machines; one cuts off the tops, and another lifts the beets from the ground.

Log Cabin Syrup

Pure maple sugar and syrups were expensive liquid sweeteners, even in the late 1800s. Supplies were not always sufficient to meet the demand, even though prices were high for the average consumer. People started using alternative products such as corn syrup or molasses.

A St. Paul, Minnesota, grocer named Patrick J. Towle decided that if he could blend cane sugar syrup and maple syrup, he could provide his customers with true maple flavor in a syrup that they could afford. In 1887 he invented a successful formula, thereby pioneering the blending of syrups.

Towle gave the name Log Cabin to his new product. He packaged it in a tin can shaped like a log cabin in honor of his boyhood hero, Abraham Lincoln. The tin became as much a tradition at Sunday breakfast as pancakes, waffles, and French toast. During World War II, when tin "went to war," the familiar little cabin was replaced with a reproduction of an antique glass bottle. The Towle Syrup Company joined General Foods in 1927 and is now a part of Kraft General Foods.

Ethnic Food Heritages

The people of Minnesota are from a very diverse ethnic heritage—British, Germans, Scandinavians, Finns, Italians, Slavs, and more recently, refugees from Southeast Asia. The Scots, Welsh, and Canadians were some of the earliest settlers of Minnesota, while the greatest number of British arrived in 1890 to work in the mines on the Vermilion and Mesabi Iron Ranges.

Those of British heritage still cook some of their traditional dishes. They are fond of puddings and fruitcakes, and fish is still an integral part of the British cookery. Bubble and Squeak is a unique British combination of cabbage and mashed potatoes. The name is derived from the noise it makes while being sautéed.

Some British baking traditions still exist in Minnesota. Cooks of British heritage flavor many of their breads with saffron. The Scots make shortbread, a mixture of butter, flour, and sugar, which was traditionally mixed by hand. Early British Minnesotans also adapted some of their neighbors' baking practices. They observed that their neighbors decorated their cookies with sugars, candies, and other toppings and soon followed suit.

The Germans are Minnesota's largest ethnic group, having immigrated to the area from the 1830s to the present day. Nineteenth-century German immigrants found the land suitable for raising the type of food they enjoyed.

Many of the early German settlers baked rye bread every Saturday and as a special treat also made *Zwiebelkuchen* (onion pie). On Saturday nights most German families dined on cold, sliced German sausages, bread and cheese, fruit *kuchen* (pastry), and homemade beer.

Sunday dinner was usually special—a roast, chicken, or Wiener schnitzel; dumplings or *Spätzel;* and a sweet-and-sour salad. If Wiener schnitzel was served it was accompanied by a warm potato salad.

Maultaschen, a speciality of Württemberg, Germany, continued to be a favorite dish of many German settlers in Minnesota. The pockets of noodle dough resembled a large ravioli and were filled with ground, smoked ham mixed with onions, eggs, and parsley. As a special treat spinach was added to the filling.

The Scandinavian immigrants—Norwegian, Danish, Swedish, and Finnish—found Minnesota to be very similar to Scandinavia, with fir trees, bright lakes, long winters, and deep snows. The housewives were delighted with the new white flour that yielded cakes and bread much lighter than those of their native land. Meatballs of beef and pork, American-style bacon, corn, and a strange fruit called watermelon became a part of the immigrants' diet.

Initially, Norwegians in Minnesota did not have their native dish, *Lutefisk*—a type of cod that was preserved with lye and thoroughly rinsed before boiling. Once salted cod from Massachusetts became available, the pioneers again prepared their native dish. *Lutefisk* is steamed, served with melted butter and boiled potatoes, and often is served with *Lefse,* the Norwegian flat bread. Leftover cold *Lutefisk* is eaten the next day wrapped in *Lefse.*

The Danish immigrants found many of their traditional cooking ingredients in Minnesota. Their kitchen gardens had large patches of parsley, carrots, peas, and kale, since Danish cooking makes liberal use of vegetables, especially in soups.

Parsley predominates Danish cookery, not only as a garnish but as a flavoring in cooked dishes, soups, and spreads. Fish in the Danish household was often boiled and served with a sauce, preferably a *Sennep Saus* (mustard sauce).

The Danish tradition of smorgasbord, also adopted by other Scandinavians, is one that has been passed down through generations of Danish Minnesotans and is often used at community fund raisers. The smorgasbord is credited with being the forerunner of our buffet dinner.

At a smorgasbord most of the foods are thinly sliced, including the underlying bread. The combination of ingredients is flexible but must be eaten in a certain order—herring to fish, to chicken or egg salads, next meats, pâté, sausages, and *Frikadeller* (meatballs); and finally cheeses with *Havarti, bleu,* and *Camembert* being most commonly served. Danish open-faced sandwiches are never eaten with the fingers but with a knife and fork. Traditionally, ice-cold aquavit, a colorless Scandinavian liquor distilled from grain or potatoes and flavored with caraway seeds, is served with the first and last course, and beer is served in between.

The pioneer Swedes, many of whom were refugees from poverty and adversity in their homeland, depended on staples for their diet. Homemade soups, potatoes, fish, and various grains were the mainstay of their early cuisine. Soups, such as pea, cabbage, ox-tail, and chicken (usually with dumplings) are still favorites of Swedish-Minnesotans' cuisine. In the summer they enjoy cold fruit soups.

Swedish-Americans still serve some of their traditional dishes, such as herring with flat bread, smoked fish, and *Limpa* (yeast bread) flavored with raisins and anise. They also serve *Kroppkaka,* which is a dumpling made from potatoes and flour and boiled in ham-flavored water, Swedish meatballs, and a variation of them called *Fiskbollar* (steamed fish balls).

The earliest Finnish immigrants in Minnesota homesteaded in the south-central part of the state in 1864. They also settled in the northern iron ranges, where they combined farming with work in the lumber camps and iron mines.

Finnish food was plain and basic, influenced by both Sweden and Russia. The staples of Finnish cooking were hardy root crops and salt fish, which would last through the winter. The Finnish soups, stews, and casseroles were based on hearty ingredients, such as rutabagas, potatoes, rice, milk, and fish combined with minimal seasonings.

The early Finnish-Minnesotans ate little meat, preferring fish, either fried, baked, or in a stew with onions, potatoes, and milk or water. They did make cabbage rolls filled with ground meat, and meat *Mojakka,* a stew of short ribs or cubed beef, carrots, potatoes, rutabagas, cabbage, and other seasonal vegetables.

The great variety of Finnish breads indicates that bread was a most important part of the meal. Rye and barley were the popular flours for bread, since both grains grow in the short growing season in Minnesota. Wheat flour, unknown to Finns, was not used by the early Finnish immigrants.

Minnesota posed a culinary challenge to most Italians, since much of their native ingredients were not available and could not be grown in the short growing season. The early Italian immigrants relied heavily on what they called peasant food—polenta, rice dishes such as *risotto,* and pasta. Polenta is a traditional Italian dish made from a hot cornmeal mush that is cooled on a board, sliced, and baked or fried. Their preferred meats were veal, chicken, and some pork, although they used ground beef for meatballs and meat sauces.

Once established, Italian settlers tried to recreate the food habits of their native land. They gathered mustard and dandelion greens on the banks of the Mississippi River and raised gardens of tomatoes, squash, peppers, beans, and herbs. They built community ovens to bake bread, made their own pasta, and bought grapes to make wine.

The Italians also established food companies to produce their native foods. In 1889 the Italian Macaroni and Vermicelli Company was founded in St. Paul, and 20 years later, the Duluth Macaroni Company began marketing its pasta throughout northeastern Minnesota. Today, the Stella Cheese Company, founded by Italian immigrants, is one of the largest producers of Italian cheeses in the United States. Jeno's, Totino's, and Mama Vitale's frozen foods are also Minnesota food companies of Italian heritage.

Southern Slavs, mostly Croatians, Slovenians, and Serbs, settled in Minnesota between 1900 and 1920. They came either to St. Paul to work in the meat-packing industry or to northern Minnesota to work in the iron mines. Being accustomed to fresh fruit, they planted apple, cherry, apricot, and olive trees. Because of the harsh climate, the apricots and olives did not survive. Slavic cooking is primarily based on soups, stews, and other combination dishes. Most of the South Slavic recipes blended Turkish and classic Eastern European cooking. The former used stuffings in vegetables and pastries, and the latter was famous for soups, stews, sauerkraut dishes, sausages, grilled meats, and filled pancakes.

The kitchen was the center of the Slavic home, where women worked all day to feed their families and their boarders. They knew how to prepare meals cheaply and how to stretch their meat supply.

Many Southern Slavs became boardinghouse operators, first welcoming a member of the family from the old country, then people from their old village. In the late 1800s five to ten dollars a month was charged for a room, laundry, and three meals—two at the boardinghouse and a lunch pail for work. Often there were two 12-hour shifts of workers who exchanged beds—one slept while the other worked.

Cooking for a crowd day in and day out was hard work and most Slavic women had only their children to help them. The day started at five a.m. Some women slept in their clothes in order not to waste a moment. Breakfast had to be prepared for both shifts and lunch pails packed. Breakfast consisted of eggs, pork chops, potatoes or hot cereal, and bread. When breakfast was over, the women started on the day's cooking and the baking of bread and pastry. The evening meal usually began with soup, followed by two meats accompanied by potatoes, vegetables, and a salad. The meal typically ended with a dessert of fruit and pastry.

At the close of the Vietnam War, some of the Hmong people of northern Laos, aided by various organizations, came to Minnesota (about 10,000 now live in the Twin Cities). These people brought yet another dimension to the varied cuisine of Minnesota. Although the staple of their diet is rice, they have learned to adjust to the foods of America, mixing it with their own native Asian dishes. One thing that makes Hmong meals unique is the absence of desserts or sweets.

OHIO

OHIO WAS SETTLED by veterans of the Revolutionary War who were given land grants (called bounty lands) in recognition of their service to the new nation. Settlers from New England began flocking westward along the Buffalo-Cleveland route soon after the Greeneville Treaty of 1795, which promised safety from Indian attacks.

Immediately after the Revolutionary War, Congress persuaded the states to cede their rights to western lands to the federal government "to be disposed of for the common benefit of the United States." Thus land disputes would be settled, and revenue from the sale of these lands would aid the impoverished young country. As soon as population growth warranted, new states would be formed and admitted to the Union.

Certain areas were retained by the states. Virginia kept the Virginia Military District in the southwestern part of Ohio, and Connecticut reserved three million acres in what is now northeastern Ohio. This land became known as the Western Reserve.

Half a million acres of Connecticut's Western Reserve were set aside as the "Sufferer's Tract" or "Firelands" and were given to those whose homes had been burned by the British during the Revolution. Eighteen hundred and seventy people from Connecticut relocated to the Firelands, bringing with them their New England customs and cuisine. These settlers were industrious and ambitious people and rapidly turned the fertile soil of North Central Ohio into rich farmland. They helped build turnpikes, canals, and later, railroads.

THE OLD RED MILL by Jasper Francis Cropsey, oil, 48 1/2 x 84 1/4 inches, courtesy of The Chrysler Museum, Norfolk, Virginia.

Ohio Pioneers

The pioneers in Ohio experienced many of the same lifestyles as their forefathers had when they settled the East Coast. Cooking was done in iron pots in the open hearth. Food was raised or hunted. The pioneer women baked once a week in the hearth oven. Cookies and bread were baked first, followed by cakes and pies. By the 1850s many Ohio homes, including some of the log cabins, had a wood-burning, cast-iron stove for cooking.

These early settlers of Ohio were innovative in providing labor-saving devices for food-producing tasks. Even the family dog contributed. Dog-tread power was used to churn butter, winnow the grain, turn the cooking spit, and wash the clothes.

Almost every farm home had a bean separator, since beans were a major ingredient in the farm diet. This handmade machine, which threshed dried beans, could be operated by dog power. A primitive corn sheller was invented in 1860. Other items of the early Ohio kitchens were sausage stuffers and a lard press.

In the developing years of Ohio, flour mills were the first signs of stability in a new settlement. There was a mill on nearly every stream, with a huge waterwheel powering a grindstone that turned the farmers' wheat and corn into flour and meal.

Mills were meeting places where isolated farmers were glad to wait for their flour or meal by enjoying gossip and companionship. To avoid a long ride, many people settled near a mill, thereby forming communities. Mills were dry and dusty, and in the early days many were destroyed by fire but were rebuilt again and again.

UPSIDE-DOWN APPLE TART

Johnny Appleseed crisscrossed the Ohio Valley and Indiana in the early 1800s planting apple seeds, which created the first orchards in that region. He believed that fruit was second only to religion.

The apple trees were a welcome addition to the settlers of the new Northwest Territory, because they provided fresh or dried fruit year-round for pies, tarts, apple butter, and cider.

Serves 8

8 tablespoons (1 stick) butter or margarine

1 1/4 cups all-purpose flour

2 teaspoons sugar

1/2 cup ground almonds

1 egg yolk

3 tablespoons ice water

■

Cut the butter into the flour in a bowl until the mixture resembles fine crumbs. Stir in the sugar and almonds. Combine the egg yolk and water and slowly stir into the flour mixture with a fork. Stir well to combine. Then, using your hands, shape the dough into a ball. Place the dough between two large sheets of plastic wrap and, with a rolling pin, roll the dough 1 inch larger than a 9-inch round cake pan. Carefully place the dough in the refrigerator to chill for 20 minutes, while preparing the apples.

Apple Topping

3 tablespoons butter or margarine

1/4 cup sugar

5 large tart apples such as Granny Smith, peeled, cored, and sliced very thin

1/2 teaspoon cinnamon

1/2 teaspoon nutmeg

Whipped cream, for garnish

■

Place the butter and sugar in a 9-inch round cake pan and melt the mixture over low heat. Continue cooking, stirring constantly with a wooden spoon, until the mixture is a light golden brown. Remove from heat, cool slightly, and add the apple slices, making sure that the top is reasonably flat. Sprinkle the apples with the cinnamon and nutmeg.

Unwrap the pastry and fit it over the apples, tucking the edges under the crust. Bake in a preheated 400° F. oven for 30 to 35 minutes, or until the crust is lightly browned.

After removing the tart from the oven, immediately turn it upside down on a serving plate. Leave the pan on the tart for a few minutes to let all of the juice permeate the crust; then remove. Serve warm or cool with whipped cream, if desired.

Many settlers brought their native customs and cuisines to Ohio. The transplanted New Englanders brought with them their recipes for baked beans with salt pork and molasses. Dumplings made with sour milk, chicken potpie, fudge cake with boiled frosting, and other Yankee dishes soothed the homesick pangs of the early pioneers. Some of the early settlers used bread stuffings for pork and beef, mainly to stretch a meal. Today, stuffings are still popular in Ohio cuisine.

The Germans brought their love for sausages, sauerkraut, and hearty meat and potato meals. Czech immigrants brought one of their favorite dishes—fish boiled with spices and served with a black sauce of prunes, raisins, and almonds.

Johnny Appleseed

No fruit was more important to pioneer life than the apple. A valuable addition to the pioneers' limited diet of pork and corn, apples could be used in many different ways—eaten fresh, cooked, dried, or fermented for cider, applejack, and vinegar.

John Chapman, better known as Johnny Appleseed, left a trail of apple orchards throughout Ohio, Indiana, and Illinois. Born in Massachusetts in 1774, he was a vegetarian and a religious disciple of Emanuel Swedenborg, a Swedish mystic and philosopher. Chapman spent 40 years in the wilderness planting apple trees and preaching the Gospel. He is said to have gone barefoot most of the time, clad only in a coffee sack.

Johnny Appleseed, carrying a spade and a burlap bag of apple seeds, began planting and pruning apple trees through-out the Ohio Valley at the age of twenty-seven. This strangely clothed visionary was seen wandering through the countryside planting apple orchards in whatever fertile areas he could find. On return trips to these areas, he tended and transplanted the young trees so that even the most primitive cabin had an orchard surrounding it.

He traveled alone, carrying his kitchen, an inverted saucepan, on his head. Johnny Appleseed never married, but he hoped that for his life of celibacy, he would be granted two wives in heaven. He preached that "fruit is next to religion."

Although apple trees are most often propagated by grafting, Johnny Appleseed denounced this method of cultivation as sinful. He grew his trees only from seed, most of which he obtained from the waste material of the cider presses in western Pennsylvania.

Cincinnati Cuisine

Many of the first permanent settlers of Ohio were Germans from Pennsylvania. In the nineteenth century more than 10,000 Germans settled in Cincinnati, and the community was nicknamed "Over the Rhine." Beer gardens, German restaurants, and bakeries were prevalent. The area had an average beer consumption of 30 gallons per person per year, more than any other city in the country.

Cincinnati was established after the War of 1812 and became an elegant metropolis. Oysters were the luxury food there, arriving by "oyster express." This involved shipping oysters from Baltimore, Maryland. The freshly harvested oysters were packed in straw soaked in seawater, then driven in fast wagons to Pittsburgh, where the barrels of oysters were loaded on riverboats. After arriving in Cincinnati the oysters

were kept alive for weeks in tanks of saltwater sprinkled with cornmeal. The oyster craze, which swept not only Cincinnati but the entire country, resulted in hundreds of fancy oyster parlors selling oysters raw, stewed, fried, baked, and in pies. Rich people ate them year-round, even for breakfast.

In the mid-nineteenth century Cincinnati was the world's greatest pork-packing center, turning hogs from Ohio, Indiana, and Kentucky into hams and sausages. Many German recipes were used for the sausages. The city also produced related products such as lard, oil, soap, and candles.

Ohio Wine

The most important historical agricultural contribution of Ohio was the creation of America's first wine industry. Ohio's winemaking history can be traced to the early 1800s, when the first vineyards were planted along the banks of the Ohio River near Cincinnati. In the 1820s Nicholas Longworth began experimenting with the Catawba grape for winemaking, and by 1830 wine had become an important product for Ohio. In 1860 Ohio led the nation in wine production. Many of the German immigrants brought old-world winemaking skills to Ohio and founded numerous wineries in the state.

At the turn of the century, the shores of Lake Erie became recognized for their optimum grape-growing conditions, with the lake acting as a temperature regulator and breezes from the lake providing the necessary ventilation to keep the vines free of disease. Today, Ohio's wine industry has grown to every region of the state, encompassing 50 wineries with about 2,000 acres of vineyards growing both European varieties and American hybrids.

Other Ohio Foods

Until after the Civil War, yeast for bread baking was primarily made at home from potato skins or leftover beer. The result was a haphazard product that varied from batch to batch, often producing a bread that was barely edible.

A young Austrian, Charles Fleischmann, revolutionized the American baking industry. Fleischmann had come to the United States in 1865 to attend the wedding of a sister. Astonished by what he called the poor taste of American bread, he went back to Austria to collect samples of the yeast used in making Viennese breads.

When Fleischmann returned to America with his brother Maximilian, they took their yeast samples to James M. Gaff, a well-known Cincinnati distiller. The three went into business together and in 1868 began manufacturing the country's first standardized yeast. The advantage of the new yeast was that it was created under rigid controls and compressed into cakes of uniform size and effectiveness. Two years after the first yeast production, the partners used their expertise in the distilling field by forming The Fleischmann Distilling Company and producing America's first gin.

Liederkranz cheese, the ripe, soft, strongly odorous cheese in the cardboard box, was first commercially produced in Van Wert, Ohio, in 1926 when the Monroe Cheese company of Monroe, New York, moved there. The move was prompted by the company's search for a more dependable supply of rich, fresh milk. Three years later, the Borden Company acquired the business and has been producing Liederkranz cheese ever since.

Liederkranz cheese, an American invention, was perfected by one of Monroe's New York employees. In the 1880s Emil Frey, a young Swiss

CHICKEN AND CHESTNUTS

The buckeye chestnut for which Ohio is nicknamed is not edible. At one time, however, edible chestnut trees were plentiful in the state. Most of these trees were killed by a disease brought into the country in 1904 with some Chinese chestnut trees. Efforts are now being made to grow edible chestnuts in Ohio and several other states.

Serves 4

3 slices bacon, cut into 1-inch pieces

1 medium onion, chopped

1 cup sliced mushrooms

2 1/2 tablespoons butter or margarine

1 frying chicken (3 to 3 1/2 pounds),

   cut-up

Salt and pepper, to taste

1 teaspoon dried rosemary, crumbled

1/2 teaspoon dried thyme, crumbled

3/4 cup medium (Golden) sherry

1/3 cup chicken broth

10 chestnuts, skinned and peeled

   (see method below)

Flour and water for gravy thickening

   (optional)

■

Gently fry the bacon in a large skillet or flameproof casserole until most of the fat is rendered. Add the onions and mushrooms. Sauté until soft, about 3 to 4 minutes. Remove the vegetables and bacon bits and drain the fat from the pan.

Add 1 1/2 tablespoons of the butter to the skillet and, when melted, add the chicken pieces. Brown them on both sides. Then sprinkle each piece of chicken with salt, pepper, rosemary, and thyme. Top the chicken pieces with the mushroom mixture. Combine the sherry and chicken broth and gently pour the liquid over the chicken. Cover and place in a preheated 325° F. oven for 30 minutes.

Melt the remaining tablespoon of butter in a small skillet and add the chestnut halves, tossing them lightly and taking care that they do not brown. Add the chestnuts to the chicken casserole, cover, and return it to the oven. Continue baking the chicken for another 25 to 30 minutes or until tender. Thicken the pan juices with a little flour and water, if desired.

■

Chestnut Preparation

Cut the chestnuts in half, vertically. Place them in a small saucepan and cover with water. Bring to a boil and boil over medium-high heat for 7 to 8 minutes. Drain and, as soon as the chestnuts are cool enough to handle, remove the outer shell and the skin.

cheesemaker, was trying to duplicate an imported cheese called Bismarck *Schlosskaese,* for the German delicatessens in New York City. He never succeeded but instead created a golden crusted, very pungent, spreadable cheese that he sent to Adolph Tobe, a New York delicatessen owner. He, in turn, gave it to his fellow members of the Liederkranz Singing Society in Manhattan for tasting. They approved the product, and Tobe sent a telegram to the Monroe Cheese company saying, "It's better than Bismarck. Send more."

Ice cream had been eaten for at least 400 years, but no one thought of eating it on a stick, like a lollipop. That is until one January night in Youngstown, Ohio, in 1920, when the Burt family stumbled upon the invention. They subsequently commercialized their treat under the name of Good Humor, which quickly became part of American life.

Harry Burt was a confectionery manufacturer and merchant who had invented a candy lollipop that he called Good Humor Sucker. Shortly before that night in January 1920, he had heard that a high school science teacher in Iowa had succeeded in getting melted chocolate to adhere to a block of ice cream. (This product, first called "I-Scream Bar," later became famous as the Eskimo Pie.) Burt began his own experiments and one night tried out a sample of chocolate-coated ice cream on his daughter. She said it was "too messy to handle." Harry Jr. suggested putting a lollipop stick into it.

The stick stuck in the ice cream and the Good Humor Ice Cream Sucker was born. The name was later shortened, and the Burts obtained a broad patent to market their product. A Tennessean, Tom Brimer, helped franchise Good Humor rights throughout the country.

WISCONSIN

WISCONSIN was off the main path of the westward settlement that followed the Revolutionary War. The region's first frontier communities had developed around the fur trade. In 1820 there were only 1,451 white civilians and soldiers living in Wisconsin. However, the discovery of valuable minerals and the rich, fertile land brought settlers from the East and abroad.

The first pioneers subsisted largely on salt pork and cornmeal, embellished occasionally with baked beans and whatever meat the men hunted. Passenger pigeons, cooked in clay in the Indian style, was a popular game dish. Many families survived the winter on just a few bushels of potatoes. Other families, too poor to buy flour to make bread, survived by foraging for fish, wild onions, and roots.

The earliest settlers had little trouble finding a homesite, since water abounded and there was ample timber for home building and fuel. Vegetable gardens and commercial crops were soon established, and surpluses were either traded or sold.

By the end of the 1830s, the new settlers had firmly established Wisconsin on its economic course as an agricultural state, with urban centers along Lake Michigan. The northern area remained largely untouched, but agriculture developed rapidly in the central and southern regions of the state.

After clearing the land and bringing in the first garden crops, the typical farm family acquired a cow and a few chickens, which provided homemade butter and fresh eggs. The more precious commodities—tea, coffee, flour, sugar, and salt—had to be obtained in town, primarily through barter since money was scarce.

Two years after Wisconsin attained statehood in 1848, the population numbered 305,390. Nearly two-thirds were American born, and more than a third of these Americans were farmers from New York state. Others came primarily from the New England states and Pennsylvania, Ohio, and Indiana. Most of the New Yorkers had been wheat farmers, and they planted it in Wisconsin, where wheat became one of the chief crops.

The foreign immigrants came mainly from England (particularly Cornwall), Switzerland, Germany, Ireland, Wales, the Netherlands, and Norway. Most arrived by railroad or by boat from New York via the Erie Canal and the Great Lakes. European immigrants, who came via the Great Lakes, usually disembarked at Milwaukee and tended to settle nearby in tight-knit communities.

Once established, immigrants planted kitchen gardens with vegetables as well as herbs for their familiar old-world dishes. Most German gardens had chives. Currant bushes were popular with the English, Scandinavians, and Germans. Sage was planted by the Scots and English; dill by the middle and northern European settlers.

Frequently a family's meager cash was used to buy the traditional herbs and spices that could not be grown in Wisconsin. Poppy seeds were favored by the Poles and Russians. The Norwegians used cinnamon and almonds for their baking, the Cornish liked saffron, the Bohemians purchased caraway, and the Germans preferred savory, bay leaves, and nutmeg for their cooking.

Ethnic Cooking Styles

Each ethnic group tended to retain the cooking styles of its homeland. The German settlers, for example, considered a cabbage cutter and a crock for making sauerkraut as indispensable in their kitchens. In the fall the women and children harvested the cabbages and filled the crock with sliced cabbage until it was full. Pickling liquid and some caraway seeds were added, and the crock was covered with a clean cloth, a board, and a heavy stone. The Germans had a tradition of cooking sauerkraut with spareribs every Thursday. The Scots, Irish, and English kept a supply of gingersnaps and white sugar cookies, and the Cornish miners had their sweet tea cake.

The Scandinavians loved herring and used either those from the Great Lakes or salt herring imported from Europe in five or ten-pound wooden kegs. They cut and cleaned the herring and then marinated them in a mixture of vinegar, onions, and spices for 24 hours. The marinated herring was served with boiled potatoes and homemade sour cream. The Danes kept an earthenware crock filled with fried cakes, while the Swedes and Norwegians continued to enjoy their pot of rice pudding and the Finns their hardtack.

Butchering time in the fall involved the whole family. All farmers made their own sausages and smoked hams. Every housewife had her own recipe for the mixture that went into the natural casings or that was packed into crocks or pans.

The German settlers, in particular, produced a wide range of sausages.

German sausage making is still an important industry in Wisconsin. The city of Sheboygan celebrates an annual Bratwurst Festival each August, and many other areas are noted for their German-style smoked sausages.

Hogs were important to the German settlers and presented quite a problem to Milwaukee in the 1830s, when the first German settlers arrived. These new settlers let their pigs wander wherever they chose, as they had done in Germany. The inhabitants of Milwaukee complained about the great numbers of pigs running at large on the sidewalks, attacking small children, and frightening ladies off the streets. Ordinances were soon passed to eliminate this practice.

Logging Camps

In Wisconsin's logging camps hearty and plentiful food was indispensable, and the cook was king. Logging in those days was strenuous and required gargantuan meals. A good cook meant a contented crew and that meant a good cut of timber.

The day began for the cook and cookee (his assistant) at about 3 a.m., when they prepared breakfast of buckwheat pancakes. There was also oatmeal, ham, potatoes, fried salt pork, beans, blackstrap molasses, fried cakes, and lots of black coffee sweetened with brown sugar.

The noon meal was brought out to the loggers by the cookee, who carried about an 80-pound barrel-pack on his back. The pack was filled with pork and beans, homemade bread, fried cakes, and cookies. The cookee summoned the men with a tin whistle, or he blew into the neck of a whisky bottle.

Dinner was served back at the camp and consisted of such dishes as potatoes with gravy, fresh meat, salted beef, pea soup, stewed prunes or dried apples, rice pudding, fried cakes, and a pie of dried apples, prunes, or raisins. Homemade bread was baked in such quantities that the dough was mixed in a large pine trough, which could hold a half barrel of flour.

Food for one week for a logging camp of 100 men required the following supplies: 6 barrels of flour, 2 $1/4$ barrels of beef, 2 $1/2$ barrels of pork, 8 bushels of potatoes, 3 bushels of onions, $1/4$ barrel of pickles, 1 barrel of sugar, 5 pounds of tea, 16 pounds of coffee, 50 pounds of butter, and 40 pounds of lard. Fresh game and fish caught locally were additional.

Cookbooks

Nineteenth-century Wisconsin housewives enlarged their culinary horizons by reading cookbooks and newspapers, much as cooks do today. When Wisconsin was settled cookbooks had become generally available. The first American cookbook, entitled *American Cookery* by Amelia Simmons, had been published in 1796, forty years before Wisconsin became a territory.

Henriette Davidis, a cookbook author living in Germany, published several books on cooking and homemaking in the 1860s. Her works, which were widely read in Wisconsin's German community, were translated into English in 1897 by C.N. Caspar, a Milwaukee publisher.

In the late 1800s reformers and social workers in Milwaukee were giving courses to the urban poor to improve their diets and teach them the use of new cooking ingredients. One cookbook that grew out of such classes was *The Settlement Cook Book,* authored by Elizabeth (Lizzie) Black Kander, who was born in Milwaukee in 1858. As president of the Milwaukee Jewish Mission and its social house, The Settlement, Mrs. Kander organized classes for immigrants dealing with all of the household arts, in addition to cooking.

At each class session, Lizzie Kander used to write the day's recipes on the blackboard for each student to copy. To expedite her classes, Lizzie Kander decided to get her recipes printed. A friendly printer helped Mrs. Kander solicit advertisements to cover the cost of printing, and in April 1901 a 174-page cookbook of Kander's lesson recipes was published.

The Settlement Cook Book was one of the first cookbooks to bring together some of the ethnic dishes of America and it was also the first to include Jewish cookery. Since its first printing in 1901, *The Settlement Cook Book* has gone through 33 revisions, the latest being in 1976.

Cookbooks were a natural promotional device for manufacturers of nationally distributed food and kitchen products. In Wisconsin the Malleable Iron Range Company of Beaver Dam, manufacturers of Monarch stoves, published the *Monarch Cook Book* by Helen Tomson in 1906. Four years later, the rival stove company, Caloric of Janesville, came out with the *Caloric Book of Recipes.*

One of the most famous cookbooks of all time is the *Betty Crocker Cookbook,* which was originally published to promote Gold Medal Flour, produced by the Gold Medal Flour Company of Wisconsin. The company, now a part of General Mills, was founded by Cadwallader C. Washburn, former governor of Wisconsin.

Dairying

Even during wheat's heyday, the more farsighted Wisconsin farmers knew that the boom could not last. They turned to dairying as a logical alternative, since it could make use of Wisconsin's grasses and grains, its transportation network, and the practical dairying experience many immigrants had brought with them from New York and Europe.

In 1844 an almost total crop failure occurred in Switzerland. As a result the Swiss government subsidized emigration of some of its farmers to Wisconsin, where they established the community of New Glarus. Experienced in livestock breeding, the Swiss settlers began to build their dairy herds and make cheese from the milk.

By the 1860s cheesemaking had moved from the home to commercial operations. The first Wisconsin cheesemaker was Chester Hazan, who had come from New York State and opened his establishment in Ladoga in 1864. He and several other farmers started scientific breeding and feeding programs for their cattle. Their success inspired others, although one factor delayed the acceptance of dairying as a way of life: even as late as 1870, farmers thought of tending and milking cows and the making of butter and cheese as woman's work.

The cream separator, a Wisconsin development in the 1870s, took butter making out of the home and into commercial creameries. In 1890 Stephen Moulton Babcock, a researcher at the University of Wisconsin, developed a standard test for butterfat content in milk. This development helped set pricing standards for milk, encouraged farmers to improve their herds, and set standards for the butter making industry.

All types of cheese have been made in Wisconsin over the years, but only one can be called a native Wisconsin variety—Colby. This moist, mild yellow cheese was developed in 1885 by Joseph Steinwand, whose father had opened a cheese factory west of the Clark County town of Colby. Brick cheese, a variation of a German-Swiss cheese in which the curds are pressed under glazed brick for six days, was developed in the 1870s by John Jossik in Dodge County, Wisconsin.

One of the largest modern Wisconsin cheese producers is Tolibia, Inc., of Italian-Spanish descent. In the 1920s José Ramon Tolibia found that the grass on the shores of Fond du Lac in northern Wisconsin were similar to those of his native Italy, and consequently, he believed that the milk production would also be similar. The area is now the

CEDARBURG FARM by Dan Gerhartz, oil, 8 x 12 inches, courtesy of Mongerson Wunderlich Galleries, Ltd., Chicago, Illinois.

center of American-Italian cheese production, and a million and a half pounds of milk per day are processed there into provolone, mozzarella, Gorgonzola, and Romano.

In the 1940s Wisconsin cheesemakers near Milwaukee and Green Bay developed outstanding cheddars and an excellent *kummelkase*, or caraway cheese. Discovery of limestone caves near Milwaukee started the production of Wisconsin blue cheese.

Today, Wisconsin dairy farmers milk almost two million cows daily, with 60 percent of the milk being made into more than 200 different types of cheese. Wisconsin cheese has also influenced the cookery of the state, which is often referred to as white cookery, since many of the dishes are based on milk, cream, white cheese, butter, white sauces, or milk-fed veal. White sausages, white noodles, white cabbage, and meringues add to the connotation.

Meat and Sausage

The pioneers and early settlers used every scrap of the animal after butchering to make all types of sausages. When urban settlements developed, meat-market operators took over sausage making. Each of the ethnic groups who settled in Wisconsin had their own recipes for sausage. These sausages, each with its own flavoring, had various names, such as frankfurter, bologna, *bockwurst,* bratwurst, knockwurst, *mettwurst, theuringer,* liverwurst, and *cervelatwurst.* "Homemade" sausages are still a tradition with many butcher shops in Wisconsin. Some even specialize in custom-made sausage, such as venison sausage for hunters.

Almost from its founding, Milwaukee became a center of pork meat packing and at one time ranked fourth among the nation's pork-packing cities. While most meat packing has moved out of Wisconsin, the state continues to be known for meat processing, especially for the processing of sausages. Industry leaders such as Patrick Cudahy, Hillshire Farms, Jones Dairy Farm, and Oscar Mayer & Company are all located in Wisconsin.

In 1852 two Milwaukee butchers, Frederick Layton and John Plankinton, formed a packing firm, which became the forerunner of Chicago's giant Armour and Company. In 1863 Plankinton invited young Philip D. Armour to become a partner in the enterprise. Armour envisioned that Chicago's transportation network and geographic advantages were far superior to Milwaukee's and persuaded the partners

HERRING SALAD

The Scandinavian settlers of the Great Lakes region enjoyed herring salad as part of their smorgasbords. Among the Finnish settlers, herring salad was traditionally served as a Christmas treat, while the German settlers enjoyed it on New Year's Eve. Some used pickled herring and others preferred salt herring. The Norwegians often added pieces of cooked beef or veal, while the Germans added pieces of salami or *cervalat wurst.*

Serves 8 to 10

2 cups chopped pickled herring

3/4 cup cooked leftover beef or veal roast

1 cup diced cooked potatoes

1 cup diced cooked beets, 1/4 cup beet
   juice reserved

1 dill pickle, diced

2 apples, cored and diced

1/3 cup chopped onions

2 hard boiled eggs, sliced

■

Combine the herring and the next 6 ingredients in a large bowl. Pour the dressing over the salad and refrigerate for at least 3 hours. Garnish the top of the salad with hard-boiled egg slices and serve.

Dressing

5 tablespoons white-wine vinegar

3 tablespoons sugar

1/4 teaspoon pepper

1/2 cup whipping cream

1/2 cup sour cream

1/4 cup beet juice

4 tablespoons finely chopped fresh dill

■

Whisk together the vinegar, sugar, and pepper in a bowl. Stir in the whipping cream, sour cream, and beet juice. Fold the dill into the dressing.

to open a Chicago branch under his own personal direction. Armour ultimately took over the firm and made it into one of America's food giants.

Most sausage makers started as butchers, although there is one exception: Milo C. Jones of Jones Dairy Farm in Fort Atkinson. Jones, who owned a dairy, cheese, and butter business, had been ill for a number of years. Getting involved in making sausages in the family kitchen like his Vermont mother used to make helped restore him to health. The first batches were turned out in 1889 and sold locally. As the operation expanded it moved from the Jones kitchen to a modern factory. Soon Jones' "little pig-sausages" were found in markets throughout the country.

Fishing Industry

Commercial fishing in Lake Michigan by non-Indians dates back to the 1830s. The first large-scale attempt at fishing in Lake Superior was made by Ramsey Crooks, who after buying the American Fur Company from John Jacob Astor in 1834 decided to diversify into fishing. Hoping to keep his men busy in the fur trade's off-season, he established fishing stations in Michigan, Minnesota, and Wisconsin and marketed his catch in Eastern cities.

The fishermen were largely French-Canadians, but there were also Swedes, Norwegians, and some Indians. About a fourth of the fishermen on Lake Superior came from Wisconsin.

By 1870 Lake Superior fishermen found certain species in short supply. Whitefish catches started to decline, and the lake sturgeon was nearly extinguished. The sea lamprey depleted the lake trout and made inroads on the

BAKED WHITEFISH

Whitefish weighing more than 20 pounds were the norm in Lake Superior when the first settlers arrived in the 1820s. Today, 4-pound whitefish are considered to be "jumbo" size.

The quick baking of this dish brings out the delicate flavor of the fish.

Serves 4

4 whitefish fillets

Lemon juice

1 teaspoon paprika

Salt and pepper, to taste

2 tablespoons chopped fresh parsley

1 1/2 tablespoons chopped fresh tarragon
　　or 3/4 teaspoon dried tarragon

1 medium onion, sliced

1/2 lemon, thinly sliced

1/4 cup dry white wine

1/3 cup melted butter

4 lemon wedges, for garnish

■

Place the fish fillets in a single layer in a large, flat, buttered baking dish. Sprinkle with lemon juice, paprika, salt, pepper, parsley, and tarragon. Arrange onion and lemon slices on the fish. Drizzle the wine and melted butter over the fish and bake in a preheated 400° F. oven for 10 to 12 minutes, or until the fish flakes easily with a fork. Serve each fillet with some of the pan juices and a lemon wedge.

whitefish before it was brought under control. This situation changed little until the introduction of new species changed the fishing dramatically in the 1950s and 1960s. Smelt, a newcomer to the Great Lakes, started competing with herring. Fishermen also started concentrating on chub.

Compared with other states bordering the Great Lakes and Mississippi River, Wisconsin's commercial fishing industry has fared well over the years. The state ranks first in freshwater fishing. Commercial fish farms have also been established in the state.

Vegetables and Fruit

Wisconsin's climate and soils are well suited to the growing of certain vegetables, primarily peas, sweet corn, snap beans, lima beans, cabbage, cucumbers, and carrots. Although other states produce more vegetables (particularly in the South and California), Wisconsin has more cultivated land in vegetables than any other state.

Except for peas, vegetable cultivation is a recent phenomenon in Wisconsin. It started in the first two decades of the twentieth century and was given a boost by World War II. Most of Wisconsin's produce reaches the market canned or frozen. For decades Wisconsin has produced more canned vegetables than any other state and regularly accounts for one-fourth of the national output. Wisconsin's canning industry has declined in recent years as frozen foods became popular.

Peas were first grown in Wisconsin in 1875, when Albert Landreth, a Pennsylvanian, came to Manitowoc to grow seed peas for his family's seed company in Pennsylvania. In 1883 he began experimenting with canning green peas. The following year he produced the first commercial pack in the kitchen of the hotel owned by his mother-in-law. Three years later, Landreth built a canning plant and started producing under the Lakeside label.

By the early 1890s Landreth was shipping canned peas and other canned vegetables across Lake Michigan in railroad cars on car ferries. By the time Landreth died, the plant was producing two million cans of peas annually. Lakeside Packing still exists and now cans and freezes a variety of vegetables.

Wisconsin's leading fruit crop, the cranberry, started as a wild berry. This marsh berry was known to local Indians, who dried it for food and also brewed it for tea as a remedy for nausea. The settlers found that the leaves were a good diuretic and that the berries prevented scurvy.

Commercial cranberry cultivation started when Edward Sacket came from Chicago to inspect 700 acres near Berlin that he had bought for speculation. When he found that the land was a bay covered with marsh grass and cranberry vines, he decided to commercialize the cranberries using New England's methods

of cultivation. Sacket's sons and neighbors followed his lead. The first harvest of Wisconsin cranberries was in 1865 and totaled 938 barrels. They sold in Chicago for the grand sum of $13,000.

Honey

Since pioneer days, settlers and Indians alike have collected honey from hollow trees where the bees swarmed. Later, farmers captured and kept a few bees in order to guarantee the pollination of their crops as well as a supply of honey.

By the 1880s scientific methods of bee culture had been developed. One of the pioneers in the field was Adam Grimm of Jefferson County, Wisconsin. Born in Bavaria in 1824, Grimm immigrated to Wisconsin in 1849. His father had kept bees, and he followed the tradition. By 1863 Grimm had 60 colonies of the difficult-to-handle German black bees. Literature at the time was filled with the superior merits of the Italian honey bee, a better tempered and more productive bee. By 1865 Grimm had expanded to 440 colonies, and he installed Italian queens in each. He soon began selling bee colonies and in 1869 sent 449 colonies to Utah beekeepers. By the time he died in 1876, Grimm was making a handsome living from his honey production.

In the years since Grimm's death, bee culture has grown into an important agricultural enterprise in Wisconsin. Not all Wisconsin honey producers rely entirely on their summer output. Quite a number pack up their bees with the first frost and take them to Florida, Texas, or California for the winter. California, in particular, benefits from this practice, since it suffers from a shortage of bees, which are essential to the pollination of many fruit and nut trees.

Beer

Beer is another product for which Wisconsin is famous. Like many other Wisconsin industries, brewing started in the southwestern part of the state. In 1840 there were two breweries in the state, both of which made the heavier malt liquors—ale, stout, or porter, which were popular at the time among the English population. These beers were potent, unlike the lager beers favored by the German immigrants.

By 1850 ten firms, seven of which were German-owned, were making beer in Milwaukee. In 1855 Frederich Miller purchased one of the local breweries, and in 1866 Captain Frederich Pabst acquired another. Miller called his pilsner the "Champagne of Beers." At the same time Pabst began to win numerous blue ribbons, so he called his beer "select" and tied blue silk ribbons around the neck of every bottle. During this period Joseph Schlitz was working as a bookkeeper at another local brewery, which ultimately acquired.

William Rahr, a German immigrant, arrived in Manitowoc in 1847, where he built a brewery and malt house. When he died in 1880, his three sons took over and enlarged the facilities. By 1909 the company, William Rahr's Sons, boasted that it supplied three-fourths of the breweries in America with their patented malt. After Prohibition the Manitowoc plant was the largest single malt plant in the world. In 1961 it was sold to Anheuser-Bush.

Drinking beer was an important part of the customs of Germans and other European settlers in Wisconsin and beer making was an important commercial enterprise in the state. At one time 242 towns and cities in Wisconsin had breweries, and in the late nineteenth century, there were 300 active breweries in Wisconsin. Seventy-three breweries survived Prohibition mainly by making ice cream, cheese, near-beer, and soft drinks. Through increasing competition and mergers, by 1979 only eight breweries remained. The three in Milwaukee—Pabst, Miller and Schlitz—had become international concerns.

Ice Cream

The ice cream sundae originated in Ed Berners' ice cream parlor in Two Rivers in 1881. It seems that one summer evening one of Berners' customers, George Hallauer, dropped in and ordered a dish of ice cream. Hallauer saw a bottle of chocolate syrup, which Berners used to make sodas. "Why don't you put some of the chocolate on the ice cream?" Hallauer asked. Berners complained it would ruin the flavor of his ice cream, but Hallauer insisted he wanted to try it anyway.

Chocolate-topped ice cream became the rage of the town, and Berners began experimenting with other flavors and with toppings of nuts or a generous dash of apple cider.

The name sundae, however, was born in the neighboring town of Manitowoc. George Giffy, also the owner of an ice cream parlor, served the embellished ice cream dishes only on Sundays. One weekday, a little girl ordered a dish of ice cream "with stuff on it." When told that he only served it on Sundays, the child said, "This must be Sunday, for it's the kind of ice cream I want." Giffy gave it to her, and from then on the dish was called Sunday. How the spelling evolved into sundae is not known.

STUFFED BREAST OF VEAL

The Wisconsin dairy industry was started by Swiss immigrants in the mid-1800s. Cheese and milk-fed veal have influenced Wisconsin cooking ever since.

In this recipe a breast of veal is baked with a cheese and herb stuffing.

Serves 6

■

5 slices white bread, rinds removed and
   cubed

1 1/2 cups milk

4 tablespoons butter or margarine

1 small onion, finely chopped

1 egg, lightly beaten

2/3 cup grated Swiss cheese

1/2 cup chopped mushrooms

1/4 teaspoon nutmeg

1/2 teaspoon salt

1/4 teaspoon pepper

2 tablespoons chopped fresh parsley

2 tablespoons chopped fresh basil

1 boned breast of veal (about 4 pounds)
   with a pocket cut for stuffing

Salt and pepper, to taste

Paprika

1 1/2 cups chicken broth

1/3 cup whipping cream

2 tablespoons sour cream

Soak the bread in the milk in a bowl for 10 minutes and then squeeze dry. While the bread is soaking, heat 1 tablespoon of the butter in a small frying pan and sauté the onion until limp. Add the onion, egg, cheese, mushrooms, nutmeg, salt, pepper, parsley, and basil to the soaked bread and mix gently. Lightly stuff the breast of veal and either sew the opening closed or secure it with metal skewers. Season the veal with salt and pepper and dust with paprika.

Heat the remaining 3 tablespoons of butter in a roasting pan over medium heat and brown the veal on all sides. Add the chicken broth, cover the pan, and bake in a 325° F. oven for 1 ½ hours. Uncover the pan and bake for another 20 minutes.

Remove the veal to a platter and keep it warm. Skim any fat off the pan juices. Add the whipping cream and reduce to sauce consistency over medium heat or thicken with a combination of 2 tablespoons of all-purpose flour dissolved in 1/4 cup water. Blend in the sour cream. Slice the meat and serve with the sauce.

HUSKING by Eastman Johnson, lithographic print, 22 ¹/2 x 28 inches, published by Currier and Ives, 1861, courtesy of Gilcrease Museum, Tulsa, Oklahoma.

MIDWEST

THE MIDWEST is America's bread basket, as it grows most of the grains used to make the nation's bread. In years past there has been so much wheat in Kansas and corn in Iowa that they overflowed the barns and silos.

The Midwestern countryside is dotted with simple farmhouses; however, many small farms have merged into larger ones. The country store has given way to the supermarket. Yet an atmosphere of small town America still exists in the Midwest, with uncluttered main streets, wooden houses, state fairs, and church socials.

Midwestern cooking is no-frills home-cooking at its best. It consists of good meats, simply seasoned, such as stuffed pork loins and spareribs; rich stews, thick with root vegetables; and hearty soups and corn chowders. Swedish meatballs, Polish stuffed pike, spareribs with sauerkraut, and German hot potato salad are still prepared by descendants of the immigrants who settled the area in the mid-1800s.

Many Midwestern food traditions have remained through the years. Canning and freezing of fruits and vegetables is a carry-over from pioneer days, when food had to be preserved for the winter. Midwestern cooks still bake seasonal pies such as rhubarb in the spring, berry in the summer, and apple and green tomato in the fall. They also bake a variety of breads.

Midwesterners are hospitable people, often welcoming unexpected guests to "pot luck"—sharing already prepared meals with visitors. On such occasions extra vegetables are quickly added to the pot, and homemade preserves are put on the table to be spread on freshly baked bread.

Buffet dinners are prevalent in the Midwest and consist of a myriad of dishes, many of which are brought by the guests. The buffet tradition stems from the days when itinerant farm laborers worked their way through the Midwest at harvesttime to help bring in the crops. These dinners were also known as "Thrashers' dinners." Farmers' wives would prepare enormous spreads of meats, pies, cakes, jams, and jellies to satisfy the tremendous appetite of the field workers.

Breakfast, too, has remained a large meal in many rural sections of the Midwest. It still consists of a stack of pancakes with syrup, three eggs, a quarter pound of bacon, fresh corn bread, and coffee.

The population of the Midwest can be divided into two segments. One is those of German, Scandinavian, Polish, Bohemian, and Eastern European origin who came directly to the Midwest because they heard that land was there for the taking. The others migrated from New England and the mid-Atlantic states.

Many Midwestern settlers took advantage of the Homestead Act of 1862, which provided that a qualified head of the household could become the owner of a farm or homestead of 160 acres if he lived on it and farmed it for five years. With this act, the end of the Civil War, and the development of the transcontinental railroad, settlements began in the Dakotas, Nebraska, and Kansas.

When the early settlers came to the Midwest, they were baffled by the thick, tangled grasslands. Encouraged by the fertility of the region, they developed plows to conquer the tough grass roots. Over the decades these people invented reapers, binders, tractors, and harvesters to master the soil, converting the Midwest into the most fertile grain land in the world.

Due to the lack of wood and metal resources in the Midwest, farm implements, tools, cooking utensils, and even the smallest piece of tableware had to be brought from a former household or purchased from a passing peddler. Water was also scarce. Deep wells had to be dug, since the water source was often 300 feet below ground.

The settlers who came to farm brought with them their simple culinary traditions from the East and from Europe. Thus, sausage, smoked fish, dark breads, and coleslaw joined Yankee pot roast and baked beans. The English, Irish, and Scots brought recipes for pork pies and home-cured bacon and hams. German baking ran a close second in importance to German sausage making in the Midwest. Most of the early baking was done at home, where recipes for bread, rolls and coffee cakes had been passed down from one generation to the next.

By the late 1800s most Midwestern towns with a German population had commercial bakeries, where hefty loaves of rye and pumpernickel bread, onion buns, crisp caraway salt sticks, and fat poppy-seed rolls could be purchased. Coffee cake; *Stollen; Streuselkuchen,* a yeast cake with a crumb topping; and apple or other fruit-decorated yeast cakes were also offered. Cheesecake, however, rich in cream and cottage cheese, was usually baked at home.

Czech, Polish, and Hungarian immigrants introduced paprika and such dishes as Chicken Paprika and Goulash to the Midwest. The Czechs cooked dumplings in soups or steamed them in fruit juices. Their *Svestkove Knedliky,* plum dumplings, were made from Italian-American prune plums. These same central Europeans brought various recipes

171

GOULASH WITH SPÄTZLE

Europeans who settled in the Midwest brought their recipes for Goulash with them. Known as *gulyãs* in Hungary, this stew consists of beef, veal, or pork, or a combination thereof, and is flavored with Hungarian paprika. It is served with buttered noodles or *spätzle,* which are similar to small dumplings and are of German origin.

This Goulash uses veal and is flavored with bacon, caraway seeds, and Hungarian sweet paprika. If hot paprika is used, cut the amount in half.

Serves 4

2 tablespoons butter or margarine

2 pounds veal stew, cut in 1 1/2-inch pieces

1 large onion, halved and sliced

3 slices bacon, cut into 1-inch pieces

2 tablespoons all-purpose flour

1/2 teaspoon pepper

2 1/2 tablespoons Hungarian sweet paprika

1 1/4 cup beef broth

1 tablespoon caraway seeds

1 carrot, diced

6 ounces mushrooms, thickly sliced

■

Melt the butter in a Dutch oven; add the veal, onion, and bacon and sauté until the meat loses its red color. Sprinkle the flour, pepper, and paprika over the top of the meat and mix to combine. Slowly add the beef broth, stirring constantly. Stir in the caraway seeds, carrot, and mushrooms. Bake, covered, in a 325° F. oven for 1 1/2 hours. If desired, thicken the gravy with some flour and water. Serve over *spätzle*.

Spätzle

2 eggs

1 cup all-purpose flour

1/4 cup milk

Dash each of salt, pepper, and nutmeg

1 tablespoon butter or margarine

■

In a bowl combine the eggs, flour, and milk to form a medium-thick batter. Add the salt, pepper, and nutmeg. Bring lightly salted water to a boil in a large pot. When the water is boiling, add the butter.

Use a colander with large holes to create the *spätzle*. Holding the colander a few inches above the boiling water, pour the dough into the colander and press it through the holes using a rubber spatula. Short pieces will form and fall into the water. Or place the batter on a board, hold it at an angle, and with a sharp knife scrape off small pieces of batter, dropping them into the water.

When the *spätzle* rise to the surface, cook them for another minute. Remove them with a slotted spoon to a plate. The *spätzle* may be kept, covered, in a warm oven for 10 to 15 minutes. If doing so, add a tablespoon of butter to prevent them from sticking together.

for stuffed cabbage with them.

Distances were great in the Midwest, and social events were eagerly anticipated. The strawberry social at strawberry-picking time and the Fourth of July celebration were special events. The strawberry social was usually held at a church or a school, where a picnic lunch or supper was served with strawberry shortcake for dessert. The base of the shortcake was a rich, thick biscuit, split and buttered while hot, then covered with crushed strawberries and whipped cream.

The Fourth of July picnic, considered by many to be the high point of the year, was often a "box social," where young women packed boxes of wonderful food to be passed on to their beaus or auctioned off to the highest bidder. It was then customary for the lady who packed the lunch to join the winning gentleman in eating it. Fried chicken, baked ham, potato salad, deviled eggs, homemade relishes, homemade bread, and angel food cake or layer cake for dessert were neatly packed into the lunch boxes.

Later in the summer there were corn roasts. Fresh, green roasting ears were cooked in smoldering hickory fires. Roasted corn, dripping with butter, was eaten with barbecued pork or fried chicken.

Since corn was readily available as feed, the Midwest also became a center for livestock. Today, the massive steers, which are fattened in feedlots in Kansas and Iowa, are a far cry from the stringy, muscular animals that were trail-driven from Texas and Oklahoma until late in the nineteenth century. Although beef is raised in the Midwest, very little veal is eaten. Hogs, however, were a part of pioneer life, as pigs needed very little care. Pork is still a prime meat in the Midwest.

IOWA

"THE CORN IS AS HIGH as an elephant's eye and it looks like it's climbin' clear up to the sky," is a song lyric from the Rogers and Hammerstein musical *Oklahoma* that seems close to the truth, because the corn in Iowa often grows more than seven feet tall. Almost half of the state's farmland is planted in corn and almost half of this corn reaches the market in the form of pork.

The cultivation of corn in Iowa is at least 2,000 years old. Native Americans had developed many varieties of it before the white man came to the prairies. The appearance of trained agricultural experts and modern farm machinery in the 1930s, however, contributed most to Iowa's success with corn.

The hybridization of corn in the early 1900s has had the greatest impact on Iowa agriculture in this century. Hybridization was based on the selection of the best ears each fall for the next spring's seeds. The abundant Iowa corn crop is attributed not only to the fertile soil but also to the work of an Adair, Iowa, native, Henry A. Wallace, who served as Secretary of Agriculture and Vice-President under Franklin D. Roosevelt. When Wallace was an undergraduate at Iowa State College, he developed a hybrid seed corn. His family formed the Hi-Bred Corn Company to market this seed corn, and today, about one-third of the nation produces the Wallace corn. Furthermore, the original experiments used by Wallace have made it possible to produce seed corn for almost any type of soil.

Iowa farms are large, and today one farmer can operate a 150-acre farm alone. This is possible because corn is planted with a driller or seeder machine in as

MIDSUMMER'S SUNSET by Clyde Aspevig, oil, 48 x 54 inches, courtesy of Thomas Nygard, Inc., Bozeman, Montana.

many as eight rows at a time. The distance between the rows and the spacing of the seeds is set to exact specifications by the farmer. A large combine harvests the corn, leaving the stalks in the field, where they are later plowed under for fertilizer.

Other Iowa Agricultural Specialties

The introduction of soybeans from the Orient added another important crop to Iowa's agriculture. The Iowa State Experiment Station tested more than 300 varieties of soybeans in 1910 to find the one best suited for Iowa. At first soybeans were used largely as a forage crop, but during World War II they became a source of oil and a high-protein food. Soybeans also became a rotation crop for corn. Today, Iowa is number one in the nation in soybean production.

Iowa is a major hog producer, with 25 percent of all the pork produced in this country coming from that state. The total value of hogs in Iowa is greater than that of beef in Texas. Hogs and corn go together since swine consume a great amount of corn. It takes four pounds of corn to produce one pound of pork.

STUFFED IOWA PORK CHOPS

Hogs and corn are Iowa's major agricultural products. From the time the Midwest was settled, pork has been the primary meat of the region. Iowans developed their own specifications for a pork chop. According to John Wall, one of the leading pork producers of the state, "To be a true Iowa chop, it should be a lean center-cut or rib chop that is an inch and a quarter or an inch and a half thick." This stuffed pork chop recipe combines two Iowa products.

Serves 4

4 rib pork chops, 1 $1/4$ to 1 $1/2$ inches

   thick

1 cup crumbled corn bread

$1/2$ cup fresh or canned corn kernels

$1/4$ cup chopped onion

$1/4$ cup chopped celery

$1/4$ cup chopped green pepper

3 tablespoons melted butter

1 egg, beaten

$1/4$ teaspoon salt

$1/8$ teaspoon pepper

$1/2$ cup ketchup

2 tablespoons light brown sugar

2 teaspoons prepared mustard

$1/2$ teaspoon Worcestershire sauce

■

Cut a pocket in the chops along the rib bone, first making a 2-inch cut along the rib. Then insert the knife into the opening and cut a pocket without cutting through the other side of the chop.

Lightly toss together the corn bread, corn, onion, celery, green pepper, butter, egg, salt, and pepper. Fill the pockets of the chops, dividing the stuffing evenly. Place the chops in a shallow baking dish.

Combine the ketchup, sugar, mustard, and Worcestershire sauce and brush over each chop. Cover the dish with aluminum foil and bake in a preheated 350° F oven for 50 to 55 minutes, or until done Spoon some of the glaze over the chops before serving.

At Maytag the cottage-cheese-like curds are still stirred by hand with large wooden forks until they firm up like gelatin. After draining, the cheese is placed into large stainless-steel hoops and inoculated with the mold that gives it a special flavor and creates the blue streaks. After six months of aging, the cheese is ready for market.

One of the nation's most famous apples, the Red Delicious, was first discovered in Iowa by Jesse Hiatt, a farmer in Madison County. In the late 1860s he found an unknown apple seedling in his orchard and cut it down. The next year it came up again stronger than before, and Hiatt decided that if the tree was so determined to live, he would nurture it. When the tree began to bear, however, the apples did not resemble any other variety. They were strawberry-colored, streaked with dark red, and very sweet and flavorful.

For years Hiatt took samples of his mysterious apples, which he called Hawkeyes, to various horticultural shows. In 1893 Hiatt entered four Hawkeyes in a competition in Louisiana, Missouri, sponsored by Stark Nurseries. The apples won first prize, and Stark Nurseries negotiated the propagating rights for the trees. They also renamed the apple Red Delicious.

The Sioux Honey Association, founded in 1921, is a cooperative of 550 beekeepers whose headquarters are located in Sioux City, Iowa. The co-op markets more than half of the nation's commercially packaged honey under the Sue Bee and Aunt Sue labels. Farmers from throughout the country who either raise bees as a hobby or as a commercial venture supply the company's honey, which totals more than 40 million pounds annually.

Almost everyone has heard of Maytag washing machines through the "lonely repairman's" television commercials, but that is not the only product that has made Newton, Iowa, famous. Located almost adjacent to the Maytag plant is Maytag Dairy Farms, a producer of blue cheese. Many, including the late food-writer James Beard, have rated the Maytag blue cheese far above its European competitors.

Maytag Dairy Farms was started in 1920 by Frederic Maytag, grandson of the washing machine magnate. Maytag raised dairy cows and had heard of a new process to make American blue cheese that had been formulated by scientists at Iowa State University. An agreement was concluded with the university, and today, the company produces about a quarter of a million pounds of blue cheee annually.

One such farmer, Bob Van de Hoef, produces about 100,000 pounds of honey annually from hives that he has placed in northeast Iowa and parts of Minnesota. The Iowa honey, which is lighter in color, is from bees who feed on soybeans, alfalfa, and white clover. The Minnesota honey, derived primarily from bees who feed on sunflowers, is much darker. Van de Hoef gathers his honey from August until mid-October and has it delivered to the Sioux Honey Association. He sells the wax to candle makers and manufacturers of floor polishes.

Iowa Immigrant Foods

Due to the lack of ingredients, many of the first European immigrants to Iowa found it difficult to maintain their native food customs. As one young Scandinavian minister's wife who immigrated to Iowa from Norway in the early 1850s wrote, "It is hard to get used to the monotony of the food. The dishes vary from boiled to fried pork. Potatoes and homemade bread and sometimes fried onions are added to this staple meal. Milk is scarce and Tykmelksuppe, milk soup, has become a delicacy."

In Iowa German descendants still make Westphalian hams. They are prepared by soaking the pork in brine for four weeks and then slowly smoking the hams, which have been liberally dusted with finely ground black pepper, over a hickory fire. Afterwards, they are hung in a dry place for several months to ripen.

There is a standing invitation in Swedish communities to "come for coffee." This is particularly true in the town of Stanton in southwest Iowa, where a pot of freshly brewed coffee and Swedish pastries, such as Spritz Cookies and *Mandal Skorper* (Swedish Rusks)

SAUERBRATEN

The German settlers of the Midwest brought recipes for many versions of Sauerbraten. Some were made with pork, others with beef, some included wine in the marinade, and still others used gingersnaps or a piece of pumpernickel to flavor the gravy. In the Dakotas it was made with buffalo meat. This version of Sauerbraten is typical of those served in the Midwest and has its origin in the Rhineland of Germany.

Serves 8

Marinade

1 cup red wine vinegar

1 cup red wine

2 cups water

2 onions, sliced

1 celery stalk, chopped

1 carrot, chopped

2 bay leaves

6 peppercorns, lightly crushed

4 whole cloves

6 whole allspice

1/2 teaspoon mustard seeds

1/2 teaspoon dried thyme

1 rump roast of beef (about 4 pounds)

■

Combine the marinade ingredients in a large earthenware bowl. Add the meat, making sure that the marinade covers the meat. If not, add equal amounts of vinegar, wine, and water. Cover and refrigerate for 3 to 4 days, turning the meat occasionally. The marinade and meat may also be placed in a large plastic bag.

Sauerbraten

1/2 teaspoon salt

1/4 teaspoon pepper

2 slices bacon, cut into 1-inch pieces

1 medium onion, chopped

6 crushed ginger snaps

1/3 cup raisins

1 tablespoon molasses

3 tablespoons all-purpose flour

1/4 cup water

2 tablespoons sour cream

■

Remove the meat from the marinade, wipe dry, and sprinkle with salt and pepper. Reserve the marinade.

Fry the bacon in a Dutch oven or roasting pan until slightly crisp and most of the fat has been rendered. Add the meat and brown on all sides. Then add the onion and 2 cups of the marinade. Cover and bake in a preheated 325° F. oven for 2 1/2 to 3 hours or until the meat is very tender. Add the gingersnaps during the last half hour of cooking. Remove the meat to a platter and keep warm.

Skim any excess fat off the pan juices. Add the raisins and molasses to the pan juices and cook over medium heat for 5 minutes. Combine the flour and water and slowly add to the gravy to thicken to desired consistency. Whisk in the sour cream. Carve the meat into thick slices and serve with the gravy.

STREUSELKUCHEN WITH PLUMS

Both *Streuselkuchen,* a yeast cake with a crumb topping, and plum cakes were favorites of the early German settlers of the Midwest. Today's descendants of these early settlers still bake a combination plum and crumb cake. The *Streusel,* or crumbs help retain the moisture of the plums during baking.

Serves 10 to 12

Dough

1 package dry yeast

1 cup lukewarm milk (110° to 115° F.)

3 1/2 cups all-purpose flour

1/3 cup sugar

4 tablespoons (1/2 stick) butter or

    margarine, softened

1 egg, slightly beaten

■

Sprinkle the yeast into 1/4 cup of the milk and let it stand until dissolved. Mix the flour and sugar in a large bowl. Stir the yeast, butter, egg, and remaining milk into the flour and beat until it forms a soft ball. Knead into a soft dough (additional flour may be necessary). Let the dough rise in a warm place for 40 minutes. Punch the dough down and roll on a lightly floured board to fit into a 9 x 13-inch greased pan. Push the sides of the dough up to form a 1-inch rim. Let rise for 30 minutes.

Filling and Crumbs

2 pounds Damson or Italian plums,

    washed, pitted, and halved

1/2 cup all-purpose flour

1/3 cup sugar

1/2 teaspoon cinnamon

5 tablespoons butter or margarine

1/2 cup coarsely chopped almonds

Whipped cream, for garnish

■

After the dough has risen the second time, arrange the cut plums on top of the dough, overlapping the pieces slightly.

Combine the flour, sugar, and cinnamon in a bowl. Cut in the butter until the mixture resembles fine crumbs. Mix in the chopped almonds. Sprinkle the crumb mixture over the plums. Bake the cake in a preheated 350° F. oven for 40 to 45 minutes. Serve warm with a dab of whipped cream.

provide a good excuse for a get-together. Swedes have always been known to be big coffee drinkers. One of Stanton's native daughters, Virginia Christine, was once the symbol of coffee. Most television viewers in the 1960s and '70s knew her better as "Mrs. Olson," the Swedish lady on Folger's coffee commercials.

Iowa Amish

Life in the Iowa Amish-Mennonite settlements is not much different than it was a century ago. An offshoot of the sixteenth-century Mennonites, the Amish were among the first settlers in Iowa. They came from Pennsylvania, Maryland, and Ohio in the early 1840s.

Today, in the rich, rolling countryside of eastern Iowa, there is a 200-square-mile area centered around Kalona known as Iowa's Amishland. The horse and buggy are the means of transportation. The Amish have a close attachment to the land and receive great pleasure from watching things grow. Daily farm work is regarded as a pleasure, not as a chore.

Food is hearty for these large, hard-working families, which usually have six to eight children. Breakfast usually consists of meat, fried potatoes, eggs, and sometimes pies if there is company.

Hearty fare continues at dinner, which is served in the middle of the day. There is meat, which has been home-butchered, or poultry; thick cheese slices; lots of fresh vegetables; a dessert; and fruit. Homemade bread or corn bread is served with most meals. Meat dishes are usually stretched with potatoes or pasta. "We eat a lot of hash—potatoes and peas and meat all mixed up together," said Ruth Beachy, an Amish woman in Kalona. In the summer there are many meatless meals with vegetables from the garden.

The evening meal is similar to breakfast, and one of the favorites is corn bread with a tomato gravy made from the juice of canned tomatoes. Dessert is frequently tapioca pudding with some fruit on top.

Store-bought groceries are at a minimum since the Amish preserve most of their food. All of the fruits and vegetables are raised in Amish gardens. They butcher their meat, stuff sausages, and bake all of their own bread. If the produce is not eaten fresh or canned, it and the meat are sometimes frozen in a local shop, although this deviates from the strict Amish principals of not using electricity.

The Amana Colonies

A group of Lutherans broke away from the church in Germany in the late 1700s and emigrated to the Buffalo area of New York in 1842 to escape religious persecution. As the area became over-crowded, they decided to seek a new home that was more conducive to their self-sufficient, God-fearing lifestyles. Under the direction of Christian Metz, who had led them to the New World, they came to Iowa in 1859 and established a cluster of seven villages. Each village was centered around a church and a communal kitchen. Collectively, these villages became known as the Amana Colonies.

These settlers, known as True Inspirationists, bought and tilled 26,000 acres and lived a communal lifestyle. Their colonies lasted for more than 80 years, longer than any other communal group in America except the Shakers. They achieved a happy balance between the demands of communal living and the desire for personal possessions. The land, mills, factories, and livestock belonged to the community. People worked in the fields. Although the colonists had their individual homes with their belongings, they ate in the common dining room. To make the colonies self-sufficient, young men were trained in a variety of occupations, including umbrella making and lamp-shade making.

Many of the homes did not have kitchens of their own, thus it was more efficient to cook as a community. Those that did have kitchens served portions of the community. The residents were assigned to a "home kitchen," where they, in association with about 40 other True Inspirationists, ate all of their meals—breakfast, lunch, and dinner, and two coffee breaks. Each kitchen had a boss who made up the menus and supervised a staff of ten young girls who did the cooking. The kitchen bosses were very frugal and stretched the ingredients whenever possible. For example, bread crumbs were used to extend stewed tomatoes and spinach, and apples were mixed with pickled herring to stretch a herring salad.

The menus followed a strict pattern. On Tuesdays the desserts were *Mehlspeisen*, puddings made with cream of wheat or flour. Boiled beef was the main course on Wednesdays, and on Thursdays there was always a special dessert, such as lemon or custard pie.

Meals were huge. A dinner favorite was a large pork chop, dipped in batter and fried in a cast-iron skillet. There were lots of fresh vegetables and potatoes. Fruit pies made with apples, wild plums, or wild gooseberries were a favorite dessert. Other typical German dishes included liver dumplings, Sauerbraten, and *Streuselkucken*, a crumb cake baked with a yeast dough.

The Amana Colonies have now opened their doors to tourists and carry on their food traditions in several large restaurants, which serve the typical German-American cooking of the communal kitchens. The bakery still bakes breads and coffee cakes in a brick oven but now also sells them to outsiders. The meat markets still have hand-stuffed sausages, and wineries produce local wine from dandelions and elderberries.

Other Iowa Food Traditions

The city of Pella, Iowa, was founded in 1847 by 800 Dutch immi-grants, who had left their homes to seek religious freedom. To preserve their Dutch heritage, the community decided in 1935 to celebrate an annual Tulip Day. What started out as a one-day event has blossomed into a week of festivities with parades and special foods at the churches and restaurants. The meat markets do a brisk business selling Dutch-style bologna. Split pea soup, fish fillets, and Dutch Lettuce (wilted lettuce salad) are the delicacies of the day.

Each spring the Tulip Festival draws thousands of visitors, not only to see the colorful tulips but also to partake of tasty Dutch pastries, especially the "Dutch letters." During the festival Ralph and Howard Jaarsma work busily in the family bakery filling sweet dough with almond paste and shaping the dough into Dutch letters. Originally baked to represent each family's initials, the letters have now been simplified into S-shapes or straight strips. During festival week 12,000 letters are sold in the bakery and at roadside stands.

In addition to the letters, the Jaarsmas bake other Dutch delicacies from recipes passed on to them by their grandfather, who had a bakery in Hol-land. These include St. Nick cookies, rye bread, meat-filled *Saucijzebroodjes* (similar to pigs in a blanket), crunchy Holland rusks, and *Olie Bolen* (deep-fried currant fritters). Everything is made from scratch, including the jams and jellies for the doughnuts and coffee cakes.

Iowa's Czech population, which is centered around Cedar Rapids, also celebrates its national heritage with Houby Days, or mushroom-hunting days.

KOLACHE WITH PRUNE FILLING

The Czechs who settled in the Great Lakes region continued to bake their native pastries, particularly strudels and *Kolache,* which were frequently served as a holiday dessert.

Although this recipe calls for a prune filling, poppy seed or cheese fillings are also used for *Kolache.*

Makes 2 dozen

2 packages dry yeast

1/2 cup lukewarm water (110° to 115° F.)

12 tablespoons (1 1/2 sticks) butter,
  softened

1/2 cup sugar

1/2 teaspoon salt

1 teaspoon grated lemon zest

4 egg yolks

1/2 cup milk, scalded and cooled to room
  temperature

4 1/2 cups all-purpose flour

■

Dissolve the yeast in the lukewarm water. With an electric mixer beat the butter, sugar, salt, lemon zest, and egg yolks in a bowl until light and smooth. Stir in the dissolved yeast, cooled milk, and 2 cups of the flour. Beat 5 minutes with the electric mixer at medium speed. Stir in the remaining 2 1/2 cups of flour to make a soft dough. Place the dough in a lightly greased bowl. Cover the bowl with a towel and let the dough rise in a warm place until double in size, about 1 hour.

Gently punch down the dough, turn it out on a lightly floured board, and knead for about 3 minutes. Divide the dough in half and roll on a lightly floured board to 1/4 -inch thickness. Cut into 12 rounds with a cookie cutter. Repeat with the other half of the dough. Place the dough rounds on an ungreased cookie sheet, about 2 inches apart. Cover and let rise in a warm place for 45 minutes, or until double in size.

Using fingertips, make a large depression in the center of each *Kolache.* Place a tablespoon of filling in each and bake in a preheated 350° F. oven for 12 to 15 minutes.

Prune Filling

12 ounces pitted prunes

2 cups water

2 tablespoons sugar

2 teaspoons grated lemon zest

1/2 teaspoon cinnamon

■

Chop the prunes and combine them with the water and sugar in a medium-size saucepan. Cook over low heat, stirring constantly, until very thick, about 10 minutes. Cool the mixture; add the lemon zest and cinnamon.

Mushrooms, considered the "Poor Man's Bread" in Czechoslovakia, are a staple of the Czech diet. Houby Days, which occur in May just before Mother's Day, are one of two national Czech festivals held in Iowa. The other is the Czech Village Festival on the weekend after Labor Day. For both occasions Czech food is served, starting with a *Kolache* breakfast. *Kolaches* are individual pastries or buns made with a sweet yeast dough and have a cheese, prune, poppy seed, or apple filling. Throughout the period such native foods as Goulash, sauerkraut, mushroom fritters, and mushrooms with scrambled eggs are served.

There are still many festivals in Iowa that unite people whose parents and grandparents came from other countries. For example, 75 percent of the 10,000 people in Carroll, Iowa, are of German heritage. Bratwurst and beer are the main attractions at local functions in this leading pork- and beef-producing city. The locals prepare bratwurst in many different ways—on a bun with lots of mustard, with eggs for breakfast, grilled with "kraut on the side," or boiled and topped with a barbecue sauce.

Harvest meals are still very much a tradition of Iowa. While the men and machines are working in the fields, the women are preparing big meals. At harvesttime there are long tables set with all kinds of food—ham, roast chicken, mashed potatoes with butter, baked beans, macaroni and cheese, watermelon-rind pickles, home-baked bread, and raisin, apple, custard, and berry pies for dessert.

KANSAS

EARLY PIONEER SETTLERS of the Kansas territory found life and any type of agriculture to be primitive. Kansas was part of the treeless Great Plains, known at the time as the "Great American Desert." Shelter for the settlers consisted of dugouts or sod huts, which were often shared with the animals the pioneers had brought with them. Lucky were the ones who had found enough wood to build a log cabin, which usually had a dirt floor and was so drafty that buckets of water froze a few feet from the fireplace.

Cornmeal, the staple of the early settlers' food, was baked into various types of bread and was the basis of puddings. If the settlers grew some wheat, they also baked wheat bread. Pork was the popular meat, and in season green vegetables were available from the garden. Root vegetables were stored in a dugout cellar for winter use. There was no fruit, since there were no fruit trees.

Men struggled to break fields out of the stubborn prairie sod and to cut any available wood for building and fuel. The women worked equally hard. They did all of the cooking, sewing, soap making, candle making, and preparing of food for winter storage. Indian raids and illness often interrupted the daily chores of the pioneer farm family.

Kansas fever, otherwise known as malaria, was prevalent in the lowlands. Thus, many preferred the less-fertile higher ground. Occasionally, the weather went on a rampage with sleet storms in the winter and droughts in the summer to further hinder the farmers' progress.

THE REAPER by Winslow Homer, watercolor, 19 1/2 x 13 3/4 inches, courtesy of Taggart & Jorgensen Gallery, Washington, D.C.

Shipping of Cattle

No city in the Midwest in the mid-1800s was willing to become a rail center for Texas cattle. Their great fear was the tick carried by the cattle, which brought a disease known as Texas fever. Hannibal, St. Joseph, Kansas City, and numerous other cities said no to the railroads wanting to ship cattle to Chicago. Finally, Abilene, Kansas, said, "Well, all right," after the Kansas legislature revised a bill prohibiting Texas cattle in all but the northern part of Kansas.

Abilene had nothing to lose. It was a small dead place consisting of a dozen or so log huts. With excellent grass and good water, the surrounding countryside, however, was well-suited to holding cattle. Abilene was also the furthest point east for a good depot for the cattle drives from Texas.

The idea of creating a rail depot in Abilene for the shipment of Texas and western cattle originated with Joseph McCoy, a livestock dealer and entrepreneur from Illinois. He persuaded the Kansas governor to lift the quarantine restrictions in Abilene so that Texas cattle could be shipped from there.

McCoy felt that a shorter journey for the cattle would conserve their weight. Additionally, he believed that

179

the cowboys would welcome Abilene as the end of their journey. Having Kansas as the stopping point of the cattle drives meant that they would no longer be terrorized by the cattle rustlers who were prevalent in Missouri and Arkansas.

When Abilene agreed to become a rail junction for cattle shipments, McCoy purchased the whole town for $2,400. He quickly installed cattle yards, barns, scales, and other necessary equipment to handle up to 3,000 head of cattle. Upon completion of the facilities, McCoy sent riders to the trails to intercept the drives that were in progress and entice the cowboys to come to Abilene.

The first rail cattle shipment of 20 cars left Abilene on September 5, 1867, and by the end of the year, 35,000 head of cattle had been shipped. By the end of the cattle drive period in the early 1880s, more than four million cattle had been shipped east from Abilene and other points in Kansas.

Although there are no more cattle drives coming into Kansas, the state has become an important beef producer. Beef is the number one agricultural commodity in the state, with cattle being raised in every one of the 105 counties.

Turkey Red

When the German Mennonites from Russia arrived in Kansas in the 1870s, they found parched land. Local farmers who were depending on spring wheat were almost starving. Being frugal people, each Mennonite family had brought with them seeds of a special wheat that they had been growing on the steppes of Russia. These new wheat seeds flourished and made wheat growing in Kansas viable.

The Mennonites were originally pacifist Germans, who had fled their native country to escape compulsory military service. Some of them immigrated to America to become part of the Amish communities. Others went to Russia in 1783 at the invitation of Catherine the Great. She wanted them to settle in the Crimea, which she had taken from Turkey, hoping they would be examples of industrious, hard-working people for the shiftless Tatars, then predominating the Crimea.

Ninety years later, the Crimean Mennonites realized that their century of military-conscription exemption was about to expire and began searching for a new home. They sent scouts to Canada and the United States. As a result of their findings, 500 families moved to Kansas. The first 24 families arrived in 1874; others soon followed.

While living in the Crimea, the Mennonites had found that the Turks grew a dark, hard wheat, which was excellent for use in baking. Over the years, with careful selection of seeds, the Mennonites improved the wheat strain and named it Turkey Red. Each family brought a small amount of Turkey Red seed with them to Kansas. Since the Mennonites could carry very little on the long journey, each seed was hand-picked, a grain at a time, to insure that none but the finest was taken to the new land.

These new immigrants, who had bought inexpensive land from the newly built railroads, proceeded to plant a small patch of wheat beside each of their cabins. The new variety of wheat was successful where no other variety had grown. Neighbors started buying seeds from the Mennonites, and Turkey Red spread all over the plains.

Over the years experimentation and research in wheat breeding have improved the original Turkey Red brought by the Mennonites. These improvements have resulted in a hard, red winter-wheat variety that is well suited to Kansas. The principal use of this wheat is commercial bread production.

Today, wheat is no longer planted or harvested by hand as it was when the Mennonites arrived in Kansas. Depending on whether or not the wheat is planted on irrigated land, it is planted either in rows or in circles. Much of the circular planting is dry farmed or uses circular irrigation sprinklers that turn around a controlled axis. Harvesting takes place with large combines that cut the wheat and thresh it, separating the straw from the seed grains.

Early Food in Kansas

The early Mennonites shared many of their recipes with the Kansas settlers, such as *Pirozhki,* a Russian dish which the Germans grew to like. It is a flaky pastry filled with ground meat and eaten with sour cream. Buttermilk pie, cinnamon-flavored apple pie, and *Bubbat* (hot rolls with smoked-sausage fillings) also became part of Kansas cuisine. Another Mennonite dish was a meat roll filled with onions, bacon, and sweet pickle and then baked with sour cream. It is similar to the German *Rouladen.* In the summer cold plum soup with raisins and milk was a refreshing repast.

Many early pioneers, however, did not have the food variety of the Mennonites. Pancakes were the typical staple of early Kansans. Served with sorghum and gravy, they were dinner for many of the pioneers who very rarely had meat. When they ate meat, it was usually dried buffalo. Later, when beef was available, barbecues and chuck-wagon stews became a part of Kansas cuisine, especially in cattle country. Hamburgers were usually served with a barbecue sauce.

One pioneer's memoirs recalled how an apple pie was made before there were apple orchards in Kansas. The filling consisted of sorrel, dried currants, and crackers treated with tartaric acid. She also recalled living in a sod house with her family, where her mother made homemade noodles, which she fried to a deep golden brown, then served with a gravy and bits of bacon sprinkled on top. In order to supplement precious butter, many settlers made egg-butter, which was a creamy mixture of eggs and molasses. It was served with freshly baked bread. Buttermilk pastry became the accepted pie crust.

Like those in other Midwestern states, Kansas immigrants retained some of their food traditions—Swedish almond cakes, Bohemian beer and sausages, English pancakes, and Scottish scones. When Mexican cowboys and railroad workers came to Kansas, they brought their own style of cooking. There was even a small French culinary influence in Kansas.

In 1868 a Frenchman named Ernest Valeton de Bissière set up a French socialistic colony in Franklin County to raise silkworms. Unfortunately, the settlement soon discovered that raising silkworms was not profitable in Kansas and shifted to wheat farming. The French wives, however, continued to cook their native dishes with ingredients available in Kansas. According to early diaries, some of the dishes were quail with garlic sauce, stews of turkey and new potatoes, and rich bean soups.

PIROZHKI

Recipes for *Pirozhki,* which are small meat- or vegetable-filled pastries, were first brought to the Midwest by the German Mennonites from Russia. The *Pirozhki* dough can be either yeast or a flaky pie pastry. Even puff pastry can be used. Traditionally *Pirozhki* were eaten with soup; today, they are often served as hors d'oeuvres.

In this recipe a flaky pastry is filled with a meat and cabbage combination.

Makes about 20 pastries

Pastry

2 cups all-purpose flour

8 tablespoons butter or margarine

4 tablespoons vegetable shortening (or lard)

5 to 6 tablespoons ice water

1 egg, beaten with 1 tablespoon water

■

Place the flour in a bowl and, with a pastry blender, cut in the butter and shortening until the mixture resembles fine crumbs. Gradually add the ice water, a tablespoon at a time, until the dough can be formed into a ball. Wrap the dough in plastic wrap and refrigerate for 1 hour.

Roll the dough on a lightly floured board into a rectangle about 21 x 6-inches and 1-inch thick. Fold the dough into thirds to make a three layered package 7 x 6-inches. Turn the pastry around and roll again into the same size rectangle and fold into thirds. Repeat the process twice more. Wrap the dough in plastic wrap and refrigerate for another hour.

Roll the dough on a floured board into a circle 1/8 inch thick. Cut into 3-inch rounds. Put 2 tablespoons of filling in the center of each round, pull the ends of the

dough together over the filling and pinch them closed. Place on a lightly greased baking sheet, seam side down, and brush with the egg wash. Bake in a preheated 400° F. oven for 30 minutes, or until nicely browned.

Filling

3 tablespoons butter

1/2 cup finely chopped onions

3/4 cup finely shredded cabbage

1/2 pound lean ground beef

2 hard boiled eggs, chopped

1/4 cup minced dill

1/4 cup sour cream

Salt and pepper, to taste

■

Melt the butter in a skillet over medium-high heat and add the onions and cabbage. Sauté for about 5 minutes, until the vegetables are limp. Add the beef and continue sautéing until the meat is no longer pink. Remove the skillet from the heat and stir in the eggs, dill, sour cream, salt, and pepper. Let the mixture cool and then fill the pastry.

MISSOURI

THE FIRST AMERICANS to settle in what is now Missouri were 70 Virginians. In 1789 they founded New Madrid; the name was probably selected because the territory belonged to Spain at the time.

Many of the early settlers of Missouri came in covered wagons from Kentucky, Virginia, and other regions of the Upper South. The men built log cabins, cleared land, and planted crops. The women used their Southern recipes to make buttermilk biscuits, fried chicken with cream gravy, cooked greens with bacon, and baked apple dumplings topped with cinnamon, brown sugar, and thick cream.

French traders and eventually French families from Canada came down the Mississippi into Missouri. They, too, brought their favorite recipes for thin French crêpes and cookies of sweet and bitter almonds called *croquignoles*. The French women made a special soup of dried peas, turnips, celery, and onions that was flavored with mint and thyme. They also brought recipes for *brioches* to St. Louis.

German immigrants also settled in Missouri, bringing their food traditions with them. New Year's in the German communities was ushered in with herring salad, which consisted of herring mixed with apples, beets, pickles, eggs, onions, and spices. Sometimes cooked chicken or a mild wurst (sausage) was also added. Other German specialties included raw potato pancakes crisply fried in lard and cheesecakes, which abounded in every German community. Germans also brought the brewing industry to St. Louis.

Angel food cake, named for its fluffy whiteness and delicate texture, is said to have been "invented" in St. Louis. As the average angel food cake requires a dozen eggs, its creation needed an area where eggs were plentiful. Angel food cakes also required abundant hand labor to whip the egg whites. Since Missouri was one of the slave states, it is assumed that the first angel food cakes were baked by Negro slaves who were brought up the Mississippi from the Deep South to work the cotton plantations of Missouri.

Missourians remember that food was not always plentiful in the region. Wasting food of any sort still goes against the Midwestern grain. During "hawg killin'" time in the late fall in rural Missouri, every part of the hog is used. Ribs and sliced sides of the pig are fried or baked; the liver, heart, and kidneys are boiled together; and much of the remaining small scraps of meat are ground into sausage meat.

The Germans and central Europeans brought their sausage-making ability to the Midwest. One of their sausages, *wienerwurst*, became the most American of all. The wiener, wrapped in a long, soft roll, was the fast-food sensation at the St. Louis World's Fair in 1904. At the time a local newspaper cartoonist drew a dachshund with a body that looked like a sausage, and the words "hot dog" have been used ever since to describe *wienerwurst* on a bun. Another famous German and central European sausage, *Leberwurst* (liverwurst), became a very popular sandwich spread.

Missouri Nuts and Other Foods

Missouri is the largest producer of black walnuts in the world. Nearly 50 percent of the world's black-walnut crop, more than 40 million pounds, is harvested in Missouri during October and November each year. There is also a sizeable crop of pecans and hickory nuts in Missouri.

Famous for their rich, tangy flavor, Missouri's black walnuts are grown in deep, well-drained soil throughout the state. They are popular baking ingredients and have a much stronger flavor than the milder English walnuts.

Black walnuts have a green exterior husk, which turns brown when ripe and contains a dark dye. Inside the husk is a hard inner shell. Both are extremely difficult to remove. All of the husking used to be done by hand, which stained the workers' fingers black for weeks. Machines have now been developed to remove the husk and crack the shell.

Pecan trees grew wild in Missouri and were a source of food for the Missouri Indians long before the white man came. Today, pecan orchards are located in the well-drained bottomlands of the Missouri and Osage rivers. There are more than two million pounds of pecans grown commercially in the state each year.

The pecan-growing process begins in April when the trees bloom. Spring rains help set the blooms into nutlets, which later become a green husk with a nut inside. By September the pecan-nut meat has matured. With the first frost of the season, the outer husk darkens and opens, exposing the nut. Mechanical shakers then wrap around the tree trunk and vibrate the tree so that the nuts will fall to the ground. Most commercial growers use mechanical harvesters to gather the fallen nuts, which are washed in their shells and graded by size. The cracked nut meat is sorted into pecan halves and pieces, packaged, and put in cold storage until shipment.

Honey has been a part of Missouri history. Before Missouri became a state, there was a battle, called the Honey War, to determine the territory's northern boundary. Missouri and Iowa officials had disagreed over the boundary for years. In 1839 when a Missouri man cut down three hollow trees containing bee hives in the disputed area, Iowa tolerance reached its limit, and the Honey War began. Missouri won, and the border was established in Missouri's favor. Today, there are 7,000 beekeepers in Missouri.

The peak of honey production by Missouri bees is from June through August and tapers off with cool weather. When the honey is collected from the hive, it is very thick. At the processing plant the honey is heated to make it free flowing, then sterilized, and filtered. It is then packed into jars and capped.

While Missouri is not a leading producer of wheat, it has become famous for a product made from Missouri-grown wheat—Aunt Jemima Pancake Mix. Self-rising pancake flour, or what is known today as pancake mix, was created in St. Joseph, Missouri. It was first packaged in 1889. Four years later, one of the inventors of the mix saw a black-faced comedian in an apron and red bandana perform a song called "Aunt Jemima." He liked the tune and the character and decided to name the mix after it. Aunt Jemima pancakes were introduced at the Chicago World's Fair in 1893.

APPLE-NUT CAKE

The black walnut is a native American nut and was used extensively for food by the Indians. Black walnuts are now grown commercially in Missouri. They are rarely eaten by themselves and are better when used in combination with other foods. Since the black walnut is a very oily nut, its flavor improves as the oils diminish after being stored for a while.

If you prefer a stronger black walnut taste, use all black walnuts in this cake, and conversely, if you do not like the taste of black walnuts, use all English walnuts. This cake is an adaptation of an old European recipe and needs no frosting. It keeps well for several days.

Serves 10 to 12

16 tablespoons (2 sticks) butter

1 3/4 cups sugar

3 eggs, lightly beaten

1 cup whole-wheat flour

1 cup all-purpose flour

2 teaspoons baking soda

1 teaspoon nutmeg

1 teaspoon cinnamon

1/4 teaspoon salt

4 cups peeled and diced apples

1/2 cup chopped English walnuts

1/2 cup chopped black walnuts

1 cup raisins, lightly floured

Confectioner's sugar, for garnish

Cream the butter and sugar in a bowl until smooth. Add the beaten eggs and mix until creamy. Sift together the flours, soda, nutmeg, cinnamon, and salt and add to the egg mixture. Fold in the apples, nuts, and raisins. Pour the batter into a well-greased and floured 10-inch tube pan and bake in a preheated 325° F. oven for 1 1/4 hours. When cool, remove the cake from the pan and dust with confectioner's sugar.

NEBRASKA

IN 1804 THE LEWIS AND CLARK expedition inventoried the edible resources of Nebraska. The list included deer, "turkies," grouse, elk, geese, ducks, buffalo, catfish, and "other" fish. They also noted an abundance of wild grapes, three kinds of plums, wild cherries, and gooseberries. Meriwether Lewis and William Clark observed that the two most popular foods of the nomadic Indian tribes of Nebraska were jerky (dried beef preserved with salt) and pemmican (finely pounded dried meat mixed with fat).

Like the native Indians, the early traders, trappers, explorers, and missionaries who traversed Nebraska were able to live off the land. They carried only the basic food items, such as salt pork, sugar, flour, and coffee. Salt pork, a staple food because it would keep indefinitely, was soaked for a few hours to remove some of the excess salt and then fried. The sugar was usually in loaves or coarsely crushed brown sugar, and the flour was unbleached. Coffee, which was green, had to be roasted in a skillet over an open fire before it could be ground and brewed.

When Fort Atkinson was established in the Nebraska Territory in 1820, it was the western-most outpost of the United States. The War Department issued a daily ration list, which included the following items for each soldier and civilian inside the fort: 3/4 pound of pork or bacon, or 1 1/4 pounds of fresh or salted beef; 18 ounces of bread or flour, or 20 ounces of cornmeal; and 1 gill (2 glasses) of whiskey per man. Additionally, 2 quarts of salt, 4 quarts of vinegar, and 12 quarts of dried peas or beans were allotted for each hundred soldiers or civilians.

To see if the fort could be self-sufficient, the occupants were allowed to grow gardens to supplement their rations. Not only were they able to raise vegetables, but they also raised cattle and hogs. This first experiment in farming in Nebraska proved to be a success, even though the fort was abandoned after seven years.

Peter Sarpy's Trading Post in Bellevue, at the border of present-day Iowa, became a place where immigrants stocked provisions for the long trip west. It offered such items as crushed and loaf sugar, several types of molasses, tea, coffee, sassafras, ginger, nutmeg, vinegar, and homemade pickles. On very rare occasions oysters in cans could be obtained. The trading post also supplied the surrounding settlement, the oldest in Nebraska. These trading-post staples supplemented the garden produce, beef, venison, and wild game of the settlers.

From the time of the establishment of the first settlements and farms in Nebraska, corn and cornmeal became the major item of the diet. Since corn was abundant, cornmeal was used instead of expensive wheat flour. Even the corncobs were used for fuel in cooking and heating. After the corn was ground at a local mill, the cook sifted out the hulls with a wooden-rimmed sieve. An article in a 1861 issue of the *Nebraska Farmer* told of the superiority of cornmeal over wheat and potatoes. It gave 33 recipes for the use of cornmeal, including Indian dumplings, apple corn bread, and baked Indian Pudding.

The Homesteaders

The coming of the railroads to Nebraska in the mid-1860s attracted homesteaders by the tens of thousands. Most came from agricultural areas of the East, and a large portion emigrated from Europe, especially Germany, Bohemia, the British Isles, and Scandinavia. Many started out with nothing but hope and literally built their homes from the land—sod houses or dugouts were the norm.

Pioneer life on the plains was hard and posed special problems. There were few trees and consequently no wood for building or fuel. The pioneers, however, cut and used "Nebraska marble," large, thick, rectangular chunks of sod, to build cabin walls. The floors were hard-packed dirt, and the roofs consisted of more sod supported by poles and rafters taken from the few trees that were available. Some of the sod houses were dugouts built into an embankment and required only a front and a partial roof of sod. The life of a sod house was only six or seven years, after which, with luck, the pioneers could afford to build a more permanent log residence with lumber shipped from the East or the northern Great Lakes region.

Although the sod houses were cool in summer and warm in winter, they tended to leak in rainy weather. Sometimes cows wandered on the roof, thinking it was grazing land, and fell through to the one room below.

One of the first items the new settlers installed in their sod houses was a stove that could burn hay, corncobs, and buffalo or cow chips. The stoves had to be stoked almost continuously to keep the fire burning. One early account tells of stoking the stove five times during the preparation of biscuit dough and continuing the process while the biscuits were baking.

Homemakers brought their recipes and familiar methods of cooking with them, but the new circumstances on the frontier required them to make many adjustments. Until a settler could plant a garden and acquire livestock, the family had to do without eggs, milk, butter, or lard. Settlers improvised recipes for pancakes without eggs, biscuits without lard, and used water instead of milk in baking. Salt-risen bread became popular with housewives who had no yeast. The term "salt-risen" refers to the practice of keeping a bowl of starter nested overnight in a warm bed of salt, which retained a uniform heat. The starter contained warm milk or water, flour, cornmeal, sugar or molasses, and salt. At the time sorghum molasses was used extensively instead of expensive sugar.

Later, when milk became available, cream was used to make butter, which often turned rancid in the heat of the summer. Consequently, many used the cream to make cheese, which kept better. Excess eggs were preserved in a number of different ways: coated with paraffin, stored in brine, packed in barrels of sawdust, or preserved in borax.

Pork in its many forms became the most important ingredient in the settlers' diet. It could be salted, smoked, or made into sausage and headcheese (jellied loaf of chopped pork parts). A smokehouse

for the pork was often made from a barrel with holes punched in the sides for the insertion of sticks from which to hang the hams. The barrel was placed

over a fire in a trench. After the hams were smoked they were placed in gunnysacks that had been coated with a flour paste to make them airtight. The

MEAT LOAF

Meat loaf, a staple of Midwest cookery, is said to have originated with the German settlers of the area. The original ingredients of meat loaf consisted of ground meat, usually beef, veal, or pork; onions; bread soaked in milk or water; and seasonings. Some of the German settlers added sauerkraut for moisture. Rye bread was frequently used as a "stretcher."

This meat loaf is a modern variation with a combination of meats and tomatoes with milk added for moisture.

Serves 6

1 1/2 pounds ground meat, consisting of
    1/2 pound beef, 1/2 pound veal,
      and 1/2 pound pork

1 cup coarsely chopped mushrooms

1/2 cup chopped celery

1/3 cup chopped red pepper

1/2 cup chopped green pepper

1 large onion, chopped

3/4 cup crushed soda crackers

1 can (8 ounces) stewed tomatoes

1 can (5 ounces) condensed milk

1 large egg

2 tablespoons ketchup

1/2 teaspoon salt

1/4 teaspoon pepper

■

Lightly combine the meats, mushrooms, celery, peppers, onion, and soda crackers in a large bowl. Then add the stewed tomatoes with their juice, the milk, egg, ketchup, and salt and pepper. Mix lightly, but thoroughly. Turn the mixture into a flat casserole, shaping the meat loaf into a long mound. Bake in a preheated 350° F. oven for 1 hour and 15 minutes. Occasionally remove any accumulated liquid fat.

hog was also the principal source of lard for shortening and soap.

The Food of Nebraska

Nebraska's immigrant settlers from the older parts of the United States and from many European countries combined their favorite dishes into what is today the state's cuisine. When the right ingredients were available, nineteenth-century Nebraska housewives generally cooked the native dishes with which they were familiar.

Swiss immigrants made small, delectable plum tarts, using the wild plums of the area. The tiny tarts were first filled with a custard, then topped with pieces of plums and dabs of thick, sweet cream dusted with nutmeg or cinnamon. When the oven had been heated to just the right temperature, the tarts were quickly baked; then they were cooled and eaten almost immediately.

Another Nebraska Swiss specialty was *Thuna*. It was made from creamed spinach or other greens thickened with sweet cream and a little flour. The spinach mixture was placed in bread-dough lined corn-stick pans, and the spinach was dotted with sour cream, which browned nicely when the sticks were baked. Since the spinach filling was firm, the *Thuna* could be picked up and eaten like corn sticks.

The Bohemians added Chicken Paprika, Goulash, tiny dumplings, and almond cakes to Nebraska cuisine. Danish pears, Swedish fish mousse, and pork pancakes were attributed to the Scandinavians who helped settle Nebraska. The Swedish cooks used snow for leavening in their waffles, which they served with cherry jam.

Settlers from other parts of the country brought their favorite recipes for buttermilk spoon bread, apple-bran rolls, lemon-flavored cornmeal cookies, and raisin oatmeal bread—all of which became part of Nebraska's cookery.

Apple Pie, a favorite American dish of settlers from the Northeast, was also well-liked in Nebraska. Nebraskans, however, preferred their pies made with fresh apples, as the following Nebraska-originated ditty attests: "Spit in my ears and tell me lies, but give me no dried-apple pies." Unfortunately, in the 1800s drying apples was the simplest way to preserve them for later use. The apples were peeled, sliced into round rings, threaded, and hung in the sun to dry. Peaches, pumpkins, squash, string beans, and even rhubarb were preserved by drying.

Beginning in the 1840s, the Platte River Route through Nebraska became the main road for settlers and prospectors going to Oregon and California. Within ten years, tens of thousands had come through Nebraska, although only a few settled permanently in the Nebraska Territory. As late as 1854 there were still only 2,700 permanent inhabitants in Nebraska.

There is a Nebraska tale that biscuits saved an entire immigrant family. It seems that the family was traveling west in a covered wagon when a band of Indians rode into their camp one evening. Frightened that they would be scalped, the father of the family looked the Indians straight in the eye and said calmly, "Mother, those boys look hungry. Fix 'em a batch of your biscuits."

Mother did and also hurriedly cooked a rasher of bacon while Father milked the cows. The Indians sat down to an unusual feast. While other caravans were subjected to Indian raids, the "Biscuit Caravan" continued peacefully across Nebraska, with the Indians dropping in at odd times for a meal.

Dining on the Railroad

With the passage of the Homestead Act in 1862 and the completion of the Union Pacific Railroad across Nebraska in 1868, tourists started coming to the territory. Thousands of prominent Europeans came to visit the American West and hunt buffalo. Among the buffalo hunters was the Grand Duke Alexis of Russia, who came in a private railroad car in 1872.

The trains from Chicago to Omaha had dining cars. Railroad food was primarily a choice among various wild game, although there were also such delicacies as suckling pig and lobsters from Maine. Beyond Omaha to the west, unless the traveler had a seat in the hotel car, he or she ate at stations spaced at appropriate distances along the railroad. The food was substantial, well-prepared, and sufficient time was allowed to eat—about 30 minutes. A warm meal at these stations cost a dollar.

Those who could afford first-class accommodations traveled in a hotel car consisting of two drawing rooms and six open sections of double berths. Each hotel car had a kitchen at one end, which was fully equipped with everything needed for cooking. There was also a wine closet, a linen closet, and space for provisions for 30 people traveling from Chicago to California.

In the hotel car a porterhouse steak cost 75 cents, but if topped with mushrooms the price was increased to a dollar. A dollar was also charged for a whole spring chicken; two broiled lamb chops cost 50 cents. A plate of eggs was 30 cents, and any vegetable accompaniments or breads were 10 cents each. Desserts were limited to preserved fruits, which were 25 cents per serving.

By the mid-1870s dining cars replaced station restaurants, and hotel cars were refurbished for sleeping only. Thus, dining cars became more elaborate in their meals and their mode of service. Massive silver services were provided, including the traditional duck press and individual chafing dishes, egg boilers, and toasters. Individual coffee percolators were set at each table.

Nebraska Agriculture

Early fur traders and trappers reported that the plains of Nebraska were almost a desert and not fit for agriculture. These early soothsayers did not take into account that vast herds of buffalo had been feeding on the lush, thick grass of Nebraska for centuries.

There were times when later Nebraskans agreed with the traders and trappers, however, particularly after the first plague of grasshoppers invaded the state in 1856. The Indians had dealt with the grasshoppers by grinding them into meal, but this solution did not appeal to the white settlers. During the next 17 years, the grasshoppers reappeared six times.

Although the area was once known as the "Great American Desert," it has developed into rich agricultural land. Irrigation has permitted crops to be grown in areas once considered too dry for farming. A valuable source of irrigation water is a vast underground water table called the Ogallala Aquifer. Lying below the central and west central regions of the state, it covers about one-third of Nebraska. Surface water is also channeled to the farms from rivers and streams. More than eight million acres of Nebraska cropland are irrigated from these two sources.

Nebraska has a diversity of soil and agriculture. For example, the loess soil (composed of small silt particles) that covers most of the state is well-suited to corn and soybeans. Sandy soil in the north-central region of the state is ideal for hay to feed the cattle. The southwest and the panhandle are wheat-growing country. Corn is Nebraska's major crop, and the state is the second largest cattle feeding station in the nation.

ConAgra

Nebraska Consolidated Mills, the predecessor to ConAgra, was formed in 1919 by the merger of four leading flour mills in Nebraska. The company's headquarters was established at Grand Island, where the largest of the four mills was located.

For the next several decades, each mill continued to use a different name for its flour, such as Mary Ann, Mother's Best, and Tip Top. Realizing that each housewife was loyal to one brand of flour and seldom switched to another, the company adopted the most well-known label, Mother's Best, for all of the mills. One of them decided to keep its loyal customers by printing Mother's Best on one side of the bag and their house label on the other.

Flour, at the time, was packed in 25-pound cotton sacks. The bags had pretty printed designs on them so that housewives could wash the sacks and make them into tea towels, pillow cases, and even clothing. One mill offered bordered sacks designed especially for transformation into pillowcases, or two could be sewn together for a bordered skirt. It was not unusual for a mill to offer several different designs on the sacks. Homemakers frequently chose their flour according to the beauty of the designs.

In the late 1940s Arlee Andre, chief chemist of Nebraska Consolidated Mills, started experimenting with cake mixes and developed a successful one. The company hired the noted restaurant critic and author, Duncan Hines, to promote three versions of this new cake mix, and the Duncan Hines division of Nebraska Consolidated Mills was born. Over the years Nebraska Consolidated Mills continued to diversify its operations with expansions and acquisitions, such as Dalton Poultry of Georgia, and in 1971 Nebraska Consolidated Mills changed its name to ConAgra.

Having diversified, today ConAgra is one of the largest food companies in the world. It is well-established in the frozen-foods field with its Banquet and Healthy Choice products. ConAgra continues in the poultry business and has an aquaculture division that produces catfish and shrimp. ConAgra's deep-sea fishing operations are Singleton Seafood Company and Sea-Alaska Products. In 1983 ConAgra acquired Armour, with its 19 meat-processing plants and beef and pork slaughtering houses. Throughout this expansion and diversification, ConAgra has maintained its headquarters in Grand Island, Nebraska.

NORTH DAKOTA

MORE THAN 10,000 YEARS AGO, bands of nomadic Indians, who probably were descendants of those who crossed the Bering Strait to Alaska and migrated south, camped in Dakota. They hunted bison, mastodon, and other big game. The arrival of white explorers, trappers, and traders altered the established Indian cultures. Though contacts between Indians and whites were usually peaceful, there were conflicts that led to armed struggle.

Few settlers came to the North Dakota region before the 1870s. Transportation was poor, and there were threats of Indian attacks. The first settlements along the northeastern Red River Valley were carry-overs from fur-trading posts that had been established by the British in the early 1800s.

After 1870 thousands of settlers entered the Northern Dakota Territory drawn by fertile farm lands "practically free for the taking." The U.S. government and the railroads that traversed the Northern Dakota Territory encouraged settlers from the eastern United States and abroad. Immigration officers distributed optimistic literature and even organized colonies of immigrants to come to America. The literature touted Dakota as a delightful place, and offers of free or cheap land ready for the plow encouraged many Europeans to immigrate. Some of the early settlers arrived by wagons, which contained their families and household goods. Most, however, came by railroad in immigrant trains. Settlers from Norway, Germany, and Russia predominated. Many of those from Russia were of German heritage, who had settled in the Ukraine many decades previously.

The population of North Dakota grew from 2,400 in 1870 to 63,000 in the early 1900s. During these boom years the prairie changed dramatically. Hundreds of "claim shacks" began to dot the grasslands of the plains. Towns were built and farmers cultivated the land.

New farming developments helped build the agriculture of North Dakota. These included durable, efficient, and inexpensive steel plows. Factory-made windmills provided access to water. Inexpensive fence wire defined grazing lands and farms. Railroads expanded to provide a mode of transporting agricultural products to market.

Buffalo

Thirty to forty million buffalo once roamed across North America. Although they wandered over almost all of the United States, the grasslands of the Great Plains provided an excellent habitat. There they fed on grama, a highly nutritious native grass, which dries during the summer without losing its food value. In the winter buffalo herds broke up into small groups, because only a limited amount of grazing was available. With abundant food and few natural enemies, the buffalo had a life span of about 25 years before the white man arrived.

The buffalo herds of the plains played a key role in the frontier life and food supply of early North Dakota. Both the Indians and the settlers were dependent on these animals in different ways. The Indians of the northern Great Plains obtained such necessities as food, clothing, shelter, and fuel from the buffalo. As a food source the buffalo provided fresh meat, tallow, bone marrow, pemmican, and dried or jerked meat. The Indians considered tongues, dried and smoked, as a delicacy. They converted buffalo horns into spoons, and dried buffalo dung was an important source of fuel.

The buffalo was also a source of meat for the early white visitors to the Dakota territory. To the fur trader the buffalo represented a fur commodity to be sold in Eastern and European markets. Professional fur hunters seldom preserved the meat from their kills, leaving the carcass on the ground to rot. They often took the buffalo tongues, however, which they sold for 30 cents apiece.

Later, the pioneers considered the buffalo as obstacles to western settlement and encouraged the slaughtering of the herds. The U.S. military seized the opportunity to control the Indians by controlling the availability of buffalo. As a result professional hunters were allowed to destroy the herds under the protection of the army present in the Dakota Territory. They continued to operate until the end of the nineteenth century.

Bonanza Farms

North Dakota has had an agricultural economy since the time the territory became a state. It is probably the most rural state in the country, with about 90 percent of the land in farms. The cultivation of spring and durum wheat and barley, along with the raising of cattle and hogs and dairy operations, constitutes the state's agriculture.

Western North Dakota is known as grazing country. The first important use of these western prairies was by English and Scotch "beef barons," who made extensive investments in land and cattle.

The eastern part of the state has been traditionally dominated by crop farming. Large-scale farming began in North Dakota in the 1870s. Eastern corporations and some wealthy eastern families established huge wheat farms covering thousands of acres in the Red River Valley. The farms made such enormous profits that they were called "bonanza" farms.

The "bonanza farmers" came at the instigation of the Northern Pacific Railroad, which wanted to encourage settlement by demonstrating the profitability of farming in North Dakota. The bonanza farms were short-lived, however, since they were broken up and sold to small farmers during the depression of the 1890s. These farms specialized in wheat and planted enormous acres with extraordinary yields. Terms such as "incredible," "unlimited," and "inexhaustible" were used to describe the Red River Valley wheat crops at the time.

"Wheat is King," wrote many of the new farmers to their friends and families back East and in Europe, encouraging them to come to North Dakota. A typical wheat farm was that of Oliver Dalrymple, whose holdings in 1886 contained 75,000 acres: 32,000 in wheat and the rest in pastureland. The following description by Mr. Dalrymple appeared in the March 15, 1886, issue of the *New York Mail and Express*:

"In addition to its being cultivated by the most improved machinery, the farm requires at certain seasons between 600 and 800 men in plowing, harvesting, threshing, and moving the wheat. We own 500 horses, which are also used on the farm, and in the busy part of the season, we employ 300 more. The yield

INDIAN BUFFALO HUNT by Charles M. Russell, watercolor, 21 1/2 x 33 1/2 inches, courtesy of Mongerson Wunderlich Galleries, Ltd., Chicago, Illinois.

averages 20 bushels to the acre and is spring wheat that is sown in the spring and taken off in the fall. During the harvest season it takes 175 self-binders to cut and bind it and 25 steam threshers to thresh it."

North Dakota Wheat

North Dakota grows three types of wheat—spring, durum, and winter wheat. The hard, red spring wheat is North Dakota's major crop, and the state leads the nation in that type of wheat production. It is planted in March or April and harvested in August. Spring wheat has a high protein content and makes an ideal flour for baked goods.

The state is also the nation's leading producer of durum wheat, supplying 80 percent of U.S. needs. Durum, also a spring wheat, is milled into semolina and durum flour. These flours are used to

make macaroni and other pastas.

Winter wheat is seeded in the fall and starts to grow, then lies dormant over the winter and resumes growing in the spring. It is harvested in the summer. Winter wheat is important to bread-making. The soft winter wheat is used in flat breads, cakes, crackers, and noodles.

Dependent on its flour mills, the little town of Grand Forks, North Dakota, experienced a severe economic depression during the Panic of 1893. Not only were flour prices depressed, but the demand for flour had been greatly reduced. The Diamond Milling Company, owned by Emery Mapes and George Bull, was processing fewer than a thousand bushels of wheat a day and was getting only two dollars for a hundred pounds of flour.

One of Diamond's employees, Scotland-born Tom Amidon, was in the habit of taking home the unused hearts of

DAKOTA BREAD

In 1988 the North and South Dakota Wheat Commissions jointly developed a recipe for a new bread called Dakota to honor the 100th anniversary of their statehood. The bread recipe was inspired by bakers from both states and uses grains grown in North and South Dakota. The recipe is being reproduced by permission of the South Dakota Wheat Commission.

Makes 1 loaf

1 package active dry yeast

1/2 cup warm water (105° to 115° F.)

2 tablespoons sunflower oil

1 egg

1/2 cup cottage cheese

1/4 cup honey

1 teaspoon salt

2 to 2 1/2 cups bread flour

1/2 cup whole-wheat flour

1/4 cup wheat germ

1/4 cup rye flour

1/4 cup rolled oats

Cornmeal

1 lightly beaten egg white

Wheat germ, sunflower kernels, or
   oatmeal, for garnish

■

Sprinkle the yeast over the warm water in a small bowl; stir to dissolve.

Mix the sunflower oil, egg, cottage cheese, honey, and salt in a large bowl. Add the dissolved yeast and 2 cups of bread flour, beating until the flour is moistened. Gradually stir in the whole-wheat flour, wheat germ, rye flour, and oats, plus enough bread flour to make a soft dough.

On a floured surface knead the dough about 10 minutes, or until the dough is smooth and elastic. Place the dough in a greased bowl; cover loosely with oiled plastic wrap. Let rise in a warm place until doubled in size, about 30 minutes.

Punch down the dough. Shape into one round loaf. Place in a greased glass pie pan sprinkled with cornmeal. Cover with oiled plastic wrap and let rise until doubled in size, about 1 hour.

Brush the loaf with egg white and sprinkle with either wheat germ, sunflower seeds, or oatmeal. Bake in a preheated 350° F. oven for 35 to 40 minutes. If the crust becomes too dark during baking, cover loosely with foil the last 10 to 15 minutes of baking. Remove from pie pan and cool on a wire rack.

For the hundredth anniversary of their statehood in 1988, the North and South Dakota Wheat Commissions jointly developed a recipe for a new bread called Dakota. The bread, which is now commercially produced, was inspired by favorite recipes from bakers in the two states. It is a high protein bread and utilizes many of the grains grown in both states.

Other Agricultural Products

In recent years other agricultural products besides wheat and barley have been developed in North Dakota. Sunflowers have become an important crop, and the state leads the nation in their production. There are two types of sunflowers: those raised for their oil and those raised for human consumption. Both are raised for their seeds. The oil seeds are used in margarines and salad oils, while the confection seeds are for snacks and food garnishes.

Although edible sunflowers have been grown in North America by the Indians for centuries, their cultivation as a major crop is a rather recent phenomenon. Following World War II farmers focused on growing sunflower-oil seeds and tended to ignore the confection sunflower. As nutritional values of the seeds were recognized, confection-sunflower production increased, and it became an important crop in the early 1970s. At about the same time, the demand for oil seeds from foreign markets increased, causing the production of both types of seeds to expand rapidly.

Two other notable agricultural products of North Dakota are dry, edible beans and potatoes. The dry bean varieties include pinto, navy, and Great

wheat, or middlings, as they were called, and cooking them into a breakfast porridge. Since he liked the cereal so much, Amidon persuaded Mapes and Bull to package some of it and include ten cases in a shipment of flour to a customer in New York City.

At the suggestion of another employee, they had called the product "Cream of Wheat." Three hours after the shipment arrived in New York, a telegram was received at the Diamond Milling Company. It said, "Forget the flour. Send us a car of Cream of Wheat."

Northern. Early Scandinavian, German, and Irish immigrants brought seed potatoes to the Red River Valley by ox cart. Once the settlers discovered the rich soil of the valley, which is partly in eastern North Dakota and partly in western Minnesota, they began to seek better varieties of potato plants. Potatoes were one of the mainstays of Midwestern meals.

Ethnic Foods of North Dakota

The pioneers who came to Dakota in wagons brought potatoes, squash, rice, preserves, pickles, and eggs. The fragile items such as eggs were packed in cornmeal for the rough journey. However, the supply of both eggs and cornmeal was usually exhausted at journey's end.

In 1812 a small group of Scottish Highlanders established a settlement in the Red River Valley and ignored the eating habits of the area, which were primarily based on the food of the Indians. The Highlanders had brought with them salt pork and beef from England, as well as oatmeal for porridge, salt fish, and shortbread. Scottish food is still available in North Dakota, especially at Scottish festivals. Those of Scottish heritage make *Free Kirk*, a pudding with spices, raisins, and currants; *Bannocks*, orange flavored cakes; and oatmeal porridge, which is often served with fresh berries.

The largest group of Icelandic settlements in this country is in North Dakota. *Skyr*, a version of yogurt, was made by many of the Icelandic housewives and was served with blueberries. At Christmas, Icelandic holiday tables featured *Handikjot*, smoked mutton served cold with creamed green peas.

The North Dakota mutton was especially prized for its flavor, which was acquired by pasturing the sheep on wild herbs.

The Norwegians still bake many of their native cookies and pastries at Christmas time, such as *Krumkaker*, a very thin rolled cookie, and *Fattigmannbakkel*, a deep-fried sugar cookie flavored with brandy. At holiday time many other Norwegian specialities are served, including *Rullepolse*, rolled, spiced beef that is served cold; *Spekekjott*, smoked dried lamb; *Lefse Risgrot*, a rice pudding; and *Rommegrot*, a sour-cream pudding.

Some of the other ethnic dishes brought to North Dakota include a Scotch-Irish mashed potato dish called *Colcannon*. Sometimes mashed rutabagas were also added to the dish which contains onions and cabbage or kale. Moslem immigrants brought a sweet stew made with meat, vegetables, and durum wheat. The Finns made a type of blood sausage. Those of French Canadian heritage still serve *Cassoulet*, Vichyssoise, and croissants.

COLCANNON

Although the Swedes were probably the first to bring rutabagas to the Midwest, it was the Scotch-Irish settlers in North Dakota who popularized this root vegetable in their native Scottish dish, *Colcannon*. The basis of the dish was mashed potatoes with onions and cabbage to which rutabagas were often added.

Serves 6

1 1/4 pounds potatoes, peeled and cut in large cubes

1 pound rutabaga, peeled and cut in large cubes

2 cups finely shredded cabbage

7 tablespoons butter

1/3 to 1/2 cup half-and-half

Salt and pepper, to taste

3 scallions, finely chopped

■

Cook the potatoes and rutabagas in lightly salted water in a large saucepan until tender, about 25 minutes. In the meantime blanch the cabbage in boiling water for about 4 minutes until crisp-tender. Drain the cabbage. When the potatoes and rutabagas are done, drain them and return them to the pan. Shake over low heat until they are dry.

Mash the hot potatoes and rutabagas with 4 tablespoons of the butter and 1/3 cup of the half-and-half. Add more half-and-half, if necessary, to make a thick, smooth purée. Season with salt and pepper, to taste.

Melt 2 tablespoons of the remaining butter in a large ovenproof skillet over medium heat, add the cabbage and cook, stirring constantly, for a minute or two. Stir in the mashed potatoes and scallions. Dot the top with the remaining tablespoon of butter and bake in a preheated 350° F. oven for 15 minutes. Serve immediately.

SOUTH DAKOTA

FOLLOWING THE DISCOVERY of gold in the Black Hills of South Dakota in the mid-1870s, miners, prospectors, and merchants swept into the state with visions of quick wealth. Towns sprang up overnight. One trader delivered a load of supplies to a small group of tents called

DEATH OF BEAUTY - PHEASANT by John S. Curry, oil, 48 x 33 1/2 inches, courtesy of Mongerson Wunderlich Galleries, Ltd., Chicago, Illinois.

Deadwood Gulch, and when he returned a few months later, he found 25,000 people were living there.

One of the main problems of the gold seekers was food. Every single bite of food that fed the hungry multitude had to be transported across miles of open prairie and into the hills. The story of the food supply in the Black Hills probably had more romance and drama connected with it than the gold strikes. More fortunes were made in supplying the necessities of life than were made with a pick and a pan.

The basis of much of the food was the hog. In almost every phase of American history, the stubborn hog, which eats almost anything, has provided food for the American pioneers. The hog also came to the Black Hills. Slung in a crate beneath a covered wagon or waddling, grunting, and rooting behind the slow-moving oxen of the wagon train, the hog became the staple diet of the prospectors. After slaughtering, the meat was salted down in barrels or smoked.

Although food was of vital importance, there was not a great deal of care in its preparation. Anyone who could soak beans and fry bacon was a cook, until a more profitable means of making money came along. The food was monotonous. The menus did not vary and consisted of fried bacon and beans, corn bread in various forms, and sourdough bread. In the gold camps one ate to keep alive, and anything that kept body and soul together was acceptable.

"Store boughten" bread cost a dollar a loaf, about $10 in today's values.

The miners' bread was unleavened or sourdough. Fresh vegetables, as well as fresh milk or dairy products, were very rare. There was an occasional chicken, but eggs were a great luxury that only a few could afford.

Cattle

In 1876, when the gold fever was at its height in South Dakota, there were no cattle on the lush prairies. Only a few remaining buffalo and a few oxen, which had been abandoned by settlers moving west, roamed the vast grazing lands. Two years later when the value of the grazing land became apparent, however, there were 100,000 head of cattle in South Dakota. Five years later the number had risen to 800,000.

The original cattle brought to South Dakota were rangy longhorns from Texas. They had walked up the Chisholm Trail, herded by whooping cowboys. Pioneer ranchers paid $25 for each head of cattle delivered to South Dakota.

The new cattle industry appealed to European investors, particularly the Scottish, as there was money in food. They acquired large landholdings and had hundreds of cowboys on their payrolls. In the late 1800s a Scottish accent was all that was needed as collateral for a mortgage to start a ranch and raise cattle in South Dakota.

Along with the Scots came their cattle—Scottish Highlanders, Aderdeen Angus, and white-faced Herefords. Many returned to Scotland as meat. In 1883 South Dakota shipped 50,000 dressed beef carcasses on ice to Glasgow. Even with all of the cattle on the range, however, the population mainly ate pork. Beef steak, like store-bought bread, was a luxury that few could afford. Also, the penalty for rustling was severe, and the easiest way to avoid suspicion of cattle rustling was to sell the cattle outside of the area, sticking to beans and bacon for sustenance.

Life and Food in South Dakota

Although the food of the South Dakota pioneers was not too different from that of pioneers in other parts of the country, South Dakota settlers added their own recipes to America's cuisine. There is still gold in the Black Hills, and the miners favorite meat continues to be pork. Pork roast with baked sweet potatoes and a rhubarb pie always put a glint of gold in any miner's eye.

The South Dakota homesteaders at the turn of the century subsisted primarily on potatoes, plus salted pork, and whole-wheat bread. It they had a cow, they also had milk, butter, and cheese to add to this diet. Water was often scarce. Bundles of hay tied tightly together, called hay ties, and buffalo or cow chips were used for fuel. During threshing time, the women spent days preparing food for the hungry workers, with dumplings and baked goods being special treats.

Coffee breaks were the norm twice a day for the Scandinavian families who settled South Dakota. At mid-morning and mid-afternoon the women carried steaming coffeepots and baskets of almond cakes, spice cookies, and yeast crullers out

HAM AND POTATO CHOWDER

Recipes for chowders were transported by the New England settlers to the Midwest. Instead of being based on seafood as they were in New England, Midwest chowders were created with readily available smoked pork, potatoes, and other vegetables.

This chowder is a good way to use the last of a ham and the ham bone. Small pieces of fresh green beans are added at the end of the cooking time. For a variation add fresh corn kernels during the last 7 minutes of cooking.

5 large carrots, diced

4 stalks celery, diced

1 medium onion, diced

5 large potatoes, diced

6 cups water

1/4 teaspoon pepper

1/2 teaspoon dried thyme

1 ham bone

3/4 cup 1-inch pieces of green beans

2 cups diced ham

1/3 cup half-and-half

■

Place the vegetables in a stock pot and add the water, pepper, and thyme. Bring to a boil and cook over medium-low heat for 25 minutes, or until the vegetables are tender. Mash about half of the vegetables with a potato masher. Add the ham bone and bring the soup back to a boil. Then continue simmering for 2 1/2 to 3 hours. Add the green beans and cook on medium-low heat for 15 to 20 minutes, or until the beans are done. Add the ham and the half-and-half to smooth and thin the soup. Heat through and serve.

to the men in the fields.

The Swedes introduced rutabaga to this country, and in South Dakota it is still cooked with apples and brown sugar. It is also combined with sautéed mushrooms and green peas. The Swedes also continued to have smorgasbord meals with herring in cream; hot, spicy meatballs; vegetable salad; and headcheese, a well-seasoned molded sausage made from the meaty bits of the head of a calf or pig. When cool the sausage was

unmolded and served at room temperature, thinly sliced.

The German Mennonites from Russia, who established farms in South Dakota, brought recipes of both countries with them. Poppy-seed cakes came from their homes in Germany, and pastries filled with ground meat were brought from their stay in Russia. One sect of these Mennonites in South Dakota is the Hutterites, who still live communally and practice much of their

ROASTED PHEASANT

Each fall hunters from throughout the nation flock to South Dakota to hunt pheasants. The sport is so popular that game farms stock local hunting areas through government contracts. Pheasants are also commerically available from game farms in many states throughout the country.

In this recipe the pheasant breast is covered with bacon to provide additional moisture during roasting. The juniper-flavored cabbage is a good flavor contrast to the tarragon and the slightly sweet glaze of the pheasant.

Serves 2

1 pheasant (2 to 2 1/2 pounds)

1/3 pound sausage

1/2 tart apple, peeled, cored, and
    chopped

2 tablespoons chopped onion

3 large mushrooms, chopped

1/4 cup golden raisins

1/4 cup chopped walnuts

1/4 cup chopped parsley

1 egg, beaten

1/2 teaspoon celery seeds

Salt and pepper, to taste

1 large sprig fresh tarragon or 1 teaspoon
    dried tarragon

3 slices bacon

1/2 cup dry sherry

2 tablespoons red currant jelly

■

Rinse the pheasant and pat it dry. Combine the sausage, apple, onion, mushrooms, raisins, walnuts, parsley, egg, celery seeds, salt, and pepper. Stuff the bird with the sausage mixture.

Place the pheasant in a shallow roasting pan. Put the tarragon sprig on the breast of the bird or sprinkle it with dried tarragon. Then place the bacon slices over the breast and roast the bird in a preheated 350° F. oven for 1 hour, or until the bird is almost tender. Pour off the fat. Combine the sherry and jelly, mixing well to blend. Baste the bird several times with this glaze and continue roasting it for another 15 minutes, or until the pheasant is tender.

To serve, spoon some cabbage on each of two plates. Cut the pheasant in half and place each half on top of the cabbage.

Savory Cabbage with Juniper Berries

1/2 medium head savory cabbage

2 tablespoons butter

1/3 cup chopped onion

10 juniper berries, slightly crushed

1/4 cup chicken broth

1/4 cup white wine

Salt and pepper, to taste

■

Shred the cabbage. Melt the butter in a medium-size saucepan, add the onions, and sauté them until they are a light brown. Add the rest of the ingredients. Cover and bring to a boil, then cook over low heat for 15 to 20 minutes, or until the cabbage is done.

German-Russian cooking.

The Germans are the most widespread ethnic group in South Dakota, and many settled around Freeman. They have an annual *Schmeckfest*, food-tasting festival, where many of the ethnic German and Russian dishes are available.

An area north of the Black Hills has a strange black soil called gumbo, which wrinkles when dry and looks like a murky sea when wet. The grass on the gumbo is exceedingly rich and the lambs that graze on it are known throughout the state for their delicate flavor. An extra-special Sunday dinner in South Dakota consists of roast leg of gumbo lamb seasoned with nutmeg, crusty brown roasted Dakota potatoes, and chokeberry jelly.

The most exotic game bird in South Dakota is the Chinese ring-necked pheasant. It was imported from China in the 1890s and became the state bird of South Dakota. The natural habitat and climate of the state proved suitable for the pheasant, and the first official hunting season opened in 1919 with a one-day, two-bird limit.

Longer now, the pheasant-hunting season in October attracts hunters from all over the country to Redfield and Huron, South Dakota. Local restaurants and lodges prepare special pheasant meals. The birds are roasted with salt pork, braised with a tangerine stuffing, or cooked in a casserole with onions and mushrooms.

South Dakota Agriculture

Farming is not new to South Dakota. For centuries the Arikaras Indians cultivated corn, melons, beans, and squash. Utmost care was taken to preserve the seeds for the following year. The Arikaras would rather starve than eat the last ear of corn. They used food scraps and horse and buffalo dung for fertilizer. Produce was not only important to the Indians for food but also for barter with their neighbors and with white traders for goods and horses.

Farming was not extensive in South Dakota until an agricultural population began settling the Indian lands in the southeast. The farms were not large and usually consisted of a few acres for vegetables, corn, and spring wheat. Although the early pioneer farmers in southeastern South Dakota mixed the raising of cattle with farming, the raising of livestock did not develop rapidly as a separate industry since it required a large investment.

There was, however, extensive livestock raising on the unoccupied ranges west of the Missouri River. The cattle were turned loose without shelter and at the end of the summer were rounded up and sorted out by brand. This method of raising cattle was only profitable if there was a mild winter. Raising livestock increased when a ready market developed as settlers, gold prospectors, and the army arrived.

After 1878, when the railroad extended into the prairies, agriculture became the chief industry of the state. Since corn became a major crop in the southern part of the state, pork production increased. The raising of livestock and the cultivation of wheat, rye, and sunflower seeds comprise the major agriculture of the state today.

John Morrell & Co.

The largest single meat-packing plant in the nation is located in Sioux Falls, South Dakota. The Morrell family started in the meat-packing business in England in 1827, and came to Chicago in 1871 to open a plant. In 1878 the Morrell meat-packing operation was moved to Iowa, and another plant was opened in South Dakota in 1909. The Iowa plant closed in the early 1980s and has been consolidated with the one in South Dakota.

WARM POTATO SALAD

Wilted lettuce salads with wild greens and rendered salt pork were often prepared in the 1800s by the Dutch pioneers of the Midwest. The early German settlers enjoyed their warm potato salads.

This salad combines wilted lettuce and potatoes in a warm salad prepared with bacon instead of salt pork. Serve with Bratwurst or thick dinner franks.

Serves 4

4 medium potatoes (about 2 pounds)

1 stalk celery, sliced

4 radishes, sliced

3/4 cucumber, pared and sliced

2 green onions, chopped

1/2 large head romaine lettuce, torn into
   bite-sized pieces

5 slices bacon

2 tablespoons all-purpose flour

1 1/4 cups water

1/2 cup cider vinegar

1/8 teaspoon pepper

■

Boil the potatoes until just tender, about 25 minutes. Cool the potatoes just enough to handle; peel and slice them.

Combine the celery, radishes, cucumbers, and onions in a bowl. Place the lettuce in another bowl.

While the potatoes are boiling, place the bacon in a large cold skillet and fry over medium heat until crisp. Drain the bacon and retain 1/4 cup bacon drippings in the skillet. Break the bacon into small pieces and set aside. Add the flour to the bacon drippings and stir over medium-low heat until smooth. Then stir in the water and vinegar and cook until there is a smooth sauce. Season with the pepper. Reduce heat to simmer.

Add the potato slices and lightly toss them with the sauce. Then add the vegetables and lettuce and lightly toss to combine. Return heat to low to warm the salad and serve immediately. Do not let the mixture boil, as the lettuce will become too limp.

Beef, pork, and lamb are slaughtered in the South Dakota plant and shipped fresh and processed to 46 states. Several years ago Morrell acquired the Rath Company, well-known for its bacon, canned hams, and sausages.

COME AND GET IT by Charles "Charlie" R. C. Dye, oil, 29 5/8 x 39 1/2 inches, courtesy of The Rockwell Museum, Corning, New York.

THE SOUTHWEST

THE REGION KNOWN as the Southwest extends from Texas and Oklahoma across New Mexico to Arizona. It is a vast land of plains, desert, gorges, and mesas with cacti, yucca plants, and mesquite.

Although much of the land is without trees and water, some of the early Indian tribes who inhabited this area were predominantly farmers. They grew corn, squash, beans, melons, and pumpkins.

Hunting was secondary to agriculture for some of these tribes, including the Hopi, Zuni, Mojave, and Yuma. They often traded for meat with their more nomadic neighbors, who went north to hunt buffalo. Jerky was a favorite form of preserved game and was the basis of stews to which a little cornmeal was added.

Some 50 years before the English settled Jamestown, the Spanish were exploring the Southwest from Mexico. They were looking for the seven legendary cities of gold and silver. Instead the Spanish discovered the fertile, green valleys of the upper Rio Grande River in what is now New Mexico.

Early Agriculture

By 1609 the Spanish had established a mission-fort at Santa Fe, New Mexico. During the next 200 years, Spanish priests founded missions throughout the Southwest. These missions ministered to the spiritual welfare of the Indians and trained them in farming. At first only the Indian vegetables of corn, beans, and squash were raised, along with a little wheat.

Later, Spanish missionaries and settlers brought vegetable seeds and fruit seedlings from Mexico to the area. Tomatoes, sweet potatoes, avocados, oranges, and lemons began to flourish in the Southwest with the aid of the primi-tive irrigation systems developed by the Indians hundreds of years previously. The Spanish also brought cuttings to grow grapes for sacramental wine.

Although some livestock and poultry were raised on the missions, it was the wealthy Spanish cattlemen who established the first large ranches using Mexicans as cowboys. Some of the first cattle in the Southwest were longhorns, descendants of the Andalusian cattle brought to Mexico from Spain as early as the 1520s. These longhorns were raised primarily for their hides, since the meat was very tough.

In the mid-1800s when Texas longhorns were shipped north and east, they sold at low prices. Their meat was used primarily by immigrant European sausage makers. "Western beef" was not favored until shorthorns and Herefords, both English varieties of cattle, were brought from the East, and the breeding stock improved. Longhorn hides, however, continued to be in demand by New England shoe factories.

Spanish and Mexican Influences

The bland cooking of the Southwestern Indians provided an excellent base for the flavorful and spicy foods introduced by the Spanish. The Spaniards, who ruled Mexico and the Southwest for more than 300 years, wanted to recreate the dishes of Spain and Mexico in this new territory they called *Nuevo Mejico*. They brought the foods of the Mexican Indians to the Southwest—peppers of different varieties, tomatoes, tomatillos, and chocolate. In addition they introduced Spanish foods such as olives, garlic, chorizo (a spicy sausage), and citrus fruits to embellish the corn and beans of the Southwest.

Mexican cookery is based on the tortilla, a flat cake made with specially prepared cornmeal. The tortilla is the basis of several Mexican dishes, including enchiladas, tacos, and tostados.

Avocados, which grew wild in the tropical regions of the Americas, became a favorite of Mexican and Southwest cuisine. Avocados add a touch of coolness both in color and flavor to contrast the hot chilies in many dishes. They are served either as an accompaniment or as a topping. Rice was brought to the area by the Spanish and also became a part of the Southwestern meal.

There are several other main ingredients of Southwestern cookery. Cheeses such as Monterey Jack, Cheddar, or the traditional Mexican *Queso Fresco* are used as fillings and toppings. The dry pinto bean is popular since it remains firm after cooking. Lard has long been the shortening of choice, but it has almost been replaced by vegetable oils.

Chocolate, derived from the Mexican cocoa bean, not only became the base for a popular beverage, but also the main ingredient in desserts and *mole* sauces. Chocolate and exotic spices from the Far East were brought into the Rio Grande Valley by traders from Chihuahua, Mexico.

New Settlers Arrive

After the end of the Mexican-American War in 1848, American settlers came to the Southwest. The majority had become dissatisfied with life in the East or were looking for new adventure. Some were only passing through on the way to California for the Gold Rush. Those who settled were primarily of English, Irish, and Scottish descent and brought their own food preferences. They tried unsuc-

MEATBALLS IN MOLE SAUCE

Mole sauce is of Mexican origin. This rich, dark-brown sauce is a blend of several varieties of chilies, onions, garlic, ground sesame or pumpkin seeds, and a small amount of chocolate. The chocolate contributes to the richness of the sauce without adding sweetness. Mole sauce is usually served with chicken or turkey.

In this recipe, meatballs are cooked in a mole sauce and then served with rice.

Serves 6

1 pound ground beef

3/4 cup crushed corn chips

1 egg, lightly beaten

1/2 cup milk

3/4 teaspoon salt

1 1/4 tablespoons chili powder

1 tablespoon sugar

1 teaspoon cumin

1 teaspoon coriander

3/4 teaspoon dried oregano leaves

3 1/2 tablespoons all-purpose flour

2 tablespoons butter

1 large onion, sliced

1 clove garlic, minced

1 can (16 ounces) tomatoes, juice reserved
    and tomatoes chopped

1 square unsweetened chocolate

Salt and pepper, to taste

■

Combine the beef, corn chips, egg, milk, and salt in a bowl. Refrigerate, covered, for 30 minutes. In the meantime, combine the chili powder, sugar, cumin, coriander, oregano, and the 1/2 tablespoon of flour. Set aside.

Shape the meat mixture into 12 meatballs, using a little more than 2 tablespoons of the mixture for each. Roll the meatballs lightly in the remaining 3 tablespoons of the flour. Melt the butter in a large skillet and brown the meatballs on all sides. This may have to be done in two batches. Remove the meatballs. Add the onions and garlic and sauté for 3 to 4 minutes, stirring occasionally. Then add the spice mixture, the tomatoes and their juice, chocolate, and 1 cup of water. Bring to a boil, stirring constantly. Reduce heat and cook the sauce, covered, over low heat for 30 minutes, stirring occasionally. Season with salt and pepper, to taste. Add the meatballs and simmer covered for an additional 20 minutes. Serve with rice.

flour and learned which peppers were sweet and which were pungent.

The Americans brought beef and dairy cattle. Herds began to roam the open plains. With the shortage of range grass, cattle were kept constantly on the move. Thus, the cowboy and his source of food—the chuck wagon—came into existence.

Cattle have long predominated the agriculture of the area, and beef is still the focal point of much of the cuisine of the Southwest. To produce the leanest and tenderest cuts of beef possible, the breeding and raising of cattle has become a fine art in the Southwest. That is one reason why today no food event is more popular than the barbecue. It is the scene of political rallies, business and civic affairs, as well as purely social events. Equally as important as the meat is the barbecue sauce with which the meat is basted during cooking. Over the years the sauce has been strongly influenced by Mexican spices. Most sauces contain tomatoes, chili peppers, garlic, onions, vinegar, oil, cumin, and various other spices. Many are secret recipes.

In addition to the many versions of chili con carne, there are a variety of stews in the Southwest. *Posole,* a hominy and pork stew, is spiced with chilies. A hearty dish, it is served in the mountains of New Mexico at Christmas. In Arizona beans are stewed with cumin and cilantro.

Today, traditional Southwest cuisine is based on the crops of the Indians—corn, squash, and beans. It has been enhanced by the Spanish, who brought fruits and vegetables, and has become more spicy with the chilies from Mexico. American settlers added their own culinary preferences to the mélange of Southwestern cuisine.

cessfully to grow cabbages, potatoes, and turnips. These new settlers had grandiose plans to make the desert in the Southwest productive. Many years later with modern irrigation, they succeeded.

In order to survive, the new settlers used many of the Indian and Mexican cooking ingredients, including the reputedly poisonous tomato. They baked bread with corn flour instead of wheat

ARIZONA

BECAUSE OF ITS ARID CLIMATE, Arizona has always suffered from a water shortage. There was little commercial agriculture in the state before irrigation canals were built at the beginning of this century.

Many of these canals parallel those built by the ancient Hohokam Indian culture almost 2,000 years ago. The Hohokam developed extensive canal networks and created an agricultural society around the beginning of the Christian era. The early pioneers built new canals along the route of these ancient canals.

Modern Indian tribes did not undertake extensive farming. The Apache and Yuma Indians in the southern part of what is now Arizona subsisted on the plants of the Sonoran Desert. The Mojave and Hopi Indians in the north hunted game, and gathered wild berries and roots in the mountainous areas.

Arizona's grapefruit and other crops grow in man-made oases that were developed by Spanish missionaries. Later, the Mormons increased the productivity of these oases. Still growing around some of the adobe Spanish missions are descendants of wheat and fruit brought to the area in 1687 from Mexico by Father Kino, a Spanish missionary whom many consider to be the Father of Arizona Agriculture.

Father Kino, an Italian named Eusebio Chini (Kino is the Hispanization of Chini), received his Jesuit education in Austria. His goal was to go to the Orient, where the Jesuits influenced that region's science and learning. In anticipation of the transfer, he studied Chinese. When it came time to draw lots with a fellow priest to see where they would go, Kino lost and was assigned to Mexico. His subsequent achievements as an explorer,

MAKING NAVAJO FRYBREAD by Ray Swanson, oil, 30 x 48 inches, courtesy of Miner's Gallery Americana, Carmel, California.

cartographer, astronomer, developer of agriculture and animal husbandry, and founder of Christian missions contributed immensely to the development of the Spanish Southwest. He led a very productive, although austere life and had a great love for the Indians and their well-being.

Early Settlers and Their Foods

Due to its remoteness, Arizona was not settled until the 1850s, when copper, silver, and gold were discovered. Arizona became a territory in 1862, principally because President Abraham Lincoln thought the area's silver deposits could help the Union cause. It was not until 1912, however, that the territory had sufficient population to qualify for statehood.

The copper and silver mines in Arizona brought Slav and Cornish immigrants to work in the mines. Although these early settlers could not get many of the necessary ingredients to cook their favorite native foods, most managed to prepare some of their native dishes at holiday time. A roasted suckling pig with a necklace of berries frequently graced the Slavic Christmas table.

Prairie chicken (grouse) with spiced gravy, baked noodles, plump dumplings, and an assortment of poppy-seed tarts, sweet rolls, and cookies were often served in Slavic homes. Cornish cooks kept busy baking crisp pasties, a turnover made with a pie dough and filled with meat and vegetables. These pasties provided lunch for the miners, as well as dinners for the families.

Beans, a staple food of the Indians,

also became an everyday dish for settlers. They were served along with meat, baked potatoes, homemade rolls or sourdough biscuits with syrup, and coffee with goat's milk.

In the late 1840s a group of 400 Mormons with wagons and animals crossed into Arizona from Utah. They established settlements, planted trees, and tilled the land. Despite the difficulty of obtaining water, the persistent Mormons prevailed, and they played a major role in the agricultural development of Arizona.

Agriculture

Spanish missionaries established the first farms on irrigated oases, which became the basis of Arizona agriculture.

In the late 1600s Father Kino brought cattle to Pimeria Alta (southern Arizona). The Spanish missionaries also brought horses and sheep. The Apache Indians at first welcomed this enrichment of their lean economy, since the cattle provided them with food and the horses, a means of raiding other villages.

Although some cattle were raised by American settlers during the 1850s and early 1860s, the Apache threat prevented any large ranching operations. Once the Apaches were substantially subdued in the early 1880s, large-scale cattle raising became viable. By then the ranges were heavily stocked with Mexican and Texas cattle. The great herds driven in from Texas and the Mexican state of Sonora were used to supply the army and the reservation Indians with beef. The meat was also designed to be a trade-off with the Indians to curtail their hunting and raiding of the settlements. By the turn of the century, cattle grazing declined due to depletion of the grasses.

Modern Agriculture

The Sonoran Desert covers more than a quarter of Arizona. With the aid of irrigation, however, parts of this desert have become farmland. The heat of the desert provides a long growing season of about 240 to 300 frost-free days, depending on the elevation. Most of the agriculture of the state is located in the middle elevations of the desert in Maricopa County, around Phoenix. The city was founded about 100 years ago as an Anglo farming community.

Although the majority of Arizona's farmland is planted with cotton, one-fourth of the acreage produces vegetable and fruit crops. Winter iceberg lettuce is the leading food crop; citrus and cantaloupes are also significant. The area around Phoenix supplies the nation with many fresh vegetables in the winter when they cannot be grown elsewhere.

The remainder of the state raises a variety of food products. White corn for *masa* (corn dough) to make tamales and several varieties of mild chilies are grown in the southern part of the state. With the aid of irrigation, large fruit, pecan, and pistachio orchards thrive. Black mission and Turkey figs are a speciality. A variety of dates that do not have to be pollinated by hand are also grown in orchards. Arizona's oldest industry, livestock raising, remains a significant part of the state's agriculture.

Arizona has had to fight hard to obtain water for its agriculture, competing with Nevada and California. Many of the

JICAMA SALAD

Jicama has been called the Mexican potato. Although it is a root vegetable and has a brown skin like a potato, its texture is crisp even after it is cooked. Jicama is used most often raw as a salad ingredient, where its bland flavor provides a contrast to more assertive spices, such as the mint in this salad.

Serves 6

2 pounds fresh peas, shelled

1 cup of peeled and chopped jicama

1/4 cup chopped red pepper

3/4 cup toasted pine nuts

1/4 cup chopped fresh mint

1 clove garlic, finely chopped

1/8 teaspoon cayenne pepper

1/4 teaspoon salt

1/4 cup mayonnaise

3/4 cup sour cream

Lettuce leaves

■

Blanch the peas in boiling water for 3 to 4 minutes. Rinse them under cold water and drain. In a bowl combine the peas, jicama, red pepper, and pine nuts.

Place the mint, garlic, cayenne pepper, salt, mayonnaise, and sour cream in the bowl of a food processor. Process until the ingredients are well blended. Add the dressing to the vegetables and toss. Serve on lettuce leaves.

farmers have become water brokers, selling the excess water they have on their farms. The water for irrigation comes primarily from the White Mountains, the Colorado River, and the Salt River.

Unique Arizona Foods

Cacti are an integral part of Arizona's cuisine. The prickly-pear cactus thrives in Arizona. The bumpy prickly pear, a favorite food of the Indians, was called a fig by some. Its skin varies from green to purple; however, the flesh is always a purplish red and contains small, hard seeds. It has the consistency of a cucumber and was used by the Indians in stews. It is still cooked in stews but is also eaten fresh and is the basis of some candies and jellies.

In the spring the *nopalitos,* or tender, new green pods of the prickly pear cactus, are included raw in salads, cooked as a green vegetable, or combined in egg dishes. Their taste is similar to green beans.

The magnificent giant saguaro cactus, which abounds only in the Sonoran Desert, has long supplied a sweet red fruit that the Pima and Papagos Indians harvested in the summer. About the size of a hen's egg, the fruit was made into jam or syrup by the Indians. Today the fruit is eaten raw with ice cream and continues to be used for jams and syrup. The juice is the basis for a chiffon pie. As the population of Arizona has grown, it has become necessary to protect these cacti. Harvesting of the fruit is supervised by the state.

Two other special foods of Arizona are jicama and tomatillos. Jicama, a tuberous vegetable brought from Mexico and now grown in Arizona, is crisp like an apple and has a slightly sweet taste. It is primarily used in salads and can be shred-

SWEET POTATO SOUP

Sweet potatoes, which were brought to North America by migrating Indians from Peru, are combined with traditional chili peppers and corn in a soup with Southwestern flavors.

Serves 4

■

2 tablespoons butter or margarine

1 medium onion, chopped

1 1/2 pounds sweet potatoes, peeled and cut in large cubes

1/4 teaspoon pepper

5 cups chicken broth

1 3/4 cups fresh corn kernels

1/3 cup chopped red bell pepper

1 jalapeño pepper, seeded and finely chopped

1 teaspoon chopped fresh oregano

Fresh cilantro leaves, for garnish

Melt the butter in a medium-size saucepan, add the onion, and sauté until the onion is limp, but not brown. Add the sweet potatoes, pepper, and chicken broth. Bring to a boil and cook, covered, over low heat for 25 to 30 minutes, or until the potatoes are tender.

Strain the soup and purée the solids in a food processor. Return the liquid and purée to the saucepan and add the corn, red pepper, jalapeño pepper, and oregano. Bring to a slow boil and simmer 5 to 7 minutes until the corn is tender. Ladle into soup bowls and garnish with cilantro leaves.

ded as a topping for chili. Tomatillos were used by the Aztec Indians and were transplanted to the Southwest. Today, this small green tomato with a paper-thin covering is grown commercially in Arizona. Its lemon-herbal flavor adds zest to sauces and salsas.

Arizona Cuisine

Arizona cuisine, like that of other Southwestern states, was strongly influenced by the native Indians, Spanish conquistadors and padres, as well as Mexican settlers. Indian and Spanish dishes are still prevalent in Arizona's cuisine, since 20 percent of the population is Native American and 16 percent of the population is of Spanish descent.

The dishes of southern Arizona have been strongly influenced by Sonora, the Mexican state directly south of Arizona. In Sonora more wheat than corn is grown. Consequently, Arizona tortillas are more often made of wheat flour. Another Sonoran influence is that dishes are less spicy than in other Mexican and Southwestern cookery. Beef, lamb, and goat are the main meats of both Arizona and Sonora. A dish that Arizonans have adopted from Sonora is *munodo,* a soup containing tripe, green chilies, onions, and mint, which grows profusely in Arizona.

Until the middle of this century, Mexican and Indian dishes were predominant. With the great influx of retired people from all over the country, however, the food of Arizona has become more all-American, with many Midwestern dishes prevailing.

NEW MEXICO

NEW MEXICO was the first area in the Southwest to be settled by the white man. Spaniards from Mexico came to the fertile Rio Grande Valley in 1598 and established outposts along the river. New Mexico had long been the domain of communal Pueblo Indians, so named by the Spaniards because they lived in cliff dwellings and adobe villages.

The Spaniards found these Indians—the Tewa, Tiwa, Towa, and Keres—had a sophisticated trading relationship with neighboring tribes. They had established a trading network using turquoise from northern New Mexico, buffalo meat from the plains, and seashells from what is now California. They also had a complex structure of government, religious rituals, and a well-developed agricultural economy. They raised beans, squash, corn, and pumpkins along with wild cotton.

The Spanish established Santa Fe, which is on the upper Rio Grande River, as a royal city in 1609 and made it the center of government for their holdings in the Southwest. They also set up missions in the region. Although the Spanish attempt to Christianize the Indians was not very successful, they introduced the Indians to horses and cattle. The previously barren lands around the missions were turned into farms, orchards, and even vineyards.

Early white settlers in the Rio Grande Valley soon found that a vast stretch of desert and hostile Indians isolated them from Spanish Mexico. After Spanish power declined in Mexico, aid to the Spanish settlers in the Rio Grande Valley was almost nonexistent. The settlers were forced to become self-sufficient. They built fortresses against the hostile Indians and grew their own food. They adhered to Spanish traditions in their food preparations, embellishing them with local ingredients.

The only domestic animal the Indians had in pre-Spanish days for eating was the dog. With the coming of the Spaniards, however, they quickly added lamb, beef, and goat to their diet. The settlers, in turn, started growing and using Indian corn, particularly blue corn.

Through the years, the Indians had learned that once dried, yellow or white corn could be stored almost indefinitely without spoiling if sprinkled with lime. The corn was ground into flour when needed. Blue corn, popular in New Mexico and the Southwest, was treated differently. Blue corn was smoked in an adobe oven with piñon (a species of pine) wood, giving it a unique, rich flavor. The corn was then ground with a lava wheel into flour. The same process is still being used, and blue cornmeal is the key ingredient in New Mexican corn bread, tamales, and tortillas.

The Spaniards and Indians lived together for almost 200 years in New Mexico. Although there were conflicts between them, there was a melding of their foods. The large landowners who settled along the Rio Grande River preserved their Spanish heritage as much as possible. They imported chocolate and spices from Mexico; however, Indian foods also began to appear on their tables. Corn bread was served more often than white bread.

Agriculture

From early Indian days, there has always been an interest in agriculture in the area that is today New Mexico. As early as 1598 members of the *Onate* expedition brought 7,000 head of rangy Moorish cattle up the *Camino Real* (royal road from Mexico) to begin raising stock. As settlements were founded, large tracts of grazing land were set aside. During the Spanish and Mexican colonial period, sheepherding surpassed cattle raising. Families owned a milk cow, oxen for plowing, and several head of cattle for meat, tallow, and hides. As early as 1630 small farms called *ranchos* and *estancias* were established along the Rio Grande to take advantage of the dependable water supply and fertile bottomland.

A series of Indian wars, which culminated in the Pueblo Revolt of 1680, drove white settlers out of the area. In 1693 settlers began to return to the middle Rio Grande Valley to reclaim old farms and establish new ones. In the early 1700s most of the good farm land had been taken.

By 1776 the agricultural lands of the Rio Grande Valley had very wide irrigation ditches called *acequias*. They were maintained by the citizens of the communities. This system of irrigation made it possible to grow fruits, vegetables, and cereals in the area around Albuquerque in the late eighteenth and early nineteenth centuries. A great variety of fruits and vegetables is still being grown in the valley. Now, however, wheat, sorghum, corn, and beans are primarily dry farmed.

The early farm tools in New Mexico were hand tools, which required long hours in the field. The first mechanical harvester did not appear in New Mexico until the 1870s, because it was too expensive for the average farmer in this isolated region.

By the 1880s truck farms, called market gardens, were established near Albuquerque. As a result the produce grown in the Rio Grande Valley was shipped by railroad throughout the Southwest.

NAVAJO CORN GRINDER by Ray Swanson, oil, 30 x 40 inches, courtesy of Miner's Gallery Americana, Carmel, California.

Early New Mexico

Life in the early days of Spanish settlement in New Mexico did not present some of the hardships encountered by settlers in other parts of the United States. Although typical dwellings were small and built of adobe bricks with a well-packed earth floor, many settlers possessed Chinese blue export porcelain, silver, and furniture. They cooked with spices that had been brought to Mexico from the Far East by Spanish galleons. These finer things of life had to be bought to Santa Fe by mule train from Chihuahua, Mexico, until the Santa Fe Trail opened in 1821.

The fireplace was used for cooking in early New Mexico homes. One of the most common household cooking utensils was an iron griddle, which was used for making tortillas and other flat breads. It was placed on an iron trivet over the coals in the fireplace. Trivets also supported the bean pot and other cooking kettles. Skewers were used for roasting freshly butchered pieces of venison, sheep, chickens, and rabbits. Larger pieces of meat, such as beef, were suspended by means of hooks on a rod over the fire.

Some of the more popular early New Mexican dishes that were cooked in the fireplace included chick-peas and lamb. The chick-peas were baked into a chili flavored soufflé or pudding. Stewed lamb shanks were flavored with saffron or

ZIA DESIGNS by Gayle Nason, oil, 13 x 20 inches, courtesy of Legacy Galleries, Scottsdale, Arizona.

pieces of hot sausages. Roasted lamb was served with a sauce made from red and green chili peppers.

In the early 1800s the favorite beverage of New Mexican settlers was chocolate, prepared from blocks of unsweetened chocolate imported from Mexico. It was shaved and cut into small chips, placed in pitchers or mugs, and mixed with hot water. Spices and sugar sweetened the bitter taste.

Chilies and Nuts

Chilies, members of the pepper family, were originally brought from Mexico four centuries ago. They have become a main ingredient in Southwestern cuisine and an integral part of the agriculture of New Mexico. There are festivals for the harvest of red and green chilies, chili clubs, and an organization of International Connoisseurs of Red and Green Chili.

New Mexico is known for its profusion of chilies—red, yellow, and green. Much of the chili crop is dried and ground into pure chili powder. The packages are marked with the words "no spices added" to distinguish them from commercial chili powders.

Chilies became an ingredient of Spanish Southwestern cooking when they were introduced to the Spanish by Mexican Indians. Early settlers in New Mexico found that the taste of hot peppers contrasted nicely with the bland beans and rice of the area. In Indian times chilies were also used to preserve and tenderize meat.

There are more than 200 varieties of chili grown in New Mexico; however, only 25 varieties are in common use. Their names vary with the places where they are grown. The milder ones are usually known as *poblano* or *ancho* and some of the hotter ones are *jalapeño, pequin,* and *seranno.* In the early fall ropes of brilliant red chili peppers can be seen drying along the roads in the upper Rio Grande Valley. Chili peppers are the major crop of the local Indian-Spanish farmers.

The piñon tree is the state tree of New Mexico. Its seeds have been used for food by both the native Indians and Spanish. In Indian times the trees' pinecones were harvested in the fall and spread on the ground to dry and open. The nuts were removed by thrashing or trampling the pinecones. These pine nuts, along with the beans of the wild mesquite, were ground into flours from which small cakes were baked in the sun. The nuts were also added to stews. Today, in the Southwest the piñon nut is combined with other ingredients to stuff tomatoes and avocados and is used in rice salads, as well as in chocolate and prune cakes.

CAPIROTADA

Capirotada, a New Mexican bread pudding, is made with a caramelized wine sauce instead of the usual milk and eggs. The sauce plus the melted cheese gives this pudding a custard-like texture.

Serves 6

3/4 cup sugar

1 1/2 cups water

3 tablespoons butter

1/3 cup maple syrup

1/2 cup sweet white wine, such as Tokay

8 slices white bread, toasted and cut into
   2-inch square pieces

3/4 cup raisins

3/4 cup pine nuts or slivered almonds

1 cup grated mild Cheddar cheese

Whipped cream, optional

■

Spread the sugar in the bottom of a medium sauce pan and place it over medium heat. Cook without stirring until the sugar turns a light gold. Turn heat to low and continue cooking sugar until it is a medium brown, stirring constantly. Slowly add the water, stirring to dissolve any lumps. Cook until the syrup is smooth. Remove from heat and add the butter, maple syrup, and wine.

Butter an oblong baking dish that will accommodate the bread in 2 layers. Place half of the bread in the dish and sprinkle with half of the raisins and nuts. Then sprinkle half of the cheese into the dish. Top with the remaining bread and sprinkle with the remaining raisins, nuts, and cheese. Carefully pour the sauce over the bread and bake in a preheated 350° F. oven for 20 to 25 minutes or until the syrup is absorbed. Serve warm or cold, topped with whipped cream, if desired.

Classical New Mexico Cuisine

New Mexico is an area of mixed cultures—Pueblo Indian, Spanish, Mexican, and pioneer Anglo-American. From this mixture of cultures a unique cuisine has developed.

Those of Spanish descent still prepare a variety of traditional dishes, particularly desserts, which incorporate some of the exotic spices used by the early Spanish settlers. Anise cookies are a favorite at Christmas and *Sopaipillas,* small hot breads, are served with a cinnamon sauce. *Flans,* egg custards of Spanish origin, are often flavored with nuts or chocolate, and uncooked meringues are served with a flavored custard sauce.

Cinnamon is also used in the Spanish bread pudding, *Capirotada.* This pudding is made with toasted slices of white bread, which are put in a casserole with pine nuts, raisins, and grated mild Cheddar cheese. The mixture may be sprinkled with cinnamon, is then covered with a wine-based caramel syrup, and baked in the oven. If brandy or whiskey is added just before serving, the dish is called "drunken" bread pudding.

Panocha, similar to a traditional Indian Pudding, was topped with a dash of cinnamon by the Spanish settlers. This pudding was made with sprouted wheat, which gave it a slightly sweet flavor.

Pumpkin seeds, nuts, wild celery, and poultry also figured predominantly in Spanish-Indian cooking, such as the classic Spanish *Arroz con Pollo*—chicken with saffron rice. The dish took on another dimension when the Spaniards used chopped chilies instead of the traditional peas. Pumpkin seeds, as well as almonds, cumin seeds, and garlic were also added to this chicken dish. The wild celery that grows near Chimayo, New Mexico, is used to season chicken and pork. Its root is dried and is the basis of a Christmas drink known as *Mistela de Chimaja.*

New Mexican cuisine is a simple one, based on corn and chilies. The most popular flavorings are onion, garlic, tomato, cumin, oregano, and cilantro. Beef, pork, and chicken are the standard meats, although fish and seafood have been added to New Mexican cooking in recent years. Breads, too, are simple, with tortillas being the most popular. Indian fry bread, which today is deep-fried, is another favorite. Fresh citrus, which was originally planted by the Spaniards, provides an unusual accent to many New Mexican dishes.

FLAN

Flan, or baked custard, is a light, creamy dessert that is typical of Mexican and therefore Southwestern cooking. Some of the custards of the region are made with citrus juice in addition to the customary milk and eggs. This *Flan* is flavored with brandy and nutmeg.

Serves 4

Caramel

1/2 cup sugar

3 tablespoons water

■

Heat the sugar and water in a small skillet over medium-low heat, stirring occasionally until golden brown. Immediately pour the caramel into a medium-size custard dish with a straight bottom or pour 2 tablespoons of the mixture into 4 individual custard cups.

Flan

2 cups milk

1 teaspoon vanilla

1 tablespoon brandy

1/2 cup sugar

3 whole eggs

2 egg yolks

1/4 teaspoon nutmeg

■

Mix the milk, vanilla, and brandy together in a saucepan and warm, but do not boil. Mix together the sugar, eggs, egg yolks, and nutmeg in a small bowl. When the milk mixture is warm, slowly and carefully add it to the eggs. Strain the mixture through a fine sieve to remove any egg particles that may have formed. Pour into the caramel-lined custard dish or divide among the 4 individual custard cups. Place the custard in a baking pan and fill the pan with hot water half way up the sides of the custard dish or cups. Bake in a preheated 350° F. oven for 50 to 60 minutes or until a knife inserted in the center comes out clean. Cool and invert the custard onto a serving plate. (The *Flan* may be prepared early in the day, stored in the refrigerator, and then inverted onto a serving plate.)

OKLAHOMA

AFTER HIS FIRST HUNT by Charles M. Russell, watercolor, 18 1/2 x 23 inches, courtesy of Mongerson Wunderlich Galleries, Ltd., Chicago, Illinois.

UNTIL LATE in the nineteenth century, the history of Oklahoma was closely tied to its Indian population. In the 1700s twenty distinct groups of Indians inhabited the Oklahoma Territory. The Prairie tribes lived in small groups and practiced both hunting and farming. In the summer, they traversed the prairie, hunting buffalo, and using every part of the animal for food, clothing, shelter, fuel, and tools. In the fall, the prairie Indians returned to their small villages to harvest their crops. They again hunted some buffalo to add to their store of food for winter. The Plains Indians in the western part of the Oklahoma Territory were also buffalo hunters, but they did not maintain permanent villages.

By the early 1800s the largest portion of Oklahoma was occupied by five major Indian tribes—the Creek, Choctaw, Chickasaw, Cherokee, and Seminole—who had been forcibly moved there from the Southeast.

These five tribes were primarily agricultural, and their principal crop was corn. They used hollowed-out tree stumps and wooden pestles to grind corn into meal. A favorite dish of the Cherokees was *Tafala*, a boiled porridge of cracked corn. Creeks and Seminoles enjoyed a cornmeal mush called *sofky*. The Indians' diet was supplemented with beans, pumpkins, squash, wild game, and fish. Although much of the Indian economy was based on tilling the soil, livestock raising became part of their economy when the settlers came to Oklahoma.

Settlers

Oklahoma was the last of the Great Plains regions to be settled and homesteaded. The area had been set aside in the 1820s as Indian Territory to house those tribes that had been removed from more thickly populated southern states east of the Mississippi River. For the next 60 years, white settlers made inroads into the lands reserved for the Indians. Although the settlers were fined and evicted by the army, it was impossible to stop the immigration. In 1889 the U.S. government paid the Indians for the "Unassigned Lands."

At noon on April 22, 1889, Oklahoma was opened for settlement, and the rush for land began. People came by covered wagon, cart, and on horseback to stake their claims. It was reported one man rode an ostrich. In a few days all of the land was claimed. Over time, some of the Indians sold their allotted land to land-hungry white settlers.

The majority of the homesteaders were small-scale farmers and ranchers. Their first houses were made of sod or they lived in clay dugouts in the side of a hill. A few very fortunate settlers had enough timber on their property to build a log cabin. Unlike their ancestors on the East Coast 250 years earlier, however, these new settlers were not met by a wilderness. The region had many of the amenities of life, which had been brought there by the military, railroads, and cattle ranchers.

Settlers spent the first few years raising subsistence crops and bartering for necessities. When wheat was raised a few years later, they earned enough money to build houses. However, the drought of 1890 forced many of the settlers to return to their home states. Those who stayed eventually experienced prosperity from plentiful harvests.

Early Oklahoma Cooks

Most of the women who helped settle Oklahoma had brought with them their silver and good English china, onion sets, and packets of seeds. They carried in their heads recipes for sugar cakes, gingerbread, Brunswick Stew, and carrot fritters. Unfortunately, they did not realize that their new homes would be located in a land of red dirt, rattlesnakes, and swirling winds.

BARBECUE SAUCE

Barbecue sauce has been traditionally used for basting meat or poultry to add flavor and moisture while the meat is grilling. It may also be used as a sauce for the grilled meat after it has finished cooking.

Makes 1 quart

4 tablespoons butter

1 large onion, chopped

2 cloves garlic, chopped

2 cups ketchup

1 can (8 ounces) tomato sauce

1 tomato diced

1 medium green pepper, chopped

1 jalapeño pepper, seeded, and very finely
   chopped

3 tablespoons fresh oregano leaves,
   chopped

1 1/2 teaspoons salt

1/2 teaspoon black pepper

4 tablespoons Worcestershire sauce

1/3 cup dark brown sugar

2 tablespoons paprika

3 tablespoons cider vinegar

1 tablespoon cumin

2 teaspoons chili powder

1 can (12 ounces) beer

■

Melt the butter in a large saucepan over medium heat and add the onions and garlic. Sauté until the onions are limp. Add the remaining ingredients along with 1 cup of water and mix well. Bring to a boil, then simmer over low heat for 1 1/2 hours, stirring frequently, until thickened. If the mixture becomes too thick, add a little more water. Cool sauce and store in the refrigerator for up to 2 weeks.

The pioneer women of Oklahoma adjusted and made biscuits and corn bread. They invented a stew of rabbit, turnips, and flour gravy. They combined grains of hard Spanish wheat with beef and named it Oklahoma Stew. Wild pecans were used in pie fillings, and Pioneer Pecan Pie became famous all over the state. Pickles and preserves were made from watermelon rinds. Watermelons originally grew on Indian farms and were later raised by the settlers.

The Dust Bowl of the 1930s provided yet another challenge for Oklahoma cooks. Farm women, who were constantly fighting the dust, put milk, butter, water, and other liquids in covered fruit jars. They mixed biscuit dough in partly closed bureau drawers, whose openings were covered with a cloth. Holes cut in cloth coverings accommodated the hands so that they could knead the dough in the drawer. Black Blizzard Cake, similar to a pound cake made with sour cream, spices, and pecans, originated at that time.

Times have not been easy in Oklahoma. "Alfalfa Bill" Murray campaigned for governor in the 1930s on rat cheese and crackers, foregoing the typical political luncheons and dinners. He drove through the depression-ridden farm country in his Model-T Ford declaring that people could eat anything. He enamored the female population by declaring that the "cooks of the state could write as good a history any day as the sociologists and the militarists."

Oklahoma's Food Heritage

A variety of ethnic groups settled in Oklahoma, including Native Americans, African Americans, Germans, English, Italians, Spanish, Poles, and Czechs. Although each group brought some of their native dishes with them, they soon melded into the cooking of Oklahoma with its strong Tex-Mex flavorings.

Some Native Americans still go to great lengths to gather and prepare traditional foods. They forage for poke greens and dig sassafras roots, even though these items can be purchased in specialty stores. Poke greens are served with scrambled eggs accompanied by fry bread. To Native Americans the gathering of food is a renewal of their traditions and their heritage.

African-Americans had come involuntarily to America, and they came involuntarily to Oklahoma on the Trail of Tears, the forced march of the Indians from the East, as slaves of the Indians. After emancipation, the Indians agreed to free the slaves and give them an allotment of land. A number of free blacks also came to Oklahoma.

At first most African-Americans farmed the land and ate what they grew or could buy, which was often what no one else wanted. They found tasty ways to prepare pig's feet, chitterlings, and hog jowls. Pork was a staple of their diet. Since they had no refrigeration, pork was stored by curing it with salt. Greens, sweet potatoes, and black-eyed peas from the garden were part of their cooking. They ate a great amount of watermelon since there was usually a surplus of it.

Czechs, Poles, and Germans from Russia comprised the majority of the Eastern European population who settled in Oklahoma. Most came in the late 1800s, and the Germans established large Mennonite and Lutheran communities in the state. Many of the Germans were farmers who planted some of the first wheat in western Oklahoma.

All of the Eastern Europeans still retain their culinary heritage through annual folk festivals serving such dishes as *Keelkje,* dumplings with onion gravy; *Poertzelki,* hot caraway sauerkraut; and *Kolaches,* filled yeast pastries. Traditionally, *Keelkje* was always prepared on washday.

There were more German immigrants in Oklahoma than any other nationality, and many lived in close-knit communities, where they retained their food traditions. The Italians also established communities and kept many of their national dishes. The Krebs area, in southeastern Oklahoma, is noted for its Italian food. A number of the restaurants are managed by third-generation Italian-Oklahomans. Potato soup, Italian meatballs and spaghetti, German breads, Sauerbraten, and corned beef are among the repertoire of many Oklahoma cooks.

The Mexicans came to Oklahoma in the late 1800s to work on the railroads. They added to the Tex-Mex style of cooking, which was already familiar to many of the settlers. The latest wave of immigrants came from Vietnam in the late 1970s. They, along with other Asians, have added curries, stir-frys, egg rolls, and a variety of seafood.

TEXAS

IN THE EARLY SIXTEENTH CENTURY Spanish conquistadors came to Texas to seek treasure, find a short route to the Orient, and civilize and Christianize the native Indians. For the next 300 years, the Spanish ruled the region, until ceding it to Mexico in 1821.

When the Mexican government began to rule Texas, it adopted a policy of encouraging Americans to settle there. Some of these early settlers received large land grants from the government; others purchased land. Although land was cheap, back-breaking work was necessary to extract a living from it. Corn became the basic commodity, providing not only a vegetable but also meal for various breads. The pith from the corn stalks was made into molasses to provide a sweetener. Meat was plentiful, consisting of wild cattle and game, such as buffalo, turkey, and deer.

The first American settlement was founded by Moses Austin, a St. Louis banker and businessman, who was granted permission by the Mexican government to bring 300 American families into central Texas. Unfortunately, he did not live to see the settlement established. The project eventually came to fruition under the leadership of his son Stephen. The settlement later became known as Austin.

Texas gained independence from Mexico in 1836 and existed as an independent republic for ten years before joining the United States in 1846. By the late 1830s there were 30,000 Americans in Texas and only 7,500 Mexicans.

When Texas joined the Union, the state possessed two distinct segments—the settled east with its seaports and plantations and the wild western frontier. The leading port of Galveston reflected European and Southern influences in its culture as well as its cuisine. In contrast,

CANTALOUPE, JUG, CHERRIES by Harl Nobles, oil, 12 x 16 inches, courtesy of Miner's Gallery Americana, Carmel, California.

log cabins were the common dwellings on the western frontier, and stewed game provided a subsistence diet.

Early Cuisines of Texas

The heritage of Texas cuisine is like a five-pronged star. Each of the five regions of Texas was settled by pioneers from different parts of the United States and Europe. Each had different food heritages.

In northeastern Texas the new settlers learned how to plant corn and use wild plants from the Indians. Consequently, they adopted many of the Indians' cooking techniques. They also supplemented native foods with produce grown from seeds they had brought with them. The Dutch oven became the stew pot and the utensil for baking various types of corn bread. When wheat flour became cheap, corn bread gave way to biscuits.

Deep East Texas was settled by inhabitants of the lower southern United States—Alabamians, Georgians, Mississippians, and Louisianians. Some were poor whites, who existed on wild berries, fruits, edible weeds, and whatever game they could hunt. Others were plantation owners, who brought the tradition of fine foods and southern hospitality to their Texas plantations, located along the rivers that flowed into the Gulf of Mexico.

Plantation owners served their guests fish and game, followed by an assortment of cakes, pies, and puddings. Plantation ladies were able to purchase spices, which, along with herbs from their gardens, enhanced their foods. The majority of the cooking on these Texas plantations was done by black cooks in a separate kitchen behind the main house. Cajun and Creole cookery also became part of the Deep East Texas cuisine, and shrimp from the Gulf was used in jambalayas.

The third prong of the Texas star, Central Texas, was originally settled by the 300 people Stephen Austin brought to his colony. Until they could establish farms, many lived on wild greens, berries, game, and the little cornmeal they brought with them. Toward the end of the 1800s, immigrant communities of Germans, Czechs, and Poles developed in central Texas.

While the European settlers cooked beef and lamb, they favored roast pork, which they served with dumplings or mashed potatoes and gravy, and cooked garden vegetables. Fresh pork was consumed only during the winter months, and each farmstead had its own smokehouse to preserve the meat for the rest of the year. Although these European settlers preferred rye bread, they learned to accept corn bread as a substitute. It often accompanied hearty soups, which provided a whole meal. The Europeans baked a wide variety of pastries including *Kolaches*, sweet yeast buns of Czech origin, which were a favorite dessert.

South Texas, the fourth prong of the Texas star, was influenced by the cuisine of Mexico and Spain. By the mid 1850s Mexican cooking had become popular in Texas. Tamales, made of cornmeal filled with chopped meat and hot peppers, then wrapped in a corn husk and steamed, were more appealing than the settler's Johnnycakes. Tacos, guacamole, enchiladas, and tortillas became the daily foods of many settlers. They used Mexican chilies and Spanish spices, such as cumin, for flavorings. The new population of Texas adopted Mexican ways of cooking eggs and meat.

The fifth prong of the Texas star is West Texas. Until the discovery of oil in the area, beef was king. Beef is still the primary meat of the region. West Texans adopted one of their essential foods—beans—from the Mexicans. Thus beef, beans, and corn bread or tortillas became the staple food of West Texas.

SPICY TEXAS SHRIMP

The Gulf Coast is renowned for its shrimp. In this dish the spices of Southwest cookery blend with the milder-tasting shrimp. Serve with warm flour tortillas or with rice.

1 large onion, chopped

2 cloves garlic, chopped

2 tablespoons olive oil

3 tomatoes, skinned, seeded, and chopped

1 can (4 ounces) chopped chilies, drained

2 pounds medium shrimp, peeled and
   deveined

1/4 cup fresh lime juice

1/3 cup chopped cilantro

1/2 teaspoon salt

Warm flour tortillas

Guacamole, optional

Sour cream, optional

■

Sauté the onion and garlic in olive oil in a large skillet over medium heat until translucent. Add the tomatoes and chilies and cook over low heat for 5 minutes. Add the shrimp and cook, stirring gently, over medium heat until the shrimp turn pink and opaque, about 5 to 8 minutes. Stir in the lime juice, cilantro, and salt and heat through. Serve shrimp wrapped in warm flour tortillas with guacamole and sour cream, if desired.

Pintos, often called strawberry beans, became a main ingredient in chili and other dishes. Chicken-Fried Steak originated on the cattle drives in that part of Texas. A pounded (cubed) boneless beef steak, it is fried in a skillet and then smothered in gravy. On their cattle drives cowboys found that the meat was tough and a good pounding was necessary to break down the meat fibers to make it tender.

Texas Cattle

When Mexican ranchers fled south after Texas gained independence in 1836, they left behind free-roaming longhorns, which were descendants of the Andalusian cattle the Spanish had brought with them. There are still some longhorns in Texas, but they have been mostly replaced by other breeds, such as Herefords.

By 1840 the Shawnee Trail, the first of the great cattle trails, had opened from Brownsville at the Gulf through Dallas to Missouri. The most heavily traveled was the Chisholm Trail to Kansas, with half of all the cattle moved from Texas using it. The heyday of the cattle drives lasted about 20 years, from 1865 to the mid-1880s. During this period five million cows were moved from Texas to rail heads in Kansas and Missouri. The great cattle drives came to an end with the expansion of the railroads. Eventually refrigeration made it possible to slaughter closer to the cattle ranches and ship meat instead of live cattle.

Chuck-Wagon Cooking

One of the unique contributions to American cooking of the Southwest is the chuck wagon. Praised in literature and still used in modern rodeo races, the chuck wagon has become one of the

TWILIGHT by Olaf Wieghorst, oil, 24 x 29 inches, courtesy of Mongerson Wunderlich Galleries, Ltd., Chicago, Illinois.

symbols of the American cowboy. Literally a kitchen on wheels, the chuck wagon first came into use in the 1860s, when the long cattle drives from Texas to the railheads in Kansas were started. "Chuck" was the cowboy word for food.

Often as many as 3,000 head of cattle were slowly driven on the 700-mile journey, which usually took several months. On the long trip three meals a day had to be provided for the dozen cowboys and the trail boss.

Probably the first chuck wagon was taken "up trail" in 1866 on one of the first large cattle drives to the railroad. Oliver Loving and Charles Goodnight, who were partners in a cattle operation in the Texas panhandle, drove 3,000 cattle and a wagon made to Goodnight's specifica-

tions. It was a large wagon, on the back of which was mounted a tall box with a drop door. The box was a traveling pantry containing shelves with food staples such as flour, cornmeal, coffee, sugar, and dried beans. There were usually enough provisions for a two-month journey.

The drop door of the chuck-wagon box had a dual purpose: when the wagon was traveling it kept the provisions from spilling; when the wagon was parked and the door was let down, it became a table. On this the cook, who was known as "cookie," prepared the food.

The cookie ruled his domain with an iron hand. Cowboys were not allowed to stand around his fire and had to ride into camp downwind from his chuck wagon. He usually arose at 3 a.m. to

CHUCK-WAGON STEW

Chuck-Wagon Stew was strictly a cowboy dish, its ingredients determined by what was slaughtered on the trail. The meat ranged from venison or other wild game to beef. The cook's ingenuity concocted the flavor of the stew, given whatever ingredients were available. In making a beef stew, some cooks used everything except the horns, the hoofs, and the hide. Others used only the meat and discarded the innards. Stews are still cooked by cowboys out on the range and are also popular fare in ranch dining halls.

Serves 6

2 1/2 pounds chuck (beef) cut into 1-inch
  cubes

Salt and black pepper, to taste

2 tablespoons vegetable or olive oil

3 medium onions, chopped

3 tablespoons all-purpose flour

2 cups beer

2 cups canned tomatoes

3 carrots, cut in large cubes

1 tablespoon molasses

2 teaspoons chili powder

1 bay leaf

1/4 teaspoon oregano

1 can (1 pound) kidney beans

■

Season the beef with salt and pepper. Heat the oil in a Dutch oven over moderate heat. Add the onions and sauté until lightly browned. Add the beef and let it brown lightly. Sprinkle the flour over the beef and stir well to coat the meat. Slowly stir in the beer, scraping any brown particles from the bottom and sides of the Dutch oven. Then add the remaining ingredients, except the beans, and stir well.

Bring the stew to a boil, then reduce heat to very low. Cover and cook for 2 to 3 hours or until the beef is tender. The stew may also be cooked in a preheated 300° F. oven. Just before serving, add the beans and heat through.

The menus for most chuck-wagon meals were the same, and as one cowboy remarked, "with your eyes closed you couldn't tell the difference between breakfast, dinner, or supper." The trail cook usually served up great slabs of beef basted with his own brand of hot sauce, a mess of beans, and biscuits. Desserts were rare. When offered they were either a pie of dried fruit or a rice pudding.

Chuck-Wagon Stew was a favorite meal on the trail. It consisted of tongue, heart, kidneys, liver, and lean meat, along with onions, chili peppers, and salt. Steaks were another favorite. Since the meat was on the hoof alongside the wagon, it was eaten three times a day. Green vegetables were not available on the trail. Consequently, the only vegetable served from the chuck wagon was dried beans, cooked with salt pork and seasoned with onion, garlic, and chili powder.

By the early 1880s the railroads had replaced the cattle drive, but for many years the chuck wagon continued to be used on the vast cattle ranches of the Southwest.

Barbecue

Roasting meats over an open fire has been a cooking technique for many centuries and was used by the Indians and early settlers alike. When the Spanish came to Texas, they attached the word "barbecue" to it, which came from the Spanish word *barbacoa*. It, in turn, came from an old Arawak Indian word describing a framework of green-wood twigs placed over a hole in the ground containing heated stones on which game or fish was cooked.

Although the barbecue was an early Spanish tradition, Texans expanded on it. It is now not uncommon to feed 300 to

cook breakfast and then continued to work for long hours. He would plan ahead, and when camp was to be moved, he would cook the next day's meals the night before.

One of the most prized possessions of the chuck wagon cook was his small wooden cask of sourdough starter from which the daily biscuits and hotcakes were

made. Sourdough is a mixture of flour, salt, and water to which sugar, molasses, or boiled mashed potatoes have been added for fermentation. On the trail the cook rolled out the biscuit dough on the table and cut it with an empty tin can. The biscuits were left to rise and then baked in a heavy Dutch oven over an open fire.

400 people at such an event. Lyndon Baines Johnson, our 35th president, loved to entertain visiting dignitaries at his LBJ Ranch with a barbecue. His favorite meat accompaniment was black-eyed peas, which were served with pork ribs, short beef ribs, chicken, sausages, and sometimes a suckling pig. Other barbecue accompaniments included steamed ears of corn, potato salad, cole slaw, pickles, and biscuits. Barbecues of beef and chicken accompanied by rice, okra, and crayfish dishes have become popular in East Texas.

No Texas barbecue is authentic unless two sauces are applied to the meat. The first is the "sop" or "mop," a marinade applied to the meat before and during cooking, often with a kitchen mop—hence the name. The second sauce, called barbecue sauce, is for splashing over the meat after it is served. The main ingredients for these sauces vary, but they usually are based on either ketchup or beef stock with numerous spices, including chili powder.

Chilies

Chili con Carne, known as a "bowl of red," is considered to be the national dish of Texas. It is believed to have been developed in San Antonio after the Civil War. The popularity of the dish grew after the invention of chili powder in 1902 in New Braunfels, Texas, by a German. Most chili powders are a combination of ground dried chilies, cumin seed, oregano, and garlic.

Texans have always boasted about how hot they like their chilies. For years chili peppers have been one of the fundamental ingredients of Chili con Carne, which Texans say should be hot enough to make a man weep. They have now discovered a red berry, called

chiletepin, which is hotter than chili, and has become very popular. The Indians made a powder from *chiletepin* and used it to coat buffalo jerky. However, the Indians always carefully washed it off before eating the meat.

Originally chili was made with cheaper cuts of beef, pork, or venison, plus chili peppers, suet, cumin, and garlic. Later additions to chili have included oregano, tomatoes, and beans. In true chili con carne, beans are not included in the dish but are served on the side, along with rice. Venison is still the traditional meat in the chilies of West Texas and parts of New Mexico.

Tex-Mex Cuisine

Texas cuisine has always been heavily influenced by Mexican cooking. Texas cooks have adapted many Mexican dishes to their own tastes, resulting in a style of cookery known as Tex-Mex. Many of the original Mexican dishes now contain more meat. Chili peppers are used in almost every dish from corn bread to salads to stews.

Tex-Mex cooking began in the southwestern corner of Texas and has been described by historians as the only food that is native to this country. Although Tex-Mex cooking was originally regarded as a poor-man's Mexican cuisine, today it has become very sophisticated while adhering to Mexican traditions. It uses many of the ingredients indigenous to the Southwest, such as corn, pinto beans, tomatoes, and chili peppers. Tortillas are the bread accompaniments and serve as containers for various meat and cheese fillings. Many of the tortillas are made with blue corn, since Texas grows more blue corn than any other state. Some of the more innovative dishes are crab enchiladas and seafood tostadas.

Other Texas Cooking

There are a variety of other influences on the cookery of Texas. Many Texans are predominantly Anglo-Saxon who came via the antebellum South. Consequently, they like flavorful meat dishes with gravy, served with greens, green beans, and accompanied by rice or potatoes and coleslaw. The southern influence has also added spoon bread, grits, and sweet potato pie.

European immigrants have influenced Texas cooking too. Texans of Polish origin often serve Polish sausages. Fredericksburg, in the central part of the state, was settled by German immigrants at the end of the 1800s. Here one can get sauerkraut, although frequently mixed with bell peppers and hot chilies.

Beef is still king in Texas, although chicken is also popular. In Texas cuisine, soup is a rarity. San Antonio is known for its black bean soup, however, flavored with garlic and topped with sausages. Salads are served as a first course or main course accompaniment but never following the meat. Iced tea is the usual Texas refreshment.

Seafood and Agriculture

There is more to Texas than beef, chili, and barbecue. The state produces a variety of fresh produce and seafood. Texas is also known for its pink grapefruit, cantaloupes, and other melons, as well as pecans and sweet figs. Wheat is grown in northern Texas, particularly the panhandle, which is the southern extension of the Great Plains.

On the Gulf Coast seafood is as much a part of traditional Texas cuisine as chili and Chicken-Fried Steak. More than 100 million pounds of shrimp, oysters, crabs, and finfish are harvested

TACO SALAD

Hearty salads are popular in the warm climates of the Southwest. They often include a large amount of cool, crunchy head lettuce. This Taco Salad features a spicy taco filling with lots of lettuce.

Serves 4 to 6

1 pound lean ground beef

1 medium onion, chopped

1 can (8 ounces) tomato sauce

1/2 cup water

1 teaspoon chili powder

1 1/2 teaspoons dried Mexican seasonings

1/2 teaspoon cumin

1 can (16 ounces) kidney beans, drained and rinsed

1/8 teaspoon crumbled red pepper flakes

1/2 medium head lettuce, torn into bite-size pieces

2 medium tomatoes, cut into chunks

1/2 medium green pepper, chopped

1/4 medium red pepper, chopped

1 can (2.2 ounces) sliced black olives

1 Haas avocado

3/4 cup shredded sharp Cheddar cheese

3/4 cup shredded Monterey Jack cheese

1 cup broken corn chips

Additional corn chips

Bottled taco sauce, optional

■

Cook the beef and onions in a large skillet over medium-high heat until the meat is no longer pink. Drain any accumulated fat. Add the tomato sauce, water, chili powder, Mexican seasonings, cumin, kidney beans, and red pepper flakes. Stir well to combine and cook over low heat for 10 to 15 minutes until the sauce is smooth, stirring occasionally.

Gently combine the lettuce, tomatoes, green and red peppers, olives, and avocado in a large bowl. Spoon the sauce over the lettuce. Top with the cheeses and then corn chips. Serve immediately and pass additional corn chips and taco sauce, if desired.

annually from the Gulf of Mexico by commercial fishermen in Texas. Catfish and trout are caught in the rivers, as well as cultivated in ponds.

One of the newest crops in the Lone Star State is the Texas 1015 Super Sweet onion, developed in 1985 by Texas A&M University. As big as a grapefruit and as sweet as an apple, the Texas 1015 onion grows during the short winter days in the Rio Grande Valley of south Texas and is harvested in the spring. Because of its high moisture content, it cannot be stored for long periods and is only available from late April to early June.

Commercial production of apples is a recent addition to Texas agriculture. It was made possible by Dr. Loy Shreve, a horticulturist at Texas A&M, who experimented with dwarf apple trees that would not be susceptible to the cotton root rot which had killed Texas apple trees in years past. The majority of Texas apples come from dwarf espaliered trees. Varieties include Yellow Delicious, Red Delicious, Jonathan, and Molly Delicious.

Rice growing and milling have become important agricultural activities in Texas. Four generations of the Godchaux family have been involved in rice production in Louisiana and Texas to such a great extent that they have become known as the First Family of Rice. Gustave (Gus) Godchaux was born of French parents in the late 1800s in Franklin, Louisiana, and settled first in New Orleans and then in Abbeville, where he operated a store and a brickyard. By the turn of the century Godchaux had acquired considerable land holdings and two newly mechanized rice mills.

Over the years the family introduced new methods of rice production and rice merchandising. They were the first to launch a brand name, "Water Maid," into the market. The idea of merchandising rice in consumer packages under the brand name was the next step. By 1926 Americans were buying Water Maid and the new long-grain "Mahatma" rice in small cardboard boxes.

After the Second World War, the great grandson of Gus Godchaux introduced a new rice milling process at their Louisiana State Rice Milling Company plant in Abbeville, Louisiana. The process retained the proteins in rice bran and also yielded a rice oil.

In 1965 the River Brand Rice Company of Houston, Texas, merged with the Godchaux rice interests. With this merger Riviana Foods was born. Since then Riviana has built a plant which produces only instant rice, and the company has acquired various other enterprises in the food field. Today Riviana, under the leadership of the Godchaux family, is the largest distributor and marketer of branded packaged rice in the United States under the Mahatma, Carolina, Water Maid, River, and Success labels. The latter is a boil in the bag rice product.

Rice grows in the low, marshy coastal plains of eastern Texas near the Gulf of Mexico. Some of the rice grown in Texas has an aromatic natural flavor. Texmati rice, introduced in 1970, is a cross-breed of white, long-grain and Indian aromatic rice. It is similar to the *basmati* rice of India and Pakistan. Texmati rice is grown on 50,000 acres owned by the Farms of Texas Company, a joint venture of the International Paper Company and The Prince of Liechtenstein Foundation.

CRAB AND CHEESE ENCHILADAS

Enchiladas are one of the basics of Mexican cookery. They were brought to the Southwest by the Mexicans and have become part of that region's cuisine.

An enchilada may be based on a corn or flour tortilla. If the softer flour tortilla is used, it does not need to be fried before it is filled with meat, seafood, and/or cheese. Enchiladas are baked in either a cheese- or tomato-based sauce.

Texas fishermen harvest a variety of seafood off the Gulf Coast of Texas. One of their catches, crab, is an ingredient in these enchiladas with a white cheese sauce.

Serves 4

5 tablespoons butter or margarine

1 medium onion, chopped

3 cups crabmeat

1 can (4 ounces) chopped green chilies

1/4 cup all-purpose flour

2 1/4 cups milk

3 tablespoons chopped cilantro

1/4 salt

1/4 teaspoon pepper

1/2 cup sour cream

2 1/2 cups shredded Monterey Jack cheese

8 (6-inch) flour tortillas

■

Melt 1 tablespoon of the butter in a medium-size skillet, add the onions and sauté until soft. Then add the crabmeat and chilies and gently stir to combine; set aside.

Melt the remaining 4 tablespoons of butter in a medium-size saucepan. Add the flour and stir until smooth. Slowly stir in the milk. Add the cilantro, salt, and pepper and cook the mixture over medium heat until it thickens. Stir in the sour cream and 1/2 cup of the cheese until it is melted. Remove from heat.

Add 1 cup of the cheese and 1 cup of the cheese sauce to the crab mixture. Spoon 1/4 cup of the sauce into the bottom on an oblong baking dish. Fill each tortilla with 1/8 of the crab mixture and place seam-side down in the baking dish. Pour the remaining sauce over the enchiladas and sprinkle with the remaining cup of cheese. Bake in a preheated 350° F. oven for 25 to 30 minutes, or until hot and bubbly.

MEAT'S NOT MEAT 'TIL IT'S IN THE PAN by Charles M. Russell, oil, 23 x 35 inches, courtesy of Gilcrease Museum, Tulsa, Oklahoma.

THE MOUNTAIN STATES

THE FIRST EXPLORERS of the Mountain States were the Spanish, who in 1540, under the leadership of Francisco Vásquez de Coronado, came looking for the fabled Seven Cities of Cibola in search of gold. The next major exploration did not occur until 1804, when Meriwether Lewis and William Clark passed through the region looking for the shores of the Pacific.

During the first half of the 1800s, fur traders and trappers traversed the mountains gathering pelts for eastern markets. Many fur trappers ultimately settled in the mountains and lived among the Indians. Several of these mountain men eventually became guides and led numerous wagon trains across the mountains and along the Oregon Trail.

The eastern section of the Mountain States adjoins the Great Plains, where large herds of buffalo grazed in years past. Trappers usually stocked up on buffalo-meat jerky, pemmican, and sausage before heading into the mountains. Later, buffalo became the meat source for the settlers as well.

The Mountain States area was not a friendly or inviting place, since it was inhabited by hostile Indians. Its treacherous rivers and mountains also presented great obstacles. No substantial maps of this region were created until 1870.

After the Gold Rush in California declined in the 1850s, miners drifted into the Mountain States region looking for gold and other minerals. Soon, other miners came from eastern mining regions; they, in turn, were followed by farm settlers. Miners lived in tents, sod huts, or even shacks made from poles. Everything was in demand, and everything commanded a high price. Eggs sold for a dollar each in Colorado in the 1860s. Fortunes were gambled away in the saloons.

Slowly, however, homesteaders lured by the promise of land began to take over. Settlers came in their wagons bringing their belongings—potbellied stoves, bedsteads, quilts, cradles, and chamber pots. They carried cuttings of plants kept moist in moss. They brought seed potatoes from former farms and planted them in Idaho and Colorado. A pot of goose grease and turpentine was brought along to ease coughs.

Pioneer women lived with a stew pot in one hand and a rifle in the other to shoot a rabbit for dinner or an unfriendly Indian. Wild game was plentiful, so the women cooked whatever was on hand—rabbit, squirrel, fowl, or bear. Settlers preserved the game meat by salting it down in barrels or smoking it. They soon learned which berries were edible and which could be dried for winter use. Pioneer women combined potatoes, water, and a little salt in a bowl and set it out to trap wild yeast from the air. In a few days they had a sourdough starter for biscuits.

Root cellars were often dug before a home was built. Settlers were more concerned with preserving turnips, squash, and potatoes than they were in building a permanent dwelling, since they could continue to live in their wagons.

Wild Game

The Indians hunted deer, elk, and other big game, as well as beavers and other small animals. They fished the mountain lakes and rivers. The Ute and Northern Shoshoni, many of whom lived on the eastern side of the Rocky Mountains, also hunted buffalo on the Great Plains.

Drying was the Indians' only means of preserving meat. When a kill was made, the entire tribe ate its fill of fresh meat, then the rest was cut into strips and sun-dried for jerky. Pemmican made with finely ground meat, suet, marrow, and dried fruits also sustained the Indians.

For the early pioneers anything that flew, leapt, or swam was netted or shot for food. Wild game provided meat for the winter and was the main ingredient in sausage. Thick steaks of venison or buffalo, accompanied by hardtack biscuits or corn bread, was typical fare.

Agriculture

Although the Mountain States were not considered prime agricultural land, settlers used irrigation to cultivate all types of produce. The Idaho potato, which is now known throughout the country, is only one of the early crops developed through irrigation.

In the early 1870s farmers began diverting large amounts of water from the rivers for irrigation. The government did not help the situation when they offered water rights to settlers living in areas where no water existed. Farmers started guarding the floodgates with shotguns. Elsewhere, rustlers and outlaws roamed freely. It was indeed the Wild West.

In addition to crop production, livestock has played an important part in the economy of the Mountain States. Beef has always been number one in livestock production in the region, and 50 percent of the lamb eaten in America is raised in the high mountains in these states. Typically, sheep are taken directly to market from mountain pastures, resulting in a more flavorful meat. Traditionally, most of the sheepherders in the Mountain States are of Basque origin or have come directly from the Basque region of Spain.

STUFFED TROUT

For the early pioneers to the Mountain States, rivers and streams were obstacles to over-come. They were forced to forge the treacherous streams with their wagons, risking their lives and family belongings. The settlers soon discovered, however, that these streams held a valuable delicacy, fresh fish—a welcome relief from their diet of beans and wild game. Rainbow trout is the best-known fish of the Mountain States' rivers and streams.

The delicate flavor of trout is complemented with a simple bread stuffing in this baked-fish recipe.

Serves 2

2 small trout, pan-ready

3 slices soft white bread, torn into small
     pieces

1/2 cup chopped celery

1/2 cup coarsely chopped mushrooms

1/4 cup chopped onions

2 tablespoons finely chopped green pepper

1/2 teaspoon dried thyme

1/2 cup chicken broth

3 tablespoons melted butter

Salt and pepper, to taste

■

Rinse the fish and pat dry. Combine the bread, celery, mushrooms, onions, green pepper, and thyme in a bowl. Add the chicken broth and stir to moisten the stuffing ingredients. Stuff the cavities of the fish and secure with toothpicks. Place the fish in a well-buttered, shallow baking dish. Brush with the melted butter and sprinkle with salt and pepper. Bake in a preheated 400° F. oven for 15 to 20 minutes, or until the flesh flakes easily with a fork.

High-Altitude Cooking

The high elevation presents a major problem to cooking in the Mountain States. The thin, dry air causes quick evaporation, which makes water boil at a lower temperature and makes baking difficult. Regional cookbooks recommend that the amount of sugar used in baking be reduced to allow room for more liquid to help the evaporation problem. Cakes tend to rise higher, thus the cook must reduce the amount of leavening. Eggs are beaten less, and baking temperatures are increased by 25 degrees to set the sides of the cake quickly. Many food companies design special recipes for use in the Mountain States.

Mountain States Cuisine

Although the region was bypassed for many years and often considered unfit for settlement, the cuisine of the Mountain States has a great deal of variety. The early settlers from the East and Midwest brought their style of cooking with them. Russian, Slavic, German, and Scottish immigrants soon added another dimension to the cooking. Basque sheepherders and Chinese and Mexican railroad workers contributed their food preferences. There is also a strong Spanish culinary influence in the southern part of the Mountain States, where chilies are used as liberally as they are in the Southwest.

The spirit of pioneer days is still prevalent in many dishes of the Mountain States. Game is prepared both at home and in many restaurants. Roast leg of lamb and steak on the grill are enjoyed by many of the modern "mountaineers." Steak and eggs with a side order of Idaho potatoes has remained a popular breakfast dish.

COLORADO

AS LATE AS 1877 wagon trains of immigrants from the Midwest were still coming into the Colorado Territory. They came from the Missouri River to Denver over a trail so rugged it was named the Unmarked Grave Route. A fifteen-year-old girl from Maine rode on one of these wagon trains, and after looking at the hungry, disheveled travelers, reportedly decided that what the road really needed was a wayside inn.

The following year she married, and the couple opened the Twelve Mile House in what is now Denver, where she cooked for the hungry travelers. In addition to stirring gallons of oyster stew and making buckets of coffee, her average day consisted of baking 36 cakes, churning butter, and baking bread. She also roasted whole hams, sides of beef, and loins of pork. The inn became so famous that the elite society of Denver dined there. When the railroad came she reportedly baked a thousand biscuits in a day for the railroad workers and crew.

Life in the early settlements of Colorado was rather primitive. In Central City 4,000 people were sleeping under pine-bough shelters and in tents. The grocery store consisted of boards laid across some barrels. Customers paid for their purchases in pinches of gold dust measured between the thumb and the forefinger. Potatoes cost $15 a bushel and oysters were $16 a gallon. Beaver-tail soup became the local delicacy.

Some prospectors soon discovered that a good crop of grain and a few bushels of apples brought in more gold than agonizing hours of panning and digging. By the 1890s Colorado farms produced more income than the mines. Sugar beets, introduced into the South Platte Valley in the early 1890s, became a particularly profitable crop.

PIKI BREAD MAKER by Ray Swanson, oil, 40 x 30 inches, courtesy of Miner's Gallery Americana, Carmel, California.

The sugar-beet industry commenced in Colorado after a French-designed, sugar-manufacturing plant, which was brought to America by the Mormons, failed to work in Utah. The soil and climate of Colorado proved to be good for sugar beets, and the plant was moved to Colorado. By 1900 there were two other refineries in Colorado.

One of the pioneers in the sugar-beet industry was a shrewd German immigrant, Charles Boettcher. He had made a fortune with a chain of hardware stores in Colorado and returned to his native Germany to retire. There, he became interested in the sugar-beet industry and decided it would do well in Colorado. At the turn of the century, he brought back a number of his countrymen to help build six German-style sugar refineries along the South Platte Valley. At the same time many Mexicans moved into Colorado to work in the beet fields.

Agriculture

Although mining attracted the first settlers, the ranchers and farmers played the key role in the development of the state. They discovered that Colorado's diverse climate and geography made many different types of agriculture possible: high mountain meadows for sheep and cattle grazing, warm valleys for fruit orchards, land suitable for growing wheat, and a sufficient supply of water for irrigation where needed.

Sixty percent of Colorado's land is devoted to agriculture and livestock. The northwest boosts a thriving sheep industry. In the extreme southwest pinto beans are grown in the hot, arid climate. Potatoes, barley, and lettuce flourish in the San Luis Valley, which is nestled between two mountain ranges. Sugar beets and vegetables are primarily grown in the eastern part of Colorado on irrigated fields.

The sheltered valleys of western Colorado have traditionally been the fruit-growing regions of the state. Irrigation ditches, canals, and pumping stations, originally built in 1870, transformed this region into a major agricultural area. The coming of the Denver and Rio Grande Railroad helped establish markets for

STUFFED CROWN ROAST OF LAMB

Colorado is the largest producer of lamb in the nation. Today, "spring lamb" has become a marketing term, since most of the lamb is slaughtered in the early fall. Lamb is often served for Easter dinner, since it is closely associated with Christianity. This Stuffed Crown Roast of Lamb makes an elegant presentation for a holiday dinner.

Serves 8

1 crown roast of lamb consisting of 14
   to 16 chops

Stuffing

1/2 cup dark raisins

1 teaspoon grated lemon zest

1 tablespoon grated orange zest

1 tablespoon lemon juice

3 tablespoons orange juice

1 pound ground lamb

1/4 cup chopped walnuts

2 tablespoons pine nuts

3/4 cup coarsely chopped fresh mushrooms

1 medium onion, chopped

2 slices white bread, torn into small pieces

1/4 cup finely chopped fresh parsley

1 1/2 tablespoons chopped fresh rosemary

1/2 teaspoon ground coriander

1 egg, beaten

1/2 teaspoon garlic powder

Salt and pepper, to taste

For garnish

6 cherry tomatoes

4 mushroom caps

4 walnut halves

■

Have your butcher prepare a crown roast, Frenching the bones, from two or three racks of lamb, depending on their size.

To make the stuffing, place the raisins in a bowl, add the fruit zests and juices. Allow the mixture to stand for 30 minutes. Combine the remaining stuffing ingredients in a large bowl and add the soaked raisin mixture.

Lightly coat the bottom of a roasting pan with olive oil. Season the roast with salt and pepper, place it in the pan, and spoon the stuffing in the center of the roast. Garnish the top of the stuffing with the cherry tomatoes, mushrooms, and walnuts.

Protect the ends of the bones with foil. Also put foil over the stuffing for the first 30 minutes of cooking time. Roast in a preheated 400° F. oven for 15 minutes, then reduce the oven heat to 375° F. and continue roasting for a total of 1 1/4 to 1 1/2 hours, depending on the weight of the roast. A meat thermometer inserted into the meatiest part of the lamb chop should read 135 degrees for pink lamb. Remove the meat from the oven and place it on a platter. To serve, cut the lamb into chops between the bones and serve with the stuffing.

Colorado fruits.

There was a new aspect to Colorado agriculture after World War II. The Japanese who were interned in Adams and Weld Counties northeast of Denver remained in the area and became vegetable growers on small plots of land. In addition to the familiar vegetables, they also grew such items as bok choy and snow peas for their Oriental cuisine. Now these truck farmers supply the majority of fresh produce to the Denver area.

Along with new agriculture there is also a revival of the growing of quinoa, an ancient grain grown high in the Andes by the Indians of Peru. Quinoa is now being cultivated in Colorado, although in limited quantities, at altitudes above 7,000 feet. This ancient grain looks like millet and can be cooked like rice. Most of the quinoa, however, is used in cereals or ground into flour and added to bread or pasta flour to give a different taste. Since quinoa has no gluten, it can never be used as the sole flour in baking or pasta making.

Beef and Lamb

Ranching began in western Colorado in the 1870s and boomed in the 1880s, following the removal of the Ute Indians to Utah and the coming of the railroad. Despite devastating winters, droughts, overgrazing, and range wars, ranching became a vital enterprise in various parts of the state. The range wars involved conflicting claims between cattlemen, sheepherders, and homesteaders.

Beef is raised in many areas of the state. Colorado has numerous feedlots to fatten both local and out-of-state cattle. More than two million head of cattle go through Colorado feedlots annually.

Colorado is famous for its Rocky

Mountain lamb and is number one in the nation in lamb production. The age of the lamb is not as important as the weight in determining its marketability. Lambs are usually processed when they weigh between 105 and 115 pounds, although some markets and restaurants prefer 135-pound animals, since they have larger chops. Spring lamb is not prevalent in the Mountain States, since most lambs are born between January and March and slaughtered between August and October.

Buffalo

Buffalo once roamed the Great Plains and the Mountain States, providing meat for Indians and settlers alike. While their numbers were greatly depleted in the late 1800s, today, herds of buffalo roam public lands such as Yellowstone Park and other government tracts in Montana, Wyoming, and the Dakotas. Two-thirds of the estimated 80,000 buffalo in existence are privately owned herds being raised on ranches, mostly in northern Colorado, Wyoming, and Montana.

Bob Dineen of Rocky Mountain Natural Meats in Denver, Colorado, processes about 40 privately raised buffalo per month and sells the meat to restaurants and shops all over the country under his Great Range Bison label. He works closely with the producers as to size and fat content of the animals. Although buffalo are much lower in fat content than beef, the meat is only popular as a novelty food.

One advantage to raising buffalo is that they have a great ability to withstand extremely cold temperatures and are not as susceptible to disease. On private lands the buffalo are allowed to roam freely, keeping the wild instinct alive. They are grain fed just before slaughter, but only the bulls are slaughtered.

Orchards

In the late 1800s Jesse Frazier, traveling west from Missouri to open a coal mine, brought along some of his favorite apple seedlings. About the same time, other pioneers also brought seedlings of their favorite fruit trees. By the late 1890s fruit orchards had been established in Western Colorado, and Mesa County became the center for fruit growing.

Marion Bowman, the daughter of one of these orchard pioneers, wrote an account of the early days, recalling her father's invention, which made apple harvesting more efficient. It seems that Mr. Bowman decided to make a picking bag for the fruit, which he later patented. The bag is filled from the top, and when full, the bottom is unsnapped to let the fruit roll into a basket or bin. Straps were used to tie the bag onto the backs of the workers, leaving both hands free for picking.

Pioneer Food

In pioneer days "eating out" did not mean going to a restaurant. Rather, it meant that the women prepared food to be carried outdoors and eaten on a table made from planks laid across two sawhorses. A "mosquito" fire was made from twigs and leaves to keep the bugs away. In hot weather the fire was smothered with green weeds pulled for the occasion. "Eating out" kept the house cool.

When women settlers arrived in Colorado, they could not figure out how to make a good cake. The high altitude of the mountains prevented cakes from rising properly. The pioneer women were distressed that their beloved cake recipes failed constantly, until the correct proportions of sugar, leavening, and shortening were worked out and high-altitude baking was born. It eventually produced one of the most famous cakes in America—Denver Red Chocolate Cake.

Many a Colorado cowboy had his own special biscuit mix. Before starting out on the range, he would mix together flour, salt, and leavening in a sack and tie the sack to his saddle. At mealtime he took some of the mixture, added water to achieve the right consistency, and dropped the biscuit dough into a skillet greased with lard or bacon drippings.

In the 1890s Russians from the Volga region came to Colorado to become sugar beet farmers. They brought with them recipes for their favorite foods, such as sausages encased in rich dough; a sponge cake made with lemon; cucumber salad with sour cream; *Piroshki*, meat baked in small turnovers or tarts; and *Golbutzi*, cabbage leaves stuffed with a mixture of meat, rice, and sour cream. A great number of Germans also came to grow sugar beets, bringing with them recipes for sauerbraten and dumplings.

Mexicans came later to work on the railroads and in the sugar-beet fields, adding their spicy dishes to Colorado's cuisine. These included *Pollo con Mole*, chicken with chocolate and seasonings; Tamale Pie with a cornmeal mush topping; and *Flan*, a rich custard.

It is said that the Chinese cooks working on the transcontinental-railroad construction invented the Denver sandwich, also known as a Western sandwich. It was simply Chinese Egg Fu Yung prepared with green peppers, onions, and usually chopped ham. The cooked omelet was put between two pieces of bread and eaten as a sandwich. Green pepper had made its way to Colorado with the Mexicans.

IDAHO

BEARS FOR BREAKFAST by O. C. Seltzer, oil, 23 x 31 inches, courtesy of Mongerson Wunderlich Galleries, Ltd., Chicago, Illinois.

FUR TRAPPING AND TRADING with the Indians provided the first source of wealth in Idaho in the early part of the 1800s. By the 1840s, however, the beaver had vanished, trading was over, and settlers began to arrive to farm the land. Gold was discovered in 1860, and with the opening of the transcontinental railroad, the population of Idaho increased rapidly as mining became the quickest way to get rich.

Along with the miners came Chinese immigrants, who took up the claims of Caucasian miners after they had moved on to more productive claims. The first Chinese miners arrived Idaho in 1864, and by 1870 they owned more half of all Idaho mines. Almost every frontier community had a cluster of Chinese workers' houses called Chinatown.

As mining declined for the hardworking Chinese, they moved into trades and vegetable farming. Idahoans began to rely on their local Chinese vegetable farmer to deliver fresh vegetables door-to-door. The Chinese raised vegetables on terraced mountain terrain, because the land was cheaper. For their Cantonese style of cooking they had brought with them their woks, cleavers, and chopsticks.

Some of the first European settlers in Idaho were Finns, Welsh, and Basques, who came to work in the mines and to raise sheep. The Finns brought with them a love for *Lobimuhennos*, a salmon chowder, and the Welsh brought *Bara Brith*, a raisin and currant bread. The Basque preferred lamb stew and split pea soup. *Chorizo*, a spicy sausage, attributed by some to Basque origin, is still being produced in Idaho.

In the early days Basque sheepherders made a sourdough bread on which they slashed the sign of the cross before baking. This act reflected their devout religious feelings. The first piece of the baked bread was always given to their invaluable sheepdog.

The primary food of the early settlers was bread and beans. They occasionally relieved the monotony with a pie made of elderberries from a bush called the "Tree of Music." The Indians had given this name to the bush because the wood was a favorite with Indian flute makers.

Most small settlements had a mom-and-pop general store in which the smell of kerosene and coffee beans permeated the air. It was a place to meet and chat with friends and neighbors around the warm potbellied stove. The store was stocked from ceiling to floor with household items, farm implements, and packaged grocery items. The storekeeper was often paid in barter or trade, although eggs were rarely accepted as barter because they were fragile.

Volcanic Land

At the time that Idaho was admitted to the Union in 1890, the potential of the state to produce food was considered to be next to nothing, because the land primarily consisted of mountains or volcanic deserts. Most of Idaho's land was used for cattle and sheep grazing. Although Idaho still raises a considerable amount of livestock, including dairy cattle and sheep in the northern part of the state, field crops have become the state's main source of farm income.

Time proved that these volcanic tracts were cultivatable with adequate irrigation, which was introduced to parts of Idaho in 1894. Some 50 years later the state had 15,000 miles of irrigation canals and 360 reservoirs. Nitrogen in the form of plowed-under alfalfa and clover enriched the soil for vegetable cultivation. By the 1950s agriculture became the main source of income for the state.

Idaho Potatoes

The first potato grower in Idaho was Henry Harmon Spalding, a Presbyterian missionary, who planted potatoes in 1836 to teach the Nez Percé Indians how to provide food for themselves other than by hunting. Homesteaders grew potatoes to sell to the miners who came through the state. The Mormons, however, were the first to grow potatoes commercially. By the time Idaho was admitted to the Union in 1890, its potatoes were famous for their superior quality.

Luther Burbank, the great horticulturist, developed the Russet Burbank potato that is today called the Idaho® Potato. In 1872 he perfected a long white potato with a rough russet skin. Adapted to the Northwest, the Russet Burbank has made Idaho the leading potato producer in the nation. The Idaho Potato Board calls the Russet Burbank potato the "Tiffany of Tubers." Because of its low moisture content, this potato can easily be stored for long periods of time.

The volcanic soil and the climate of warm days and cool nights provide the ideal conditions for potato cultivation, much of which is along the Snake River. With these growing conditions, the starch stored in the leaves of the potato plant drops down to the tuber. Water from irrigation helps control the shape of the potato.

In Idaho, cut pieces of potatoes containing a sprout or "eye" are planted in rows from by May 15. During the 150-day growing season, the plants reach a height of about two feet, and each plant has eight to ten tubers. The potatoes are harvested by October 15 with a mechanical harvester, which can work four rows at once. The harvester separates the potatoes from the earth clods and vines.

After the potatoes are harvested, they can be stored for 12 months. Originally potatoes were stored in dirt cellars, but now they are stored in darkened warehouses, called garages, where they are piled 20 feet high. Air is piped through the warehouse to maintain proper ventilation and a temperature of 40 to 45 degrees Fahrenheit, which keeps the tuber dormant. Darkness and controlled temperatures prevent the starch in the potato from turning to sugar. Before potatoes are shipped they are washed, sorted, graded, and boxed according to size.

The 2,300 Idaho potato growers produce 100 million 100-pound bags of potatoes annually. Sixty percent of Idaho potatoes are processed for either french fries, dehydrated potatoes, or potato flakes. It takes five pounds of potatoes to make one pound of potato flakes. There are several mills in Idaho that produce

COUNTRY POTATOES

Although Henry Spalding planted the first potatoes in Idaho in 1836, it was Joe Marshall, a potato farmer, who instituted modern marketing techniques in the early 1900s. In order to deliver the potato to the consumer in the best condition, he cleaned the potato with a brush, since washing deteriorated it. He was also the first to market them in bags.

These country-style potatoes are reminiscent of the skillet home-fried potatoes of the settlers of the Mountain States.

Serves 6 to 8

4 large Idaho® potatoes

2/3 cup chopped red pepper

1 medium onion, chopped

Butter

Pepper

Paprika

■ Peel the potatoes and slice them 1/4-inch thick. Butter a 11/2-quart casserole. Place a layer of potatoes in the casserole and sprinkle with some of the red pepper and onions. Dot with some butter flakes. Continue layering the potatoes, red pepper, and onions, and dotting them with butter until all of the ingredients are used. Sprinkle top with pepper and paprika. Cover casserole and bake in a preheated 400° F. oven for 1 hour.

northerly region of Idaho has a climate similar to that of Germany and produces fine hops on a 10,000-acre tract leased by Anheuser Bush.

Because of the climatic and atmospheric conditions in Idaho, a major seed industry has developed in the state. Six major seed companies, including Burpee, produce 90 percent of all sweet-corn seed in the nation, as well as bean and pea seeds.

Herbs and spices, broccoli, and a small amount of asparagus constitute the remainder of the crops in Idaho. In the mid–1900s asparagus was a major crop, but it was abandoned for broccoli, which proved to be more profitable. Treasure Valley in Canyon County is known for its mint and spearmint cultivation—all planted from root cuttings. Both mints are distilled for their oils, which are sold to the confection industry.

Trout

Today nearly every state in the Union has trout farms; however, in Idaho's Magic Valley more trout is raised per square mile than anywhere else in the world. It seems that the slightly warmer water in the streams of the area is conducive to trout production. Idaho supplies over half of the country's trout. Rainbow trout are the major farm crop, but many other varieties are also available, including one of the best tasting, the pink-fleshed cutthroat trout.

Recreational fishing provides another source of food in Idaho. Both the Salmon and Snake rivers yield a plentiful supply of bass and rainbow and steelhead trout. There was a time on the Snake River when white sturgeon weighing as much as 1,000 pounds were caught. They had to be hauled from the river by mule teams. Taken to Boise, the

potato flour, which is used primarily in baking cakes and doughnuts.

Other Agriculture

Northern Idaho is mostly dry farmed, and wheat, dry peas, and lentils are the predominant crops. Originally immigrants from the Mediterranean area and Armenia settled the area and grew lentils. Today, Idaho and Washington produce most of the lentils in this country. They are grown in a 50-mile-wide strip of land along the Idaho-Washington border. The arid climate of this region, historically inhabited by the Palouse Indians, makes it possible to dry lentils and peas in the field before harvesting. The majority of the Idaho lentil crop is sold internationally. Pinto, lima, and Great Northern beans are also raised and dried in the area.

Barley and hops for making beer are grown in northern Idaho. Much of the malt barley is under contract to the Adolph Coors Company. The most monster fish would be pulled through the streets on a wagon and sold to residents piece by piece for a few nickles each until the fish was whittled down to the bare bones. As recently as 35 years ago, a 394-pound sturgeon was caught in the Snake River.

Some Idaho Food Specialties

Idaho, with its diverse climate and agricultural products, has a number of food specialties. Many homegrown apples are combined with ham in a casserole. The apples are also used to make jelly, which is mixed with mayonnaise for a salad dressing. Prunes, another home-grown orchard product, are often used for prune butter, prune-whip pies, and spicy prune puddings.

During hunting season Idaho cooks prepare venison with a prickly currant sauce or a huckleberry sauce made from berries that grow wild in the woods. Huckleberry pie is an Idaho speciality.

Idaho's dried beans, lentils, and split peas are used in a variety of dishes, such as a casserole of white beans baked with pimento, bread crumbs and cheese, or split pea soups made with ham or sausage. Lentils are cooked in a casserole with sausages, in a soup with lamb, or are served cold in a salad. The latter is a recent innovation.

LENTILS WITH RED PEPPER SAUCE

Lentils were introduced to the Iroquois Indians along the St. Lawrence River by French Jesuit missionaries in the late 1600s. The missionaries tried to grow the legume but were not successful. Almost 200 years later, immigrants from the Mediterranean area and Armenia settled in Idaho and started growing lentils.

Lentils are traditionally used in soups and stews. The following lentil dish may be served hot in the winter as a meat accompaniment or cool in the summer as a luncheon salad.

Serves 6

3/4 cup lentils

3 cups water

3/4 teaspoon salt

1/8 teaspoon black pepper

1 teaspoon cumin seeds

1 bay leaf, crumbled

Sauce

2 tablespoons olive oil

1 clove garlic, minced

2 red bell peppers, skinned and chopped

3 green onions, chopped

1/4 cup chopped fresh parsley

2 tablespoons chopped fresh cilantro

■

Combine the lentils with the water, salt, pepper, and herbs in a medium-size saucepan. Bring to a boil and cook covered over medium heat for 15 to 20 minutes or until the lentils are just tender. Keep testing for doneness so that they do not overcook. Drain the lentils, removing the bay leaf and any visible cumin seeds. While the lentils are cooking, start the sauce.

■

Heat the olive oil in a medium-size skillet and sauté the garlic until soft but not browned. Add the chopped red peppers and cook on low heat for 30 minutes. Near the end of the cooking time, add the remaining sauce ingredients and continue cooking over low heat for 5 minutes. Pour the sauce over the lentils and mix gently.

If serving as a summer salad, add 2 to 3 tablespoons of vinaigrette to the red pepper sauce and serve at room temperature.

MONTANA

THE NAME MONTANA is derived from the Spanish word *montañoso,* meaning mountainous. While the Rocky Mountains cover two-fifths of the state, the majority of the land is part of the Great Plains, with gentle rolling hills suitable for livestock grazing.

Montana had been left to the Indians until gold and copper mining swept the Western frontier and the Rockies. Only a few trappers, Jesuit missionaries, and daring traders ventured into the wild canyons and high ridges of Montana's Rockies in the early 1800s. David Thompson, a trader in Montana in 1808, described a meal the Indians offered his party. It consisted of dried carp, muskrat, shoulder of venison, and moss bread, "which gave us a bellyache."

In the heyday of fur trading, Montana was inhabited by millions of buffalo, but with the gold and copper strikes, the coming of the railroads, and the growth of sheep and cattle ranches, the buffalo gradually disappeared. Hunters frequently killed buffalo for the fur and left the meat, except for the tongue which was considered a delicacy. It is said that an Indian named Walking Coyote realized that the buffalo was in danger of extinction and saved two males and two females. From them came the government-protected herds of present-day Montana, although there are also a number of privately owned herds of buffalo in the state.

Ranching and Agriculture

Milk cows were brought into Montana in 1833, and by the 1850s missionaries had brought in a few beef cattle. Montana's livestock industry can be credited to Nelson Story, who in 1866 drove a thousand longhorns from Texas to Montana. Soon thereafter other Texas cattle followed. Eight years later cattle were being driven from Montana to Eastern markets, because they had fared so well on Montana pastures. The arrival of the Northern Pacific Railroad in 1883 made it easier to get cattle to market.

Sheep came into the Montana territory at about the same time as the railroads. They increased from 250,000 head in 1880 to more than one million head in 1900. This made Montana the largest wool-producing state in the nation, as well as a provider of lamb and mutton.

The loneliest of all livestock men are the sheepherders, who spend months on the solitary high ranges with their flocks. Montana's ranches are particularly lonely since they stretch for miles up the valleys and onto the mountain slopes. Montana sheepherders may be of Turkish, Russian, Romanian, or Basque origin, but if you look into their canvas-topped wagons at mealtime, you'll find that the majority of them are eating the typical simple-to-

BORSCHT

The Russian immigrants brought their famous cabbage soup to the Mountain States. In Russian homes meat-filled *pirozhki* (similar to small turnovers) often accompanied the soup.

This meatless Borscht can be served as an appetizer or as a main course. Although regular cabbage can be used in this recipe, the savory cabbage is more flavorful. If fresh beets are unavailable, canned ones may be substituted.

Serves 6 to 8

8 cups beef broth

5 cups chopped savory cabbage (1/2 large head of savory cabbage)

1 1/2 stalks celery, chopped

1 carrot, chopped

1 1/2 cups diced beets (about 4 beets)

1 large onion, chopped

1 bay leaf

4 tablespoons red wine vinegar

2 teaspoons Worcestershire sauce

3 tablespoons light brown sugar

Salt and pepper, to taste

Sour cream, for garnish

■

Place the beef broth, cabbage, celery, carrot, beets, onion, bay leaf, vinegar, Worcestershire sauce, and sugar in a large stock pot. Bring to a slow boil and simmer the soup for 1 hour. Long, slow cooking improves the flavor. Add salt and pepper, to taste. Ladle into soup bowls and serve with a dollop of sour cream.

MONARCH OF THE PLAINS by Jerry Thrasher, oil, 18 x 24 inches, courtesy of Miner's Gallery Americana, Carmel, California.

prepare meal of American livestock herders—beans and salt pork. Today, many Basque sheepherders work on Montana ranches for a period of three years and then return to Spain.

In the early 1900s there was a shift in Montana's agriculture from livestock to wheat farming. Wheat has now become the state's top agricultural crop. The state also grows large quantities of barley, sugar beets, oats, and potatoes.

Montana's Food Traditions

The various ethnic groups who settled Montana brought their native recipes with them. Many Russian immigrants became wheat farmers in Montana.

They retained their traditional foods, such as beet soup and a cheese tart called *Vatroushki*. Just before Lent they made stacks of *blinis*, buckwheat pancakes served with melted butter or sour cream. Hot tea served in glasses usually accompanied the meal. For company there was a pudding of Montana cherries, bread crumbs, and cinnamon or a pie called

227

Smettanick, which had a filling of cherry jam, almonds, and sour cream.

The Croatians and Slavs settled Butte, Great Falls, and Anaconda. They traditionally observed Christmas on the sixth of January, and their holiday fare included poppy-seed pudding and very thin pancakes rolled around tangy cherries and dusted with sugar. The holiday turkey was stuffed with an almond dressing, while cabbage was served with savory meat, rice, and a sour-cream sauce. A variety of dumplings, including ones made with fruit and cottage cheese, were also served.

In the Scandinavian settlements of Montana a special porridge with heavy cream was served at Christmas. An almond was hidden in the porridge, and the girl finding it was destined to be the first to marry. Thin pancakes and Swedish Christmas bread with a touch of rye and molasses enlivened Christmas dinners. The Scandinavians served cold fruit soups in the summer.

The Irish celebrated Easter by preparing a dish called Golden Bread, which consists of thick slices of home-made white bread dipped in egg and fried in butter. Hot Cross Buns with a cross of icing on top were baked for Good Friday.

The Scots enjoyed scones, mulli-gatawny stew made with mutton and curry seasonings, and barley broth, as well as sweet, tender Montana carrots and split peas from neighboring Idaho. Many women of Scottish decent still stir their oatmeal with an heirloom wooden porridge stick.

Montana's cuisine is also based on ingredients indigenous to the state. White honey, perfumed with clover, is spread on huckleberry bread. Montanans have easy access to huckleberries since they grow wild in the woods.

In the hunting season many dishes center around elk, moose, and deer. Montana cooks serve ground venison meatballs with a hot, spicy tomato sauce, which was first introduced to Montana cuisine by the Mexicans, who came to Montana to help to build the railroads in the late 1870s.

RED CABBAGE

Red cabbage was a favorite meat accompaniment of the German immigrants of the Mountain States. They served it with meats, particularly wild game. The longer the cabbage slowly cooks, the better the flavor.

Serves 6

1 medium red cabbage

1 tablespoon butter or margarine

1 medium onion, chopped

1 Pippin apple, cored and cut into 1-inch cubes

6 pitted prunes, quartered

1/2 cup chicken broth

1/2 cup red wine

1/4 teaspoon ground cloves

1/4 teaspoon cinnamon

Pinch of nutmeg

■

Remove any wilted outer leaves from the cabbage. Cut the cabbage in quarters, remove the core, and shred it.

Melt the butter in a large saucepan over medium heat. Add the onions and sauté until the onions are limp. Add the cabbage and the remaining ingredients. Stir the mixture, cover, and bring to a boil. Reduce heat and cook on low heat for 1 hour. Check occasionally to see if there is enough liquid to keep the cabbage moist. If not add some more wine. There should be enough liquid to keep the cabbage moist but not soupy. Reduce heat to simmer and continue cooking for another 30 minutes.

NEVADA

NEVADA BECAME A STATE in 1864 but brought little to the country of gastronomic significance. The land, basically desert, was so poor that it could barely support its Shoshone Indians, nicknamed "diggers," who had to dig for roots and rodents for nourishment. Nomads with no permanent villages, the Shoshones lived off the land collecting berries, seeds, and nuts.

The first white people to cross Nevada on their way to the California Gold Rush had no suspicion of the gold, silver, copper, and other minerals they were passing over with their creaky wagons. At first the Paiute Indians, who inhabited the northern part of Nevada, looked kindly upon the few whites crossing their territory. They showed the women how to crush the pulp of the barrel cactus for juice since there was no water to drink. They also taught them how to grind pine nuts into flour.

The Indians of Nevada ate very little meat since it was rarely available in this desert. They supplemented what little meat they could find with pine nuts in the winter, leaves and stems in the spring, berries and herbs in the summer, and roots in the fall. Indian women used hot stones to cook soups or pine mush, a favorite dish made with roasted, shelled pine nuts that were gently crushed with a stone.

Grasshoppers, captured when they became entangled in the sweet sap of the cattail, were a delicacy for the Paiutes. While the Indians introduced their delicacy to the travelers coming through the area, the dish never caught on, except in an emergency.

Mormon Farming

One of the first settlements in Nevada was formed by a group of Mormons who came from Salt Lake City in 1850 and built

GARLIC STALK by Harl Nobles, oil, 16 x 12 inches, courtesy of Miner's Gallery Americana, Carmel, California.

Mormon Station, a crude trading post in the western wilderness of the then Utah Territory. They traded with the gold miners and settlers on their way to California. During the next decade Brigham Young sent more Mormons to establish settlements along well-traveled trails so that the stream of gold seekers could get food and supplies. However, the settlements were few and far between.

It is believed that Nevada's first town was Genoa, a roofless stockade built in the western part of Utah Territory in 1851. The first house was a log cabin built in 1853 by Mormons John Reese and Jacob Dinsey, who brought seeds and cattle with them and began farming. Soon hungry immigrants and prospectors were paying as much as a dollar apiece for turnips.

The Mormons who settled in Carson Valley in western Nevada at about the same time started with 30 cattle and a few hogs. Although these settlers were recalled to Utah within a few years, their methods of irrigation and crop rotation set the pattern for Nevada agriculture. As one observer in the 1880s noted, "the Mormons don't skim the cream off the country with a six-shooter and a whiskey bottle." Mormon grapes, melons, potatoes, corn, wheat, and squash helped Nevada mining camps survive the days of boom and bust.

Gold Rush Food

The discovery of the Comstock Lode at what became Virginia City in 1859 brought a huge migration of prospectors to Nevada. Rambunctious mining towns sprang up everywhere and collapsed when the Comstock Lode was depleted.

Prospectors survived on sourdough biscuits and sourdough bread, which descendents of pioneer families still bake. When women arrived in the mining camps, they started trading recipes, which eventually became the basis of Nevada cuisine. Meat-stuffed Cornish pasties and tripe stewed with onion, celery, and parsnips and flavored with mustard and Worcestershire sauce became favorites. Saffron Cake and Potato-Caramel Cake topped the list of desserts.

In the rough first days of prospecting, the miners ate and drank anything that came their way. Legend says that one town subsisted an entire winter on whiskey. The result of this diet was that 75 people were shot before anyone died a natural death.

No one could predict where gold would be found. A cook dressing chickens for dinner is reported to have found gold nuggets in their craws. One night in

WESTERN BAR by Tibor "Stibor" Silberhorn, oil, 36 x 24 inches, courtesy of Kertesz Fine Art Galleries, San Francisco, California.

the 1860s, three men claim they found that the walls in their rock-house shelter glistened. It turned out that the walls were veined with silver and worth $75,000. Finds of this magnitude were necessary for survival since a handful of crackers at the time cost 75 cents.

During the gold and silver rush of the 1860s, prospectors who had struck it rich liked any type of food, as long as it "cost a lot." Black-tie dinners in Virginia City sparkled with French champagne that had crossed the ocean, rounded the Horn, and come over the Sierras from California. They ate from imported china and drank from glasses that twinkled under huge crystal chandeliers.

Virginia City boasted fine restaurants, clubs, and hotels, many of which had imported internationally known chefs. West Coast oysters became a delicacy for the newly rich; oyster loaf and oyster stuffing for quail became the showpieces of dinner parties.

Ranching and Agriculture

Many Nevada towns still retain a frontier flavor. If there is a railroad going through the town, livestock corrals often line the tracks. Shipping time is noisy and dusty with shouting cowboys, howling steers, bleating lambs, and the piercing whistle of Basque sheepherders.

The stand-up bars in the saloons are lined at day's end with cowboys in scuffed, high-heeled boots, faded Levi's, and big hats and sheepherders with weathered faces wearing short brimmed Stetsons. Talk around the bar centers on their daily livelihood.

"I got me a good price for them steers," one cowboy says to another. "That's a benefit of dealing with a buyer you like." A few steps away a Basque sheepherder says, "Them coyotes don't bother me. They don't eat grass. They eat rabbits, and rabbits eat grass."

Nevada grazing land is home to cattle and sheep. The Basque sheepherders, who constantly fought the cattlemen over land use, came to Nevada at the turn of the century and were a closely knit group.

As soon as a man had accumulated enough money, he sent for other male relatives from Spain to help with the sheep. Eventually the women also came and ran boardinghouses, which became gathering places for the herders.

Meals on the range for the sheepherders were simple and varied depending on whether they were out for only a day or for weeks at a time. Many Basque women followed their husbands into the mountains and became camp cooks. Breakfast usually consisted of strong, steaming-hot coffee with condensed milk, sourdough bread, and a strong cheese.

Lunch, the main meal of the day, was often eaten in the shade of an aspen grove. It varied from stews or roasted meats to an omelet filled with bacon and potatoes. At the end of the day, the sheepherders were often too tired to cook anything and were happy with some warmed-over beans or stew.

The tradition of annual Basque festivals in Elko, Ely, Winnemucca, and Reno was born in the friendly atmosphere of their Basque boardinghouses. Festival dinners feature soup made with potatoes, cabbage, and ham; lamb stew; fried steak; various vegetables and potatoes, plus pie and cake for dessert.

Even though Nevada's state seal pictures a plow and shield, there is little agriculture. Nevada is primarily a desert. What little agriculture there is depends entirely on irrigation. Nevada grows some fruit and vegetables, mainly for local consumption. A great quantity of garlic is cultivated, however, much of which is shipped to California for processing. Nevada ranchers raise deer, and as a result venison is commercially available.

When Nevada became a territory in 1861, nearly one-third of its population had come from foreign lands. By 1900 the foreign born population had increased to 50 percent. Living in a desert, the diverse ethnic groups who came to Nevada found it difficult to maintain their culinary traditions. Since most of their native ingredients were not available, they had to meld their cooking with the supplies at hand.

Many of the Chinese and Hindus who laid rails for the new railroads traversing Nevada stayed to operate small farms. Italians and Swiss burned charcoal for mine smelters, founded ranches, and established dairy herds in the valleys near Reno. The Cornish and Irish worked in the mines of the Comstock Lode; the French-Canadians were lumberjacks in the forests around Lake Tahoe; and the Germans farmed to produce food for many of these people. Later Slavs and Greeks worked in the mines, and Basques and Scots herded sheep in the desert and mountains.

Today, Las Vegas and Reno have extravagant hotels and restaurants with some of the most cosmopolitan cuisine in the country. Any type of food—from corned beef, to lobster and escargot—is available almost 24 hours a day. These gambling towns never sleep.

BASQUE LAMB STEW

Lamb stews were popular with Basque sheepherders and were served at Basque boardinghouses and restaurants. Many Basque restaurants still serve family-style meals, where diners sit at long tables and are served Basque specialties, such as lamb stews.

Serves 6

1/4 cup olive oil

3 pounds lean lamb, cut into 1 1/2-inch pieces

2 strips very lean bacon, cut into small slivers

1 large onion chopped

1 stalk celery, chopped

3 cloves garlic, chopped

1 medium green pepper, coarsely chopped

1 medium red pepper, coarsely chopped

2 large tomatoes, peeled, seeded, and chopped

2 tablespoons tomato paste

1 1/2 tablespoons paprika

1/2 teaspoon salt

1/4 teaspoon pepper

1 bay leaf, crumbled

1 cup red wine

Chopped fresh parsley, for garnish

■

Heat the olive oil in a large, deep skillet or Dutch oven over medium-high heat. Add the lamb, in batches if necessary, and brown on all sides. Remove the lamb to a plate and discard all but 1 1/2 tablespoons of the fat.

Add the bacon, onion, celery, garlic, green peppers, and red peppers to the skillet and sauté over medium heat for 5 minutes. Add the tomatoes and cook for 2 to 3 more minutes. Stir in the remaining ingredients and mix them well. Add the lamb along with any juices that have collected on the plate. Bring to a boil, reduce the heat, cover, and simmer the stew until the lamb is tender, about 1 1/2 hours. Uncover and increase the heat to medium-low and cook to evaporate some of the juices so that the sauce will thicken slightly. Skim off any accumulated fat. (The stew may also be thickened with a little flour and water combined.) Garnish with chopped parsley and serve.

UTAH

WHEN THE MORMONS arrived in the Utah Territory in 1847, the area was inhabited by three major Indian tribes—the Utes in Utah Valley, the Paiutes in southern Utah, and the Northwestern Shoshone in northern Utah. The Indians raised beans, squash, and corn and supplemented their diets with wild berries, nuts, and seeds. They hunted buffalo and other wild game. Even though part of Utah was fertile land, the Great Salt Lake Valley was considered a no-man's-land where tribal wars were fought. This valley became the Mormons' first home.

Spanish explorers and missionaries had passed through Utah in the seventeenth and eighteenth centuries while exploring a route from New Mexico to California. Several expeditions had even skirted around the Salt Lake Basin, with its strange lake that is five times saltier than the ocean. Only the Mormons, members of the Church of Jesus Christ of Latter-Day Saints, found the isolated valley around the Great Salt Lake to be the land they were seeking. Upon seeing this valley on the edge of the desert, their leader, Brigham Young, declared, "This is the place."

The Mormons had come to stay. Driven from their homes in the East and Midwest because of their religious beliefs, which included plural marriages, they packed their wagons with plows, seeds, fruit saplings, and household necessities and headed West. The Mormons also brought cattle, horses, hogs, and crates of chickens.

Early Mormon Food

The first years were hard for the Mormons. They tried unsuccessfully to pan for gold and to convert the Indians. Isolated from civilization and finding food difficult to obtain, many of the settlers subsisted on sego-lily buds, thistle greens,

GREAT SALT LAKE WITH GARDEN by Janet Millikan, oil, 16 x 20 inches, courtesy of Kertesz Fine Art Galleries, San Francisco, California.

hawks, owls, and crows. Their first homes were either dirt dugouts or lean-tos made of wooden branches. Many of the settlers became discouraged and wanted to go to California to prospect for gold. Brigham Young, however, told them that their form of gold was in the land and asked everyone to plant crops.

The area around Salt Lake City soon flourished, and Mormon expeditions were sent to other parts of Utah, Idaho, Nevada, and Arizona to create similar centers. One group of Mormons walked to San Diego and back. They returned with seeds for wheat and peas.

Obtaining water from the streams flowing out of the mountains, the Mormons soon established irrigated farming communities. The men planted fruit orchards and field crops. Women learned to cook with wild plants, such as lamb's-quarters, milkweed, and wild spinach, until the crops matured. Wild lettuce was cooked together with salt pork for a stew. If a small neighborhood had only one pig, everyone saved scraps to feed it. At butchering, the contributors were given their share of fat, liver, and bits of pork.

The story has been told that when grasshoppers descended on the fields in a black storm in the early days of settlement, the Mormons prayed that their crops might be saved. They looked up in the sky and saw sea gulls, 1,000 miles from the ocean, diving down to devour the grasshoppers.

As the towns grew and the crops prospered, Utah women started cooking some of their family's favorite dishes. Home-cured ham with mustard sauce and buttermilk biscuits, along with roast beef and fried chicken with green peas, potatoes, cheese, and bread were often served. Mormon gravy made with browned flour, ham grease, milk, and black pepper was served with buttermilk biscuits. For dessert there might be a jelly layer cake; bread pudding made with stale bread, applesauce, and cream; or dried apple pie and Brigham Young Tea—hot water, milk, and sugar.

Mormon Food Customs

The early years in Utah were very difficult for the Mormons because there was a continual shortage of food. Ever since those early days, the Mormons have been instructed by their church to keep one-year's food supply on hand in case of a natural disaster or other emergency.

Although Utah is in little danger of famine now, the custom of stockpiling food is still strictly observed by Mormon families. Thus, most Utah cooks preserve food at home. Dried fruit is one of the mainstays of the Mormon food supply. The typical Mormon pantry includes shelves of home-canned fruits and vegetables, unground wheat, cereal grains, and a freezer filled with meat, as well as game. Food supplies are rotated so that nothing becomes stale or spoils.

Encouraged by the Mormon church, breadmaking with freshly ground flour is an almost daily activity in many Mormon homes. In order to provide fresh flour to its parishioners, the church operates large flour mills. Mormon brides often receive small hand-operated flour mills as wedding presents. Many housewives still bake a whole-wheat bread from an early

Mormon recipe that includes honey and molasses.

Tea, coffee, and alcoholic drinks are not allowed in strict Mormon households. In the absence of a quick "pick-me-up," the Mormons have turned to other stimulants, including sugar. Utahans consume nearly twice as much candy per capita as the rest of the country. They are also one of the highest per capita consumers of ice cream. It is no wonder that the Utah Agricultural Experimental Station was a pioneer in making improvements in commercial ice-cream production, perfecting many of the exotic flavors used today.

The church encourages Mormons to have a family evening once a week. A popular entertainment for children and grownups alike is candymaking—anything from popcorn balls to "pioneer fruit" candy. The fruit candy is made with raisins, figs, dates, prunes, and orange peel ground together and blended with orange juice and chopped walnuts. The mixture is then shaped into balls. For an extra treat the balls are dipped in melted chocolate.

Utah Agriculture

Upon discovering that most of the land suitable for cultivation had to be irrigated, the early settlers decided to concentrate their efforts on raising livestock. Since grazing does not depend heavily on the availability of water, livestock raising became the main agricultural activity of Utah. Today 87 percent of the land in Utah is devoted to the pasturing of animals; as a result beef and dairy products predominate.

When Utah became a state in 1896, farmers sought markets for their products

ZUCCHINI SPICE COOKIES

Recipes for spice cookies were brought to the Mountain States by the pioneers. Garden vegetables, an essential ingredient in Mormon cooking, are used here in a cookie recipe.

Makes 4 to 5 dozen cookies

8 tablespoons (1 stick) butter or margarine

3/4 cup sugar

1 egg

2 cups all-purpose flour

1 1/4 teaspoons soda

1 1/4 teaspoons cinnamon

1/2 teaspoon cloves

1/4 teaspoon nutmeg

1 1/3 cups grated zucchini

1 cup chopped walnuts

1 cup raisins

■

Cream together the butter and sugar in a large bowl. Add the egg and beat well. Combine the flour, soda, cinnamon, cloves, and nutmeg. Gradually stir the flour mixture into the batter. The dough will be very stiff. Slowly add the grated zucchini, incorporating it into the batter, which will become lighter with the moisture of the zucchini. Stir in the nuts and raisins. Drop by heaping teaspoonfuls onto a lightly greased cookie sheet. Bake in a preheated 350° F. oven for 15 minutes.

PRUNE WHIP

Dried fruits were commonly used in pies, puddings, and whips in pioneer days. Puddings were either cooked or baked, while whips were uncooked, fluffier, and retained their texture with beaten egg whites. Today, gelatin helps hold the shape of whips.

Serves 6

24 large pitted prunes, soaked overnight
    in 3 cups cold water

3/4 cup prune juice

1/3 cup sugar

1 envelope unflavored gelatin

2 tablespoons lemon juice

2/3 cup chopped walnuts

3 egg whites

1 cup whipped cream

■

Place the prunes and the soaking water in a saucepan. Bring to a boil and cook on low heat for about 20 minutes or until tender. Drain the prunes and purée them in a food processor.

Heat 1/2 cup of the prune juice and the sugar in small saucepan. Soften the gelatin in the remaining 1/4 cup of cold prune juice and let stand for 5 minutes. Add the gelatin to the hot prune juice and stir to dissolve. Add the prune purée and lemon juice. Cool the mixture over ice water or in the refrigerator until slightly thickened. Stir in the nuts.

Beat the egg whites until stiff and gently fold them into the prune mixture. Spoon into a 4-cup mold and chill until firm, about 3 hours. Serve with a dollop of whipped cream.

---

outside of the state's boundaries. Crop patterns were changed to suit available markets. Sugar beets, dairy products, wheat, vegetables, and fruit became Utah's principal agricultural commodities.

After an earlier attempt to establish a sugar refinery failed, the Mormon church sponsored the construction of a sugar plant in Lehi, Utah, in the late 1890s. Sugar beets provided farmers with the means of converting family labor to cash, and by 1917 there were 9,000 farms raising sugar beets. Generations of young people grew up working in the beet fields. The routine of planting, growing, and harvesting sugar beets determined school vacations and local holidays.

Fruit orchards did not become an integral part of Utah's agriculture until the turn of the century, although early settlers had planted orchards and berries almost immediately upon arrival in the Utah Territory. Farming, however, remained a rural, slow-paced way of life, with family orchards, home gardening, a cow, and a few chickens being the norm for most Utah farmers. Any excess fruit and produce was sold locally.

By 1900 fruit growing was commercialized. Orchard associations were organized and fruit raising became a scientific venture. Today, Utah orchards grow a variety of fruits and are leading producers of tart cherries. Many of the tart cherries are processed for cherry raisins, a new snack food. Much of the local fruit crop goes into the baking of pies. Wine grapes are grown in the southern part of Utah and are used to make jelly, since the Mormon church does not approve of their use in wine.

Utah's Cuisine Today

Mormon cooking is still very much the traditional fare of the past. Oatmeal breads fresh from the oven, fragrant stews, spicy pot roasts, strawberry shortcake, fruit pies, and light, fluffy cakes continue to be some of the basics of Mormon cooking.

Since many of the early Mormon converts came from Europe, much of Utah's cuisine has been influenced by European immigrants. German spiced red cabbage is just as popular as sour-cream raisin pie. Scandinavian pepper cookies, *Pepparakor,* can be found in many Utah lunch boxes.

There is also a Southwestern influence in Utah's cooking. The recipe for a lima-bean and pork-sausage casserole spiced with a little chili powder has been handed down from mother to daughter for generations. Many of the Spanish recipes have been Anglicized, however, since few Mormon dishes include chili. Some say that Hamburger Bean Goulash, a Utah favorite, is merely a milder version of Chile con Carne.

At the turn of the century, many Italian immigrants came to Utah to work in the mines and on the railroad, settling in Carbon County. The merchants of the area still stock basic Italian food items. Even today Italian families grow their own vegetables, have fruit orchards, make wine, cure olives, and make special Italian sausages.

Barbecuing and Dutch-oven cooking are indigenous to the state, starting with the early settlers. Today, Utahans bring meats for barbecuing; casseroles, which were prepared ahead of time; homemade breads; pickles; and pies to their outings.

WYOMING

BY 1851 WAGON TRAINS carrying prospectors and a few settlers began coming to Wyoming. The prospectors were heading west in search of gold, and the settlers came to establish farms.

For many the long journey from the Midwest was a hard one. Although the women frequently started the trip preparing fried chicken and corn bread, they soon learned to cook simpler food over a camp fire. As the journey got rougher, salt pork, jerked venison, sourdough biscuits, and beans became the basic foods. Fried deer liver was a rare treat. By the end of the journey, when food supplies were low, cornmeal mush had become the daily fare for all.

While the settlers were building their homesteads and planting crops, they subsisted on braised bear meat, venison steak, hominy cooked with dried beef, and sometimes rice with honey and cinnamon. Pioneer women soon became experts at improvising. For coffee they roasted anything that would turn brown over a fire. They used the Dutch oven for everything from boiling water to baking cakes. Pies were baked in the Dutch oven and were often made of edible roots.

People came to Wyoming from all over the world. Before 1900 there were already 47 different nationalities represented in Rock Springs, Wyoming, in the southwestern part of the state. There was a French bakery that made fluffy croissants and rich éclairs. The owner of the Greek candy shop baked almond cakes, spice bars, and made *halvah*, a type of pudding. The Chinese restaurant served sweet-and-sour pork and wonton soup. The Germans made Wiener schnitzel and cheesecake, and the Norwegians prepared cold fruit soups.

HUNTING, CABIN DOOR by Richard La Barre Goodwin, oil, 58 1/2 x 35 1/2 inches, courtesy of Richard York Gallery, New York, New York.

Since the late 1800s, when the Chinese came to work on the railroads, there has been an Oriental influence on Wyoming's cooking. This influence expanded when the Japanese, who were interned in Wyoming during World War II, began to farm the land. Today, a variety of Oriental vegetables are grown and cooked in Wyoming, and there are Chinese restaurants in many towns.

Cattle in Wyoming

Many of the immigrants who settled in Wyoming brought their own cattle. Raising cattle was an especially attractive venture for the settlers, since most of the land was public and free for pasturing until 1868, when the Wyoming Territory was created.

Wyoming had no gold, silver, or copper to offer settlers, but it had another precious resource—vast stretches of lush green grass. The grass was not only well suited for summer grazing of cattle, but it was so thick that herds could be kept in the pastures almost all year.

The Wyoming cattle industry grew rapidly. In 1866 the first cattle drives from Texas to the Union Pacific railheads began. Many cattle trails crossed into Wyoming on their way to markets further north and east. Wyoming had become a grazing ground for Texas cattle, since the range was free and much of Texas grass had been depleted. Cheyenne, the center of Wyoming cattle enterprises, was one of the wealthiest city per capita in the world in the late 1870s.

Cowboy food was unadorned. The bunkhouse kitchen provided meals of beef, beans, and chili, which was sometimes made with venison. Out on the range, the cowboys' fare was even simpler, consisting of chuck-wagon beans and beef often enriched by a bread twist. This was biscuit dough twisted on a stick, baked, stick removed, and the hole filled with honey or jelly.

Cattlemen were prosperous until the winter of 1886-87. More than six inches of snow covered the pastureland that year, and the watering holes were frozen solid. As a result 400,000 of the one million cattle in the state died. The depletion of pasture in Wyoming hindered the recovery of cattle raising. At the time the governor of Wyoming, Thomas Moonlight, encouraged the breakup of the open range into small farms. His plan did not succeed.

Even with a steady decline of cattle over the years, Wyoming still produces more than one and a half million head of cattle each year. Livestock, both cattle and sheep, remains an important part of Wyoming agriculture, occupying about 85 percent of the farmlands.

Although cattle have been relatively easy to raise, at one time their teeth were a problem. Grazing animals often picked up dirt, bits of stone, and other abrasive materials together with grass. With steers this was no problem, since they went to market at a fairly young age, but over the years the teeth of valuable breeding stock wore down. Unable to chew, they might eventually starve. Dentists fitted the cows with stainless-steel crowns that covered the lower incisors.

Sheep

In the 1880s sheep began coming into the state. For many years there was a constant battle between the cattlemen and the sheep farmers. After the winter of 1886, many ranchers realized that there was not enough grass to sustain cattle. Sheep could exist on poorer pasture and could feed at higher elevations.

In pioneering days raising sheep and cattle together would have been unthinkable. For years Wyoming cattlemen accused sheep farmers of denuding the range and draining water holes with their hungry, thirsty flocks. In the late 1800s there were vicious skirmishes between sheep raisers and cattlemen. Now most ranches are fenced, and sheep and cattle graze separately on what used to be open range.

The advent of sheep raising in Wyoming also brought Basque sheepherders from the Spanish plateaus near France. They introduced new types of food to Wyoming, such as spicy chorizo sausages, garlic to flavor stews, chick-peas, lamb stews, and hard-crusted bread to dip into gravy.

Agriculture

Farming started in Wyoming in the mid-1850s, when a group of Mormons arrived in a wagon train at Fort Supply in the southwestern corner of the state. They brought seeds, herds of cattle, flocks of chickens, and plentiful food supplies.

The Wyoming climate and a short growing season have lent themselves to several crops, which have become the mainstay of the state's agriculture. Dry-farmed winter wheat is the major grain crop in Wyoming. Planted from mid-August to mid-September, the wheat is harvested the next year from mid-July to mid-August. Wyoming grows sugar beets, since the cool climate helps to bring up the sugar content. Barley, pinto beans, and Great Northern beans also grow in Wyoming.

Hunting

Soon after settlers arrived in Wyoming, hunting lodges became popular. Great hunting parties came from the East and as far away as Europe in search of big game. One English nobleman brought a hunting party overland with 6 wagons, 121 carts, 112 horses, 14 dogs, and 40 servants.

Today, Wyoming is considered to be one of the prime game-hunting states. Big game—deer, bear, elk, moose, and mountain sheep—is still available in the mountains. Sage grouse and pheasants top the list of game birds. The cold mountain streams provide excellent fishing with several varieties of trout.

A number of farmers in Wyoming are raising game birds, particularly wild turkeys, which many Wyomingites claim taste far better than the bland commercial varieties. Wild duck, fattened on wild grains, is another Wyoming speciality, as is wild pheasant and partridge.

Big game and game birds have become an integral part of Wyoming cuisine. The big game is broiled, roasted, or stewed. Venison is often marinated in wine, vinegar, and spices and then slowly braised in the oven. Game birds are stuffed with wild rice, roasted, and served with a wild mushroom sauce. Pheasant is cooked with apples and also is the basis of a pie.

Wyoming's Tea Party

On Election Eve of 1869, Ester Morris invited the two rival candidates for president of the First Territorial Legislative Assembly in Wyoming to tea. She filled their palates with an array of cakes, cookies, muffins, and jams. Well-fed, the gentlemen asked what they might do to show their appreciation for such fine fare. Ester Morris extracted from each of them a promise concerning the revolutionary law she wanted passed. As a result of the new law, Wyoming became the first state in the United States to give women the right to vote.

BRAISED LOIN OF VENISON

The first fur trappers in the Mountain States in the early 1800s and the settlers who followed them lived off the land. Wild game provided the meat, and venison was preferred by many. The Mountain States are still well known for their abundant supply of wild game.

A combination of buttermilk and milk is used in this recipe to soften the gamey taste of venison and also to help tenderize the meat. If a more gamey taste is desired, omit the marinade. The red wine aids in making the meat more tender.

Serves 4

1 loin of venison (about 1 1/2 pounds)

3/4 cup milk

3/4 cup buttermilk

1/2 teaspoon salt

1/4 teaspoon pepper

1/4 teaspoon dried thyme

1/4 teaspoon dried marjoram

1/4 teaspoon dried rosemary

1/4 teaspoon dried sage

2 tablespoons butter or margarine

1 medium onion, chopped

1 slice bacon, diced

6 juniper berries

1/2 cup sliced shiitake mushrooms

1/3 cup finely diced carrot

3/4 cup red wine

1/3 cup fresh cranberries

2 tablespoons sour cream

■

Place the venison loin in a small, oblong bowl. Combine the milk and buttermilk and pour over the venison to just cover the meat. Cover the dish with plastic wrap and store in the refrigerator for 24 to 36 hours.

Remove the meat from the marinade and pat it dry with paper towels. Discard the marinade. Combine the salt, pepper, and spices and pat them onto the meat.

Melt the butter in a small roaster or oven-proof casserole over medium heat. Add the venison, onion, and bacon and lightly brown the meat on both sides. Add the juniper berries, mushrooms, carrot, and wine. Cover the roaster and bake in a preheated 325° F. oven for 45 minutes to 1 hour or until the meat is no longer pink on the inside.

In the meantime, cook the cranberries in a little water just until they burst. (This may be done in a microwave oven.) Remove the venison from the pan to a warm platter and keep it warm. Add the cooked cranberries to the pan juices, then add the sour cream and stir to combine. If necessary thicken the pan juices with a little flour and water combination. Slice the venison and serve with the gravy.

SALMON BOAT by Armin Carl Hansen, oil, 15 3/4 x 19 1/2 inches, courtesy of Montgomery Gallery, San Francisco, California.

PACIFIC NORTHWEST

THE PACIFIC NORTHWEST originally included both Oregon and Washington, plus portions of Idaho, Montana, Wyoming, and British Columbia. At the time it was first settled the area was known as the Oregon Territory. The region is divided by the Cascade Mountains into a wet western area and a dry eastern one. At the base of the western slope of the Cascades, fed by rainfall from the Pacific Ocean, lies some of the most productive farmland in the West.

The mild climate of the coastal Northwest is moderated by the warm offshore Japanese Current. Cool winters and long growing seasons are conducive to growing a wide array of fruits and vegetables.

The land east of the Cascades is used principally for raising cattle and sheep. Due to the lack of sufficient rain, only 15 percent of the land is under cultivation through the use of irrigation. These irrigated lands, however, produce exceptional agricultural products.

Along the coastline of the Northwest there is a variety of seafood. In peaceful weather clams can be dug on the beaches, and smelts can be gathered with a rake. Dungeness crabs are harvested off the coast of Oregon and Washington. While the native Olympia oysters are rare and so tiny that two will fit into a thimble, they are considered a delicacy by Northwesterners. The very abundant Pacific oysters from Yaquina Bay in Oregon and Willapa Bay in Washington grow up to ten inches in length and are frequently enjoyed broiled. Red, pink, and silver salmon are caught in Oregon and Washington waters, as well as sturgeon, rockfish, sablefish, and cod.

The first white men in the fertile Pacific Northwest were French and British fur traders, who came from Canada in the late eighteenth century. They found the Chinook, Clatsop, and Kwalhioqua Indians living on the rich coastal land. They gathered wild fruits and berries, hunted deer, and fished for giant halibut and salmon. Food was so abundant in the wild that there was no need for the Indians to farm. They were not avid hunters, since killing a deer or antelope with a bow and arrow required far more effort than taking salmon in baskets or dip nets.

The Oregon Territory first began to attract settlers in the early 1840s. They were restless Midwestern farmers who had emigrated from northern Europe or were only a generation removed from emigrants from England, Scotland, Sweden, and Denmark. Soon thereafter Chinese, Japanese, and Italians came to help build the railroads. Many settlers were attracted by the opportunity to claim huge tracts of land under the Land Act of 1850. By 1853 the territory had developed sufficiently for Congress to create a separate Washington Territory.

After completion of the railroads in the 1880s, many of the Italian, Chinese, and Japanese stayed and sent for their families. The Italians bought land, particularly near Portland, and began truck farming vegetables. The Japanese established farms along the Hood River, where they worked hard to cultivate the steep hillsides. The Chinese continued to settle in the area, and by 1900 Portland's Chinese population rivaled that of San Francisco.

The abundance of resources in the Northwest continued to attract immigrants, such as Swedish and Finnish lumberjacks; Italian, Greek, and Japanese fishermen; and European fruit growers. By 1900 most of the farmland had been claimed.

The coastal pastures of the Northwest began to produce excellent milk cows, whose milk was used to make cheese and other dairy products. The land at the western foot of the Cascade Mountains became pasture for beef cattle and farmlands for wheat and hops. During this same period, the late 1800s, Basque farmers started to raise sheep in the southeastern part of Oregon.

The Northwestern fruit industry flourished in the mild climate and rich soil of the region. According to some records, the first apple tree in the Pacific Northwest came from seed brought from London in 1824 by a Captain Aemilius Simpson. Commercial orchards of Oregon started in the Willamette Valley in the 1840s with seedlings brought from Iowa.

The central part of the Pacific Northwest became orchard and berry country. Today, many varieties of berries are cultivated in the Northwest, including blackberries, raspberries, strawberries, and cranberries. Currently, Oregon and Washington produce 90 percent of the nation's raspberries. The berry production, in turn, has spawned a cottage industry specializing in jams and preserves.

The commercial fishing industry has thrived. At the turn of the century, competition from Alaskan salmon packers was keen. Fortunately, several inventions in the Northwestern fishing industry reduced labor costs and helped keep it competitive. Axel Johnson developed an automatic can-making machine, and Edmund A. Smith invented the "Iron Chink." The latter device cut, cleaned, and packed salmon automatically, a job that otherwise required the work of 50 cannery workers.

In 1877 the canneries started their own fish hatchery, and by 1888 the U. S. Fish and Game Commission started

ASPARAGUS WITH CRABMEAT SAUCE

Oriental cooking techniques have become an intricate part of Northwestern cuisine. Dungeness crabs, both alive and cooked, are available in the Northwest from November through March.

In this recipe fresh asparagus is served with a crabmeat sauce prepared in a wok for a meatless entrée.

Serves 4

1 1/2 pounds asparagus, cleaned and
   trimmed

1 cup chicken broth

1 tablespoon cornstarch

1/4 teaspoon sugar

1 tablespoon peanut oil

2 teaspoons dry white wine

8 ounces crabmeat

2 egg whites

Pinch of salt

3 cups steamed rice

■

Blanch the asparagus in boiling water until just tender, about 3 to 4 minutes. Drain and keep warm while preparing the sauce.

Mix the chicken broth with the cornstarch and sugar in a small bowl. Heat the wok over medium-high heat and add the peanut oil. Lower the heat, add the chicken broth mixture, and stir the sauce until it is clear. Stir in the wine and add the crabmeat. Quickly beat the egg whites with a pinch of salt until frothy and stir them into the sauce. Stir gently over low heat until the sauce thickens.

To serve, divide the steamed rice among four warm plates. Top with equal portions of asparagus and cover with the crabmeat sauce.

parts of Burgundy, France. Fine Rieslings, Chardonnays, and Pinot Noirs are being produced.

Foods of the Northwest

Fish and seafood cookery is the outstanding feature of the cuisine of Oregon and Washington. Salmon, a staple of the Chinook Indians, is still widely eaten but prepared in a great many more ways than the Chinooks ever imagined. Today, salmon is baked, fried, grilled, broiled, smoked, pickled, and barbecued. Other fish such as lingcod, Pacific snapper, halibut, squid, and whiting are also popular.

Shellfish are plentiful. Dungeness crab is famous for its tender, delicate flesh. Oregon shrimp have become a major industry in the last 20 years. Olympic oysters are now farmed in several coastal bays, and mussels are outpaced by the demand. Clams are there for the digging.

The abundance of fresh fruit has contributed to the variety of foods in the Northwest. Scandinavian immigrants made cold fruit soups popular. Russian settlers contributed a form of Western pot roast prepared with dried apricots and prunes. A wide variety of bakery goods, such as pies, tarts, and even bread, contain apples, pears, cherries, and other fruit.

The most famous confections of the Pacific Northwest are the sugar-coated Aplets and Cotlets. They are made with apples or apricots plus sugar and walnuts.

Pacific Northwestern cuisine, with its abundant use of fresh fruits, vegetables, and seafood has been at the forefront of the new American food styles, which feature lighter and zestier foods. The Asian influences of quick stir-frying and the Scandinavian influences of fruit cookery are characteristic of the cooking of the Pacific Northwest.

stocking the Columbia River with fish. Today, fishing is one of the great industries of the Pacific Northwest. Fishing towns with fleets of boats and canneries speckle the coast.

The most famous of the Pacific Northwestern fish is, of course, salmon. Five species abound in the Pacific Ocean along the West Coast from Alaska to California. There are other commercially important fish in the Pacific Northwest, however, including halibut and a dozen varieties of flatfish. Most prevalent of the flatfish are the petrale, sand dab, lemon, and Dover sole. In the Pacific Northwest

Dover sole is the common name for Pacific flounder, a large flatfish weighing up to ten pounds. There are also about 50 species of rockfish, as well as cod and smelt off the coast of Oregon and Washington.

Wine, another food product, has brought fame to areas of Oregon and Washington. The cool Pacific Northwest has a mild, damp climate and ample sunshine, which lets the grapes ripen gradually, making deep-flavored red wines and light delicate whites. These growing conditions have been compared to the Rheingau of Germany and the cooler

OREGON

IN 1840 THERE WERE only 150 Americans in Oregon. Then "Oregon Fever," the lure of a new frontier, began the move westward for New Englanders, Southerners, and even settlers in the Missouri and Mississippi valleys. During the next 20 years, tens of thousands of settlers came over the Oregon Trail to the Pacific Northwest. They settled in the fertile valleys to begin a frontier existence, adapting their recipes to the ingredients of the region. After clearing land and building homes, the pioneers planted crops and fruit orchards.

The Oregon Trail

The trek to Oregon over the Oregon Trail is considered to be the largest and longest migration by land in the history of mankind. It entailed a six- to eight-month journey of 2,000 miles over the inhospitable Great Plains and through the almost impassible Rocky Mountains. Historians have commented that had the Great Plains been more conducive to settlement, there would have been no need for the Oregon Trail.

Most immigrants brought little more than the clothes on their backs with them on the difficult journey. Those who brought cattle and other farm animals lost most of their stock, including the animals needed to pull their wagons. In spite of having to travel light, some immigrants succeeded in bringing cows, pigs, chickens, seeds, and tree-root stocks to start their farms. They also carried saws and axes to clear the land and tools to cultivate the fields.

The journey began in Independence or St. Joseph, Missouri, or in Council Bluffs, Iowa, all towns along the Missouri River. There the immigrants and their covered wagons, which they called prairie schooners, gathered during the late winter and early spring. Finally, when the spring grass was high enough on the plains so that livestock could graze en route, the wagons departed.

Although game and wild plants could be relied upon to provide some nourishment along the way, the covered wagons were loaded with enough food to last the journey. Food for the trip had to be compact, lightweight, and non-perishable. Each family brought along such staples as flour, sugar, cornmeal, coffee, dried beans, rice, bacon, and salt pork. Some also brought dried fruit.

Mealtime on the Oregon Trail was governed by the sun, since the immigrants traveled from sunup to sundown. Breakfast had to be completed by 4 a.m. so that the wagon train could be on its way by daybreak. Beans, cornmeal mush, Johnnycakes or pancakes, and coffee were the usual breakfast. Fresh milk was available from the dairy cows that some families brought along, and pioneers took advantage of the rough rides of the wagon to churn their butter.

"Nooning" at midday meant stopping for a rest and a meal. Little time could be spent preparing the noonday

COLD CHERRY SOUP

Both sweet and sour cherries are grown in Oregon's Willamette Valley near The Dalles on the Columbia River. Recipes for cold fruit soups were originally brought to the Northwest by the Scandinavians and are still popular.

Serves 4

3/4 cup sugar

3 cups water

3 cups pitted sour cherries

1 cup pitted sweet (Bing) cherries

1 tablespoon cornstarch

2/3 cup dry red wine

1/3 cup whipping cream

■

Combine the sugar and water in a saucepan. Bring to a boil, reduce heat, and gently boil the syrup for 3 to 5 minutes, stirring constantly, until smooth. Add the cherries and simmer, partially covered, for 30 minutes. Remove half of the cherries and purée them in a food processor. Return the puréed cherries to the soup. Mix the cornstarch with 2 tablespoons cold water and stir the mixture into the soup. Cook on low heat for another 5 minutes or until slightly thickened.

Chill the cherry soup for at least 6 hours. Before serving, add the wine and cream.

THE BERRY PICKER by John George Brown, oil, 18 x 12 inches, courtesy of Montgomery Gallery, San Francisco, California.

If the wagon train halted for a day to make repairs, the women and children gathered wild berries and other wild fruits while the men worked on the wagons.

Agriculture

Two young Iowans, Henderson Luelling and William Meek, can be considered the "Johnny Appleseeds" of the Pacific Northwest. Both Meek and Luelling came to Oregon with nursery stock in soil-filled boxes in their wagons; Meek arrived in 1846 and Luelling a year later. Transporting plants was not an easy task, since they had to be watered frequently. The two men settled in the Willamette Valley, teaming up to form a partnership and start a nursery. Their trees were the forerunners of today's Rogue River pears, Willamette Valley plums and prunes, Hood River apples, and Dalles cherries.

In those early years fruit was so scarce that settlers came from all over the region to see the first apple trees. By the 1850s, however, enough trees had been planted and were bearing sufficient fruit to supply local needs. The surplus was sent by ship in theft-proof iron crates to the growing San Francisco market. A shipment of four bushels of apples sold for $500 in San Francisco in 1853.

The coming of the railroads made it possible to transport Oregon fruit to eastern markets. As the tree-fruit industry grew and prospered, orchards spread from the fertile valleys to the drier parts of the state where irrigation made fruit growing possible. Pear orchards, in particular, expanded rapidly, since pears can be picked green and shipped across country without spoiling. Since pears do not ripen properly on the tree, they are picked slightly immature and ripen at room

meal, since the wagon train could only travel by daylight. Usually a piece of meat was fried over a camp fire. Longer-cooking stews were left for the evening meal. The women made bread dough while riding in the wagons and timed the rising so that it would be ready to bake

when evening camp was made.

In the evening the wagon train camped in a circle, forming a barricade against Indian raids. In dangerous Indian country fires could not be lit after dark, and supper usually consisted of a cold biscuit or Johnnycake and any leftover cold meat.

temperature. If the pear is left on the tree too long, it becomes mushy and gritty.

Bartlett pears, which are hardy and keep well, became Oregon's major crop. Anjou, Bosc, Comice, Winter, and Seckel pears are also grown in the state, primarily in the Rogue River Valley.

Cherries and berries comprise a major portion of Oregon's fruit crops. The cherries are grown in the Willamette Valley near The Dalles (or rapids) on the Columbia River and are sold to the fresh market and to canners. Most of Oregon's berries—strawberries, blackberries, raspberries, and blueberries—are sold for processing and are marketed frozen, canned, or concentrated.

Ninety-eight percent of the hazelnuts used in this country are grown in Oregon. The first American hazelnut trees were planted in 1858 in Scottsburg, Oregon, by David Gernot, a Frenchman. When he arrived in the lush Willamette Valley, he found it very similar to his native Loire Valley in France. Gernot planted the 50 young hazelnut seedlings he had brought with him, and from these trees a major agricultural commodity developed in Oregon. Today, there are more than 1,100 hazelnut growers in the state.

Unlike other nut trees, hazelnut trees bloom and pollinate in mid-winter. Nuts begin to form in June, then mature, and are harvested in the early fall. After the nuts have fallen to the ground, mechanical harvesters sweep the nuts into windrows. They are then picked up by another machine and taken to processing plants.

Since Oregon has a diverse topography and climate, ranging from fertile valleys to rangelands, forests, and deserts, the state has a varied agricultural industry. It consists of more than 100 different crops and livestock enterprises, including cattle grazing, dairying, and sheep-raising.

The early Oregonians found that cattle could be raised on the wild bunch grass in western Oregon without the need for supplemental feeding. One of the first dairymen was Joe Champion, who in April 1851 sailed down the Oregon coast from Astoria, at the mouth of the Columbia River, to settle his small herd in the Tillamook Bay area. The land was uninhabited at the time he arrived, so he lived in a hollow tree for a month. That same year other rugged pioneers arrived with herds of dairy cows and cattle that became fat on the thick grass and produced an abundance of quality milk.

At the time there was no transporta-

GREEN SALAD WITH HAZELNUTS

This green salad, flavored with Oregon hazelnuts, exemplifies the lighter style of Northwestern cuisine. The tartness of the watercress is contrasted by the sweetness of the mustard in the salad dressing.

Serves 6

1 bunch red lettuce, washed, dried, and
    torn into bite-sized pieces

1 head butter lettuce, washed, dried, and
    torn into bite-sized pieces

1 bunch watercress, washed, dried, and
    coarse stems removed

1/3 cup dry white wine

1 1/4 tablespoons sweet mustard

1/8 teaspoon salt

1/4 teaspoon white pepper

1/4 cup hazelnut oil

1/4 cup vegetable oil

1 1/4 cups hazelnuts, lightly toasted and
    coarsely chopped

■

Combine the lettuces and watercress in a large bowl. Whisk together the wine, mustard, salt, and pepper. Slowly whisk in the oils until well blended. Pour the dressing over the salad and toss. Arrange the salad on six serving plates and sprinkle each generously with the chopped hazelnuts.

POACHED PEARS

Oregon is known for its Bartlett, Anjou, and Bosc pears. In this recipe Anjou pears are poached in a ginger-flavored liquid and then served with a brandy chocolate sauce.

Serves 4

Grated zest of 1 medium lemon

1 piece (1-inch) ginger, finely chopped

3/4 cup dry white wine

1/2 cup water

2 tablespoons lemon juice

2 tablespoons sugar

1/4 cup applesauce

1/4 teaspoon cinnamon

1/4 teaspoon cloves

4 firm ripe Anjou pears

■

To make the poaching liquid, combine all of the above ingredients, except the pears, in a medium-size saucepan. Bring to a boil, reduce heat, and simmer covered for 10 minutes.

In the meantime, peel the pears, leaving the stems intact. Cut the bottom of each pear flat so that it will stand upright when served. Add the pears to the poaching liquid, placing them on their sides. Bring to a boil, reduce heat, and simmer, covered, for 7 minutes. Turn the pears and cook for another 5 to 7 minutes, or until the pears are tender. Remove the pears, transfer them to a shallow dish, and let them cool for 10 minutes.

Reduce the poaching liquid to one cup and pour over the pears. Refrigerate, covered, until well chilled, about 4 hours.

Place each pear upright in a serving dish and spoon some of the liquid around each. Top with the chocolate sauce.

Chocolate Sauce

3 ounces semi-sweet chocolate

1 tablespoon butter

1 tablespoon light corn syrup

2 tablespoons brandy

■

Combine the sauce ingredients in a small saucepan over low heat and cook just until the chocolate is melted. Stir to combine the ingredients. Let the sauce cool to room temperature and serve.

tion to ship the milk out of Tillamook, since boats were undependable and slow and milk was bulky and perishable. The only land route was an Indian trail over the Coast Range. A railroad from Tillamook to Portland was not constructed until 1911.

In order to keep their excess milk from spoiling, the Tillamook dairymen began making cheese. In 1855 the Tillamook pioneers built a ship, the *Morning Star,* to transport their cheese up the Columbia River to the Portland market.

Soon small cheese factories sprung up throughout Tillamook County. In 1894 Peter McIntosh, a cheesemaker from Ontario, introduced a cheddar process he had learned in the East. The unique Tillamook Cheddar, aged for up to two years rather than the standard six to seven months, became popular for its sharper, more mature flavor.

In 1909 the Tillamook cheese producers formed the Tillamook County Creamery Association in order to standardize production, create a trademark, and increase marketing of the product. Today, Tillamook cheese is not the old-fashioned variety. Consumer tastes have changed and cheesemakers have adapted to the preference for milder flavors. Medium cheddar is aged only for three months and sharp for seven months.

Although traditionally sheep were raised in Oregon for their wool, lambs are now being raised for meat. Oregon lambs are often a crossbreed of white-faced ewes with black-faced Suffolk lambs. The offspring, which are neither white- nor black-faced are called "smut-faced" lambs. They mature rapidly, making it possible to market the lambs earlier. Since Oregon has an abundant supply of grass, lambs do not have to be fattened in feedlots.

Harvesting Seafood

Fishing has been a way of life as well as an economic enterprise in Oregon since the first pioneers arrived. With the discovery of the Columbia River in 1792, this vast river system, more than 1,200 miles long, has yielded an abundant amount of salmon.

The Chinook (king) salmon is the largest of the varieties found along the Oregon Coast, weighing between 15 and 20 pounds. It roams the waters from California to the Bering Strait, but the largest concentrations of Chinook salmon are found in the Columbia River. The coho or silver salmon is smaller, weighing between 8 and 12 pounds, while the pink salmon is the smallest, averaging only 3 to 5 pounds. The sockeye salmon, about the same size as the Chinook, is preferred by canneries because it is redder in color, flakes easier, and is oilier. The color and ability to flake easily appeals to the consumer, and the oil helps in preservation.

Smoking salmon was an old method of preservation used by the Indians, as well as by the early settlers, and it is still used. Some of the first Oregon smoked salmon was sent around Cape Horn to Boston in 1831. When it arrived, the Treasury Department ruled that it was a foreign-caught fish and imposed a duty on it. At that time most eastern Americans regarded the Oregon Territory as a satellite of the United States, inhabited by Americans but not actually part of the Union. When California achieved statehood in 1850, it was difficult not to admit Oregon, since at the time it provided much of the food consumed in California. Oregon finally became a state in 1859.

Other Seafood Specialties

More than two dozen varieties of clams inhabit the sandy tidelands of Oregon and Washington—butter, Japanese littleneck, horse, sand, surf, razor, and geoduck, to name a few. The Japanese littleneck, or Manila clam, is the most common; the geoduck is harvested mainly by clam diggers for sport.

The five-inch razor clams live on sandy, wave-washed beaches from Pismo Beach, California, to the Aleutians. A rather bizarre-looking creature, it can only be hunted at low tide, but it has a tasty flesh.

The geoduck clam digs deep into the sand and reveals its presence by squirting water in the air. Named by the Nisqualli Indians, these "gooey-duck" clams have an enormous neck. They have almost become an endangered species, so their take is limited.

Most of the squid harvested in the Pacific Northwest come from the coast of Oregon. Squid travel in large schools and are fished commercially by a unique method. They are tracked by a depth recorder during the day. Then at night,

SALMON SEASON BEGINS by Nicky Boehme, oil, 34 x 48 inches, courtesy of Nicky Boehme Gallery, Mendocino, California.

SALMON WITH DILL SAUCE

Dill is still a favorite herb with the Scandinavians of the Pacific Northwest. Serve this salmon entrée with small boiled red potatoes and green beans.

Serves 4

4 salmon steaks

1 small onion, sliced

1/2 lemon, thinly sliced

3/4 cup dry white wine

■

Place the salmon steaks in a large skillet; cover with the onion and lemon slices. Add the wine and sufficient water to barely cover the fish. Cover the skillet and bring to a boil. Reduce heat and simmer for 10 minutes, or until the fish flakes easily with a fork.

In the meantime, prepare the dill sauce. When the salmon is done, remove it to 4 warm plates and top with the sauce.

Dill Sauce

3 tablespoons butter or margarine

1 1/2 tablespoons all-purpose flour

2 teaspoons Dijon mustard

1 1/4 cups milk

1/4 cup chopped fresh dill

1 egg yolk

3 tablespoons lemon juice

Salt and pepper, to taste

■

Melt the butter in a medium-size saucepan over medium-low heat. Stir in the flour and then the mustard. Gradually add the milk, stirring constantly. Cook until the sauce is smooth and then add the dill. Beat the egg yolk, stir a little of the hot sauce into it, then add the egg mixture to the dill sauce. Blend in the lemon juice and season to taste with salt and pepper.

As with most regions of America settled by pioneers, Oregon's cuisine reflects a rich and varied ethnic and regional heritage. The Southerners who settled in Oregon after the Civil War brought with them recipes for fried chicken, hot breads, hominy grits, and baked ham. Aurora was first settled by Germans, who made the region famous for its sage sausages served with fried potatoes. Basque cooking is found in eastern Oregon, where Basque sheepherders settled. Descendants of Scandinavian and Russia immigrants use dried fruits in their Oregon cookery. French immigrants contributed Golden Oregon prunes, which were derived from plum-tree cuttings brought from France in the 1850s. The prunes are often used in poultry stuffings.

Few know that one of our country's most famous gourmets, James Beard, was born and raised in Portland, Oregon. His father had come west in a covered wagon from Iowa at the age of five. Beard's mother was English, and the family employed a Chinese cook. All three cuisines, American, English, and Chinese, influenced James Beard's cooking.

James Beard, who died in 1985, was one of the country's most distinguished food experts. He conducted a successful cooking school in New York City, wrote numerous magazine articles, frequently appeared on television, and was a consultant to many food companies. He also authored more than a dozen books on various aspects of cooking. Many considered Beard to be the father of modern American cookery. In all of his writings and teachings, he advocated using fresh ingredients, particularly fruits and vegetables—part of his Oregon heritage.

when the squid come to the surface to feed, they are netted or siphoned into fishing boats by means of a large hydraulic pump.

Oregon Cuisine

Oregon cuisine is a unique combination of foods based on fresh ingredients—seafood, fruits, and vegetables—as well as adaptations of recipes the early settlers brought with them. Many of the state's food traditions are still being practiced. Pioneer sourdough biscuits and pancakes are eaten by today's fishermen and hunters, for example, and some still eat Prospector Soup, which is made with flour, bacon fat, canned milk, and onions. Apple turnovers, are a carry-over from Oregon Trail days when they were made with dried apples. Today, they are served with thick cream, while on the trail it was an extra treat if cream was available.

WASHINGTON

THE DISCOVERY OF GOLD in 1855 brought a rush of prospectors to what is now the state of Washington. Close on the heels of the prospectors came settlers, attracted by reports of lush valleys and free land grants. Most of these pioneers were of English, Dutch, German, and Scandinavian origin. Although each ethnic group had its own distinct culinary traditions, they were melded into the cooking of Washington state.

Salmon had been the main sustenance for coastal Indians of the Northwest since prehistoric times. These Indians lived at the mouth of the Columbia River, and over the years they had perfected intricate fishing techniques and various rituals honoring the salmon. The Indians believed that salmon were spirit-people who took the form of fish to feed the tribe and then returned to the depths of the sea after being eaten.

For bait and hooks the Indians used natural materials such as bones, roots, and pieces of human hair. They caught the fish in small stone dams built on the rivers, using long run-out lines, harpoons, traps, or baskets. During the migration of salmon up the river to their spawning grounds, the fish were so plentiful that the Indians speared them from the banks or scooped them up with their hands. In the years the rivers were teeming with salmon, the survival of the Indians was guaranteed.

The Indians of the Northwest learned centuries ago to cook salmon by butterflying a whole fish, attaching it to a green branch, and holding it over a fire of aromatic alder wood. They also roasted and baked their fish either in an open shallow pit or in a sealed earth oven. The

POINT OF VIEW by Nicky Boehme, oil, 24 x 30 inches, courtesy of Nicky Boehme Gallery, Mendocino, California.

latter method of cooking was used to cook a large amount of fish during bad weather. The Indians filled a deep pit with hot stones, which they covered with greens and fish. They then sealed it with earth and left the food to cook for 12 to 24 hours, depending on the amount being cooked. Periodically, water was poured through hollow poles into the sealed pit to generate steam.

Since salmon fishing was seasonal for the Indians, most of the year they ate the fish smoked or dried. In many tribes the chieftain's wife had the task of smoking fish in a specially constructed smokehouse made of cedar shingles. The Indians also prepared pemmican with salmon, wild berries, and a little flour made from wild roots. Pemmican was stored in bags

holding approximately 100 pounds. About 500 pounds of fresh salmon were processed to make one bag of pemmican. An Indian lodge frequently had more than 100 bags of pemmican to tide them over during the winter months.

Salmon eggs were an important part of the Indians' diet. They obtained this delicate food by laying trays made of branches underwater in shallow places. When the trays were covered with eggs, they were carefully removed from the water. Fish eggs that were not consumed immediately were dried and stored for later consumption or to be used in soups.

Salmon became a commercial enterprise in the early 1800s, when the white traders added the dried or smoked fish to their bundles of pelts before

MUSSELS STEAMED IN WINE

Aquacultivation of mussels, a new enterprise for Washington state fish farmers, has been expanding each year.

In this recipe mussels are steamed in a dry white wine with a pinch of saffron. Serve with French bread to dip up the sauce.

Serves 4

1 3/4 pounds mussels

2 tablespoons butter

1 clove garlic, crushed

2 tablespoons minced shallots

1 1/2 cups dry white wine

1/4 teaspoon freshly ground pepper

Pinch of saffron threads

1/4 cup whipping cream

2 tablespoons finely chopped fresh parsley

2 tablespoons finely minced chives

■

Clean the mussels and discard any that have opened.

Melt the butter in a large skillet, add the garlic, and cook until it begins to change color. Remove the garlic and add the shallots, sautéing them lightly. Add the wine and the pepper. Bring mixture to a boil and reduce the liquid by one-third. Add the saffron and the mussels. Cover the pan and cook over low heat, shaking the pan gently from time to time, until the mussels open, about 2 to 3 minutes. Stir in the cream, parsley, and chives and continue cooking for another 2 minutes.

Remove the mussels with a slotted spoon to warm serving bowls and keep them warm while reducing the sauce. Continue cooking the sauce over medium-high heat until reduced to a rich consistency. Pour over mussels and serve.

either to seafood markets and restaurants or to smokehouses and canneries for processing.

Other Washington Seafood

In addition to salmon there are more than 30 species of fish harvested off the coast of Washington, including rockfish, cod, lingcod, sablefish, and smelt. After salmon and oysters, crabs are the most abundant seafood harvested.

More than 90 percent of all West Coast oysters are grown in Washington, and more than half of these come from Willapa Bay off the southwestern coast. Although there are more than a hundred species of oysters worldwide, only three are commercially grown and harvested in the Northwest: the native Olympia oyster, the Pacific oyster, and the European flat oyster.

The native Olympia oyster is a little more than an inch long and has very tasty meat. The Pacific oyster, brought from Japan in 1902 and now the mainstay of the Pacific Northwestern oyster industry, is about three times the size of the Olympia oyster. Since the Pacific oyster does not reproduce well in the cold waters of the Northwest, seed or young oysters are imported annually from Japan to maintain the crop. The European flat oyster raised in Washington has a milder taste than those raised along the coast of New England.

At the turn of the century, whole communities of oyster gatherers lived and worked on floating homes in the tidal inlets of southern Puget Sound near Olympia. Steamers came periodically to pick up the oysters that had been put in large burlap sacks. To fill the sack oystermen and their families worked through the night when the tide was out,

returning East. The Hudson Bay Company, a British trading firm, shipped pickled salmon in barrels to Eastern markets, as well as to Europe, Hawaii, and Argentina. Fresh iced salmon was shipped to Europe, where it was cold-smoked and then returned to American markets. By 1860 the Hudson Bay Company's monopoly on salmon was broken by American packers, who had begun to experiment with other curing methods.

In 1884 one of the first canneries in Washington was built on the Columbia River near The Dalles to take advantage of the fish wheels that had been built there by the Indians. By the time the fish reached The Dalles, they were upstream far enough that fresh water had rid them of sea lice, their stomachs were empty, and their flesh was firm. During the peak canning years of the 1880s, canners packed 6.5 million pounds of salmon annually.

Salmon are also fished commercially in the ocean off the coast of Washington. In recent years many Washington fishermen have started using the established Norwegian practice of preserving the fish at sea. Soon after the salmon are caught, they are bled and the innards removed to prevent spoilage. The fish are then quick-frozen at minus 35 degrees Fahrenheit, to retain the firm flesh. The more traditional fishermen simply ice down their fish. Once the catch reaches shore, it is shipped raking oysters from the mud flats. By the 1890s artificial beds were constructed and diked so that water would shelter the seeded oysters from extremes of heat and cold. From the mid-1800s to the early 1920s, more than 100,000 bushels of Olympia oysters were harvested each year.

Although industrial pollution has destroyed some of the Washington oyster beds, Pacific oysters, which can withstand the ravages of pollution, continue to be grown in the Sound. Additionally, several new methods of oyster culture have been perfected in the last 15 years. Randy Shuman, president of Shoalwater Bay Oysters in Bay Center was the first to use the so-called "French Table" method of oyster cultivation, whereby the oysters are grown in heavy mesh bags that sit on metal racks above the tidal flats. Free of mud and silt, the oysters grow quickly and can be harvested in about ten months instead of the usual three years it takes in tidewater beds.

Bill Webb at Wescott Bay in the northern part of Puget Sound grows the delicately flavored Olympia oysters in large round nets tied to buoys and hanging 30 feet under water. The oysters grow to maturity in about a year. Since these oysters have fragile shells, transporting them without breakage was a problem. To toughen the shells Webb now exposes his oysters to air several hours a day for two weeks before shipping.

In recent years Olympia oysters on the half-shell have become a popular first course in Washington restaurants. The market and supply of Olympia oysters has grown to the extent that shucked Olympia oysters are now available in local markets.

Mussels are raised in Penn Cove on the eastern shore of Whidbey Island, about 45 miles north of Seattle. It seems that this tiny area is ecologically perfect for mussel cultivation. Mussels are attached to 14-foot polypropylene lines, which are anchored to buoys or rafts. Since the mussels are always in water, they can feed continuously and grow to maturity in one-third of the time required by non-cultivated shoreline mussels. Mussel farms are new to Washington state.

The Dungeness crab is named for the town of Dungeness on the Olympic Peninsula in Washington, where commercial fishing for this crab started. In Washington a Dungeness crab must measure at least six and one-quarter inches across the shell before it can legally be harvested. As they grow young crabs molt and replace their shells with larger ones. This occurs as many as 20 times during the four years it takes the crabs to reach maturity.

Dungeness crabs are caught off the Washington and Oregon coasts from December through August, with the winter months being the peak season. Mature crabs are harvested in crab pots on the ocean floor, brought to shore, and shipped live to processing plants, where they are prepared for sale to restaurants, seafood markets, and grocery stores. Most

ROAST LOIN OF PORK WITH PRUNE AND APPLE STUFFING

Prune-plums are tree-ripened in the Willamette and Umpqua valleys of Oregon. Northwesterners often use them in stuffings, as in this pork roast. The fruit stuffing has a pleasing contrast of sweet prunes and tart apple, flavored with ginger.

Serves 8

8 ounces pitted prunes

1 cup hot water

1 large tart apple, cut into 1/2-inch cubes

1 whole boneless pork loin

3/4 teaspoon salt

1/2 teaspoon pepper

1 teaspoon ground ginger

3 tablespoons butter

1 cup apple cider

2 tablespoons all-purpose flour dissolved
   in 1/3 cup water

■

Quarter the prunes and soak them in the hot water for 30 minutes. Drain and reserve the liquid. Combine the prunes and apple.

Cut the pork loin open lengthwise, but do not cut through. Sprinkle the meat with the salt, pepper, and ginger. Arrange the fruit down the center of the meat. Roll the roast and tie it in several places.

Melt the butter in a heavy skillet or roasting pan. Add the pork loin and brown it on all sides. Then add the apple cider and the reserved prune liquid. Cover the pan and bake in a preheated 350° F. oven for 1 1/2 to 1 3/4 hours, or until the roast is done. Remove the roast to a platter and thicken the gravy with the flour and water combination.

of the crabs are sold cooked—either whole, in sections, or as picked-meat removed from the shell—though live crabs are available in many markets along the West Coast.

One of the most under-used fish resources of Washington State is the shad, which like salmon journey up the Columbia River each year. A native of the Atlantic Coast, shad arrived in the West a few years after the Civil War. The California Fish Commission had become aware that shad roe was a

READY FOR PICKING by Levi Wells Prentice, oil, 12 x 10 inches, courtesy of Richard York Gallery, New York, New York.

gourmet delicacy and requested international fish expert, Seth Green of Rochester, New York, to procure some shad for the California coast. On June 19, 1871, Mr. Green loaded 12,000 young shad that had been hatched the night before into four 8-gallon milk cans and brought them by train across the country. The journey took seven days, and the 10,000 shad that survived the trip were transplanted into the Sacramento River.

Soon some of the original shad transplants migrated north and made the Columbia River their freshwater home. In 1885 additional shad were planted in the Columbia River. Today, the shad run on the Columbia River from May through July.

Agriculture

Although fishing is one of the main food-related, commercial activities of Washington, agriculture is also of prime importance. Washington is known for its fruit and is the top apple-producing state in the nation, growing about half of America's crop.

In the 1890s, the Red Delicious, a transplant from Jesse Hiatt's orchard in Iowa, became Washington's main commercial apple because of its taste and hardiness. Currently Red Delicious apples make up almost 70 percent of the crop and Golden Delicious 25 percent. Granny Smith apples have replaced the Winesap in third place. Romes and Newtons make up the remainder of Washington's apple crop.

Pioneer apple farmers discovered that apples growing on the eastern slope of the Cascade Mountains grew bigger and were better-tasting than those on the western slope. This has turned the Wenatchee Valley into one of the state's prime apple-producing regions. The area

APPLE SOUP

Fruit soups were a specialty of the Scandinavian settlers of Washington and Oregon and are still popular. This slightly tart apple soup may be served either warm or lightly chilled.

Serves 6

3 tablespoons butter

1/2 cup chopped onion

4 large tomatoes, unpeeled and chopped

4 large tart apples, cored, unpeeled, and chopped

5 stalks celery, chopped

2 tablespoons dry sherry

4 cups mild chicken broth

Salt and pepper, to taste

■

Melt the butter in a 3-quart saucepan, add the onion, and sauté until the onion is limp. Then add the tomatoes, apples, celery, and sherry. Cover and simmer for 7 minutes. Add the chicken broth and continue to simmer covered for 25 to 30 minutes, or until the vegetables are very tender.

Cool the soup mixture and then purée the solids in a food processor. Put the purée through a fine sieve to remove any skins that may be left. Add the purée back to the broth in the saucepan and season to taste with salt and pepper. Heat through to serve.

is arid, so massive irrigation systems are required to sustain the orchards. Long periods of sunshine and warmth and deep, fertile soil contribute to making the Wenatchee Valley ideal for growing Red and Yellow Delicious apples.

Growning apples in this dry climate requires a lot of care. Orchards are laid out carefully, and old trees are periodically uprooted and replaced. In the spring beehives are taken into the orchards to pollinate the blossoms. Through a careful process of thinning, only the large "king blossom" is left in a cluster. The result is the production of large, beautifully shaped apples. Any small apples that appear on the tree after the fruit has set are removed in order to provide more nourishment for the larger apples. When ripe, the apples are picked by hand and then individually wrapped in tissue for shipment.

In addition to its apples, the state has become famous for Walla Walla sweet onions, which contain 12-percent sugar as compared to the 8-percent sugar in regular onions. The original seeds for the Walla Walla onions are said to have come from Italy but were planted in the sandy soil of the Walla Walla Valley by an unknown Frenchman. Subsequent Italian immigrants developed today's Walla Walla sweet onion by many years of selective breeding.

The cherry season in Washington lasts from mid-June through early August. Bing cherries are the first to ripen, followed by Lamberts, and then tart pie cherries. Because of its ideal weather, Washington grows more cherries than any other state in the nation.

Washington has also become known as a producer of fine wines. Chardonnay, Riesling, Gewürztraminer, and Chenin Blanc are the main wine grapes grown in the state, mainly in the Columbia and Yakima valleys, east of the Cascade Mountain range. The huge vineyards in these

FOUR-BEAN SALAD

Vegetable salads are a light accompaniment to grilled meats in the Northwest.

Fresh and canned beans are combined in this salad with an herb dressing. If fresh wax beans are unavailable, canned ones may be substituted.

1/2 pound thin green beans, trimmed and cut into 1 1/2-inch pieces

1/2 pound wax beans, trimmed and cut into 1 1/2-inch pieces

1 can (7 1/2 ounces) kidney beans, drained and rinsed

1 can (7 1/2 ounces) garbanzo beans, drained and rinsed

1/3 cup chopped celery

1/4 cup chopped red pepper

2 green onions, finely chopped

1/3 cup raspberry vinegar

4 tablespoons water

2/3 cup olive oil

2 tablespoons chopped fresh basil

1 tablespoon chopped fresh thyme

1/2 tablespoon chopped fresh oregano

■

Cook the green and wax beans in boiling water until just tender, 6 to 8 minutes. Drain and rinse under cold water. Drain again. When the cooked beans have cooled, combine them with the kidney and garbanzo beans in a bowl. Add the celery, red pepper, and green onions.

Whisk together the vinegar, water, and oil in another bowl. Stir in the chopped herbs and then combine the dressing with the beans. Refrigerate for 3 hours to blend flavors before serving.

semi-dry valleys rely heavily on extensive irrigation systems. Days in the growing season are long, and nights are chilly, a perfect combination for growing wine grapes. The large production of wine grapes has contributed to making Washington one of the leading states in table wines.

Food Heritage

Whatever their heritage, many of the early settlers quickly learned to adapt their recipes to ingredients available in Washington. The New Englanders who settled near Puget Sound, for example, found that chopped clams could be substituted for beef in corned-beef hash. They sautéed the chopped clams with crumbled bacon and onions, combined them with diced potatoes and beaten eggs, and then baked the mixture in the oven. Clam chowder, a dish familiar to New Englanders, became another mainstay of many pioneer diets.

The pioneer women learned to go out at low tide and gather the large geoduck clams, which they sliced and fried like chicken. They also learned from the Indians how to cook salmon and other fish over an open fire.

Today, the cuisine of Washington is not defined by a specific culinary style. Rather it is one that blends fresh produce, seafood, and locally raised meats into a light style of cooking, simply prepared and unadorned by heavy sauces.

FARM by Nils Gren, oil, 32 x 36 inches, courtesy of George Stern, Fine Arts, Encino, California.

CALIFORNIA

CALIFORNIA'S greatest culinary contribution to this country has been the state's ability to grow a wide variety of fruits and vegetables year-round. Today, California supplies more than 50 percent of the nation's produce and 70 percent of its wine. Mediterranean type climate and diverse soils have made California self-sufficient in most foods.

California Indians

Before the Spanish explorers arrived in California in 1542 and until the late 1700s when the Franciscan friars attempted to domesticate them, the native Indians of California lived in isolation. The complex topography of this land of mountains, deserts, and rugged coastlines split the area's 300,000 Indians into about 100 small village-states, each with its own language. Villages had little contact with one another and none with the outside world. The natural abundance of berries, nuts, and game was sufficient to meet their needs.

The mainstay of the Indian's diet was whole or coarsely ground acorns, which were used in soups or as a mash. Both were cooked in watertight baskets with hot stones. The soup often contained meat or seafood.

The Klamath River Indians in the northern part of California stirred their acorn mash with a wooden paddle that had a beautifully carved handle. They used a dipper to spoon the mash into individual eating baskets, which varied in size according to the user's age and sex. Decorative elk-horn spoons were used by the men, while women and children ate with mussel shells, fingers, or cupped leaves.

In Southern California most of the Indian tribes lived near the sea, where food was plentiful. They dug for clams and mussels, gathered fish, and hunted sea otters, sea lions, and seals. Due to the lack of rainfall, the interior of Southern California was less populated because food was scarce. The primary foods of the inland Indians in Southern California were pine nuts and mesquite seeds. They also hunted and trapped wood rats and rabbits.

Following the arrival of the Spanish missionaries around 1770, the native Indian population quickly declined. White man's diseases and changes in diet

MARINATED FLANK STEAK

Because of California's mild climate, cooking outdoors on the grill has been popular for more than a century. The early Spanish landowners held large outdoor barbecues, which frequently lasted for several days. Barbecued beef was eaten with tortillas or sliced and used in tacos and enchiladas.

Oriental flavorings, which were brought to California by the large number of Chinese and Japanese who came to work on constructing the railroads in the latter part of the 1800s, did not come in general usage until the 1960s. In this recipe they are used to flavor a flank steak.

Serves 8

1 flank steak, about 1 1/4 to 1 1/2 pounds

Marinade

2 tablespoons vegetable oil

2 tablespoons Oriental sesame oil

2 tablespoons light brown sugar

1/3 cup lite soy sauce

3 green onions, chopped

1 piece (2-inches) fresh ginger, peeled and chopped

1 large clove garlic, chopped

1 tablespoon lemon juice

4 tablespoons water

2 tablespoons balsamic vinegar

1 tablespoon honey

1/3 cup dry sherry

■

Score the flank steak in large diagonals on one side. Place in a shallow dish. Combine the marinade ingredients and pour over the steak, lifting it so that the liquid runs underneath the meat. Cover and refrigerate for 4 to 6 hours, turning once.

Grill over medium-hot coals for 3 to 4 minutes per side for medium rare, or to desired doneness. Slice the meat on the diagonal.

LIMAS WITH CHILIES AND CHEESE

California bean growers concentrate on the specialty dried beans that are not readily produced commercially in other farming areas of the United States. Among these varieties are both the baby and large limas. Others include garbanzos and dark red kidney beans. Most dry beans are grown around Tracy, California, where the Dry Bean Festival is held each August.

Before the turn of the century, many California dishes were influenced by Mexican cooking. The spicy flavor accents popular in the hacienda kitchens of the Spanish and Mexican settlers were often combined with large lima beans, as they are in this casserole.

Serves 6 to 8

1 pound large dry lima beans

1 tablespoon butter

1 teaspoon onion powder

1/8 teaspoon garlic powder

1/4 teaspoon pepper

1 1/2 cups chicken broth

1/4 teaspoon dried basil

1/4 teaspoon dried thyme

1/8 teaspoon dried oregano

2 cans (4 ounces each) whole green chilies
   (mild)

1/2 pound Monterey Jack cheese

3/4 cup sour cream

Chopped fresh parsley, for garnish

Additional sour cream, for garnish

■

Soak the beans overnight in water. The next day, place the beans in a saucepan with the butter, onion powder, garlic powder, pepper, and chicken broth. Add 1 1/2 cups water. Bring to a boil and boil gently with the lid tilted until tender, about 45 minutes to 1 hour. Add more water, if needed, to keep the beans covered. Drain the beans, saving the cooking liquid and adding water, if necessary, to make 1 1/2 cups.

Spread 1/3 of the beans in a shallow 2 1/2-quart casserole. Sprinkle with half of each of the herbs. Cut each chili in half lengthwise and then cut crosswise into 1/2-inch strips. Cut the cheese into 1/4 x 1-inch pieces. Layer half of the chilies and one-third of the cheese over the beans. Repeat the process for the second layer. Top with the remaining beans and cheese.

Stir the bean liquid into the sour cream until smooth. Pour over the beans and bake uncovered in a 325 ° F. oven for 30 to 40 minutes, or until bubbling. Garnish with parsley and additional sour cream.

for those herded into the missions wiped out most of the Indian tribes.

Early California Settlers

The first white man to set foot on California soil reportedly was the Spanish explorer, Juan Rodrigues Cabrillo, in 1542. The first permanent settlement in California was not established, however, until 1769 when a group of Spanish colonizers led by Junipero Serra, a missionary, and Gaspar de Portola, a soldier, founded a mission in San Diego. Their intent was to build a chain of missions northward through the state at one-day-journey intervals in order to Christianize the local Indians and turn them into Spanish subjects. The Spanish also decided to settle California at this time to thwart Russian, English, and French designs on the territory. The last of the 21 missions was completed north of San Francisco, in Sonoma, in 1823.

As each mission was founded the friars immediately set out to become self-sufficient. Wheat, corn, beans, and squash were grown, and every mission had a vineyard. Climate permitting, some missions had olive groves and pear, apricot, fig, pomegranate, orange, and lemon orchards. They grew tomatoes at a time when white settlers in the rest of North America still thought them to be poisonous. These missionaries are also credited with bringing the taste of cumin and coriander to California from Mexico.

Each mission was charged with integrating the local Indians into mission life. The Native Americans were given food and lodging, along with other amenities. In exchange they were required to cultivate the fields, tend the sheep and cattle, harvest the crops, and tan the cattle hides. Few of the Indians who lived on these mission farms are reported to have converted to Christianity.

Once the missions were established, a secular society began to develop. The backbone of the California economy shifted from Spanish missionaries to Spanish landowners, who had been given huge tracts of land by the Spanish governor for services to the government. They built extravagant haciendas, which became the social as well as economic centers of the society.

These landowners, called rancheros, raised cattle for hides and tallow. The beef meat was discarded except for that roasted at great outdoor barbecues. When a ranchero announced a barbecue, guests traveled 100 miles on horseback or by stagecoach to attend. These barbecues frequently lasted three to four days and featured barbecued beef flavored with chilies, cilantro, cumin, and oregano and served with tortillas. The roasted meat was also used in tacos and enchiladas.

The rancheros enjoyed food made from the finest ingredients, all imported from Mexico and other parts of the world. Spanish ways and cuisine predominated in California long after the territory became part of the United States.

Early American Settlers

Spain lost California when Mexico gained its independence in 1821. At the

CALIFORNIA OR OREGON by F. T. Johnson, oil, 30 1/2 x 40 inches, courtesy of Gilcrease Museum, Tulsa, Oklahoma.

FRANCISCAN APPLE PIE

When the Franciscan fathers started establishing missions in California in 1769, they planted orchards, particularly citrus and apple trees. The padres used both fresh and dried apples in various dishes. They often added wine to apple pies for moisture, as in this tart apple pie recipe based on an old Franciscan one.

Serves 6 to 8

Pastry

2 cups all-purpose flour

1 tablespoon sugar

5 tablespoons butter

3 tablespoons solid vegetable shortening

1/4 cup ground almonds

5 to 6 tablespoons ice water

■

Combine the flour and sugar in a bowl. Cut in the butter and shortening until the mixture resembles fine crumbs. Mix in the almonds with a fork and then add the ice water, 1 tablespoon at a time, until the mixture forms a dough. Form the dough into a ball, wrap in plastic wrap, and refrigerate for 1 hour.

Filling

6 large tart apples

1/2 cup canned apple juice

1/4 cup sugar

1/4 cup dry sherry

1 tablespoon butter

1 1/2 tablespoons tapioca

1/2 teaspoon lemon juice

1/4 cup chopped walnuts

1/4 cup raisins

■

Peel and core the apples and cut them into eighths. Combine the apple juice, sugar, and sherry in a large saucepan. Add the apples and bring to a slow boil. Lower the heat and cook gently until the apples begin to get tender. Do not let them get too soft.

Remove the apples from the liquid to a bowl with a slotted spoon and set them aside. Add the butter, tapioca, lemon juice, walnuts, and raisins to the liquid. Cook for a few minutes until the mixture begins to thicken. Combine the sauce with the apples, which have accumulated additional liquid.

Roll out half of the pastry to fit a 9-inch pie plate. Place the filling in the pie crust. Roll out the other half of the pastry dough and place it on top of the filling, seal, and flute the edges. Cut small slits in the top of the crust. Bake in a preheated 425° F. oven for 35 to 40 minutes until the crust is crisp and golden brown.

time few Americans showed any interest in this hard-to-reach, far-off place, despite occasional descriptions of California's spring-like climate, exotic fruits grown in mission gardens, and cattle that roamed the grass-covered countryside.

No one knows exactly when the first American came to California. However, records show that in 1824 Joseph Chapman planted a vineyard on land that is today downtown Los Angeles. William Wolfskill, a Kentucky trapper, was making wine in Southern California in the 1830s.

By 1840 there was considerable trade between the United States and California, and by the mid-1840s there were more than 500 Americans farming in the San Joaquin Valley. In 1846 these and other groups attempted to establish an independent Republic of California. It took another two years, however, before Mexico formally ceded California to the United States. In 1850 California was given statehood.

The Gold Rush

Gold was discovered at John Sutter's Fort near Sacramento in 1848. John Sutter was a Swiss who had come to California by ship in 1839. Three years later, he purchased a large tract of land near Sacramento and established a colony he named New Helvetia. Sutter grew wheat, raised cattle, operated a river boat carrying freight to San Francisco, and felled trees for lumber. In April of 1848 while building a sawmill along the creek on Sutter's property in the California foothills, an employee, James Marshall, discovered a gold nugget in the clear water.

Despite slow communications, news of the Gold Rush spread quickly, and by the next year California was inundated

GOING TO MARKET by Douglas Parshall, oil, 27 x 43 inches, courtesy of Peregrine Galleries, Montecito, California.

with prospectors. In 1849, eighty thousand people came overland or by ship around Cape Horn in search of gold. By July of 1850 five hundred deserted ships were anchored in San Francisco Bay, because their crews had gone prospecting for gold.

With the discovery of gold in 1848, California changed from a strictly agrarian society to one of gold-mining frenzy. Unlike preceding waves of pioneers moving westward, gold seekers did not build settlements and did not bring families. During Gold Rush days only eight percent of the California population were women.

Living conditions of the prospectors were very crude, and food was outrageously expensive. Although most food supplies had to be brought to California from the East at great cost, profits for food importers were enormous. Whiskey that cost 5 cents a drink in St. Louis cost 50 cents in San Francisco. Bartenders poured the whiskey from a pitcher on the bar and served it in a tin cup.

Bread was a mainstay of the San

Francisco diet, and onions were the primary cooking ingredient of San Francisco cooks as well as of the miners in the gold country. Both bread and onions cost $1 per pound. One enterprising individual planted two acres of onions and sold them for $8,000. A loaf of bread, which one newspaper reporter referred to as a "fair-size biscuit," cost 50 cents. Eggs were half a dollar each and even as high as ten dollars a dozen. Most of the eggs came from the East and took three months to arrive in San Francisco. Butter, or what passed for butter, was manufactured by various means using beef, sheep, or bear tallow and some lard.

In San Francisco miners from the gold fields were willing to pay almost anything for different food. Chickens were a rarity. The half-wild Spanish cattle, which were raised by the rancheros for their hides and tallow, became a coveted source of meat. Professional hunters brought their game to San Francisco and sold it for just a little less than its weight in gold. Four boxes of apples shipped from New England were auctioned at $500 each. Potatoes sold for a dollar apiece, cooked. One man milked his cow twice a day and sold a whiskey-bottle full of the milk for a dollar.

Life in the mining camps was very rough. Since the camps were in the mountains, the norm in the winter months was snow, bitter cold, and wind. Most of the miners carried bacon, flour, coffee, and sourdough starter for biscuits and bread with them. In the winter the flour was kneaded with snow into a stiff dough and baked over an open fire into a type of bread. Bacon fat was dripped onto the bread to make it a little more tasty. Coffee was often made from beans crushed in a sack between two heavy stones. The grounds were used repeatedly.

By the early 1850s prices had moderated at San Francisco hotels and boarding houses. At the boarding houses everyone sat at a long table and ate family style. For those who had really struck it rich, there were a number of French restaurants in San Francisco. One of the most notable was Le Poulet d'Or, whose name many pronounced "Poodle Dog." The restaurant adopted that nickname and used it until after the Second World War. By then its patrons referred to the restaurant as the Ritz Old Poodle Dog.

The gold seekers who had struck it rich coveted luxurious food. Oysters became a prized item. Tiny Olympia oysters from Puget Sound were brought regularly by sailing ships to San Francisco. These delicate oysters became the ingredient for one of California's earliest dishes—Hangtown Fry, which was a meal considered fit for a king and cost almost a king's ransom in gold dust.

Hangtown, in the California foothills, was the supply base for much of the mining region at the time. The place, originally known as Old Dry Diggins, was called Hangtown when five men were hanged there on the same day from the same tree.

Legend has it that a miner who had struck it rich came into Hangtown one day and demanded the best food he could get. Since cost was no object, he was served a huge meal of fried oysters, fried eggs, and bacon. Thereafter, any miner who ordered Hangtown Fry was showing his prosperity.

Early Agriculture

As more and more of the rich mining claims in California became exhausted, many miners gave up. Some went to Nevada and Colorado to prospect: others stayed in California and became tradesmen

and farmers. Soon orchards and grain fields were planted in the valley between the Sierra Nevada and the Coastal Range. In the 1880s farming replaced mining as the primary occupation in California. One old man had the right idea when he told his son, "Plant your lands; these be your best gold fields, for all must eat while they live."

Irrigation was the key factor in the development of much of California's agriculture. Efforts to irrigate California land were as old as the Spanish settlements. However, the real expansion of irrigation occurred with the coming of the Americans. The San Joaquin Valley, perhaps the greatest agricultural region in the world, was initially considered a desert. Irrigation by American settlers made this valley a producer of all types of fruits, nuts, and vegetables. In the more than 150 years of California's statehood there have been many bitter verbal as well as physical battles fought over water rights and irrigation.

The first dominant commercial crop in California was wheat. Much of the Central Valley was suited to growing wheat. It grew well in this area where annual rainfall varied considerably and where there were hot, dry summers. Wheat was a major crop in California until 1879, when a worldwide overproduction of wheat occurred. Fortunately for California, irrigation and railroad transportation had developed to the point that it was possible to grow other crops.

California Canneries

The agricultural business in California grew to include food processing and many cooperatives. One food processing firm was founded by an Ohio physician named James Dawson, who suddenly decided to give up his practice and heed

Horace Greeley's call to go west. He took a train to California and arrived in San José in 1870, where he resumed his medical career. However, Dr. Dawson spent a great amount of time wondering how to preserve the fruits being grown in the area's orchards.

A confirmed tinkerer, he was in the process of developing a metal container when he was joined by his son Thomas, who was an expert in metals. Together the Dawsons handcrafted tin canisters for several of the new canning firms in San Francisco. Not long after, they went into the fruit-canning business themselves. By 1872 with James cooking the fruit and Thomas sealing the canisters with a soldering iron, they were packing a hundred cases of peaches, pears, apricots, and plums each month.

A year later the Dawsons discarded the backyard wash-boiler in which they had done the cooking and built a cannery. In 1875 they incorporated the business as the San José Fruit Packing Company, thus becoming the first major cannery in California.

In 1886 the Oakland, California, catering firm of Tillman and Bendel started preparing a special blend of fine coffees for a new client, the prestigious Hotel Del Monte on the Monterey peninsula. Five years later, when Fred Tillman founded the Oakland Preserving Company, he adopted the Del Monte label for his own products. When Oakland Preserving became part of the California Fruit Canners Association in 1899, so did the Del Monte name. The Association introduced the familiar label with the red shield and "Del Monte" printed in old English letters that is still in use.

By 1900 eighteen canneries had joined the California Fruit Canners Association, increasing the number of plants producing under the Del Monte label to 28 with a production capacity of more than two million cases annually.

Another well-known enterprise in California was started by a former sheriff who traded his badge for a kitchen apron. His name was Emile Ortega, and he was a direct descendent of a member of the expedition that founded the Spanish persidio and mission on San Francisco Bay in 1776. In the late 1800s, after a term as sheriff of Ventura County, Emile Ortega built a career out of his two hobbies, cooking and inventing. He found a way to make the canning of green chilies commercially feasible.

In 1898, he established the Ortega Canning Company in Ventura and in 1906 moved the operation to Los Angeles where it was expanded to include pimientos and salsas. After a subsequent move to Oxnard, a line of taco products and other Mexican foods was added, making Ortega one of the biggest purveyors of Mexican foods in the United States. The company was acquired by Heublein in the 1970s and by Nabisco Brands in 1987.

California Wine

When Father Junipero Serra and the other Franciscans started the string of California missions in 1769, they assumed that wine for the celebration of Mass could be readily obtained from headquarters in Mexico City. They soon found that the distance and terrain made shipments of wine from Mexico City virtually impossible to obtain. Consequently, the fathers started making wine from indigenous grapes but found it undrinkable.

After years of frustration, the Franciscan fathers finally procured vine cuttings from Mexico City and started their own vineyards. These first vines, of a variety called the Mission grape, were planted at the Mission San Juan

TWO TIERS OF FRUIT by Severin Roesen, oil, 29 1/4 x 24 1/4 inches, courtesy of Taggart & Jorgensen Gallery, Washington, D.C.

Capistrano around 1780. The climate of Southern California was well-suited to the Mission grape, and winemaking quickly became part of mission life for the Spanish priests. As each new mission was established, the priests planted cuttings of the Mission grape and started making wine.

Winemaking, however, was never meant to be a significant function of the missions. The objective was to produce only enough wine for use at Mass and for drinking with the evening meal—an established custom with the Spanish priests. In spite of this objective, by 1820 the San Gabriel and San Fernando Missions in the Los Angeles basin had become the two largest wine producers in California. As the population grew, however, the missions were unable to fill the needs of local inhabitants, and a secular wine industry began in Los Angeles in the early

1820s. With the secularization of the missions by Mexico in 1834, mission vineyards were abandoned.

The first commercial vineyard was planted in 1833 by a Frenchman from Bordeaux named Jean Louis Vignas in what is now downtown Los Angeles. Soon afterward European immigrants and settlers from the eastern part of the United States began planting commercial vineyards around Los Angeles.

Vineyards of Mission grapes also began to proliferate in Northern California, although the southern part of the state continued to dominate wine production until the late 1800s. Wine production in Southern California declined at that time because the vineyards suffered damage from a bacterial infection called Pierce's Disease. The hot southern climate also was not conducive for the growing of the more refined European varietals.

The Northern California wine industry received its start when Lt. Mariano Guadalupe Vallejo was sent to Sonoma by the Mexican government to secularize the missions and colonize the northern part of the state in 1835. Vallejo found the mission vineyards in great disrepair and restored them. By 1840 he was making wine, and 15 years later Vallejo, by then a general, was winning statewide medals for his wines.

While a number of individuals made contributions to the development of the Northern California wine industry, none had the impact of Agoston Harazthy de Moskesa. Born in 1812 in Yugoslavia of Hungarian ancestry, Harazthy came to America in 1839 as a political fugitive. He settled in Wisconsin and immediately started several businesses.

In 1849 Harazthy packed his family and belongings into wagons and made the long trek to San Diego. Within a year he was farming 160 acres, had become county sheriff, and was elected to the state legislature. In 1852 he again pulled up stakes and moved to San Francisco, where he planted grapes on 200 acres he had purchased in South San Francisco.

The weather on the San Francisco Peninsula was too cool for grapes, and in 1857 Harazthy moved to Sonoma, where he planted 400 acres in grapes. He rebuilt an existing, run-down winery and employed Chinese workers to dig wine-storage caves into the hillside. Harazthy called his estate Buena Vista, a name that is still used by the winery currently operating on the original site.

Harazthy imported large quantities of superior grape varieties from Europe. The resulting wine caught the attention of the governor of the state, who sent Harazthy abroad in 1861 to gather information about winemaking techniques. Harazthy returned not only with information but also with 100,000 meticulously packed cuttings, representing nearly 300 varieties of *Vitis Vinifera,* from the major wine-producing countries of Europe.

Within a few years financial losses forced Harazthy to flee to Nicaragua, where he died in an accident in 1869. During his tenure in California, Harazthy was influential in establishing the state

GRAPES IN AN INDIAN BASKET by Edith White, oil, 12 x 18 inches, courtesy of Peregrine Galleries, Montecito, California.

agricultural school at the University of California at Berkeley, and he wrote the first definitive books on grape growing and winemaking.

In the mid- to late-1800s, there were many other wine pioneers in California, including Charles Krug, Jacob Schram, Carl Wente, Jacob Beringer, Jacob Gundlach, Pierre Mirrasou, Charles Lefranc (Almaden), and Lefranc's son-in-law, Paul Mason. Many of these names have been carried on to the present day by their descendents or through the label on well-known premium wines.

Prohibition in 1919 put a virtual end to winemaking in California. After its repeal in 1933, it took another 35 years for the industry to reestablish itself. In the 1970s the American public discovered California wines, and production expanded rapidly. In the Napa Valley, for example, grape acreage and wine production doubled during the 1970s. Today, there are eight major wine-growing areas scattered throughout California, from San Diego County to Mendicino County and into the foothills of the Sierras where formerly gold was mined. Wine is being made by hundreds of small, family-owned boutique wineries as well as by multi million dollar corporations—more than 800 wineries in total.

Agricultural Experimenters

Luther Burbank, born before the Civil War in Lancaster, Massachusetts, was a self-taught botanist, who devised methods of crossbreeding fruit and vegetable varieties. His first commercial success was the Burbank potato, which he developed while still in Massachusetts. This development netted him $150, enough to get him to Santa Rosa, California, for a visit. There he found the climate and the soil ideal for his experi-

MINTED LEMON SOUFFLÉ WITH PISTACHIO NUTS

Most of this country's lemons are grown in California. They were introduced into the state by the Franciscan fathers in the 1700s. Lemons did not become a commercial crop until the 1880s, when farmers learned to ripen the fruit in cold storage before shipping them to the East.

The hint of mint is a refreshing compliment to the acidity of lemon in this cold soufflé. Toasted pistachio nuts add another flavor component.

Serves 8

3/4 cup shelled, unsalted pistachio nuts

1 envelope unflavored gelatin

6 large eggs, separated

1 cup sugar

3/4 cup fresh lemon juice

4 tablespoons grated lemon zest

1 1/2 tablespoons finely chopped fresh mint

Pinch of cream of tartar

1 1/4 cups very cold whipping cream

Mint leaves, for garnish

■

Place the shelled pistachio nuts on a baking sheet and toast them in a preheated 350° F. oven for 8 to 10 minutes. Cool the nuts slightly and then rub them together in a kitchen towel to remove the skins. Coarsely chop the nuts in a food processor.

Make a 5-inch piece of doubled aluminum foil long enough to go around a 6-cup soufflé dish. Brush the foil with flavorless vegetable oil or lightly spray it with a flavorless oil spray. To form a collar for the souffle dish, fit the oiled side of the foil around the dish, extending it 2 1/2 inches above the rim. Secure it with either string or a rubber band.

Soften the gelatin in 1/4 cup cold water for 10 minutes.

Combine the egg yolks, sugar, lemon juice, and lemon zest in the the top of a double boiler or in a large bowl. Set the double boiler or bowl over gently boiling water and beat the mixture with a hand-held mixer for 15 minutes, or until it falls in a ribbon when the beaters are lifted.

Remove the egg yolks from the heat and add the gelatin, stirring until completely dissolved. Transfer the mixture to a glass or ceramic bowl. Cool to room temperature or set in a pan of ice water to cool. Do not let it congeal. Fold in the chopped mint.

Beat the egg whites until frothy, then add the cream of tartar and beat until the egg whites hold stiff peaks. Fold the egg whites into the lemon mixture. Beat the cream in a chilled bowl until it holds stiff peaks and then fold it into the lemon mixture.

Spoon one third of the soufflé into the prepared soufflé dish. Sprinkle with one third of the nuts. Spoon another third of the soufflé on top and top with another third of the nuts. Then add the remaining soufflé mixture, smoothing out the top, and sprinkle with the remaining nuts. Chill for 4 hours. Garnish with mint leaves just before serving.

261

TAKE ONE by Stanley S. David (pseudonym for De Scott Evans), oil, 12 1/8 x 10 1/8 inches, courtesy of Richard York Gallery, New York, New York.

began in California in 1880, although they were introduced by the Franciscan fathers a century earlier. For years California lemons were regarded as inferior to those imported from Italy. This was blamed on the fact that growers did not "cure" the fruit before shipping, which was a common practice in Italy.

The curing process consists of picking the fruit while still somewhat green and allowing it to ripen in a cool storage facility before shipment. After adopting this practice the California lemon industry grew rapidly, and today the state grows 80 percent of the country's lemons. They are grown primarily in Southern California in counties near the coast, where the Pacific Ocean moderates both winter cold and summer heat.

Tillie Lewis is a name much respected among tomato growers and farmers of the Delta region, northeast of San Francisco in the upper reaches of San Francisco Bay. Tillie grew up in Brooklyn and as a teenager worked part-time in a wholesale import market. She often wondered why American tomato paste was less piquant than Italian. The secret, she decided, was the pear-shaped Italian tomato called *pomodoro*.

"It won't grow in this country," she was told. In 1935, after traveling in search of soil and climate like those of Naples and Palermo, she borrowed $10,000 and leased 20 acres of Delta farmland near Sacramento to plant *pomodoros*. Her venture proved phenomenally successful and in 1966 she sold her firm to New York's Ogden Corp. for $14.5 million.

"I used to climb up on a box to watch the tomatoes roll down the conveyor belt into the processing plant," she recalled. At the plant one day in 1936, at the height of the harvest, a man ran up to her and said: "The boilers are down! It'll take 36 hours to fix them. What will we

mentations, and he decided to stay. By using skillful breeding techniques, Burbank created more than 800 new strains of fruits, vegetables, and flowers. Among others, he introduced the Burbank cherry, 113 new varieties of plums and ten new varieties of berries.

There were others who experimented in improving California foods. Lyman Bruce came from Canada to improve his health in the warmer California climate. He settled in Petaluma (Marin County) and started raising chickens. Bruce, perplexed by the number of diseases his chickens acquired, began experimenting with diets and medicines for his brood. His success ultimately made Petaluma known as the world's egg basket and chicken coup.

Commercial production of lemons

do?" In that time enough tomatoes would have spoiled to eat up the year's profits.

Tillie had to get steam from some-where, so she ran down to the local Sante Fe railroad station. They rented her two locomotives for $15. Since there were rails alongside the plant, she got the locomotives to the plant, strung up a pipe, and saved the crop. "In this business you can never give up," was Tillie's motto.

Dates

Date palms were introduced into California by the Spanish in the second half of the eighteenth century. However, it was not until the early part of the twentieth century that a commercial date industry was established. By 1960 there were more than 5,000 acres of date trees around Indio in the Coachella Valley of California. Since then, however, date-plantation acreage has declined greatly due to the cost of the intensive manual labor involved in date cultivation.

Two of the pioneers in American date production were Mr. and Mrs. Floyd Shields of Indio, California, who planted their first date orchards in 1924. Today the Shields' orchards contain more than 1,200 date palms and 700 citrus trees (which grow beneath the palms). Many of the original date palms still produce fruit.

The Shields started their date orchard with 25 trees imported from Algeria and over the years have propa-gated additional trees. There are now 119 different kinds of dates in their orchards, with Black Beauty being the newest. These black dates, which are bright red when they are immature, have a more intense flavor than their brunette cousins.

It takes 5 to 10 years for an offshoot of the date palm to develop a root system

FRESH FIG AND PEACH COMPOTE

The Spanish introduced the fig tree to California in the early 1700s. Today, California produces 99 percent of all the commercially grown figs in the United States. One of the most famous varieties of figs is the black-purple mission fig, which has very tiny seeds. They are available fresh from June to October and dried throughout the year.

Poached peaches are combined with fresh figs for a light summer dessert.

Serves 4

4 large ripe, firm peaches

3/4 cup white wine

1/4 cup peach brandy

1 teaspoon vanilla extract

1 tablespoon sugar

6 large ripe figs

2 tablespoons lemon juice

2/3 cup very cold whipping cream

1 tablespoon rum

Chopped pistachio nuts, for garnish

■

Peel the peaches and cut each in half vertically and remove the pit.

Combine the wine, peach brandy, vanilla extract, and sugar in a small saucepan. Bring to a low boil and add the peach halves. Cook over low heat, turning the peach halves after 1 minute, and continue cooking for another minute or two. The peaches should still be slightly firm to the touch. This poaching may have to be done in two batches. Remove the peaches and set them aside and continue simmering the poaching liquid for another 5 minutes. Remove from heat and cool slightly.

Cut the figs in half and sprinkle them with lemon juice. Place the figs in a deep, narrow bowl. Top them with the peach halves and pour the poaching liquid over the fruit. Cool to room temperature, cover with plastic wrap, and refrigerate at least 4 hours before serving.

Just before serving, whip the cream until it holds stiff peaks. Add the rum and blend well. Place 2 peach halves, cut side up, in each of 4 compote dishes. Arrange 3 fig halves on top of the peach halves and divide the liquid equally among the dishes. Top with a dollop of whipped cream and sprinkle with some chopped pistachio nuts.

CALIFORNIA BROCCOLI

Fields of broccoli abound in the Salinas Valley of California, where harvesting is a precision operation. After the broccoli stalks are cut, they are trimmed, packaged in bunches, and boxed in the field. Within an hour after harvesting, broccoli is rushed to the warehouse, where ice is added immediately. The broccoli is then held in a cooler for 24 hours before shipment.

This broccoli dish, with its citrus sauce, can be prepared ahead and refrigerated before baking.

Serves 8

2 bunches broccoli with small stems

5 tablespoons butter, melted

1/3 cup freshly grated Parmesan cheese

Sauce

4 tablespoons butter

4 tablespoons all-purpose flour

1/8 teaspoon white pepper

1/4 teaspoon ground celery seeds

1 1/4 cups milk

1/3 cup whipping cream

1/3 cup fresh orange juice

1 1/2 tablespoons lemon juice

1 1/2 tablespoons grated orange zest

1 teaspoon grated lemon zest

1/3 cup slivered almonds, lightly toasted

■

Trim the broccoli stems to a total length of 5 inches, including the top of the florets. (Save stem pieces for soup.) Then cut the florets and stems lengthwise into 2 or 3 pieces, depending on the thickness of the stem and florets. There should be 16 pieces.

Place the broccoli pieces in a deep saucepan and barely cover with water. Cover and bring to a boil, reduce heat to medium, and boil for 5 minutes or until crisp-tender. Drain and rinse the broccoli with cold water and then drain again. Place the broccoli in a long baking dish, overlapping broccoli pieces slightly. Drizzle the melted butter over the broccoli and sprinkle with the Parmesan cheese.

To make the sauce, melt the butter in a small saucepan over medium-low heat. When melted, remove from heat and add the flour, stirring vigorously to make a smooth paste. Stir in the pepper and ground celery seeds. Return the saucepan to the heat and slowly add the milk, stirring constantly to combine into a thick sauce. Stir in the whipping cream, orange juice, lemon juice, and orange and lemon zests. Continue stirring the sauce until it is creamy. Spoon the sauce over the broccoli. Sprinkle the almonds on top. (The broccoli may be refrigerated at this time for up to 6 hours. Bring to room temperature before baking.)

Bake the broccoli in a preheated 375° F. oven for 10 to 12 minutes, or until bubbly. The casserole may also be heated in a microwave oven at full power for 7 minutes.

of its own, at which time it may be planted in another spot. After planting, an additional 8 to 15 years are required before the palm will bear fruit.

The date palm has often been described as living with its feet in the water and its head in the sun. In spite of the fact that the date palm is a desert plant, it requires as much water as a willow tree. The Shields's date orchards contain irrigation ditches between each row of trees.

Because of their unique method of pollination, dates have never been gathered wild but have always been cultivated. Date palms are either male or female. Nature did not make the male blossoms attractive to pollen-carrying insects, thus there is no natural pollination of the date trees. In ancient times date growers relied on the wind to distribute the pollen, which was a very unreliable process.

Today, the male flowers are cut, and the pollen is shaken out and placed on small cotton powder puffs. These puffs are then attached to long sticks and used to pollinate the female blossoms twice a week during February, March, and April. When the fruit is the size of small olives, the bunches of dates are thinned, covered with a sheer cloth, and tied to the major branches to prevent the stems from breaking.

Since the dates in the clusters do not all ripen at the same time, the fruit must be picked individually. Dates begin to ripen about the first of September and, from then until Christmas, are handpicked once a week. Pickers climb the palm tree with the same leg spikes used by telephone linemen, sometimes to the height of 100 feet. After the dates are picked, they are cleaned, graded, and packed for shipment.

Mechanized California Agriculture

Innovation has been a tradition in California agriculture. Machines have been developed to plant and harvest most of the major crops grown in California. The University of California at Davis (UC Davis) has been the principal source of this innovative farm machinery.

The tomato harvester, which took more than 15 years to develop, was created at UC Davis. First, G.C. Hanna, a plant breeder at UC Davis, had to develop a hybrid tomato plant sturdy enough to survive handling by a machine. In addition, the plant had to be one on which all of the tomatoes ripen at the same time so that the whole vine can be harvested at once. The harvesting machine that followed, which was developed by Coby Lorenzen of the Department of Agricultural Engineering at UC Davis, eliminated the need for most field workers in the California tomato harvest.

The tomato harvester looks like an open-air trolley. Behind the driver and the machinery that picks the tomatoes sit 14 women busily sorting tomatoes. They are shaded by awnings and serenaded by taped music. The harvester picks and bins 15 tons of tomatoes an hour, once the backbreaking work of 100 migrant laborers.

The machine cuts the plants underground, pulls them up with metal fingers, and then gently shakes off the fruit. As the women sort the tomatoes, a conveyor feeds them into bins strategically placed in the field.

Planting tomatoes, as well as many other vegetables, has also been modernized. Factory assembly lines slip tomato seeds into plastic tapes at designated intervals. Reels of the tape are threaded through a digging tube on a planter that places the tape in predetermined rows. Within minutes of planting, the moisture in the soil dissolves the tape. Pulling a six-tape rig, a single operator can plant 30 acres a day.

To see a field of produce being harvested in the Salinas Valley of California is like watching a mobile factory at work. Many of the harvesters, which are used for iceberg lettuce, broccoli, celery, and cauliflower, look like a single-wing airplane. Mechanical lettuce-picking is a "once through" operation that picks a lettuce field clean in one pass. The same is true for broccoli and cauliflower.

The crew needed to operate such a machine works like a precision team. In the case of iceberg lettuce, men stoop and cut the heads, gently throwing them onto the conveyor-belt wings as the machine

ASPARAGUS SOUP

California asparagus, which is grown primarily in the Salinas Valley, is harvested manually. When the asparagus stalk reaches the designated height, it is cut slightly underneath the soil with a special tool and immediately packed in boxes in the field.

Rice helps give this asparagus soup a smooth texture and also softens some of the harsh asparagus taste. The soup may be prepared a day ahead and served either warm or cold.

Serves 6

2 pounds asparagus

1 tablespoon butter

1 small onion, chopped

1/2 cup rice

5 cups chicken broth

Salt and white pepper, to taste

1/4 cup cream

■

Trim the asparagus and cut it into 1-inch pieces. Set aside 12 tips and blanch them in boiling water for 2 minutes. Refresh the tips under cold water and reserve them for garnish.

Melt the butter in a medium saucepan over medium heat. Add the onion and sauté for 3 minutes, or until the onion is translucent. Add the rice, the asparagus pieces, and the chicken broth. Bring to a boil, reduce the heat, and simmer, covered, for 25 minutes.

Purée the soup in batches in a food processor or blender. Then strain the soup through a sieve over a large bowl. Add salt and pepper, to taste, and blend in the cream. Refrigerate the soup, if serving it cold, or heat it to warm, but do not boil. Ladle soup into soup bowls and garnish with the asparagus tips.

FUYU PERSIMMON AND KIWI SALAD

The Fuyu persimmon was first brought to the United States by Commander Perry in the middle of the nineteenth century and now grows in California. This variety of persimmon is orange in color and shaped like a tomato. Tannin-free, it is usually eaten when crisp. The kiwifruit, originally imported from New Zealand, has become a significant crop in northern California. The fruit is named after New Zealand's native hairy, flightless bird.

In this salad the sweetness of the persimmon is a good contrast to the kiwi.

Serves 6

6 Fuyu persimmons

6 kiwifruit

1 head Boston lettuce

2 tablespoons raspberry vinegar

2 tablespoons dry white wine

1/2 cup olive oil

1/2 teaspoon sugar

Salt and pepper, to taste

■

Peel and slice the persimmons and kiwis into 1/4-inch slices. Divide the lettuce among 6 salad plates. Place alternating slices of persimmon and kiwi on the lettuce. Whisk together the vinegar, wine, oil, sugar, salt, and pepper. Spoon some of the dressing over each salad.

crawls along at one and one half miles per hour. Women riding the wings of the harvester cut off the outer leaves and wrap each head in transparent plastic. A heated shrink-wrap machine tightens the wrapper. Men in the center section of the harvester pack 24 heads to a carton. When full the cartons are left in the field, picked up by truck, and rushed to the warehouse to be cooled.

Some Unusual California Fruits

Because of its favorable growing conditions, California has always been a leader in the growing of unusual fruits and vegetables. Some are unique to California, while others have been perfected there, yet are grown in various parts of the country.

The California prune industry began in the mid-1800s when a Frenchman, named Pellier, immigrated to the Santa Clara Valley south of San Francisco and grafted French prune-plum cuttings to root stock of the native wild plum. The resulting plum dries perfectly without fermentation around the pit, an essential requirement for any prune. In California plums suitable for drying are called prunes even while they are still on the tree.

Apricots are also a major part of California's agriculture. A considerable amount of the apricot crop is marketed in dried form. After ripening in mid-July, the apricots are picked, cut in half, and pitted. They are then placed centers-up on shallow wooden trays and immersed for about four hours in sulphur smoke, which preserves their color. The apricots are then sun dried for another two to six days, depending on the weather.

The mission fathers introduced olive trees to California, where they grew as well as in their native Spain. Olives are green when unripened and turn black when fully ripe. The majority of both green and black California olives are marketed pickled, instead of being pressed into oil. Since most of these olives have a bitter taste, they are soaked in a lye solution to destroy this taste and are then washed thoroughly. Both types of olives are cured in a pickling and salt solution and canned.

Avocados have become a great favorite of California cooks. A native of central and South America, the avocado was brought to California by the Spanish. The avocado was slow to become accepted as a food because it was rumored that the fruit was an aphrodisiac. Sales increased when the Avocado Association hired a public-relations firm to tout the avocado's nutritional properties and promoted it as a chic new addition to salads and other dishes.

For years avocado groves blanketed much of the coastal area of Southern California, where the sandy soil and temperature moderated by the ocean favored their growth. Avocado ranches were major investment properties in the 1960s and 70s. Over-planting and flooding of the market, however, forced many growers to tear out their groves and turn to other agricultural crops.

Traditionally, the yellow-green flesh of the avocado is mashed and combined with spices for a Mexican appetizer known as Guacamole. Use of the avocado has now expanded to where it has become the basis for soups and salads. It is also included in many light entrees.

Kiwifruit has been grown in California as a backyard curiosity since about 1936. However, when New Zealand kiwifruit began flooding the West Coast markets in the early 1970s, California farmers also began growing it. Since New Zealand and California seasons complement each other, kiwifruit is available throughout the country year-round. California farmers have also started cultivating *feijoas,* another small exotic tropical fruit. It has a green skin, and its flesh tastes like a combination of strawberries, lemons, and hazelnuts. Many predict it will one day be as popular as the kiwifruit.

California Seafood

The California coast offers a unique univalve mollusk called abalone. These giant mollusks, which may weigh as much as ten pounds and measure almost a foot across, cling to rocks with a broadmuscular foot that occupies the shell. Divers pry the abalone loose with a flat bar. The flesh of the muscular foot is eaten, while the irredescent inner shell is a source of mother-of-pearl.

In the early days of white settlement, the rocky shores of the California coast were abundant with abalone. The Indians were the first to eat them and taught the early settlers how to harvest them. When fishermen discovered that dried abalone meat brought high prices in China, the supply of the mollusk was almost depleted. Unfortunately, abalone has been over-harvested and today is very expensive, when obtainable. The state has

taken steps to protect the abalone, but so far with only moderate success.

To prepare abalone for cooking, the meat must first be tenderized by pounding it with a mallet. Abalone steaks can be broiled, fried, or baked. The meat can also be combined with onions, potatoes, fried bacon, and milk or cream into a chowder similar to New England fish chowders.

Dungeness crabs are the most

AVOCADOS FILLED WITH SEAFOOD

Avocados were brought to California from Mexico by the Spanish padres and Mexican settlers in the 1700s. Archaeological excavations have found traces of avocado cultivations in Mexico dating back at least 7,000 years B.C. Today, avocados are used primarily in soups and salads. Avocado halves are frequently stuffed with seafood or cold cooked vegetables. If small bay shrimp are not available, substitute medium cooked shrimp and cut them into small bite-sized pieces.

Serves 4

2 avocados

1/2 pound crabmeat

1/4 pound bay shrimp

1/4 cup minced celery

2 tablespoons minced red pepper

1 teaspoon lemon juice

3 tablespoons mayonnaise

1/4 teaspoon curry powder

Lettuce leaves

2 hard-boiled eggs, chopped

Paprika

■

Cut the avocados in half and remove the seed. Pick over the crabmeat to remove any cartilage and combine with the shrimp, celery, and red pepper in a bowl. Sprinkle with the lemon juice. Combine the mayonnaise and curry powder and mix with the seafood. If the mixture is not moist enough, add a little more mayonnaise and a dash more curry powder, to taste.

Fill the avocado halves with the seafood mixture and place on lettuce leaves. Sprinkle each half with some chopped egg and dust with paprika before serving.

SAN FRANCISCO FISHERMAN'S WHARF, by Nicky Boehme, oil, 26 x 36 inches, courtesy of Nicky Boehme Gallery, Mendocino, California.

favorite of California seafoods. These delicate crabs are usually steamed and then served cold. The meat is picked out of the crab shell and often topped with a Louis sauce, similar to a Thousand Island Dressing. Dungeness crabs are also a favorite ingredient of *Cioppino,* a fish stew. During crab season, which runs from November to March, crabs are cooked in big caldrons on the sidewalk at Fisherman's Wharf in San Francisco. "Walk-Away Crab Cocktails" can literally be eaten as you stroll along the colorful wharf.

Dungeness crab is not the only crustacean along the coast of California. Delicate small shrimp and bay scallops are harvested near the coastline as well. The shrimp meat is sold cooked and shelled, ready for salads.

California has what is called a "cold

water" coast, which makes for excellent fishing. This cold water emanates from the Alaska current that sweeps down the coast of California. It has created huge kelp beds that provide food for a variety of shell- and finfish. The most popular finfish is rex sole. There are also sand dabs and 52 varieties of rock fish, including the popular Pacific red snapper — no relation to the Gulf Coast red snapper.

Tuna abounds in California waters and is commercially fished with huge scoop nets that can raise a ton of tuna at a time. Of the four varieties of tuna harvested off the California coast, albacore, yellowfin, skipjack, and bluefin, the yellowfin is the most popular with fishermen because it is preferred by canners. The albacore has moist, flaky, white flesh and is prized for cooking.

California Cuisine

California cuisine has been influenced both by the great abundance of fruits and vegetables grown in the state and also by the immigrants who settled there. The chilies, corn tortillas, tomatoes, avocados, olives, and citrus fruits brought by the Spanish priests and early Mexican settlers have become everyday cooking ingredients in California. Later immigrants from Italy, China, and Japan (to name the most significant) have made major contributions to California cuisine. Most recently, immigrants from Vietnam have added another dimension.

The Chinese first came to San Francisco in 1847 to help build the transcontinental railroad. Some of the Chinese were cooks for the railroad workers, others became cooks in lumber and mining camps. Still other Chinese became housemen in upper-middle class Northern California homes. Although they were not allowed to prepare their

SUKIYAKI

Sukiyaki is a Japanese dish that has become very popular in California. It uses the Oriental stir-fry technique of cooking in a wok. Originally the dish was prepared in Japan by the farmers in the fields who used the metal part of their plow as a cooking utensil. *Suki* means "plow" and *yaki* means "broiled." Since sukiyaki originated as an impromptu dish, it consisted of whatever ingredients were available. Today, either beef or chicken can be the basis of this Japanese stew, and a variety of vegetables can be used.

Sukiyaki cooks very quickly, thus all of the ingredients should be sliced, arranged on a platter, and ready to use. Cut or break the cellophane noodles into several pieces, since they are long and folded into a short package. The sauce ingredients should also be combined before cooking commences. The sukiyaki may be cooked in two batches, if desired.

Serves 4 to 6

3 tablespoons peanut or vegetable oil

1 1/4 pounds beef tenderloin or sirloin, cut into paper-thin 1 x 2-inch slices

1 medium onion, cut in half diagonally and then sliced 1/4-inch thick

3 green onions, cut into 1-inch pieces

2 stalks celery, cut into 1/2-inch pieces

8 ounces white or crimi mushrooms, sliced

4 ounces shiitake mushrooms, sliced

1 can (8 ounces) sliced bamboo shoots, drained

1 can (8 ounces) sliced water chestnuts, drained

Broth (recipe follows)

1 bunch spinach, well-washed, drained, tough stems removed, and torn into large pieces

3 ounces cellophane noodles *(shirataki)*, broken or cut into several pieces

■

Pour the oil into a wok and preheat to 375° F. if using an electric wok, or to moderate-high heat. Add the meat and stir-fry for 1 or 2 minutes until the meat starts to lose its red color. Do not over cook. Remove the meat and add the onions, celery, mushrooms, bamboo shoots, and water chestnuts. Stir fry for 2 minutes. Add half of the broth and cook until the vegetables are crisp-tender, about 4 minutes. Add more broth if necessary to give a soup-like consistency. Then add the spinach and the noodles. Cook covered for 2 to 3 minutes until the noodles are translucent. If necessary add more broth. Return the meat to the wok and heat through. Serve the meat and vegetables in bowls with some of the broth.

Broth

1 can (14 ounces) beef broth

2 tablespoons sugar

1/3 cup dry sherry

1/4 cup soy sauce

1/2 cup water

■

Combine all of the broth ingredients in a pitcher.

native Chinese dishes for their employers, they did manage to prepare vegetables in the Chinese tradition. No longer were overcooked, bland vegetables served in these homes. Quick cooking or stir-frying vegetables soon became popular in California.

The Japanese began arriving in California in considerable numbers after the Chinese exclusion acts in the 1880s, which limited Chinese emigration. Initially, California farmers welcomed the Japenese because they came with their families and provided cheap labor to work in the fields. The thriftiness of the Japanese, however, enabled them to purchase land and compete with their former employers. By 1941 the Japanese raised more than 40 percent of California's truck-garden crops. During World War II Japanese farmers were placed in internment camps. After the war, many went back to farming, but only a portion came back to farm in California.

Japanese cuisine, with its interesting preparations and colorful presentations, became very popular in California in the 1960s and has remained so. The almost theatrical showmanship of teriyaki, sukiyaki, tempura, and sushi preparations

FRUIT SELLER by Enoch Wood Perry, oil, 12 x 13 1/2 inches, courtesy of Montgomery Gallery, San Francisco, California.

enthralled diners in California as it has diners throughout the world. Sukiyaki is a meal in itself, consisting of beef or chicken cooked in a broth with vegetables; and it has become a popular informal meal in many California homes.

Italians came to California during the Gold Rush of 1849, first to pan for gold and then to open restaurants or boarding houses. Every gold mining town in California had at least one Italian boarding house, most of which served pasta and tomato sauce at the main meal.

About the time of the Gold Rush, Giuseppe Buzzara, a Genoan sailor, emigrated to San Francisco, where he supposedly invented a new fish stew known as *Cioppino*. The origin of the name *Cioppino* is unknown, but is thought to be the Italian version of "chip-in," where each fisherman added something of his day's catch to the stew pot.

Cioppino was prepared with whatever the catch happened to be and could have as many as 12 or as few as two different kinds of fish, mussels, shrimp, crab, and oysters. The fish was cut into pieces and cooked in a tomato sauce to which garlic, onions, green pepper, celery, and Italian herbs had been added. The shellfish was cooked either in the shell or out of it. Depending on the cook, red or white wine, or even sherry, was added to the stew. At the turn of the century, *Cioppino* was served with polenta (a cornmeal mush); however, it was never served with pasta. *Cioppino* was and still is traditionally served with crusty sourdough bread. Today, California *Cioppino* typically includes Dungeness crab.

Another Italian contribution to California cuisine is the artichoke. For many years artichokes were rejected by non-Italian Californians because they were too much trouble to eat. As the Italians taught their neighbors how to eat

CIOPPINO

Cioppino was supposed to have been created in San Francisco by Italian fishermen and is now consumed in almost very fishing port in California. The ingredients of this Italian-based fish stew vary with the day's catch, and seasonings vary from port to port. California *Cioppino* typically includes Dungeness crab, shrimp, and mussels or clams.

In this recipe the sauce is prepared first and then the seafood, including an uncooked crab, is cooked in it. However, if only cooked crabs are available, add the crab pieces after half of the cooking time has elapsed, just to thoroughly heat them. If Dungeness crabs are not available, lobster may be substituted.

Serves 4

Sauce

3 tablespoons olive oil

1 large onion, chopped

4 green onions, chopped

1 green pepper, chopped

2 cloves garlic, chopped

1 can (1 pound) tomatoes

1 can (8 ounces) tomato sauce

1/2 teaspoon dried oregano

1/2 chopped fresh basil

1/4 cup chopped fresh parsley

Salt and pepper, to taste

2 1/2 cups dry white wine

■

Heat the olive oil in a medium-size saucepan. Add the onions, pepper, and garlic and sauté until the vegetables are limp. Chop the tomatoes coarsely and add them with their juice, together with the tomato sauce, oregano, basil, and parsley, to the vegetables. Bring to a slow boil and simmer the sauce, uncovered, for 30 minutes. Season with salt and pepper and add the wine.

Seafood

1 large or 2 small live Dungeness crabs

2 pounds skinless and boneless firm fish, such as Pacific snapper or sea bass

1 pound shrimp

1 dozen clams, in the shell

1 dozen mussels, in the shell

■

Have the fish market remove the top shell of the crab, cut the body in 4 pieces (2 pieces if using small crabs), and crack the legs. Cut the fish into 2 to 3-inch pieces. Shell and devein the shrimp and clean the mussels and clams.

Place the crab, fish, clams, and mussels in a Dutch oven or large saucepan. Pour the sauce over the seafood, cover, and bring to a boil. Reduce the heat to medium-low and cook for 12 minutes, or until the clams and mussels have opened. After half of the cooking time has elapsed, add the shrimp and finish cooking, checking to see that the mixture is slowly boiling. Serve in deep soup bowls with French bread.

PASTA SALAD WITH BLACK OLIVES

Pasta salads are very popular in California. There are take-out shops that specialize in these salads. They may have an Oriental, Italian, or a Mexican flavor, such as this one has.

Serves 4 to 6

8 ounces fusilli (corkscrew pasta)

1 tablespoon olive oil

2 medium tomatoes, peeled

1 can (2.2 ounces) sliced black olives, drained

1/2 cup sliced celery

1/3 cup chopped red pepper

1/3 cup chopped green pepper

3/4 cup blanched broccoli florets

1 jalapeño pepper, seeded and finely chopped

2 tablespoons chopped fresh cilantro leaves

Dressing

2 tablespoons white wine vinegar

2 tablespoons lemon juice

1 tablespoon water

3/4 teaspoon Dijon mustard

Dash of garlic powder

1/4 teaspoon cayenne pepper

7 tablespoons olive oil

■

Cook the fusilli in boiling salted water until al dente, rinse in cold water, and drain. Transfer the pasta to a serving dish and toss with the 1 tablespoon of olive oil.

Chop the tomatoes into bite-sized pieces and add them with the olives, celery, red pepper, green pepper, broccoli, jalapeño pepper, and chopped cilantro to the pasta. Toss well to combine.

Whisk together the vinegar, lemon juice, water, mustard, garlic powder, and cayenne pepper in a small bowl. Gradually add the oil, while continuing to whisk.

Pour the dressing over the salad and combine well. Refrigerate at least 1 hour before serving.

farmers in California are also credited with the first commercial growing of fava beans, bell peppers, eggplant, Savoy cabbage, and broccoli.

Many salad recipes have originated in California, one of the famous being the Caesar Salad. Its originator was Caesar Cardini, a Beverly Hills restauranteur. It seems that on a Fourth of July weekend Cardini ran out of salad ingredients and searched the pantry for something to feed his clientele. All he found were eggs, romaine lettuce, stale bread, and Romano cheese. Cardini rubbed a bowl with garlic, soaked the bread in olive oil, and lightly sautéed it. Then he beat the eggs and stirred them into a mixture of vinegar and oil. This dressing was poured over the torn lettuce and topped with the bread cubes and grated Romano cheese. Anchovy filets have since been added to the basic recipe, and grated Parmesan cheese is used instead of the Romano.

The Cobb Salad also originated as a solution to a restaurant menu problem. In the late 1920s, Bob Cobb, then manager of the Brown Derby in Hollywood, was becoming tired of his own daily meals, which consisted primarily of hamburgers and hot dogs. One day he chopped up an avocado, along with some lettuce, tomato, and bacon. He added dressing, and this salad became his dinner. A few days later Cobb embellished his creation by adding other ingredients—chicken breast, chives, hard-boiled egg, watercress, and cheese—all chopped into small pieces. Cobb salad became a menu staple at the Brown Derby.

Fine dining has been important to Californians since the Gold Rush days, particularly to the residents of San Francisco. For years the gentlemen members of the city's Chit Chat Club

them, they started growing bigger and better varieties of artichokes, which could be more easily eaten and were large enough to stuff. Today, most of the artichokes are still grown in the region along the coast from Half Moon Bay south to Watsonville, which has become the artichoke capital of America.

Many of the Italians who settled in California were from Southern Italy, where much of the cooking was based on the use of the tomato. Camillo Pregno, an Italian immigrant, improved tomato cultivation in California and opened a factory to produce canned tomato puree for his fellow countrymen. The Italian met monthly to hear a paper being read and enjoy a sumptuous meal. Not even the great earthquake and fire of 1906 disrupted their repast. As San Francisco lay smoldering, the determined members hired a chef to cook in an outdoor kitchen, and they ate in the bedroom of the remains of a home. The subject of the paper was quickly forgotten, but the menu was recorded for posterity—oysters on the half shell, *Crab à la Poulette*, Roman Punch, dessert, and coffee.

Today California sets the pace in cuisine for much of the nation. The state, with its readily available fresh ingredients, interesting ethnic influences, and innovative chefs, has presented an entirely new cuisine to the nation. The cuisine is not limited by strict rules, and unusual ingredients are combined to create new dishes. California cooks continue to experiment with unusual food combinations—slices of grilled duck on salad greens, ravioli with nasturtium blossom filling, goat cheese *flan* with grilled eggplant, chicken breasts with raspberry sauce, or chocolate-cranberry torte.

The so-called new American Cuisine originated in California with such chefs as Alice Waters, Bradley Ogden, Jeremiah Tower, and Joyce Goldstein. The California Culinary Academy, located in San Francisco, has become a renowned training ground for chefs in this new cuisine. This style of cooking was influenced by France's *nouvelle cuisine,* but its strongest attraction is the myriad of fresh ingredients available in California year-round. To paraphrase an old political saying, "As California food styles go, so go those of the nation."

CHICKEN WITH ARTICHOKES

The globe variety of artichokes is cultivated primarily along the coast of California between Watsonville and Monterey. Every winter several artichokes grow on the thistle-like plant and are harvested between March and May. They are still picked by hand and put into a basket tied onto the picker's back.

The use of frozen artichoke hearts makes this chicken dish easy to prepare.

Serves 4

1 chicken (3 to 3 1/2 pounds), cut into
   serving pieces

2 tablespoons butter

1 tablespoon vegetable oil

12 small white boiling onions, skinned

1 teaspoon lemon juice

1 package (10 ounces) frozen artichoke
   hearts, defrosted and drained

1/2 cup dry or semi-dry white wine

1/2 cup chicken broth

Salt and pepper, to taste

1/4 teaspoon dried thyme

1 bay leaf, broken in small pieces

■

If desired the chicken pieces may be skinned.

Heat the butter and oil in a 10-inch skillet over medium-high heat and add the chicken and brown it on all sides. Remove the chicken from the skillet and place in a 13 x 9-inch baking dish.

Sauté the onions in the same skillet until golden brown. Place the onions in the dish with the chicken. Add the lemon juice to the skillet and sauté the artichoke hearts lightly. Arrange them in the baking dish with the chicken and onions. Combine the wine, chicken broth, salt, pepper, thyme, and bay leaf. Pour this mixture over the chicken. Bake uncovered in a preheated 350° F. oven for 50 minutes to 1 hour, or until the chicken is done.

ARTICHOKE KALEIDOSCOPE by Virginia Paul, watercolor, 19 x 21 1/4 inches, courtesy of the artist, Charlottesville, Virginia.

273

THE STAR FLEET IN BRISTOL BAY, 1909 by Nicky Boehme, oil, 24 x 35 inches, courtesy of Nicky Boehme Gallery, Mendocino, California.

THE NEWEST STATES

WHILE VOLCANOES played a major role in creating both Alaska and Hawaii, the states are entirely different in climate, culture, and food heritage. Alaska, much of which is a cold wilderness, is best known for its seafood. Hawaii, a tropical paradise, is known for its exotic fruits, nuts, and sugarcane. Despite their distance from the mainland, however, both are important suppliers of food to the rest of the nation.

Sailing ships plying the Pacific Ocean first brought the white man to Hawaii and Alaska. In the late 1700s and early 1800s, Yankee whaling ships hunted whales in Alaska and used Honolulu as a repair port. American fur traders along the coast of Alaska also visited the Hawaiian Islands (then known as the Sandwich Islands) to obtain supplies and make repairs.

Hawaii was an independent nation until it gave up its sovereignty in 1900 to become a U.S. territory. Starting in 1870 Hawaii was drawn closer and closer to the United States, because the islands depended on the American market for the sale of their two principal products—pineapple and sugar.

The United States purchased Alaska from Russia in 1867 for $7.2 million. At the time the only settlements of Caucasians were Russian fur traders, who had established settlements along the southern coast in the late 1700s. Russia agreed to sell the territory to the United States because of the decline of the fur trade and its fear of a British takeover. The American people were slow to appreciate the value of the vast new land, which they nicknamed "Seward's Folly" after the Secretary of State at the time. Both territories became states in 1959.

Even though the soils of Hawaii and Alaska are volcanic in origin, climatic conditions have dictated entirely different agriculture for each state. Both states supply the rest of the United States with their specialty foods. Hawaii exports pineapple, sugar, and tropical fruit, while seafood is Alaska's main export. Ironically, both of these important food-exporting states receive most of their food staples from the mainland.

GRILLED SALMON

Alaskans frequently grill their salmon over alderwood and charcoal, however, any aromatic wood may be added to the charcoal to impart extra flavor. The basting sauce, which caramelizes during cooking, adds a slightly sweet flavor to the salmon.

Serves 4

4 salmon steaks

Vegetable oil

5 tablespoons butter or margarine

1/2 cup brown sugar

1 teaspoon dark rum

Lemon juice

■

Very lightly brush the steaks with oil so that they will not stick to the grill.

Combine the butter, brown sugar, and rum in a small saucepan. Cook over low heat until the butter melts and the ingredients are combined. Add enough lemon juice to the mixture to cut the sweetness and make it the consistency of a sauce.

Grill the salmon steaks on a charcoal grill until just done, about 5 minutes per side, depending on the thickness of the steaks. Just before the steaks have finished grilling, brush one side with the sauce and continue grilling for another minute or two. Turn and brush the other side with the sauce and grill for another minute.

ALASKA

ALASKA is a land of many contrasts. Its southeastern panhandle lies between steep coastal mountains and the sea. Due to the warm Japanese Current, the harbors of the cities located in this region hardly ever freeze over.

The top third of Alaska lies within the Arctic Circle and has vast stretches of treeless tundra, which are crusted with deep snow most of the year. Once the sun goes down in the middle of November, it does not reappear for two months.

The Alaskan interior, known as the Yukon River Basin, has a slightly more pleasant atmosphere. Although winters can be extremely cold, with temperatures dropping to minus 30 degrees Fahrenheit, they are followed by mild springs and hot summers. Even with these extreme temperatures, the Yukon River Basin is suitable for some farming.

South-central Alaska is sheltered from Arctic winds by the Alaska Range to the north and is warmed by the Japanese Current to the south. This is the region of the Matanuska Valley, where two-thirds of Alaska's farm products are grown.

The Aleutian Islands appear like stepping stones leading to Asia. The island chain, part of an ancient land bridge between the two continents, is basically unfit for agriculture, except for some sheep farming.

Native Alaskans

When white fur traders and whalers arrived in the eighteenth century, they found that the native Alaskans—Indians, Eskimos, and Aleuts—had adapted remarkably well to this varied habitat. The Indians who lived in the panhandle and along the southern coast had the most favorable environment. They did not farm since seafood, as well as berries and roots, was plentiful. Like their Pacific Northwest Indian neighbors, they depended on salmon as the mainstay of their diet.

They also made long journeys out to sea in oversized canoes. In the deep waters the Indians hunted seals, sea otters, porpoises, and whales. Fish was preserved for year-round eating by drying it and making a form of jerky. Since wood was plentiful along the coast, they used it to create wooden boxes, which, when filled with water and heated stones, served to cook their food.

Inland Indians, however, relied on caribou as their main source of food. The caribou provided not only food but also clothing, fuel, and oil for lamps. At one time great herds of caribou covered Alaska, but over the years the herds have been depleted.

In years past most Eskimos ate their food raw since there was little fuel available for cooking. They ate *Muktuk*, whale skin with a thick coating of blubber, raw. It was a nourishing food, and as recent studies have shown raw meat and fish best meet the body's demands for fat in a cold climate. The Eskimos, however, did some cooking over a fire of precious seal oil, which also provided light and warmth. Wild game such as mountain goats, polar bears, caribou, and Dall sheep, a relative of the bighorn, were also part of the Eskimo diet.

Today, the Eskimo diet is a mixture of old and new foods. Eskimo children enjoy chewing on a raw walrus kidney just as much as a chocolate candy bar. Eskimo fishermen can be observed sipping hot Brazilian coffee from a thermos while sitting on a chunk of ice awaiting a catch.

A modern Eskimo meal might consist of dried or smoked fish, reindeer stew, and a dessert of fresh or preserved Arctic berries with sugar and canned milk. If the dessert is served in the traditional manner, the berries are topped with seal oil. *Alitol*, Eskimo "ice cream," which is a mixture of cranberries and fish eggs beaten to a fluff, is still popular.

The Aleuts of days past also endured a hard life. They lived along the shore of the Aleutian Islands in either driftwood or whalebone dwellings, subsisting mainly on seafood and some birds. They supplemented their diet with berries and edible plants.

Today, there is some sheep-raising in the Aleutians. Native grasses and herbs provide pasture for the sheep nearly 12 months of the year. The cool summers and absence of sunshine for part of the year are not deterrents to raising sheep. Aleutian sheep produce excellent wool, and the meat is of superior flavor.

Russians and "Sourdoughs"

In 1741 Captain Vitus Bering, a Dane in the employ of Russia, was the first white man to set foot on Alaskan territory. He had discovered the strait that now bears his name in 1732 but had not landed. Shortly after he came ashore in 1741, Bering died of scurvy. At that time the beneficial properties of the scurvy grass that grows along the Alaskan coastline were unknown. Russian sailors later discovered that eating this ascorbic grass raw would prevent scurvy and took great quantities of it aboard their ships.

Russian settlers in search of furs established the first permanent settlement in Alaska on Kodiak Island in 1784. In order to make the area self-sufficient, the Russians tried to grow grain. This effort failed, so they established farms on the coast of California, north of San Francisco, to grow food for the Alaskan territory. By the middle of the 1800s, the stock of fur animals in Alaska had been greatly reduced, and Russia sold the territory to the United States.

Russian culinary influences are still evident in Alaska, particularly in Sitka, where at Easter time Russian foods and customs prevail. *Kulich,* the Russian Easter bread, and decorated eggs are part of the Easter celebration. Traditional Russian *Piroghi,* rectangular pies filled with rice, silver salmon, celery, and cabbage, are still served as a main course. Beef Stroganoff and *Kasha,* a porridge of buckwheat groats served with fruit and nuts, are favorites.

In 1896 the Klondike and other gold fields were discovered, and prospectors from the lower "Forty-Eight" streamed into Alaska. Along with the gold rush came sourdough starter, which was used as leavening for biscuits, bread, and pancakes in the days before commercial yeast became available. Made of a mixture of sugar, flour, water, and usually a few boiled potatoes, a little sourdough starter was added to each batch of dough to make it light and fluffy. Every time some of the starter was used, it was replaced with an equivalent amount of flour, salt, and lukewarm water. If the mixture was kept at the right temperature, it would remain active for years.

Many Alaskan cooks still bake sourdough bread, frequently from starter that is many decades old. Sourdough bread has a rich flavor and a denser texture than other breads. Alaskan sourdough specialties include poppy-seed potato-bread, caraway-studded rye bread, whole-wheat bread, and French bread.

Other food necessities of the "Sourdoughs," the nickname given to the Alaska gold prospectors, were bacon, salt pork, lard, flour, and coffee or tea. Most miners' food was dull and monotonous,

PIROGHI (SALMON PIE)

Piroghi are large, traditional Russian pies, which in Alaska were primarily filled with fish, such as the abundant salmon. The addition of rice and some vegetables created a one-dish meal.

This modern version of *Piroghi* is baked in a square pan. The pie may be served with a light Cheddar cheese sauce, if desired.

Serves 6

Pastry

2 1/2 cups all-purpose flour

6 tablespoons butter or margarine

5 tablespoons solid vegetable shortening

5 to 6 tablespoons ice water

■

Place the flour in a bowl. Cut in the butter and shortening until it is the texture of coarse crumbs. Add the water, a tablespoon at a time, and mix with a fork until the dough can be formed into a ball. Wrap the dough in plastic wrap and chill for at least 1 hour.

Filling

2 tablespoons butter

2 medium onions, thinly sliced

2 cups cooked rice

3/4 cup dill cream sauce (recipe follows)

1 1/4 pounds skinless fresh salmon, cut
　　into 1 1/2-inch pieces

1 stalk celery, finely diced

1 cup finely shredded cabbage

2 hard-boiled eggs, finely chopped

■

Roll out half of the pastry to fit an 8-inch square pan with 1/2 inch overlapping the sides. Refrigerate until ready to fill.

Melt the butter in a medium-size skillet over medium heat; add the onions and sauté until golden. Combine the rice with the cream sauce and spread half of the mixture over the bottom of the dough. Place the salmon pieces over the rice and then distribute the onions, celery, cabbage, and eggs over the salmon. Cover with the remaining rice.

Roll out the other half of the dough and place it over the rice. Bring the pastry edges together and seal with a fluted edge. Make a few slits in the top of the crust to let steam escape. Bake in a preheated 350° F. oven for 1 hour.

Dill Cream Sauce

1 1/2 tablespoons butter or margarine

1 1/2 tablespoons all-purpose flour

Dash of pepper

3/4 cup milk

2 tablespoons chopped fresh dill

■

Melt the butter in a small saucepan over medium-low heat. Add the flour and pepper and stir until well blended and smooth. Slowly add the milk, stirring constantly, and cook until smooth and thickened. Add the dill and cook 1 more minute.

FISHING SMACKS
by Armin Hansen, oil, 16 x 21
inches, courtesy of George Stern,
Fine Arts, Encino, California.

since little food was grown in Alaska at the time and only the basic necessities were shipped from the lower "Forty-Eight." Alaskan pioneers created substitutes for foods not readily available in Alaska. Sea-gull eggs replaced chicken eggs. Clover and other flowers were boiled into a syrup to produce squaw honey, since there were no bees in Alaska. Relishes were made from kelp, and moose fat was often used in cooking.

Seafood

Alaska fishing has consistently provided food for its inhabitants, as well as contributed to the economy of the state. Although a variety of fish are harvested in Alaska waters, salmon, particularly pink and sockeye, represent the majority of the catch. Other varieties of salmon in Alaska waters are chinook, coho, and chum. Japan imports salmon roe from Alaska because the Japanese consider it a great delicacy.

In 1878 the first salmon cannery, the Cutting Packing Company, was established near Sitka. Others followed, and soon there were salmon canneries along the panhandle and at Kodiak Island. By 1929, there were 156 salmon canneries in Alaska, and canned salmon had flooded

the American market.

In order to conserve the supply of salmon, Congress passed the White Act in 1924, which regulated the times and areas for commercial salmon fishing. The act also fixed the size of the fish that could be caught and the type of fishing gear that could be used. Strict regulation has helped increase salmon runs.

Because of the limited salmon season, in recent years many fishermen have turned to other catches such as halibut, black cod, and sablefish. Eighty percent of the 60 million pounds of halibut harvested annually along both the Atlantic and Pacific coasts is caught in the Gulf of Alaska during the spring and summer. Halibuts weigh between 100 to 300 pounds at maturity.

Shellfishing is primarily a winter activity, since many of the finfish have migrated to warmer waters. Some salmon fishermen have outfitted their boats with shellfishing equipment to harvest crabs during the off-season. It is not unusual during the winter months to see Dungeness crab pots on decks where salmon had lain the previous summer.

Until the early 1980s Kodiak Island salmon fishermen harvested king crab in the winter months. When the king crab harvest was depleted, the Alaska Depart-

ment of Fisheries closed most of the king crab fishing grounds. A few have recently been reopened on a limited basis.

With the depletion of the king crab, Alaskan crab fishermen are now harvesting the Tanner, or snow crab, and the smaller and more delicately flavored Dungeness crab. The annual Alaska crab harvest is about 200 million pounds, with Tanner crabs predominating. Like the king crab, the Tanner crab has long spindly legs but a much smaller body. To be harvested legally, it must measure five and one-half inches across the body.

All of the crabs harvested off the coast of Alaska are caught in large traps dropped from fishing boats. The traps are usually baited with fish heads, and when the ship's sonar detects that the traps are full, they are raised by hydraulic lift. The crabs are then placed in holding tanks, where cold seawater is constantly circulated in order to keep them alive. Some ships process the crab harvest aboard ship. A large boat can butcher, clean, cook, box, and freeze 40,000 pounds of crabmeat per day.

Agriculture

Alaska is not considered a farming state, but it does raise some produce for local consumption. Even though the early Russian settlers did not succeed in growing wheat in Alaska, the Alaskans now grow it, as well as rye, oats, and barley. The strain of wheat grown in Alaska is a hardy winter type whose first seeds were imported from Siberia.

The main farming region of Alaska is the Matanuska Valley, which stretches inland from Anchorage. It is protected from severe northern winds by the Alaska Range and is warmed by offshore breezes generated by the Japanese Current.

Farming began in the Matanuska

Valley as an experiment in 1935. During that depression year the federal government transported 200 families—most of whom were on relief in Minnesota, Wisconsin, and Michigan—to Alaska to begin a new life. Each of the pioneering families received a tract of land, basic farm buildings, and livestock. Even with this head start, the settlers found life to be very difficult during the first several long winters. The experiment eventually proved successful due to fast-growing crops and a sound financial return.

More than 50 years later, the Matanuska Valley, with its intense growing season, produces wheat and other grains, root and leafy vegetables, and tasty potatoes. Many of the vegetables grown in the valley reach phenomenal proportions. Fifty-pound cabbages, fist-size strawberries, four-foot-high rhubarb, and sunflowers ten feet tall are not unusual. The most famous of the large vegetables are the hybrid cabbages that weigh up to 70 pounds.

The gigantic size of the produce is thought to be caused by the long periods of daylight between spring and autumn. These long daylight hours not only increase the size of produce but, along with relatively cool temperatures, also help the plant store starch and sugar, which produce intense flavors. Turnips, potatoes, and other root vegetables, as well as green vegetables, flourish under these conditions. Since rhubarb grows quickly in Alaska, it must be planted in a separate plot or it will overpower anything growing near it.

Alaska grows a great variety of berries, including blueberries, strawberries, raspberries, wild gooseberries, and a type of cranberry entirely different from those grown in Massachusetts and Wisconsin. The Alaskan high-bush variety of cranberries produces small, red, currant-like fruit;

RHUBARB-STRAWBERRY TART

In Alaska the short summer growing season with long days of sunshine produces some of the most magnificent fruits and vegetables in North America. Rhubarb is so prolific in the far north that many Alaskans use it for desserts and preserves instead of conventional fruit. In this recipe it is combined with strawberries to soften the tart flavor of the rhubarb.

Serves 8

Tart Shell

1 1/4 cups all-purpose flour

1/4 cup sugar

1/2 cup butter or margarine

4 to 6 tablespoons ice water

■

Combine the flour and sugar in a bowl. Cut the butter into 8 pieces and then cut them into the flour until the mixture resembles fine crumbs. Add the water, a little at a time, until a dough forms and can be gathered into a ball. Wrap the dough in plastic wrap and refrigerate for 1 hour.

Filling

1 1/2 pounds rhubarb, trimmed and cut into 1-inch pieces

2/3 cup sugar

8 large strawberries, quartered

3 eggs, separated

1/4 cup whipping cream

Grated zest of 1/2 lemon

■

Place the rhubarb in a bowl and sprinkle it with half of the sugar. Let it sit for 30 minutes to draw out the juice.

In the meantime, roll out the pastry and fit it into a 10-inch tart pan. Prick the tart shell bottom and sides with a fork and line the dough with aluminum foil, shiny side down, and pie weights or beans. Bake in a preheated 375° F. oven for 10 minutes. Remove the pie weights and foil. Then bake for another 7 minutes.

Drain the rhubarb, reserving the juice, and arrange it with the strawberries in the tart shell. Sprinkle with half of the remaining sugar and bake for 20 minutes. Remove from oven.

Just before the baking time has elapsed, beat the egg yolks with the remaining sugar and mix in the rhubarb juice, cream, and lemon zest. Beat the egg whites until stiff and fold them into the egg yolk mixture. Pour the custard over the rhubarb and return the tart to the oven. Bake for another 20 minutes until the custard is set and the top is brown. Serve warm or cold.

the low-bush variety's berries are known as lingonberries. Alaskans use both varieties for relishes, ketchup, jellies, and wine. Salmonberries, similar to raspberries but lighter in color, are eaten raw or used to make jelly.

Alaska has a growing dairy industry. The cattle feed on the region's rich grasses. Today's Alaskan butter is a far cry from the spread the early pioneers made

BUCKWHEAT PANCAKES

Buckwheat and sourdough pancakes were a favorite breakfast food of the Klondike gold miners in the 1890s. They used buckwheat flour because wheat flour was scarce.

Leaving the pancake dough to rest overnight gives it a sour taste reminiscent of a sourdough starter. Omitting the dissolved soda will also give the pancakes a more sour flavor, but it will make them chewier.

Serves 4 to 6

2 cups buckwheat flour

1 cup all-purpose flour

2 tablespoons sugar

1/2 teaspoon salt

1 package dry yeast

1/4 cup warm water (110° F. to 115° F.)

2 cups warm milk

2 tablespoons molasses

1 teaspoon baking soda

1/4 cup lukewarm water

4 tablespoons melted butter or margarine

1 egg, lightly beaten

■

Combine the flours, sugar, and salt in a bowl. In another bowl, dissolve the yeast in the warm water and let it stand until bubbly, about 10 minutes. Add the warm milk and molasses to the yeast and then add the mixture to the flour, beating until smooth. Cover and let the batter stand at room temperature overnight.

The next morning, dissolve the baking soda in the lukewarm water and add it, along with the melted butter and egg, to the pancake batter. Using about 1/3 cup of batter for each pancake, cook the pancakes on a hot griddle until bubbles form on top. Turn the pancakes and brown the other side. Serve with butter and maple syrup or honey.

from fat skimmed off the surface of water in which caribou horns had been boiled for three days.

Game is abundant in Alaska and is hunted throughout the year. Caribou, over-hunted in the late 1800s, is still available. Currently, the federal government is experimenting with raising reindeer commercially. At present the meat is sold through local markets in the autumn. At the end of the nineteenth century, 1,200 reindeer were imported from Siberia to Alaska by Sheldon Jackson, who hoped to domesticate them and establish a

reindeer meat industry. By the 1920s there were a quarter of a million reindeer, and the meat was being shipped to the United States. The project failed, however, because the reindeer quickly depleted existing grasses and the herds died.

Alaskan Food

Alaska has been considered the last frontier of the United States, conjuring up images of gold prospecting, oil strikes, and pioneer living. There is still more

wilderness than civilization in Alaska and cooking retains some of the influences of the pioneering American past.

Although Dutch, Germans, and Scandinavians helped settled Alaska and brought some of their own cooking preferences, the limited variety of ingredients dictates simple, unadorned cooking. Pot roasts and stews are accompanied by potatoes, fresh vegetables in season, or cooked dried beans. Homemade pickles and relishes, bread or rolls, and pie for dessert complete the typical meal.

Most of the Alaskan meals are based on seafood and game, including salmon, crab, herring, moose, and elk. Caribou sausage and reindeer steak are Alaska specialties. Moose, a more common meat, is broiled, roasted, or ground for hamburgers. The meat can also be marinated and then broiled or fried.

Game, fish, and wild-berry dishes abound in Alaska. Some specialties include venison stew, caribou Swiss steak, breast of ptarmigan in sour cream, and red and blue huckleberry pie. Snow ice is made with evaporated milk, sugar, vanilla, and sufficient fresh snow to produce a mixture with the consistency of ice cream.

Local meats such as lamb chops and roasts from the Aleutians, beef from Kodiak Island and the Matanuska Valley, and hams, sausages, and pork roasts from the growing number of Alaskan pork farms are available. Nevertheless, a great deal of food is still brought by boat, mainly from Seattle.

Local communities of foreign immigrants continue to celebrate their native ethnic festivals. The Russian community in Sitka serves traditional Russian food at holiday time. In Petersburg, also in the panhandle, families of Norwegian descent have outdoor smorgasbord feasts in the summer months.

HAWAII

LEGEND HAS IT that the Hawaiian Islands were created by the goddess Pele, whose sleepless wandering produced volcanoes below the ocean floor. However created, the volcanoes continued to erupt over tens of millions of years, producing lava formations that gradually built up until they emerged as steaming mountain tops.

Black and barren, these mountains became the core of the islands we know today as the state of Hawaii. Wind, rain, sun, and waves gradually pulverized the rock into the fertile soil that now supports a wide variety of agriculture.

Over the years the volcanoes have become dormant, with the exception of Kilauea on the "Big Island," Hawaii. It is indeed an awesome sight to walk through bare, burnt land to the tip of the Kilauea crater and look down into molten lava boiling and churning. One imagines that Pele is still at work.

The Hawaiian Islands, located about 2,000 miles west of the U.S. mainland in the Pacific Ocean, are linked by tradition and early history to the Orient, the Far East, and the East Indies. The first settlers in Hawaii were Polynesians from Samoa, the Indo-Malayan region, and other southwestern archipelagoes. Historians believe that they arrived between the sixth and eighth centuries A.D.

Early Hawaiian Food

The early Polynesians had learned from their many voyages that food on even the greenest of the South Seas' islands was scarce. Thus, on their voyages to Hawaii, they took not only provisions for the journey but also roots and seeds to grow food. In addition to bananas and coconuts, the Polynesians brought taro, a root from which poi is made; plantain, the starchy cooking banana; breadfruit, a globe-like fruit that is eaten cooked; yams; and sugarcane. Although the Polynesians had no way of making sugar from sugarcane, they considered the cane a form of candy.

For meat the Polynesians brought along pigs, dogs, and possibly chickens. It was fortunate that they did, as there was no wild game on the islands.

Fish became the mainstay of the early Hawaiian diet, supplemented by the foods the Polynesians had brought with them.

Salmon was so plentiful that the Hawaiians referred to it as "the pig of the sea." Mullet, a particular favorite, were placed in specially constructed ponds, where they could be bred and harvested easily.

The early Hawaiians caught fish by netting, spearing, hooking, and trapping. Their traps were slanted wooden cages that caught a variety of fish, including dolphin, tuna, snapper, and barracuda, as well as shellfish and turtles. Hawaiians ate small fish raw but cooked the larger ones in underground ovens.

The Hawaiians grew no grains or rice and depended on poi for their starchy

PAPAYA SOUP

Spanish and Portuguese explorers brought papayas from the West Indies to the Hawaiian Islands in the eighteenth century. Today, Hawaii is one of the leading growers of the fruit.

The density of this Papaya Soup is governed by the amount of papaya flesh, which in turn dictates the amount of light cream added at the end. Since papaya has a very delicate taste, do not add too much cream or it will be overpowering.

Serves 4

5 ripe papayas

2 cups dry white wine

6 tablespoons fresh lime juice

1/4 cup honey

1/2 teaspoon cinnamon

1/2 teaspoon ground ginger

3 tablespoons brandy

1/2 to 1 cup half-and-half

Mint leaves, for garnish

■

Cut 4 papayas in half, scoop out the seeds, and discard them. Then scoop out the pulp. Place the papaya meat and all the other ingredients, except the half-and-half and mint in a blender or food processor. Blend until smooth. Add 1/2 cup half-and-half and blend again. Add more cream if the mixture is too thick. Chill the soup for several hours.

To serve, slice the flesh of the remaining papaya. Ladle the soup into soup bowls and garnish with papaya slices and mint leaves.

HAWAII LAHAINA WATERFRONT, MAUI by Nicky Boehme, oil, 28 x 38 inches, courtesy of Nicky Boehme Gallery, Mendocino, California.

food. Although considered their "bread," poi is really a thick, bland-tasting, pasty pudding prepared from the root of the water-loving, lily-like taro plant. This plant has heart-shaped leaves that taste like spinach when cooked. The purple-brown root is baked, peeled, and then pounded into fine granules. As it is pounded, water is added until the mixture is similar to bread dough.

Legend says that an early native king originated poi. He had grown tired of baked taro root, pounded it with his fists, and threw it aside in disgust. The smashed mixture began to ferment. Out of curiosity, the king tasted it, liked it, and from that time on the taro root was ground into a pudding-like mixture.

The early Hawaiians stored their poi in gourds or other vessels and let it ferment slightly. Before serving, a little more water was added. The natives ate poi with their fingers and called it one-, two-, or three-finger poi, depending on its consistency.

Coconut milk was also used in poi, as well as in other food preparations. To the Hawaiians coconut milk is the juice pressed from the meat of the coconut, not the liquid inside of the nut. Since there were no milk animals in Hawaii, coconut milk became the alternative. The meat of the coconut was used as a sweetener before sugar was refined from sugarcane and is still used in a wide variety of Polynesian dishes.

The early Hawaiians were happy eaters. They made no distinction between breakfast, lunch, and dinner, or hot and cold foods. Since no regular meal-times were observed, eating took place throughout the day. It was not unheard of for one person to eat as much as 18 pounds of poi in a 24-hour period.

With continuous eating, it is no wonder that the early Hawaiians were more than on the chubby side. Until the nineteenth century, stoutness was considered to be a sign of wealth, for it meant that the person did not have to work and could engage in the more pleasurable things of life, such as eating. As a result many Hawaiian rulers and kings weighed more than 400 pounds.

Since the Hawaiians did not possess eating utensils, the people ate with their fingers. They used their teeth to tear apart stringy seafood and roasted pork. Coconut milk was the common drink. Gourds, coconut shells, and hollowed-out wooden bowls were used as drinking vessels. Large palm or banana leaves served as plates.

Early Hawaiian cooking methods were very limited, since there was no metal on the islands, and the Hawaiians made no pottery. They did boil some food using hot stones in hollowed-out wooden vessels or gourds.

The most popular cooking device was the underground oven or *imu*, a pit lined with kindling wood and heat-retentive stones. The food was wrapped in large banana or palm leaves and placed in the pit to cook. Water-soaked leaves and handwoven mats covered the *imu* to steam the food. Meats, as well as vegetables, were cooked in their own juices. The early Hawaiians cooked pigs, chickens, and dogs in this manner.

In accordance with ancient Polynesian customs, Hawaiian women were not allowed to eat pork, turtles, bananas, coconuts, and certain varieties of fish, nor were they allowed to cook them. Not being able to cook these forbidden foods kept them from nibbling on these delicacies. Hence, the men did the majority of the cooking. Men and women were also not allowed to eat together, and in some areas they were not permitted to cook their foods in the same ovens. Men sat or squatted while they ate. The women carried vessels of food with them, eating while they performed their various tasks. This segregated eating ended in 1819, when King Liholiho sat down to dine with the queen at a public feast.

European Influences

In the centuries following the Polynesian settlement of the Hawaiian Islands, travelers and traders brought ginger, guavas, papayas, and Hawaii's most famous crop, pineapple, to the islands.

In 1788 Captain James Cook, searching for a route across North America that would connect the Atlantic and Pacific oceans, discovered the Hawaiian Islands for the Western world. He named them the Sandwich Islands, after his patron, the English Earl of Sandwich.

The Hawaiians became interested in the food of Cook's sailors—salted beef and biscuits, the latter known as hardtack. These two food items provided the natives with their first taste of beef and bread. When he sailed away, Cook left European species of pigs and goats, which

MAHIMAHI WITH GINGER SAUCE

Mahimahi is another name for a variety of dolphin that is found in Hawaiian waters. It has become synonymous with Hawaiian cuisine, although it is somewhat scarce in the waters around the islands.

In this recipe mahimahi is oven-poached in coconut milk, the traditional cooking liquid of the Hawaiian Islands. Ginger adds an oriental flavor. Unsalted peanuts may be substitued for the macadamia nuts.

Serves 6

2 pounds mahimahi fillets

Salt and pepper

All-purpose flour

4 tablespoons butter

1 tablespoon minced fresh ginger

2 cups coconut milk

1 tablespoon cornstarch

1/2 cup chopped macadamia nuts

■

Season the mahimahi fillets with salt and pepper and coat them in the flour. Melt the butter in a large skillet and quickly sauté the fish over medium-high heat until golden. Transfer the fish to a flat baking dish. Combine the ginger, coconut milk, and cornstarch and pour over the fish. Bake in a preheated 350° F. oven for 8 to 10 minutes or until the fish flakes easily with a fork. Place the fish fillets on a platter, spoon some of the sauce over them, and sprinkle with the chopped nuts.

CHINESE BEEF

There is a large Oriental influence in Hawaiian cuisine. Oriental spices are used to season meats and seafoods, as well as marinades and sauces. This oven-braised beef recipe includes Chinese five-spice powder, which consists of equal parts of cloves, cinnamon, fennel seeds, star anise, and szechuan peppercorns.

Serves 4 to 6

2 tablespoons peanut oil

1 3/4 pounds lean stew beef, cut into

    1-inch cubes

1/4 cup lite soy sauce

3 tablespoons dry sherry

1 1/2 tablespoons sugar

4 slices (1/4-inch) fresh ginger root

1 clove garlic, minced

2 teaspoons Chinese five-spice powder

1 3/4 cups beef broth

2 cups thickly sliced fresh mushrooms

1 tablespoon cornstarch mixed with 2

    tablespoons cold water

Boiled rice

■

Heat the oil in a Dutch oven, add the beef, and brown well on all sides. Combine the soy sauce, sherry, sugar, ginger, garlic, five-spice powder, and beef broth in a bowl. Pour the mixture over the meat and add the mushrooms. Stir to combine the ingredients. Cover and bake in a preheated 325° F. oven for 1 1/2 hours or until the meat is tender. Skim any fat off the sauce and place the Dutch oven over low heat while thickening the sauce with the cornstarch mixture. Serve with boiled rice.

Eager to develop their livestock, the Hawaiians imported fast-riding cowboys from Mexico, longhorn breeding stock from Texas, and ranch-trained quarter horses from California. The Hawaiian-style cowboys were called *Paniolas*. The herd thrived on the rich grasslands on the slopes of Hawaii's Mona Kea volcanic mountain. Their diet of native grasses was supplemented with molasses and coconuts. King Kamehameha was so fascinated with the cattle that he decreed none should be slaughtered for a period of ten years.

Japanese, Filipinos, and Portuguese settled in Hawaii in the nineteenth century. The first American missionaries, a Protestant group from New England, came to the islands in 1820. Missionary schools and churches were established by the New Englanders, who also introduced Western foods, particularly vegetables, grains, and the eating of beef.

Agriculture

Commercial agriculture started in Hawaii in the middle of the nineteenth century, and as a result of a favorable soil and climate, agriculture has become the leading economic factor in the state's economy. The soil produced by Hawaiian volcanoes is rich in nutrients and well suited to the growing of fruits and vegetables. Northeastern trade winds, combined with abundant rainfall on the eastern slopes of most of the islands, have produced lush plantations.

Kauai, the northernmost of the Hawaiian Islands, receives the most annual rainfall, with as much as 600 inches on some parts of the island. Sugarcane, a water-loving plant, thrives on Kauai, which is called the "Garden Island."

The western sides of the Hawaiian Islands, however, have sparse rainfall and support only low-moisture vegetation

proceeded to run wild. Unfortunately, when he returned the next year, Cook was killed by the natives over a dispute regarding a missing boat.

In 1792 George Vancouver, a young midshipman who had been in the Cook expedition, returned to the island of Hawaii with his own expedition. He had been there several times before and had grown fond of the Polynesian people. As a token of friendship, Vancouver brought a number of trees and plants, three American Hereford cows, and a bull.

Although the animals were rather disoriented after the long journey, Vancouver presented his live cargo as a gift to King Kamehameha. The king graciously accepted this strange-looking herd, but at first sight of the animals, he grew very concerned that the "great hogs" would bite him. The cattle thrived, multiplied, and became the basis of one of the largest and finest cattle ranches in the world—the famous Parker Ranch, which is exceeded in size only by the mighty King Ranch in Texas. Today, the Parker Ranch consists of 250,000 acres and 60,000 head of cattle.

such as cacti. In these areas many fields are irrigated so that crops will grow. On the western side of the Big Island, dry, grassy plains support the gigantic ranching industry, much like those of the western plains on the mainland.

Hawaiian agriculture today is different from the days when land was assigned to landholding family groups. The old landholdings were triangular in shape, starting with the apex at the top of a mountain and expanding in width out into the sea. In this way the landowner had the best of all worlds—wood at the top, taro in terraced land further down the mountain, yams and bananas below the taro, domesticated animals and vegetable plots on the flatlands at water's edge, coconuts from the beach, and seafood from the sea. Many of the landowners built pools with semicircular walls to retain fish.

Sugar

Today, Hawaii's most important agricultural product is sugar, and the state supplies about one-fourth of U. S. needs. Hawaii also produces three-fourths of all the pineapple sold in the world and most of the world's supply of macadamia nuts. It is also the only state in the union that grows coffee.

Commercial growing of sugarcane changed the life of the islands. It brought American planters; Chinese, Portuguese, Japanese, and Filipino cane-field workers; and Welsh and Scottish plantation managers to Hawaii. All of these people influenced the cuisine of the islands.

Sugarcane was not native to Hawaii but was brought by the Polynesians who used it to fence their taro patches. They loved chewing on the stalks to obtain the sweet juice.

The Hawaiian sugar industry began in 1835 with the establishment of a 25-acre sugar plantation by Ladd & Company, at Koloa, Kauai. The first sugar mill was also built on Kauai that same year. Because of scientific farming, Hawaii's sugar plantations are the most productive in the world—producing 100 tons of cane per acre. Today, more than 170,000 acres of sugarcane are under cultivation throughout the islands.

Sugarcane, planted from cuttings, takes two years to mature. Since a great deal of moisture is vital to the growth of sugarcane, most fields are irrigated. Before the cane is harvested, the fields are burned to remove unwanted foliage. Modern mechanized equipment then cuts the sugarcane into short lengths, which are transported to a mill where every drop of juice is extracted. Sugar is not refined in Hawaii but is shipped to California in a moist, brown, lumpy state for refinement into white or brown granulated sugar.

Pineapple

The second most important crop in Hawaii is pineapple, which is believed to have originated in Brazil and was discovered in the New World by Christopher Columbus. The exact date when the fruit came to Hawaii is unknown. Records show that in 1813 pineapples and oranges grew in the garden of Don Francisco de Paula y Marin, a friend and advisor to King Kamehameha.

The mainstay of today's pineapple industry is the "Smooth Cayenne" variety. In 1886 one thousand of these plants were imported from Jamaica by Captain John Kidwell. Although having excellent taste, the fruit did not keep well on the long voyage to San Francisco, which is Hawaii's principal market for fresh pineapple. In order to preserve the fruit, Kidwell opened the first pineapple cannery in Hawaii in 1892. Unfortunately, it did not fare well and soon closed.

James Dole, a young Harvard graduate, came to Hawaii from Boston in 1899 and pioneered the modern pineapple industry. He found that pineapple will grow on slopes too cool for sugar.

Dole began with a 64-acre homestead and, as he said, with "two horses, a plow, a harrow, a wagon, and a 16-year-old Chinese, complete with pigtail." At that time pineapple was not commonly known in America. One of Dole's first ads read, "Pineapple—you eat it with a spoon, like a peach!"

In 1901 Dole organized the Hawaiian Pineapple Company at Wahiawa on Oahu and planted more fields of pineapple. He built a small cannery, which was the forerunner of a giant factory in Honolulu. In 1903 Dole's cannery produced 1,600 cases of canned pineapple per year. Today, the plant produces the same amount in ten minutes.

Employing mechanized cultivation and research, Dole's venture skyrocketed to success. Probably his most daring move occurred in 1921, when he purchased the whole island of Lanai and converted 15,000 acres of its pastureland to pineapple, establishing the world's largest pineapple plantation in the process.

Labor problems and excessive shipping rates to the mainland forced Dole to sell his company to Castle and Cooke in 1932. Castle and Cooke acted as the holding company for the reorganized Hawaiian Pineapple Company, and Jim Dole remained chairman of the board until his retirement in 1948. He died in Hawaii in 1958.

Today Dole operates one of the largest fruit canneries in the world. During canning season each year, about ten million pineapples are washed, graded,

PINEAPPLE CHICKEN

A pineapple and chicken combination is often served in Hawaii and is frequently presented in half of a hollowed-out pineapple.

In this dish, Maui's pineapple wine intensifies the fruit's flavor. If unavailable, however, a fruity semi-sweet wine may be substituted. To intensify the browning of the chicken, sprinkle it with paprika before putting it in the oven and after adding the additional wine.

Serves 4

1 broiler (3 to 3 1/2 pounds), cut into
   4 pieces

1/4 cup lite soy sauce

1 tablespoon honey

1 medium green pepper, cut into 2-inch
   pieces

1/2 medium red pepper, cut into 2-inch
   pieces

10 large mushrooms, cut in half

1 medium onion, cut into 8 pieces

1/2 large pineapple, cored, skinned, and
   cut into 2-inch pieces

1 cup pineapple wine or semi-sweet white
   wine, at room temperature

■

Place the chicken in a 13 x 9-inch glass baking dish. Combine the soy sauce and honey and brush the chicken with the mixture. Add the peppers, mushrooms, onion, and pineapple to the dish, distributing them evenly around the chicken. Tuck some of the vegetables and pineapple underneath the chicken if there is not enough room in the dish. Sprinkle half of the wine over the vegetables. Bake in a preheated 375° F. oven for 30 minutes. Sprinkle the remainder of the wine over the chicken and vegetables and return to the oven. Bake an additional 30 minutes. Cut chicken into serving pieces and serve with the vegetables and pineapple.

peeled, cored, sliced or crushed, and canned daily. The mass production of canned pineapple was made possible by an invention of Henry G. Ginaca, a Dole employee. The machine, which bears his name, mechanized the peeling and coring operation.

Oahu, where pineapple was first planted, remains the center of the industry, with large plantings around Wahiawa. Honolulu continues to be the canning center; however, pineapple companies operate on five of the six major islands. Almost 700,000 tons of pineapple are produced annually on approximately 34,000 acres. Although the majority of the crop is still canned, converted to juice, or frozen, refrigerated ships and air transportation have made it possible to ship fresh pineapple from Hawaii to the mainland.

Since pineapples are virtually seedless, they grow from shoots taken from the mother plant. Before planting the fields are plowed, disked, and carpeted by machine with tar paper to raise soil temperature, save moisture, and check the growth of weeds. On each acre about 17,000 shoots are planted by hand through holes punched in the paper.

When the plant is 12 to 14 months old, a bud grows at the top of the plant, which eventually becomes the fruit. Pineapple plants bear fruit in about 20 months. Each two- to three-foot plant produces only one pineapple. When the fruit is ripe, the pickers work day and night between the rows, cutting the ripe pineapples and tossing them onto conveyor belts, which extend from the harvester.

Macadamia Nuts, Coffee, and Wine

The third largest agricultural commodity in Hawaii, the macadamia nut, was first brought to Hawaii from Australia in 1881 by William H. Purvis, a Hawaiian sugar-plantation owner. Today, there are 650 macadamia nut growers, making the state the world's leader in both the growing and processing of these nuts.

The macadamia nut grows on an evergreen tree that can easily reach 65 feet in height and width, has bright green foliage, and likes a lot of moisture. The tree flowers in the early spring with long racemes of creamy white flowers that hang down like tassels from the tree's branches. Although there can be several hundred flowers on a raceme, very few set fruit.

The nuts are encased in a thick green-colored husk. At maturity the nuts fall to the ground, and the husk splits open, exposing the hard-shelled nut. On the larger plantations the shells are cracked by machine in the field, and then the nuts are sent to processing plants.

Coffee is one of Hawaii's important

smaller agricultural crops. It is believed that Samuel Ruggles, a missionary, planted the first coffee trees on the Kona coast of the island of Hawaii in 1828. Nearly all of the coffee produced in Hawaii is grown on the Kona coast of the Big Island. Some is roasted and ground in small mills near the coffee plantations, but most is shipped to Honolulu for processing.

Most of the coffee plantings on the Kona coast are found in five- to ten-acre plots at elevations of 1,000 to 2,000 feet above sea level. At this altitude there is sufficient warmth and moisture to assure good growing conditions. Coffee beans are picked by hand when they are cherry-red and put through a pulper to remove their outer skins. Then the beans are spread out in the sun to dry.

There is also a winery in Hawaii. In the late 1970s Emil Tedeschi, a vineyardist from Napa Valley, California, started experimenting with a wide variety of grapes on leased mountainside land on the southern side of Maui. Today, the vineyard consists primarily of Carnelian grapes, a red hybrid developed at the University of California at Davis for use especially in hot climates. While waiting for the grape vines to start producing, Emil Tedeschi made a dry pineapple wine for several years. It became very popular, and Tedeschi still produces it. As the vineyard came into full production, he started making a full range of wines, including champagne by the traditional *méthode champenoise*.

Hawaiian Foods

Seafood is still an important part of Hawaiian cuisine. Ocean fishing is a multimillion dollar business, with bonito, tuna, and mahimahi being the fish most frequently caught and eaten. Hawaiian

MACADAMIA NUT PIE

Because of their extremely hard shells, macadamia nuts are usually sold shelled, either raw or roasted. Honey roasting brings out the delicate flavor of macadamia nuts, which are used in this light vanilla-custard pie.

Serves 6 to 8

Pastry

1 cup all-purpose flour

3 tablespoons butter or margarine

2 tablespoons solid vegetable shortening

3 to 4 tablespoons ice water

■

Place the flour in a bowl and cut in the butter and shortening until the mixture resembles coarse crumbs. Add the water, a tablespoon at a time, and stir with a fork until the dough can be formed into a ball. Wrap the dough in plastic wrap and chill for at least 1 hour. Roll out the dough and fit it into a 9-inch pie pan. With a fork prick the bottom and sides of the dough. Place aluminum foil, shiny side down, and pie weights or beans on the pie dough and bake in a preheated 425° F. oven for 10 to 12 minutes or until nicely browned. Remove the foil and pie weights and cool the pie shell before adding the filling.

Filling

1 jar (3 1/2 ounces) honey-roasted
    Macadamia nuts

1/4 cup cold water

1 tablespoon unflavored gelatin

4 egg yolks

1/2 cup sugar

1 cup milk, scalded

1 1/2 teaspoons vanilla extract

2 egg whites

1 1/4 cups very cold whipping cream

2 1/2 tablespoons rum

Shaved semi-sweet chocolate, for garnish

■

Spread the macadamia nuts onto a towel and rub off any salt adhering to the nuts. Then put the nuts in the bowl of a food processor and chop into small pieces. Place the water in a small bowl, add the gelatin, and let it soften for 10 minutes.

Beat the eggs with the sugar in a bowl until lemon colored and the mixture falls in ribbons. Slowly pour the scalded milk into the egg mixture, stirring constantly. Transfer the custard to a saucepan and cook over medium-low heat, stirring continuously with a wooden spoon, until it starts to thicken and coats the spoon. Do not let the custard start to boil. Remove the pan from the heat and stir in the vanilla and the gelatin until completely dissolved. Cool the custard.

Fold the chopped nuts into the custard. Then whip the egg whites until stiff and fold them into the mixture. Whip the cream in a chilled bowl until thick, then add the rum and continue beating the cream until soft peaks form. Fold the cream into the custard and gently pour it into the baked pie shell. Refrigerate 3 hours before serving. Garnish with shaved chocolate.

cooking also includes such specialties as cuttlefish, squid, bonefish, and crabs. Convict fish, another favorite, takes its name from its vertical black stripes. Having such a large variety of seafood from which to choose, Hawaiians seldom prepare a one-fish meal.

The traditional Hawaiian feast is the luau. The centerpiece of this feast is a pig, which is still roasted in the same manner as it was centuries ago. The body cavity of the pig is stuffed with hot lava rocks so that cooking will take place from within as well as without. It is then wrapped in banana leaves and buried in a pit with hot lava rocks. After six to eight hours, the pig is fully cooked. In modern times chickens have also been added to the pit and roasted for several hours.

The slices of roast meat are served with poi; *Lomi-lomi*, fillets of raw salted

STILL LIFE WITH MAJOLICA BOWL by Geneve R. Sargeant, oil, 18 x 24 inches, courtesy of George Stern, Fine Arts, Encino, California.

salmon; and Opihi, a salty, clam-like mollusk. Bananas with toasted coconut and pieces of pineapple soaked in rum conclude the feast—unless it is a birthday celebration. Then a coconut cake topped with macadamia nuts is usually served.

In addition to poi, pork, and pineapple, there are several other key components of Hawaiian cooking. Plantain, breadfruit, and yams have remained a staple of the Hawaiian diet. The plantain looks like a large green banana, but it must be cooked to be edible. Breadfruit, which is about the size of a child's head, has flesh that resembles fresh bread. It must be baked before eating. Hawaiian yams are sweeter and more waxy than mainland sweet potatoes.

During the nineteenth century the new emigrants to Hawaii introduced their native foods and their own styles of cooking. The New England missionaries, for example, brought stews, chowders, corned beef, and corn bread. The Welsh and Scots brought scones and shortbread. The Chinese introduced stir-frying and Oriental vegetables and brought ginger, litchi nuts, and Chinese dumplings to Hawaii. (Fresh litchi nuts have been cultivated in Hawaii by the Chinese since 1873.) The Portuguese and Filipinos contributed spicy pork sausages. The East Indians added a myriad of curries.

The influx of Japanese in the last 40 years has greatly influenced the cuisine of Hawaii. They brought noodles, soy sauce, and charcoal-brazier cooking and introduced sashimi (thinly sliced raw fish) as an appetizer at Hawaiian dinners. Japanese noodle soups known as saimin are sold at sidewalk cafes and noodle shops, just as they are in Japan. Sushi is available at sushi bars, and shrimp and vegetables are prepared tempura-style.

To reflect the ethnic influences in Hawaiian cuisine, the Hawaiians have created *Pupu*, an array of international delicacies that include Chinese-style barbecued spareribs, Japanese *Kumaki* which is marinated chicken, meat, or seafood grilled on a stick, Korean meatballs, Hawaiian *Lomi-lomi* salmon, glazed pineapple, and roasted macadamia nuts. The *Pupu* tray is usually kept hot over a hibachi.

The foods of modern Hawaii have great variety. Chicken, which is often served in a pineapple shell, and mahimahi are both flavored with Oriental soy sauce. Chicken is frequently combined with pineapple or coconut and Oriental spices. Meats are prepared with a variety of sauces and marinades and are usually grilled or roasted. There are such dishes as Japanese-style Teriyaki Beef, Polynesian Meat Loaf, and Pork Lelani, barbecued pork with oriental vegetables. Vegetables are often part of a stir-fried dish. Coconut and macadamia nuts are key ingredients in desserts. Papaya is used in desserts, as well for breakfast.

Hawaii's cuisine, like its population, is a meeting of East and West. Both are influenced by the climate and the natural food resources.

288

ARTISTS

CLYDE ASPEVIG (1951-) was born and raised in rural Montana. He started painting at the age of twelve, guided by his artist uncle. After receiving a degree in art education from Eastern Montana College, he taught for a short time before dedicating himself full-time to painting, specializing in landscapes.

WARREN BAUMGARTEN (1894-1963), a Missouri native, studied at the Chicago Art Institute and the Grand Central School of Art in New York City. A watercolorist, Baumgarten spent much of his life illustrating national magazines. He used Connecticut backgrounds for many of his paintings and exhibited in numerous national shows, including those by the Society of Illustrators and the Maine and Baltimore Watercolor Societies.

NICKY BOEHME (1938-) is a native of California. Boehme studied technical art drawing at the Oakland Art Institute in California and later became art director of several national advertising agencies. At that time she received numerous awards as an illustrator and graphic designer. Boehme is an artist-member of the American Society of Marine Artists and has exhibited her paintings throughout the country. She specializes in painting old cannery towns, fishing boats, and the tall ships of the past.

A.D. BROWERE (1814-1887) was born in Tarrytown, New York, and was a self-taught painter. He journeyed around Cape Horn to California in 1852 as a gold prospector, remaining there for four years. Browere's paintings of the gold miners and majestic landscapes of the Sierra Nevada range are some of California's finest artistic heritage. His works are exhibited in major California art museums.

JOHN GEORGE BROWN (1831-1913) was one of the most popular painters of nineteenth-century everyday life. He was born in England and received his art training there. In 1855 he settled in Brooklyn, New York. Throughout his early career Brown specialized in painting children in rural settings. About 1880 he began painting street urchins, such as bootblacks, newsboys, and young fruit vendors, who were poverty stricken, but cheerful and clean.

BYRON BROWNE (1907-1961) was born in Yonkers, New York; studied art with C.W. Hawthorne; taught at the Art Students League; and was a charter member of the American Abstract Artists. He had numerous one-man shows, and his work is included in the art collection of the Boston Fine Arts Museum.

DOROTHY COGSWELL (1909-) was the first woman to receive a Master of Fine Arts degree from Yale University. She did her undergraduate work at the same institution. Cogswell taught art at Mt. Holyoke College from 1939 to 1974, where in the last ten years she was chairman of the art department. Some of Cogswell's paintings are semi-abstract, and she often presents a somber mood in her paintings.

MAX A. COHN (1903-) was born in England and came to America at an early age. He studied under John Sloan at the Art Student's League in the 1920s. Like the Ash Can School of painters earlier in the century, Cohn also painted the "unbeautiful" elements of modern cities; however, his paintings were more idealized. Cohn painted many New York City scenes while working as a W.P.A. artist from 1936 to 1939. A decade later he concentrated on the painting of landscapes and then turned to abstract art.

LUCILLE CORCOS (1908-1973) was born in New York City, studied at the Art Students League, and began painting professionally in 1928. She divided her career between commercial and fine art. Her commercial career centered around book illustrations and included *A Treasury of Gilbert and Sullivan* and a four-volume edition of *Grimm's Fairy Tales*.

JASPER FRANCIS CROPSEY (1823-1900) was born in Staten Island, New York; graduated from the New York Mechanics Institute; and became an apprentice to an architect. Cropsey took watercolor lessons from an English artist, Edward Murray, and also took classes in life drawing at the National Academy of Design. He opened his own architectural firm in New York and designed everything from subway stations to private mansions. By 1854, however, he was painting landscapes full-time. Cropsey's popularity

crested at the Philadelphia Centennial Exposition of 1876, where he exhibited three paintings, including *The Old Red Mill,* which later became one of the most popular prints ever produced in the United States.

JOHN S. CURRY (1897-1946) was born in Kansas, the son of a Scottish Presbyterian farm family. He studied art at the Kansas City Art Institute. After successfully starting a career as a magazine illustrator in the East, Curry went to Paris to further his art studies. Upon his return to the United States in 1927, he painted a series of canvases based on midwestern themes, which established his reputation.

FELIX O.C. DARLEY (1822-1888) was born in Philadelphia and worked primarily as an illustrator. He is credited with bringing illustration into the mainstream of art. After moving to New York in 1848, Darley began to exhibit book illustrations and bank note designs at the National Academy of Design. He illustrated Washington Irving's *Sketch Book* (1848) and the *Knickerbocker History of New York* (1850), both of which brought him wide popularity.

STANLEY S. DAVID was the pseudonym used by De Scott Evans (1847-1898), a midwestern artist. He studied in Paris and later taught at the Cleveland Academy of Fine Arts before moving to New York City in 1887. David was primarily a painter of portraits and genre pictures, including many small interior scenes with attractive young women. He is also known for his still life paintings.

ROBERT SPEAR DUNNING (1829-1905) was born in Brunswick, Maine, and founded the Fall River School, which emphasized still life paintings. After working in a cotton mill and as a seaman, Dunning studied at the National Academy of Design in New York City. Upon finishing his art education, he returned to Fall River and by 1865 devoted his time primarily to still life painting. Fruits were his best subjects.

GEORGE HENRY DURRIE (1820-1863) studied portraiture in New Haven, Connecticut, and became an itinerant portrait painter, traveling throughout the Middle Atlantic states. Durrie turned to landscape painting in the mid–1840s, and his winter scenes became and have remained his best-known works. At the end of his life, his landscape paintings became well-known through lithographic reproductions by *Currier & Ives*.

CHARLES R. C. DYE (1906–1973) was born in Canon City, Colorado, and was raised on a ranch. He studied art at the American Academy in New York City. Dye was one of the founders of the Cowboy Artists Association in 1964, and many of his western paintings served as cover illustrations for national magazines.

JOHN F. FRANCIS (1808–1886), a Philadelphia native, specialized in still lifes in the tradition of the Charles Wilson Peale family. He began as a portrait painter, but in 1850 Francis turned to still lifes exclusively. He was one of the country's leading specialists in "luncheon" or "dessert" still lifes, featuring a whole meal consisting of fruits, cakes, cheeses, nuts, and other sweets.

DAN GERHARTZ (date of birth unknown), a contemporary American artist, is a painter of landscapes, portraits, and still lifes in oil. He studied art at the American Academy in Chicago and with Richard Schmidt. Gerhartz paints only on location to take advantage of natural lighting.

SANFORD ROBINSON GIFFORD (1823–1890) was a landscape painter whose studies of light resulted in him being considered to be the founder of American luminism. A native of Hudson, New York, he attended Brown University and studied art in New York City. In 1846 he made a walking tour of the Berkshire and Catskill mountains and began devoting his energies to landscape painting. Gifford continued to travel widely, making several trips to Europe.

RICHARD LA BARRE GOODWIN (1840–1910) was born in Albany, New York, and was a leading painter in the *trompe l'oeil* style of still life painting. He, like many others at the time, started as a portrait painter but turned to still lifes, particularly paintings with wild game. He is also known for his "kitchen" paintings of cooking ingredients.

NILS GREN (1893–1940) was born in Sweden, then moved to Australia, and immi-grated to the United States after the First World War. Gren worked as a designer for a pattern manufacturer in New York City until 1925 when he moved to Southern California to study art. In the late 1920s he changed his residence to San Francisco and destroyed all of his previous canvases, because he wanted to make a new start. Gren is known for his still lifes, a few landscapes, and scenes of San Francisco.

CHARLES J. HAMILTON (dates unknown), a nineteenth-century artist, recorded in considerable detail a variety of activities associated with mercantile enterprises in Charleston, South Carolina, during the 1870s.

ARMIN CARL HANSEN (1886–1957) was born in San Francisco, California, and received his early art instruction from his father, Herman, a famous painter of the old West and frontier life. After visiting the art centers of Europe, Hansen became a deckhand on a Norwegian trawler. Upon returning to California he settled in Monterey, where he founded the Carmel Art Institute. He is recognized for his etchings and paintings of marine and coastal scenes and the fishing industry of the Monterey Peninsula.

WILLIAM MICHAEL HARNETT (1848–1892) was born in Ireland but raised in Philadelphia. He received some of his art education at the Philadelphia Academy of Fine Arts and in 1871 moved to New York where he attended night classes at Cooper Union while working as a silversmith. He set up a studio in 1874 and began painting small still lifes of such objects as mugs, pipes, books, and ink bottles. Harnett took *trompe l'oeil* to its greatest lengths.

EDWARD HICKS (1780–1849) was a Quaker folk painter and preacher. Born in Bucks County, Pennsylvania, he was appren-ticed to a carriage maker and eventually became a sign painter. In his paintings Hicks created a pictorial record of Bucks County farm life. As a prominent Quaker minister, he doubted the moral worth of art but needed its financial rewards.

WINSLOW HOMER (1836–1901) was born in Boston, Massachusetts, and received his early art training from a lithographer. He worked as a freelance illustrator, contributing to *Harper's Weekly* and other publications. When the Civil War started, *Harper's Weekly* sent him on assignments to the front. Not interested in the drama of war, Homer depicted soldiers in mundane activities. While living in England in 1881, Homer became fascinated with the sea as the subject for his paintings. After returning to the United States, he settled in Maine, where the sea still held a fascination for him.

LEE JACKSON (1909–) was born in New York City where he studied painting. In 1941 he was awarded a Guggenheim fellowship. In the 1950s Jackson exhibited his works in galleries and major museums including the Metropolitan Museum of Art and the Whitney Museum. Jackson paints primarily circus scenes, markets, and city street scenes.

EASTMAN JOHNSON (1824–1906) was born in Lovell, Maine. His very early works consisted of portrait drawings before he was apprenticed to a Boston lithographer. Largely self-taught and eager for more formal training, Johnson left America to study at the Royal Academy in Düsseldorf, Germany. Upon returning to the United States, Johnson settled in Nantucket, Massachusetts. He painted a large number of scenes depicting nineteenth-century American life.

FRANK TENNY JOHNSON (1874–1939) was born in Iowa and studied at the Art Student's League in New York City. Johnson, a successful illustrator of *Zane Grey* books, later gained fame as an painter of western scenes.

WALTER KUHN (1877–1949) was born in New York City and studied in Paris and Munich. He worked as an illustrator and cartoonist for many publications, including *Life* and *Puck*. Although he painted primarily family scenes, between 1918 and 1923 Kuhn painted a history of the West, featuring cowboys and Indians.

PHILLIP LITTLE (1857–1942) was born in Swampscott, Massachusetts. He attended the Massachusetts Institute of Technology and began working for his father's cotton and woolen mill. After working for a short time in the design department, Little entered the Lowell School of Design and then worked as a lithographer.

He eventually studied painting and in 1903 set up a studio in Salem, Massachusetts. Many of his paintings were either of Salem or coastal New England.

LUIGI LUCIONI (1900-1988), the son of a coppersmith, was born in Malante, Italy. As a child he demonstrated an ability to draw and was sent to a local art school. When Lucioni was ten years old, he emigrated to the United States with his family and studied art at Cooper Union. By the time he was twenty, Lucioni was supporting himself as a newspaper and magazine illustrator. He also attended the National Academy of Design and studied for several months in Europe. His still life compositions often included an odd assortment of objects, ranging from copper utensils to early American glass bottles.

JANET MILLIKAN (date of birth unknown), a contemporary artist, is a native of Iowa. She received her formal art education at Drake University and the State University of Iowa. In 1975, in celebration of the "Year of the Woman," Millikan was selected to exhibit one of her paintings at the World Trade Center in New York City. An avid gardener, Millikan often paints still lifes of fruits and vegetables, as well as landscapes using French Impressionistic techniques.

LEWIS MILLER (1796-1882) compiled a sketchbook of his drawings of the period 1853-1867. Many of the 147 drawings in the book depict Virginia towns and everyday life in the 1850s and 1860s.

PATRICIA BUCKLEY MOSS (1933-) was born in New York City. She studied art and design at Cooper Union in spite of her severe dyslexia. After graduation, marriage, and six children, she moved to Waynesboro, Virginia, in the Shenandoah Valley, where her artistic reputation evolved. Moss's distinctive artistry has become synonymous with images of the Amish and Mennonites, rural scenery, and the depiction of traditional rural values.

GAYLE NASON (1948-) is an Arizona artist who is known for the clarity and jewel-like quality of her southwestern still lifes. She incorporates many artifacts and Indian food staples into her oil paintings.

HARL NOBLES (date of birth unknown), a contemporary American artist, was born in Sydney, Australia, and came to the United States at the age of six. He studied art at the Pennsylvania Academy of Fine Arts in Philadelphia. In the 1950s he became a lithographer. After moving to California, Nobles became a well-known, full-time painter. He paints traditional still lifes in the *trompe l'oeil* style.

DOUGLAS PARSHALL (1899-1990) was born in New York City and as a child began to draw. He briefly studied art in New York, Paris, and Boston before settling in Santa Barbara, California. Parshall traveled extensively, seeking subject matter in the remote corners of the world. Using mixed media, he painted very diverse subjects, including landscapes, figures, portraits, and horses. Parshall's works have been exhibited extensively and won many awards.

VIRGINIA PAUL (1930-) specializes in watercolors. She studied with watercolorist Barbara Nechis at the Parson School of Design in New York City and now resides in Charlottesville, Virginia.

ENOCH WOOD PERRY (1831-1915) was born in Boston and lived in New Orleans before going to Düsseldorf, Germany, in 1852 to study painting. Upon returning to America in 1859, he settled in New Orleans. During an extended stay in the San Francisco area, he painted many scenes of the city, including several views of San Francisco's Chinatown before the 1906 earthquake. In later life he was influenced by the paintings of the French Impressionists.

MARIE ADRIEN PERSAC (ca. 1822-1873) was born in Lyons, France, and married Odile Daigre of Baton Rouge, Louisiana, in 1851. Persac operated an apple orchard in Indiana with money he inherited from his mother's estate. He was a partner in a photography business, as well as an artist and lithographer. In the 1850s Persac painted a series of scenes and boats on the Mississippi River for which he is best known.

JOYCE PIKE (date of birth unknown) is a contemporary artist and a sixth-generation Californian. She has taught art throughout the United States and in Europe. Pike has published more than 40 articles and created 45 one-hour video tapes on painting. She is the author of *Painting Floral Still Lifes* and *Oil Painting: A Direct Approach*.

LEVI WELLS PRENTICE (1851-1935) was born in New York state and is remembered principally for his Adirondack mountain and lake landscapes. He began his career as a decorative painter of ceilings and portraits. In the 1880s he moved to Brooklyn, where there was a community of still life painters. Prentice painted still lifes with almost photographic accuracy.

WILLIAM F. REESE (date of birth unknown) is a contemporary artist who studied at the Art Center College of Design in Los Angeles, California. He is a member of the National Academy of Western Art. Reese lives in Woodinville, Washington, and works in oil, watercolor, pastel, bronze, and etchings.

RENE RICKABAUGH (1947-) received her art education and later taught at Pacific Northwest College of Art in Portland, Oregon. Rickabaugh has had numerous one-woman shows in the Pacific Northwest.

SEVERIN ROESEN (1815-1871) was one of the most important still life painters of the mid-nineteenth century. His canvases overflowed with fruits and flowers and reflected Victorian opulence. Although little is known of Roesen's life, it is thought that he was born in 1815 in the German Rhineland and emigrated to the United States in 1848. Roesen settled first in New York City and then in Williamsport, Pennsylvania. During his lifetime he painted about 400 canvases, all similar, with fruits mixed with flowers, wine glasses, and ceramic objects.

CHARLES M. RUSSELL (1864-1926) was born in St. Louis, Missouri, and left his home at sixteen to work on his uncle's ranch in Montana, where he promptly got fired. He worked as an itinerant ranch hand in Montana and began to sketch scenes of cowboy and Indian life. Russell also spent some time with the Blackfoot Indians. More than probably any other painter, Russell brought the cowboy to life for the American public. Almost from the beginning his paintings told stories, many of which Russell was either involved in or witnessed. For a brief time Russell maintained a studio in

Pasadena, California, but in the early 1920s he returned to Montana.

GENEVE R. SARGEANT (1868-1957) was born in San Francisco and studied art in that city's School of Design. She continued her studies at the Art Student's League in New York City, and after her marriage to Winthrop Sargeant, she lived in the Midwest and California. Mrs. Sargeant was a productive and highly respected artist in the San Francisco area.

O.C. SELTZER (1877-1957) was born in Copenhagen, Denmark. After coming to the United States, he traveled to Great Falls, Montana, where he found work as a machinist on the Great Northern Railroad. He became friends with Charles M. Russell and after Russell's death traveled to New York City to fulfill some of Russell's last commissions. Seltzer continued painting and produced a series of works about Montana's history.

TIBOR "STIBOR" SILBERHORN (1928-1981) was born in Hungary and emigrated to the United States in 1971. Silberhorn had studied art in Hungary and became famous as a mural painter and classical illustrator. He was an advisor to the Hungarian movie industry from 1957 to 1967. Silberhorn is known for his excellent composition and faultless color coordination.

LILLY MARTIN SPENCER (1822-1902) was the best-known woman artist working in the middle decades of the nineteenth century. Born in England, she came to America in 1830 and settled in Marietta, Ohio, later moving to Cincinnati, where she studied art privately. While living in New York City in 1849, she started painting genre pictures based on her own family life.

"QUEENA" STOVALL (1887-1980) was born Emma Serena Dillard in Lynchburg, Virginia. Her nickname came from her childhood attempts to pronounce Serena. Stovall was a self-taught artist, who portrayed the vanishing lifestyle of the rural Virginia she knew. Through her paintings, Stovall showed day-to-day life—farm chores, household chores, and family gatherings.

RAY SWANSON (date of birth unknown) is a contemporary American artist with a highly successful painting career of more than 30 years. He is a member of the Cowboy Artists of America. Swanson is considered to be one of this country's most distinguished painters of the Native Americans of the Southwest—the Navajo, Hopi, and Zuni Indians.

JERRY THRASHER (date of birth unknown) is a contemporary artist who was born in Paris, Texas, and has had a love affair with American wildlife for as long as he can remember. Thrasher is an avid sportsman, hunter, and fisherman, and spends many months of the year in the field studying, sketching, and photographing nature first-hand. Thrasher gained national recognition in 1970 when his painting of a mallard scene entitled *Greenhead Pitch-In* was featured on the cover of *Ducks Unlimited* magazine.

JOSE TRINIDAD (date of birth unknown) a contemporary artist who was born in the Philippines, studied fine art at the University of the Philippines. He started his career as a mural artist. For more than 20 years, Trinidad has studied trends in American art in the United States and Canada. His garden scenes are vibrant with color and light and show the influence of Monet and Renoir, two artists whom Trinidad greatly admires.

JAMES BARRE TURNBULL (1910-1976) was born in St. Louis, Missouri, and studied art at the St. Louis School of Fine Arts; Washington University School of Fine Arts, Seattle, Washington; and the Pennsylvania Academy of Fine Arts in Philadelphia. During the 1930s Turnbull headed an art project to reproduce early Missouri household objects. He was an artist correspondent for *Life* magazine during World War II and was also an artist correspondent for Abott Laboratories.

MARY ANN VESSEY (1946-) is a contemporary, self-taught American artist, who specializes in Americana, primarily farm scenes. She won the 1991 and 1992 *Virginia Ducks Unlimited* Artist of the Year Award.

EDITH WHITE (1855-1946) was born in Iowa and at age four came across the Great Plains with her family in an ox-drawn wagon. Upon arriving in California the family settled in a mining camp in Nevada City. After graduation from Mills College in Oakland, California, White studied art at the School of Design in San Francisco. Her paintings included portraits, floral still lifes, missions, and landscapes with flowers.

OLAF WIEGHORST (1899-1989) was Danish by birth and had an early interest in painting, particularly in painting horses. After coming to the United States shortly after the First World War, he worked on a ranch in Arizona and then became a mounted policeman in New York City. Upon retirement in 1944, Wieghorst moved to Southern California, where he painted primarily western scenes.

N.C. WYETH (1882-1945) took art lessons from well-known illustrator Howard Pyle and settled in Chadds Ford, Pennsylvania, in 1908. He continued in Pyle's tradition, establishing himself as one of America's greatest illustrators. Wyeth also worked in oils. He painted more than 3,000 illustrations for hundreds of articles and books. Many of these include vigorous depictions of working farmers. His best-known book illustrations include Robert Louis Stevenson's *Treasure Island, Kidnapped,* and *Black Arrow;* James Fenimore Cooper's *Deerslayer* and *The Last of the Mohicans*; and Daniel Defoe's *Robinson Crusoe.*

BIBLIOGRAPHY

Adams, Marcia. *Cooking in Quilt Country*. New York: Clarkson N. Potter, 1989.

_____. *Heartland*. New York: Clarkson Potter, 1991.

Adams, Ramon F. *Come an' Get it, The Story of the Old Cowboy Cook*. Norman, Okla.: Univ. of Oklahoma Press, 1952.

Adolph Coors Company. *Coors® Taste of the West*. Des Moines, Iowa: Meredith Corporation, 1981.

American Cancer Society, Idaho Division. *Idaho Sampler Cookbook*. Memphis, Tenn.: Wimmer Brothers Books, 1984.

McCully, Helen and Helen Duprey Bullock, eds. *The American Heritage Cookbook*. New York: American Heritage Publishing Company, 1964.

Beard, James. *James Beard's American Cookery*. Boston: Little, Brown and Co., 1972.

Beck, Bruce. *The Official Fulton Fish Market Cookbook*. New York: E .P. Dutton, 1989.

Beck, Warren A. and David A. Williams. *California, A History of the Golden State*. New York: Doubleday & Company, 1972.

Belk, Sarah. *Around the Southern Table*. New York: Simon & Schuster, 1991.

Belsinger, Susan and Carolyn Dille. *The Chesapeake Cookbook*. New York: Clarkson N. Potter, 1990.

Betz, Bob, ed. *Star Spangled Cooking*. New York: Stewart, Tabori & Chang, 1987.

_____ . *Taste of Liberty*. New York: Stewart, Tabori & Chang, 1985.

Bifani, Kenna Lach and Miranda Whyte. *American Home Cooking*. Mississuaga, Ontario: Cupress, 1987.

Billard, Jules B. "The Revolution in American Agriculture." *National Geographic* Vol. 137, No. 2 (February 1970): 147-185.

Blatti, Jo. "Farming in Minnesota, The Settlement Years." *Roots* Vol. 15, No. 3 (Spring 1987): 3-18.

Booth, Letha, comp. *The Williamsburg Cookbook*. Williamsburg, Va.: The Colonial Williamsburg Foundation, 1975.

Bowles, Ella Shannon and Dorothy S. Towle. *Secrets of New England Cooking*. New York: M. Barrows & Co., 1947.

Boyer, David S. "Wyoming: High, Wide, and Windy." *National Geographic* Vol. 129, No. 4 (April 1966): 554-594.

Bradley, Susan. *Pacific Northwest Palate*. Menlo Park, Calif.: Addison-Wesley, 1989.

Brown, Dale et al., eds. *American Cooking*. New York: Time-Life Books, 1968.

_____. *American Cooking: The Northwest*. New York: Time-Life Books, 1970.

Brown, Ellen. *Southwest Tastes*. Tuscon, Ariz.: HP Books, 1987.

Butel, Jane. *Fiesta!* New York: Harper & Row, 1987.

Cameron, Shelia MacNiven. *The Best from New Mexico Kitchens*. Santa Fe: New Mexico Magazine, 1978.

Chenchar, Shirley M. and Paula Chenchar Hanus. *Recipes from the Heart of Iowa*. Audubon, Iowa: S.M. Chenchar Productions, 1988.

Chesnel, Connie. *The Rocky Mountain Cookbook*. New York: Clarkson N. Potter, 1989.

Clements, Carole, Martha Lomask, and Norma MacMillan. *American Tradition*. New York: Gallery Books, 1989.

Collin, Rima and Richard Collin. *The New Orleans Cookbook*. New York: Alfred A. Knopf, 1987.

Copeland, Pat, ed. *Oklahoma Cooks*. Oklahoma City: Oklahoma Folk Life Council, 1989.

Davis, Kenneth S. *Kansas, a History*. New York: W. W. Norton & Co., 1976.

Davis, Nancy and Kathy Hart. *Coastal Carolina Cooking*. Chapel Hill, N.C.: Univ. of North Carolina Press, 1986.

DeBolt, Margaret Wayt and Emma Rylander Law. *Savannah Sampler Cookbook*. West Chester, Pa.: Schiffer, 1978.

DeBolt, Margaret Wayt, Emma Rylander Law, and Carter Olive. *Georgia Entertains*. Nashville: Rutledge Hill Press, 1983.

Dille, Carolyn and Susan Belsinger. *New Southwestern Cooking*. New York: Macmillan, 1985.

Dent, Huntley. *The Feast of Santa Fe*. New York: Simon & Schuster, 1985.

Eberly, Carole, ed. *Our Michigan, Ethnic Tales and Recipes*. East Lansing, Mich.: Eberly Press, 1979.

Ellis, William S. and Dean Conger. "High-Stepping Idaho." *National Geographic* Vol. 143, No. 3 (March 1973): 290-317.

English, Sandal. *Fruits of the Desert*. Tucson: Arizona Star, 1981.

Fehrenbach, T. R. *Lone Star, a History of Texas and the Texans*. New York: Macmillan, Collier Press, 1968.

Feibleman, Peter S. et al., eds. *American Cooking: Creole and Acadian*. New York: Time-Life Books, 1971.

Findley, Rowe and Robert W. Madden. "Old Salem, Morning Star of Moravian Faith." *National Geographic* Vol. 138, No. 6 (December 1970): 818-837.

Frantz, Joe B. *Texas, a History*. New York: W. W. Norton & Co., 1976.

Gibbons, Boyd. "Easygoing, Hardworking Arkansas." *National Geographic* Vol. 153, No. 3 (March 1978): 396-427.

Gilley, Mickey. *Mickey Gilley's Texas Cookbook*. New York: Simon & Schuster, 1984.

Glenn, Camille. *The Heritage of Southern Cooking*. New York: Workman, 1986.

Gluesing, Laurie and Debra Gluesing. *Recipes from Iowa with Love*. Chanhassen, Minn.: New Boundary Designs, 1986.

_____. *Recipes from South Dakota with Love*. Chanhassen, Minn.: New Boundary Designs, 1985.

_____. *Recipes from Wisconsin with Love*. Chanhassen, Minn.: New Boundary Designs, 1984.

Godbey, Marty. *Dining in Historic Ohio*. Kuttawa, Ky.: McClanahan, 1987.

Graber, Kay, comp. *Nebraska Pioneer Cookbook*. Lincoln, Nebr.: Univ. of Nebraska Press, 1974.

Greer, Anne Lindsay. *Cuisine of the American Southwest*. New York: Harper & Row, 1983.

Hachten, Harva. *The Flavor of Wisconsin*. Madison, Wis.: State Historical Society of Wisconsin, 1986.

Hamilton, Virginia Van der Veer. *Alabama, a History*. New York: W. W. Norton & Co., 1977.

Heller, Edna Eby. *The Art of Pennsylvania Dutch Cooking*. Garden City, N.Y.: Doubleday & Co., 1968.

Hein, Peg. *Tastes and Tales from Texas with Love*. Austin, Tex.: Hein & Associates, 1984.

Howard, B.C. *Fifty Years in a Maryland Kitchen*. New York: Dover, 1986.

Huck, Virginia and Ann H. Andersen, eds. *100 Years of Good Cooking*. St. Paul: The Minnesota Historical Society, 1958.

Hughes, Stella. *Chuck Wagon Cookin'*. Tucson: University of Arizona Press, 1974.

Ingle, Schuyler and Sharon Kramis. *Northwest Bounty*. New York: Simon & Schuster, 1988.

Jardine, Winnifred C. *Mormon Country Cooking*. Salt Lake City: Bookcraft, 1983.

Jones, Evan. *American Food, The Gastronomic Story.* New York: E.P. Dutton & Co. 1975.

Jones, Judith and Evan. *The L.L. Bean Book of New New England Cookery.* New York: Random House, 1987.

Junior League of Albuquerque. *Simply Simpático.* Albuquerque: Junior League of Albuquerque, 1981.

Junior League of Baltimore. *Hunt to Harbor.* Baltimore: Junior League of Baltimore, 1985.

Junior League of Charleston. *Charleston Receipts.* Charleston, S.C.: Junior League of Charleston, 1986.

Junior League of Monroe. *Celebrations on the Bayou.* Monroe, La.: Cotton Bayou, 1989.

Junior League of Salt Lake City. *Heritage Cookbook.* Salt Lake City: Junior League of Salt Lake City, 1975.

Kaplan, Anne R., Majorie A. Hoover, and Willard B. Moore. *The Minnesota Ethnic Food Book.* St. Paul: Minnesota Historical Society, 1986.

Keating, Bern. "Today Along the Natchez Trace." *National Geographic* Vol. 134, No. 5 (November 1968): 641-667.

Kerr, Mary Brandt. *America, Regional Recipes from the Land of Plenty.* Secaucus, N.J.: Chartwell Books, Inc., n.d.

Kitching, Frances and Susan Stiles Dowell. *Mrs. Kitching's Smith Island Cookbook.* Centreville, Md.: Tidewater Publishers, 1981.

Kyle, Evelyn and Emma McCreanor, eds. *Mesa County Cooking with History.* Grand Junction, Colo.: Museum of Western Colorado Press, 1980.

La Fay, Howard. "Alabama, Dixie to a Different Time." *National Geographic* Vol. 148, No. 4 (October 1975): 534-569.

Lambert, Walter N. *Kinfolks and Custard Pie.* Knoxville: Univ. of Tennessee Press, 1988.

Langlois, Stephan and Margaret Guthrie. *Prairie, Cuisine from the Heartland.* Chicago: Contemporary Books, 1990.

Larson, Barbara and Helga Gonzalez, comp. *The Prairies Collection Cookbook.* Bismarck, N.D.: Bismarck-Mandan Symphony League, 1983.

Laxalt, Robert. *Nevada, a History.* New York: W. W. Norton & Co., 1977.

Laxalt, Robert and William Belknap, Jr. "Lonely Sentinels of the American West: Basque Sheepherders." *National Geographic* Vol. 129, No. 6 (June 1966): 870-888.

League of Women Voters of Bemidji Area. *Favorite Wild Rice Recipes of Minnesota's North Country.* Bemidji, Minn.: League of Women Voters, 1983.

Leonard, Jonathan Norton et al., eds. *American Cooking: New England.* New York: Time-Life Books, 1970.

_____. *American Cooking: The Great West.* New York: Time-Life Books, 1971.

Linck, Ernestine Sewell and Joyce Gibson Roach. *Eats, A Folk History of Texas Foods.* Fort Worth: Texas Christian Univ. Press, 1989.

Longstreet, Stephen and Ethel. *A Salute to American Cooking.* New York: Hawthorn Books, 1968.

Loomis, Susan Herrmann. *The Great American Seafood Cookbook.* New York: Workman, 1988.

Magness, J.R. "How Fruit Came to America." *National Geographic* Volume C, Number Three (September 1951): 325-377.

Marshall, Lillian Bertham. *Southern Living® Cooking Across the South.* Birmingham, Ala.: Oxmoor House, 1980.

Martha White Foods. *Martha White's Southern Sampler.* Nashville: Rutledge Hill Press, 1989.

McBride, Mary Margaret. *Harvest of American Cooking.* New York: G. P. Putnam's Sons, 1956.

McClane, A. J. *The Encyclopedia of Fish Cookery.* New York: Holt, Rinehart & Winston, 1977.

McConnaughey, Gibson Jefferson, *Two Centuries of Virginia Cooking.* Amelia, Va: Mid-South Publishing Co., 1977.

Miller, Amy Bess and Persis Fuller. *The Best of Shaker Cooking.* New York: Macmillan, 1985.

Morgan, H. Wayne and Anne Hodges Morgan. *Oklahoma, a History.* New York: W. W. Norton & Co., 1977.

Morgan, Judith and Neil. "California's Surprising Inland Delta." *National Geographic* Vol. 150, No. 3 (September 1976): 409-430.

Morgan, Nina, ed. *Favorite Recipes of the South.* Guilford, Surrey, England: Colour Library Books, 1988.

Patteson, Charles and Craig Emerson. *Charles Patteson's Kentucky Cooking.* New York: Harper & Row, 1988.

Patout, Alex. *Patout's Cajun Home Cooking.* New York: Random House, 1986.

Perl, Lila. *Red-Flannel Hash and Shoo-Fly Pie.* Cleveland, Ohio: World Publishing Co., 1965.

Penner, Lucille Recht. *The Colonial Cookbook.* New York: Hastings House, 1976.

Peterson, Charles S. *Utah, a History.* New York: W. W. Norton & Co., 1977.

Poseley, Judy, ed. "Flour Milling." *Roots* Vol. 3, No. 2 (Winter 1974): 4-28.

Powell, Lawrence Clark. *Arizona, a History.* New York: W. W. Norton & Co., 1976.

Powell, William S. *North Carolina, a History.* Chapel Hill: Univ. of North Carolina Press, 1977.

Puckett, Susan. *A Cook's Tour of Iowa.* Iowa City: Univ. of Iowa Press, 1988.

Rhoades, Robert E. "The Incredible Potato." *National Geographic* Vol. 161, No. 5 (May 1982): 668-694.

Riordan, Kay, comp. and ed. *Historical Cookery of the Black Hills.* Keystone, S. D.: Mountain Co., 1971.

Root, Waverley. *Food.* New York: Simon & Schuster, 1980.

Root, Waverley and Richard de Rochemont. *Eating in America, a History.* New York: Ecco Press, 1976.

Schulz, Phillip Stephen. *America the Beautiful Cookbook.* San Francisco: Collins, 1990.

Shenton, James P. et al., eds. *American Cooking: The Melting Pot.* New York: Time-Life Books, 1971.

Southern Living. *The Deep South Cookbook.* Birmingham, Ala.: Oxmoor House, 1980.

Stamm, Sara B. B. et al., eds. *Yankee Magazine's Favorite New England Recipes.* 2d ed. Dublin, N. H.: Yankee, 1979.

Taylor, John Martin. "Food and History in the Carolina Low Country." *The Journal of Gastronomy* Vol. 4, No. 3 (Autumn 1988): 3-17.

The 1006 Summit Avenue Society. *Wild Rice.* New York: McGraw-Hill, 1986.

Tolley, Lynne and Pat Mitchamore. *Jack Daniel's The Spirit of Tennessee Cookbook.* Nashville: Rutledge Hill Press, 1988.

VanCronkhite, Mary Joanne, ed. *The Ethnic Epicure, a Treasury of Old World Wisconsin Recipes.* Wauwatosa, Wis.: Wauwatosa Junior Woman's Club, 1973.

Volunteers of the Colorado Historical Society. *Pioneer Potluck, Stories and Recipes of Early Colorado.* Boulder, Colo.: Johnson, 1963.

Waldman, Carl. *Atlas of the North American Indian.* New York: Facts on File, 1985.

Walter, Eugene et al., eds. *American Cooking: Southern Style.* New York: Time-Life Books, 1971.

Wennersten, John R. *The Oyster Wars of Chesapeake Bay.* Centreville, Md.: Tidewater, 1981.

White, Bruce M. "Life In Minnesota Territory." *Roots* Vol. 13, No. 2 (Winter 1985): 22-25.

Wilson, José et al., eds. *American Cooking: The Eastern Heartland.* New York: Time-Life Books, 1971.

SUBJECT INDEX

RECIPE INDEX

METRIC CONVERSION CHART

U.S. Measure	Metric Equivalent
¼ teaspoon	1.25 milliliters
½ teaspoon	2.5 milliliters
1 teaspoon	5 milliliters
2 teaspoons	10 milliliters
3 teaspoons	15 milliliters
1 tablespoon	15 milliliters
2 tablespoons	30 milliliters
1 fluid ounce	15 milliliters
2 fluid ounces, ¼ cup	59 milliliters
4 fluid ounces, ½ cup	118 milliliters
8 fluid ounces, 1 cup	236 milliliters
16 fluid ounces, 2 cups	472 milliliters
1 cup	.24 liter
2 cups	.47 liter
1 ounce	28 grams
2 ounces	56 grams
4 ounces, ¼ pound	112 grams
8 ounces, ½ pound	225 grams
16 ounces, 1 pound	450 grams
18 ounces	500 grams, ½ kilo
24 ounces, 1 ½ pounds	675 grams
32 ounces, 2 pounds	900 grams
36 ounces, 2 ¼ pounds	1000 grams, 1 kilo

Oven Temperature Equivalents

Fahrenheit	Gas Mark	Celsius	Heat of oven
225°	1/4	107°	very cool
250°	1/2	121°	very cool
275°	1	135°	cool
300°	2	148°	cool
325°	3	163°	moderate
350°	4	177°	moderate
375°	5	190°	fairly hot
400°	6	204°	fairly hot
425°	7	218°	hot
450°	8	232°	very hot

DATE DUE

12/3/94 11:45 6892		